ON CONSTITUTIONAL GROUND

ON CONSTITUTIONAL
GROUND

John Hart Ely

PRINCETON UNIVERSITY PRESS   PRINCETON, NEW JERSEY

Library of Congress Cataloging-in-Publication Data

Ely, John Hart, 1938–
On constitutional ground / John Hart Ely.
p.   cm.
Includes index.
ISBN 0-691-08644-3 (cloth : alk. paper)
ISBN 0-691-02553-3 (pbk. : alk. paper)
1. United States—Consitutional law.   I. Title.
KF4550.A2E46   1996
342.73—dc20   [347.302]   95-48113

This book has been composed in Times Roman

Princeton University Press books are printed
on acid-free paper and meet the guidelines
for permanence and durability of the Committee
on Production Guidelines for Book Longevity
of the Council on Library Resources

Printed in the United States of America
by Princeton Academic Press

10   9   8   7   6   5   4   3   2   1

10   9   8   7   6   5   4   3   2   1
(Pbk.)

The one important thing I have learned over the years is the difference between taking one's work seriously and taking one's self seriously. The first is imperative and the second is disastrous.

 —Margot Fonteyn

They liked to begin a paper with some formula like "I want to raise some questions about so-and-so" and seemed to think they had done their intellectual duty by merely raising them. This manoeuvre drove Morris Zapp insane. Any damn fool, he maintained, could think of questions; it was *answers* that separated the men from the boys. If you couldn't answer your own questions it was either because you hadn't worked on them hard enough or because they weren't real questions. In either case you should keep your mouth shut.

 —David Lodge, *Changing Places*

"What's new?" is an interesting and broadening eternal question, but one which, if pursued exclusively, results only in an endless parade of trivia and fashion, the silt of tomorrow. I would like, instead, to be concerned with the question "What is best?", a question which cuts deeply rather than broadly, a question whose answers tend to move the silt downstream.

 —Robert Pirsig, *Zen and the Art of*
  Motorcycle Maintenance

Contents

1. The General Theory   3
The Chief (1974)   3
Excerpt from *Another Such Victory: Constitutional Theory and Practice in a World Where Courts Are No Different from Legislatures* (1991)   5
Democracy and Judicial Review (1982)   6
On Protecting Fundamental Interests and Powerless Minorities under the United States and Canadian Constitutions (1986)   18
The Rule of Clear Mistake: "A Great and Stately Jurisdiction"? (1993)   25

2. Federalism   31
Remarks at American-German Bicentennial Symposium on Constitutional Law (1976)   31
Excerpt from *The Limits of Logic: Syntactic Ambiguity in Article I of the U.S. Constitution* (1963)   33
Excerpt from *The Irrepressible Myth of Erie* (1974)   35
Excerpt from *Legislative and Administrative Motivation in Constitutional Law* (1970)   36
The Irrepressible Myth of Erie (1974)   39
Choice of Law and the State's Interest in Protecting Its Own (1981)   61
Another Spin on Allegheny Pittsburgh (1990)   86

3. Separation of Powers   89
United States v. Lovett: *Litigating the Separation of Powers* (1975)   89
The Bounds of Legislative Specification: A Suggested Approach to the Bill of Attainder Clause (1962)   111
Excerpt from *Legislative and Administrative Motivation in Constitutional Law* (1970)   136
Memorandum to Special Prosecutor Archibald Cox on the Legality of Calling President Nixon before a Grand Jury (1973)   137
Letter to *The New York Times* (1973)   140
Letter to *The New York Times* (1994)   142
Whose War Is It, Anyway? The Gulf and the War Powers Act (1988)   143

Perspective on the Persian Gulf: "War by Default" Isn't
   the Law (1990) 146
Clinton, Congress, and War (1993) 148
Now Bosnia (1994) 150

4. Freedom of Expression 152
Trial by Newspaper and Its Cures (1967) 152
Flag Desecration: A Case Study in the Roles of Categorization
   and Balancing in First Amendment Analysis (1975) 173

5. Religious Freedom 188
Memorandum to Chief Justice Warren Concerning *United States*
   v. Seeger (1965) 188
Excerpt from *Legislative and Administrative Motivation in*
   Constitutional Law (1970) 190
Letter to *The New York Times* (1984) 197

6. Criminal Procedure 198
Excerpts from Memoranda to Abe Fortas Concerning *Gideon v.*
   Wainwright (1962) 198
Remarks at American University Conference Marking the
   Thirtieth Anniversary of *Gideon v. Wainwright* (1993) 203
Letter to Anthony Lewis (1990) 207
Harris v. New York: *Some Anxious Observations on the*
   Candor and Logic of the Emerging Nixon Majority (1971)
   (co-authored with Alan M. Dershowitz) 211
The Proposed "Good Faith" Exception to the Exclusionary
   Rule (1983) 228
Sure Money Talks, but That's Precisely the Reason We Need
   the Reasonable Doubt Standard (1995) 230
Letter to Stanford *Campus Report* (1991) 232
Memorandum to Other Members of Yale University Police
   Advisory Board (1971) 233
What Counts as Liberal? Some Observations on French
   Criminal Procedure and the "Projet Peyrefitte" (1980) 235

7. Racial Discrimination 247
Excerpts from *Legislative and Administrative Motivation in*
   Constitutional Law (1970) 247
School Desegregation: A Sense of Déjà Vu (1977) 258
Excerpt from *Professor Dworkin's External/Personal Preference*
   Distinction (1983) 261
The Constitutionality of Reverse Racial Discrimination (1974) 267
Excerpt from *Legislative and Administrative Motivation in*
   Constitutional Law (1970) 275

8. "Substantive Due Process"   279
Memorandum to Chief Justice Warren Concerning *Griswold v.*
    Connecticut (1965)   279
The Wages of Crying Wolf: A Comment on Roe v. Wade (1973)   281
Excerpts from Testimony on S. J. Res. 119 and 130 before the
    Senate Judiciary Committee, Subcommittee on Constitutional
    Amendments (1974)   297
Let There Be Life (1981) (co-authored with Laurence H. Tribe)   301
Abortion for the Rich (1977)   303
Letter to Justices Kennedy, O'Connor and Souter Concerning
    Planned Parenthood v. Casey (1992)   304
Democracy and the Right to Be Different (1981)   306
Excerpt from *Professor Dworkin's External/Personal Preference*
    Distinction (1983)   311

9. Candor   329
Letter to Attorney General Levi (1975)   329
About the Evidence (1975)   331
Draft Letter to "the Media" Concerning the Warren Commission
    (1992)   333
On Living Lies for Professional Reasons (1992)   334
Letter to *The New York Times* (1988)   338
Letter to *The New York Times* (1989)   338

10. In Conclusion   340
Another Such Victory: Constitutional Theory and Practice in a
    World Where Courts Are No Different from Legislatures
    (1991)   340
Author's Comment on Legislative and Administrative Motivation
    in Constitutional Law *and* The Wages of Crying Wolf:
    A Comment on *Roe v. Wade* (1991)   361
Excerpt from *On Constitutional Nihilism* (1980)   363

Notes   367

Index   497

ON CONSTITUTIONAL GROUND

1

The General Theory

The Chief (1974)[1]

The image of Earl Warren often conveyed by the popular press was that of a glad-handing politician whose accomplishments resulted very largely from his winning personality. A sunny, even jolly man: a sort of lovable uncle. Thus while he may not have been a great scholar, the theme seemed to run, he sure did have a "way with people" and that's what accounted for his success as Chief Justice. But somehow that just doesn't add up to greatness, and this was, unmistakably, a great man.

Don't get me wrong: the Chief went out of his way to show respect for everyone with whom he came in contact, regardless of station, and he was deeply sensitive to the feelings and insecurities of others. But no one who ever saw him pounce on a dissembling or callous lawyer would ever again think "lovable" quite the right word. No one who heard him on the phone with one of his colleagues—"No, Bill, we can't consider that. . . . No. It's all been decided. . . ."—could imagine that this was a man who "led" by going along. No doubt the Court was more cohesive because he was Chief Justice, but that had little to do with charm in any cheap sense of the word. It had to do with the man's tireless devotion to his work, with his unusual ability, legal as well as administrative, and most of all with the unmistakable purity of his motives. Sure, he knew how to shake your hand, and even ten years after his appointment to the Court, he instinctively waved back at people who waved at his car. But those were just the leftover reflexes of a prior life in politics: anyone who thought they were the way the Chief Justice did business would soon learn his mistake. He was a leader because he was a man with a mission, and because the mission was good.

If a law clerk's tribute is supposed to be full of anecdotes that demonstrate what a fascinating private character his boss was, then this tribute will be a disappointment. Oh, the Chief was a great sports fan—that's not made up—and a close and prescient student of the political process. But that's not so terribly interesting, and it was all secondary. There was simply too much important work to leave room for the cultivation of engaging eccentricities. I suppose it may be a little dull after all, but Earl Warren did not add up to a great deal more than the public record makes him—one of the greatest single forces for right the nation has ever known. The public man was the man, and that was a good deal more than the rest of us can even hope to be.

The public man was, always was, a democrat. The image often conveyed by the academic press of Chief Justice Warren and the Court he led was that of an unprecedented willingness—rightly or wrongly, depending on the commentator's biases—to superimpose the judiciary's value judgments on those arrived at by the political processes. There was some of this, to be sure, when liberty genuinely hung in the balance. But like any good lawyer, the Chief was preoccupied with questions of process—not simply of the criminal process, which he so thoroughly understood, but more importantly of the democratic process as well. His concern lest those in power freeze others out of that process was most obvious in his voting rights opinions. But privately at any rate, he saw First Amendment cases in much the same terms. He could expound on the values of self-expression and the marketplace of ideas as eloquently as the next person, but what the cases really involved for him were efforts on the part of the in's to make sure the out's stayed out. The racial discrimination and other equal protection cases were this too, if less obviously: the institution of representation, the Chief realized, will work only if the representative is made to understand that he cannot hurt the relatively powerless without at the same time hurting himself, or at least broad segments of the constituency on whose support he depends.

The Chief used to say that if *Reynolds v. Sims* had been decided before 1954, *Brown v. Board of Education* would have been unnecessary. The claim seems somewhat oversimplified, but it bespeaks a view of the judicial role that tells us much about the man and gives unity to much of his work. The Court's proper work, he was telling us, consisted not so much in second-guessing legislative value judgments as in tending the machinery of the democratic process to keep it from being captured, from becoming the self-serving organ of some privileged segment of society. A concern with process, seriously pursued, can lead in some quite "activist" directions.

The items that kept the Chief's death from being headline news remind us (as if we needed reminding) that those who love the Constitution have had much to mourn of late. But while we should weep for the absence in public life of men like Earl Warren, we need not weep for him. He lived the American Dream. Quite a number of men have done that, however. The Chief did something that few will ever do: he did what he set out to do. And that was to make the American Dream more broadly accessible than it had ever been before.

Like most tributes, this one is about the tributor as well as the tributee, summarizing not only what I take to have been the Chief's underlying concerns but also the then-emerging themes of my own work. The core of my theory was presented in my 1980 book *Democracy and Distrust: A Theory of Judicial Review* (Harvard University Press). It is developed more fully, and applied to numerous new issues, in the instant volume. I certainly don't want to dissuade you from reading (or, more importantly, buying) *Democracy and Distrust*, but its principal theses are summarized in the two excerpts that follow, the first comprising two paragraphs from a footnote to an article I wrote for a symposium on that book published in 1991,[2] the second a lecture I gave at Lehigh University in 1982.

Excerpt from *Another Such Victory: Constitutional Theory and Practice in a World Where Courts Are No Different from Legislatures* (1991)[3]

Approached philosophically—I have previously approached it more through an analysis of the Constitution—my general theory is that a group of equals in the "original position" attempting to frame a government would start from the presumption that no sane adult's values are to count for more or less than any other's, which would lead rapidly to the conclusion that public issues generally should be settled by a majority vote of such persons or their representatives—with two, perhaps three, exceptions: (1) where a majority of such persons votes to exclude other such persons from the process or otherwise to dilute their influence on it; (2) where such a majority enacts one regulatory regime for itself and another, less favorable one, for one or another minority; or (3) where other side constraints seem sufficiently important (and vulnerable to majority sentiment) that the framers decide by supermajority vote to designate them in a constitutional document and thereby render them immune to displacement by anything short of a similar supermajority vote in the future. The third exception seems to me more problematic than the first two for a liberal theorist. In the context of the American Constitution, however, that is an observation that is somewhat beside the point, as all three exceptions plainly characterize that document to a degree.

It seems to me to follow further that precisely because of their tenure, courts are the appropriate guardians of at least exceptions (1) and (2):

> Obviously our elected representatives are the last persons we should trust with identification of either of these situations. Appointed judges, however, are comparative outsiders in our governmental system, and need worry about continu-

ance in office only very obliquely. This does not give them some special pipeline to the genuine values of the American people: in fact it goes far to ensure that they won't have one. It does, however, put them in a position objectively to assess claims—though no one could suppose the evaluation won't be full of judgment calls—that either by clogging the channels of change or by acting as accessories to majority tyranny, our elected representatives in fact are not representing the interests of those whom the system presupposes they are.[4]

That judges are to be the principal enforcers of the collection of provisions that make up exception (3) is entirely settled by history, and I have no quarrel with it: indeed the supposition that no right is to be thus designated unless it is unusually vulnerable to majority sentiment makes judicial enforcement appropriate. What does not follow from anything said above, or in my opinion from anything sensible said ever, is that judges are also to be given a license to create or "discover" further rights, not justified by exceptions (1) or (2) nor ever constitutionalized by a supermajority, and protect them as if they had been.

Democracy and Judicial Review (1982)[5]

Two years ago I published a book called *Democracy and Distrust*. I know a number of you have read it (because you told me you did) but I want to take a few moments to sketch its outlines for the others. It is not the subject of this evening's talk, but a brief description should help set the stage. I argue in the book that whereas many, in fact most, of the provisions of the Constitution are reasonably specific—not in the sense that they mechanically generate answers, but rather in the sense that one at least knows by reading them what their general subject matter is—there are a few that are inescapably open-ended. That is, the document contains clauses whose content cannot be discerned from either their language or their legislative history. For example, the Fourteenth Amendment provides that "no state shall make or enforce any law which shall abridge the privileges or immunities of citizens of the United States," and the Ninth Amendment (this one is applicable against the federal government) provides that "[t]he enumeration in the Constitution, of certain rights, shall not be construed to deny or disparage others retained by the people."

Most of the book is about how the courts should give content to these Delphic provisions. The answer I give is not the prevailing one, that appointed judges should overrule elected officials essentially on the ground that what they did is wrong or even outrageous or, what is the same thing, that they should overrule elected officials on the ground that those officials have violated some right, not mentioned elsewhere in the Constitution, that the judge thinks is precious. For some years this has been the dominant academic view of what judicial review should comprise, and we know that at various times (apparently including the present) it has also been the view entertained by a majority of the members of the Supreme Court. One notable judicial episode occurred early in this century when something called "liberty of contract" (which translated into the right not to pay your employees the minimum wage or to work them more than the maximum hours) was vigorously protected by the Supreme Court, even though it is nowhere mentioned in the constitutional document. The Burger Court has created a modern counterpart of liberty of contract by constitutionally enshrining the right to have an abortion, although, of course, that right too is nowhere suggested in the document. (I might add parenthetically—if only because the dominant view is one that blurs the distinction—that I agree that the political branches should grant women the right to have an abortion. Indeed, I suppose it is not even clear that minimum wage laws do a great deal of good—it is at least asserted that they actually have the effect of keeping some people from being employed at all—but that judgment too, in my opinion, is properly left to elected officials.)

What, then, *should* the courts protect constitutionally? To begin with, they should protect those rights that are designated with some specificity in the constitutional document as entitled to protection. That much may seem easy. The harder question is what should be protected under open-ended provisions of the sort I mentioned. To that question the book suggests two answers. The first is that the courts should protect rights of political access: the right to vote, to have one's vote counted equally, to run for office, to organize politically, to speak, and so forth. That cannot be the whole story, however. I go on to argue in the book that the duty of our representatives to represent all their constituents also implies certain equality rights, or rights of various minorities not to be treated by a set of rules different from that which the majority has prescribed for itself.

Platonic Guardians

The system I have sketched can be seen as self-policing: if we all have a right to significant political input, and if at the same time a majority cannot treat various minorities worse than it treats itself, it will follow that none among us will be treated very badly. (If I have to do to myself what I am prepared to do to you, I am not likely to treat you outrageously.) I was informed that the one hundredth review of my book was published just last week. (Now if we could just get the sales figure up as high as the review figure, we might have something.) Its title caught my eye. It was a review by Professor Samuel Estreicher in the *New York University Law Review*, and it was entitled "Platonic Guardians of Democracy."[6] It was not an especially friendly review, but I do think the title captures my general idea rather well. Whereas Plato's platonic guardians (the real platonic guardians) actually were to take substantive control of the government decision making process, my "guardians" (as Estreicher's title suggests), while they do indeed sit largely apart from and immune to the political process, sit primarily to safeguard democracy, to make sure that political incumbents do not manipulate things so as to deny others an effective right to participate in either the democratic process or its outcomes.

Obviously the book's discussion proceeds at some length; let me close my summary by listing the three general arguments I make for this "participation-oriented" form of judicial review. The first is that the sorts of rights I have designated—access rights and equality rights—are those with whose protection we should least trust elected officials. Such officials have every incentive to bar the access of various insurgent and dissident groups to the process (for the obvious reason that such access is likely to turn said officials out of office). And they have a similar incentive to cooperate with some dominant majority of their constituency (enough to return them to office) so as to tyrannize, or at least to discriminate against, certain minorities whose continued support they do not need. To be contrasted in this regard is judicial protection of "society's fundamental values," the favored recipe of academic theorists. For if it is truly "the values of the people" that the theorists want enforced, elected officials have strong incentives to define them correctly (and thereby to insure their return to office), and thus the intervention of the judiciary cannot be justified.

The second argument involves a rather lengthy review of the constitutional document and is one, you will be relieved to learn, I do not intend to repeat here. Its overall claim, however, is that the general concerns of the Constitution (to the extent it is not concerned simply with housekeeping details) are with just the sort of rights I have mentioned, rights of access and rights of equality. I might add that this claim is particularly strong with respect to the amendments that have been ratified since the Civil War, most of which have been concerned precisely with increasing the access to the process of groups that had previously been denied it. (Lest you be tempted to dismiss that as not "our real Constitution," I would note that the period since the Civil War constitutes more than half of our national history.)

Finally, I argue, again distinguishing my position from the dominant academic theory, that my representation-reinforcing approach on judicial review is more consistent with the underlying democratic theory of our institutions. It is, I suggest, entirely incompatible with democracy for courts to define their mission as one of correcting elected officials who have strayed too far either from what the judges think is right or from what they claim they know (and the legislators do not) that "the people" really think is right. The theory I propose, on the other hand, is one that is geared to making democracy work by insuring the access of all groups to the process and insuring, further, that the dominant majority coalition will not prescribe one set of rules for itself and another, less favorable set for groups that are not part of that coalition.

Why Are We a Democracy?

I mentioned that there had been a number of reviews of my book, a gratifyingly large number in fact. And most of them have been quite flattering. Unsurprisingly, however, the flattery generally is followed by a healthy dose of criticism. One recurrent theme of the criticism is that the last argument I mentioned, the argument from democracy, is ipse dixit. Why can one not, the critics ask, just as well announce that the preservation of certain rights that judges or philosophers think are important flows from the true meaning and rationale of "democracy"? What right, they ask, has Ely to announce that the form of review he favors is any more consistent with democracy? Isn't this simple question-begging? It's that question I've been pondering of late and concerning which I want to share my at least tentative thoughts. In particular, I want to spend some time this evening asking why we're a democracy—that is, what are the various rationales, or at least the various plausible rationales, for democracy—and what each of these various rationales seems to imply for the appropriate role of judicial review.

An account of democracy that one finds in Rousseau, and in a number of contemporary theorists as well, is that it is a system of government that enhances the autonomy of the citizen and thus puts her in a position where she can behave morally.[7] (The notion here is that a robot or a slave can be judged neither moral nor immoral—that is, she simply is not a moral being—because her actions are controlled by another: only by being granted autonomy or control over a range of significant decisions is one placed in a position where she has the option of behaving morally.) Democracy, the argument continues, increases the range of significant decisions for which the citizen has responsibility and thus increases her opportunities to behave in a moral manner. To the extent this rationale is valid, it should lead to a form of judicial review that increases the opportunities of the citizenry to participate in politics and political decisions and, having done that, leaves the product of their decisions alone. (If there is a judicial veto over the substance of the citizenry's choice, that obviously will decrease the autonomy of the citizenry.) This first account of democracy is thus not simply in the position of not generating judicial authority to overrule the democratic process on grounds of substantive disagreement: it is incompatible with such authority.

The second rationale for democracy to which one commonly hears reference is that it is an unusually stable form of government, that if change can come peacefully through the system, there is a lessened chance of violent revolution. This account too seems quite clearly to generate a form of judicial review that facilitates popular decision (including the equal representation of all citizens) and seems incompatible with any judicial or other elite veto with authority to thwart such decision.

The third sort of account of democracy would take the following general form: "democracy is a system of government that is likely to generate laws of type x, and laws of type x are good." Finally we have an account that would generate a mode of judicial review different from that recommended in my book. For it would seem to follow from the account just given that the courts too should pursue goal x and correct the product of the legislature when it has failed to pursue that goal or has done so with less efficiency than the courts think appropriate. To flesh the concept out even that far, however, is to begin to indicate the reasons why we do not often hear any such rationale for democracy. For if the idea is to produce policy decisions of a certain type, one is not likely to select democracy as the preferred governmental system. Much more efficient would be some sort of dictatorship or oligarchy which could quite straightforwardly and efficiently pursue the goal in question. Democracy is a form of government ill-suited to the efficient generation of laws of a certain type; people differ and thus the products of democracies differ as well.

It is precisely for such reasons that we hear a great deal more of a quite distinct, indeed opposite, rationale for democracy—that everyone should have a say in how we are governed because no one can be sure that she knows what's right (and even if she thinks she does, she has no right to impose her notion of what's right on others who think differently). This attitude was perhaps put most succinctly by the distinguished political scientist E. E. Schattschneider: "Democracy is a political system for people who are not sure that they are right."[8] Thus in a recent article in *Political Theory*, Michael Walzer argued for a theory of judicial review that was gratifyingly similar to that which I had proposed.[9] (It's true he credited it to Richard Ely, but at least that keeps it in the family. It might, after all, have been credited to Ron Ely, television's first Tarzan, who unfortunately is not a relative.[10]) The reason the adoption of such a theory of judicial review by Walzer merits special mention is that he has for some years been an explicit and forceful spokesman for a socialist perspective. Walzer is a person who does have an answer, an admirably well-articulated one at that, to our various public policy choices. And yet, to his credit, he feels—despite this confidence—that he has no right to impose that preference on the rest of us through the judgments of politically unaccountable judges.

This fourth account of democracy can thus be stated under at least a couple of rubrics which, though different, in this context come to much the same thing. One is the rubric of equality, the idea being that although it is obvious that we are not all equal in all respects, we are equal as regards our right to decide what is the right policy for our government to pursue.[11] The other is utilitarianism, the theory that defines as moral that course of action that conduces to the greatest good or greatest happiness of the greatest number of people.

"Utilitarianism" has become of late something of a dirty word,[12] but it certainly bears noting that it is a moral philosophy that proceeds from the same underlying impulses as democracy, namely, a skepticism that any among us has the "right answer" to questions of public policy and the tenet that the opinion of everyone on such questions is entitled to equal consideration. And indeed democracy can be viewed as a form of "applied utilitarianism."[13] It is possible, I suppose, to imagine our appointing someone to make an estimate of what will make most of us most happy, but that would be a roundabout and obviously disingenuous way of pursuing utilitarianism. The more efficient (and candid) way of making that estimate is to give everyone a vote. There are many subjects on which I am prepared to yield to the expertise of others, but the subject of what makes me happy is not among them.

Utilitarian Calculus and Democratic Process

I just noted, and of course you knew it already, that utilitarianism has been subjected to a good deal of recent criticism. What I want to do next is briefly look at the various objections that have been made to utilitarianism and ask how many of them remain applicable when that philosophy is translated into a democratic political system. We will find that some of the standard objections are simply inapplicable when we are talking about democratic public policy decisions as opposed to individual moral decisions, and that others among them actually operate to *strengthen* the argument for democracy. We will also find, I think, that one of the most often cited objections to utilitarianism—that it is indifferent to considerations of distributional equality—while it is an objection that can fairly be leveled at some theories, including some theories of democracy, is not one that can legitimately be directed, or at least so I will argue, at the utilitarian account.

There exist a number of familiar objections to utilitarianism as a guide to personal morality—among others, that it occasionally counsels lying or breaking promises, and that it ignores the distinction between positive and negative responsibility. (What is meant by this last objection, for example, is that utilitarianism would counsel a person to shoot one innocent person in order to keep another from shooting ten innocent persons, an outcome the critics think unacceptable.[14]) My own view, though this is not the subject of tonight's talk, is that such objections are invalid—that a sensible utilitarian would lie or break a promise only very rarely indeed (the maintenance of such conventions is not only entirely justified, but required, on utilitarian grounds) but that she should on rare occasions be prepared to do so. (For example, one should lie to keep a deranged killer from finding an innocent child he is intent on slaughtering. I expect this is how most of us would in fact behave, and I cannot for the life of me see how it is immoral.) As for shooting one person to save ten, I would note first that it is not a problem that is likely often to arise. (I am older than most people in this room, and I can assure you that it has arisen for me only rarely.) And should a real-world situation arise, we probably would conclude, correctly, that there was serious doubt that ten people would in fact be shot if we did not shoot the one. But given the unrealistic laboratory conditions necessary to set up the dilemma, my view would be that the moral course of action would be to shoot the one person to save the ten, and that my admitted likely refusal to do so testifies more to my squeamishness and powers of rationalization than to any reasoned moral conclusion. Having already commented too long on something that is not really to the present point, I should get to the point that is to the point, namely that such considerations, although they bear in interesting ways on personal moral codes, have little or nothing to do with this evening's question, which is how governmental policy decisions should be made.

I react much the same way to two objections that have been stated by various people, recently and forcefully by Charles Fried: first, that utilitarianism is "suffocatingly universal" in that it makes every decision on how to act a moral decision and second, that in enjoining us to treat the happiness of others as equal in moral terms to our own happiness, utilitarianism thwarts human nature and thus is an "unreasonable" morality.[15] He's right to a point: there is no doubt that each of us often places our own happiness somewhat above the happiness of other human beings. That does not mean, however, that we are behaving in a morally admirable way when we do so, and I do not believe we are. And while I certainly agree that people generally lack the stamina to treat every decision as a moral decision—at least not without the help of various "rules of thumb"—it seems to me that every decision that affects the happiness of other people *is* a moral decision, and at least when the effects are serious and the computation is doable, we should behave on precisely that assumption. Again, however, I've strayed from the relevant point, one with which I'm sure Charles would agree, that every governmental choice is a choice with moral implications.[16] (I also assume that no one would argue that it is morally right, though unfortunately it is common, for those who govern to favor their own welfare above that of the rest of us.)

Other common objections to utilitarianism are not simply irrelevant, they strengthen the argument for a democratic system. The first objection I would cite is one made by Marshall Cohen, that utilitarianism would justify the suppression of political rights, such as voting and free speech.[17] If, however, the way we do our utilitarian calculus (and it is certainly the most sensible way) is by a democratic political process, it follows inexorably that such rights must be preserved. To be taken more seriously is a threshold issue in utilitarianism, namely the question of what it is that should be maximized. Is it happiness? Pleasure? Lack of pain? What do we say to the person who says that the commodity to be maximized is wisdom, or physical prowess?[18] These are hard questions, but democracy provides us with an institutional way out by letting each individual decide for herself what the commodity to be maximized should be. That objection leads straight to another commonly made to utilitarianism, however, that there is no workable way of measuring various individuals' intensities of feeling or degrees of happiness.[19] When utilitarianism is translated into democracy, the objection becomes that the vote does not reflect such intensities.[20] It can tell us how many prefer ballet to basketball, and vice versa, but not by how much.

That, however, is true only on certain assumptions: that there is only one issue before the voters, that everyone is obligated to vote on it, and that the vote is taken immediately after the question is announced (leaving no time for preelection politicking). Those assumptions are patently untrue. We are not required to vote, and if one does not care about the issues on the ballot, one need not—indeed I am tempted to commit the heresy of saying one should not—vote. If one cares, one should vote. If one cares more intensely, she should urge others to vote as she does, acquire the information necessary to become a source to whom others will turn to find out how they should vote, and so forth—in short, one should politick. Moreover, things are rarely decided by one-issue referenda. Instead we vote for *packages* of views and attitudes—packages we call candidates. Of course candidates tell us (sometimes) how they stand on the various issues, but more often than not we will be confronted with a choice among candidates who all hold some positions with which we disagree. How, then, do we choose? In large measure by placing greatest stress on those issues about which we care most, that is by taking into account our various intensities of preference. Beyond that, at the stage at which laws are actually made in our legislatures, our representatives allocate their persuasive energies, even trade votes, in accord with the intensity with which they (and their estimate of the intensity with which we) care about the various issues. The reflection of intensity is certainly far from perfect, money being the most obvious distorting element (which, parenthetically, is why the decisions in *Buckley v. Valeo*[21] and its progeny seem questionable to me), but nonetheless our democratic system is one that is in various ways programmed, at least roughly, to register intensities of preference.

Equality and Democracy

At least in a representative democracy—which is all we're realistically going to encounter nowadays—equality poses serious theoretical and practical problems.[22] Of course it is often inevitable that numerical minorities must bear some special burden, and I am not talking about a situation where everyone's happiness has been taken into account, but it has been decided that the greater good requires some regrettable but unavoidable sacrifice from some minority. I mean to pose instead a situation where a controlling majority of our representatives have weighed some sacrifice by a minority as a good or, if not that, have treated it as a matter of indifference. One answer, which seems to have been given by James Madison as well as certain modern pluralist theorists, is that that won't happen, given our system of shifting political alliances and, in particular, the realization on the part of the various subgroups that make up the majority on a given issue that they will in future battles need the help and friendship of some or all of those who make up the present minority. This is often an accurate description of the process, but we know perfectly well that there are exceptions, as is tragically evidenced by the role that racial prejudice has played throughout our history, politically dividing groups that have much in common (such as poor blacks and poor whites) and uniting groups that actually lack substantial common interest (for instance, poor whites and more affluent whites).[23]

This sort of possibility is an objection to a "pure" representative democracy—some safeguard does indeed seem necessary—but I do not think it is a valid objection to utilitarianism. I have in mind here particularly John Stuart Mill's famous dictum that "each is to count for one, and none for more than one." (One also finds this thought in Bentham and Sidgwick.)[24] Nor is that an accidental or a nonessential appendage to utilitarian theory: remember that the critical impulse underlying utilitarianism is that no one is to be counted as superior to anyone else. Interestingly, therefore, a "utilitarian" theory of democracy will yield a brand of judicial review that is richer on the subject of equality than would be yielded by a theory of democracy that is geared to equality simpliciter. A pure "equality" account might be satisfied by giving everyone one vote. If, however, one is serious about Mill's dictum, a stronger form of review would seem to follow. Of course we cannot expect judges to figure out whether our representatives have really considered everyone's interests equally—indeed, it would be overly intrusive if they tried—but we can, I think, identify the extreme cases of malfeasance, cases where the welfare of some people has been valued negatively (what in the book I call first degree prejudice) and cases where the welfare of some minority has been valued at zero or wholly ignored. (This would include the case of the overdrawn stereotype whose incidence of counterexample is significantly higher than the political decision makers thought it was—as in "There's no point in letting women be police officers since none of them are big or strong enough").

"Hiding the Car Keys"

The final objection one is likely to encounter to "utilitarian democracy" is that it is indifferent to rights. Note that I am not now talking about political or other rights that are prerequisite to participation in the political process: those must be protected on a theory of utilitarian democracy. Nor are we talking about guaranteeing to politically disadvantaged minorities the same rights that the people in power have seen fit to grant themselves: those too will be substantially protected, by the "each to count as one" aspect of utilitarian democracy. Instead this last objection must focus on those nonpolitical rights that the majority has denied to everybody, including themselves.

Some nonpolitical rights undoubtedly should be protected. They should, as an initial matter, be protected by the political process (and if, in fact, there is a consensus to support such a right, they *will* be protected by the political process). But I agree that that probably won't be enough. We should have some method for protecting ourselves and our progeny, majorities and minorities alike, against the hasty or ill-considered acts of future legislatures. There must be some way of "hiding the car keys" to protect us from ourselves in future times of anticipated drunkenness. In fact our system does provide a method of hiding the car keys, when there really does exist a calm consensus (as opposed to the mere preference of some elite) in favor of the right in question, and that is to enact it into the constitutional document. Nothing I have said would suggest (and indeed most of my career has been devoted to the contrary proposition) that there is anything at all improper in vigorous judicial protection of those various rights that are marked for shelter in the constitutional document.

Thus we must add a third qualification. The objection must posit the protection of rights that (a) are not to be found in the Constitution, (b) are not prerequisite to political participation, and (c) are not among those that the controlling majority has assured to itself. That kind of judicial review not only does not follow from any of the theories of democracy we have

canvassed but indeed is incompatible with them. We are a democracy precisely because we do not as a society believe that any of us has a greater
right than any other of us to dictate what is ultimately important, that no
elite's definition of what is right and good is entitled to any special deference. Thus I say to courts: Enforce those rights that have inspired sufficient
popular consensus to secure a place in the document. Enforce those rights
that are needed to let us all freely and equally register our preferences.
Enforce for minorities those rights that the majority has seen fit to guarantee for itself. Enforce all those rights with all the vigor you can muster. But
beyond that, you simply have no right in a democracy—no more than philosophers or law professors or anyone else has—to tell the rest of us that we
have made a mistake and that you know better.

*I suppose it is partly because of this discussion[25]—partly also, of course,
because today's dominant biases thus make it an easier target—that my
theory of judicial review is often described as if it were necessarily rooted
in a utilitarian political philosophy, or in its second cousin, a "pluralist"
model that describes the political process as a sort of marketplace in which
various groups engineer trades designed to protect their own interests. In
fact I do try to behave substantially in accord with utilitarian principles. (I
am, for example, a vegetarian because I believe the unrelentingly miserable
lives ordinarily inflicted on animals in raising them for slaughter cannot
remotely be justified by the pleasure you and I take from eating them.*) I
thus can corroborate Charles Fried in one respect: treating every decision
as a moral decision is hard work, so hard in fact that I know I sometimes cut
corners.*

*And so too I suppose my political philosophy can be described as sub-
stantially utilitarian, albeit with serious "corrections," principally for
equality. Of course one should always be wary of someone who says he
believes both x and y but the two aren't connected, but at the same time
we'd expect his critic to demonstrate that they are. And think as I may (and
I've thought about this a lot), I don't understand any respect in which my
approach to judicial review—at least any of the limitations I would place
on judicial review, and it is they that are attacked under the "indictment"
that I am a utilitarian—is inextricably tied to utilitarianism. That of course
is one of the things the foregoing piece is about, and in it I believe I have
demonstrated that no plausible account of democracy supports a stronger
theory of judicial review. I suppose I don't blame the critics for ignoring it,*

---

* A special circle in hell should be reserved for those who say they can see my point but
"*really* like meat," the implication apparently being that were my capacity for enjoyment the
equal of theirs I'd join them on the selfishness train. I actually love the taste of cows, pigs, and
lambs; I just can't understand how on any civilized moral philosophy that can justify the
infliction of lifelong torture on the critters I end up eating.

as (in my capacity as Dean) I saw fit to publish it in an alumni magazine; maybe putting it here will help.

As regards pluralism, my reaction is stronger still, in that I have never regarded pluralism as anything approaching an adequately complete description of the way groups interact in the United States (or for that matter anywhere else). Thus I not only have at no point connected my theory of judicial review to pluralism even to the degree that the foregoing piece connected it to utilitarianism (i.e., as compatible) but indeed have from the beginning conceived and characterized my theory as a reaction to the ways in which pluralism *fails* to protect minorities. In *Democracy and Distrust* I wrote:

> Not long ago the assurances of pluralist political theory, that any group whose members were not denied the franchise could protect itself by entering into the give and take of the political marketplace, dominated academic political science. Recently, however, pluralism has come under powerful attack, as more stress has been placed on the undeniable concentrations of power, and inequalities among the various competing groups, in American politics. Of course the pluralist model does work sometimes, and minorities can protect themselves by striking deals and stressing the ties that bind the interests of other groups to their own. But sometimes it doesn't, as the single example of how our society has treated its black minority (even after that minority had gained every official attribute of access to the process) is more than sufficient to prove. (p. 135; footnotes omitted)

See also Ely, "Another Such Victory: Constitutional Theory and Practice in a World Where Courts Are No Different from Legislatures," 77 Virginia Law Review 833, 840 n. 15 (1991):

> The theory of judicial review articulated in *Democracy and Distrust* was intended to be as compatible with "republican" legislative and community behavior as with a "pluralist" model. See, e.g., id. at 80–82, 135. Indeed, by constitutionally condemning the infliction of "inequality for its own sake—[treating] a group worse not in the service of some overriding social goal but largely for the sake of simply disadvantaging its members," id. at 153—it counseled a significant judicial push away from bare-knuckled pluralism in the direction of "public values." Thus my point here is only that anything resembling a full-scale attempt to impose a "republican" political mentality seems badly out of place under contemporary conditions, and also would be unwarranted as a matter of constitutional interpretation, as no coherent account of the document supports it. This is hardly surprising, as the "republican" and "pluralist" models contended at the time of the framing, and if one had to pick a "winner," it would have to be the latter (personified perhaps most fully by James Madison), while the former is conventionally identified with the antifederalists, whose attempt to defeat ratifi-

*cation failed. This certainly doesn't mean republicanism is a forbidden model—
the document defeats that claim as well—only that it cannot properly be imposed
as constitutional law.*

On Protecting Fundamental Interests and Powerless Minorities under the United States and Canadian Constitutions (1986).[26]

Je ne suis pas preparé à presenter mon discours en Francais—it will be sufficiently incomprehensible if I do it in English.

"Protecting fundamental interests and powerless minorities," the assigned topic. Those are two very different tasks, and my punch line, succinctly put, is that the protection of minorities, specifically under Section
15.1 of the Charter, is a job the judiciary can do in a principled manner, but
that the former task, protecting fundamental interests or fundamental justice under Section 7, at least if you give it a substantive reading, is one you
can't do in a principled way. Consequently, you should consider strategies
for escaping the apparent instruction of the latter provision.

Section 15.1, as you all know better than I, provides that every individual is equal before and under the law and has the right to equal protection
and equal benefit of the law without discrimination—in particular, without
discrimination based on race, national or ethnic origin, color, religion, sex,
age, or mental or physical disability.

It seems pretty clear that any sensible system has to incorporate two tiers
of review for equality. If you try for more than two it gets overly manipu-
lable, dissolving into a situation where the decision makers can do whatever they want. But you do need two. One must be a weak or "rationality"
test, lest all legislation be unconstitutional because, of course, all legislation treats some people better than it treats others. On the other hand, some
laws must be subject to a more intensive review than this because virtually
all laws, in fact I would say—as I know Judge [Hans] Linde [another
speaker] would say—all laws that are actually enacted are *rational*, though
some of them are impermissible: that is, they pursue rational but impermissible goals. It is rational to want to incarcerate your political enemies, but
that doesn't mean that it is something that is allowed under the Constitution. Thus for some laws there must be a demand more intensive than one
for mere rationality.

What does "more intensive review" mean? Colloquially (at least in
American terms) it means you "nickel and dime" the law, you nit-pick it.
That can be done to any law—"Gee, if that were really the goal, then, why
would this provision be here? And that over there could have been done
more precisely"—a first-year student is capable of worrying a law to death

in such ways. I suppose more specifically what strict scrutiny should mean is that legislation by stereotype or surrogate, using certain characteristics as shorthand for other characteristics, is ordinarily not to be permitted. If it is possible to do so, there must be a more individualized hearing to make sure that the person being disqualified is individually incapable of performing the task in question.

The hard question is how to decide which classifications go into which category. *Democracy and Distrust*, my book, which Justice Seaton was kind enough to mention, sets forth a theory sometimes referred to as a "we-they" theory, meaning that the classifications of which courts should be suspicious are those classifications that favor groups that are dominant in the legislature, which is to say classifications that favor whites, that favor males, that favor (at least in this country) Protestants, that favor heterosexuals—in other words, classifications that favors those possessing any characteristic that is shared by most members of the legislature. Such a classification is one of which I believe we should be suspicious, for the simple psychological reason that we are all attracted by generalizations that flatter ourselves. We are considerably more likely, perhaps unconsciously, to accept generalizations that reassure us that the groups to which we belong are superior.

Admittedly that can get tricky, and to your credit you seem to have avoided the problem in Canada. Section 15.1 appears on its face—although this can be disputed, I know it has by Professor Hogg—to list for you the classifications that are to be treated as suspect, those that are to get special scrutiny—namely, race, national or ethnic origin, color, religion, sex, age, and mental or physical disability. This is pretty much the same list that would be generated by the kind of test that I was talking about, especially when you factor in Section 2, which permits affirmative action, or *favoring* those groups (even racial groups and so forth) that are not dominant in the legislature.

Section 7 is the one that scares me, where it says that everyone has the right to life, liberty, and security of the person and the right not to be deprived thereof except in accordance with the principles of fundamental justice. There certainly will be, I know there already has been, a temptation to give "principles of fundamental justice" a substantive content, that is, to require not simply that certain procedures be observed but that *substantive* "principles of fundamental justice" be complied with.

The temptation is understandable. We all have political preferences and are understandably inclined to think of those we hold strongly as "principles of fundamental justice." What else would they be? Thus the temptation for you as judges and justices to impose them even in the teeth of a contrary legislative judgment must be very strong indeed. It could hardly be otherwise.

The history of what has happened in this country bears out the strength of this temptation. Our "comparable" clause actually isn't all that comparable on its face. It says that nobody can be "deprived of life, liberty or property without due process of law." Due *process* of law—a procedural injunction if ever I heard one, and yet it has not been limited to that construction. Yours thus seems an a fortiori case. If our clause has been given a substantive interpretation, yours *surely* will be, given that yours on its face is at least responsibly susceptible to a substantive reading.

My view, defended at length in chapter 3 of *Democracy and Distrust*, is that identifying substantive "principles of fundamental justice" is, if not an impossible task, at the very least one respecting which courts should not overrule popularly elected legislatures.

How might one attempt such definition? There are several possible formulas. One, of course, is that you could simply impose your own political choices. That is a possibility, but one I don't think anyone in this room would overtly choose. One very practical reason for not doing so is that once you start down that road, there is no guarantee that you are going to win. The other party or bloc or whatever may get the chance to appoint more judges than yours, and you may lose. What's happening respecting the issue of abortion seems to me to demonstrate this. Our Supreme Court, under a Constitution that says nothing even remotely about abortion, has held that abortion is a strenuously protected constitutional right; the West German Constitutional Court, as you are undoubtedly aware, under a strikingly similar provision, has held precisely the opposite—that it is constitutionally mandatory that there be laws seriously *restricting* abortion. Each court ignores what seems to me the correct solution, that the question ought to be left to the legislatures. Thus in this country now, *Roe v. Wade* is under attack largely not by people who want to go back to the status quo ante and say that the legislature should be able to decide the issue. Rather, the constitutional push is to say the Constitution must be written or read to say that states cannot *allow* abortions. Once you start playing the fundamental values game, you may lose, big-time.

More fundamentally, your judiciary, like at least our federal judiciary, is appointed essentially with tenure, except for personal misbehavior. It seems to me simply inconsistent with the theory of either of our governments that judges appointed on those terms should have authority to impose their own political values on those of elected officials.

Section 33 of your Charter, permitting legislative overrides—which I notice Chief Justice Dickson did not yesterday put on the list of provisions that are different from the American Bill of Rights—may mitigate the situation a little. At least I can understand that provision's becoming the predicate for an argument that it is all right for judges to impose their own political views, because after all they can be overruled by the elected branches.

That route seems ultimately fraught with peril, however, the danger being that there will develop a spiral of exchanged insults between the legislature and the courts. One can easily imagine a court holding that a legislative override of its judgment was done in the wrong form, or was too general or something like that, and throwing it back at the legislature; and one can in turn imagine the legislature's responding, "Oh yeah, well, smoke this," and trying it again in a different form. Et cetera and at least partially ad infinitum. At least it's a danger. Thus I'm pleased to be unaware of anyone's using Section 33 as the predicate for an argument that courts should (at least overtly) employ their own values to overrule the legislature.

Thus courts everywhere proceed in other terms, although I think it often amounts to the same thing. They will say, "No, no, it's not *my* values I'm imposing; it's values I have (objectively) discovered somewhere outside myself, in history or, perhaps, in the true hearts and minds of my fellow countrymen." My admittedly fun-killing suggestion is that such values aren't really "out there" to be found, at least not by judges. A far more reliable (though certainly not perfect) test of what "the people" really think is to be found in the words of the legislation that is before you, not in any supposition on your part that you are better at figuring out popular morality than elected officials are.

In order to stay within the half-hour, I won't talk long about natural law, although that source is certainly suggested by the provision's reference to "natural justice." I expect most people, albeit not all, would say that natural law is a philosophically obsolete notion. Indeed, it is hard even to imagine what it might *mean* unless you adopt a rather specific religious metaphysic. I can understand the view that God has made a list of the precepts of natural law, and here they are on stone tablets or in a particular scripture. That is a coherent notion. Once you move away from that, as most would, it is hard to know what you could mean by natural law, unless it be those principles that most everybody in the world would agree on if they sat down and talked it out—a sort of consensus notion, which I will talk about in a moment. In this country at least, natural law has been invoked (when it has been invoked at all) in support of all manner of causes, some noble, others nefarious. It was, for example, conspicuously invoked on both sides of the slavery issue, as it is today regarding abortion.

Tradition, the true traditions of, in our case, the American people, is a reference one sees quite often. There are a number of problems with it. The first is that in this country, as in yours, there are all sorts of traditions. Some of them are the traditions of rascals. Lynching is a tradition; riding people out of town on a rail is a tradition; keeping blacks from voting is a tradition. Well, those don't count, it will be answered. Those are bad traditions. Well, how do you decide which count and which don't? Not simply by asking whether it is a tradition, that much has to be clear. And even if we could agree on which traditions count and which don't, there is always a question of how broadly one articulates a tradition, what kind of scope you give it. Here I want to quote from Professor Laurence Tribe, one of our most distinguished constitutional scholars, arguing that homosexual sex is protected by American tradition. (I can understand lots of arguments that would protect such behavior, but tradition, that's a tough one. But, here goes.)

> It makes all the difference in the world what level of generality one employs to test the pedigree of an asserted liberty claim. Plainly, the history of homosexuality has been largely been a history of disapproval and disgrace. . . . It is crucial in asking whether an alleged right forms part of a traditional liberty, to define the liberty at a high enough level of generality to permit unconventional variants to claim protection along with mainstream versions of the protected conduct.[27]

Thus there is a tradition of sexual freedom in this country. (Even that seems a trifle debatable.) True, it hasn't specifically covered homosexuality. But define it broadly, and lo and behold, tradition protects homosexual acts.

In *Bowers v. Hardwick*, a very recent case holding that such activity is not protected by the Constitution, Justice White, in what seemed to me a somewhat insensitive opinion for the Court—no, actually, it *was* an insensitive opinion, whether right or wrong—pointed out that it had been argued that tradition protected homosexual acts and dismissed the argument as "at best, facetious." Neither side is right. If you construe our traditions narrowly, of course Justice White is right (though we could have done without the allegation of facetiousness); if you give them greater scope, Professor Tribe has an argument. But there isn't any talisman that tells us how broadly to read our traditions.

I have probably lingered on this point too long. As our critical legal studies colleagues would say, the test of tradition is radically indeterminant. You can't tell (a) which traditions count, or (b) how broadly to define them even if you could. Beyond that, there are a couple of other things wrong with tradition as a source for filling in, say, Section 7. Why, for openers, should the values of our grandparents act as a limit on what our democratically elected legislators can do? I just don't understand the argument that makes that follow. Second, the point of provisions like section 7 is obviously to protect dissenting individuals, nonconformists, from the power of the state. However, if you fill in Section 7 by looking at tradition, it would seem, if you play it straight and try to take the traditions as you find them, it is going to end up protecting those people who least need protection, people who live in traditional ways. But it is *un*traditional types who need this type of protection. So, it seems to me a rather illogical source, invoked by liberals largely on the basis of wishful thinking.

The other source that is commonly mentioned is a kind of consensus. "No, we are not looking backward, but instead, to find our fundamental principles of justice, we look out into our society today and discover the true values of the people." In other words our courts are to put themselves forward as better judges of popular morality than the legislatures are. This, you will not be surprised to learn, seems to me equally unacceptable. Courts are good at many things, but one thing they are not constructed to do is measure popular morality. The legislatures are much better designed to do that and are much more likely to get it, well obviously not exactly right, but something closer thereto.

In 1972 a case called *Furman v. Georgia* seriously limited (albeit temporarily) the extent to which the death penalty could be imposed. Justices Brennan and Marshall, concurring, employed essentially this popular morality rationale. Popular morality, they asserted, had evolved to the point where it had rejected capital punishment, and therefore, essentially in the name of the people, it had to be struck down. Well, that was wishful thinking on their part, unfortunately.[28] There was really quite a backlash to this decision, and it appears the people in this country today are quite in favor of capital punishment, and have reenacted it with a vengeance. I think that is a tragedy, but I invoke the example here as instructive of what happens when judges say to legislatures, "Look, you've got it figured wrong; *we* know what the people out there really think; and what they really think is the opposite of what you have done." That is a very risky claim; seldom will it be right. If you are serious about measuring popular morality, elected officials are a much more reliable gauge.

Also, think again of the overall purpose of a provision like Section 7. It is to protect minorities against the value judgments of the majority. Well, it just doesn't make sense to protect minorities against the value judgments of the majority by imposing on the legislature what purport to be the value judgments of the majority. In fact that's zany, suggesting, again, that people who say that's what they are doing, if they thought about it, would realize they weren't really serious.

Judges will often say to me, "Gee, I agree with your criticism of each and every one of those sources, but you haven't laid a glove on me, because I don't rely on any of them—I use a mixture of all of them. I take tradition and throw in a dash of popular morality. . . ." [Laughter] The laughs show you understand. Eclecticism makes the operation even *more* malleable and subjective.

Well, what do you do with Section 7? (I know you're just dying to have an American give you the answer to that.) On its face, it seems to invite an inquiry of the sort I am advising against. There are two obvious strategies for escaping this awesome delegation. One, and this appears in some

Canadian cases, is to give a relatively narrow construction to the terms "liberty" and "security of person"—that is, to restrict the scope of the provision by saying that the class of interests protected by the principles of fundamental justice is not so broad as one might suppose on first reading.

I don't think that's the way you should go. There are at least two problems with it. First, it avoids the problem only sporadically. Sure you have reduced the number of occasions on which you must exercise this frightening authority to define fundamental justice, but you haven't eliminated it altogether. Second—this has happened here, to our Due Process Clause—if you narrow the meaning of "liberty" and "security of the person" you deprive certain interests of even *procedural* due process protections. That is, if something is declared in one case not to be a case of liberty or security of the person, you have then taken it totally out of Section 7, which means, I take it, that it can be denied without procedural due process too (which I trust is a frightening outcome for us all).

The second strategy, and this would be my impulse, would be to give "life, liberty, and security of person" a broad reading, to cover just about any serious deprivation imposed by the government, but to hold "principles of fundamental justice" to be a procedural reference, referring basically to the kind of hearing to which one is entitled before a deprivation is visited upon him. Surely the language of the provision bears that construction.

An American observer might say of this answer, "Look, the Canadians have picked this broad language, inviting substantive construction, and what's more, they did so knowing that in the United States, just to their south, there has been a hundred-year debate on whether due process of law has substantive content, and in fact it has (at least periodically) been held to. If the framers of the Charter of Rights had meant Section 7 to be merely procedural, they would, in light of the United States experience, have been very careful about saying that that was what they meant. Because they didn't narrow it, they must knowingly have been inviting the broader interpretation."

I can't dismiss that as crazy. On the other hand it does seem to represent a United States–centered perspective, assuming the entire world has its eyes fixed on what's going on here and acts in light of it. Now I'm a Yankee Doodle Dandy, but that seems to me overstated. Because I see such a transparent lack of principle to be inevitable in any search for constitutionally unstated fundamental principles of substantive justice, I would give Section 7 a procedural reading only. Unlike the protection of powerless minorities from the self-serving generalizations of legislative majorities, this, the identification of constitutionally unmarked principles of fundamental substantive justice, doesn't seem to be a task that can be performed by the judiciary in a principled manner.

The Rule of Clear Mistake: "A Great and Stately Jurisdiction"? (1993)[29]

Sometimes I am compared to turn-of-the-century constitutional theorist James Bradley Thayer, not simply because we are both often characterized as "moderates," but also because we both were (are) somewhat lonely apostles of limiting judicial review in eras where the Supreme Court was more "conservative" than the political process.[30] The latter has something to it in the sense that I've always been concerned—as I believe any constitutional theorist should be—with giving a general veto over the political process to any unelected group, whether it be to the right or the left of the country (and yes, you've caught me; I am aware that of late the threat has been from a right-leaning Court, and yes, you've caught me again; it does strike me as odd that liberals today seem generally want to increase the Court's authority). But there, I think, any serious similarity ends.

I was told the theory on which I was invited was—no, not that Thayer and I both use our middle names—but rather that we were (are) both "moderate constitutional theorists." Well, maybe, but the differences between us seem plainly to predominate. To the extent Thayer was a moderate (and I'll suggest that may be something of an overstatement), it was because of the limited *force* of his principles (or principle) of judicial review, whereas to the extent that I'm a moderate (equally an overstatement, I think, in the other direction), it's because of the limited *range* of my principles of review. Oldsters among you will remember a similar disagreement, between Justices Frankfurter and Black, though Thayer wasn't Frankfurter and I'm not Black. But one can justly caricature Frankfurterism as a view that everything should be judicially reviewed . . . tepidly. Black, on the other hand, was of the view that only some things should be reviewed, and some things not at all, but those things that do merit review should be reviewed with a vengeance.

I feel a little like the Grinch that stole Christmas, but in preparation for this evening I have reread Professor Thayer's landmark article with great care, and while I'm sure he was a great guy, I have to confess I don't understand why the article continues to elicit such fascination. I say that knowing the enormous respect in which the man is held by people for whom I in turn have enormous respect. Alex Bickel, who along with the rest of the Yale faculty was my teacher of constitutional law, thought Thayer was a great man, and Bickel surely was a great man. Michael Perry, another man worth taking seriously, also tells me Thayer is worth taking seriously. A blurb on the back of *Democracy and Distrust* from Henry

Monaghan says, of my book, that it is "the single most important contribution to the American theory of judicial review written in this century." Well, some of the stuff that Tom Merrill sent us quoted Monaghan to the effect that Thayer's was the most influential essay *ever* written on American constitutional law. So I now know why Henry's praise for me was limited to this century. I never doubted for a minute that it should be, but I now know the reason . . . Thayer. (And here I thought it was *The Federalist*.)

Thus I seem to be one of the few who doesn't get it, but I'll nonetheless forge fearlessly ahead. "The Origin and Scope of the American Doctrine of Constitutional Law" . . . not the American doctrine of judicial review, but the American doctrine of constitutional law. Thus Thayer meant to be talking about *what the Constitution means*, not just about the way judges should behave. It seems to me the article can be read a couple of different ways: I don't think Thayer himself was clear about which he meant. I'll suggest, however, that either reading, played straight, means essentially no judicial review and second, that each is indefensible in principle.

I guess Thayer's definitive formulation of his thesis was that the Court

> can only disregard the Act when those who have the right to make laws have not merely made a mistake but have made a very clear one—so clear that it is not open to rational question.[31]

The first possible meaning of this is that if a rational person could vote for a law, it is constitutional. That, I think, is what Bickel read it to mean and thus, since he was the one who introduced me to Thayer, it's what I've always assumed Thayer meant. But there's another possible reading, namely that if a rational person *could think a law is constitutional*, it is constitutional. In theory, obviously, these are not the same. For example, one could quite rationally favor a law saying members of the House of Representatives should serve three-year terms, but one could not rationally suppose that law to be constitutional.

Now, it may be that Thayer at no point intended the first meaning. I doubt that. He said things that sound very much like it—"Whatever choice is rational is constitutional,"[32] for example—and a number of intelligent people have read him that way. I think, rather, he didn't see the difference between the two formulations. Not that he couldn't, had he focused on it; obviously he could have. But he was writing in an era whose principal emerging threat was Lochnerism, which must have inclined him to want to say that rationality is the test the Constitution imposes. But if rationality is the constitutional test, then the question whether a law is rational and the question whether one can rationally suppose it to be constitutional come very close to converging.

The problem with that, of course, is that it's never been widely held that all provisions of the Constitution require no more than rationality. That doesn't quite have it, though. The two are the same if one can *rationally construe* all provisions of the Constitution to require only rationality, but one can't even do that. My House of Representatives example again suffices. One obviously cannot even rationally imagine the provision setting two-year terms to require only that terms be of some rationally defensible length.

I probably should here be explicit that Thayer did not limit his remarks to "substantive due process" or other doctrines that can plausibly be construed as demanding only rationality. He wrote in all-inclusive terms, and indeed the article specifically mentions ex post facto laws, bills of attainder, double jeopardy[33]—all of which prohibitions can be violated with entire rationality (in the first sense). Given the appropriate malefactors, a rational person could vote for an ex post facto law, a bill of attainder, or to subject certain people to double jeopardy. So I guess I end up thinking that although his two formulations are plainly different, Thayer missed the difference. This is hardly a big deal: we all are susceptible to focusing overmuch on our central concern and thus to overstatement of our reaction.

Meaning one, it seems to me—if a rational person could vote for it, it's constitutional—has little plausibility. As I have almost made a career of noting, irrational laws simply don't get enacted. Legislatures sometimes do things for bad, paranoid, or self-dealing reasons. They don't do things for no reason. Professor Bickel gave the following example of an "irrational" law—I think it's his only one—indeed he gave it precisely to prove the converse of what I am asserting here, namely that the rule of clear mistake does *not* lead to a total abdication of judicial review:

> I take as one fairly recent example a decision of some consequence, *Wyman v. Updegraf*, handed down in 1952. The state of Oklahoma, exercising its power over the public service, set out "to make loyalty a qualification to hold public office or to be employed by the State." In pursuance of this purpose, the state required its employees to swear that in the five years immediately preceding the taking of the oath they had not been members of any group whatever that had been listed by the Attorney General of the United States as a Communist-front or subversive organization.[34]

That's the law Bickel claimed to be irrational and therefore to flunk his version, that is reading one, of Thayer's rule of clear mistake. He explained:

> But obviously, as the Supreme Court pointed out, membership in one of these organizations might have been quite innocent. A man might have joined a proscribed organization without being aware of its true nature . . . . The group itself

might have been innocent at the time of affiliation and have come to have an illegitimate purpose later . . . . Or, conversely, it might have cleansed itself by the time of his affiliation, having previously been dedicated to subversive activity. The required oath did not take account of these discriminations . . . . And so the Court struck down the oath requirement as arbitrary. It was irrational to consider that the end of a loyal public service would be served by dismissing people who had innocently belonged to organizations that might themselves have been totally innocent at the time of membership. That was simply absurd—lunatic if one feels a need for a stronger word . . . .[35]

Now these arguments obviously constitute very good reasons not to pass such a law. They are also very good reasons to strike such a law down as unconstitutional, and it would take me about three-quarters of a second to do so. But to say that it is *irrational* not to admit to public service anybody who has belonged to an organization on the Attorney's General list within the last five years strikes me as, well, lunatic if one feels the need for a strong word.

In addition to its emptiness, I think reading one is wrong in principle. Thayer says that we should attribute to Congress virtue, sense, and competent knowledge.[36] We can grant that . . . at least for the sake of argument. But even doing so, Congress like all of us is subject to conflicts of interest. I grant I am verging dangerously close to talking about my own theory here, but there are certain issues that we shouldn't trust Congress with, most obviously those affecting their own job security. It would be *rational* to weight the votes of college graduates or lawyers—in other words people like us—at several times those of working people. (One reason we know that's rational is that John Stuart Mill, a great hero of many of us, proposed doing exactly that.) It would also be *rational*, in the interest of stability, to limit political speech and organization to a fairly narrow spectrum of opinion, but obviously either move would be unconstitutional and should be voided in very short order.

Thus reading one—if a rational person could vote for the law, it is constitutional—not only isn't going to invalidate anything if you play it straight, it's indefensible in principle. But maybe you think reading one, despite the fact it's fairly common, is a straw man. I'll therefore move on to reading two, which is that if a well-informed and rational person could think a law is constitutional, it's constitutional. As we said earlier, that's different. It still has problems. First, it seems to me the question of what a constitutional provision means is exactly the sort of question on which the Court should *not* defer to others. Perhaps on factual judgments, connections between facts and policy, even the meaning of a specialized statute— but not the meaning of the Constitution. (Also don't forget to whom the deference is here supposed to be given—*any* rational person, even if all other rational persons on earth disagree with her.)

Moreover, like the first reading, the second, played straight, is not likely to lead to any real judicial review. Respecting any constitutional provision, or at least those that have been most often featured in judicial opinions, there are likely to be a *host* of rational interpretations, at least one of which will end up upholding any real law you can cite. In this company I need not belabor this point. Let's just take section 1 of the Fourteenth Amendment, specifically due process and privileges or immunities. I assert that none of the following interpretations is irrational: that they constitute an open-ended warrant to do the right thing (that's not my favorite theory, but we can infer it's not irrational from the fact that it is held by just about everyone *but* me); that they incorporate the Bill of Rights and do nothing else (Justice Black thought that); that they incorporate the Bill of Rights *and* constitute a warrant to do the right thing (essentially the Murphy-Rutledge view); that they do not incorporate the Bill of Rights (Professor Fairman, inter alia); that they constitute fairly determinate references to certain well-understood and broad commands taken from the platforms of the Republican and Free Soil parties (Professors Graham and tenBroeck); or that all they meant was to replicate the 1866 Civil Rights Act (Raoul Berger). Now those obviously can't all be correct—they contradict each other in sixty-three ways—but they are all rational. Not simply because they were advocated by rational people, although that's not bad evidence. But additionally, I have looked at the history here, as I know many of you have as well, and some support for each of these views can be found there.

Some of you may by now be dying to point out that Thayer was quite explicit that he was talking only about acts of Congress, not those of state legislatures. Okay, I've been ignoring that, supposing that today anyone who bought Thayer's doctrine for Congress would buy it for state legislatures as well: remember, for example, Bickel's example was one involving a state legislature. But of course I could just as well give examples of multiple rational interpretations of prohibitions that apply to the states. It is rational to read the Establishment Clause to prohibit only the creation of a (real) established church: "the official religion of the United States shall be X." Indeed it seems likely that's all they meant. It's not irrational to think that Leonard Levy was right in his first book about the meaning of the First Amendment and that it should be limited to that meaning; neither half of that view is irrational. Or that Richard Epstein is right about the meaning of the Takings Clause. In fact, I would argue, actually this must have occurred to everyone in the room, that under this second reading—that laws are constitutional unless they are unconstitutional beyond a reasonable doubt—invalidation should have to be unanimous; it should take a 9–0 vote, on the theory that if one justice of the Supreme Court votes the other way, the provision can be rationally construed not to invalidate the law. Or, I suppose, one federal judge. One magistrate? One bailiff? One Beowulf? (Just checking to see if you're awake.)

Thayer gives an example of a law that cannot rationally be regarded as constitutional, one vesting the executive power of the United States not in the president but in a committee of the House of Representatives.[37] Of course a law that said henceforth "the executive power of the United States shall be vested in the House Ways and Means Committee" could not rationally be supposed to be constitutional, but that is not a realistic case. More likely Congress would provide for a legislative veto or something like that, which a majority in *Chadha*[38] characterized as precisely amounting to vesting the executive power of the United States in a legislative committee, or in that case one house. But the dissent's reading of the Constitution in *Chadha* was hardly irrational, to put it mildly—some of us even think it was right. Okay, my earlier example, three-year terms for House members: you can't rationally think that is constitutional. But obviously the Court won't be called upon to decide that case because the constitutional command is so clear the law would not be passed.

Thus it doesn't seem to matter much whether we adopt reading one or reading two. There are times we can trust Congress and there are times we can't, and in the latter class of cases we require a Constitution and a practice of judicial review that, first, requires of a law that it be more than rational (because all real laws, even those passed in areas where we should distrust Congress, are rational) and second, requires more than that there be a rational reading of the Constitution pursuant to which the law is constitutional (because as to any real law there will be a rational reading of the Constitution that will uphold it). The alert among you notice that despite my efforts I have lapsed into talking about myself—I suppose a psychiatrist would say I never had a choice—so I'll conclude my remarks and thank you for your attention.

Now you've heard an after dinner speech about James Bradley Thayer. I'll bet you never hear another.

2

Federalism

Though contemporary commentators tend to forget it, the two principal means by which the framers of the original Constitution sought to protect our liberties from governmental tyranny were the state-federal division (the subject of this chapter) and the separation of powers at the federal level among legislature, executive, and judiciary (the subject of the next). On the rare occasion that either subject should come up today—actually the latter does with increasing frequency—it has become fashionable to respond that we needn't worry, as the branch whose authority has allegedly been usurped (generally in the one case the states, in the other the Congress) can be counted on to take care of itself. I agree that state and federal legislators will take care of themselves, if by that we mean their personal prerogatives: the problem is that that doesn't necessarily mean they will be moved to exercise independent law-making authority (indeed political survival increasingly depends precisely upon avoiding that) and consequently provides no assurance whatever that they will take care of us.

Thus I've spent much of my career searching for enforceable principles of federalism and the separation of powers. On the latter I think I've made some headway. However, the search for enforceable principles of federalism has proved considerably more elusive, with the result that at least as of 1996 I remain in the large army of those who suppose that the preservation of state legislative prerogatives must be left substantially to the federal political branches—though the enlistment in my case has been not on principle but rather by default. I don't suppose for a moment that either the president or Congress is likely to be concerned about the growth of federal power; it's just that (along with everyone else) I haven't been able to locate any determinate and defensible principle of federalism on whose basis an outside agency, specifically the courts, could responsibly assume jurisdiction to limit them.

Remarks at American-German Bicentennial Symposium on Constitutional Law (1976)

It's something of a blur, but I do recall enough to know this entire enterprise was weird. Rather than spending the bicentennial in this country like a sensible patriotic American—actually I was General Counsel of the U.S.

Department of Transportation at the time and thus could have spent July 4,
1976, on a Coast Guard cutter watching the "tall ships" sail into New York
Harbor—I, along with approximately twenty other American constitu-
tional law teachers who by some mysterious process had been rated dis-
tinguished, spent the bicentennial as guests of the German government,
being bored by German professors and boring them in return. (I believe this
is called an exchange program.) The excerpt that follows resulted from one
of the conference's organizers approaching Professor Charles Black and
me to advise that we had not yet spoken for the transcript—that was indeed
true, in fact the only thing that had kept either of us even semi-comatose
was the "Nuremberg" aura created by the tangle of earphone connections
and simultaneous translators—and "asking" us to say something. Our re-
sponse was to flip a coin—unobtrusively; we're not complete boors—the
loser to speak first, the winner then to disagree with whatever the loser had
said. I won, and serendipitously even got to say something I believed.

I would like briefly to disagree with Professor Black's view, and many
people embrace it, that we need not worry about the federal government's
taking over subject matters that are properly left to the states, because after
all, the states are adequately represented in the Congress. Though I used to
think that too, my recent year of federal service has made me skeptical. As
Professor Black mentioned, congressmen develop a certain institutional
allegiance to the federal government and to the Congress itself. There are
few United States senators who are not running for president and have that
more in mind than they do the interests of the constituents. I think congressmen tend to worry about the home folks in terms of what we call pork
barrel, that is, in terms of actual tangible benefits for their home territory.
I do not think they worry much about whether subjects that they are asked
to control might better be left to state regulation. The staffs of congressmen
have, I think, still less allegiance to local interests; they are distinctly
Washington-oriented people. The analysis also leaves out of account the
gargantuan nature of the executive branch of the federal government. It is
hard for us to convey to our German hosts the hugeness of our executive
establishment. Indeed, it is hard for many of us to believe that we are in a
capital city when we are in Bonn, as—to put it mildly—it is not obviously
dominated by an immense federal establishment.

I think the framers of our Constitution were right to see some value in
diversity, in things being done locally and being done differently, even
though that will inevitably cause all of us to put up with some results we do
not like. I would therefore not be as chagrined as Professor Black or as
most of my colleagues if the Supreme Court were to move somewhat back
into the business, although I know it is almost heresy to say it, of keeping
the federal government from attaining plenary legislative power.

I would add, however, that that issue is not what is usually debated in the name of states' rights in the United States. Frequently the debate is rather over the states' ability to thwart constitutionally guaranteed individual rights, over whether the states can have prayer in schools, over whether the states can keep people in prison despite the fact that they were convicted on the basis of an unlawful search, and so forth. State legislative competence, by contrast, is not a popularly debated issue. Even our law school curricula sometimes tend to mislead in this way. I teach a course at Harvard, and it is taught at many schools, called The Federal Courts and the Federal System. It is an interesting course, but it may lead people to think that the true battleground of federalism is over the extent to which federal courts will protect individual rights. It is a mistake, however, to suppose that that is where federalism really hangs in the balance. To believe that the existence of states as independent entities somehow importantly depends on the degree to which individual rights are enforced in federal courts is to miss the point. The issue, it seems to me, is where legislative competence lies.

Excerpt from *The Limits of Logic: Syntactic Ambiguity in Article I of the U.S. Constitution* (1963)[1]

So federalism won't take care of itself and thus the Constitution's guardians need to worry about it. One conceivable reading of the document rightly rejected quite early on was that Congress possessed a free-standing power to promote the general welfare. However, as the following excerpt goes on to suggest, other, facially more limited provisions have been read in a way that functionally gives Congress much that authority. I confess I include this excerpt partly because the piece from which it is drawn is strange—don't worry, this instinct for the bizarre will cease—a course paper written for "Symbolic Logic and Legal Communication" that my teacher (Layman Allen) submitted to a journal entitled Modern Uses of Logic in Law. (So okay, he was the editor and the competition wasn't that stiff. I'm not likely soon to forget "editing" the piece, though: the galleys arrived for my "review" while I was in basic training . . . . On second thought this won't be describable to anyone who didn't have that pleasure, and doesn't need to be described to anyone who did.) Anyhow, this is one of the few parts of the article written in something approaching prose. If you want to see the formulas and truth tables, you'll have to consult the original.

Article I, section 8, clause 1 provides that "The Congress shall have Power To lay and collect Taxes, Duties, Imposts and Excises, *to pay the Debts and provide for the common Defence and general Welfare of the*

United States . . . ." The issue here, which might have proved to be of great importance, is whether the "common defence and general welfare" language is a grant to Congress of a general power to legislate for the common defense and general welfare, or whether it merely limits the purposes for which Congress can spend. That is, does it mean:

(A) Congress has power
      (1) to lay and collect taxes, duties, imposts, and excises
  &OR (2) to pay the debts of the United States
  &OR (3) to provide for the common defense and general welfare of the
      United States,

or

(B) Congress has power to lay and collect taxes . . . in order to get money to spend so as to pay the debts and provide for the common defense and general welfare of the United States.

It might be argued that if the words I have italicized had been intended to qualify the spending power, the comma before "to pay" would have been omitted; the comma, it might be argued, implies that the clause following it represents the grant of an independent power. But if this is true, why was the section not worded, "to lay and collect taxes, to pay the debts, and to provide . . . ."? Further, the proviso that follows the underlined words also refers to the taxing power[2]: should not the whole clause be read as a "Taxing and Spending Clause"? And looking beyond syntax, would not the grant of a power "to provide for the general welfare of the United States" entirely negate the Constitution's overall approach of enumerating the national government's powers?

Interpretation (B) has been accepted by all courts and most commentators. It was expressed in Jefferson's opinion on the Bank:

[T]he laying of taxes is the power, and the general welfare the purpose for which the power is to be exercised. [Congress] are not to lay taxes ad libitum for any purpose they please; but only to pay the debts or provide for the welfare of the Union. In like manner, they are not to do anything they please to provide for the general welfare, but only to lay taxes for that purpose.[3]

Hamilton and Madison disagreed over whether the general welfare language should be limited by the specific powers spelled out in the remainder of section 8; but what is significant for our purposes here is that they agreed that the clause defined the scope of the spending power. The Supreme Court has adopted the broader (Hamiltonian) view, paying no attention to the threshold question whether the general welfare language is a limitation on the spending power of any sort.[4] Interpretation (B) is therefore the law of the land.

Professor Lawson has devoted an entire book to trying to prove that interpretation (A) is correct.[5] His arguments, based on the intent of the framers as reflected in Madison's report of the Convention, are worthy of attention. But they are not irrefutable, particularly in view of the fact that the following clause was proposed but not adopted:

> The Legislature of the United States shall have power to pass all laws which they shall judge necessary to the common defence and general welfare of the Union.

The fact of the matter, however, is that Professor Lawson's efforts are (or at least have been since the mid-1930s) superfluous. For essentially nothing hangs on whether the common defense and general welfare language is interpreted as an independent grant of power or as a limitation on the spending power. In the first place, many of the other grants of power contained in section 8—notoriously the Commerce Clause—have been construed so broadly as to give Congress what is functionally a power to legislate for the general welfare.[6] Second, if one accepts—as the Court has—the Hamiltonian view that the general welfare reference is not limited by the remainder of section 8, then even if the clause is regarded as a "mere" definition of the scope of the power to tax and spend, Congress has broad power to legislate for the general welfare. For the power to lay and collect taxes and use the revenues obtained therefrom to provide for the general welfare is not very different from the naked power to provide for the general welfare.

The final sentence strikes me in retrospect as overdone: even an open-ended spending power cannot justify, say, the criminalization or even civil discouragement of whatever behavior Congress wishes to discourage. The earlier point, however, is valid: given the range of the commerce power the question whether Hamilton or Madison was right about the spending power doesn't much matter.

Excerpt from *The Irrepressible Myth of Erie* (1974)[7]

Okay, so what meaningful federalism-based limits might courts enforce? One tempting possibility is to define a domain of exclusive state power and not let the federal government mess with it. However, even if a clear definition were here possible, this approach also wouldn't fit our Constitution.

The Constitution is of course a sort of checklist, enumerating in a general way those things the central government may do and by implication denying it power to do anything else. For a time, however, the Court operated as though there were in addition a second line of constitutional defense against federal overreaching, a sort of enclave of "local affairs" committed exclusively to state regulation and therefore, whatever the checklist might imply,[8] beyond the reach of the central government:

> Thus the act *in a twofold sense* is repugnant to the Constitution. It not only transcends the authority delegated to Congress over commerce *but also* exerts a power as to a purely local matter [manufacture] to which the federal authority does not extend.[9]

The problem with this approach is not so much that it is impossible to give meaning to the notion of a fenced-off domain of exclusively local affairs; there is no a priori reason to suppose that over time this concept could not be fleshed out as intelligibly as any other. The real and dispositive problem is that the enclave theory does not accurately reflect the Constitution's plan for allocating power between the federal and state governments. The Constitution in no way defines the content of any enclave of exclusive state authority[10]—except, of course, by a process of inference from what is not on the checklist of federal powers. And the Tenth Amendment, sometimes, incredibly, cited in support of the state enclave approach,[11] in fact flatly rejects it. That amendment certainly proves what would have been fairly obvious anyway, that the framers felt there were some powers that the central government was to be denied. But it could hardly be clearer that the question of what matters are to be left exclusively to the states is to be answered not by reference to some state enclave construct but rather by looking to see what is not on the federal checklist:

> The powers not delegated to the United States by the Constitution, nor prohibited by it to the States, are reserved to the States respectively, or to the people.[12]

Beginning in the late 1930s the Court returned to the plan thus indicated,[13] and since that time it has consistently construed the Constitution as leaving totally up to the states only what it did not entrust to the central government.

Excerpt from *Legislative and Administrative Motivation in Constitutional Law* (1970)[14]

Congressional motive, then? Well, no—not because I don't think the motivation with which a law was passed can invalidate it (the article from which this is taken argues that it can[15]) but rather because finding an unconstitutional motive to have underlain an apparent case of federal overreaching would seem to require adoption of one of the theories of federalism we've already laid to rest.

An attack on a given Act of Congress on the ground that power to enact it is not granted in Article I, section 8 or elsewhere in the Constitution is one to which the motivation of Congress is irrelevant. [However, t]his is not to say that there will not be occasions, in the context of what are typically but myopically approached as scope of authority cases, when motivation is relevant. If, for example, Congress were to create a tax rate discrepancy in order to disadvantage negroes* or liberals, its motivation would indeed be relevant—not because the illicit motivation proved that the taxes in question were "beyond the taxing power," but rather because . . . Congress had decided whom comparatively to advantage and disadvantage on an unconstitutional basis. The taxes are no less "real" because of that, but the distinction must nonetheless fall under the logic of *Gomillion*.[16]

Of similar contour are cases like *McCray v. United States*,[17] which involved the taxation of white oleomargarine at one quarter cent a pound and colored oleomargarine at ten cents a pound. While both taxes are "real," no examination of legislative history is needed to tell us that the discrepancy between them was designed to discourage the coloring of oleomargarine. And that is a goal difficult to justify in terms of any independent constitutional grant of congressional power. The theory this article proposes would therefore seem potentially applicable, in that the challenged distinction was created in order (1) to control behavior whose control is left exclusively to the states, or in the alternative (2) to achieve a goal encompassed by no other constitutional grant of power. The Court in fact upheld the taxes, asserting that motivation simply is not relevant to questions of congressional power. But that answer will not bear analysis, for properly conceived McCray's objection was not that Congress had exceeded its power by taxing oleomargarine, but rather that the discrepancy in rates had been un-

---

* [This at the time was the only safely nonderogatory word for African-Americans. You'll see that more recently authored pieces use "black" (which the original publisher sometimes capitalized but the Princeton University Press has decapitalized—each with my approval, as the critical point in that regard has always seemed to me that "black" be treated the same as "white") or, more recently still, "African-American." I have not sought 1996 political correctness by updating these usages for this volume. I would hope it would go without saying that none was derogatory at the time it was used, and retention of the original usage—in addition to being the usual policy of the book—may help convey a sense of the history we have traversed over the past three and a half decades.

Gender has been even trickier. For a while I said "he or she," but that can be a real space-taker. ("Whenever he or she has a choice, he or she should choose whatever favors his or her own personal interests.") For several years I used "she" exclusively, but few followed suit, and thus the "she"s stuck out like sore thumbs. My present practice is essentially to alternate "he" and "she," though not with respect to the same hypothetical (or real) person. And while that's the best yet, I expect it too is a little jarring. Maybe we all should cave and start using "they" as a singular personal pronoun, though for some time it will turn our stomachs and make our fourth-grade teachers roll over in their graves.]

constitutionally motivated. The attack was one sounding not in scope of authority, but in the "equal protection" of *Gomillion*.

There is, nonetheless, a serious problem with the argument: it is difficult to maintain—today, at any rate—that either of the asserted motivations is unconstitutional. The notion that the Constitution fences off some enclave of "local affairs" and entrusts them exclusively to the states was long ago resoundingly (and rightly) laid to rest; what is left exclusively to the states is now seen as a function of what has not been granted to the central government. There is, however, also James Madison's view that taxing and spending provisions can constitutionally be manipulated in order to promote only those goals that are entrusted to Congress by some grant of power independent of the taxing and spending clause. This position is by no means without appeal, primarily because without some such limitation federal power is virtually limitless. But in view of the mass of federal legislation built upon the contrary assumption, it is probably too late in the day to consider exhuming it.

In retrospect I'm inclined to think I had this partly wrong too. The fact that Hamilton was "right" (in any case the Court agreed) that Congress can spend for any purpose it regards as conducing to the general welfare (whether or not that purpose is otherwise listed in Article I, section 8) by no means implies it can manipulate tax rates in order to achieve results it is not otherwise empowered to achieve. (It's true that before the Revolution excise taxes were used at least in part to discourage disfavored behavior, but not, and this seems critical to the question before us, behavior the government in question could not lawfully discourage by more direct measures.)

However, in today's world that error—if that's what it is—also turns out to be harmless. It may, as I said, be "difficult" to justify discouraging the coloring of oleomargarine as an exercise of the commerce power, but in the context of today's cases it is far from impossible—"protecting the interstate market in butter" (which of course is what the exercise in fact was about) would undoubtedly suffice. Thus although the logical conundrums surrounding the taxing and spending powers may fascinate more (which undoubtedly is why I've revisited them so often), the root explanation of runaway federal power, once again, is the seeming illimitability of the commerce power, for which no one has been able to define a principled cutoff, at least not one with serious teeth. (I personally would enforce the requirement that putative regulations of "commerce" be "commercial" in purpose and effect. That may be more than the Court appears to have been doing of late,[18] but admittedly it isn't much: most congressional regulations have economic effects sufficiently serious that they cannot be dismissed as part of the probable congressional point.[19] Thus although in my opinion there are a few Commerce Clause cases the Court might do well to overrule,[20] by and large—why do I get embarrassed when I agree with the conventional wisdom?—the protection of our federal system must be left to the president and Congress (neither of which, *contrary to the conventional wisdom, is generally likely to do a very good job*).

The Irrepressible Myth of Erie (1974)[21]

Once it has a perceived evil in its sights it wishes to eradicate, Congress tends to ignore considerations of whether the area in question might better be left to state regulation. When it isn't focused on a particular problem, however, it sometimes moves to protect state prerogatives even in ways the Constitution doesn't require (as we have seen, it essentially never does). It is important to bear in mind, however, as the commentators rarely do, which protections of state prerogatives are statutory and which are constitutional.

> Sometimes a great poem can do more than legislation.
> —Herbert Hoover[22]

The ones I feel sorry for are the people who paid $150 for the cassette tapes explaining the Federal Rules of Evidence.[23] It is hard to say it was their own fault: everything certainly seemed to be going according to plan. The Rules had been forwarded to the Supreme Court by the Advisory Committee, and the Court had duly blessed them and sent them on to Congress. That meant that unless something went wrong, they would automatically take effect on July 1, 1973. Something went wrong, however. A statute was passed preventing the Rules from taking effect unless another statute approved them, and they were referred to committee.

Most of the objections were directed at the provisions refusing, even in diversity cases, to recognize the privileges created by state law and substituting a set of privileges defined by the Rules themselves. The narrowness of the husband-wife privilege provided and the virtual elimination of the doctor-patient privilege were thought to threaten personal privacy. The refusal to recognize any sort of newsman's privilege was seen by many as a threat to the freedom of the press. Nor did these restrictions appear to have been informed by any coherent evidentiary philosophy, given the effusive protection the Rules extended to trade secrets and a broad category of "official information." The misgivings went beyond the merits of the proposals, however. There was also a qualm sounding in federalism—a feeling that by refusing to recognize in diversity cases the privileges provided by local law, the federal government was making law that should be made by the states.

The Advisory Committee's attempt to meet this latter objection built upon a general vision of the relevant demands of federalism that is widely shared by courts and commentators. Of course there are variations, but the account goes generally like this:

All questions of whether to apply federal or state law to a given issue in a diversity case should be decided in accord with Erie. Man took his name for Erie from *Erie R.R. v. Tompkins*,[24] decided in 1938, but Erie is by no means simply a case.* Nor would it do it justice to call it a rule or even a principle, for it implicates, indeed perhaps it is, the very essence of our federalism. Thus, although the case involved the construction of the Rules of Decision Act of 1789,[25] applicable where there is no relevant Federal Rule of Civil Procedure, Erie has to do with much more than that. It also inhabits and gives shape to the Rules Enabling Act of 1934,[26] which controls the Federal Rules, and indeed determines the validity of Acts of Congress directly defining the law to be applied in diversity actions.[27] For although it first revealed itself in statutory form, it has an unmistakable, if only vaguely definable, aspect of the constitutional about it. Of course shadows on cave walls have a way of shifting, and the Court's attempts to describe Erie have varied over time. Originally it was believed that Erie simply commanded the application of state law to substantive issues, but permitted federal courts to handle procedural problems their own way. Beginning in the mid-1940s and continuing into the late 1950s, however, the Court described Erie as considerably more protective of state prerogatives than this, requiring the application of state law whenever applying federal law instead might generate a different outcome.[28] In 1958, in *Byrd v. Blue Ridge Rural Electric Cooperative, Inc.*,[29] the Court qualified this extreme description somewhat, announcing that Erie really required that the state's interests be balanced against whatever interests the federal government might have in the application of its rule. The Court could not leave such sensible moderation alone, however, and in 1965, the pendulum that had begun in *Byrd* to swing back toward the teaching of Erie swung too far, indeed perhaps beyond its 1938 starting place, in Chief Justice Warren's opinion for the Court in *Hanna v. Plumer*.[30] There, Erie was described as establishing what amounted to a presumption in favor of the application of federal law. It is true that there was some attempt in the Court's opinion to suggest that Erie might mean different things in different contexts, but that should not be taken too seriously: what *Hanna* really gave us, whether the Court was fully aware of it or not, was yet another rendition of Erie. And a singularly hard-hearted rendition it is: any

---

* Indeed, the case was originally referred to as *Tompkins*. See, e.g., Clark, "The Tompkins Case and the Federal Rules," 24 J. Am. Jud. Soc'y 158 (1941). This helpful distinction has unfortunately not been maintained in the literature. Nor has Professor Kurland's suggestion that Erie be renamed "York" found wide acceptance. See Kurland, "Mr. Justice Frankfurter: The Supreme Court and the Erie Doctrine in Diversity Cases," 67 Yale L. J. 187, 187–88 (1957).

federal rule (or at least any Federal Rule[31]) that is even arguably procedural is to be applied in a diversity action, state law to the contrary notwithstanding. This surely does not seem even remotely to capture Erie's true meaning. But the Supreme Court is the Supreme Court, and seven is a majority of nine even when Justice Harlan is one of the two. *Hanna* therefore may not be Erie, but it seems to be the law.

Since the privilege provisions of the Evidence Rules are surely at least arguably procedural, the Advisory Committee, following the commentators, concluded that they satisfy Erie's present demands and therefore must be valid.

My suggestion in this article will be that the indiscriminate admixture of all questions respecting choices between federal and state law in diversity cases, under the single rubric of "the Erie doctrine" or "the Erie problem," has served to make a major mystery out of what are really three distinct and rather ordinary problems of statutory and constitutional interpretation. Of course there will be occasions with respect to all three on which reasonable persons will differ, but that does not make the problems mysterious or even very unusual. The United States Constitution, I shall argue, constitutes the relevant text only where Congress has passed a statute creating law for diversity actions, and it is in this situation alone that *Hanna*'s "arguably procedural" test controls. Where a nonstatutory rule is involved, the Constitution necessarily remains in the background, but is functionally irrelevant because the applicable statutes are significantly more protective of the prerogatives of state law. Thus, where there is no relevant Federal Rule of Civil Procedure or other Rule promulgated pursuant to the Enabling Act, and the federal rule in issue is therefore wholly judge-made, whether state or federal law should be applied is controlled by the Rules of Decision Act, the statute construed in *Erie* and *York*. Where the matter in issue is covered by a Federal Rule, however, the Enabling Act—and not the Rules of Decision Act itself or the line of cases construing it—constitutes the relevant standard. To say that, however, and that is one of the things *Hanna* said, is by no means to concede the validity of all Federal Rules, for the Enabling Act contains significant limiting language of its own. The Court has correctly sensed that that language cannot be construed to protect state prerogatives as strenuously as the Rules of Decision Act protects them in the absence of a Federal Rule. However, the Court's recent appreciation that the Enabling Act constitutes the only check on the Rules—that "Erie" does not stand there as a backstop—should lead it in an appropriate case to take the Act's limiting language more seriously than it has in the past.

But if the inquiries are really discrete—and that much at least I am confident I can demonstrate—how are we to account for the widespread acceptance of the account related above of "Erie" as a monolithic doctrine? Part of the fault has surely been the commentators': to one accustomed to the savagery of constitutional criticism, writers on procedure seem strangely, if refreshingly, accepting. But most of the blame must be laid at the door of the Court, in particular the Court of the 1940s and 1950s. By essentially obliterating the Enabling Act in *Sibbach v. Wilson & Co.*[32] in 1941, it created a need for limits on the Rules, a need it subsequently filled not by reconsidering *Sibbach*, but rather by an undefended application of the *Erie* line of precedents.[33] That step made the next one quite natural: if Erie is controlling outside the context of the Rules of Decision Act, that must mean it is a constitutional doctrine, which implies in turn that it determines the validity of acts of Congress directly defining the law applicable in diversity actions.[34] Thus did "the Erie doctrine," despite the more modest ambitions of the decision from which it took its name, gain control of all choices between federal and state law in diversity actions. Whenever a new question presented itself for which the existing Erie lore seemed inadequate, the Court reacted not by considering whether a distinct test might be appropriate—that is, whether Erie might not be relevant or at least have different implications for the new question—but rather by reevaluating Erie's true meaning.

All that should have changed in 1965, however, with the decision in *Hanna v. Plumer*. For whatever *Hanna*'s other merits or demerits, the major point of the Court's opinion was its separation for purposes of analysis of the Rules of Decision Act, the Enabling Act, and the constitutional demands to which the *Erie* opinion had alluded. How, in light of that, can we account for the monolithic "Erie doctrine's" continued pervasion of the literature? Surely one reason has to do with the prestige of Justice Harlan, who concurred separately in *Hanna*. The clear assumption of his otherwise sensitive discussion was that all choices between state and federal law in diversity actions are controlled by a single doctrine, the Erie doctrine, and that that doctrine is of constitutional magnitude and therefore indiscriminately applicable whether there is a Federal Rule covering the point in dispute or not. Of probably more significance to the subsequent commentary is the fact that he gave no sign of recognizing that the majority had clearly rejected that assumption, that it had sought to separate the various issues. Instead he proceeded simply by detailing the respects in which he agreed with what he took to be the majority's rendition of Erie and those in which he disagreed. And this, one has to suppose, is just what many commentators were waiting to hear. After all, if Justice Harlan thinks it is still a single question, one cannot be very far off in supposing that it is and getting on with the business of touching up one's picture of Erie. But "Erie" is really about several things, or at least so this article will argue.

The Constitution

Central to Justice Harlan's attack on the majority opinion was the charge that it had "misconceived the constitutional premises of *Erie*" by setting forth an "arguably procedural, ergo constitutional" test. Instead, building upon the Hart and Wechsler casebook,[35] he proposed the following:

> To my mind the proper line of approach in determining whether to apply a state or a federal rule, whether "substantive" or "procedural," is to stay close to basic principles by inquiring if the choice of rule would substantially affect those primary decisions respecting human conduct which our constitutional system leaves to state regulation. If so, *Erie* and the Constitution require that the state rule prevail, even in the face of a conflicting federal rule.[36]

As will be noted later, the considerations Justice Harlan touched on here are of some help in approaching cases that, like *Hanna*, involve Federal Rules. However, in asserting that the test suggested was one of constitutional magnitude, he helped perpetuate a constitutional misapprehension that the majority had striven mightily to allay—the misapprehension of the state enclave theory.

The Constitution is of course a sort of checklist, enumerating in a general way those things the central government may do and by implication denying it power to do anything else.[37] For a time, however, the Court operated as though there were in addition a second line of constitutional defense against federal overreaching, a sort of enclave of "local affairs" committed exclusively to state regulation and therefore, whatever the checklist might imply, beyond the reach of the central government:

> Thus the act *in a twofold sense* is repugnant to the Constitution. It *not only* transcends the authority delegated to Congress over commerce *but also* exerts a power as to a purely local matter [manufacture] to which the federal authority does not extend.

The problem with this approach is not so much that it is impossible to give meaning to the notion of a fenced-off domain of exclusively local affairs; there is no a priori reason to suppose that over time this concept should not be fleshed out as intelligibly as any other. The real and dispositive problem is that the enclave theory does not accurately reflect the Constitution's plan for allocating power between the federal and state governments. The Constitution in no way defines the content of any enclave of exclusive state authority—except, of course, by a process of inference from what is not on the checklist of federal powers. And the Tenth Amendment, sometimes, incredibly, cited in support of the state enclave approach, in fact flatly rejects it. That amendment certainly proves what would have been fairly obvious anyway, that the framers felt there were some powers that the central government was to be denied. But it could hardly be clearer that the question of what matters are to be left exclusively to the states is to be answered not by reference to some state enclave construct but rather by looking to see what is not on the federal checklist:

> The powers not delegated to the United States by the Constitution, nor prohibited by it to the States, are reserved to the States respectively, or to the people.

Beginning in the later 1930s, the Court returned to the plan thus indicated, and since that time it has consistently construed the Constitution—outside of "Erie contexts" at any rate—as leaving totally up to the states only what it did not entrust to the central government.

The opinion Justice Brandeis wrote for the *Erie* Court in 1938 was a creature of its time,[38] and it understood all this perfectly well. It has been faulted for failing to indicate precisely what constitutional provision *Swift v. Tyson*'s[39] interpretation of the Rules of Decision Act violated,[40] but the lack of a relevant provision was precisely the point. The prior interpretation was unconstitutional,[41] but not because the federal common law rules that had been developed under it were encroaching on areas of "state substantive law" or "state law governing primary private activity"; it is on precisely those areas that new federal domestic legislation inevitably encroaches. It was unconstitutional because nothing in the Constitution provided the central government with a general lawmaking authority of the sort the Court had been exercising under *Swift*.[42] The Constitution's reference to a diversity of citizenship jurisdiction had been intended as that and no more—a grant of power to provide courts for diversity cases and to prescribe the rules of practice and procedure by which they would manage their business, but not to go on and provide them, or let them provide themselves, with rules that could not fairly be characterized as procedural.

The Court therefore made no allusion to an enclave of exclusive state concern either entirely immune to, or in some sense entitled to be "balanced" against, claims of federal competence. The question, here as with respect to any other question of federal power, was whether anything in the Constitution provided a basis for the authority being exerted—and the answer was no:

> Congress has no power to declare substantive rules of common law applicable in a State whether they be local in their nature or "general," be they commercial law or a part of the law of torts. And no clause in the Constitution purports to confer such a power upon the federal courts.[43]

That point having been made, and the interpretation of "rules of decision" expanded to cover "general common law" as well as statutory and "local" common law, the Constitution's utility as a point of reference was ended. After *Erie*, the Act itself protected the prerogatives of state law as fully as (in fact more fully than[44]) the Constitution does. It is therefore not the least bit surprising that the Court did not mention the constitutional basis of the *Erie* decision again for eighteen years.

But all the while the myth of Erie was abuilding, and with it the belief that it carried some special constitutional magic of a sort that transcended ordinary issues of federal power. The myth took its toll in 1956, in *Bernhardt v. Polygraphic Co. of America*. There the Court—in construing the Federal Arbitration Act not to apply in diversity actions[45]—relied on the consideration that if the Act were construed the other way, it would probably be unconstitutional under *Erie* for invading the "local law field."[46] But *Erie* did not fence off a "local law field" constitutionally immune to federal influence; it was quite clear that exclusive state power takes up only where federal power leaves off. The Arbitration Act, even as applied to diversity cases, would be in peril of unconstitutionality only if it were so plainly nonprocedural as to fall outside Congress's undoubted power to formulate procedure for federal courts, which it quite clearly is not.[47] *Bernhardt's* ultimate conclusion, that state law applied, seems correct. The language and legislative history of the Arbitration Act, quite unaided by any supposed constitutional pressure, suggest that it was not intended to apply in diversity cases like *Bernhardt*. Since, therefore, no other federal law covered the matter in issue, the Rules of Decision Act became the relevant statute, and under that statute the Court's choice of state law was quite proper. But in suggesting that as a matter of constitutional law restrictive of Acts of Congress, a "local law field" limits the federal government's exercise of powers no one doubts it has—and further that this "local law field" is defined by the series of cases construing the Rules of Decision Act—the *Bernhardt* Court sowed only needless confusion.

The *Hanna* majority was therefore well advised to bring the Constitution into its discussion, if only to usher it back out again—to demonstrate that its function in "Erie contexts" is no different from its function respecting other issues of federal power, and thereby to attempt to restore it to its rightful place of functional irrelevance in cases covered by the Rules of Decision and Rules Enabling Acts.

> We are reminded by the *Erie* opinion that neither Congress nor the federal courts can . . . fashion rules which are not supported by a grant of federal authority contained in Article I or some other section of the Constitution; *in such areas state law must govern because there can be no other law*. But the opinion in *Erie*, which . . . dealt with a question which was "substantive" in every traditional sense (whether the railroad owed a duty of care to Tompkins as a trespasser or a licensee), surely neither said nor implied that measures like Rule 4(d)(1) are

unconstitutional. For the constitutional provision for a federal court system (augmented by the Necessary and Proper Clause) carries with it congressional power
to make rules governing the practice and pleading in those courts, which in turn
includes a power to regulate matters which, though falling within the uncertain
area between substance and procedure, are rationally capable of classification as
either. Cf. *M'Culloch v. Maryland*, 4 Wheat 316, 421.[48]

The fact that the state enclave model is not that of the Constitution need
not, of course, imply that it is not a model Congress might by legislation
impose on federal courts. And Congress has—twice.

The Rules of Decision Act

Originally enacted as section 34 of the Federal Judiciary Act of 1789, the
Rules of Decision Act provides:

> The laws of the several states, except where the Constitution or treaties of the
> United States or Acts of Congress otherwise require or provide, shall be regarded
> as rules of decision in civil actions in the courts of the United States, in cases
> where they apply.[49]

Despite the fact that *Erie R.R. v. Tompkins* seems to be a mandatory citation in any case raising an issue of whether federal or state law is to be
applied to a given point in a diversity case, the Court's opinion in that case
provides little guidance on such issues. A considerable body of nostalgic
literature to the contrary, *Erie* did not indicate that "substance" and "procedure" were the keys to interpreting the Act.[50] The Court's attention
was obviously focused elsewhere, and in fact it did not even explicitly
acknowledge that federal courts would be applying some of their own rules
of practice in diversity cases. Thus any "answer" in the *Erie* opinion will
have to be found in the reasons given for overruling *Swift* and not in anything resembling an attempt at a test.

A brief comment in *Sibbach v. Wilson & Co.* indicated that at least as of
1941 the Court was assuming that substance and procedure were the critical concepts.[51] We shall see that this assumption about the workings of the
Rules of Decision Act was of some importance in shaping the Court's construction of the Enabling Act.[52] However, the remark was hardly considered and little noticed, as the *Sibbach* discussion was predominantly directed to the latter statute. The first significant attempt to formulate a test
for the Rules of Decision Act came in 1945, in Justice Frankfurter's opinion for the Court in *Guaranty Trust Co. v. York*. The Court did not question
the assumption that the difference between substantive and procedural
rules bore some relevance to the concerns of the Act, but it noted that the

line that separates them must vary with the legal context. Building upon the Act's apparent concern lest the "accident" of diversity be permitted to make a material difference, it proposed the "outcome determination" test, which required that the state rule be followed whenever enforcing the federal rule in its stead was likely to generate a different outcome.[53]

But although it held sway for quite a time, *York*'s outcome-determination test seemed overbroad. As the *Hanna* Court later noted, pushed to an extreme it would imply that a litigant in a diversity action could insist on filing his responsive pleadings in accord with the state rather than the federal timetable, on the theory that enforcement of the federal timetable would cause him to lose, and thereby undeniably determine the outcome of the suit.[54] And once there was added to the apparent overbreadth of the test itself the "realization" that it controlled not simply judge-made rules, but Federal Rules of Civil Procedure and even other federal statutes as well, some sort of backlash was inevitable. It came in 1958, in *Byrd v. Blue Ridge Rural Electric Cooperative, Inc.*[55] The question presented—whether to apply federal law, which required that a jury decide the issue in dispute, or state law, which had a judge decide it—could have been decided, at least if the subsequent decision in *Simler v. Conner*[56] is to be believed, on Seventh Amendment grounds pure and simple. The Court shunned this straightforward course, however, and indicated that choices between state and federal law were thenceforth to be resolved by balancing the relevant state and federal interests. The opinion exhibits a confusion that exceeds even that normally surrounding balancing tests, and lower courts understandably experienced considerable difficulty in applying it.

Thus, when *Hanna* reached the Court the Rules of Decision Act was in some disarray. The majority's main point, that the Rules Enabling Act alone was the appropriate measure of a Federal Rule of Civil Procedure, was sufficient to decide the case. It saw fit, however, to add a considered dictum on the question of what law would have been applicable had there been no such Rule and thus had a genuine *Erie* problem been presented.

Since "rules of decision" is hardly self-defining and the legislative history is sparse, the Court approached this issue by seeking "the policies underlying the *Erie* rule." It noted that the *Erie* opinion had evidenced concern with federal-state forum shopping, and gone on to lay considerable stress on that concern in construing the Rules of Decision Act. But while the likelihood of forum shopping may turn out to be a handy touchstone for identifying those situations exhibiting the evils against which the Act was directed, forum shopping is not an evil per se. It is evil only if something evil flows from it; indeed, the very idea of the diversity jurisdiction was to provide an alternative to state court. Thus, unless the Rules of Decision Act was a pointless exercise, the First Congress must have seen something else wrong with allowing federal courts to formulate their own rules of decision and thereby to create a separate regime for those nonresident plaintiffs who wish to avail themselves of it.

A good deal of critical attention has focused, in Justice Harlan's phrase, on "the debilitating uncertainty in the planning of everyday affairs" that would confront potential resident defendants—which is to say everyone— because of the possible applicability to their conduct of two different sets of legal rules.[57] Of course precisely this possibility is created by much modern thinking respecting interstate conflicts of law,[58] and the extent to which people consult the law before acting varies. But we can all agree that a situation where a person cannot predict or control where he will be sued, and will lose in one court if he does X and lose in the other if he doesn't, is one we should certainly try to avoid:

> People repeatedly subjected, like Pavlov's dogs, to two or more inconsistent sets of directions, without means of resolving the inconsistencies, could not fail in the end to react as the dogs did. The society, collectively, would suffer a nervous breakdown.[59]

The prospect is frightening, but the picture is overdrawn. The directives involved in the line of cases under discussion have generally (though not inevitably, as *Erie* itself demonstrates) been requirements of dubious relevance to "the planning of everyday affairs" and indeed of major concern to legal advisers—who presumably are in a better position than laymen to "resolve the inconsistencies" or at any rate to cope with them without serious distress. That there is usually a way of doing so is suggested by the concession made in a footnote to Justice Harlan's discussion: "Since the rules involved in the present case are parallel rather than conflicting, this . . . rationale does not come into play here."[60] For I am not aware of a single case in the line under discussion in which a similar concession would not be in order. Of course compliance with one of the two contending rules (the one in fact complied with) fell short of compliance with both; that is what caused all the shouting. However, in every case compliance with the *other* rule would have constituted compliance with both. One rule was simply more demanding than the other; in none of the cases did one rule require behavior that the other penalized. Of course such predicaments are theoretically possible even if they are practically unlikely. And more importantly, Justice Harlan's concession may have been a bit hasty; being told by an apparently authoritative source that X is sufficient and later finding out it was not may not be as bad as being confronted with two apparently authoritative rules with which simultaneous compliance is impossible, but it is bad enough. Whether the possibility of this mitigated form of debilitation could alone have accounted for the enactment of the Rules of Decision Act need not detain us, however. The *Erie* opinion did not allude even obliquely to the "conflicting orders" rationale. Something more important, and more obvious, is at stake.

What *Erie* mentioned[61] and *Hanna* picked up[62] was simple unfairness. The Court was referring to the unfairness of affording a nonresident plaintiff suing a resident defendant a unilateral choice of the rules by which the lawsuit was to be determined.[63] But there is another unfairness, one not tied to the vicissitudes of the removal provisions—the unfairness of subjecting a person involved in litigation with a citizen of a different state to a body of law different from that which applies when his next door neighbor is involved in similar litigation with a cocitizen.[64] The *Erie* opinion suggested a denial of equal protection was involved,[65] but surely that was a metaphor.[66] It would not be irrational to fight bias against out-of-staters by giving them access to a body of law, developed by persons beholden to no particular state, unavailable in suits between cocitizens.[67] Not irrational, but the founders of our Republic—by not including any such power in the Constitution, and even more clearly by enacting the Rules of Decision Act—refused to do it. Bias against out-of-staters was to be resisted, but only by providing an unbiased tribunal. To provide more, or at least so it was felt, would create an unfairness in the other direction.

The point of the *Hanna* dictum is that it is difficult to find unfairness of a sort that would have troubled the framers of the Rules of Decision Act, or of a sort whose elimination would justify disrupting a federal court's routine, when the difference between the federal and state rules is trivial, when their requirements are essentially fungible. The problem with the previously prevailing rhetoric was that it is possible to speak of enforcing a rule in either of two senses—exacting compliance on the one hand, or sanctioning a noncomplying party on the other. Thus, whenever the sanction for noncompliance is dismissal, there is a sense in which "enforcement" of the rule can be outcome determinative. But it is a backhanded sense, and one that implicates the concerns that gave rise to the Rules of Decision Act only when the underlying mandate thus enforced is sufficiently more or less burdensome than its state counterpart to support a plausible claim of unfairness. The Court therefore suggested by its examples that a federal court may adhere to its own rules in diversity cases insofar, but only insofar, as they are neither materially more or less difficult for the burdened party to comply with than their state counterparts,[68] nor likely to generate an outcome different from that which would result were the case litigated in the state court system *and the state rules followed.*

Thus, state rules controlling such things as burden of proof, presumptions, and sufficiency of evidence should be followed where they differ from the federal court's usual practice;[69] but those regulating such matters as the form of pleadings, order of proof, time limits on responsive pleadings,[70] and the method by which an adversary is given notice can ordinarily be disregarded,[71] though of course there is no reason they must. The difference between the federal and state rules with respect to these matters will be outcome determinative only in the backhanded sense the Court

rejected—a litigant who despite his presence in one court insisted on following the other court's procedure would lose. But discrepancy in the regulation of such matters is unlikely to lead to forum shopping. And more to
the point—though it now appears that the likelihood of forum shopping
does furnish a useful touchstone[72]—discrepancy that will not alter outcome
for, or otherwise materially affect, litigants who comply with the forum's
rules is hard to condemn as unfair.

Thus, although it indicated some reservation about certain extreme statements of the outcome determination test, *Hanna* was far from discarding it
altogether. The Court overruled no prior application of the test and indeed,
by dusting it off and adding a couple of qualifications that should have been
there all along, resurrected it from the uncertain situation in which *Byrd*
had left it.[73] There was nothing wrong with *York* but oversimplification;
what was seriously wrong was its subsequent and understandably frightening transplantation to situations involving Federal Rules and even other
statutes. But in the context of the Rules of Decision Act, a rejuvenated
outcome determination test—augmented a little and clipped a little, so as to
intercept the more preposterous implications of its earlier formulations[74]—
was just what was called for. And that is what *Hanna* provided.

The Rules Enabling Act

Hanna's main point, however, was that when the application of a Federal
Rule is at issue, the Rules Enabling Act—and not the Rules of Decision Act
as construed by *Erie R.R. v. Tompkins* and other cases—should determine
whether federal or state law is to be applied. Although it is a different
question how closely the two statutes should be read to track each other,
this point seems plainly correct. The Enabling Act provides that "[a]ll laws
in conflict with" Rules promulgated under its authority "shall be of no
further force or effect,"[75] and the Rules of Decision Act is a law. But even
if that language were not there, the Enabling Act is much more recent; it is
specifically designed to control the validity of the Rules; and it contains
language directed to the same general concern—protection of the prerogatives of state law—as the Rules of Decision Act. It indicates it is the only
statutory test of a Federal Rule, and there is every reason to believe it
means it.

Enacted in 1934, the Enabling Act provides:

> The Supreme Court shall have the power to prescribe by general rules the
> forms of process, writs, pleadings, and motions, and the practice and proce-
> dure of the district courts and courts of appeal of the United States in civil
> actions . . . .[76]

In thus delegating authority to the Court, the Act begins with a checklist approach—anything that relates to process, writs, pleadings, motions, or to practice and procedure generally, is authorized; anything else is not. Thus far, no limitation is imposed that was not imposed by the Constitution. The second sentence, however, provides that "Such rules shall not abridge, enlarge or modify any substantive right. . . ." The Act therefore contains, as the Court used to say the Constitution contained, limitations of both the checklist and enclave variety. Not only must a Rule be procedural; it must in addition abridge, enlarge or modify no substantive right.

You would never know it from the case law, though. In the landmark Enabling Act case, *Sibbach v. Wilson & Co.*, the Court construed the Act as a checklist only:

> The test must be whether a rule really regulates procedure,—the judicial process for enforcing rights and duties recognized by substantive law and for justly administering remedy and redress for disregard or infraction of them. That the rules in question are such is admitted.[77]

And indeed, petitioner had admitted that; but she had read beyond the first sentence of the statute and did not understand her hardly avoidable admission that Rule 35 was procedural to amount to a concession of its validity.

> [P]etitioner admits, and, we think, correctly, that Rule 35 and 37 are rules of procedure. She insists, nevertheless, that by the prohibition against abridging substantive rights, Congress has banned the rules here challenged.[78]

Yet despite the fact that it was precisely the situation to which the Act's draftsmen were addressing themselves in the second sentence, the possibility that a Rule could fairly be labeled procedural and at the same time abridge or modify substantive rights was one the Court was unwilling to accept; by its lights, either a Rule was procedural *or* it affected substantive rights.[79] Thus, the Act's two questions were collapsed into one: "*The test* must be whether a rule really regulates procedure . . . ."[80] This construction has been widely accepted by the literature and has continued to inform the Court's discussions.

Nor was the *Hanna* opinion much help in this regard. It should be noted that what Justice Harlan termed the "arguably procedural" test was set forth in the Court's discussion of the Constitution and not in relation to the Enabling Act. But the Court's demonstration that the state rule in question was properly regarded as procedural was relegated to a footnote,[81] and the text of the opinion did little more, so far as the interpretation of the Enabling Act was concerned, than point to *Sibbach*. This comparative lack of attention to the Enabling Act is not too surprising, since the opinion's main point was to dismiss the Rules of Decision Act precedents, which were the ones on which the court below and the respondent had relied and indeed the only ones remotely threatening to the Federal Rule in controversy. Once those were cleared away and the Enabling Act established as the only relevant statutory test, the case was a relatively easy one. But whatever the reason, the willingness to reexamine and clarify that the Court demonstrated respecting other issues was not really in evidence in its treatment of the Enabling Act.

The Court did make one significant statement about the Enabling Act—that it should be read to protect the prerogatives of state law against incursions by a Federal Rule with somewhat less vigor than that with which the Rules of Decision Act protects them in the absence of such a Rule.[82] It is true that there is no evidence to suggest that those responsible for the passage of the Enabling Act—which was finally enacted in 1934 (four years before *Erie*) after many years of skirmishing—had the Rules of Decision Act in mind as a guide to the boundaries of the Supreme Court's rule making authority. But the possibility that the two Acts should be read to provide identical standards cannot be dismissed quite so easily.[83] The limiting language of the Enabling Act's second sentence ("abridge, enlarge or modify") is strong and on its face might be taken to command the application of state law in any situation covered by the refined outcome determination test that *Hanna* suggested for the Rules of Decision Act. For the outcome of a lawsuit surely affects importantly the substantive rights the parties are effectively to be granted.

Applying the broad standard of the Rules of Decision Act to the Federal Rules as well as to wholly judge-made procedures would doubtless strike many as an entirely sensible approach to the diversity jurisdiction: if that jurisdiction exists to provide an unbiased tribunal, it is surely arguable that that is all of significance that should be provided. But as an interpretation of the Rules Enabling Act, it would seem that this approach must fail, since it would eviscerate the Rules[84] and thereby render the Act almost entirely self-defeating. About all we can be sure of respecting the Enabling Act's intendment is that it was designed to authorize a comparatively enlightened set of Federal Rules of Civil Procedure to be applied in all federal courts, in diversity actions as well as others. While the precise content of the set of Rules promulgated four years later was not known or even very precisely predicted prior to the law's enactment, the set that emerged was consistent with what predictions there had been,[85] and there is no evidence of a reaction of betrayal or even surprise at the time of promulgation. The Rules are replete, however, with provisions whose implementation in lieu of state law can be outcome determinative even in *Hanna*'s refined sense. To take just two examples, the provisions for discovery of an opponent's case in advance of trial[86] and those that ensure the liberal construction and amendment of pleadings[87] have doubtless often meant the difference between winning and losing a lawsuit. Thus, were they not part of the Rules, the

Rules of Decision Act would require federal courts to follow state practice. To import the Rules of Decision Act's standard into the Enabling Act would therefore be to invalidate not only these provisions, which are obviously central to the Rules' design,[88] but many others as well. If this wholesale defeat of the Enabling Act is to be avoided, its interpretation must be geared not to the lawsuit's ultimate outcome, but rather to the character of the state provision that enforcement of the Federal Rule in question will supplant, in particular to whether the state provision embodies a substantive policy or represents only a procedural disagreement with the federal rulemakers respecting the fairest and most efficient way of conducting litigation.[89]

Those dread words "substantive" and "procedural" obviously need, and will receive, further attention, but we are now in a position to clarify the difference between the analytic framework appropriate to the Rules of Decision Act and that imposed by the Enabling Act. When there is no Federal Rule, and as a result the Rules of Decision Act constitutes the controlling text, the court need ordinarily[90] not concern itself with whether the federal rule urged by one party, or the state rule urged by the other, is most fairly designated substantive or procedural. The test is whether the choice between the two is material in the sense *Hanna* indicated, and that is not a function of the goals the rule makers on either side were pursuing. Consider a disagreement between the state practice and that of the local federal court over whether receipt of a letter should be presumed from proof that it was properly addressed and mailed. This is a very rare situation so far as presumptions are concerned, in that neither of the contending rules seems designed to further any substantive goal and the difference of opinion apparently respects only the most likely way of approximating the truth.[91] It thus seems a strictly procedural disagreement. The difference in approach could nonetheless quite obviously be outcome determinative. A litigant—even the litigant made relevant by *Hanna*, who follows the rules of the chosen forum to the best of his ability—might well, if the federal court persisted in its disagreement, lose in one court a case he would have won in the other. Thus, the state rule, though by hypothesis wholly procedural, should be followed where there is no Federal Rule promulgated pursuant to the Enabling Act. Where there is such a Rule, however, the designations substantive and procedural become important, for the Enabling Act has made them so. Its first sentence, tracking the constitutional requirement, demands that the Federal Rule be procedural. Its second sentence (the one the Court and the commentators have ignored) adds to this checklist restriction the further, and considerably more significant, enclave-type proviso that the Rule not abridge, enlarge, or modify any substantive right. The proviso is not significant in the case hypothesized, however, since the state rule entails no substantive policy. Consequently a Federal Rule could displace it.[92]

We were all brought up on sophisticated talk about the fluidity of the line between substance and procedure. But the realization that the terms carry no monolithic meaning at once appropriate to all the contexts in which courts have seen fit to employ them need not imply that they can have no meaning at all. And they are the terms the Enabling Act uses.[93] We have, I think, some moderately clear notion of what a procedural rule is—one designed[94] to make the process of litigation a fair and efficient mechanism for the resolution of disputes.[95] Thus, one way of doing things may be chosen over another because it is thought to be more likely to get at the truth, or better calculated to give the parties a fair opportunity to present their sides of the story, or because, and this may point quite the other way, it is a means of promoting the efficiency of the process. Or the protection of the process may proceed at wholesale, as by keeping the size of the docket at a level consistent with giving those cases that are heard the attention they deserve. The most helpful way, it seems to me, of defining a substantive rule—or more particularly a substantive right, which is what the Act refers to—is as a right granted for one or more nonprocedural reasons, for some purpose or purposes not having to do with the fairness or efficiency of the litigation process.[96]

Thus, in attempting to give content to the notion of substance, the literature has focused on "those rules of law which characteristically and reasonably affect people's conduct at the stage of primary private activity."[97] That is a good place to start, but it seems to me it is not enough. For one thing, we probably should give "conduct" a coverage somewhat broader than that the term most naturally suggests, to include along with the encouragement of actual activity the fostering and protection of certain states of mind—for example, the feeling of release, the assurance that the possibility of ordeal has passed, that a state seeks to create by enacting a statute of limitations. Beyond that, we surely would want to count as substantive various sorts of immunizing laws—such as sovereign immunity and abatement laws,[98] married women[99] and spendthrift statutes[100]—which surely are not calculated to encourage those immunized to engage in the conduct involved, conduct for which the rest of us would be liable.[101] They are, instead, based upon a judgment that although the conduct involved is undesirable and indeed ought to be deterred, other and, in context, more important goals will be served by immunization from liability. Yet the laws remain substantive: in none is the "greater" goal to which the interests in deterrence and compensation are subordinated a procedural goal concerned only with the most sensible way to manage a litigation process.

Of course it is not at all unlikely that with respect to a given rule the legislature or other rulemaker will have had two (or more) goals in mind—one relating to the management of litigation and one relating to some other concern. Under the definitions suggested above, such a rule would be both procedural and substantive. That conclusion strikes me as not at all trouble-some, however, and indeed fits precisely what I am suggesting is the proper interpretation of the Enabling Act. Thus, statutes of limitation are passed not simply for the substantive purpose of relieving people's minds after the passage of the designated period, but also for procedural purposes, to keep down the size of the docket and to ensure that cases will not be tried on evidence so stale as to cast doubt on its trustworthiness. They are therefore procedural, which means, first, that Congress could constitutionally enact a statute prescribing a limitation period for diversity cases, and second, that a Federal Rule prescribing such a limitation would satisfy the Enabling Act's first sentence. It should not get by the second sentence, however,[102] for the substantive rights established by state statutes of limitations would be abridged by applying such a Federal Rule. Thus, the image of a "sub-stance-procedure line" is somewhat misleading here. In the context of the Enabling Act at any rate, the predicament reported by Justice Rutledge simply does not exist:

> [I]n many situations procedure and substance are so interwoven that rational sep-aration becomes well-nigh impossible. But, even so, this fact cannot dispense with the necessity of making a distinction. . . . Judges therefore cannot escape making the division. And they must make it where the two constituent elements are Siamese twins as well as where they are not twins or even blood brothers.[103]

The quoted passage is from Rutledge's dissent from three decisions ren-dered in 1949, decisions that by the rarest of coincidences provide fertile ground for further exploration of the approach proposed in this article. In one of them, *Woods v. Interstate Realty Co.*,[104] the Court held applicable in a diversity action a Mississippi statute providing that corporations that had not qualified to do business in the state would not be permitted to sue in its courts. The Court assumed that there was no relevant Federal Rule and that the case therefore arose under the Rules of Decision Act. Thus conceived, the case was correctly decided.[105] A somewhat harder question is whether the same result would have been appropriate had there been a Federal Rule expressly or impliedly rejecting for federal courts Mississippi's require-ment—as indeed Rule 17(b), which the Court did not so much as mention, seems to be.[106] But that question is not a great deal harder. It is true that the statute's enforcement mechanism, its club, was a denial of jurisdiction, a device that may well typically be employed for procedural ends. But a primary reason jurisdiction was denied by the state law was to encourage corporate qualification.[107] That is a substantive goal concerned with some-thing other than the way litigation is to be managed, and the Enabling Act's second sentence therefore intervenes.

In *Cohen v. Beneficial Industrial Loan Corp.*,[108] the Court directed a federal court sitting in a diversity action to apply a New Jersey statute requiring the plaintiff, as a condition of bringing a stockholder's derivative action, to post a bond securing payment of defense costs. Federal Rule 23 also dealt with the requirements for bringing a derivative action, but the Court concluded that there was no conflict between the two.[109] In his *Hanna* concurrence Justice Harlan accepted this construction of Rule 23,[110] but went on to opine that even if the Federal Rules had by implication dispensed with the bond requirement, the same result—application of the state rule—would have been in order.[111] Though he styled this a conclusion compelled by *Erie*, thereby suggesting the relevance of the Rules of Decision Act, this conclusion seems correct even under the Enabling Act. The New Jersey requirement was enacted to deter the small stockholder's "strike suit," brought not to redress any real wrong to stockholders generally but only to harass and thereby to coerce a settlement that would benefit only the plaintiff and in the process injure the interests of the other stockholders.[112] *Cohen* differs from *Woods* in that the state had closed the courthouse doors not to influence some other behavior but rather to abort the very litigation in question. But even that can be done for a substantive purpose, as the statute of limitations example demonstrates. The critical question is *why* the lawsuit was aborted. The answer—to stop the stockholder acting in bad faith from enriching himself at the expense of the rest of the stockholders—is a substantive one; in enacting the statute the New Jersey legislature was concerned with something more than improving the process by which lawsuits are conducted.

The third case, *Ragan v. Merchants Transfer & Warehouse Co.*,[113] featured a twist on the limitations problem. Kansas had a two-year statute of limitations on torts, which was tolled only by the service of the summons. Rule 3 of the Federal Rules of Civil Procedure, then as now, prescribed no limitation but provided, "A civil action is commenced by filing a complaint with the court." Needless to say, the two years ran between the filing of the complaint and the service of the summons. The Court indicated that in nondiversity cases Rule 3 should be read to mean that the filing of the complaint tolls the applicable statute of limitations.[114] It held, however, that in a diversity case arising out of a Kansas cause of action the Rule could not be so applied, because "the principle of *Erie R. Co. v. Tompkins*" demanded the application of the state tolling provision.[115]

Concurring in *Hanna*, Justice Harlan argued that *Ragan* was wrongly decided.[116] The *Hanna* majority was at great pains to distinguish *Ragan*, however, characterizing it, somewhat charitably, as a case in which the Rule in question had been narrowly construed to avoid a clash with state law.[117] This self-restraint seems justified. In the first place, an argument can be made that even if *Ragan* was wrong, the *Hanna* majority was right nonetheless in declining Justice Harlan's invitation to cast doubt on it sixteen years later; much of the point of a set of procedural rules is to let people get used to and rely on the routine of doing things in a certain way.[118] In addition—despite the *Ragan* Court's misconception of the issue before it as one involving *Erie* and the Rules of Decision Act—a strong argument can be made that *Ragan* was correctly decided.[119] Admittedly, it is conceivable that a state's choice of the service of the summons rather than the filing of the complaint as the event that tolls the statute might simply be arbitrary, signifying only the need to choose something. But arbitrariness is not the only possible explanation, and it may not even be the most likely: the choice of service as the critical event might well have been seen as directly connected with what the legislature was trying to achieve by enacting a statute of limitations in the first place.[120] Statutes of limitation have several purposes, but one of them, which cannot be dismissed as procedural, is to permit potential defendants to breathe easy after the passage of the designated period. It is hard to breathe easy, however, so long as the possibility remains that you have been sued without knowing it. Thus, the right extended by a state statute of the sort involved in *Ragan* may be seen as a right to breathe easy at the end of two years unless you have been notified otherwise.[121] It should be noted that tying tolling to service makes sense only in these terms, and bears no functional relation to either of the procedural goals of a statute of limitations.[122] There is, however, even more pointed evidence that the Kansas lawmakers regarded the rule at issue in *Ragan* as an integral part of their statute of limitations. For whereas that rule required actual service to toll the statute, another provided that "[a] civil action may be commenced . . . by filing . . . a petition, and causing a summons to be issued thereon."[123] Rule 3 closely parallels the latter provision;[124] the *Hanna* majority's suggestion that it had been construed so as to avoid a clash with the former, and thereby a serious Enabling Act problem, may not have been good history—but it does seem like good sense.[125]

It would be a mistake, however, to jump from this analysis of *Woods*, *Cohen*, and *Ragan* to the conclusion that state "doorclosing" rules generally should be treated as substantive under the Enabling Act, on some theory that they determine not how lawsuits are to be conducted but rather that certain classes of lawsuits are not to be conducted at all. The state laws involved in those cases may have barred lawsuits for reasons unconnected with the way litigation is to be conducted, but sometimes doors are closed for purely procedural reasons. A monetary jurisdictional limit designed to keep the docket clear for the careful handling of "important" cases is one example. Or a suit may be barred not out of any such concern with protecting the process generally but rather because of a concern with procedural fairness in the very case involved. Thus in *Hanna* the Court held that federal courts should follow Rule 4(d)(1), which authorizes service on any responsible adult at the defendant's home, even in a state whose rules insist that the defendant be served in hand. This was the correct result, since the state rule thus subordinated was one concerned with assuring actual notice and therefore a fair opportunity to appear and be heard.[126] This goal is terribly important, but it is a procedural goal nonetheless, and the difference between the state and federal rules was one attributable to a disagreement typical of procedural squabbles—over the relative importance, on the one hand, of bending over backwards to ensure a full and fair hearing and, on the other, of keeping the process manageable.[127] Any rule that enforces its mandate by refusing to entertain, or dismissing, a suit is a door-closing rule. Here as elsewhere the nature of the state mandate thus enforced, and more specifically the concerns that gave rise to it, must be carefully scrutinized before the Enabling Act can be sensibly applied.

We are now in a position better to understand the *Sibbach* Court's refusal, which from the perspective of 1974 seems almost willfully blindered, to take the Act's second sentence seriously.[128] Denigrating Mrs. Sibbach's argument that the right not to be subjected to the sort of physical examination contemplated by Rule 35 was one recognized as substantive, the Court asked: "Recognized where and by whom? The state courts are divided . . ."[129] But didn't this "unanswerable" question have an obvious answer—that the character of the right, if any, that would have been abridged by applying Rule 35 should have been determined by examining the law of the state whose rule would have been applicable had Rule 35 never been promulgated? (The two realistic candidates were Illinois, the state in which the district court was sitting, and Indiana, the place of the tort.) If the state rule that would otherwise be applicable turned out to authorize physical examinations, it would seem that there was no right, substantive or otherwise, that application of Rule 35 would abridge. If, on the other hand, the otherwise applicable state law had failed to provide for such examinations, the Court could have gone on to explore the reasons for that failure. In 1941 it would not have been at all surprising to find that such an omission represented simply one aspect of an approach to civil procedure generally hostile to discovery practices, on the theory that creating and supervising them was just not worth the effort or indeed that they were more likely to disserve the cause of finding the truth than to serve it. Had that turned out to be the explanation, it would have been difficult to argue that application of Rule 35 would abridge a substantive right, since the theory or theories informing the state's refusal to provide for physical examinations would seem purely procedural. On the other hand, such examinations might not have been authorized because it was felt that any procedural or truth-finding gains that might be realized were outweighed by concern for the privacy of one's body. In such a state, the right to be free from examination would have to be counted substantive, in that it was granted for a purpose that transcends concerns about how litigation is conducted. Rule 35 itself is of course procedurally motivated—at the federal level the procedural, truth-finding goal was thought to outweigh the countervailing substantive claim—and so the Enabling Act's first sentence is satisfied. But if the state whose law would otherwise be applicable has struck the balance the other way, in favor of a right grounded in considerations of bodily privacy, the Act's second sentence should preclude the application of Rule 35.

Yet the Court did not even identify the state whose law would have been applicable in the absence of Rule 35.[130] Was that because it had not yet decided *Klaxon Co. v. Stentor Electric Manufacturing Co.*[131] and therefore had no basis for making the choice? That seems most unlikely: *Klaxon* was decided, in a brief and unanimous opinion, later the same term.[132] More probably, the explanation has to do with the comparatively primitive state of the Court's thinking, circa 1941, about the Rules of Decision Act. The reason the Court did not identify the state whose law would have been applicable in the absence of Rule 35 was, in all likelihood, that by its lights there was no such state. With *York* four years in the future, the Court was still operating on the assumption that the Rules of Decision Act divided legal problems into two separate piles marked "substance" and "procedure," and that those in the second pile could be dealt with by federal courts under their own rules. And since Rule 35 was plainly procedural, that put the problem with which it dealt, or so at least the Court assumed, in the second pile for Rules of Decision Act purposes.[133] And if the Rules of Decision Act did not mandate the application of state law, nothing did.[134] The case thus placed in historical context, it becomes easier to understand why the Court could not bring itself to take the Enabling Act's second sentence seriously. Invalidating a Rule under the first sentence, on the ground that it was substantive rather than procedural, would have rendered the law of some state applicable.[135] But invalidating a Rule under the second sentence, on the theory that although it was procedural it was void nonetheless, would only have led to what must have seemed the somewhat pointless result of shifting control from the Federal Rules to the federal courts.

Of course that situation no longer prevails. The Court's interpretation of the Rules of Decision Act has developed to the point where enforcement of the Enabling Act's second sentence in a diversity case[136] will lead inevitably to the application of state law and not simply to a shift of decision authority to a different set of federal officials. That much, however, has been true since 1945, the year *York* was decided. If the Court did not then begin to recognize the existence of the Enabling Act's second sentence,[137] is there any reason to think it might do so now? I think there is, and again it has to do with shifts in the Court's perception of the interrelationship between the two statutes. For by its ill-considered anastomosis of the Rules of Decision and Enabling Acts, and in particular its notion that the Rules of Decision Act, or at least "the principle of Erie," somehow limits the Federal Rules, the Court managed for years to shield itself from the necessity of seriously confronting the Enabling Act. Federal Rules that gave it little trouble, such as those involved in *Mississippi Publishing Corp. v. Murphree*[138] and *Schlagenhauf v. Holder*,[139] were evaluated and upheld under the Court's watered-down version of the Enabling Act. But cases where the application of the relevant Rule seemed troublesome, such as *Ragan* and *Woods*, were handled under the rubric of Erie and state law was applied. *Hanna* should have put an end to that shell game, however, by indicating that Federal Rules are to be tested under the Enabling Act alone. Thus, in one slight sense it seems a pity that Congress intercepted the Evidence Rules. For the privilege provisions might well have presented the case that forced the Court to get serious about the Enabling Act.

The Proposed Privilege Provisions

Defending its refusal to follow state law on husband-wife and physician-patient privilege, the Advisory Committee reported:

> [I]n diversity cases . . . the rules avoid giving state privileges the effect which substantial authority has thought necessary and proper. Regardless of what might once have been thought to be the command of Erie R. Co. v. Tompkins . . . as to observance of state created privileges in diversity cases, Hanna v. Plumer . . . is believed to locate the problem in the area of choice rather than necessity.[140]

Of course there is substantial authority that in the absence of a Federal Rule, the Rules of Decision Act requires the application of state privilege rules: any other result would plainly be wrong. Nor did *Hanna* even remotely suggest the contrary; its only alteration of the previous learning respecting the Rules of Decision Act was a clarification of the outcome determination test that was plainly without relevance to the question whether state privilege rules should be followed.[141]

Hanna did say, however, that where a Federal Rule (like the Rules the Committee was drafting) is in issue, the Rules of Decision Act, and therefore the *Erie* line of cases construing it, are beside the point, and the Enabling Act, specifically designed for the purpose, constitutes the relevant text. About the proper construction of that Act *Erie* said nothing at all and *Hanna* said nothing new. The case the Committee should have cited was *Sibbach*, which not only constitutes the Court's most extended exegesis of the Enabling Act, but also seems a fairly clear precedent for the validity of the proposed privilege provisions.[142]

When one reads beyond the Act's first sentence, however, it becomes clear that *Sibbach* was misconceived. A Rule eliminating or narrowing a privilege is designed to get at the truth and is therefore procedural; it passes the test of the Enabling Act's first sentence. But the converse of a procedural rule is not necessarily entirely procedural, and in those states with husband-wife or physician-patient privileges the procedural-substantive balance was struck the other way.

> On the classic analysis of Wigmore, the existence of a privilege is justifiable only where confidentiality is essential to foster a relation society believes so important that encouragement of the relation outweighs the need to have all relevant evidence in determining the truth of a matter.[143]

A Federal Rule displacing such a privilege would therefore violate the Act's second sentence.

Now, of course, the deal is changed. In blocking the Evidence Rules, Congress indicated that if any such Rules were to take effect it would have to be by statute,[144] and subsequent developments indicate an intention to proceed in that way. That takes the Enabling Act out of the picture (at least officially) and frees Congress to enact any Rules that do not violate the Constitution. A statute abolishing the husband-wife and physician-patient privileges in diversity cases would be constitutional because it would be procedural. Congress can therefore pass such a law if it wants to.[145] But it should proceed in the awareness that if it does, it will ignore a view of federalism that admittedly is not the Constitution's, but has nonetheless throughout our history been imposed on the allocation of lawmaking authority in connection with the diversity jurisdiction.[146]

Choice of Law and the State's Interest in Protecting *Its Own* (1981)[147]

This article examines the premise, widely invoked in modern American choice-of-law theorizing, that a state has a greater interest in protecting its own citizens or residents[148] than it has in protecting others. (Usually, we shall see, it is put more strongly—to the effect that a state's interest in protecting people extends *only* to protecting its own.) Recently this premise has come under some attack, notably by Professors Brilmayer and Twerski and Judges Bergan and Breitel of the New York Court of Appeals.[149] This article is an attempt to evaluate the extent to which the criticism is valid—at present it is somewhat undifferentiated—and what its implications must be for future choice-of-law theorizing.

The classic statements of the premise are from the godfather of modern interest analysis, the late Brainerd Currie.[150] Discussing the Massachusetts married women's statute involved in *Milliken v. Pratt*,[151] Currie wrote:

> Massachusetts . . . believes . . . that married women constitute a class requiring special protection. It has therefore subordinated its policy of security of transactions to its policy of protecting married women . . . . *What* married women? Why, those with whose welfare Massachusetts is concerned, of course, *i.e.*, Massachusetts married women. In 1866 Maine emancipated (its) married women. Is Massachusetts declaring that decision erroneous . . . ? Certainly not. . . . All that happened was that in each state the legislature weighed competing considerations, with different results. Well, each to his own. Let Maine go feminist and modern; as for Massachusetts, it will stick to the old ways—for Massachusetts women.[152]

Of the Wisconsin wrongful death statute at issue in *Hughes v. Fetter*[153] he had this to say:

> How should the statute be applied to cases that are not wholly domestic in order to effectuate the community's policy? Rather clearly, its benefits should be made available whenever those who are the objects of its protection are members of the community—*i.e.*, residents or domiciliaries of the state.[154]

His verdict on the New York "no damage ceiling" rule involved in *Kilberg v. Northeast Airlines, Inc.*[155] was the same:

> New York had no interest in applying its law and policy merely because the ticket was purchased there, or because the flight originated there. New York's policy is not for the protection of all who buy tickets in New York, or board planes there. It is for the protection of New York people.[156]

When one asks why this should be so, there is a tendency in fashionable conflicts circles to respond that that's just Currie talking, that statements like this do not reflect the sophistication that interest analysis has since achieved. This attempted dissociation is understandable, but it is neither accurate as description nor possible as prescription.

It is certainly true that most interest analysts are far from buying Currie's system lock, stock, and barrel. In particular, his recommendation for "true conflicts"—that where more than one state turns out to have an interest in seeing its law applied the forum should simply apply its own law—is one that has had almost no takers. Rejecting that approach to true conflicts, however, is by no means the same thing as rejecting Currie's basic method of deciding which states are interested (and consequently whether the conflict is true or false). Indeed, without Currie's basic methodological premise—that states are interested in protecting their own residents in a way they are not interested in protecting others—interest analysis is largely impotent.

The modern learning's proudest boast—one joined by virtually every contemporary writer on the subject—is that in a significant percentage of the cases (many say most), analysis of the interests of the states apparently involved will generate the conclusion that only one state is interested (and the conflict is therefore dismissible as "false") or if not that, the interests of one state will so overwhelmingly predominate that there can be no serious doubt that its law should be applied.[157] Faith that this is so is needed to maintain faith in interest analysis generally, since there is general agreement that no one has come up with a very convincing way of coping with genuine conflicts.[158]

Let's assume a case with two potentially interested states, however. Ignore the questions where the accident or whatever took place, where the parties are from, where the suit is brought, and so forth: the point I want to make does not depend on such particularities. The conflicts issue will arise, obviously, from the fact that one of the states has a rule that in one or another way is more favorable to the plaintiff (and the other has a rule that is correspondingly favorable to the defendant). *If, however, the state with the plaintiff-protecting rule is taken to have an interest in protecting the plaintiff irrespective of where he is from, and the state with the defendant-protecting rule is taken to be interested in protecting the defendant irrespective of where he is from, both states will necessarily be interested and the conflict will thus necessarily be true.* Indeed, without the device of discounting one or the other state's interest because the party its law would protect is not local, it is difficult to discern a principled basis for concluding that the interests of the two states in applying their own laws are in other than essential equipoise.

Now this could be avoided by refusing to define interests in domiciliary terms at all. The dilemma arises only if we assume, say, that a state with a plaintiff-protecting rule is interested in applying its rule in cases where the plaintiff comes from that state—at which point we will begin to wonder, at least we should, whether the state shouldn't be claiming an interest in protecting nonlocal plaintiffs as well. Why, then, don't we define interests other than in terms of protecting this or that party and say instead, for example, that the state of injury, or perhaps the state of the alleged wrongful conduct, is the "interested" state? In fact, I think that's about where we ought to end up in all of this. The problem is that despite my procrustean imposition of the label "interest," this isn't what is ordinarily meant by interest analysis; indeed, it seems to amount to nothing other than a quite old-fashioned territorial rules approach.

This isn't to say that interest analysts don't recognize that there can be interests in influencing local behavior. In fact they do—though we'll see that when it comes to the actual analysis of cases such interests tend to get ignored, or at any rate receive short shrift, as compared with the asserted interests of states in protecting their resident litigants.[159] And, indeed, when they describe their systems in the abstract, such analysts are likely to place little or no stress on the extent to which interests will be defined in terms of protecting local parties: in such summaries the reference will probably be to "interested" (or "concerned") states without going into detail about what it is that makes them interested.[160] When they get down to the actual analysis of cases, however, the premise that states have an unusual interest in applying their rules so as to benefit their own citizens will typically be quite quickly and matter-of-factly wheeled into action.

The reason for this is easily understood when one considers the alternatives. If, on the one hand, the residences of the parties are left out of account and "interests" are defined entirely in terms of the geographical locale of one or another critical event—that obviously is the only real alternative—it will soon become plain that what is being recommended is just another version of the "bad" old territorial learning. If one goes to the other extreme, however, and holds that the state with, say, the plaintiff-protecting rule is "interested" in generating a victory for the plaintiff not simply when he or she is a local resident, but also when he or she hails from another jurisdiction, it will become plain just as soon that all states with any connection with the case must be counted as interested and that the case therefore cannot be waved aside as involving a false or trivial conflict. Thus, the only way the system can operate, without reducing itself to a set of old-fashioned territorial rules, is by assuming that states are interested in applying their rules so as to generate victories for their own people in a way they are not interested in generating victories for others.

One would naturally expect writers whose analysis has hewed close to Currie's original line to follow him here, and they do. This, from Robert Sedler, is typical: "The plaintiff's home state is interested in applying its own law allowing its resident to recover, while the defendant's home state is equally interested in applying its own law to protect the defendant and the insurer."[161] Since the premise that states are unusually interested in promoting the fortunes of their own people turns out to be prerequisite to any real progress by analysis of the interests, however, one would also expect to find it in the work of those whose methodology does not so nearly parallel Currie's. And, again, one does. The premise is shared, and enunciated, by analysts as independent of Currie and of one another as, for example, Paul Freund ("The invalidating law of Pennsylvania may fairly be regarded as designed to protect Pennsylvania borrowers; New York borrowers, on the other hand, are not given that kind of protection by their own internal law");[162] William Baxter ("X lawmakers want X law to apply in cases involving X food processors, and Y lawmakers want Y law to apply in cases involving Y consumers");[163] and Donald Trautman ("If the purpose of a guest statute . . . were seen as one solely to protect the driver . . . such a statute in the place of accident should rationally have little bearing on a case in which the driver comes from a liability state . . .").[164] Professor Baade thus does not overstate badly when he asserts:

> If state *A* has [a married women's] disability and state *B* does not, all cases where the wife is domiciled in *B* will be false-conflict cases, for the application of the law of *A* will frustrate an interest of *B* without really advancing an interest of *A*.
>
> So far as I can determine, most commentators—with the significant exception of Professor Ehrenzweig and his followers—have come to accept this basic proposition.[165]

I intend in this article to evaluate the constitutionality and sense of the premise that states have a greater interest in advancing the interests of their own than they have in advancing the interests of outsiders. Having cast what seems to me significant doubt on it, I shall take a more careful look at its functional importance and conclude that it actually may not have a great deal—that in fact most of what appear on the surface to be conflicts of law are just that, and cannot be dissolved *either with or without* the premise that states are unusually interested in helping their own. Interest analysis, I shall suggest, has an important contribution to make only in cases—and actually only a subset of these—where the plaintiff and defendant hail from the same state (or states whose laws are identical). All others, I shall argue, can sensibly be resolved only by what will doubtless strike many as hopelessly old-fashioned choice-of-law rules.

The Constitutional Framework

Brainerd Currie used to argue, in essence, that the Supreme Court had constitutionalized his system, which meant, among other things, that the Court had indicated that states had no constitutionally legitimate business regarding out-of-staters as within the scope of their protective policies.[166] This claim is so plainly the result of wishful thinking that it does not merit extended rejoinder. The recent cases have indicated that essentially any contact with a case, certainly including those to which the traditional territorial rules were geared, will constitutionally support a state's application of its own law,[167] and the older cases on which Currie relied (apparently on the theory they somehow trumped the newer ones) turn out on analysis, and I must say unsurprisingly, to be if anything even less Currian in method.[168] Whether the Court *should* have constitutionalized the premise that states are legitimately interested in protecting only their own is a different question, one included within the subject of this article. That it has not in fact done so seems entirely clear.

Indeed, it is the contrary proposition—that it is *un*constitutional for a state to take the position that its protective policies extend only to its own citizens—that seems more likely to strike the contemporary observer of the constitutional scene as plausible. The clause that thrusts itself forward here, of course, is that first resort of constitutional argument, the Fourteenth Amendment's Equal Protection Clause.[169] Limiting the protection of local laws to local people is obviously "rational" under traditional tests, but somehow that seems unsatisfying. Classifications that distinguish locals from out-of-staters seem somehow, well, suspect, and therefore appropriately subject to a demand for a defense that is more than rational.[170] Since the special constitutional vulnerability of such distinctions is established quite directly by Article IV's Privileges and Immunities Clause, however, it is this clause that I shall proceed to consider.

The guarantee of Article IV that "[t]he Citizens of each State shall be entitled to all Privileges and Immunities of Citizens in the several States" was plainly intended to prevent discrimination against out-of-staters: "It was designed to insure to a citizen of State A who ventures into State B the same privileges which the citizens of State B enjoy."[171] And indeed, with minor and soon-corrected diversions, that is precisely the spirit in which it has been interpreted for the two centuries it has been in the Constitution. For example, in *Toomer v. Witsell*, decided in 1948, the Court invalidated a South Carolina statute imposing a higher shrimping license fee on non-residents than on residents, using language that made very clear its disposition to subject local/nonlocal distinctions to intensive scrutiny.[172] *Doe v. Bolton*, decided in 1973, was equally serious in its scrutiny when the subject was medical care: "Just as the Privileges and Immunities Clause . . . protects persons who enter other States to ply their trade . . . so must it protect persons who enter Georgia seeking the medical services that are available there."[173]

A different note was struck in 1978, when the Court indicated that the clause protected against discrimination regarding only "fundamental" rights,[174] and upheld a state law imposing a higher elk hunting license fee on out-of-staters than on locals in *Baldwin v. Montana Fish & Game Commission*.[175] The significance of the shift was attenuated by the fact that in the course of its opinion the Court articulated an alternative ground—that residents contribute to the support of hunting areas through other sorts of taxes (to which nonresidents are not subject)[176]—and in any event *Baldwin* appears to have been gutted a month after it was decided by *Hicklin v. Orbeck*, which invalidated an Alaska law requiring that local residents be hired in preference to equally qualified nonresidents for all local employment resulting from oil or gas leases.[177] I certainly don't mean to suggest that no responsible person could distinguish the facts in *Baldwin* from those in *Hicklin*; that would be nonsense. The reason I suggest the latter may have "gutted" the former has to do instead with the fact that Justice Brennan's opinion for the (unanimous) Court in the later case is strikingly similar to the dissent he wrote for himself and Justices White and Marshall in the earlier one, and relies heavily on *Toomer v. Witsell*, which *is* difficult responsibly to distinguish from *Baldwin*.

Whether or not *Baldwin* is here to stay is beside the present point, however, because the cases we are talking about involve not simply something on the order of the right to hunt elk (let alone the amount of the license fee for doing so), but rather questions such as whether a given state's guest statute or contractual immunity law is to be applied in a given case, and therefore whether the defendant will or will not be held liable for the damages he or she inflicted. *Baldwin* or no *Baldwin*, it is not likely to be suggested that such decisions implicate rights so unimportant that they can be dismissed as beyond the coverage of the Privileges and Immunities Clause. It is true that in our "conflicts" context we will not ordinarily be dealing with laws that on their face limit their protection to locals. However, the methodology under discussion, which counsels that in order to avoid or minimize conflict state laws should be interpreted as if they contained precisely that limitation, amounts for constitutional purposes to the same thing. A judicial assurance that "Of course California law would protect you fully, but because you do not come from California its law will not be applied in your case" is plainly the equivalent of a holding that you are outside the protection of California law, and thus equally in apparent violation of the Privileges and Immunities Clause.

In one of his early articles, Currie noted in passing that adoption of an interest analysis methodology "would give a new importance" to the Privileges and Immunities Clause.[178] It should be clear by now that that is putting it mildly. In fact few interest analysts seem prepared to take the issue seriously[179]—the prevailing assumption seems to be that nothing so sensible could possibly be unconstitutional—but, characteristically, Currie was an exception. In two lengthy articles published in 1960 and written in collaboration with Professor Herma Kay, herself a distinguished interest analyst, Currie took the privileges and immunities attack very seriously indeed,[180] in fact so seriously as to overcomplicate it substantially.

The key device Currie and Kay recommended for coping with the constitutional problem was the so-called "intermediate solution" of extending the protection of forum law to an out-of-stater if, but only if, he or she was similarly protected by the law of his or her home state.[181] That solution was subject to several restrictions, among them that it not be employed if it ended up generating a true conflict,[182] and indeed the restrictions underwent significant alteration between the first article and the second.[183] Paradoxically, however—and here the overcomplication took its toll—the intermediate solution turns out on close analysis to be a mere paper alteration, without functional significance. For if the law of a party's home state would decide the case for him, then by standard interest analysis canons that state has an interest in the application of its law. If no other state has an interest in a contrary result, the conflict is "false" and the courts of all states are instructed to find for him; no "extension" of another state's law to protect him is needed to reach that result. If, on the other hand, another state *does* have an interest in a contrary result, there exists a true conflict between the law of that state and that of the home state of the party in question. Different commentators have different ways of dealing with true conflicts, but for none will the consideration that the party is protected not only by his home state's law but also by an "extension" of another state's law make a difference. At first blush it might seem that it could make a difference for Currie, if the law whose "extension" is in issue is that of the forum. For his recommendation, not widely accepted, was that in case of a true conflict the forum, if it has an interest, apply its own law. And the "extension" of the forum's law to protect an out-of-stater will convert it from a disinterested forum into an interested one. But again, no outcome will be influenced. For Currie's recommendation was that a disinterested forum confronted with a true conflict between the interests of two other jurisdictions decide the case in accord with the law of that interested state whose law is the same as its own.[184] The same result would therefore be reached whether or not the extension of the intermediate solution was made.

It may be, however, that the linchpin of that little demonstration—the realization that the party's home state has an interest in protecting him or her whether the forum does or not—provides a more direct route out of our privileges and immunities dilemma. Perhaps we have been focusing our attention too narrowly, on the recommendation that we construe a particular state's protective policies as protecting locals only. Viewed that narrowly, it's quite true that the discrimination seems just what the Privileges and Immunities Clause forbids, one between locals and nonlocals. If we widen our horizon, however, the recommendation of the interest analysts is not simply that Californians receive the protection of California's protective policies and everyone else be denied them, but rather that everyone receive the benefit of the protective policies his or her own state has seen fit to legislate. Of course that may turn out not to be possible, if two or more states wish to protect their own in ways that cannot coexist: that is the classic true conflict situation. Currie would, in that event, tell the forum to apply its own law.[185] Most commentators reject that solution, however, refusing in their various processes of accommodation to discount the presumptive entitlement of an interested state to the application of law on the ground that it is not the state in which suit was brought. And if that is the approach, the system can be viewed not as one that flatly distinguishes locals from out-of-staters, but rather as one that "simply" sorts people out according to the states from which they hail. Whether or not they are accorded benefits equivalent to those accorded by local law, therefore, will depend on what their local legislators have seen fit to do for them, and that, the argument would run, is not a violation of the Privileges and Immunities Clause.

The argument does not run smooth, at least so far as the case law is concerned. For if it satisfied the Privileges and Immunities Clause to deny someone the benefits of local law so long as he is getting what his home state's law would give him, the proper course, before voiding any law under that clause, would be to inquire where the complainant is from and whether he would be entitled at home to the benefit he now seeks. If he wouldn't, his privileges and immunities challenge should be rejected (though the challenges of others from other states would succeed). Yet we know perfectly well that this is not the way the Court has proceeded under Article IV: indeed I am not aware of a single instance where it has asked what the challenger would be entitled to at home.[186]

The Court's assumption that the content of the challenger's home state law is irrelevant to a privileges and immunities challenge was demonstrated even more forcefully, albeit still with apparent inadvertence, in its 1975 decision in *Austin v. New Hampshire*.[187] Invalidated in *Austin* was the New Hampshire Commuters Income Tax, which applied to the New Hampshire–derived income of nonresidents, but exempted the income of residents similarly earned within the state. It thus seems like a straightforward privileges and immunities case—until we add two facts, that the law imposed a ceiling on the tax rate of whatever rate would be imposed by the taxpayer's home state on income he earned there, and included a provision that in the event the home state refused to credit the taxpayer for the taxes paid to New Hampshire they would not be imposed. The net effect, therefore, was to tax an out-of-stater at the rate his home legislature had selected. Of course it can be argued that this is something other than treating him as his home legislature would, as taxes paid at home will be spent at home whereas New Hampshire will spend its revenues, understandably enough, in New Hampshire. The Court did not so much as mention this, however—unsurprisingly, I think, since New Hampshire is a place where the commuting taxpayer spends a good deal of time even if he doesn't sleep there, and as noted the home state was given the option, which in the event was not exercised, of ensuring that the money *would* be spent at home. *Austin* thus seems to stand rather directly for the proposition that it is *not* sufficient under the Privileges and Immunities Clause to treat people as the laws of their home states would treat them.

The importance of this conclusion should not be underestimated. If *Austin* is right as written, the dominant contemporary choice-of-law theory is unconstitutional. The threat is by no means simply to Brainerd Currie's dictum that in cases of true conflict the forum should apply its own law; the point is much more devastating. It undercuts the entire methodology by indicating that whenever a state would claim an interest in enforcing its protective policy on the ground that the party its law would protect is a local resident—and that much is common to all "interest" or "functional" analysts—it is obligated by the United States Constitution to claim a similar interest in protecting out-of-staters, irrespective of what their home states' law provides. That, for reasons we have canvassed, spells the end of "interest analysis" in any recognizable sense of the term and insists instead that we direct our choice-of-law references to that state which will most often bear the strongest relation to the issue in question—relation, however, not being defined in terms of who lives where.[188]

Austin was decided only six years ago, and surely the Court has cast nothing resembling explicit doubt on it.[189] Reason to suppose its implications were not fully considered, however, is supplied by the more recent decision in *Allstate Insurance Co. v. Hague*,[190] where seven members of the Court, while they did not explicitly say that the residence of the party to be benefited could alone form the constitutional basis for the application of local law, did seem to imply that[191] and surely indicated, as the Court had in the past,[192] that such residence is a factor on which a state may constitutionally rely in applying its own law.[193] The opinions in *Hague* did not even mention *Austin*.

It seems, therefore, that the one hand is not keeping up with what the other is up to, that for some reason *Austin* did not strike the Court as "a conflict of laws case" and, more surprisingly, did not even set off alarms suggesting a consideration of the implications of what the Court was saying for more run-of-the-mill conflicts cases. For if *Austin* is right as written, and it violates the Privileges and Immunities Clause to grant everyone the benefits of his or her home state's law, then interest analysis of the sort approved six years later in *Hague*—permitting states to apply local law to benefit local citizens under conditions where they would not do likewise for nonlocals—seems unconstitutional. Which should give?

A cheap-shot sort of answer to the *Austin* inference, variations of which answer one encounters with distressing frequency, would run that it is the office of the Privileges and Immunities Clause, as it is the office of Article IV generally, to promote interstate harmony, and, after all, such harmony will not really be threatened so long as people are accorded the protections of their home states' laws. It is true that under such circumstances officials of the home state of the individual in question are unlikely to respond by vowing that "Tennessee, suh, will be ruhvainged." But *no* approach to conflict of laws is likely to have that effect, not even, to focus on the relevant comparison, out-and-out discrimination against out-of-staters without regard to where they are from. Friction and the threat of retaliation may not be the real point, however.

I argued in *Democracy and Distrust* that the Privileges and Immunities Clause was an early statement of a central concern of our Constitution, the representation of the unrepresented. Discrimination against out-of-staters is not likely to have been singled out for prohibition in the original constitutional document because the framers supposed it to be a uniquely invidious form of discrimination: under the circumstances that would have been quite perverse. The perceived distinguishing characteristic seems instead quite clearly to have been the unique political powerlessness of those with no voice in the local political process.[194] (The franchise has constituted a classic conundrum for the clause: countless courts and commentators have wondered how on earth it can be, as it plainly must be, that the clause permits a state to deny nonresidents the right to vote in local elections? In fact this conundrum seems responsible in part for the "fundamental rights" dodge we saw in *Baldwin*[195]—though it plainly forms a bizarre basis for distinction, voting being counted in most constitutional contexts as the paradigmatic fundamental right. The conundrum dissolves after a moment's reflection on the purpose of the clause, however: unless one started with the assumption that a person would be able to vote in only one state, there would be no occasion for the clause to begin with.)

Now if this account is correct, and the point of the clause is to protect people from being disadvantaged by legislatures they lack any say in electing, it should be satisfied so long as the individual is provided whatever protections his local legislature has seen fit to provide. (Of course the person may have little effective clout at home, but it's as much as a local will have locally, and locals plainly are not protected by the clause.) And while one wouldn't want to place anything resembling principal stress on a basis as shifting and questionable as eighteenth-century conflicts thinking, the view that it is constitutionally sufficient to accord everyone the protection of his home state's law is corroborated at least slightly by the fact that at least one influential conflicts thinker whose work was widely noticed in this country around the time the Constitution was framed—namely Ulrich Huber—had expressed the view that questions concerning a person's "capacity" were to be decided by the law of his domicile.[196] The relevance of that historical observation is trivial, however, compared with that of the argument that really matters, that the apparent central purpose of the Privileges and Immunities Clause is served so long as everyone is accorded the benefits of his or her home state's law.[197] And if that is right, it is *Austin* that should give way. Certainly I don't see any pressing need to rush out and overrule it, but it probably should be limited by a fact of which the

Court took no visible notice, that paying taxes to another state is not quite the equivalent of paying them at home, even assuming the rates are identical.

Obviously this conclusion is short of self-evident, and one might well side with *Austin* in supposing that the fact that a person is being treated as he would be treated at home is irrelevant to the constitutionality of treating him less well than locals are treated. (Even without resort to the fiction that interstate harmony will be significantly threatened, one might maintain that Article IV's general goal of making us more one nation is sufficiently disserved by gearing choice-of-law determinations to residence in one or another state to justify invalidating such references under the Privileges and Immunities Clause. My own instinct, as we are about to see, is to classify that as a "small c" constitutional argument, but that classification too is surely debatable.) If it *is* your inclination to accept *Austin*, however, I think there is no escape from the conclusion that an interest analysis approach to choice-of-law problems, whereby a state must be granted a greater interest in applying its law so as to generate a victory for a local resident than it has in applying its law so as to generate a victory for an outsider, is unconstitutional. For reasons that will become obvious, this is not a conclusion that would throw me into a tailspin. But for reasons I have indicated, it seems to me the less sound line of inference from the central purpose apparently informing the Privileges and Immunities Clause. It is therefore incumbent on me, though it may not be on you, to proceed further in considering the merits of the axiom that states have an unusual interest in protecting their own.

The Sense of a Policy of Construing Local Protections as Protecting Locals Only

Despite what has been said, something continues to nag: isn't there something somehow out of accord with at least our "small c constitution"—out of accord in particular with the reasons we as a nation decided to supersede the Articles of Confederation—in adopting what amounts to a system of "personal law" wherein people carry their home states' legal regimes around with them?

> Personal law was perhaps appropriate in the era following the barbarian invasions of Italy, when a Lombard or Roman in the Kingdom of Alboin obeyed only the law of his own people, largely no doubt because ethnic differences were great and because the royal authority was too weak to impose uniformity. In the modern setting there seems little reason to magnify artificially the difference between citizenship in one or another of the American states.[198]

It's true that Huber and undoubtedly some others thought that personal law was appropriate to questions of "capacity," and it's also true that clever counsel can slap the label "capacity" on just about any legal issue under the sun, but that should not be enough to legitimate a *general regime* of personal law. It is further true that the Court has done little to enforce Article IV's Full Faith and Credit Clause, which plainly is devoted to the idea that at least in a significant set of contexts conflict-of-laws questions should be determined, in all states, by some uniform reference. Perhaps it is just as well that it hasn't, as the early candidates for uniform imposition would have been gross, clumsy rules of the *First Restatement* variety. What's more, the need for uniform treatment in some areas is at least debatable, and a principled line between those occasions on which uniformity is essential and those on which it is not has proved elusive. To admit that, however, is surely not to concede that all is harmony between the unifying spirit of the Full Faith and Credit and Privileges and Immunities Clauses and a system that takes as its starting point the protection of locals only.[199] No "principled" cut-off has been found for the Commerce Clause either, yet I trust we remain free to object, indeed to object in the name of the constitution, to a theory of federalism that takes as its starting point the proposition that the central government can and should regulate anything it pleases.

This point too is surely less than clear as crystal, as I would suppose claims of "small c" unconstitutionality inevitably are. It is well to move on briskly, therefore, to consider the *sense* of the premise that state protective policies are appropriately extended only to the state's own citizens. We must ask, to begin with, exactly what it *means* to assert that states are "interested" in protecting their own in a way they are not interested in protecting others. Occasionally the suggestion is that this is the likely legislative *intent*, that states are unusually interested in protecting their own citizens because their own citizens are the only people the lawmakers intend to be covered by their various protective policies.[200] This claim need not be tarried over, since it has so recently been pulverized by Professor Brilmayer, whose search of state statutory choice-of-law provisions turned up none that were geared to benefiting forum residents.[201]

Legislators probably seldom think about the choice-of-law implications of what they are doing. Their commands generally are phrased in universal terms and so, frequently, must be their thoughts: such-and-such a practice is simply bad (or good) and it is probably the legislators' intention simply to eradicate (or encourage) it—at least insofar as it is constitutional for them to do so. Or they may be thinking in terms of the conflict-of-laws rules they learned in law school, likely quite traditional ones. Or they may simply be assuming that such questions are for the courts to decide. What we don't find, in either the statutes or the legislative history, are expressions of intention to protect only locals.[202]

The legislative intent line thus cannot be pursued seriously for very long, and it is not. Its defects become obvious so early that the argument for a local-protection premise must soon verge into the normative assertion that states have no *business* protecting anyone but their own citizens, that they are intermeddling when they protect anyone else.[203] We've seen that this isn't supported by the constitutional case law, and I suggest it isn't supported by good sense either. In the first place, states have various "interests" that are indifferent to the residence of either or both parties to a lawsuit—interests, for example, in shaping behavior that affects the environment within the state, or interests in protecting the state's judicial system in various ways. Generally speaking, these interests will not be keyed to which litigant comes from where, and it would be quite consistent with the vindication of an interest, say, in reducing dangerous behavior within the state to apply a rule whose effect in the case at bar would be to render a verdict for a foreign plaintiff.

Interest analysts do recognize the theoretical existence of these behavior-shaping and process-protecting interests, at least some of them do, sometimes. They have an annoying habit, however, of "putting such interests to one side for purposes of analysis"[204] or, more commonly, simply ignoring them.[205] The reason for this is not hard to discern: by universal agreement the real value of interest analysis lies in its ability to dismiss apparent conflicts as false—that is, as implicating the genuine interests of no more than one state—and a candid recognition of such litigant-independent interests will almost inevitably ensure that something that looks on the surface like a case involving a "conflict of laws" (a case, for example, where the situs of the critical events is not the residence of both parties) will on analysis turn out to be just that.

It is not this sort of potentially competing state interest that I want to focus on, though, if only because the point is recognized in theory. I want to focus instead on that aspect of the local-protection premise that holds that a state can be interested only in *helping* its own by applying its rules so as to assure that they will win their lawsuits, that consequently it can have no interest in causing a local to *lose* his or her case. Of course this conclusion is entailed by the definitions of "interest" quoted above,[206] but lest you think I am seizing on an unintended implication I tender some specifics: "New York has no particular interest in holding its own people liable for injuries to foreigners."[207] "The plaintiff's domicile has no interest in insulating a defendant from liability."[208]

> It seems evident that New Hampshire's protective policy is directed to the protection of New Hampshire buyers. One could scarcely expect its extension to a Massachusetts buyer even though the seller's place of business was in New Hampshire.[209]

This strikes me as simply wrong. Even assuming that there can be no state "interest" in what happens to a given litigant unless he or she is a local resident, it hardly follows that states can be interested only in generating *victories* for such persons. A state law providing *P* a cause of action against *D* (or otherwise promoting such a cause of action) would seem to serve an interest not simply in compensating *P* but also in assessing *D*. (In all likelihood it also serves some interests transcending the fate of the immediate litigants, but for now we are leaving those aside.) Such a law indicates that *P* ought to be paid, but it also indicates that it is *D* who ought to do the paying—perhaps because he misbehaved, at all events because it is felt to be right under the circumstances that he be the one to bear the cost.[210] (Absent this last impulse, of course, the law could be structured so that the government picked up the tab.) This would suggest—still accepting for the sake of argument the assumption that a litigant-affecting interest can attach only when the relevant litigant is local—that a state is as "interested" in applying a liability-promoting law when the defendant is local as it is when the plaintiff is local.[211] Can the idea be that it is somehow improper to claim an interest in sanctioning the state's own citizens? The tiniest peek beyond the four corners of the traditional turf of conflicts scholars, in particular a peek at the state's criminal code, should allay forever any suspicion that states either do not mean to impose liability, or behave improperly when they do mean to impose liability, upon "the state's own" when it is felt that such liability would be just.[212]

The converse situation may not be quite so clean. Usually a decision that the defendant shouldn't pay in a given situation is at the same time a decision that the plaintiff shouldn't collect. Surely this seems true respecting refusals to follow other states in recognizing particular causes of action. However, there may be some special defenses regarding which the point is not entirely clear.[213] When a state enacts a spendthrift statute, it may well be that no judgment is implied that the plaintiff shouldn't recover, only that the defendant shouldn't be held liable. (Of course, if the feeling were strongly held that the plaintiff should be compensated in such situations, the government could pick up the tab . . . .) Charitable and sovereign immunities may furnish other examples of the same configuration, though there it seems more arguable, since there may at the time such rules were common have been some feeling that "it just isn't right" for people to recover from charities or from "their" governments. In any event such immunities are rare, and decreasing, and today the burden must surely be on one who asserts that a state that seeks to insulate defendants from liability in a certain situation is not also trying to keep plaintiffs from recovering in that situation. Certainly the *general* proposition, that a state simply has no "interest" in invoking a liability-thwarting or liability-limiting rule so as to protect a foreign defendant from a local plaintiff, seems indefensible.

What Difference Does It Make?

One thing that should be reiterated, if only because it is so often denied, is that the damage inflicted by the foregoing discussion is *not* simply to Brainerd Currie's "apply the law of the forum" answer to true conflicts. The criticism strikes at interest analysis generally, in particular at its crucial claim that by eliminating states from the calculus (because applying their law will not result in a victory for one of their residents) it can demonstrate that most or at least many apparent conflicts are false. By focusing on the various possible configurations of law and party residence, however, we shall see that in most cases it will not in fact make any difference at all whether we accept or reject the assumption that states are interested only in promoting verdicts for their own people, that cases that would find themselves in equipoise without that limiting assumption are likely to remain in equipoise even if the assumption is made.

In a two-party situation there are three possible law/party residence configurations.[214] Shunning the usual labels in order to shed the usual baggage, I shall call these three configurations the "head-on" configuration, the "criss-cross" configuration, and the "common domicile" configuration. The "head-on" configuration is the classic "true conflict," where the plaintiff comes from a state with what is in context the plaintiff-favoring rule and the defendant comes from a state with the defendant-favoring rule. By standard interest analysis canons, each state has an interest in applying its own law because the party that would be favored by doing so is local. Obviously, this stalemate will not be broken or even alleviated by departing from the standard canon and holding that a state can be interested in applying its law so as to benefit a nonlocal party: both states are "interested" already and would simply remain so. This configuration is in any event the classic embarrassment for interest analysis, a situation that is not affected one way or another by limiting the definition of interest to the protection of locals.

The "criss-cross" configuration *should* be equally embarrassing, but here, by clever cosmetology, the embarrassment is hidden, maybe even from the interest analysts themselves. This is often referred to as the "unprovided" or "unprovided for" case, meaning that neither state is interested in the outcome. (I'm not using that label in order to leave open the question whether that is necessarily so.) The "criss-cross" is, in any event, the case where the plaintiff comes from the state with the defendant-protecting rule and the defendant comes from the state with the plaintiff-protecting rule. It surely does seem true that by ordinary interest analysis canons neither state has an interest in having its law applied and that the case is for that reason in equipoise. However, if this is admitted—and added to the confessed lack of a rational interest analysis resolution of head-on cases—the case begins to mount up that interest analysis isn't a great deal of help. As Professor Twerski put it:

> In an unprovided for case . . . we face a situation where there are no domiciliary interests to protect on the part of the contact states. New York has no domiciliary interests to protect by its pro-compensation rule since the plaintiff is not a New Yorker. Ontario has no domiciliary interests to protect by its anti-compensation rule because the defendant is not an Ontario domiciliary. Thus, the entire structure of interest analysis crumbled. Having defined the interests as domiciliary oriented when you run out of domiciliaries to protect you run out of interests. The emperor indeed stands naked for all to see.[215]

Criticism like this understandably has sent the interest analysts scurrying for fig leaves. Most frequently invoked is the "common policy" doctrine, which is exemplified by Professor Sedler's discussion of *Neumeier v. Kuehner*,[216] a 1972 case that understandably hastened the New York Court of Appeals' retreat from an interest analysis approach. (*Neumeier* is the case Twerski was talking about as well.) It involved a suit by a passenger-guest from Ontario, which has a guest statute (barring recoveries by guests in cases of ordinary negligence), against, you guessed it, a driver-host from New York, which doesn't have a guest statute. (The accident, if anybody else cares—and it turned out the court did—occurred in Ontario.) Professor Sedler wrote:

> It is unfortunate that *Neumeier*, presenting the unprovided for case, was the rock on which New York's "stormy affair" with interest analysis foundered. If the unprovided for case is approached with reference to the common policies of the involved states, sound solutions readily appear and would have appeared to the court in *Neumeier* . . . . An analysis of the policies and interests of the involved states may reveal, as in *Neumeier*, that neither state has an interest in applying its law on the issue of guest-host immunity, but when the common policies of both states are considered, this will furnish guidance on the question of whether the defense of guest statute immunity should be allowed.
>
> Approaching the problem from this perspective, I would submit that *Neumeier* is an easy case. All states have a common policy of compensating automobile accident victims for harm caused by the negligence of a driver . . . . Whether the purpose of the guest statute immunity is to protect the host from ungrateful guests . . . or to protect insurance companies from collusive suits, or simply to remove this category of cases from the insurer's liability . . . it is clear that the only state interested in extending such protection is the defendant's home state, where the vehicle is insured and where the consequences of imposing liability

will be felt. If that state does not have a guest statute, this means that the only state interested in protecting the defendant and his insurer does not do so, and the common policy of both states in allowing accident victims to recover from negligent drivers should prevail, causing the court to disallow the defense.[217]

But just what sort of entity is this "shared" interest or policy supposed to be? We are told that New York shares an interest in allowing recovery even though (and this an interest analyst should surely stumble over) the plaintiff is not from New York (or any other place that allows recovery in such situations) and the accident did not take place there. Then we are told that Ontario also shares the interest in providing recovery even though (and this *everyone* should stumble over) the cause of action is of a sort that Ontario refuses to recognize.[218] Is it any less plausible to assert that the two jurisdictions share a "common policy" of not imposing liability except in certain designated situations? This, for New York, is not one of those situations, the argument would continue, and thus recourse must be had to the shared policy of nonrecovery.[219]

It is therefore understandable that the "common policy" doctrine was not Brainerd Currie's only answer to the criss-cross configuration. He did suggest it, but he had two others he seemed to like as well.[220] His apparent favorite, that courts here (as in head-ons) simply apply the law of the forum,[221] was admittedly a Gordian knot cutter—he once analogized it to flipping a coin[222]—and it understandably has not had many takers. He also sometimes invoked a so-called "altruistic interest" in extending the protection of a state's law to parties who did not live there.[223] Obviously that is no solution if one plays it straight and "altruistically" extends the protections of *both* laws: if the deadlock is to be broken it is necessary to "extend" one law but not the other. Naturally this is what Currie did: unfortunately he didn't tell us how to decide which law to "extend" and indeed gave little sign of awareness of the problem. (Of course this method can be collapsed into the method of deciding the case in accordance with the "common policy" the two states share, and undoubtedly the two did merge somewhat in Currie's mind. We have seen, however, that that too is likely to entail an essentially arbitrary choice, so recognition of the connection is not much progress.)

There therefore does not appear a principled basis for "stretching" the interests said to underlie the one law so as to cover the out-of-state party without comparable "stretching" of the other law. To extend them *both* in this way is, of course, to reject the assumption that states are interested only in promoting verdicts for their own people. We return, therefore, to the question with which we began, whether it makes any functional difference whether or not we embrace the protect-locals-only premise, and the answer again seems to be no. Rejecting it will simply convert a situation in which neither state is "interested" to one in which they both are: an unprovided case will be converted, if you will, to an "overprovided" case, and the deadlock will persist, albeit at 1 to 1 rather than 0 to 0.

In fact I think thus far the discussion of the criss-cross case has been a little unfair to the interest analysts. We have been assuming, as the passage from Twerski and the several saving dodges all assume, that there exists no "interest" on the part of any state in anything other than promoting a victory for one or the other litigant. This assumption is surely understandable, on the part of critics and defenders alike, for we have seen that interest analysts often leave litigant-independent (behavior-shaping or process-protecting) interests out of account in their analyses of cases. That doesn't mean *we* have to, though, and factoring them in does seem to make a difference.

In some cases it is quite true, of course, that such interests don't exist, and what's more *Neumeier* seems to have been such a case. (Guest statutes arguably serve to protect forum processes by discouraging collusive perjury, but in *Neumeier* it was the forum that did not have a guest statute. Conversely, a failure to enact a guest statute may possibly help to make hosts more careful drivers, but in *Neumeier* it was the situs that *had* such a statute. All in all a textbook vacuum.) Not all criss-crosses are *Neumeier*, however, and there will be cases where the plaintiff comes from the state with the pro-defendant rule and the defendant comes from the state with the pro-plaintiff rule, *and* one or the other state also has some interest in apply ing its rule that is not geared to promoting or thwarting recovery. You might expect that exchanging the locations of the accident and the lawsuit in *Neumeier* would generate such a case, but it's not that simple. Remember that it's a perfect vacuum: such an exchange would give the situs a behavior-influencing interest and the forum a process-protecting interest, and thus generate what seems another deadlock.

Instead let's alter the *Neumeier* pattern, keeping it criss-cross, by putting both the accident and the lawsuit in the state without the guest statute (New York, in fact). Finally we have built a case in which it can at least be argued that it makes a difference whether one accepts or rejects the premise that states are interested in promoting victories only for their own people. (It can be argued, that is, on the assumption that the lack of a guest statute will make drivers more careful. I don't find that assumption very powerful, but let's make it for the moment in order to make the example work.[224]) Without the locals-only premise, the situs has, if you will, "two interests" in applying its law—increasing the local safety level and generating a victory for the (nonresident) plaintiff against the (resident) defendant—whereas the plaintiff's residence has one interest, in protecting the (nonresident) defendant from liability to the (resident) plaintiff. If, on the other hand, we adhere to the premise that protective policies extend only to locals, there is but one "interest" in the case, that of the situs in increasing the local safety level. Since the score is 1 to 0 (not 2 to 1), the argument presumably would run, the conflict is false: interest analysis has made good on its crucial claim that it can uncover "false conflicts" whose appropriate resolution will be obvious.

The point is right, up to a point. The appropriate resolution of a 2 to 1 case may indeed be questionable (depending on what the 2 and the 1 comprise), but the appropriate resolution of a 1 to 0 case—a case where no interest whatsoever supports the application of the nonsitus law—does indeed seem obvious. And sure enough, it is the locals-only premise that makes the case 1 to 0 rather than 2 to 1. Thus, although I'm not aware that the incidence of such cases will be statistically significant, a criss-cross with a single litigant-independent interest does indeed seem to be a case where the premise makes a difference. The problem is that it's also a rather good case to demonstrate the infirmity of the premise. Even ignoring any constitutional overtones, it makes no sense to assert that the defendant's home state in such a case has no interest whatever in making him pay up when his carelessness has killed or injured an out-of-state guest, or that the plaintiff's home legislature loses all "interest" in denying recovery (to what by its lights is an "ungrateful guest") simply because the person-to-be-recovered-from is an outlander.

Does that mean that it's wrong, in our hypothetical, to apply the (no guest statute) rule of the situs? Obviously that is not my point—what is wrong is the denial of any state interest in promoting a verdict for an out-of-stater against a local—and in fact I think the situs rule *should* apply. Why? Because two interests beat one? Just as obviously a mechanical counting system would be simplistic. I think, instead, the result is right because we should adopt a choice-of-law rule providing (where the parties come from states with different rules) for the application of the situs's rule relating to guest-host liability. I'm getting ahead of myself, however, and want now to turn to the third possible law/party residence configuration.

The "common domicile" configuration is often referred to as a "false conflict," a term I'm avoiding not simply because it announces a conclusion, but also because it is used, at least by some people, to cover criss-cross cases too.[225] It designates a situation where the parties come from the same state or from states whose law is identical respecting the issue in question. (Obviously the label doesn't fit the second situation as well as the first, but you get the idea.) This is another, and more common, situation in which it will sometimes make a difference how broadly we define "interest." It is obvious on ordinary interest analysis canons that the state from which both parties hail will be interested in having its law applied, since no matter which party its law favors one of its residents will be benefited. (If the parties are from two states with the same law, one of those states will be interested.) Since, by hypothesis, the case has been pigeonholed as a "conflicts" case, there must be at least one other state, whose law is different, that has some connection with it: presumably it is the forum or the situs of some part of the events giving rise to the lawsuit. It will often appear on fair-minded reflection that one or more of these states whose contacts are based on something other than residence also has a significant interest in seeing its law applied—so as either to protect its judicial processes or to influence behavior that will affect the local environment. As I've said, interest analysts tend to ignore or downplay interests that are based on something other than party residence: if attention were paid to them it would become even more difficult to dismiss substantial numbers of apparent conflicts as not genuine.

Again, however, let's assume a case in which there are no significant litigant-independent interests: there are some such cases,[226] if not an abundance. And in such a case it *does* make a difference whether we stick with the standard assumption that states are interested only in promoting the fortunes of their own people, or abandon it in favor of an approach that holds that any state with a contact sufficient to give it constitutional standing to apply its law should be deemed to be "interested" in applying it irrespective of whether the party to be benefited is local. With the usual "protect-locals-only" assumption (and the further assumption that there is no state with an interest based on something other than party domicile) a common domicile case truly is a "false conflict"; if, however, the non-domicile state is also granted an interest, the case deadlocks.

An Overdue Distinction

This seems to present us with an unfortunate dilemma. On the one hand, I have argued that the premise that states are "interested" only in generating verdicts for their own citizens—even assuming no constitutional infraction—is out of accord with any sensible notion of what lawmakers either are or should be doing. The infirmity of the premise seems to make a difference in two situations. The first is the criss-cross case where one (and only one) of the two states involved has a litigant-independent interest favoring the application of its law. I have suggested, however, that for precisely the same reasons it is wrong to deny a state an interest in promoting a victory for an out-of-stater against a local it is wrong to treat such cases as false conflicts. Rejection of the premise will therefore make an (occasional) difference in criss-cross situations, *but it should*: interest analysis does not work there, and we should not pretend it does by ignoring interests in assessing or thwarting locals.

The dilemma adverted to arises, rather, from the common domicile case, where common sense does not seem to require—and indeed it seems perversely complicating to insist—that a contact state from which neither party comes (and which has no litigant-independent interest either) must nonetheless claim an "interest" in applying its own law, thereby transforming a situation that seems to shriek for the application of the parties' common home law to one where the choice is deadlocked. Some common domicile variations on the guest statute situation should help make the point. In the first the plaintiff-guest and defendant-host both come from a state that has a guest statute (or from two states that both have guest statutes) barring liability, but the situs of the accident does not. Unless we insist that the situs assert an interest in applying its law so as to help the out-of-state plaintiff recover, the sensible resolution of such a case seems fairly obvious. This is not, as is sometimes asserted, a "false conflict" in the sense that the situs has *no interest whatever* in a verdict for the plaintiff. Assuring recoveries even when both host and guest come from another state might make some incremental contribution to the level of caution generally exercised within the state; it might also help facilitate collection by local medical creditors (if there are any) who treated the plaintiff-guest after the accident. But these "interests" seem speculative, at least to me, when compared with the interest of the parties' home state (or agreeing home states) in seeing to it that "its" guests not collect from "its" hosts in cases of ordinary negligence.[227]

The reverse case, where the parties come from a liability state (or states) and it is the situs that has the guest statute, seems even clearer. For here the situs's behavior-shaping interest is not only speculative, it is barely articulable. The notion that if the guest can't collect the host will be left with more assets against which others who may be hurt in the same accident can proceed, is one that seems quite hypothetical, though again I suppose it's enough to keep the conflict from being 100 percent false.[228] The forum would seem to have a process-protecting interest of sorts in applying its guest statute (assuming it has one)—to wit, an interest in avoiding collusive perjury by the parties. But that too is at least arguably insubstantial by comparison, and in any event it is an interest of the *forum*, which will be the situs only coincidentally. Thus once again it is possible to articulate other possible interests that will sometimes attach, but it seems reasonably clear that it is the law of the domicile of both parties that should prevail. In any event it would seem a pity were the possibility of such a resolution to be barred by a felt obligation to require the situs to assert an interest in applying its law so as to deny recovery.

The way out of the dilemma is to make explicit a distinction with which we have thus far been only flirting, to recognize the existence of a middle ground between the usual, crabbed "protect locals only" approach and a free-swinging obligation on the part of every contact state to claim an interest in the welfare of every party for whom application of its law would generate a victory. In order to deal rationally with the common domicile guest statute cases just canvassed, it is not necessary to cling to the indefensible proposition that states can be interested only in promoting victories for their own people. Such cases remain tractable[229] on the much more sensible view that a state generally should be regarded as "interested" in having its law applied whenever such application would serve a substantial litigant-independent interest (in shaping local behavior or protecting local processes) or *either* party—he who is to be advantaged *or* he who is to be disadvantaged by the application of local law—is local.[230]

Thus the parties' common domicile would be interested in applying its guest statute on two separate grounds, that of protecting "its" host from being gouged by an ungrateful guest *and* that of thwarting "its" ungrateful guest in his or her effort to collect. (Where the parties are from two states, each with a guest statute, one of the two would be interested in protecting "its" defendant, the other in thwarting "its" plaintiff.) Despite this limited extension of the definition of interest, however, the situs state would remain substantially uninterested in applying its host liability rule, since by hypothesis neither party comes from that state.[231] In the other case, the parties' common domicile would be interested in applying its rule of host liability for two reasons, to insure "its" guest's recovery and to see to it that "its" host pay his or her fair way.[232] The situs state would not, however, be interested in applying its guest statute to protect a foreign host from a foreign guest. It is thus possible to abandon the crabbed rhetoric of promoting verdicts only for the state's own, without at the same time abandoning the possibility of rationally resolving cases of the common domicile configuration.

What's more, this intermediate definition of interest would seem not to offend either common sense or "small c" constitutional values, at least not in the same way the usual "victories for locals" definition does. My earlier discussion of "flip side" interests does, I think, argue forcefully for expanding the definition of interest so as ordinarily to encompass the case where the party who would be disadvantaged by the application of local law is local, but it does not support any definition more sweeping than that. In particular nothing said there suggests that a contact state should always regard itself as interested in promoting a victory for the party its law would favor, irrespective of whether he or his opponent is local.

As for our "small c" constitution, well, who can really say? I do think, though, that at least on a comparative basis, it seems less offensive to any "spirit of our constitution" to apply to a suit between two people the law of the joint domicile (or even the joint law of the domiciles) of those two people—assuming no other state has a significant behavior-influencing or process-protecting interest—than it does to build a choice-of-law system on the notion that each *individual* carries around with him his home state's law, which will be presumptively applicable to his case (assuming it favors him)[233] irrespective of whom he gets involved in litigation with. Recall that we are here proceeding on the hypothesis that no actual violation of the Privileges and Immunities Clause or any other is involved,[234] and we are thus in the murkier realm of judicially unenforceable constitutional admonition. And there, I think, it is not the least bit troubling that constitutionality and rationality keep getting mixed up. It simply isn't sensible to suppose that states are not "interested" in generating liabilities for their own citizens. However, applying the law of the parties' common domicile when no other state is substantially interested—which means, of course, that one local will win and another will lose—seems, at least in some cases, so sensible it's hard to conclude it violates even our "small c" constitution.

Conclusion

Debates are wont to overpolarization, and this one is no exception. The interest analysts—apparently out of a belief that they have no workable choice—are generally quite forthright about pitching their calculus to the assumption that the only people for whom states can be interested in generating litigative victories are their own citizens. The critics rightly sense that this is indefensible, but seem to leap from that to the assumption that they must go the whole hog and hold that every time a state constitutionally can do so it must claim an interest in protecting the party who would win if its law were applied.[235] I have suggested a middle ground that avoids the nonsensicality (and arguable unconstitutionality) of the standard crabbed definition without at the same time rendering the system completely unworkable—namely a definition of interest that not only is more sensitive to goals other than generating a victory for one or the other party, but also goes beyond the usual definition by ordinarily claiming an interest in applying local law when the party to be *dis*advantaged thereby is local.

Unfortunately this isn't a very helpful breakthrough. On my intermediate definition of interest the only cases that remain manageable are those exhibiting the common domicile configuration (and even in those there are likely to be litigant-independent interests to muck up the works far more often than has heretofore been recognized). The via media I have suggested is no help at all with "head-on" or "criss-cross" cases, which is to say it is no help at all with cases where the parties come from states whose laws differ. All head-ons and most criss-crosses,[236] however, are deadlocked *however* you define interest: as limited to helping the state's own, as extending to everyone, or as I have suggested. The interest analysts' "ways out" of these two sorts of deadlock either are admittedly arbitrary knot cutters, or they are delusions.

Where, then, do we turn? Unsurprisingly, I am with those who counsel a return to a more rule-oriented approach. Of course the return should be a careful one: there is little point in formulating a rule unless and until the courts' experience and past analysis of the area in question can give them confidence that they will get it about right. Where they are possible, though, rules seem as preferable here as they do in other areas of law. The advantages they bring—advantages of predictability, economy, and equality of treatment as between one case and another—seem "worth the price of an occasional doubtful result."[237] In general, however, choice-of-law rules should limit their coverage to fairly discrete issues rather than trying to cover entire areas: a ballet slipper is less likely to crush someone heedlessly than a lumberjack's boot. The quest must therefore be for "that law which, under consideration of relevant policies is the most appropriate to provide the decisions for a problem, generically seen, but narrowly defined."[238] Professor Reese has described well the sort of process contemplated:

> Once an issue has been selected as a candidate for rule making, one should seek to determine whether in the great majority of situations a particular state will be that of greatest concern by reason of a particular contact irrespective of all other considerations, including the content of its relevant local law rule. If so, it would usually be appropriate for a rule to provide for the application of this state's law to the particular issue.[239]

Naturally our new rules should draw on whatever valid insights the past decades of interest analysis have been able to generate. Unfortunately, we have seen, those insights will prove valuable only in the common domicile situation. For all the ambitious writing by all the capable men and women this field has attracted, all that interest analysis has really taught us, when you clear away the terminological underbrush and discard the insupportable claims, is that when the plaintiff and defendant come from the same state, or from states whose law is identical, you should think seriously about applying that law rather than that which geography or some other "talisman" might otherwise suggest. Of course you may not, and often you should not, end up applying that law, but the interest analysts are surely right that it must at least be one of the candidates.

And indeed it does seem to me that some choice-of-law rules should be framed precisely this way. The rule regarding guest statutes, for example, should in my opinion be geared to the common home law of the parties (when there is one).[240] I would treat damage ceilings the same way (at least in cases where the *forum* has no such ceiling).[241] However, such cases, where the insights that interest analysis have generated do turn out to be of some help, are not very common (though it must be said that the two issues

I've just mentioned, guest statutes and damage ceilings, while they may not look like much to an outsider, do account for more and more of the choice-of-law business of our courts, as our system generally tends more and more toward uniform or federal law). In the main the rules necessarily will look somewhat Bealean—not in the sense that they must encompass entire areas at a single bound, but rather in the sense that they will be geared to something other than the residence of the parties.[242] In his comments on *Neumeier v. Kuehner*, Professor Twerski criticized the rules adumbrated in Chief Judge Fuld's court opinion thus:

> There is . . . a need to project a general philosophical position which emphasizes priorities in choice-of-law. The Fuld rules suffer from a basic inconsistency at this level. The first rule projecting common domicile as the controlling factor puts down territorial considerations completely. This is consistent only with pure interest analysis of the Currie variety. The second and third rules emphasize territorialism with the vengeance of the First Restatement by applying the *lex loci delicti* even in the face of strong opposing interests.[243]

I think this criticism is misguided. In my opinion Fuld was on just the right track (as indeed David Cavers had been some seven years earlier)[244] in embracing the only solid insight of interest analysis, a presumption in favor of applying the law of a *common* domicile, and as for the rest, leaning toward the old, gasp, territorial learning.

Another Spin on **Allegheny Pittsburgh** **(1990)**[245]

One final piece about the possible interrelationships between federal and state law, this time in the context of a Supreme Court decision invalidating a Pennsylvania assessor's refusal to update real estate assessments after the date of purchase, putatively because said refusal denied those who had recently bought their properties "the equal protection of the laws" guaranteed by the Federal Constitution's Fourteenth Amendment, but "actually" because it violated state law. Or are the two different? And does it matter whether they are?

As usual Professor Cohen is right:[246] the challenged practice in *Allegheny*[247] would not have been invalidated under the Equal Protection Clause had it not violated state law. That need work no massive shock to the system, however. The only occasions on which a "rational basis" test will invalidate a (nonhypothetical*) law are those on which one or more

---

* Any fool can *invent* a "law" and a "sole purpose thereof" that have no relation to each other—accordion lessons as a cure for global warming, or whatever—but no matter how low one's opinion of legislatures, that is not the way the world works.

goals (including the real one) have been excluded as potential justifiers. Sometimes goals will be excluded because they violate the Federal Constitution. Thus, for example, in *Skinner v. Oklahoma*:[248]

> Given that an admission of the real goal of the distinction in issue (a desire to punish larcenists more harshly than embezzlers) would have rendered the [sterilization] law as applied to Skinner an ex post facto law (and a strongly arguable violation of the Cruel and Unusual Punishment Clause as well), the state was disabled from relying on that goal, which left the classification without another to which it related even rationally.[249]

In theory, however, there is no reason why certain possible justifying goals should not be disabled from consideration on the ground that they violate *state* law.[250] That is what happened in *Allegheny*: two possible justifying goals of the assessment practice at issue—the promotion of neighborhood stability (by discouraging moving), and the avoidance of the (sometimes onerous) taxation of unrealized paper gains[251]—were excluded from consideration on the basis of a finding that, under West Virginia law, differences in assessed valuation are sustainable only in terms of differences in current value.

At first blush this is jarring, as we have all been taught since childhood that state courts—not federal courts, not even the Supreme Court of the United States—are the ultimate arbiters of what state law is. That remains so, and despite the fact that it reversed the West Virginia court's judgment, nothing in the Supreme Court's opinion in *Allegheny* even begins to change it. *Allegheny* was a very strange case—strange in a way that suggests there is no danger of opening any "every question's a federal question" floodgate.[252] For it was the West Virginia Supreme Court of Appeals that held that under West Virginia law, differences in assessment had to reflect differences in value. That means that petitioner was correct in its contention that the Webster County assessor's approach was illegal under state law, and nothing the West Virginia court said was to the contrary.

The reason it was necessary for petitioner to take the case to the United States Supreme Court was that the West Virginia court had some unusual remedial notions, indicating that (1) petitioner's own assessment, which *was* based on current value, accorded with state law, and (2) if petitioner wanted to do something about the inequity between its assessment and that of others, it would have to petition the Webster County Commission to raise the others.[253] It was, of course, this aspect of the decision that the United States Supreme Court reversed, indicating (in accordance with its prior decisions) that it is not sufficient for a state to respond to a proven equal protection violation by indicating that it is up to the party discriminated against to bring some sort of action to get everyone else treated as badly as he. Instead, the appropriate course is ordinarily for the court to place the burden of correcting an equal protection violation on the state authorities, confronting them with the immediate choice between treating the victorious party better or—what will usually be a politically unavailable option—treating everybody else worse.[254]

Thus the decision will open no floodgates. It is true that by the Court's logic, all violations of state law—at least those violations that end (as most do) in the treatment of some people better than others—are theoretically convertible into violations of the Equal Protection Clause. However, this is not likely to be an operationally significant development because state courts remain the final authorities on what is or is not a violation of state law—*Allegheny* itself having reached the Supreme Court only because of the state court's somewhat unusual idea of an appropriate remedy.

Still, the decision is unsettling, and I think the reason is this. It is true that in an "ordinary" equal protection case—in which the federal constitutional violation does not result entirely from the fact that state law was violated— the appropriate remedy is indeed to place on the state the immediate obligation either to treat the party discriminated against better or to treat everybody else worse. It seems to me, however, that in the (rare) *Allegheny*-type case—in which the federal constitutional violation is entirely a function of the violation of state law—the state should retain the option of awarding a remedy that is procedurally less accommodating than the ordinary federal equal protection remedy. Certainly states should not generally be granted discretion to respond to the denial of a federal right with a remedy less accommodating than that which the federal courts would grant. Where, however, the fact of a federal violation flows entirely from the fact that state law has been violated, it seems that state law should be able to set the remedy too.

If I am right about this last assertion, however, it means there should be no occasion on which the Supreme Court should grant review in an *Allegheny*-type case (in which petitioner's equal protection claim boils down to an asserted violation of state law). This is not because such an argument does not, at least in theory, make out a "real" equal protection claim: we have seen that it does.[255] The reason is instead a remedial one. If the state court has denied that state law has been violated, that judgment is binding on the Supreme Court.[256] If on the other hand the state court has done what the West Virginia court did in *Allegheny*—granted the existence of the state law violation but saddled the challenging party with a correction regimen more burdensome than the typical federal equal protection remedy—that judgment too (for the reason just given) should stand.[257] That would seem to leave no reason for the Supreme Court to take such a case.

3

Separation of Powers

The separation of powers among the branches of the national government remains an active interest of the Supreme Court. It is also a long-term interest of mine; indeed, the two pieces that follow were both written while I was in law school.

United States v. Lovett: *Litigating the Separation of Powers* (1975)[1]

Written for Professor Telford Taylor's seminar in Constitutional Litigation,[2] this piece was not published until years later. It too is rather different for a law review, focusing not on what the law is or should be, but rather on the techniques of litigating test cases. It's not too far afield, however, as I have throughout my career taught courses on how to litigate, ranging from traditional trial practice courses to a seminar on bringing test cases in the national security area. I should add that the argument bridging pages 94–95 was written by (the received euphemism is that "substantial assistance was provided by") the student who edited the piece for the Harvard Civil Rights–Civil Liberties Law Review, Jeff Gordon. Since he's now a professor at Columbia, you can probably rely on it. (His field is corporate law, but as is well known, the law is a seamless web. And a jealous mistress.)

> No part of any appropriation, allocation, or fund (1) which is made available under or pursuant to this Act, or (2) which is now, or which is hereafter made, available under or pursuant to any other Act, to any department, agency, or instrumentality of the United States, shall be used, after November 15, 1943, to pay any part of the salary, or other compensation for the personal services, of Goodwin B. Watson, William E. Dodd, Junior, and Robert Morss Lovett, unless prior to such date such person has been appointed by the president, by and with the advice and consent of the Senate.
>
> Section 304 of the Urgent Deficiency Appropriation Act, 1943.[3]

Thus spake the Congress of the United States, scarring three men and touching off the litigation left to us as *United States v. Lovett.*[4] The case is interesting politically, in that it represented the culmination of a battle between a conservative Congress and a liberal president. And it is interesting in terms of the development of constitutional doctrine, in that it was the first case in almost a century to invoke the Bill of Attainder Clause.

The *Lovett* case is also worth the attention of those interested in the techniques of constitutional litigation. Section 304 was an unconventional statute and therefore required unconventional attacks and defenses. Because the statute fit into no easily recognizable pigeonhole, each litigant's first and most important task was to get the courts to agree with him as to what issues the case presented; only then could he go on to argue the precedents bearing on those issues. In fact the case was ultimately decided on a ground that had not been, though perhaps it should have been, the primary place of battle. And an early error by one of the parties practically foreclosed what might have been a basis for victory.

But perhaps what makes *United States v. Lovett* most interesting is that both "Lovett" (by which I mean Lovett, Watson, and Dodd) and "the United States" (by which I mean the Justice Department) took the position that the statute in issue was invalid, and Congress had to intervene, by separate counsel, to fight for its handiwork. The case was therefore brought to the Court by three distinct litigant-clusters, each, we shall see, with a distinct goal. It is to the interplay among these three groups' views of the separation of powers, and the ways in which those views were reflected in the various litigation moves and countermoves, that this study is devoted.

Section 304

On February 1, 1943, Congressman Martin Dies read the House of Representatives a list of thirty-nine "crackpot, radical bureaucrats" whose political associations made them, in his view, unfit for continued government employment. All thirty-nine had been included on a list he had submitted to Attorney General Biddle in 1941; because the Attorney General and the heads of the departments employing those listed had failed to discharge them, Dies now urged that their removal was up to Congress. His method: to refuse to appropriate money for their salaries.

After an abortive attempt to put Dies' plan into operation on an agency-by-agency, appropriation-by-appropriation basis, a Special Subcommittee of the House Committee on Appropriations was created to consider Dies' charges. John Kerr was named its chairman. The Kerr Committee, drawing largely on material collected by Dies' House Un-American Activities Committee, and barring attorneys from the room, began hearings in mid-April. Only six of the thirty-nine on Dies' list were called; of these, three were found not to warrant dismissal. Three others—Watson, Dodd, and Lovett—did not fare so well.

Goodwin Watson, chief analyst for the FCC's Foreign Broadcast Intelligence Service, was the first called. A social psychologist and ordained minister, he had taught at Columbia University and written numerous books and articles. Although he belonged to no groups on the Attorney General's list of subversive organizations, the Kerr Committee, apparently convinced that his writings advocated the overthrow of the capitalist system, found him unfit for further employment.

William Dodd, Jr., editorial assistant of the Foreign Broadcast Intelligence Service and also a former professor, met the same fate. His main transgressions seem to have been membership in the Washington Bookstore and the American League for Peace and Democracy and the fact that he had let the Harry Bridges Defense Committee use his apartment for a press conference.

Robert Morss Lovett, government secretary of the Virgin Islands, had taught English at the University of Chicago for forty-five years. His numerous political associations led Dies to remark in 1940 that "Lovett holds the all-time record for fellow-travelling with Communist organizations." Lovett characterized the evidence introduced against him at the hearing as:

[M]y speech in support of Norman Thomas for president in 1936; an article in the New Masses, protesting against the favorable attitude of the State Department toward Franco; a contribution to the League for Mutual Aid; a letter to Mother Bloor of Iowa on her seventy-fifth birthday; a letter from someone addressing me as "Dear Comrade" ... [but primarily] the private letter to Jacob Gordin that referred to all governments as rotten.[5]

The Kerr Committee found Lovett also "dangerous" and therefore unfit for high federal employment. Its recommendation became part of the full Appropriation Committee's report; section 304 was submitted along with the report.

The introduction of this amended Urgent Deficiency Appropriation Bill touched off a two-month debate over Congress's power to use its control of appropriations to effect removal. Constitutional scruples were met with charges to the effect that the New Deal had made Washington a paradise for left-leaning professors. Although the record of the Kerr Committee's hearings was not available to the House, the "conservative victory" of 1940 took its toll: the amendment passed 318–62.

The Senate was somewhat less amenable. Acting on the recommendation of its Appropriations Committee, it voted 69–0 to delete section 304. Indeed, the Senate rejected section 304 four times. Not even the inclusion of the proviso "unless prior to such date such person has been appointed by the President, by and with the advice and consent of the Senate" could capture a majority. After about a month, however, it became clear that there would be no bill unless the Senate yielded on section 304. So yield it did, 48–32. "Urgent appropriations" could wait no longer.

The Senate's dilemma also faced President Roosevelt. He too yielded, but not without condemning section 304 as "not only unwise and discriminatory, but unconstitutional . . . . This rider is an unwarranted encroachment upon the authority of both the executive and judicial branches. It is not, in my judgment, binding upon them." The President refused to submit the three men's names for Senate confirmation under the proviso; to do so might have appeared to condone what he regarded as a legislative usurpation of the removal power.

The agencies employing Dodd, Lovett, and Watson, emboldened by the President's stance, at first ignored section 304. On November 21, 1943, however, Dodd took leave-without-pay status: the next day he was informed that he could be compensated only for work performed before November 15, the date set by the statute. (It seems the disbursing officers were not instructed to disregard section 304. Apparently the executive wanted to force a constitutional adjudication; withholding the salaries was the most direct way of doing this.) On November 26, Secretary of the Interior Harold Ickes urged Lovett to remain in his post, predicting that section 304 would be struck down and funds would then become available. But on March 6 Secretary Ickes, under congressional attack, requested Lovett's resignation. One week later Lovett resigned. Watson served until May 2, 1944, when an apparently unrelated reduction in appropriations eliminated the Analysis Division which he headed. He too was paid for no work performed after November 15.

Bringing Suit

Three men had been told they would receive no further salary. This monetary deprivation was, however, the least of their injuries: what cut deeper was that Congress had effectively labeled them, by name, dangerous and unfit for government employment. Because section 304 was so unorthodox and because the President himself had called it unconstitutional, legal action of some sort seemed promising. But precisely because the statute was so unprecedented, there was for these men no recipe telling them where to sue or what to argue.

WHERE?

Lovett, Watson, and Dodd had to weigh at least three separate objectives in deciding where to bring suit—their wish to attack the constitutionality of section 304, their need to maintain the justiciability of the dispute, and their desire to provide for expeditious review by the Supreme Court.

District Court

The three could have sued—after the fashion of cases like *Perkins v. Elg*[6]—in a federal district court for a declaratory judgment of the invalidity of section 304, appending a request for an injunction directing the disbursing officers not to withhold compensation because of that section. There were several problems with this way of proceeding, however. First, it was supported by fewer and less straightforward precedents than those supporting a suit for salary in the Court of Claims.[7] Moreover, the statute giving district courts jurisdiction concurrent with the Court of Claims in suits against the United States, 28 U.S.C. 41(20) (1940), excluded cases "brought to recover fees, salary, or compensation for official services of officers of the United States" from district court jurisdiction.[8] Without some sort of prayer for back pay, however, the plaintiffs risked the justiciability of their lawsuit. All three would be out of government by the time the suit was heard—one for reasons independent of section 304, another for reasons tenuously connected, and the third because 304 had cut off his salary. Without a salary claim, the battle could appear hypothetical. Thus the dilemma: plaintiffs Lovett, Watson, and Dodd needed the claim for salary to maintain a clear controversy with the United States, but a direct salary claim would seem to oust district court jurisdiction. Perhaps dressing the salary claim as a request for an injunction against continued refusal to pay would provide a sympathetic court with a way of avoiding the jurisdictional problem. But that was at least risky.

Consideration of the speed of Supreme Court review also appeared to argue against the *Perkins* procedure. It must certainly have seemed to the prospective plaintiffs desirable and not unlikely that the solution of this executive-legislative war (and hopefully the clearing of their names) should ultimately come from the Supreme Court. Following the *Perkins* procedure would probably have necessitated an intermediate stop in the court of appeals in the event the plaintiffs lost in the district court.[9]

Three Judge Court

Of course, the district judge might well have found (though the judge in *Perkins* had not) that the appended request for an injunction required the convening of a three judge district court.[10] By casting their action as one mainly directed toward injunctive relief and by specifically requesting such a court, the plaintiffs could have solved some, though by no means all, of their problems. Direct appeal to the Supreme Court would then have been available no matter who won. And such a request for an injunction would probably have been more likely to elicit a constitutional decision than a salary suit in the Court of Claims. (It remained conceivable, however, that a three judge court would deny the injunction without upholding the constitutionality of the statute, by holding that because the statute did not foreclose a suit for salary in the Court of Claims, that court was the appropriate forum for plaintiffs' redress at law.)

The same problems of jurisdiction and justiciability would remain, however. To the extent the action would be construed as an "officers'" suit for salary, the three judge court, as another species of district court, would be ousted from jurisdiction. But without a claim for salary, the plaintiffs' action could be seen as losing its quality as a controversy.

Court of Claims

A suit for salary in the Court of Claims was a well-trod path.[11] It is true that money was not really what the plaintiffs were after: Watson sued for $148.50 and Dodd for $79.95. They wanted section 304 declared unconstitutional. However, it seemed unlikely that the Court of Claims would grant them their pay without striking the section down, for the provision was clearly intended wholly to deny them their salaries. A suit for salary would avoid any questions about the existence of a real case or controversy, and certiorari could be sought directly from the Court of Claims.

There were also problems with bringing a suit in the Court of Claims, however. First, the court could duck the constitutional issues presented by relying on a line of cases that could be read to say that the mere withholding of appropriations, unaccompanied by the actual removal of the plaintiffs or the abolition of their jobs, did not affect their right to salary.[12] It was not inconceivable that the Court of Claims, in order to avoid the constitutional questions, would seize upon such precedent, ignore the intent of Congress, and grant the salaries without voiding the statute. Second, Supreme Court review of the Court of Claims was by certiorari rather than by the appeal of right allowed from a decision of a three judge court. However, the case was so "hot" that reliance on certiorari rather than appeal did not seem greatly to diminish the chances of getting to the Supreme Court.

Perhaps the most serious problem with the Court of Claims option had to do with the plaintiffs' desire that relief come ultimately from the United States Supreme Court. At the time of the *Lovett* case, the status of the Court of Claims was ambiguous: it was unclear whether it was a "constitutional (Article III) court" or a "legislative (Article I) court,"[13] and, if the latter, whether (and on what occasions) it exercised a power sufficiently "judicial" to admit of Supreme Court review of its actions.[14] Without attempting generally to solve these theoretical difficulties, the Supreme Court had followed the approach of reviewing those matters with respect to which the Court of Claims acted like an ordinary court and refusing to review those matters with respect to which it acted like an advisory body to Congress.[15] And given the usual pattern of routine congressional payment of Court of

Claims judgments, the Supreme Court was inclined to regard its affirmance of such a judgment as more than an advisory opinion and therefore generally treated such judgments as "final."[16]

The problem for the *Lovett* plaintiffs in planning their litigation strategy was that the normal assumptions regarding congressional payment of Court of Claims judgments were at least questionable. Appropriations bills, of course, must begin in the House of Representatives, and that was the body that was determined to be rid of Lovett, Watson, and Dodd. (Indeed, as part of their effort to force the courts to reach the constitutional questions in the case, the plaintiffs would have to argue that the legislative intent had been wholly to cut off their salaries. But such an argument would only underscore the dubiousness of Congress's ever making good on the judgment if awarded.)[17] A Supreme Court opinion awarding salary in a case thus brought could therefore be at least plausibly characterized as advisory.[18]

Thus the plaintiffs were faced with a serious dilemma. They probably needed a salary claim in order to maintain the matter's status as a case or controversy. But raising that claim in a direct way would oust them from the district court—single judge or three judge panel—and force them into the Court of Claims. On the other hand, the ambiguous status of the Court of Claims and the House's apparent determination to cut off salaries for the three raised questions of the justiciability in the Supreme Court of a case started in the Court of Claims.

The extent to which these various considerations in fact were weighed is unclear. In any event, on December 3, 1943, Lovett, Watson, and Dodd, all represented by Charles A. Horsky of the Covington firm, filed suit against the United States in the Court of Claims. This decision to sue there was one that in fact never returned to haunt the plaintiffs, and it may on balance have been the wisest. As matters worked themselves out, none of the three litigant-clusters—Lovett et al., the executive branch, or Congress—was satisfied with the Court of Claims' action. Thus none was disposed to raise, and none did raise, an argument that would jeopardize Supreme Court review. Fortunately, the members of that Court either missed the issue or did not see fit to raise it sua sponte.

THE INITIAL RESPONSE OF THE EXECUTIVE AND
LEGISLATIVE BRANCHES

United States v. Lovett might more accurately have been reported as *Lovett et al. and the Executive Branch v. Congress.* For on December 6, Attorney General Biddle informed the Speaker of the House and the Vice President that because he concurred with the President's judgment that section 304 was unconstitutional, he found it "impossible to advocate with conviction the views of the Congress." He therefore suggested that Congress employ its own attorney to argue in favor of the statute. Congress adopted the necessary legislation and hired John C. Gall as "Special Counsel." Though officially an amicus curiae, functionally he was counsel for the defendant (which is to say the statute). All the ingredients of a real adversary proceeding were present.

THE POSSIBLE LINES OF ATTACK

In evaluating the arguments against section 304, it must be remembered that the statute was under attack by two distinct groups of litigants with somewhat different goals. Lovett, Watson, and Dodd formed one group.[19] They wanted their reputations vindicated; the optimal decision from their point of view would therefore be one that held the statute unconstitutional because the finding of "dangerousness" had been made under improper conditions (denial of procedural due process) or by an improper tribunal (bill of attainder). Such a holding, by tainting Congress's procedure, would cast doubt on the reliability of its conclusion. The other party challenging the statute was the executive branch. Its interest was in maintaining executive control over appointment and removal. Both groups therefore wanted section 304 held unconstitutional; however, they differed as to the "best" ground of decision.

But certainly neither group wanted a victory on nonconstitutional grounds. *United States v. Langston*[20] had suggested that despite the withholding of appropriations, Lovett, Watson, and Dodd might still have a right to their salaries. It was therefore in the plaintiffs' interest to keep the Court of Claims from following *Langston*. This could best be accomplished by stressing Congress's wish to rid the government of Lovett, Watson, and Dodd by halting their remuneration. Convincing the courts that this is what Congress had meant would bar the possibility of the Pyrrhic victory: salaries *and* statute.

The First Amendment is where we now tend to look first for protection of persons sanctioned for their political beliefs and associations. Not so in 1943: the amendment was never so much as mentioned during the entire *Lovett* litigation until Justice Black (who else?) noted for the Court that it had not been relied upon.[21] Counsel's omission may have resulted from the fact that as of 1943 the First Amendment had been invoked mainly in cases involving "classic" infringements of the right to speak or express opinions and had not yet been seen as encompassing the broader right to hold dissenting opinions free from the fear of any sort of governmental reprisal. The panoply of "Communist cases" was yet to come; other challenges to section 304 were supported by more obviously relevant precedent. (It should also be noted that a First Amendment victory would directly fulfill the goal of neither of the two groups challenging the statute. It would not materially strengthen executive control over removals, nor would it really taint the trustworthiness of the congressional finding that Lovett, Watson, and Dodd were dangerous.)

The Fifth Amendment's guarantee of due process was relevant in two ways. First, a claim of denied procedural due process in the conduct of the Kerr Committee's hearings could be made. Attorneys had been excluded; no real notice (in Dodd's case, not even a formal statement of charges) of what the plaintiffs would be asked to answer had been given; much of the evidence upon which the committee based its decision had not been revealed; the identity of the three men's accusers had been kept secret. The trouble with this argument was that the committee had not purported to conduct a judicial hearing; it was, it would be answered, just a legislative committee considering legislation and therefore under no duty to afford trial-type safeguards. The counter to this was that, legislative committee or not, it was acting like a court: it was punishing. This latter argument—that the legislature was performing judicial functions—was another way of calling section 304 a bill of attainder. Therefore, although the procedural due process argument had little chance of alone winning the case, it was an argument not to be omitted, for it was another way of making the bill of attainder argument—another way of telling the courts that Congress had overstepped the separation of powers. Because the Bill of Attainder Clause had so long lain dormant, it was a wise move to try to get the bill of attainder argument in under labels more obviously alive. "Procedural due process" was one such label.

"Equal protection" was another. The argument here was that section 304, in singling out three men rather than formulating a general principle, was unconstitutionally discriminatory. It is true that *Bolling v. Sharpe*,[22] basically holding the Fourteenth Amendment's Equal Protection Clause applicable to the federal government,[23] was yet to come. However, there had been hints that the Fifth Amendment's Due Process Clause outlawed "special" or "class" legislation,[24] hints perhaps sufficient to make a quasi-equal protection argument appropriate to the *Lovett* litigation. The problem was that the singling out of Lovett, Watson, and Dodd was not "irrational"—the congressional committee had thought it had rather good reasons for naming them—and no higher standard had yet been imposed in cases not involving racial classification. Was it then folly to consider an argument bottomed on equal-protection style "due process"? It was not, for the reasons noted in connection with procedural due process. What made section 304 seem discriminatory was the fact that it *named names*. Equal protection was therefore another contemporary label under whose auspices the bill of attainder argument could be smuggled in. Though of little value by itself, it gave Lovett, Watson, and Dodd another way of telling the courts that Congress had not been content with making a rule, it had applied one.

How strong was the bill of attainder argument itself? Even making allowances for the fact that one may be influenced by the Supreme Court's ultimate holding, it would appear, even as of 1943, pretty strong. The landmark post–Civil War cases of *Cummings v. Missouri*[25] and *Ex parte Garland*[26] had broadly construed the clause to outlaw all statutes, no matter what their form, that inflicted punishment on named persons or an easily ascertainable group. Indeed, the *Lovett* situation seemed in some ways an a fortiori case, for unlike the statutes voided in *Cummings* and *Garland*, section 304 named the persons to whom the deprivation was to attach. The bill of attainder argument had the added virtue of not requiring a showing that section 304 had been designed to remove Lovett, Watson, and Dodd from office. The mere denial of salary was, under *Cummings* and *Garland*, sufficient deprivation to support a bill of attainder claim, so long as it could be shown that it was enacted in order to punish.

However, the Court had invoked the Bill of Attainder Clause against no law, federal or state, since 1872.[27] The term "bill of attainder" must therefore have seemed archaic when applied to World War II legislation. No member of the Court of the early forties had so much as mouthed the words; it was far from clear that they ever would.

A strong argument could also be made that section 304 was an unconstitutional encroachment upon the executive's removal power. *Myers v. United States*,[28] broadly stated, stood for the proposition that removal of executive branch officers was solely an executive prerogative, that Congress could neither prevent the president from removing them nor remove them itself. If, therefore, Lovett, Watson, and Dodd (or, more to the point, the Attorney General) could establish that section 304 worked a removal from office, the case would probably be theirs. The problem was that 304 was in terms not a removal, but a denial of appropriations. The obvious answers to this were that the legislative history evidenced a desire to rid the government of subversives and that cutting off a person's salary is an efficient way of dispensing with his services. Though it too was based on precedents seldom invoked, the removal power argument was promising.

However, it was at least theoretically open to the courts to conclude that section 304 did not remove, but only cut off salaries. Could an argument be fashioned to the effect that it was unconstitutional to keep a person in government employ and yet refuse to pay him? It should first be noted that this, stated so nakedly, would have been a difficult point for which to find precedent. But even if precedent had been available, the argument would have been unwise. For it would have cut away much of the force of one of the plaintiffs' strongest arguments: that this was a removal and therefore a usurpation of executive power. It therefore should not have been made a separate point but should have been saved for use in connection with the bill of attainder argument, where a showing of removal was not requisite. Plaintiffs could have given a court unconvinced that section 304 worked a removal a way of voiding it anyway, and at the same time refrained from urging the alternative "non-removal" interpretation with vigor sufficient to undercut the basic removal argument, by structuring their argument basically as follows:

> (1) Section 304 works a removal and is therefore an unconstitutional encroachment upon executive territory.
> (2) Because it removes plaintiffs by name in order to punish them, section 304 is a bill of attainder.
>> (a) Indeed, it would be a bill of attainder even if it had only cut off their salaries.

In summary, then, plaintiffs' strongest argument probably was that section 304, though purportedly an exercise of the congressional appropriations power, was in fact a usurpation of executive control over removals. Also strong, though perhaps weakened by antiquity, was the bill of attainder point. (Victory on the first point would be ideal from the point of view of the executive branch; victory on the second would go furthest toward exonerating Lovett, Watson, and Dodd.) The due process and equal protection claims, though neither could carry the day by itself, provided good buttresses for the bill of attainder point. An argument based on interpreting the statute as not removing plaintiffs but only cutting off their salaries would lessen the force of the basic removal point; such an interpretation would therefore best be suggested only as part of the bill of attainder claim. The possibility of a First Amendment claim should have been explored, though it did not have the precedential backing of either the removal or the bill of attainder argument. The argument that section 304 should be read not to foreclose plaintiffs' right to their salaries was, given the goals of both challenging groups, devoutly to be avoided.

THE ACTUAL LINES OF ATTACK

The legal claims of the three complaints were identical. Each alleged:

> (1) Section 304 is unconstitutional in that it deprives plaintiff of the right to his salary, "which right legally exists until such time as he shall have been lawfully relieved of, or shall have voluntarily relinquished, [his official] status."
> (2) Section 304 attempts to effect legislative removal of plaintiff, and is therefore an unconstitutional encroachment on executive power.

   (3) Section 304 is a bill of attainder.
   (4) Section 304 denies due process and equal protection.[29]

Were it not for point 1, this would have been a model pleading. But point 1 seems to have been a rather clear mistake. It not only should not have been placed first, it should not have been included at all. First, as noted above, by stressing that plaintiffs had not been officially dismissed, it took much of the fire from point 2, the strong removal argument. Second, although purportedly a constitutional claim, it spoke in terms of a continuing right to compensation. This terminology invited the Court of Claims to seize upon the *Langston* lines of cases and avoid the constitutional issues by holding that section 304 had not foreclosed a suit for salary.

CONGRESS'S DEFENSE

Mr. Gall's task was to preserve section 304 against the attacks of Lovett, Watson, and Dodd, and the Justice Department. The course of his argument was thus largely determined by the arguments put forth by plaintiffs.

Congress also wanted the constitutional validity of section 304 tested. A decision awarding Lovett, Watson, and Dodd their salaries without reaching the constitutional issues would, it is true, leave 304 intact with only a small financial outlay. However, the congressional purpose would be subverted if, under similar statutes, the persons named could continue to work for the government and pick up their paychecks at the Court of Claims. Under such an interpretation, measures like 304 would be of little use in ridding the government of "subversives." True, it was unlikely that such a statute could be enacted in the near future. But perhaps someday the president would be over another barrel or there would be sufficient votes in both houses to pass another 304 over the president's veto. Congress therefore wanted judicial approval of a scheme whereby it could encourage the departure of undesirables (though of course it was not "removing" them) by shutting off all salary sources. Hence, all three parties wanted a constitutional holding, though no two wanted the same one.

Section 304 could be left standing *and* the plaintiffs denied salary if the case could be kept out of the courts altogether. For this result there were two possible arguments. First, it could be argued that section 304 took away, as to Lovett, Watson, and Dodd, the Court of Claims' ordinary pay case jurisdiction. But although 304 could be read to foreclose on the merits all salary sources, it said not a word about the threshold jurisdictional question. The Court of Claims therefore gave this argument short shrift; it was not made again. The second possible argument was that the case presented no justiciable questions because Article I places appropriations wholly in the hands of Congress. Authority for this proposition was of less than overwhelming force.[30] And it was, in any event, an argument that stood or fell with Congress's main argument on the merits, that section 304 was nothing more than an appropriations measure.[31]

Mr. Gall might have considered confronting the plaintiffs' removal argument head on. *Myers'* actual holding, after all, had been that Congress could not limit the president's power to remove, not that it did not retain a (concurrent) removal power of its own. Moreover, the subsequent decision in *Humphrey's Executor v. United States*[32] had limited *Myers*, holding that Congress could place restrictions on the president's power to remove quasi-executive or quasi-judicial, as opposed to purely executive, officials. (Humphrey had been a member of the FTC.) But Lovett seems quite clearly to have been a purely executive official, and while Watson and Dodd worked for the FCC, their specific positions seem at least on the surface to have lacked legislative or judicial character. Perhaps there was an answer respecting them—that executives or not, their work was in aid of the FCC's legislative and judicial functions—but that answer did not seem intrinsically strong. Furthermore, no such answer was available in Lovett's case, and thus, at the least, reliance on *Humphrey's Executor* would have forced Mr. Gall to bifurcate his argument. Beyond that, in fashioning a "congressional removal" argument, he would have had to confront the contention that the constitutional grant of the impeachment power implies that Congress can remove officers of the United States by no other procedure. (Such a view would limit *Humphrey's Executor* to its facts, as permitting Congress to limit presidential removal of nonexecutive officers but not suggesting a congressional power to remove them itself.) And finally, the argument might appear to concede what it was critically important that Congress not concede, that section 304 could plausibly be regarded as working a removal. Thus, given its intrinsic weakness, Mr. Gall did well to omit this congressional removal power argument and single-mindedly argue that there had been no removal. It wasn't a strong argument, but it was the best available.

Congress's optimal strategy, then, was to start with an argument that section 304 was a garden variety exercise of the appropriations power. All Congress had done, it could be maintained, was something it had been doing since 1789; it had cut off certain appropriations. By leading with and stressing this positive argument, Congress could hope to make the courts view the issue in its terms. If, on the other hand, Mr. Gall had begun defensively—"Section 304 is not a removal," or "Section 304 is not a bill of attainder"—the issue of the statute's validity might have been pushed into one of the plaintiffs' frameworks.

Further, such a positive historical argument would constitute an indirect answer to plaintiffs' removal and bill of attainder arguments. For every substantial point at issue in the *Lovett* litigation was a variation on the separation of powers theme. At bottom,[33] the challenges to the statute were that Congress had, in passing section 304, trespassed on the executive (removal) and the judiciary (bill of attainder). Proof that Congress was in fact performing what had always been a legislative function (appropriations) would therefore go to the jugular of both of the plaintiffs' contentions, which were themselves rooted in considerations of what departments had traditionally performed what functions.

Only after this attempt to make the courts approach the question as one of the history and limits of the appropriations power had been made should Congress have proceeded to defend against such arguments as removal ("plaintiffs weren't removed"); bill of attainder ("not punishment, but the implementation of reasonable job qualifications"); equal protection ("not an unreasonable discrimination"); and procedural due process ("not a judicial proceeding"). Insofar as it is now possible to reconstruct the arguments made before the Court of Claims, this seems to be the general approach Mr. Gall took.[34] But we shall see that in later stages of the litigation, his Supreme Court brief in particular, he departed from this judicious course.

The Decision of the Court of Claims

The Court of Claims heard the case on stipulated facts. On November 5, 1945, it found unanimously for the plaintiffs,[35] but the four opinions delivered gave little guidance as to the legal status of section 304. Chief Justice Whaley delivered an opinion that was labeled "the opinion of the court" despite the fact that only Judge Littleton joined in it. (Judges Whitaker, Jones, and Madden rendered separate opinions, each stating that he "concurred in the result.") Whaley found that section 304 neither removed plaintiffs from their jobs nor cut off all sources of salary. Rather, he said, it merely prohibited payment out of funds generally appropriated; plaintiffs were therefore entitled to sue for and collect their salaries in the Court of Claims. The worst from all points of view had therefore happened; the court had seized upon the interpretation suggested by the claim the plaintiffs had injudiciously placed first in their complaints, followed the *Langston* line of cases, and dodged the constitutional questions.

Judge Whitaker, in a one paragraph argument, expressed the view that section 304 was a bill of attainder. Judge Jones, with considerable folksiness ("This is as fundamental as the ten commandments"; "A rose is a rose even though someone calls it a lily") but less than considerable clarity, suggested that 304 was such a flagrant transgression of the ideal of equality that it denied, although he did not use the term, equal protection. Judge Madden ventured the opinion that section 304 was both a bill of attainder and a violation of substantive due process.

Getting to the Supreme Court

The Court of Claims left no one happy. Lovett, Watson, and Dodd had officially been awarded their salaries, but the court had left the legislative label of dangerousness on the books. True, three members of the court had said the statute was unconstitutional, and all on grounds tainting the reliability of the congressional judgment. But the members of the court had been unable to agree on a single theory, none of the opinions was so overwhelming in its logic or its craftsmanship as to constitute a quasi-authoritative vindication of plaintiffs' reputations,[36] and the opinion that had left the statute standing had been labeled the opinion of the court. It is unlikely that any action by the Court of Claims could have nullified the congressional censure; the one taken surely did not. Only a constitutional adjudication by the Supreme Court could come close to clearing these three men's names (or, apparently, unlock their salaries[37]). Since all five members of the Court of Claims had voted for the plaintiffs, there seemed little risk on the merits in taking the case to the Supreme Court; certiorari was clearly in order.

The executive branch had wanted a judicial halt called to legislative tampering with the removal power, but none of the five judges had based his decision even in part on the removal argument. It is true that Lovett, Watson, and Dodd had been told they could continue to work and collect their salary at the Court of Claims, but perhaps sometime in the future Congress would be able to force by the president a law like section 304 with the added provision that the named parties were to be unable to collect their wages anywhere. (Indeed, that is the statute Congress had *meant* to pass this time.) The executive therefore also wanted Supreme Court review not of the hypothetical statute fashioned by the Court of Claims in order to avoid constitutional questions, but of the real statute Congress had tried to pass this time and might in fact pass next time.

Congress had lost. An attempt to get a reversal was not, however, its only alternative. It might, for instance, have thought of passing another statute—this one making it clear that Lovett, Watson, and Dodd were not to collect their salaries anywhere. However, the Senate probably wouldn't pass such a statute, and the president would certainly veto it. They had acceded to section 304 only because of the exigency of "urgent appropriations." Second, at least three members of the Court of Claims (where a challenge to the new statute presumably would be brought) would vote to void it. And third, the Supreme Court would probably, in the instant litigation, read section 304 as Congress had intended it; the "opinion of the court" had reached its interpretation only by disregarding the legislative intent. Thus the validity of the statute Congress wanted to pass would probably be adjudicated on certiorari in this action; there was no need to pass a statute more clearly closing all access to salary, even if it could have been done.

Congress might, of course, simply have forgotten the whole thing. That is, it could have encouraged the Attorney General (technically the losing party) not to petition for certiorari and opposed the petition had he chosen not to honor the request. After all, Lovett, Watson, and Dodd were out of the government, and the fact that their salaries had been awarded was of little moment. A reversal would make scant difference to the immediate situation. In view of the weakness of Congress's legal position (the Court of Claims had found against it unanimously) dropping the case might have been a good idea. However, counsel for Congress apparently figured that the Supreme Court would reach the constitutional issues (i.e., read the statute as it had been intended) and thereby determine the validity of legislative salary cessation as a means of weeding undesirables out of the government. Though no similar statute seemed capable of passage in the foreseeable future, it might now be well to try to establish its validity for possible future use. And as a psychological matter, Congress (in this case, the House) may not have been content with having its attack on the executive rebuffed by the Court of Claims.

On February 5, 1946, the Attorney General petitioned for certiorari. It may always be a good tactic to stress constitutional as opposed to statutory issues in certiorari petitions; in this case, there had to be no conscious decision to do so. A constitutional adjudication was all any of the parties wanted. Therefore, the Attorney General, with Congress and Lovett, Watson, and Dodd in agreement, urged that the "opinion of the court" was wrong in construing 304 not to foreclose a suit for salary. Under a proper construction of the statute, chimed all the parties in unison, the constitutional issue had to be reached. (The executive, like Lovett, Watson, and Dodd, went on to urge that 304 had worked a removal from office. Congress, of course, parted company with them here.)

The Attorney General's petition put forth the "Questions Presented" thus:

(1) Whether Section 304 . . . undertook to terminate the respondents' services, and not merely to prohibit the disbursing agencies from paying their salaries.

(2) If so, whether Section 304 is constitutional.

(3) Whether, in view of Section 304 and the failure of the president to appoint respondents thereunder, the United States incurred a legal obligation to pay respondents for services rendered after November 15, 1943.

(4) Was the Court of Claims presented with justiciable controversies.[38]

Even making allowances for the fact that this list of questions was drafted in accord with the wishes of counsel for Congress—Question 4 was explicitly acknowledged to have been formulated at Mr. Gall's request—it was a poor job. Question 3 was at the least ambiguous and probably dangerous. For it looks very much like an invitation to read the statute as the "opinion of the court" had read it, to allow a suit in the Court of Claims. This is an interpretation all the parties wanted forgotten, yet Question 3 reintroduced it.

Perhaps a more serious error was made in Question 2, in the words "if so." I argued in connection with the complaints that it was unwise to formulate an independent argument bottomed on interpreting section 304 not to remove plaintiffs; doing so would lessen the force of the removal power argument. But here the Attorney General went too far in the other direction; he essentially told the Court to act on the assumption that if there was no removal, the statute was valid. This was too great a concession for, as noted above, the bill of attainder argument would have been strong even if the Court found that 304 to have done no more than cut off all salary sources. Before the Court of Claims the Justice Department had argued that section 304 was a bill of attainder regardless of whether it removed plaintiffs or merely cut off their salaries; in formulating its certiorari questions it seems to have forgotten this two-pronged approach. It fell instead into the understandable trap of failing to see that there was a middle ground between removal from office and prohibiting payment out of funds generally appropriated—namely cutting off all sources of salary, including the Court of Claims. Counsel for Congress subsequently caught the error and attempted to hold plaintiffs to the questions as they had been formulated:

> It will be noted that the petition does not raise questions as to the constitutionality of the statute except in the event the court should conclude that Section 304 "undertook to terminate the respondents' services."[39]

It is true that the appearance of consistency demanded that a fetish not be made of suggesting that perhaps section 304 did not terminate the plaintiffs' employment. But the omission of the words "if so" would have constituted no such fetish and would have left open another way of striking the statute down.

Congress's Brief in Support of the Petition for Certiorari was short and direct. Mr. Gall, like the Attorney General, argued that the Court of Claims had erred in construing section 304 as a "bare caveat issued against the disbursing officers" but of course took issue with the Attorney General's contention that 304 worked a removal. He thus invited the Court to tread with him the tightrope between "removal" and the conclusion of the "opinion of the court" that salary remained available. If he could get the Court to come along, he could capitalize on the Attorney General's concession that if there was no removal, there was no constitutional infirmity. Mr. Gall's supporting brief wisely painted the constitutional issue as one of the limits of the appropriations power only; we shall see that his subsequent brief on the merits lacked such single-minded stress.

Lovett, Watson, and Dodd filed a memorandum of less than a page, agreeing that it had been error not to reach the constitutional questions. To no one's great surprise, on March 25, 1946, the Supreme Court granted certiorari in all three cases.

The Supreme Court Briefs

For each of the three interested groups there remained but one chore: to get the Court to accept its view of what sort of function—legislative, executive, or judicial—Congress had performed in section 304. Congress's task was the most challenging: it had to overcome the unanimous judgment of the Court of Claims and prove that 304 was merely an exercise of the legislative power over appropriations. The executive branch, speaking through the Attorney General, would be most pleased by a holding that 304 had been an unconstitutional attempt to exercise the executive power of removal. As for Lovett, Watson, and Dodd, their names could best be cleared by a finding that section 304 constituted a bill of attainder—a legislative usurpation of the judicial function. (It would, however, be an oversimplification to suggest that neither Lovett, Watson, and Dodd nor the Attorney General would have been pleased with a victory on the other's grounds.)

THE BRIEF FOR CONGRESS

Mr. Gall's brief opened with a short (four page) argument that the case presented no justiciable constitutional question because Article I entrusts appropriations to Congress. The next two sections construed section 304. The first purported to prove that the provision cut off all salary sources, the second that it did not terminate plaintiffs' employment. Twenty-three pages were then devoted to denying that the executive's removal power had been infringed. The point stressed, of course, was that 304 merely cut off salary and therefore did not dismiss anyone; an attempt was also made to capitalize on the unused proviso permitting the president to reappoint Lovett, Watson, and Dodd with the advice and consent of the Senate. About halfway through the brief Mr. Gall got around to arguing directly[40] that section 304 was a valid exercise of the appropriations power.[41] Again trying to hold his adversaries to the Attorney General's concession that 304 was valid if there was no removal, he next devoted seven pages to proving that the statute was not a bill of attainder and six pages to proving that it was not a denial of due process or equal protection.

This brief seems subject to several criticisms. The opening argument that the constitutional claims were not justiciable got it off to a weak start. As noted above, the argument was not intrinsically strong, and it had unceremoniously been brushed aside by the Court of Claims.

The second argument (the first of the two construing the statute) was entitled, "Section 304 Prevented the Executive Agencies from Creating Any Obligation to Pay Respondents for Services Performed after November 15, 1943." Unfortunately, that is not what it was about; it instead defended the proposition that Congress could, constitutionally, cut off all salary sources without removing from office. Negligible attention was paid to whether that was what Congress *did*. This failure to adhere to the heading could have impressed no one. But more important, the argument suggested by the title, but in fact never made, should not have been omitted. To be sure, it may have seemed obvious to some, given the legislative history, that Congress had intended to cut off all salary sources. However, the Court of Claims' "opinion of the court" had reached a contrary conclusion. (And so, subsequently, did Justices Frankfurter and Reed.) This omission by counsel for Congress is somewhat mitigated by the fact that the Attorney General's petition for certiorari had very forcefully argued that 304, if valid, blocked the awarding of salary by the Court of Claims; indeed, the grant of certiorari could conceivably be viewed as a tacit recognition that the constitutional issues would have to be dispositive. Nonetheless, a party eager for a constitutional adjudication, as Congress was, should not have wholly failed to confront the nonconstitutional ground of decision of the lower court.

The handling of the other issue of construction—whether section 304 worked a removal—was also inadequate. As to this claim, unlike the claim that 304 cut off all salary sources, Congress alone bore the burden of convincing the Court to construe its way. (Both the executive and Lovett, Watson, and Dodd were arguing that 304 did remove plaintiffs.) Furthermore, if Congress lost on this point, if the Court found 304 did work a removal, Congress was probably through under *Myers* and possibly under the Bill of Attainder Clause. Yet Mr. Gall's argument that "Section 304 Did Not Terminate Respondents' Services" ran only two pages! He wholly failed to face the claim that a cessation of salary is functionally a removal and was content with citing the "opinion of the court" below as authority for his conclusion. The Supreme Court must have been led to wonder why on this point he placed all his faith in the two-man opinion whose construction of section 304 he otherwise rejected; it is not surprising that six justices ultimately held that 304 worked a removal.

The central argument—that section 304 was an ordinary exercise of the appropriations power—was not badly handled, considering the precedent Mr. Gall had to work with. However, it came too late. By the time the justices got to it, they had already been told that the constitutional issues were not justiciable, that 304 cut off all salary sources but did not remove, and that the executive's removal power had not been abridged. Because it followed this succession of relatively weak arguments, the appropriations point lost much of its thrust. Further, by putting the argument regarding the removal power before the appropriations point, Mr. Gall was inviting the Court to view the issue in the Attorney General's terms. The brief might better have been ordered:

(1) The Scope of the Appropriations Power.
(2) Section 304 Is But an Exercise of that Power.
(3) Section 304 Does Not Infringe the Removal Power.
(4) Section 304 Is Not a Bill of Attainder.
(5) Section 304 Does Not Deny Due Process or Equal Protection.

By putting the appropriations argument first, Congress would have encouraged the Court to look at 304 in appropriations terms. And as noted above, by first arguing that 304 was an exercise of a historically legislative power, Mr. Gall would already have collaterally attacked the removal and bill of attainder claims.

Finally, plaintiffs' bill of attainder argument was not given enough attention. It was a strong argument and had been accepted by two members of the Court of Claims. Yet Mr. Gall devoted only seven pages of his 129-page brief to it—aside from the indirect attack made on the bill of attainder point via the appropriations argument. This brevity led to certain important omissions. For example, Mr. Gall failed to note that 304 lacked the "declaration of guilt" (that is, the specification of what acts gave rise to the deprivation) that Justices Frankfurter and Reed ended up viewing as essential to a finding of attainder.[42] Perhaps if the argument had been made, more than two votes for it could have been collected. But it wasn't, and Congress eventually lost on a point it had never really faced.

THE BRIEF FOR THE EXECUTIVE BRANCH

The Attorney General made only two arguments: that section 304 infringed the executive removal power (47 pages) and that it was a bill of attainder (15 pages). Although no member of the Court of Claims had accepted the removal argument, the Attorney General was wise to continue to stress it. For it was a strong argument, and it nicely served the goals of the executive department. The brief handled the bill of attainder argument well, too. For example, the Attorney General made an explicit attempt to explain away the lack of a "declaration of guilt,"[43] a lack Mr. Gall had failed to exploit. The brief was not, however, without its flaws. The Attorney General continued to ignore the middle ground he had disregarded in formulating his questions in the certiorari petition. That is, he failed to discern that 304 could be construed to cut off all salary sources and yet not to remove:

> It is patent that Congress by Section 304 intended to destroy the substantive obligation to pay respondents and to remove them from office, and not merely to prohibit the discharge of that obligation in a particular way.[44]

He did at one point argue that 304 was a bill of attainder "even if construed as expressing merely the judgment of Congress that respondents are unfit to hold Federal employment."[45] He thus demonstrated a willingness to stray from the concession made in the certiorari petition. Yet at no point did he argue that even if the Court found that 304 did no more than cut off all sources of salary, it was still a bill of attainder.

THE BRIEF FOR LOVETT, WATSON, AND DODD

Mr. Horsky's brief argued (1) that section 304 was intended to remove plaintiffs, (2) that it was therefore an infringement of the removal power, (3) that it was a bill of attainder, and (4) that it denied due process and equal protection. It was a good brief. The bill of attainder issue was here accorded the best treatment it received during the litigation. And for the first time one of the responding parties shook itself free from the concession made in the Attorney General's petition for certiorari; the brief argued that even if 304 did no more than kill all salary sources, it still was constitutionally invalid:

> The present constitutional objection to the rider does not, however, depend upon [a removal] construction; the question is equally presented if the provision be construed as only a permanent prohibition of payment of any compensation for the personal services of those three individuals. That much Section 304, if it be valid, certainly did.[46]

Unfortunately recognition of this alternative construction was misplaced; it was put not in the bill of attainder section, where it would have had power, but rather in the removal section, where its force seems dubious. Nonetheless, the middle ground—no removal, but total cessation of compensation—had finally been recognized by those challenging the statute. At long last the Court was told it could void the statute even if it could not find that there had been a removal. Perhaps if there had been a few more documents filed, the point might even have found its way into the right section of one of them.

Aside from moving the argument based on a nonremoval construction to the bill of attainder section, there is but one major change that should have been made: the bill of attainder argument should have been placed first.

It was the argument Lovett, Watson, and Dodd would have preferred to win on. It was at least as strong as the removal argument and had received two votes in the Court of Claims, where the removal argument had received none. Mr. Horsky reports that during the writing of the brief he had "some communication" with the Attorney General;[47] it would seem that the two could have worked out a territorial division whereby the Attorney General would stress the removal argument and Horsky the bill of attainder point.

The Supreme Court's Decision

On June 6, 1946, the Supreme Court unanimously affirmed the decision of the Court of Claims. Justice Black, writing for a majority of six, agreed with all three parties that the Court of Claims had been wrong in construing section 304 as "a mere stoppage of disbursal routine." Further, he rejected Congress's argument that all 304 did was cut off all sources of salary, thereby accepting the argument of the Attorney General and Mr. Horsky that 304 was intended to bar plaintiffs from government service. Thus this was no mere appropriations measure.

The parties challenging the statute had won their gamble or, on another view, they had not been hurt by the Attorney General's mistake. The Court had agreed that 304 had worked a removal; no harm had been done by the apparent concession that if there had been no removal, there was no constitutional issue.

Having held that section 304 worked a removal, the Court could have struck the statute either as an unconstitutional encroachment on the executive removal power or as a bill of attainder. It chose the latter course. Although most of the justices' questions during oral argument seem to have been directed to the removal issue,[48] that issue was explicitly put aside in the Court's opinion. (*Myers* was not even mentioned.) Apparently the pressures, so obviously felt a decade later,[49] to protect alleged subversives by doctrines that did not sound in civil liberties, to pick the ground that had on its face as little as possible to do with the protection of political dissenters, were still resistible. But the bill of attainder ground was not only more clearly responsive to the real outrage of section 304; its implications were also more clearly predictable. The Court's prior dealings with the removal power had not been happy,[50] but congressional statutes that punished people by name seemed unlikely to come along very often, and there seemed little danger in suggesting that when they did, they should fall.

Justice Frankfurter, joined by Justice Reed, concurred. (Justice Jackson did not participate.) Justice Frankfurter argued that the Bill of Attainder

Clause, unlike some other constitutional provisions, is strictly limited by historical definition. Section 304, he argued, did not come within this definition, for it did not recite the acts in return for which the deprivation was imposed. A harsh and technical limitation, Justice Frankfurter admitted, but there are other safeguards in the Constitution.[51] However, it is not these safeguards to which Justice Frankfurter then turned; rather, he "felt compelled" to adopt Chief Justice Whaley's "opinion of the court" and construe section 304 not to foreclose collection in the Court of Claims.[52]

Conclusion

Lovett, Watson, and Dodd had won—and on their terms.[53] The finding of attainder by the highest court in the land had salvaged as much of their reputations as could have survived the passage of section 304. Moreover, *United States v. Lovett* seems to have stilled further congressional attempts to punish people by name, at least in the form of statutes.[54] Mr. Horsky had done his job well.

The executive department had not gotten its reaffirmation of the removal power. Indeed, none of the thirteen judges who heard the case had founded his decision on removal power grounds. But *Myers* is still on the books, and *Lovett* itself outlawed one sort of legislative removal, although not in those terms. The Justice Department had little to be ashamed of; its only clear mistake had not proved fatal.

Mr. Gall had lost, 13–0. But although he could have done his job better, he could not have done it well. For when he was asked to defend the propriety of section 304, he was asked to do the impossible.

The Bounds of Legislative Specification: A Suggested Approach to the Bill of Attainder Clause (1962)[55]

Whereas the pretended Prince of Wales hath . . . (being bred up and instructed to introduce the Romish Superstition and French Government into these your Majesty's Kingdoms) openly and traitorously, with Design to dethrone your Majesty, assumed the Name and Title of James the Third . . . To the End therefore that your Majesty's good and loyal People of England, assembled in Parliament, may in the most solemn manner express their utmost Resentment of so great an indignity . . . and that the said Traitor may be brought more certainly and speedily to condign Punishment . . . be it enacted . . . That the said pretended Prince of Wales stand and be convicted and attainted of High Treason . . .
—1700

The Congress hereby finds and declares that the Communist Party of the United
States, although purportedly a political party, is in fact an instrumentality of a
conspiracy to overthrow the Government of the United States. . . . Therefore the
Communist Party should be outlawed.
—1954

Common in sixteenth, seventeenth, and eighteenth century England
were so called "bills of attainder," parliamentary acts sentencing to death,
without a conviction in the ordinary course of judicial trial, named or described[56] persons or groups.[57] In addition to the death sentence, it was usual
to decree that there was a "corruption of blood,"[58] which prevented the
attainted party's heirs from inheriting his property. Also common were
"bills of pains and penalties," which prescribed, after the fashion of bills of
attainder, sanctions less than capital. Both sorts of statute were almost always directed at persons who had attempted,[59] or threatened to attempt,[60]
to overthrow the government. The framers of the United States Constitution did not, however, have to scan the Statutes of the Realm in order to
appreciate the evils of attainder: our own pre-Constitution experience provided them with ample firsthand knowledge. The Revolutionary era was
marked by violent anti-Loyalist sentiments, which found expression in the
statute books of all the thirteen colonies. This wave of anti-Tory legislation
included numerous bills of attainder[61] and bills of pains and penalties.[62]
In 1789, having grown wary of such legislative excesses, the framers—
unanimously, and without debate—moved to insure that they should never
recur:

No Bill of Attainder or ex post facto law shall be passed [by the Congress].[63]

No State shall . . . pass any Bill of Attainder, ex post facto law, or Law impairing
the Obligation of Contracts . . .[64]

These clauses, limiting the extent to which legislatures can specify the individuals or groups to which their legislation is to apply, number among the
few specific safeguards of liberty that appear in the original body of the
Constitution, and also represent one of the few explicit limitations upon
both federal and state action. The recent spate of legislation specifically
directed at the members of the Communist Party[65] has forced the Supreme
Court to reexamine the scope and purpose of the clauses.

From the early days of the Constitution through the decision of *United
States v. Lovett*[66] in 1946, the Court treated the Bill of Attainder Clause as
a blanket prohibition of all forms of legislative punishment[67] of specific
groups. Since the decision in *American Communications Ass'n v. Douds*[68]
in 1950, however, the Court has espoused the view that the historical roots
of the bill of attainder proscription limit its scope to a narrowly restricted
and technically defined class of legislative acts.

The Functional Tradition

> If the [bill of attainder] inhibition can be evaded by the form of the enactment, its insertion in the fundamental law was a vain and futile proceeding.[69]

This "functional" view—interpreting the Bill of Attainder Clause not in the light of what "bills of attainder" were, but rather in the light of the kinds of evils they produced—was first suggested in 1810 in *Fletcher v. Peck*. Chief Justice Marshall, speaking for the Court, stated in dictum that "a bill of attainder may affect the life of an individual, or may confiscate his property, or may do both."[70] This is of course a statement that what were known at common law as bills of pains and penalties come within the constitutional prohibition of bills of attainder. The language of the Constitution does not compel such a conclusion; yet Marshall put it forth without argument. It seems quite clear that he arrived at this result because he viewed the constitutional provision not as a prohibition of a historically defined entity—"the bill of attainder"—but rather as a general proscription of legislative punishment, regardless of the type of sanction imposed.

The functional approach became law in the landmark post–Civil War cases of *Cummings v. Missouri*[71] and *Ex parte Garland*.[72] At issue in *Cummings* were certain amendments to the Missouri constitution of 1865 which provided that no one could vote, hold office, teach, or hold property in trust for a religious organization, unless he first took an elaborate oath to the effect that he had taken no part in the rebellion and would continue in his loyalty to the United States and the state of Missouri. *Garland* involved the constitutionality of a federal statute that required attorneys to take an oath, similar to the one involved in *Cummings*, as a condition of admission to practice in the federal courts. The Court invalidated both requirements as bills of attainder on the ground that they were legislative acts inflicting punishment upon a specific group—those who could not truthfully take the oath—without a judicial trial. Over the dissent of Justice Miller, the cases adopted Marshall's dictum that the bill of attainder proscription covers bills of pains and penalties.[73] Rejecting Miller's literalist tenets, the majority held irrelevant the facts that the act was in form a civil statute and that it lacked the "declaration of guilt" that Justice Miller and, eighty years later, Justice Frankfurter[74] claimed was essential. The Court specifically refused to read into the Bill of Attainder Clause the restricted definition of "punishment" advocated by counsel for Missouri, and implied that any deprivation could constitute "punishment" sufficient to render an act a bill of attainder.

In 1872 the Court, in a one sentence memorandum opinion in *Pierce v. Carskadon*, struck down as a bill of attainder a West Virginia statute conditioning access to the courts upon the taking of an oath similar to those involved in *Cummings* and *Garland*.[75] However, seventeen years later, in *Dent v. West Virginia*,[76] the Court upheld another West Virginia statute—this one requiring physicians to obtain a license in order to practice. (Appellant had argued, courageously, that because the granting of a license was conditioned upon graduating from medical school, practicing for ten years, or passing a special examination, the act constituted a legislative infliction of punishment upon those unable to achieve one of the qualifications.) The bill of attainder argument was also rejected in *Hawker v. New York*,[77] which involved the constitutionality of a New York statute barring convicted felons from the practice of medicine. In both cases, the Court accepted the *Cummings-Garland* doctrine that the Bill of Attainder Clause prohibits legislative punishment in any guise, but held that because the deprivation imposed by the statutes was reasonably related to the activities regulated thereby, the statutes did not impose punishment at all. Despite the finding of no bill of attainder, however, the absence of any reference to allegedly historical bonds suggests that *Dent* and *Hawker* can be placed in the pre-*Douds* stream of functional interpretation.

The Bill of Attainder Clause lay fallow until the 1946 case of *United States v. Lovett*, which involved the constitutionality of section 304 of the Urgent Deficiency Appropriation Act of 1943, prohibiting payment of further compensation to Lovett and two other named federal employees. The Court, per Mr. Justice Black and on the authority of *Cummings* and *Garland*, invalidated the section as a bill of attainder.

Since *Lovett* the Supreme Court has not condemned any statute as a bill of attainder,* although the issue has been raised at least twelve times. The functional approach, for which Mr. Justice Black remains the chief spokesman, has been relegated to the ranks of the dissenting opinion.

The Advent of Literalism

The decisions handed down since 1949 reject the traditional view that the Bill of Attainder Clause is a broad policy judgment condemning all forms of legislative punishment, and adopt instead the position that the prohibition embraces only a narrowly restricted, historically defined class of legislative acts.

> This position cannot be sustained; attainder is scarcely known in American law . . . . Bills of attainder had acquired an established and technical signification long before the framing and adoption of the Constitution of the United States, and was well understood by the men who framed that instrument.[78]

---

* [This statement no longer holds. See United States v. Brown, 381 U.S. 437 (1965), discussed briefly at pages 135–36.]

The historical lineage of this "literalist"—or strict historical—approach dates back at least as far as *Cummings* and *Garland*, where Justice Miller, dissenting from the holding of the Court in both cases and purportedly using history as his guide, drafted a list of "essential elements of bills of attainder."[79] The approach made its modern debut in Mr. Justice Frankfurter's concurrence in *United States v. Lovett*, an opinion that has subsequently achieved such status that it is now cited as authority.[80] One of the grounds for Mr. Justice Frankfurter's unwillingness to concur in the majority's finding that the statute in issue was a bill of attainder was the absence of a recital of the acts of which Lovett, Watson, and Dodd were guilty.[81] This requirement of a "declaration of guilt" would of course permit a legislature, merely by omitting its ground of condemnation, to avoid having invalidated as a bill of attainder a statute imprisoning named parties. The requirement accords with neither precedent[82] nor history;[83] it has not been accepted by a majority of the Court. Other literalist tenets first suggested in the *Lovett* concurrence, however, have become law, and have been reaffirmed several times.

THE REQUIREMENT OF POST FACTO PUNISHMENT

In his concurrence in *Lovett*, Mr. Justice Frankfurter stressed the fact that the legislation that the majority held to be a bill of attainder did not purport to inflict punishment for a past act.[84] This suggestion was adopted by the majority in *American Communications Ass'n v. Douds*, a case involving the constitutionality of section 9(h) of the Taft-Hartley Act, which conditioned recognition of a labor union upon the filing of affidavits by its officers that they were not members of the Communist Party. In rejecting petitioner's claim that the statute was a legislative imposition of punishment upon members of the Communist Party and therefore a bill of attainder, the Court distinguished *Cummings*, *Garland*, and *Lovett* on the ground that in those decisions

> . . . the individuals involved were in fact being punished for past actions; whereas in this case they are subject to possible loss only because there is substantial ground for the congressional judgment that their beliefs and loyalties will be transformed into future conduct. Of course, the history of the past conduct is the foundation for the judgment as to what the future conduct is likely to be; but that does not alter the conclusion that §9(h) is intended to prevent future action rather than to punish past action.[85]

The principle that in order to be invalidated as a bill of attainder a piece of legislation must be designed primarily to punish past acts rather than to prevent future action was recently reaffirmed in *Communist Party of the United States v. Subversive Activities Control Board*.[86] It is, however, a principle belied by the history from which its proponents contend it was culled. It is true that most of the English bills of attainder were passed by way of retribution for past deeds; indeed, some of them, notably that attainting Oliver Cromwell,[87] were enacted after the death of the person attainted.[88] But this was not always the case; some English bills of attainder were passed in order to prevent certain types of future conduct on the part of the person or group attainted. An example is furnished by the "Act for the Attainder of the pretended Prince of Wales of High Treason" of 1700.[89] There the announced intention of Parliament in passing the attainder was "that the said traitor may be brought more certainly and speedily to condign Punishment." That one of the reasons for their wanting him speedily executed was fear of his possible future revolutionary actions may be demonstrated by the second section of the Act, which declared anyone corresponding with the Prince or his followers to be guilty of treason.[90]

The historical inaccuracy of the requirement of post facto punishment is further demonstrated by the many colonial bills of attainder, which were enacted in order to prevent effective resistance to the Revolution by the Tories.[91] Undoubtedly the attainder of the Tories (and that of the Prince of Wales) was motivated in part by a desire for retribution for past acts, but the same can be said—as *Douds* essentially admitted[92]—of much of today's anti-Communist legislation. Nonetheless, these historical examples demonstrate that the primary purpose of some pre-Constitution bills of attainder was to prevent certain types of future action on the part of the individuals attainted.

THE REQUIREMENT OF THE INESCAPABLE CLASS

In holding that section 9(h) of the Taft-Hartley Act was not a bill of attainder, the *Douds* majority established another requirement—that of the inescapable class.[93]

> [T]here is no one who may not by a voluntary alteration of the loyalties which impel him to action, become eligible to sign the affidavit. We cannot conclude that this section is a bill of attainder.[94]

The requirement of the inescapable class also was reaffirmed in *Communist Party of the United States v. Subversive Activities Control Board*, which upheld an order of the Board requiring the Communist Party to register as a "Communist-action organization" under section 7 of the Subversive Activities Control Act. Although the Court refused to pass upon the constitutionality of those sections of the act that spell out the consequences of such registration, and restricted itself to a consideration of the validity of the registration provision alone,[95] it indulged in language broad enough to lay a foundation for holding that no section of the act is a bill of attainder:

So long as the incidence of legislation is such that the persons who engage in the regulated conduct, be they many or few, can escape regulation merely by altering the course of their own activities, there can be no complaint of an attainder.[96]

At one level, it may be questioned whether a member of the Communist Party is presented with a live option by legislation like section 9(h) of the Taft-Hartley Act. Further, those who claim to be following the dictates of history again are defeated by their own premises, for the doctrine that there can be no finding of attainder if the members of the class at which the statute is directed cannot escape the prescribed deprivation—like the requirement of post facto punishment—cannot be sustained historically. As the opinion of Judge Nicholas in the early Kentucky case of *Doe ex dem. Gaines v. Buford* stated:

> A British act of parliament might declare, that if certain individuals, or a class of individuals, failed to do a given act by a named day, they should be deemed to be, and treated, as convicted felons or traitors. Such an act comes precisely within the definition of a bill of attainder . . . .[97]

It was common for English acts of attainder to permit members of the specified class to escape the attainder. Frequently they could do so by surrendering by a specified day:

> An Act to attaint Alexander Earl of Kellie, William Viscount of Strathallan, Alexander Lord Pitsligo . . . of High Treason, if they shall not render themselves to one of His Majesty's Justices of the Peace, on or before the twelfth Day of July in the Year of Our Lord one thousand seven hundred and forty-six, and submit to Justice.[98]

The choice between attainder and surrender was not the Hobson's choice it initially appears to be. For by granting the attainted party the option of "submitting to Justice," Parliament gave him the opportunity to be tried by a court, under the existing statutory law and with all the safeguards of a judicial trial. If, on the other hand, he elected not to surrender, he could make no defense to Parliament's ad hoc determination of guilt.

Moreover, the attainder conditioned upon surrender is not the only form of conditional attainder to be found in the Statutes of the Realm. The bill against the Earl of Clarendon, passed during the reign of Charles II, perpetually banished the Earl; it further provided, however, that if he returned to England, he would then be made to suffer the pains and penalties of treason.[99] The conditional form is characteristic also of some colonial bills of attainder.[100]

In *Cummings v. Missouri* the Court observed that bills of attainder "may inflict punishment absolutely, or may inflict it conditionally."[101] Thus in establishing the requirement of the inescapable class, *Douds* and *Com-*

munist Party disregarded explicit precedent as well as pre-Constitution history. The literalists claim to derive their definition of attainder from history; yet history belies their conclusions as to both the requirement of the inescapable class and the requirement of punishment for past acts.

The Impossibility of Narrow Historical Definition

In his *Lovett* concurrence, Mr. Justice Frankfurter argued that the Constitution is an amalgam of flexible and inflexible mandates:

> Broadly speaking, two types of constitutional claims come before this Court. Most constitutional issues derive from the broad standards of fairness written into the Constitution (e.g., "due process," "equal protection of the laws," "just compensation"), and the division of power as between States and Nation. Such questions, by their very nature, allow a relatively wide play for individual legal judgment. The other class gives no such scope. For the second class of constitutional issues derives from very specific provisions of the Constitution. These had their source in definite grievances and led the Fathers to proscribe against recurrence of their experience. These specific grievances and the safeguards against their recurrence were not defined by the Constitution. They were defined by history. Their meaning was so settled by history that definition was superfluous. Judicial enforcement of the Constitution must respect these historic limits.[102]

Even granting the general soundness of the flexible-inflexible dichotomy—a distinction to which neither the Court in general,[103] nor Mr. Justice Frankfurter in particular,[104] has consistently adhered—it would appear that Frankfurter erred in its application when he concluded that "[t]he prohibition of bills of attainder falls of course among these very specific constitutional provisions."[105] "Bill of attainder" is *not* specifically defined by history. The terms "bill of attainder" and "bill of pains and penalties" (which, Frankfurter agrees,[106] fall within the constitutional prohibition) covered many types of statutes. Some pre-Constitution bills of attainder specifically named the parties attainted; others merely described the class of persons upon whom the penalties were to be levied.[107] Most recited the acts of which the attainted parties were guilty; a few did not.[108] The statutes prescribed a wide variety of sanctions, ranging from death and corruption of blood to such penalties as exile,[109] deprivation of the right to vote,[110] and the exclusion of the sons of the attainted parties from Parliament.[111] As noted above, some bills of attainder punished for past deeds; others were passed primarily to prevent future conduct. And some provided an escape from the class of those attainted, while others did not.

It thus comes as no surprise that those who have relied upon the history of attainder have been contradicted by that history. The search for a narrow historical definition of "bill of attainder" was from the beginning destined to fail, for the term lacks a narrowly restricted historical referent. It is true that many historical bills of attainder do meet the requirements propounded by the recent cases. The literalists have not misread particular statutes; their error is rather one of overextrapolation, of assuming that what is true of some bills of attainder must be true of all.

If the meaning of "bill of attainder" had been "settled by history," definition of the term in the Constitution would indeed have been superfluous. But its meaning was not settled; the variety of historical bills of attainder rendered the concept vague. Thus it would seem that if the framers had intended the constitutional provision to apply to only a rigidly defined class of statutes, they would have given the term specific content. But their writings give us no such definition; on the contrary, they demonstrate that the Bill of Attainder Clause was intended to be a broad implementation of the separation of powers, a general safeguard against the combination of the legislative and adjudicatory powers, or more simply—trial by legislature.

Bills of Attainder and the Separation of Powers

One of the ways in which the founding fathers sought to avoid tyranny was by building into the Constitution the doctrine of separation of powers. This means that each branch—executive, judicial, and legislative—has specific functions that are not to be encroached upon by the others. The doctrine thus attempts to assure that no single body can alone effectuate the total policy of government. A given policy can, in theory, be effectuated only by a combination of legislative enactment, judicial application, and executive implementation. For example, Article III's grant of power limits the judiciary to the adjudication of "cases and controversies" within the federal sphere of authority. It is of course impossible to define with precision those areas in which courts can under no circumstances act. At the outer limit such restrictions may be obvious, but in general the case and controversy limitation must be viewed as a broad judgment that a variety of types of problems are in varying degrees inappropriate for judicial resolution.

The section proscribing bills of attainder, on the other hand, establishes that there are certain types of decision that are in varying degrees inappropriate for legislative resolution, although specific definition of those limitations again appears impossible. Writings contemporary with the drafting of the Constitution express great concern lest the legislature assume the power to implement the total policy of government without the participation of the other branches, and support the thesis that the Bill of Attainder Clause should be viewed as a limitation on legislatures fully as broad, and as necessary to the effective separation of powers, as that which has been imposed upon courts by Article III.

Early formulations of the doctrine of separation of powers, notably that of Montesquieu, demonstrate that it was in large part founded upon a belief that fractionalization of the various functions of government would serve to safeguard the liberties of the citizenry:

> Again, there is no liberty, if the judiciary power be not separated from the legislative and executive. Were it joined with the legislative, the life and liberty of the subject would be exposed to arbitrary control; for the judge would be then the legislator. Were it joined to the executive power, the judge might behave with violence and oppression.[112]

The statutes of Revolutionary America bore ample witness to the dangers of the combined exercise of the legislative and adjudicatory functions.[113] Montesquieu's thought is clearly reflected in the writings of James Madison:

> The accumulation of all powers, legislative, executive, and judiciary, in the same hands, whether of one, a few, or many, and whether hereditary, self-appointed, or elective, may justly be pronounced the very definition of tyranny.[114]

A careful reading of Federalists 47, 48, 49, and 51 reveals that usurpation on the part of the *legislature* was what worried Madison and Hamilton most. As Madison noted:

> In a government where numerous and extensive prerogatives are placed in the hands of an hereditary monarch, the executive department is very justly regarded as the source of danger . . . . But in a representative republic, where the executive magistracy is carefully limited, both in the extent and the duration of its power; and where the legislative power is exercised by an assembly, which is inspired by a supposed influence over the people, with an intrepid confidence in its own strength; which is sufficiently numerous to feel all the passions which actuate a multitude, yet not so numerous as to be incapable of pursuing the objects of its passions, by means which reason prescribes; it is against the enterprising ambition of this department that the people ought to indulge all their jealousy and exhaust all their precautions.[115]

The bill of attainder prohibition was therefore looked to as a vital safeguard of the separation of powers:

> Bills of attainder, [and] ex post facto laws . . . are contrary to the first principles of the social compact, and to every principle of sound legislation. . . . Our own experience has taught us . . . that additional fences against these dangers ought not to be omitted. . . . The sober people of America are weary of the fluctuating policy which has directed the public councils. They have seen with regret and

with indignation, that sudden changes, and legislative interferences, in cases affecting personal rights, become jobs in the hands of enterprising and influential speculators; and snares to the more industrious and less informed part of the community.[116]

The dangers of attainder to which Madison had alluded were subsequently spelled out more explicitly by Story:

> In such cases, the legislature assumes judicial magistracy, pronouncing upon the guilt of the party without any of the common forms and guards of trial, and satisfying itself with proofs, when such proofs are within its reach, whether they are conformable to the rules of evidence or not. In short, in all such cases, the legislature exercises the highest power of sovereignty, and what may be properly deemed an irresponsible despotic discretion, being governed solely by what it deems political necessity or expediency, and too often under the influence of unreasonable fears, or unfounded suspicions.[117]

Thus the dual rationale of the separation of powers—fear of overconcentration of power in any one branch, and a feeling that the methods of selection and institutional trappings render the various departments suited for different jobs—is reflected in the Bill of Attainder Clause. Not only was there a general fear of legislative power on the part of the founding fathers, but there was also a specific realization that the legislative branch of government is more susceptible than the judiciary to such influences as passion, prejudice, personal solicitation, and political motives,[118] and that it is not bound to respect all the safeguards placed upon judicial trials.[119] The Bill of Attainder Clause is an implementation of their judgment that these factors render the legislature a tribunal inappropriate to decide who comes within the purview of its general rules:

> Every one must concede that a legislative body, from its numbers and organization, and from the very intimate dependence of its members upon the people, which renders them liable to be peculiarly susceptible to popular clamor, is not properly constituted to try with coolness, caution, and impartiality a criminal charge, especially in those cases in which the popular feeling is strongly excited, the very class of cases most likely to be prosecuted by this mode.[120]

A third justification for a system of separation of powers—one that was not explicitly suggested by the founding fathers—is rooted in the desirability of legislative disclosure of its purposes. When one branch may both enact and apply, it may more easily veil its real motive and even its true target. For instance, if Congress wanted to punish Catholics, it could merely enact a statute calling for the punishment of litterbugs, and by selective enforcement and veiled adjudication punish only those litterbugs who are also Catholics. If, however, the statute could be applied only by another branch, Congress could not achieve its desired purpose without articulating it at least clearly enough for the other branch to implement it. Thus separating policymaking from application has the additional virtue of requiring relatively clear and candid articulation of the legislative purpose. By requiring the legislature to expose its purpose for observation, the political processes are given a fuller opportunity to react to it. And the judiciary is better able to judge the validity of the purpose and to assure that it violates no constitutional restrictions.

Thus the Bill of Attainder Clause (coupled with the prohibition of ex post facto laws) can be viewed as serving a function analogous to Article III's restriction on judicial action.[121] Roughly, Article III, by limiting federal courts to cases and controversies, tells them, at least in theory, two things. First, they—unlike the legislature—may not create broad rules; they must content themselves with applying the law, either statutory or constitutional, to the particular disputes before them. And second, because they are restricted to adjudicating the rights of the litigants before them, they can act only retrospectively. On the other hand, the prohibition of ex post facto laws (and notions rooted in due process and the Obligation of Contracts Clause) tell the legislature that in general it can act only prospectively. The Bill of Attainder Clause, it is submitted, is a broad prohibition completing the legislative analogue of Article III. For it tells legislatures that they may not apply their mandates to specific parties; they instead must leave the job of application to other tribunals.

Article III has been construed to prevent federal courts from encroaching on the prospective rulemaking power granted the legislature by Article I; and similarly the section proscribing bills of attainder and ex post facto laws should be construed to prevent legislatures from encroaching on the power granted exclusively to courts by Article III—the power to apply the law to particular individuals. Thus Article III, when viewed against the background of the bill of attainder and ex post facto prohibitions, should be construed at once as a limitation on, and a grant of exclusive authority to, the federal courts: they can decide *only* cases and controversies, and *only* they can decide cases and controversies. As Jefferson noted:

> One hundred and seventy-three despots would surely be as oppressive as one . . . . For this reason, the convention which passed the ordinance of government, laid its foundation on this basis, that the legislative, executive, and judiciary departments should be separate and distinct, so that no one person should exercise the powers of more than one of them at the same time. . . . If . . . the legislature assumes executive and judiciary powers, no opposition is likely to be made; nor, if made, can be effectual; because in that case, they may put their proceedings into the form of an act of assembly, which will render them obligatory on the other branches. *They have accordingly, in many instances decided rights, which should have been left to judicial controversy.*[122]

Or, to put it another way, the bill of attainder and ex post facto law prohibitions, when viewed against the background of Articles I and III, may be construed as a limitation on, and a grant of exclusive authority to, Congress: *only* it can enact broad prospective rules without reference to particular persons, and it can enact *only* broad prospective rules without reference to particular persons. As Chief Justice Marshall observed in *Fletcher v. Peck*:

> It is the peculiar province of the legislature, to prescribe general rules for the government of society; the application of those rules to individuals in society would seem to be the duty of other departments.[123]

Thus an analysis of pre-Constitution bills of attainder and contemporary commentaries indicates that the prohibition of bills of attainder is not a technical provision meant to apply only to a rigidly defined class of statutes. The commentaries emphasize the evident but oft neglected fact that the separation of powers cannot be implemented unless each of the branches sought to be separated is effectively limited to its proper sphere of activity. Emphasis has frequently been placed on the necessity of limiting courts to the adjudication of cases and controversies; and to be sure this is important. But it is at least as important to prevent the legislature from exercising the judicial function. In fact the founding fathers were more concerned with legislative than judicial usurpation; the bill of attainder prohibition would seem to be their way of implementing this concern. It should be broadly construed in this spirit.

Trial by Legislature

It would seem, then, that section 9(h) of the Taft-Hartley Act, which was upheld in the *Douds* case, should have been held a bill of attainder. Congress can decree that persons who, because of their disloyalty, are likely to obstruct the flow of commerce shall not be officers of labor unions. But when Congress refuses to content itself with enacting this general rule, and goes on to say who—be it Gus Hall or all members of the Communist Party—is to be subjected to the prescribed deprivations, it oversteps its bounds.

But the Court found no bill of attainder. In upholding the statute the majority concluded that:

> It is sufficient to say that Congress had a great mass of material before it which tended to show that Communists and others prescribed by the statute had infiltrated union organizations not to support and further trade union objectives . . . but to make them a device by which commerce and industry might be disrupted when the dictates of political policy required such action.[124]

Mr. Justice Frankfurter, concurring, agreed that this sort of judgment, if made reasonably, is one properly within the legislative province:

> It must suffice for me to say that the judgment of Congress that trade unions which are guided by officers who are committed by ties of membership to the Communist Party must forego the advantages of the Labor Management Relations Act is *reasonably related* to the accomplishment of the purposes which Congress constitutionally had a right to pursue.[125]

Justice Jackson's concurrence also reiterates this theme, carefully reviewing the empirical data examined by Congress and concluding that "Congress could rationally conclude that, behind its political party facade, the Communist Party is a conspiratorial and revolutionary junta. . . ."[126]

To use "reasonableness" as a criterion for determining the validity of an application of a broad policy judgment to a particular group, however, is to employ a wholly inapposite test. The "reasonableness test" was originally devised in a quite distinct constitutional context. It was designed to define the scope of judicial review of broad legislative policy judgments. Of course a legislature can—indeed, our political system insists upon it—assemble and evaluate empirical evidence as an aid in arriving at intelligent broad political judgments. The reasonableness test was created to insure that courts would not trespass upon what is properly the legislative province—the promulgation of the rules by which our society is governed.

Thus, the due process standard of reasonableness would permit Congress to conclude that disloyal persons are more likely than not to obstruct commerce and that therefore they should not be officers of labor unions. But the *Douds* case presented a wholly different problem. The issue there was not the propriety of a general legislative rule, but the validity of the application by Congress of such a broad rule to a specific group of persons. As to this problem the implications of our traditional separation of powers are quite different. For when broad rules are applied to specific persons, in criminal or civil trials (the antithesis of rule-making proceedings), our society demands proof "beyond a reasonable doubt" or, at least, proof by a preponderance of the evidence, not mere reasonableness or rationality. Moreover, the proof offered must be subjected to all the truth-finding pressures of the adversary system.

Of course the distinction between rules of general applicability and the application of such rules to particular persons or groups is not a clear one. The separation of powers must therefore be viewed as setting up a continuum. At one extreme is the creation of broad policy judgments—general rules. These are left to the highly political, nonadversary legislative process. To demand more than a reasonable judgment at this level would be to trespass upon the legislative province. At the other extreme is the application of such a broad rule to a particular individual. Here our system demands that the decision be made under the circumstances most likely to insure fairness and certainty. This generally calls for an adversary proceeding accompanied by traditional judicial safeguards.

This continuum has been tacitly recognized by the courts in their review of the decisions of administrative agencies. Insofar as an administrative decision constitutes broad "rulemaking," courts hold the agency to no more than the legislative standard of reasonableness.[127] But when an administrative decision applies a broad rule to particular persons, the proceeding is labeled "adjudicatory" and the agency is required to accord the individual in question most of the safeguards of the judicial process.[128]

Of course the recognition of such a continuum yields no easy answer to where rulemaking ends and adjudication begins. The extreme cases—which are relatively easy to identify—establish guidelines for application of the continuum to the more difficult middle areas. As a given determination partakes more of "adjudication" and less of "rulemaking," more in the way of certainty—and thus, in most cases, more in the way of judicial safeguards—is required by the Constitution.

Thus Congress may enact a law providing that no one possessing a given characteristic (e.g., racial intolerance) shall work for the Civil Rights Division, but it may not provide that John Kasper, or the members of the Ku Klux Klan, be so restricted.[129] For in order to arrive at the conclusion that Kasper or the Klan members are racially intolerant, it is necessary to gather and evaluate empirical data pertaining to these men. The Bill of Attainder Clause is an implementation of the belief that the legislature is a tribunal unsuited to conducting such an investigation. It demands that whenever an individual is "tried" to see whether he comes within the purview of a broad mandate, he be tried in the proceeding best adapted to safeguard his rights and dispassionately seek the truth—a trial before an adjudicatory body.

This need not imply that a legislature may never phrase a statute so that it applies a restriction to a specific group of persons. For there are times when, even in the absence of a judicial hearing, application can be certain. For example, the statute "No person afflicted with grand mal epilepsy shall drive an automobile" is generally conceded to be permissible regulatory legislation. Yet it applies its restriction to a particular group of persons—grand mal epileptics. Further, in passing this law the legislature has proceeded along lines arguably similar to those outlined in connection with the Ku Klux Klan statute. Starting with the proposition that persons possessing characteristic x (the propensity to have uncontrollable seizures), when placed in situation y (in an automobile on a highway) may well cause z (an accident), the legislature has determined that persons having characteristic x shall refrain from driving (or pay a penalty). But, it might be argued, the legislature has also applied this general rule: it has determined that a specific group of persons—grand mal epileptics (a class of persons who, like the members of the Klan, could be listed at the time of the passage of the statute)—have characteristic *x* and therefore must suffer deprivation *y* (or *y'*).[130]

A return to the rationale underlying the Bill of Attainder Clause, however, discloses that the statute does not possess the evils of a bill of attainder. For the legislature has not "tried" the class of persons called grand mal epileptics at all. Starting with the principle that persons who are subject to uncontrollable seizures should not be allowed on the road, the legislature has, it is true, specified a class of persons who are to be so restricted. But the judgment that grand mal epileptics are persons susceptible to seizures (possess characteristic *x*), requires no "trial" of the persons involved, no collection and evaluation of empirical data concerning them. That "grand mal epileptics" are "persons susceptible to seizures" follows from the very meaning of the words employed. The judgment is tautological; empirical evidence about the persons is totally irrelevant to the decision. The only empirical judgment made by this legislature—that persons subject to seizures, if allowed to drive, are likely to cause accidents—was made earlier, at the general rulemaking level.

The Bill of Attainder Clause was adopted to keep the legislature from making judgments the framers considered the legislative branch unable to make in a calm, unbiased fashion; it would be nonsense to say that the legislature is subject to pressures that render it incapable of making fairly the definitional judgment—if it can be termed a "judgment"—that grant mal epileptics are subject to seizures. The legislative process is fully as capable of insuring fairness and certainty in applying its broad rule to grand mal epileptics as any tribunal would be. No evidence is relevant; no case or controversy exists; no trial is needed.[131]

Perhaps even the statute "No woman with syphilis may marry" is permissible, even though the legislature has applied its broad judgment that no one likely to bear syphilitic children shall marry to a specific class: women with syphilis. The judgment that syphilitic women are likely to bear syphilitic children is, to be sure, not definitional. Rather, it is based upon empirical observation of the children of syphilitics. But it is probably a permissible judgment for the legislature to make, because it is based upon a universally accepted empirical generalization that is capable of certain verification. Were the proposition to become relevant during a judicial proceeding, it would probably be labeled "judicially noticeable."[132] This means that no evidence would have to be adduced to support it. It is thus regarded as so certain that, even in a judicial context, it would be accepted as true without going through the customary channels of the adversary process. Since it is difficult to perceive wherein it is a judgment any less certain if made by a legislature, it would seem to be irrelevant which department makes it. The only danger in permitting legislatures to make applications of rules based upon such "judicially noticeable" propositions is that the test might be so loosely construed that it would serve as little more of a check than the inappropriate "reasonableness" test. If the right to judicial application of rules is to be preserved, the test of "judicial notice" must be construed as strictly here as it has been in a courtroom context.

Thus, when empirical evidence is irrelevant to the issue of whether a general legislative mandate applies to a particular person or group—as when the judgment is definitional or so universally acknowledged to be certain as to be "judicially noticeable"—a more specific legislative judgment is permissible, or, in other words, the legislature may apply its own rules. For a judicial hearing is not needed fairly to make such determinations. But as soon as empirical evidence becomes relevant to deciding that a broad rule applies to specific persons, the application of the rule must be left to that type of proceeding the founding fathers determined was best able fairly to execute it—a judicial trial.[133] The *Douds* opinions rightly recognized that Congress needed much empirical evidence to determine that members of the Communist Party are persons who, because of their disloyalty, are likely to obstruct the flow of commerce. For neither "disloyal" nor "likely to obstruct commerce" follows from the meaning of "member of the Communist Party," nor is the proposition that Communists possess these characteristics judicially noticeable.[134] In enacting section 9(h), Congress "tried" the class of members of the Communist Party. In so doing it overstepped its jurisdiction: "No bill of attainder shall be passed."

THE REQUIREMENT OF PUNISHMENT

It has long been the law of the land—concurred in by literalist[135] and functionalist[136] alike—that if a statute is to be held a bill of attainder, it must inflict "punishment." This requirement has been thought to be essential to distinguishing bills of attainder from regulations such as the epileptic statute considered above. But we have seen that the validity of this sort of permissible regulatory legislation can be established on grounds wholly unrelated to the concept of punishment. Further, courts have encountered endless conceptual difficulties in trying to decide whether given statutes are "punitive."

Even leaving aside the difficulties inherent in ascertaining punitive intent, the "punishment" test seems to furnish at best an inexact, emotive distinction. For it is difficult to see in what sense a typical bill of attainder calling for the banishment of a number of notorious rebels inflicts "punishment" any more than does a statute providing that no grand mal epileptic shall drive an automobile: in each case the legislature has moved to prevent a given group of individuals from causing an undesirable situation, by keeping members of that group from a position in which they will be capable of bringing about the feared events.

The breakdown of the "punishment" test is more clearly illustrated by contrasting the statutes "No one afflicted with a contagious disease shall teach school" and "John Jones, because he has a contagious disease, shall not teach school." Even proponents of the punishment test admit that the latter is a bill of attainder,[137] yet it is no more "punitive" than the former. For both the deprivation inflicted and the purpose underlying its infliction are identical. The second statute offends the bill of attainder prohibition not because of any "punitive intent," but because the legislature has taken unto itself the power to apply its general mandate to a specific individual. Thus, in pursuing the phantom "punitive intent," the courts have been focusing on the wrong issue. The Bill of Attainder Clause was directed not to the intent of the legislature, but to the preservation of the separation of powers. It was adopted not to prevent legislative "punishment," but to prevent legislative trial.

THE FORM OF DEPRIVATION

Threading the case law are holdings to the effect that the nature of the deprivation inflicted can alone determine that an act is not a bill of attainder, regardless of the fact that the deprivation is inflicted upon a specific group, and regardless of the intent with which the statute was enacted. Typical is the line of cases holding that laws providing for the deportation of alien Communists are not bills of attainder (or ex post facto laws), because deportation of aliens is simply "not a punishment."[138]

The view that the nature of the deprivation inflicted can be dispositive of whether an act is constitutional makes no sense in a bill of attainder context. Not even those who claim to draw their definition from history can rely upon such reasoning, for the bills of attainder (and bills of pains and penalties) of Revolutionary America and pre-1789 England prescribed a great variety of deprivations.[139] Indeed, banishment numbered among the more common sanctions.[140]

Also, early precedent—notably *Fletcher v. Peck* and *Cummings v. Missouri*—stands for the view that the Bill of Attainder Clause is not to be restricted to statutes inflicting any rigidly defined class of deprivations. We have seen that *Fletcher* specifically rejected the argument that the Bill of Attainder Clause applied only to statutes inflicting capital sanctions, while *Cummings* explicitly repudiated another attempt to narrow the reach of the bill of attainder clause on the basis of the type of sanction imposed:

> We do not agree with the counsel of Missouri that "to punish one is to deprive him of life, liberty, or property, and that to take from him anything less than these is no punishment at all." The learned counsel . . . does not include under liberty freedom from outrage on the feelings as well as restraints on the person. He does not include under property those estates which one may acquire in professions, though they are often the source of the highest emoluments and honors.[141]

Of course these cases accept the view, criticized above, that if an act is to be held a bill of attainder, it must inflict "punishment." What is noted here, however, is that they imply that legislative intent, and not the form or severity of the deprivation, is dispositive of whether or not punishment has been inflicted, and therefore of whether there has been an attainder.

Even more important, however, is the fact that an examination of the rationale underlying the Bill of Attainder Clause makes clear that the type of deprivation imposed by a statute is irrelevant to whether or not that statute falls within the constitutional prohibition. For the Bill of Attainder Clause is not a limitation upon the size or sort of sanctions the legislature can prescribe; it is rather a command that the legislature shall never, regardless of the type of deprivation the rule imposes, try persons to see if they come within the rule.

"MERE DENIALS OF PRIVILEGE"

There is a considerable body of state authority to the effect that a statute merely "denying a privilege" to a specific group of persons cannot be a bill of attainder. This reasoning has been applied most often in cases involving statutes denying a specific person or group the opportunity to vote[142] or to hold public office.[143]

Until very recently, the Supreme Court had consistently rejected this doctrine. The *Cummings* opinion stated that a statute depriving "any rights, civil or political" could be a bill of attainder.[144] The use of the word "rights" might suggest an endorsement of the view that a denial of a privilege cannot be a punishment. A closer reading, however, discloses that the word "right" was used by the Court to encompass what other courts have called "privileges," and that therefore the case stands for a repudiation of any dichotomy between the two:

> The theory upon which our political institutions rest is, that all men have certain inalienable rights that among these are life, liberty, and the pursuit of happiness; and that in the pursuit of happiness all avocations, all honors, all positions, are alike open to every one . . . . Any deprivation or suspension of any of these rights for past conduct is punishment.[145]

This was no inadvertent pronouncement, for among the deprivations inflicted upon those unable to take the oath at issue in *Cummings* were denials of the vote and the opportunity to hold office. And in the *Lovett* case, denial of compensation for federal employment was held to be a deprivation sufficient to invalidate the statute as a bill of attainder, despite widespread state authority to the effect that government employment is a privilege.

Since *Lovett*, however, suggestions of the doctrine that denial of a privilege cannot constitute punishment have crept into the opinions of the

Supreme Court. In *Douds* the Court observed that the deprivation imposed by section 9(h) of the Taft-Hartley Act—the preclusion of recognition by the National Labor Relations Board—would have the effect of imposing restrictions that would not exist if the Board had not been established.[146] The Court reasoned that it therefore was not "free to treat 9(h) as if it merely withdraws a privilege gratuitously granted by the Government."[147] From this statement it is not unreasonable to infer that if the Court had felt that section 9(h) did "merely withdraw such a privilege," it might have held the deprivation inflicted insufficient to invalidate the statute. And in *Flemming v. Nestor*, a 1960 case involving a statute terminating the old-age Social Security payments of aliens who had been deported for being members of the Communist Party, the doctrine was more strongly suggested. In holding that the statute was not a bill of attainder, the Court intimated that one reason underlying its finding was that the deprivation imposed by the statute was that of a "mere privilege":

> Here the sanction is the mere denial of a noncontractual governmental benefit. No affirmative disability or restraint is imposed, and certainly nothing approaching the "infamous punishment" of imprisonment . . . .[148]

Thus the doctrine that a statute "merely denying a privilege" cannot be a bill of attainder is threatening to establish itself, like the requirement of post facto punishment and the requirement of the inescapable class, as a technical limitation upon the reach of the Bill of Attainder Clause. Indeed, a recent district court decision, in upholding a federal statute against the charge that it was a bill of attainder, rested squarely upon the right-privilege dichotomy.[149]

Pre-1789 bills of attainder often inflicted deprivations that look very much like "mere denials of privilege"; there were statutes depriving the specified party the vote,[150] and denying to their sons the opportunity of sitting in Parliament.[151] Again, however, the fundamental reason that the right-privilege dichotomy must be rejected is that it does not accord with the rationale underlying the bill of attainder clause. For the clause is a blanket prohibition of legislative exercise of the adjudicating function.

Anti-Communist Legislation and the Bill of Attainder Clause

The similarity between our age and past "ages of attainder" is striking. English acts of attainder were almost always directed at persons or groups who had attempted, or seemed likely to attempt, to overthrow the government. Indeed, Parliament frequently cited as justification for its action the fact that the person or group attainted was "under the domination of a foreign power."[152] And the passage of bills of attainder in Revolutionary

America was similarly elicited by widespread fear of another "foreign-dominated" group, the Tories. John Adams' plaint, "I fear there is a chain of toryism extending from Canada through New York and New Jersey into Pennsylvania,"[153] can sound unfamiliar to no child of the era of the John Birch Society.

But mere historical similarity does not a bill of attainder make. The anti-Communist legislation presently on the books takes many forms. In order for any or all of these statutes to be bills of attainder, Congress must not only have laid down the general rule that persons dangerous to the nation's security shall be restricted in certain ways, but must also have usurped the function of the judiciary by itself applying that rule to specific persons.

The statutory provision that most clearly violates the Bill of Attainder Clause is that section of the Immigration and Nationality Act of 1952 that provides that aliens who are members of the Communist Party shall be taken into custody and deported.[154] While the Bill of Attainder Clause does not prevent [though others may] Congress from enacting a statute calling for the deportation of all persons found by a court to be disloyal, or dangerous to America's security, it does demand that the application of this rule be left to the judicial branch. But Congress has usurped this function by making the empirical determination that specific persons—alien Communists—come within the class of persons dangerous to the nation's security. Since the claim that "deportation is not a punishment" makes no sense in a bill of attainder context, the constitutional prohibition of trial by legislature has been violated.

THE COMMUNIST CONTROL ACT OF 1954

The Communist Control Act[155] also specifically names the Communist Party as the object of its restrictions. Section 3 provides:

> The Communist Party of the United States . . . [is] not entitled to any of the rights, privileges, and immunities attendant upon legal bodies created under the jurisdiction of the laws of the United States or any political subdivision thereof; and whatever rights, privileges, and immunities which have heretofore been granted to said party . . . are hereby terminated.[156]

There has apparently been an empirical determination that the Communist Party comes within the class of organizations that endanger the national security and must therefore be restricted. Indeed, Congress, in a classic example of the "declaration of guilt" that Mr. Justice Frankfurter considers essential, admitted as much:

> The Congress hereby finds and declares that the Communist Party of the United States, although purportedly a political party, is in fact an instrumentality of a

conspiracy to overthrow the Government of the United States . . . . Therefore the Communist Party should be outlawed.[157]

This is precisely the sort of "trial by legislature" the Bill of Attainder Clause was designed to prevent.

Of course, the deprivations imposed by section 3 attach to the group qua group, rather than directly to the individual members. But even leaving aside the fact that restrictions placed upon a group constitute indirect restrictions upon the actions of its members, this distinction cannot make any difference vis-à-vis the Bill of Attainder Clause. For regardless of whether individual or collective action is restricted by the statute, the fact remains that Congress has disregarded the separation of powers by applying its own general rules.

The Court's opinion in *Communist Party v. Catherwood*,[158] holding that the act does not require exclusion of Communist parties from state unemployment compensation systems, suggests that the "rights, privileges, and immunities" clause of section 3 may be construed so narrowly as to inflict essentially no deprivations upon the Communist Party. However, it can be argued that section 2[159]—the "declaration of guilt"—even standing alone, constitutes a bill of attainder. For although on its face it attaches no consequences to the announced empirical finding, it is bound to elicit community reaction that may well ultimately result in the infliction of severe deprivations upon Communists. Such a view was suggested in 1794 by James Madison when, in a debate over a congressional resolution that did no more than declare certain persons to have been involved in an insurrection, he observed:

> It is in vain to say that this indiscriminate censure is no punishment. If it falls on classes, or individuals, it will be a severe punishment. . . . Is not this proposition, if voted, a vote of attainder?[160]

THE SMITH ACT OF 1940

At the other end of the anti-Communist spectrum stands the Smith Act:

> It shall be unlawful for any person . . .
>   (3) to organize or help to organize any society, group, or assembly of persons who teach, advocate, or encourage the overthrow or destruction of any Government in the United States by force or violence; or to be or become a member of, or affiliate with, any such society, group, or assembly of persons, knowing the purpose thereof.[161]

Under the analysis suggested in this comment, the Smith Act is not a bill of attainder. In enacting it Congress contented itself with promulgating a rule of general applicability—that those who knowingly belong to a group that advocates the violent overthrow of the government shall go to prison; it did not take the further step of applying this general rule by specifying what persons or groups were to be so deprived. This job was left to the courts; one prosecuted under the Smith Act is entitled to a jury trial on the question of the disloyalty of the group to which he belongs, in addition to his membership in that group.[162]

THE SUBVERSIVE ACTIVITIES CONTROL ACT OF 1950

Situated both chronologically and along the continuum between the Communist Control Act and the Smith Act is that part of the Internal Security Act known as the Subversive Activities Control Act.[163] Section 3 defines a "Communist-action organization" as:

> [A]ny organization in the United States . . . which (i) is substantially directed, dominated, or controlled by the foreign government or foreign organization controlling the world Communist movement referred to in section 2 of this title, and (ii) operates primarily to advance the objectives of such world Communist movement . . . .[164]

Under section 7, every organization coming within this definition is required to file with the Attorney General a registration statement, which is to include, inter alia, the names and addresses of all its members.[165] From such registration (or a final order of the Subversive Activities Control Board requiring registration)[166] flow many severe deprivations.[167]

The Subversive Activities Control Act presents a difficult problem, because it does not neatly fit into either the category "rulemaking" or the category "adjudication." The analysis suggested in this comment would approach this problem by first determining what sort of judgment Congress has made in enacting the statute. It has not made a very broad judgment: "Any organization which operates primarily to aid an enemy of the United States in its efforts to defeat the United States shall . . ." Nor has it specifically applied a judgment to a particular person or group: "The Communist Party of the United States shall . . ."[168] Its judgment lies somewhere between these extremes. Thus neither the test of "reasonableness" nor the test of "certainty" should be applied to decide the validity of the enactment. It can, however, be forcefully argued that Congress has, in narrowing the breadth of its rule, made significant and not wholly uncontroversial empirical findings concerning the existence, government, aims, and power of the world Communist movement. In answer it might be urged that the enacted definition is not so far removed from the broad rulemaking level as to deny Congress the use of such uncertain empirical data.[169]

The issue was rendered moot in 1954 when, in section 4 of the Communist Control Act, Congress took the step it had refrained from taking four years earlier:

> Whoever knowingly and willfully becomes or remains a member of . . . the Communist Party . . . with knowledge of the purpose or objective of such organization shall be subject to all the provisions and penalties of the [Subversive Activities Control Act] as a member of a "Communist-action" organization.[170]

The Court has held that section 2 of the 1954 Act[171]—the "declaration of guilt"—is a mere statement of congressional purpose and cannot be read back into the Subversive Activities Control Act.[172] But this section, section 4—which explicitly refers to the 1950 Act—admits of no such interpretation. When the restrictions placed upon the members of "Communist-action organizations" by the 1950 Act are coupled with this 1954 declaration that members of the Communist Party are to be treated as members of a "Communist-action organization," there emerges the very model of a modern bill of attainder. Congress has not contented itself with its former generalization that members of organizations that possess certain characteristics shall be subject to certain restrictions; it has gone on to apply this rule specifically to the Communist Party. The separation of powers has broken down; Congress has passed a bill of attainder.[173]

Conclusion

Of late the Supreme Court, claiming it is bound by the chains of history, has limited the Bill of Attainder Clause to a degree to which it has never before been limited. But the allegedly historical assumptions of the Court do not stand up to the test of history, for pre-Constitution bills of attainder were so varied in form and effect that the formulation of any narrow historical definition is impossible.

Indeed, writings contemporary with the adoption of the Constitution indicate that the clause was intended as a broad implementation of the separation of powers—that it was designed to limit the legislature in much the same way the case and controversy requirement of Article III limits the judiciary. This broad purpose should dominate future judicial constructions of the constitutional provision.

This comment has analyzed only legislation directed at members of the Communist Party. This emphasis results not from design or sympathy, but from necessity. For it is the Communists who are the targets of today's bills of attainder. This is not surprising, for such bills have always been directed at those thought to present a threat to the security of the sovereign. Yesterday it was the Prince of Wales; today it is the Communists. As Justice Story wisely observed:

> Bills of this sort have most usually been passed in England in times of rebellion, or of gross subserviency to the crown, or of violent political excitements; periods, in which all nations are most liable (as well the free as the enslaved) to forget their duties, and to trample upon the rights and liberties of others.

*   *   *

> This is not surprising, when we consider that coolness, caution, and a strict regard for the rights and liberties of others, are the accompaniments of conscious security and strength, and are not to be looked for in times of great danger, when the people regard their all as being staked upon the issue of a doubtful contest, and when it is of the utmost importance to their cause, that by every possible means they force doubtful parties to take sides with them, and lessen the power, number, and means of offense of those opposed.[174]

It is easy to understand why Congress has not been willing to entrust to other tribunals the power to determine who is to come within the purview of its rules. But the fact that something is understandable does not make it constitutional.

We live in an age of anxiety. But so did the framers of our Constitution. We would do well to heed their warning that, in calm and anxious ages alike, the "accumulation of all powers, legislative, executive, and judiciary, in the same hands, whether of one, a few, or many, and whether hereditary, self-appointed, or elective, may justly be pronounced the very definition of tyranny."[175]

The thesis of this comment became law in United States v. Brown, 381 U.S. 437 (1965). The Court's opinion was written by Chief Justice Warren, for whom I was clerking at the time, thus raising in somewhat aggravated form (for those acquainted with both documents) the oft-raised question of how much law clerks have to do with the production of the Court's opinions. The answer is that, depending on the justice involved, quite a bit to do with the prose—but no matter who the justice is, very little to do (except in a highly subsidiary sounding-board capacity) with the outcome or even the vote of a single justice. Here, for example, there were a clear five votes to void the statute in question (an updated version of the labor union non-Communist affidavit provision discussed in the comment) and a clear four votes not to. Today one might imagine that the obvious ground of decision would be the First Amendment, which had indeed been the ground relied on by the court below. On the other hand, incredible as it may seem now, at the time Brown was written the Court had never invalidated a congressional act under the First Amendment. (It did, a couple of weeks before

Brown came down, in *Lamont v. Postmaster General, 381 U.S. 301 (1965).)* And since I'd handled a couple of sows' ears for the Chief, I think he wanted to repay me by letting me see if I could sell a bill of attainder opinion to the other four justices on his side. *(Had any of them balked and threatened to concur separately, thus making the lineup 4–1–4, we would have attempted to craft an acceptable First Amendment opinion.)* Obviously the other four joined, thereby prompting the Chief presciently to remark, "Would you believe it, John, a bill of attainder? It's so arcane I frankly doubt the case will ever be followed—but look on the bright side, it probably won't be overruled either. It'll just sit there."[176]

For the record: *Brown* was shamelessly ignored (actually "distinguished" on a preposterous ground) in *Nixon v. Administrator of General Services, 433 U.S. 25 (1977)*, upholding a statute directing the administrator to seize custody of the presidential papers and tape recordings of "Richard M. Nixon." *(The Court said the named individual constituted a "legitimate class of one.")* Attainder would also have formed a more responsible ground of decision—this was the gravamen of Justice Powell's concurrence—in *INS v. Chadha, 462 U.S. 919 (1983)*, which instead invalidated all "legislative veto" provisions.

Excerpt from *Legislative and Administrative Motivation in Constitutional Law* (1970)[177]

Seventeen years ago Professor [Henry] Hart effectively laid to rest the assumption that the provisions of Articles I and III granting Congress authority to define the jurisdiction of lower federal courts and the Supreme Court are uniquely immune to the Constitution's various prohibitory provisions.[178] It is unclear, however, because the cases are rare and the opinions are muddled, just what sort of review the Court would be willing to exercise in an egregious case. It surely is not prepared to demand that every decision to withdraw one sort of jurisdiction rather than another be rationally related to an acceptable goal. And although the Court has demonstrated a willingness to make state governments create effective procedures for protecting federal constitutional rights, it does not seem ready to make a similar demand of Congress, at least insofar as that demand would have implications for the jurisdiction of federal courts. One might, and I would, quarrel with the appropriateness of these two conclusions, but as predictions they seem reasonably safe.

However, [all this] should lead a reviewing court to examine the motivation underlying the challenged enactment. If a statute denying jurisdiction in a certain class of cases can be shown to be the product of a desire by a majority of those voting for it to deny citizens the protection of a certain constitutional right, the court should insist upon a defense of the choice in terms that rationally relate the choice to an acceptable goal and are unrelated to the inhibition of the right in issue. It would be impossible to infer such a forbidden motivation from the setting of a jurisdictional amount applicable to all sorts of cases. An inference of unconstitutional motivation might, moreover, on rare occasion be rebutted by a showing that some adequate alternative means of ensuring protection of the right exists, and Congress knew of it.[179] But where the inference of intent to curtail the enforcement of a constitutionally guaranteed right is solid, and no alternative legitimate justification suggests itself—and one seldom would[180]—the Court should invalidate the statute, "jurisdictional" though it may be.

Memorandum to Special Prosecutor Archibald Cox on the Legality of Calling President Nixon before a Grand Jury (1973)[181]

As requested, I've spent a couple of days rummaging about and wanted to let you know what I've come up with. The question with which I'd like to begin is whether the President enjoys some immunity from being called before a grand jury. In the *Boston Globe* for May 30, at p. 30, Alex Bickel states what I gather must be the sort of argument on which those supporting such immunity must rely, one generally emanating from the separation of powers:

> It is not a matter of law, but of assumed convention. The President, alone, is presumed to be immune to the judicial process.

But of course observing that there is a separation of powers does not begin to disclose its contours: the question, here as everywhere, is what powers, privileges, and immunities are distributed in what ways. Alex appeals to some historically evolved and broadly assumed convention, perhaps thereby trying to move considerations of original understanding off center stage.[182] But I cannot make out the basis for asserting that this convention exists: the matter just hasn't been litigated or even discussed much, for the obvious reason that it hasn't come up (at least not since the early nineteenth century). Moreover, the assertion that this "is not a matter of law" seems wrong. In *Mississippi v. Johnson*, 4 Wall. 475 (1867), the Supreme Court held that the president could not be enjoined from enforcing an act of Congress on the ground that it was unconstitutional. The last paragraph of the opinion may be instructive, however.

> It has been suggested that the bill contains a prayer that, if the relief sought cannot be had against Andrew Johnson, as President, it may be granted against

> Andrew Johnson as a citizen of Tennessee. But it is plain that relief as against the execution of an act of Congress by Andrew Johnson, is relief against its execution by the President. A bill praying an injunction against the execution of an act of Congress by the incumbent of the presidential office cannot be received, whether it describes him as President or as a citizen of a State.

Id. at 501. The implication may be that judicial relief would be appropriate against the president in a truly personal capacity, rather than as the enforcer of a law[183]—and thus, Professor Bickel to the contrary notwithstanding, the president is not "immune to the judicial process."[184] Much more to the point is United States v. Burr, 25 Fed. Cas. 30, 34 (No. 14692d) (C.C.Va. 1807), where Chief Justice Marshall on Circuit, with appropriate and helpful rhetoric, held that subpoenas ad testificandum and duces tecum may issue against the president. (He also held that if the president felt there were matters that should not be revealed, those specific matters should be disclosed to the court in order that a ruling could be had. 25 Fed. Cas. 187, 191–92 (no. 14694) (C.C.Va. 1807).) *Burr* involved a trial: should a subpoena to appear before a grand jury fare differently? It is hard to see why, and indeed just last year the Supreme Court assimilated the two situations. In Branzberg v. Hayes, 92 S. Ct. 2646 (1972), in arguing that "the public has a right to every man's evidence" before the grand jury, id. at 2660, the Court noted in a footnote:

> In United States v. Burr . . . Chief Justice Marshall, sitting on Circuit, opined that in proper circumstances a subpoena could be issued to the President of the United States.

Id. at 2660 n. 26.[185] More important than the application of *Burr* to grand juries, of course, is the fact that in 1972 five members of the Court, including the four Nixon appointees, saw fit to mention it at all. The question is one "of law," and in the face of *Branzberg* the "convention" that the president cannot be called before a grand jury, let alone that he is generally immune to the judicial process, seems very faint indeed.

At this point the argument would have to take the tack that it is an entirely different matter when the president is called concerning possible criminal liability on his part. The debates are rife with assertions that the president is not to be a monarch above the law, and so the argument must proceed along the line that the president must be impeached before he can be criminally prosecuted. It would then continue to the effect that a subpoena to appear before a grand jury is sufficiently part of the course of criminal prosecution that it too must await impeachment.[186] The relevant provision does, it is true, *mention* criminal prosecution second, but surely does not say it must *come* second.

Judgment in Cases of Impeachment shall not extend further than to removal from Office, and disqualification to hold and enjoy any Office of Honor, Trust, or Profit under the United States: but the Party convicted shall nevertheless be liable and subject to Indictment, Trial, Judgment and Punishment, according to law.

U.S. Const. Art. I, sec. 3, cl. 7. It must be granted, however, that a number of contemporary references quite plainly did assume that impeachment would precede any criminal prosecution, though, again, they did not argue that the Constitution required that order.[187] The policies underlying the quoted provision were two: first, that the legislature not be trusted with any penalty more serious than removal and disqualification,[188] and second, that there be no double jeopardy bar as respects the combination of impeachment and conviction. Neither policy speaks to the order in which the proceedings are to take place. Federal judges have been indicted while still on the bench. Yet the constitutional provisions draw no distinction. I suppose the assertion would be made, however, that the president is different—perhaps because his "station" is higher, perhaps because (assuming he does not resign) a criminal proceeding against him would bring virtually the entire government to a halt.[189]

Something of a problem for those who would assert that impeachment must precede criminal proceedings is posed by the fact that the prevailing view—though admittedly it is questionable—is that impeachment is limited to acts performed in an official capacity. (Proponents of this view admit it leaves open the unfortunate possibility of a criminal's remaining in office.) The argument here is fairly obvious: prosecution of a sitting (non-impeached) president must be possible, or else there would be no way to reach, say, a murder, since that would not be an impeachable offense. (And one thing that is clear is that the president does not stand above the law.) The answer to this form of argument would have to distinguish acts performed in an official capacity from others, and hold that as to the former impeachment must precede prosecution, though as to the latter it need not. My response at this point would be that the theory—forced to distinguish judges from presidents and even as to presidents among various classes of criminal acts—has abandoned any semblance of convincing derivation from considerations of constitutional history or policy and appears instead a crazy quilt stitched together by only the necessity of avoiding inadmissible implications.[190]

But even assuming its validity, I assume that at the time, if it ever comes, a decision is made to call the President before a grand jury, *some* acts on his part concerning which you will want to inquire will be fairly classifiable as not performed in an official capacity. (Indeed, it is not altogether clear where conspiracy to obstruct justice should be placed.) If so, the prevailing view, though perhaps it is mistaken, is that those acts cannot constitute grounds for impeachment. And if that is so, the criminal investigation must proceed unless the president is to be placed above the law.

More generally, the fact that you will be calling the President, if at all, for a variety of purposes (which is of course proper respecting grand jury proceedings) may serve to defeat the entire argument in response insofar as it is based on the theory that impeachment must precede criminal action against the president. If, for example, you were calling him to obtain evidence respecting the behavior of members of his staff—and surely that alone would be sufficient reason—the case would be on a par with *Burr*, in that the President's testimony would be needed respecting the criminal liability of others, and the argument based on the possibility of impeachment would seem irrelevant.

Obviously the important decisions here are political and strategic. My feeling at present, however, is that if you were to decide the President should be called, you would not lack authority on which to base an entirely respectable argument; indeed, as a legal matter, the backs against the wall would probably be those of the opposition. But obviously much research and thinking would need to be done, and it could probably be done effectively only once the context in which the attempt will be made, and the arguments likely to be interposed, are better appreciated than I would guess they are now.

Letter to *The New York Times* (1973)[191]

At this point Cox had been fired in the "Saturday Night Massacre" and the question was what to do next.

One question now is whether the inquiry into wrongdoing by close associates of the President and possibly by the President himself shall be conducted by persons entirely independent of the President—a House investigation looking to possible impeachment would be the safest way of ensuring that—or by the Department of Justice, which Acting Attorney General Bork assures us will do a thorough and independent job. Mr. Bork and I were colleagues at Yale Law School, and the high regard I had for him in that context gives me hope that there may exist circumstances of which the rest of us are unaware that can explain his willingness to be the man who fired Special Prosecutor Cox and thereby gave the act a semblance of legitimacy. But however that may be, at least one action taken by Mr. Bork during his months as Solicitor General—a position historically more independent of the president's personal wishes than the Attorney Generalship—suggests that whether or not he consciously sees himself so, he is the President's lawyer. I refer to the brief he filed concluding that the vice president could be indicted prior to being impeached.

That is a proposition with which I, and I expect most other constitutional lawyers, agree. The brief went on, however, to expound on how *the president* could *not* be indicted prior to being impeached. It argued, inter alia, that nothing in the debates at the Constitutional Convention suggested that "the immunity contemplated for the President would extend to any lesser offices." That is simply misleading. For there was no immunity contemplated by the framers—or if they contemplated it they didn't say so—for the president either! To the extent they suggest anything on the subject, the debates suggest that the immunities the Constitution explicitly granted members of Congress (which do not, incidentally, include this sort of immunity) were not intended for anyone else. The argument for presidential immunity from indictment is one that must be based on necessity—and perhaps, but only perhaps, the presidency and vice presidency are distinguishable on that score—and not on anything the framers said either in the Constitution itself or during the debates.

But more important than that is the fact that the brief's conclusion with respect to presidential immunity was entirely gratuitous. That issue simply was not presented by Mr. Agnew's case, and if a distinction was felt absolutely necessary, it could have been put in "even assuming the president is immune" form. Thus what started out as an "independent" brief on the indictability of the vice president ended up in large measure a brief for the nonindictability of the president, a conclusion that must at the time have seemed germane to the dispute over the tapes and may return to haunt us more directly in the future.

I didn't send this one, for the reasons outlined in my next day's letter to Bork:

Yesterday I wrote a letter to the *Times* arguing for an investigation independent of the Department, centering the argument around what I think was the gratuitous brief for the nonindictability of the president your office included in the Department's brief on the indictability of the vice president. I slept on it and decided not to send it, for whatever arguments exist for an independent investigation (and I think there should be one), I realized I could not make an argument that even suggested that you personally would be less than independent. God bless you in your efforts to be, and in your resignation if you find you're not allowed to be.

Admittedly, I held this back partly for reasons rooted in friendship, but friendship can give you insights into character, and I've never known Robert Bork to be a man of less than conspicuous integrity, though God *knows I disagree with him frequently. In any event, and quite without my help, a new special prosecutor was appointed who turned out to be every bit as independent as Cox, namely Leon Jaworski.**

Letter to *The New York Times* (1994)[192]

If you couldn't predict Joseph Califano's position from his background (or his piece's title) the first sentence of *Imperial Congress* (Jan. 23) set the tone: the executive branch "can no longer claim the coequal status that the Founding Fathers saw as crucial." Only two problems so far. First, the founders, understandably in light of contemporary history, intended the executive to be . . . well, an executive, not remotely the equal of the legislature so far as policy-making was concerned. Second, although Congress can still make life unpleasant for presidential aides possessed of a felt entitlement to run the country without interference, it has not since the New Deal approached anything resembling policy-making equality with the president and his legions.

Califano gets specific:

> When President Clinton lifted the ban on gay soldiers, Congress legislated a narrower change, assuring that any further moves would requires legislation rather than simply executive action. The foreign policy ax of Congress has chopped off Presidential moves in Bosnia, Haiti and Somalia.

I agree with Califano and the President that the military's ban on gays should have been abolished totally. But it's cheating to infer from that substantive preference that the decision is one the Constitution entrusted to the executive: quite the contrary, the power to "make Rules for the Gov-

---

* I subsequently got to know Jaworski when he and I represented Captain Preston in a reprise of the Boston Massacre trial staged at the 1976 American Bar Association convention in Atlanta. (Jaworski was John Adams, I Josiah Quincy.) Our opponents were two (real) Queen's Counsel from England, the presiding judge a (real) British judge, assisted by a bench comprising the Georgia Supreme Court. The witnesses—everyone was in period dress save Jaworski and me (go figure)—were professional actors, there were several thousand people (mainly litigators) in the live audience, and the proceedings were shown on PBS. To put the old tin lid on it, the entire trial, which lasted about four hours, was ad libbed. I did the direct and cross, Jaworski the opening and closing arguments. Happily the jury decided to acquit: moot court juries, aware that no real thug will walk and possibly menace them, generally do. But my willingness to take part—*to try a case without preparation in front of a few thousand trial lawyers*—does raise questions about my sanity. The cockiness born of being the only child of a broken marriage has generally served me well—"Hell yes, I can do that"—but as I walked out on that stage that night I confess to wondering whether I might in the future not think about reining it in. (Unfortunately there's no evidence that I have.)

ernment and Regulation of the land and naval forces" was given explicitly to *Congress*. (Unless of course the rule it enacts is unconstitutional on its merits—as I believe Congress's compromise is—in which case the Supreme Court should invalidate it. But that has hardly been President Clinton's claim, nor is it Califano's point, which is instead that as between Congress and the President this is the President's call, which under the Constitution it demonstrably is not.)

More conspicuously, decisions whether to use military force in situations like "Bosnia, Haiti, and Somalia"—and, as one would have hoped Mr. Califano would have learned from his service in the Johnson administration, these are very tough calls on the merits—are constitutionally entrusted to Congress, which is granted authority not simply to declare war but to decide on lesser acts of military hostility. (Were this not utterly clear from the document's language and legislative history, I'd recommend my recent book *War and Responsibility: Constitutional Lessons of Vietnam and Its Aftermath*. But it is, so I won't do anything so shameless.)

Worse yet, according to Califano, when Clinton "finally sent Congress draft legislative language" on health care reform, President Clinton was forced by our "imperial congress" to stress "his willingness to compromise on just about everything." Heaven forfend: a president forced to compromise with the legislature over a proposed piece of legislation! The founders must be fairly spinning in their graves.

Whose War Is It, Anyway? The Gulf and the War Powers Act (1988)[193]

We've blasted those oils rigs and half the Iranian navy to kingdom come, and President Reagan still refuses to comply with the law by officially acknowledging to Congress that we are engaged in hostilities. And no one in Congress seems to care.

On the surface this seems odd. The violation of law could hardly be clearer. Section 4(a)(1) of the War Powers Resolution of 1973 requires such a report whenever our armed forces are involved in hostilities or a situation "where imminent involvement in hostilities is clearly indicated by the circumstances." Even on the extravagant assumption that we weren't in such a situation before, we certainly got there on Monday, April 18. Nor would one ordinarily expect Congress to be complaisant about the usurpation of its constitutional and statutory prerogatives. True, they might not take decisive legislative action—they seem generally to be doing less of that lately—but wouldn't you at least expect a little screaming?

Some people excuse the President's failure to comply with the War

Powers Resolution by asserting that it is "unconstitutional." In fact there is one section of the resolution that might be invalidated under a 1983 Supreme Court decision—but that is Section 5(c), permitting Congress to order the president to withdraw troops from combat by concurrent resolution, which recent history almost conclusively establishes Congress never would have had the courage to invoke anyhow.

The heart of the resolution resides elsewhere, in the combination of Section 4(a)(1), requiring official notification of Congress whenever our troops are involved in hostilities or the imminent likelihood thereof, and Section 5(b), requiring that they be withdrawn 60 days later unless Congress has authorized their continued presence. There is no serious argument that these provisions are unconstitutional.

The "original intent" of the framers of the Constitution on this issue could hardly be clearer. The power "to declare War" was vested explicitly in Congress. The debates, and early practice, establish that this meant that all wars—whether declared or undeclared (yes, they knew about the latter)—had to be legislatively authorized. "The Executive," George Mason explained, was not "safely to be trusted" with such decisions, at least not alone.

Once a war was congressionally authorized, the president—as "Commander in Chief"—would assume ultimate strategic control of the way in which it would be fought. He could in addition—and this was the only exception to the proposition that he was not to take up arms without advance congressional authorization—respond defensively to "repel sudden attacks." The reason for this is obvious: it was feared that Congress wouldn't have time to respond in such case. Of course Congress can be convened faster now than it could in the late eighteenth century. But the need for swift military response may have become more important. Thus we should preserve for the president permission to act when there isn't time for Congress to do so.

The underlying principle, however, is certainly not obsolete: the decision to go to war is ultimately Congress's, and thus the president, having responded to what he takes to have been the emergency, remains obligated under the Constitution to report to Congress what he has done as soon as practicable and to await its decision whether to continue military activity. Congress is under a correlative constitutional duty to consider whether the nation is to be thus committed. In the event no affirmative authorization is forthcoming, hostilities are to be terminated.

Sections 4(a)(1) and 5(b) of the War Powers Resolution are designed to give concrete contemporary meaning to this original constitutional understanding. If anything is unconstitutional about the scheme, it is that the president gets as many as ninety free days (including a thirty-day extension for "unavoidable military necessity") in which to wage war without congressional authorization.

Certain presidents in the nineteenth century and early twentieth centuries played a little fast and loose with the Constitution in this area. But when they did so—and this is critical to the question whether practice over time might have somehow unofficially amended the original constitutional understanding—they obscured or covered up the actual facts, all the while dutifully pledging public fealty to the constitutional need for congressional authorization of military action. Shifts of constitutional power, to the extent they are possible at all, must be accomplished in the open. (It was only with the commitment of American troops to Korea in 1950 that presidents began to claim openly the right to initiate and sustain hostilities without such authorization.)

Since 1950, it is true, Congress has been mostly docile in the face of presidential claims of omnipotence—with occasional brief shows of courage, notably at the very end of the war in Indochina. But thirty-eight years of surrender—intermittent, at that—hardly seem enough to alter a century and a half of constitutional understanding to the contrary.

The War Powers Resolution, passed in 1973 over President Nixon's veto, was designed to screw the courage of future Congresses to the sticking post. It was supposed to ensure that the president would (as soon as practicable) bring military hostilities to Congress for approval and that Congress in turn would face up to its constitutional obligation to make the decision on war and peace.

Obviously it hasn't worked. Our recent presidents have been slick: they either have wholly failed to report hostilities under the resolution or have done so in terms so vague that they avoid starting the sixty-day clock. Congress has failed to react to this brazen or slippery defiance. The Persian Gulf is only the latest example of congressional inaction in the face of presidential failure to comply. (To be sure, it is one of the most swashbuckling. Anyone who can tell me with a straight face that sinking half the enemy's navy doesn't involve hostilities or the imminent likelihood thereof is someone with whom I'd just as soon not play poker—or, for that matter, associate.)

The *Wall Street Journal* was right in its April 19 editorial on the War Powers Resolution that "we haven't heard many complaints about the (military) events of Monday morning." "That absence," the *Journal* continued, "says a lot." The *Journal* thinks it says that everyone, and Congress in particular, is coming to realize that the resolution constitutes an improper interference with presidential power. What Congress's silence actually says is what Congress has been saying by its (in)actions since 1950: that it doesn't want to be accountable for deciding about war and peace. It says that Congress would rather revert to the comfortable pattern so brilliantly realized in its Vietnam performance, one of dodging responsibility and reserving the right to express the righteous indignation of an "unimplicated" party when the war in question begins not to play so well.

* * *

On other matters, dodging electoral responsibility may have become part (even the name) of the game, but this is *war* we're talking about. The framers of the Constitution thought it was a special subject, and it is. For one brief moment in 1973, when it overrode Nixon's veto of the War Powers Resolution, it actually looked as if Congress was prepared to face up to its constitutional responsibilities, daunting and disadvantageous as that can sometimes prove. Unfortunately, it hasn't looked that way since.

I am aware that if Congress were forced to decide on the events of April 18, it almost certainly would back the President. That is what makes this such a good opportunity for Congress to take a stand in support of the law. What it should do is to declare that Section 4(a)(1) of the War Powers Resolution is applicable—because at the very least there is an imminent danger of hostilities—and then go on (if so inclined) to authorize the continued presence and military activity of our Navy in the Gulf, thereby eliminating the sixty-day limit of Section 5(b). That way the Navy can stay and the President can blast oil rigs and Iranian ships when it seems appropriate to him, but a precedent will have been set that might stiffen the backbone of future Congresses in more contestable cases.

Fat chance, I suppose. But somebody should say a word in defense of Congress's constitutional role, since it seems cinch that Congress isn't going to.

Perspective on the Persian Gulf: "War by Default" Isn't the Law (1990)[194]

Two years later, and the Gulf's the same. But the enemy's now Iraq, not Iran. Hard to keep up.

The administration's position on war in the gulf is that because Congress has authority to preclude it by passing a resolution to that effect, its failure to do so is tantamount to a declaration of war. However this never was, and today it assuredly is not, a symmetrical situation. The fact that a majority of Congress can take action to stop a war if it can organize itself to do so is not remotely a functional substitute for the constitutional requirement that wars are not to be begun without Congress's affirmative approval.

The framers of the Constitution were explicit in their understanding that if Congress did not approve of our pursuance of a given war, it could end it by refusing further funding. But they also understood that once the president had committed "our boys" to the battlefield, it would become virtually impossible, emotionally and politically, to vote to cut off their "support." The Constitution requires a congressional declaration of war—it does not say that the president can commit troops to combat unless Congress takes steps to stop him—and there is every indication that this choice was deliberate.

This original decision has taken on additional validity today. The late twentieth century is in general an era of comparatively unassertive Congresses (perhaps one would better say Congresses comparatively unprepared to put their votes where their misgivings are). Today, members of Congress survive—and do they ever survive—by combining a maximum of individual services to constituents and other interest groups seen as critical to reelection with a minimum of actual legislative policymaking.

I do not wish to overstate: when the Constitution inescapably requires its assent, Congress remains capable of standing up to the president, as it did regarding the Bork nomination and the call for a constitutional flag-burning amendment. Decisive legislative action risks constituent support, though, and thus whenever there is any plausible way to avoid decision, Congress tends to take it. The most egregious example of this is probably the very subject under discussion, war-making. The Constitution tried to make that, too, a decision respecting which Congress's assent would be inescapably required. The system held for 161 years but broke down in 1950, over Korea—our clearest example, until now, of a war not authorized in advance by Congress—and it has stayed pretty much broken down ever since. (Indeed, in the Iraq case, unlike Korea, there can be nothing resembling a colorable presidential claim that the emergency came upon us so suddenly that there was no opportunity to seek authorization.)

Our lengthy, bloody war in Vietnam *was* authorized by Congress, most notably in the Tonkin Gulf Resolution, but with a maximum of obfuscation, disclaimers that the authorization being enacted certainly shouldn't be taken as indicating that those voting for it actually wanted the war to proceed.

And respecting our various smaller wars since—Grenada, Tripoli, Panama, the naval war with Iran and so forth—the president's confident assertions that such decisions are his alone, and the majority of Congress's unwillingness to take any action stronger than knitting their brows and waiting to see how the war in question plays politically, have both increased apace. For wars can go badly or wars can go well, and actually going on the record at the beginning (or for that matter any time before the end) can be risky. It is far safer to wait for the final curtain to decide whether you should applaud, or instead protest that you never really approved of the venture.

Actually the framers didn't want it to be symmetrical—but the asymmetry they sought was the exact opposite of that the administration's argument seeks to establish. George Mason said that he was "for clogging rather than facilitating war, but for facilitating peace," and Oliver Ellsworth defended the requirement of congressional authorization by saying, "It should be more easy to get out of war than into it."

Why should we care if Congress wants to surrender its constitutional prerogatives to the president? Doesn't it have ample means to get them back if it ever gets around to wanting to (or at least to make life miserable for any president who resists)? Probably it does, but the problem with the argument is that the war power wasn't given to Congress as a sort of "perk," but rather to ensure that no single person would be vested with the tragic decision to take the country into combat. Mason said he was "against giving the power of war to the Executive, because not safely to be trusted with it."

The prerogatives of congressmen aren't what's at stake here, but rather the lives of American (and other) young people—mainly, in this enlightened age of "volunteer" armies, the lives of young people whose disadvantage quota has already been filled.

This one may actually have helped a little. (Well, together with other op-eds by other authors; Judge Harold Greene's excellent opinion in Dellums v. Bush, 752 F.Supp. 1141 [D.D.C. 1990]; and [probably most important] President Bush's desire to try everything—even the extreme tactic of following the Constitution—to scare Saddam Hussein into retreating without a war.) Whatever the complex of reasons, Bush sought (and naturally got) congressional authorization for Desert Storm.

Clinton, Congress, and War (1993)[195]

There was a remarkable parody of constitutional process on Capitol Hill this week. First, the Senate Republican leader, Bob Dole, said he was introducing a bill to prevent President Clinton from committing American forces to Haiti, except for reasons of "national security." Without missing a beat, the administration's lawyers responded that such a bill would be unconstitutional because it would interfere with "the right of the President to make foreign policy." Possibly supposing he'd be president himself someday, Senator Dole backed off.

The cause of peace was then taken up by that even more notorious flower child, Senator Jesse Helms. But Mr. Helms' tougher version of the Dole bill was defeated by the Senate, 81–19 (with Mr. Dole somehow ending up among the 19). The Senate did indicate that it would be nice if the president consulted with it more often on such matters.

The surprise here is not that the Senate backed away from assuming its obligation to decide whether young Americans should be sent off to die. Congress has been dodging such politically risky decisions since 1950. The real surprise is that on the important constitutional issue at stake here, Senator Dole's original position was the correct one.

The Constitution gives the president no general right to make foreign policy. Quite the contrary. It makes sense for one person to negotiate for the country, and the president is the obvious choice. But virtually every substantive constitutional power touching on foreign affairs is vested in Congress. Specifically, the power to declare war is placed unequivocally in the legislative process.

The original debates over the Constitution, and early practice, establish that all armed hostilities, big or small, "declared" or not, had to be authorized by Congress. The "commander in chief" clause gives the president the power to direct how a war is fought, but not the power to begin one.

The framer James Wilson summarized the Constitutional Convention's thinking: "The system will not hurry us into war; it is calculated to guard against it . . . for the important power of declaring war is vested in the legislature at large."

There was one reservation. The president was granted the power, without advance congressional authorization, to "repel sudden attacks." Some scholars feel that this reservation applies only in cases of actual enemy attack on U.S. territory. Most, including myself, interpret the reservation more broadly, as applicable to any sudden and serious threat to U.S. security. Even then, however, the president must seek Congress's permission simultaneously with his commitment of American troops, and desist if such permission is not promptly granted.

The Dole proposal allowed the President the leeway to commit our troops for reasons affecting national security (which his elaboration defined broadly, including the need to evacuate Americans from Haiti). Thus, the Senator's bill wasn't unconstitutional; it replicated what the Constitution would require in any event.

Yet the administration replied, as all administrations have tended to do in recent years, that the president can start any little old war he likes because the Constitution, well, somehow doesn't count any more. Or its meaning has been flipped upside down. But given the exception for situations where there isn't time to seek congressional approval, this notion that group consensus has become less essential, as wars have become more apocalyptically threatening, seems perverse.

The administration's reply mirrored President George Bush's election campaign boast before the Texas State Republican Convention: "I didn't have to get permission from some old goat in Congress to kick Saddam Hussein out of Kuwait."

Actually he needed the permission of a congressional majority. And to his credit, he sought it and got it. Mr. Clinton should take his cue from Mr. Bush's deeds, not his reckless election hyperbole. A chorus of pundits have said Mr. Clinton is responding to criticism of his lack of military service by trying to act tough. We can only hope that the President remembers that most Americans didn't serve in the Army either. And that those of us who did, and surely those now at risk of being sent into combat, will forgive him for following the Constitution.

Now Bosnia (1994)

So next we may be going to war in Bosnia. True, the last one that started there didn't do anyone much good, but it's possible this one will: certainly the people who live there are doing horrible things to each other. So we threaten to bomb, and don't—and say we won't, and do—and given the "logic" of war we may soon put young Americans on Bosnian soil.

The problem is that the "we" in this case is President Clinton alone. Of course he consults with his foreign policy "team," may even consult briefly with the congressional "leadership," and presumably will tell the entire Congress what he's done once he's done it.

However, the Constitution requires that wars (even "little" ones like this is, so far) be authorized by (not just reported to) both houses of Congress (not just a few "leaders"). What's more (and unsurprisingly) they must, except in cases of unforeseeable emergency, be thus authorized *in advance* (not simply once there's no practical way to turn back). And this one sure wasn't unforeseeable: the plannings and warnings (and backings and forthings) have gone on for months.

Unfortunately it's obvious that short of the kind of cost in American lives that may finally make the war politically unpalatable and cause us to leave Sarajevo in the sort of condition in which we left Saigon and Mogadishu, nobody is going to stand up and stop Mr. Clinton, or even make him comply with the Constitution by soliciting congressional authorization.

Surely not Congress itself: they like the present arrangement fine—"you act; we'll play hide-and-complain"—and haven't been moved even to take up the question of authorization since the Second World War, except on the rare occasions when the president has found it advantageous to insist that they do so, notably Vietnam and Desert Storm. (An exception should be made here for President Eisenhower, who was quite scrupulous about obtaining congressional authorization before threatening the use of American troops or air power. As a former general, he (a) understood first-hand the deep horror of war and (b) lacked the need to prove his military machismo by going it alone.)

It is unlikely the courts will stand up either. For no matter what the Constitution says, and no matter how much the federal courts throughout the nineteenth century felt insisting on congressional participation to be very much their business, since Vietnam they have just as steadfastly ducked such questions.

So no, no one's likely to stand up to the man: like his immediate Republican predecessors he'll be permitted to bomb anyone and send troops anywhere he pleases. My proposal is thus a modest one, that Mr. Clinton remove from his résumé the report that he once served as a professor of constitutional law. Making war in Bosnia might be a good idea—God knows the temptation to "do something" to end the horror is one I share— but without congressional authorization it is a defiance of the Constitution.

I didn't publish this last one. For one thing, the suggestion that the President revise his résumé, though obviously a spoof (do presidents even have résumés?) might have been read by some readers as serious, and thus inordinately nasty. For another, after I wrote it, President Clinton, albeit a little late, did submit to Congress a report under section 4(a)(1) of the War Powers Resolution. I'd argue that that shouldn't suffice constitutionally where (as here) there was plenty of time to seek authorization before the bombing started, but that argument is probably too complicated for an op-ed piece; in any event Clinton's report was enough to kill a piece as pointed as this one. (Needless to say, a 4[a][1] notice filed in 1994, being good for ninety days at most, cannot legitimate either our 1995 bombing campaign or the later [and continuing] commitment of American ground troops. And no, the fact that these were conducted under NATO or United Nations "auspices" does not dispense with the constitutional requirement of congressional authorization.

However all that may be, if you found the last four pieces at all enticing, you should read War and Responsibility: Constitutional Lessons of Vietnam and Its Aftermath *(Princeton University Press 1993), which develops their themes at greater length.*

4

Freedom of Expression

Trial by Newspaper and Its Cures (1967)[1]

In 1965–66 I had a Fulbright Scholarship, and was theoretically enrolled as a nondegree student at the London School of Economics and Political Science. Despite the fact that I set foot there only twice, the year was important to me. It was the peak year of the Carnaby Street/Beatles scene, and theater tickets still cost about a dollar (and rarely required booking in advance). This also was the year I really got into what have remained to this day two of my chief cultural interests, jazz piano (playing) and ballet (watching). I did, however, also write the following piece. It obviously entailed talking with lots of journalists and lawyers, which isn't a bad way to get to know a city.

> In the *Daily Mirror* case in 1949, this newspaper, which has the largest circulation in Great Britain, was fined heavily and the editor was sent to prison for three months . . . . The newspapers have been more careful ever since, and nobody seems to have been worse off because of this.
> Professor Arthur L. Goodhart (1964)

> The press does not simply publish information about trials but guards against the miscarriage of justice by subjecting the police, prosecutors, and judicial processes to extensive public scrutiny and criticism. This Court has, therefore . . . consistently required that the press have a free hand, even though we sometimes deplored its sensationalism.
> U.S. Supreme Court (1966)

"Thank heaven we don't have trial by newspaper, as you do in America . . . ." The frequency with which such remarks appear in English discussions (both oral and written) of the press upsets me—not because we don't have a "trial by newspaper" problem in America (we do), but rather because the remark seems to imply that there is a ready and satisfactory solution to the problem (the English solution), and that in failing to seize upon it, we Americans are displaying either total indifference to the plight of the criminal defendant besieged by publicity, or monumental obtuseness. My purpose in this article is to suggest that the problem is in fact not capable of easy solution, that the English answer—contempt of court—although it goes a long way towards safeguarding the right to be tried by an impartial jury and may on balance be the best answer to the problem, in fact falls short of its goal of ensuring trials uninfluenced by publicity and, into the bargain, pays dearly by diminishing the contributions the press can make to the efficient and fair administration of justice. I shall consider my efforts successful if I am able to demonstrate that the failure of American law to adopt the English contempt rule results not from lack of concern for the rights of defendants, but rather from a judgment deeply rooted in the American constitutional tradition: that by restricting what can be printed or broadcast about a criminal proceeding, a society loses many of the benefits deriving from a free press—and is, therefore, better advised to enquire whether there aren't alternative means of safeguarding the right to a fair trial.

The English rule against contempt of court holds, fundamentally, that it is unlawful for a newspaper or other medium of communication to publish matter that tends to prejudice the course of justice in any pending litigation. In practice this means that once someone has been charged by the police or a charge is imminent, papers cannot print matter that might incline a jury towards either convicting or acquitting him. This includes the evidence against him, his prior criminal record, and editorial speculation about his guilt. Whether the report is accurate is irrelevant. These are things papers simply cannot publish. The press must keep this silence until the committal proceeding—the hearing at which a magistrate decides whether the prosecution has enough evidence to hold the accused for trial. Such proceedings are ordinarily conducted in public, and the press is free to report whatever transpires there. After the committal hearing, silence is again the order until the trial, which also can be fully reported. Even after a defendant is convicted, papers are not free to say whatever they like, for the contempt rule also bars the publication of anything that tends to prejudice the fair hearing of the appeal (although the rule is somewhat less stringent at this point than it is before trial). Should a newspaper overstep the line, it is liable to a fine and its editor may also be fined or even sent to prison. Whether a newspaper has committed contempt is decided by a judge sitting without a jury, and there is theoretically no limit to the amount of the fine or the term of imprisonment he can impose.

If we look only at its core effect—keeping from the jury factual data concerning the accused and editorial discussion of his guilt—the contempt rule makes much sense, for the English (and American) trial system is built upon the idea of a jury of twelve people who will make up their own minds, on the basis of the evidence produced before them in court. However, the rule has a number of side effects that are not so desirable, which should lead us to enquire whether the barn is not being burned to roast the pig.

Decisions as to whether it is legally safe to print a given item, like other journalistic judgments, must be made in a matter of minutes. And the penalty for a wrong guess is harsh. Thus contempt of court is an area in which particularly clear legal guidelines are needed. However, the complaint about the law of contempt I heard most often during the year I spent in London talking to journalists and newspaper lawyers is that it is so vague as to be of essentially no assistance in many to-print-or-not-to-print situations. Despite repeated journalistic cries for help, the courts have extended little. Dealing only with the specific factual situations presented by the cases before them, judges have refused to lay down guidelines for baffled editors and have contented themselves with warnings that crime reporting is a "perilous adventure." It is therefore not surprising that when there is a question as to whether an item can safely be printed, editors are inclined to err on the side of nonpublication.[2] The vagueness of the law of contempt thus gives it an "overkill" effect, deterring the publication of much that would not, if it ever came to court, be held to be within the rule's intendment. At first blush, overkill might appear a virtue, for is it not fortunate, one might ask, that the law makes papers steer far clear of prejudicing trials? That it is in fact *un*fortunate should become clear from an examination of the ways in which the vagueness of the contempt rule keeps newspapers from providing valuable assistance, in the form of positive aid as well as constructive criticism, to the agencies charged with the detection of crime and the administration of justice.

Newspaper Investigation of Crime

The British police are justly famous, but they are not omniscient. The crime rate in England, as elsewhere, is rising rapidly, and less than 40 percent of the crimes committed are solved. Any assistance the press could lend would, I am sure, be welcomed by the police as well as the public. (The possibility that the police will, for one reason or another, decline to take action against certain offenders is also not to be disregarded.) Moreover, stories exposing criminals are the sort that many papers would like to be able to run, because of their obvious potential for increasing circulation. In fact the English press has historically been of real assistance in investigating and uncovering crime.[3]

Such activity is, however, on the decline. There are isolated instances, such as *The People*'s exposés of football bribery and dog doping. But the view taken by most Fleet Street editors today is that the law's restrictions make exposure an activity too precarious to be undertaken. The possibility of a libel suit is the most obvious deterrent. But even if the paper can prove its allegations (proof would constitute a defense to a libel charge), the contempt rule, which does not recognize truth as a defense, can discourage criminal investigation.

In 1956 *The People* printed an article calling for the arrest of one Micallef, who, the paper argued, was engaged in the business of managing prostitutes. In fact, unknown to the paper, Micallef had already been arrested. The Queen's Bench Divisional Court found that the article was likely to prejudice Micallef's trial, held to be immaterial the fact that those responsible for its publication did not know of the arrest, and fined the publisher £1000 and the editor and reporter £500 each. The deterrent impact this ruling could have upon newspaper crime investigation is obvious. In its 1959 Report on Contempt of Court, Justice (the British Section of the International Commission of Jurists) sharply criticized this case; and a year later Parliament provided that no person or paper is to be held in contempt if he can show that, having taken all reasonable care, he did not know and had no reason to know that proceedings were in progress or imminent.

Though a step in the right direction, the 1960 Act has fallen far short of ending the newspapers' dilemma. For one thing, there is great uncertainty among journalists as to the meaning of "imminent." It seems clear that once a person is taken into police custody (once he is "assisting the police with their enquiries," to use the press euphemism), newspapers must assume that proceedings against him are imminent. But how much more does "imminent" mean? Does it cover the situation where a person will be arrested and charged soon, and if so, how soon? Does the fact that a person is likely to be charged one day (e.g., after completing a prison term for another offense) make proceedings against him imminent?[4] And even if the meaning of "imminent" were clear, difficulties in determining the status of a case would cause hesitation. There is no central register of summonses issued or committals ordered throughout the country; nor, of course, is there any reliable way of checking whether the police are about to take action. Editors are reluctant to publish on the basis of a limited enquiry, for fear of being found not to have exercised the reasonable care the statute requires.

Even if the point at which proceedings become imminent could be defined and determined with certainty, the financial risk produced by the contempt rule would deter much criminal investigation. It takes a good deal of time and money to investigate a scandalous situation, particularly since the paper must be prepared to defend a libel suit and therefore must amass impeccable proof of every assertion it makes. The realization that before the results of the investigation are ready for publication, the police may discover and charge the wrong-doer, thereby barring further press comment, makes newspapers hesitate to risk the financial investment. During

The People's football-bribery and dog-doping investigations, the police cooperated by not proceeding against the parties in question until the stories were printed (thus mirroring a realization that the press can assist them in uncovering and proving crime). There is, however, no assurance—nor should there be—that the police will always be able and willing to withhold action in this way. The fact thus remains that in undertaking a criminal investigation a newspaper is, thanks to the contempt rule, risking a good deal of money.

Visibility of Police Techniques

The law is clear that once someone is taken into custody by the police, the press must not probe and publicize the progress that is being made towards proving the case against him. Yet in many cases it is while he is in custody that the rights of the accused are most in need of protection. Investigation techniques—interrogation, identification parades, etc.—may be misused. From time to time investigators, out of zeal or hope of promotion, may embellish or even manufacture evidence against an individual. Mary Grigg, in her book on *The Challenor Case* (1965), has suggested that if the press had felt free to speak out sooner, Detective-Sergeant Challenor, whose strange habit it was to plant evidence on innocent men, might have been stopped before thirteen of his victims were sent to prison.

Though Challenors are rare, the temptation for the police to be selective in their enquiries, pursuing those lines of investigation that are likely to implicate the prime suspect and discarding those that are not, is ever-present. This is not blameworthy; it is an inevitable result of the fact that it is the policeman's job to come up with a suspect and a case against him. Naturally, he will at some point begin to select his facts to fit his theory rather than vice versa. But though the impetus is understandable, the fact must be faced that from time to time—even in England—innocent men are convicted. Surely Leslie Hale has demonstrated this in his book *Hanged in Error* (1961).

Newspapers, unlike the police, are not institutionally committed to the task of proving the case against the chief suspect. It is largely due to the investigations and protestations of the press that the question of Oscar Slater's guilt was re-opened in 1928, and the culpability of Timothy Evans has just been reconsidered and an official pardon issued. But Evans was executed seventeen years ago, and Slater spent nineteen years in prison before his conviction was quashed and he was awarded £6,000 for his trouble. It does not seem too courageous to suggest that if the press had felt free to conduct its probing prior to trial, these men might never have been convicted.

It might be argued that it is invalid to infer from the fact that the press is at times willing to take up someone's cause *after* conviction that it would, if it could, be interested in doing so *before*. For, the argument runs, whereas the public likes to read about how an innocent person has been unjustly convicted and punished, there is no market for stories favorable to the defense before conviction. Even if one is prepared (and I am not) to assume that newspapers are never motivated by noneconomic considerations, it plainly is not the case that all the public wants are stories implicating the chief suspect. (What a dull world it would be if the police were always right.) The experience in the United States, where reporters are permitted to cover the investigative process between arrest and trial, demonstrates that in its search for stories that will sell papers, the press will, given the chance, sometimes perform services that have the effect of protecting the rights of the accused. For example, stories exposing unfair police investigation methods both interest the reading public and benefit potential defendants. "There is hardly a jurisdiction in this country in which newspapers in the last 50 years have not discovered violations of the rights of accused persons in the period preceding trial," asserts James Russell Wiggins, the editor of the *Washington Post*—a bit overstated, perhaps, but it does not miss the mark by much.

Another sort of story that is both readable and helpful to the accused is one that argues that the police are holding the wrong person, that in fact someone else is responsible for the crime in question.

In 1964 in New York City, a young man confessed to the murder of two women, and most people, understandably, concluded that the case had been solved. Several months later a crime reporter for the *New York Daily News* (widely regarded as one of America's more "sensational" newspapers), by talking to police officers and others with information about the case, learned that the man who had confessed had an alibi and that in fact another seemed a far more likely suspect. For two months the *News* refrained from printing what it had learned, lest it interfere with the investigation. Finally it printed a story suggesting that the authorities were proceeding against the wrong person. The other man was arrested a week later, and subsequently convicted. In the United States this case has been widely noted as one that tells us something about the reliability of confessions. It also tells us something about the ways in which the press—even the "sensational" press—can help protect the rights of the accused.

A prosecutorial technique common in England (as well as the U.S.A.) is to offer one of the persons responsible for a crime a concession (a reduced charge or no charge at all) in exchange for his testimony against the other wrong-doers. Though perhaps pragmatically defensible, isn't this the sort of practice that papers should, and would if they had the chance, bring to light?

In 1965 a reporter for an English press association saw a tipstaff leading a man off to gaol. (In fact the man had just been sentenced, in a closed hearing, to ten days for violating a wardship order.) The reporter asked the judge to give him some information about the charge and sentence, but the judge refused (as he was entitled to under the law as it then existed). This led to a general outcry in the press against such secret proceedings; eight M.P.s introduced a motion deploring the procedure; and the court rules were amended to require disclosure of the name of the person sentenced, the nature of his offense, and the length of the sentence. This is an example of the kind of thing reporters can and will do in areas they are permitted to probe and publicize—in this case, the judicial process. It is reasonable to infer that if they were given the chance, they could perform similar services for the integrity of the investigative process.[5]

A newspaper can aid the administration of justice not only by conducting its own probes but also simply by publicizing the progress the police have made. For example, publishing a description of the criminal given the police by an eye-witness can lead to some reader's identifying the person or disclosing his whereabouts. So it is with photographs. When Scotland Yard was seeking John Henry Cole for attacking and robbing a number of women, they requested the press not to publish photographs of him on the ground that such publication might undercut the value of identification testimony given subsequently at the trial. Disregard of such a request subjects a paper to a real threat of a contempt citation. Nonetheless the *News of the World* (6 million circulation) printed Cole's picture. Two days later Cole was recognized and captured, although the *Police Gazette* had run his picture for weeks without result.

Similarly, press reports of committal proceedings and trials, both of which are permitted under present law, have on a number of occasions caused new witnesses to come forward—sometimes with information that helps the prosecution, sometimes the defense. Is there not every reason to suppose that permitting coverage of the events between arrest and charge would have a similar effect? (Indeed, the earlier in the process a witness can be brought forth by publicity, the more useful he will be in terms of saving police investigation time.)[6]

The law of contempt is also unclear, and therefore has a great deterrent impact, with regard to what can be said about a case after trial but while it is still on appeal. Once again the fact that the press is confused and constrained is unfortunate, for comment on such cases can greatly aid the judicial system. Whether it is desirable that newspapers comment on the factual issues of a case pending on appeal—e.g., whether the appellant in fact committed the crime, or whether his mental condition is such that he deserves to be punished—is a difficult question. Both the English and American legal systems theoretically suppose that appellate judges, like juries, are to decide such factual questions on the basis of only the evidence contained in the record, and the arguments of counsel. But we are not entirely consistent in our thinking. For we applaud Emile Zola's efforts to prove Dreyfus innocent, Sir Arthur Conan Doyle's lifelong struggle to free Oscar Slater, the efforts of the British press to get a reprieve for James Hanratty (the convicted "A-6 murderer") and Ludovic Kennedy's recent efforts on behalf of Stephen Ward. But if such crusades are desirable after the judicial process has run its course, are they not even more desirable while there is still time to avoid the alleged injustice? It is, unfortunately, not uncommon for a trial lawyer, because of inexperience or inattention, to fail to get into the record all the data the appellate court needs fairly to decide the case. Perhaps the press should be free to help remedy such omissions.

But even if we don't want appellate judges to read newspapers in order to inform themselves about the factual issues in cases coming before them, there can be no question that we should encourage press comment on issues of law, i.e., suggestions as to what the appellate court should find the controlling rule to be. I hope we have left far behind the notion that "The Law" is a list of rules deduced in vacuo from some set of celestial principles to which the courts have access, and therefore the bringing to bear of empirical data, and arguments as to what practical effects the adoption of a given rule would have, are somehow out of order. I hope, too, that neither the bar nor the public ever gets talked into thinking that lawyers (and their legal periodicals) are the only ones qualified to bring such considerations to bear. Law that does not respond to social needs cannot, nor should it, long remain law. The press is an organ well suited to articulating those needs.

However, the distinction between factual and legal discussion is not a clear one. A newspaper might, for example wish to argue that a certain rule of law acts to exclude evidence that should be heard, e.g., that the MacNaghten ("right and wrong") insanity test keeps out of the trial evidence the jury needs fairly to decide whether the mental condition of the accused is such that he ought to be imprisoned. Few would deny a paper the right to make such an argument. But unless it can point to the effects the rule under attack is having in a specific case, is it really able to argue in terms that will either interest or persuade its readers? It must, I think, be accepted that if we are going to give newspapers an effective right to editorialize on questions of law, factual data relating to pending cases will from time to time find their way into print.

This does not, however, to me seem to present a serious danger of prejudicing the right to an unbiased hearing. For appeals are decided by judges, who, while they are not supermen, have been trained to disregard facts and arguments that are irrelevant or for some other reason unworthy of consideration. Such an approach was suggested by the Queen's Bench Divisional Court in 1960. The case involved an article, published in the *Daily Sketch* while a criminal conviction was on appeal, which referred to the convicted man as a "hooligan" and a "thug." While the court suggested that this would have been contemptuous if it had been printed prior to the jury's verdict, it refused to hold the *Sketch* in contempt, on the ground that when it ran its article the only people left to consider the case were judges. The court stated that the test to be applied in such cases is whether the article "creates a real risk, as opposed to a remote possibility" of prejudicing the hearing.

Though the court thus indicated that papers can say more after a trial than before, it gave them no clear idea of how much more. The "real risk" test is hardly a model of precision, and whatever solace journalists might have found in the refusal to hold the *Sketch* in contempt was largely neutralized by the court's incantation of the time-honored caveat that "newspapers publish such articles at their peril." It is, therefore, not surprising that most editors and newspaper lawyers still act on the assumption (the criticism of the Mail Train Robbers' sentences is a notable exception) that it is dangerous to comment on a case, or to publish letters containing such comment, until the appeal has been disposed of—that is, until it is too late to do any good.

Criticism of Judges

Another facet of the law of contempt limits criticism of judges by making it an offense to "scandalise" or offend the dignity of the court. The rationale underlying this part of the rule has been stated by Lord Denning:

> The judges must of course be impartial; but it is equally important that they should be known by all people to be impartial. If they should be libelled by traducers, so that the people lost faith in them, the whole administration of justice would suffer. It is for this reason that scandalising a judge is held to be a great contempt and punishable by fine and imprisonment.

Thus the restrictions on press criticism of judicial behavior—which obtain all the time and not merely during the pendency of the case to which the criticism is addressed—are also related to the goal of safeguarding the course of justice. But the relation is indirect and long-range. Like the doctrine of contempt of Parliament, they stem from the idea that the tarnishing of a tribunal's image will, in the long run, decrease its capacity to do its job.

The 1959 Justice report took the position that the cases relating to scandalizing the court, properly read, place no restriction on criticism of a judge's competence. They mean only that a paper cannot allege judicial partiality. Most journalists and newspaper lawyers accept this as an accurate, if rough, statement of the existing law. But does it really benefit the administration of justice to keep the press from calling attention to what it takes to be partiality on the part of a judge? Judges are human, and it is sometimes difficult for them to avoid unconsciously importing their personal loyalties and political convictions into their work. The English judiciary is rightly renowned for its fairness, but that is no reason to take from the press the right to object in the rare case where partiality is displayed. Indeed, the secure position in the public's esteem the judiciary has earned suggests that the confidence of the people, and therefore the effectiveness of the judicial process, will not be destroyed when the rare transgression is brought to light.

During the first three decades of this century, English courts gave newspapers wide latitude in criticizing judges. However, in 1928, after Dr. Marie Stopes had lost a libel action that had arisen from the refusal of one of the national dailies to publish her advertisement advocating birth control, the *New Statesman* said of the libel trial that the presiding judge had permitted prejudice on his part concerning Dr. Stopes's views to influence his summing-up. The editor was found guilty of contempt, though no fine was levied.

Three years later the magazine *Truth* said of Lord Justice Slesser, who was at the time presiding at a trial involving an Act of Parliament that, as Attorney General in the previous Labour Government, he had guided through the House of Commons: "he can hardly be altogether unbiased about legislation of this type." The King's Bench Divisional Court held that the article in question assailed Lord Justice Slesser's impartiality, and fined the editor for contempt (against Lord Justice Slesser's wishes, it should be added). The press has been scared ever since. But wouldn't the integrity of the legal process benefit from a press free to argue that a judge who has expressed strong feelings about an area should not preside in a case involving that area—provided it can prove its factual allegations? (If a paper cannot back up what it says, it is susceptible to a libel suit.)

No one has recently been held in contempt for criticizing a judge. Ludovic Kennedy, in his book on *The Trial of Stephen Ward* (1964), seems to have got away with suggesting that the trial judge, by the tone and content of his summation and remarks made during the trial, prejudiced Ward's cause. Nonetheless, the bulk of the press continues to feel the restriction.[7] One London journalist told me of having written an editorial suggesting that a certain judge, because of past political affiliations that might lead him unconsciously to favor one side in a case he was trying, should have recused himself as to that case. Even though the editorial did not assert that the judge had in fact conducted the trial unfairly, the editor, fearful of a contempt citation, unhesitatingly killed it. Another told me of wishing to

editorialize to the effect that a certain judge had been appointed largely in
return for favors rendered to those responsible for the appointment. This
comment was not even set down on paper, the journalist fearing (reasonably, I think) that a court might find it to be a personal attack on the judge
rather than a criticism of his competence, and hold it to be contemptuous.

Nor does the rule bar only charges of partiality. Because the line dividing
such allegations from allegations of incompetence is a fuzzy one at best,
the rule has the (unintended) effect of discouraging the latter as well. What
of the judge who announces that he thinks a certain law unfairly ties his
hands by keeping him from giving sentences as severe as he thinks appropriate?[8] Is a paper that suggests that this attitude will keep him from applying the law in the spirit Parliament intended charging incompetence or a
kind of partiality? And what of the judge who, in the belief that one litigant
has little to support his case, interrupts and generally makes things unpleasant for that party's counsel? Occasionally a paper will criticize a judge for
chronic interruption. One such attack, launched by *The Observer* in 1957,
was followed a few months later by the judge's resignation. But such criticism is rare, a situation that led the 1959 Justice report to suggest that
there should be more of it. There has, however, been no appreciable response to these suggestions. This is understandable. For the Justice reports
of course lack the status of binding authority, and it is not at all unreasonable for an editor to fear that a court confronted with the issue might hold
that criticism of a judge's interference with one litigant's attorney constitutes a charge of partiality rather than incompetence, and therefore deserves
a contempt citation.

Most journalists feel that the atmosphere surrounding this area of contempt law has somehow changed, that a paper could now get away with
more criticism of judicial behavior than it could have thirty years ago. Unfortunately, they have no way of telling how much more. Once again, the
line dividing the permissible from the impermissible is unclear, with results unfortunate for the administration of justice. Little has changed since
Cecil H. King, the chairman of the *Daily Mirror* Group, observed in 1962:

> The actual operation of the rules against contempt of court, however, has meant
> that of recent years no serious criticism of judicial proceedings above the level of
> magistrates' courts has been thought to be possible. In fact there has been little or
> no such criticism, though a good deal from time to time would have been in the
> public interest. As judicial proceedings are not criticised in the House of Com-
> mons this means that there is no criticism of proceedings in the higher courts.

Thus the contempt rule, in seeking to curtail trial by newspaper, in fact has
much wider effects and deters newspapers from performing services of potentially great aid to the administration of justice. The obvious next ques-

tion is whether the good the rule does is sufficient to justify these losses. This entails an examination of the extent to which it accomplishes its goal of guaranteeing the right to a trial by a jury unaffected by publicity. For if the pig is not being roasted, the burning of the barn is surely unjustifiable.

A Jury Unaffected by Publicity?

The feature of English press law that is most surprising to an American lawyer is that in this country a person's conviction is permitted to stand on appeal, no matter how strong a showing of prejudicial publicity he is able to make. In 1949 the *Daily Mirror* published inflammatory stories about one Haigh, who was about to be tried for the "acid bath murder" of a Mrs. Durand-Deacon. On the basis of those stories the *Mirror* was held in contempt and fined £1,000, and its editor was sent to prison for three months. In so holding, the court said:

> To quote Lord Hardwicke, it was a case of "prejudicing mankind against persons before their case is heard." Anyone who had had the misfortune to read the articles must be left wondering how it could be possible for the applicant to obtain a fair trial after what had been published. Not only did the articles describe him as a vampire and give reasons for that description of him, but, after saying that he had been charged with one murder, went on to say not merely that he was charged with other murders but that he had committed others, and gave the names of the persons whom, it was said, he had murdered. In the long history of the present class of case there had never, in the opinion of the court, been one of such gravity as this, or one of such a scandalous and wicked character.

Not surprisingly, Haigh was convicted of murder and sentenced to death. In view of the language just quoted, to the effect that the *Mirror*'s articles rendered negligible Haigh's chances for a fair trial, would it not appear that justice required a reversal of his conviction? Had the trial judge admitted into evidence the matter printed in the paper, the conviction would surely have been reversed. It is difficult to see how the fact that it came to the jury's attention in another way—via the press—made it less prejudicial to Haigh's cause. In fact, however, it was so clear under English law that the prejudicial impact of the *Mirror*'s stories did not merit a reversal of the conviction that Haigh's lawyers did not even bother to appeal (and he was promptly executed). By holding the *Mirror* in contempt, the court may have rendered more likely impartial hearings for other defendants, but it is impossible to say that in Haigh's case the system made good its guarantee of a jury unbiased by newspaper publicity. Guilty he may well have been; but isn't the reason we want unbiased juries that we don't trust biased ones?

We have seen that the law deals harshly with papers that publish prejudicial material during certain segments of the criminal process—the periods between arrest and committal, and committal and trial. There are, however, "gaps" in the contempt rule, segments of the process during which the press is free to make public material that may have the effect of influencing the jury's verdict—the periods preceding the arrest, and during the committal proceeding and the trial itself.

One of the first things to strike an American visitor is the great volume of publicity given in this country to the discovery that a crime has been committed and the early (pre-arrest) stages of the investigation. This undoubtedly results in part from the fact that there are fewer violent crimes here; but it appears that the contempt rule also has something to do with it. For editors know that once someone is charged, they will be able to print essentially nothing more about the case until the committal proceeding. More than one Fleet Street journalist has told me of how he has worked especially hard to get a crime story ready for one edition for fear that someone will be charged before the next deadline. Although the difficulty of determining whether police action against a given person is imminent makes papers shy away from pointing an accusing finger at anyone, it is perfectly safe (and extremely common) to print a detailed description of the corpus delicti. (The Moors murder investigation and the discovery of various women's torsos in the Thames are two conspicuous recent examples.) Louis Blom-Cooper—although arguing for a different point, the abolition of committal proceedings—has pointed out the potential prejudicial impact of such descriptions:

> Could any juryman remain untouched by the details of the crime? It was bad enough that the horrible details would be presented at the trial, but the other elements of judicial impartiality and their constant warnings on burden of proof, etc., from judge and counsel could to some extent provide the necessary antidote.

Newspapers also commonly publish descriptions of the person the police are after. For example, of the man sought in connection with the theft of the World Cup, the *Evening Standard* said: "The man was about 5 ft. 10 in. tall, had a sallow complexion, black hair brushed back and greased down, dark eyes. He might also have a scar on his face." Though such detailed description undoubtedly helps the police find the person they are after, it can at the same time implant in the mind of a prospective juror an image of what "the guilty party" is like.

Another way matter prejudicial to the accused can find its way into print without infringing the law of contempt is in connection with a prior and seemingly separate proceeding. The prior proceeding may have involved the accused himself, as in the case of Albert Jones, who in 1960 was convicted—in a widely publicized trial—of the rape of one girl, and then shortly after charged with the murder, after sexual interference, of another. The publicity accorded the first trial was not contempt, since reports of judicial proceedings do not fall into that category, but there can be little doubt that it decreased Jones' chances of an unbiased trial on the second charge. Or the prior proceeding may have been one that was focused on another person or other persons and touched the accused only tangentially. The paradigm recent example of this is Stephen Ward, who, before he was charged, was caught on the fringe of the publicity spotlight trained on John Profumo et al.

Once a person is charged the press must keep silent. When, however, the case reaches the committal proceeding, it is again open season. Newspapers can report whatever transpires at the committal hearing, which in most cases means that they will report only prosecution evidence and arguments, since the defense generally declines to put on a case at this point.

The case most often cited in this regard is that of Dr. John Bodkin Adams, in which evidence was adduced at the committal proceeding, and therefore reported in the press, purportedly tending to show that he had killed three of his patients. In fact he was subsequently charged with (and acquitted of) only one of these supposed murders. It has also been argued that the publicity given to Stephen Ward's committal proceeding— including damaging evidence which at the trial was withdrawn by the witness—was so extensive that it probably had an effect on the jury that ultimately convicted him. In the Moors murder case, the committal hearing commenced in private; the magistrates decided after one day to throw it open to the public, however, which meant that it could be fully reported. In fact the news media exercised great self-restraint in reporting this hearing (which featured much evidence of a most grisly character); but enough managed to get into the papers to lead many people to doubt whether it would be possible to convene a wholly unbiased jury. In any of these cases, had the prejudicial matter been published one day prior to the committal proceeding, the paper would have been in contempt. Yet it is difficult to see how the fact that it was printed during the proceeding lessened its probable impact on the jury.

Paradoxically, press coverage of the trial itself can also have the effect of impressing on the jury's consciousness matter prejudicial to the accused. Newspaper stories on criminal trials almost invariably stress the prosecution's case. For one thing, the prosecution's evidence is presented during the first few days of the trial, when public interest in (and therefore newspaper space devoted to) the trial is greatest. Moreover, whereas the prosecution's job is to paint a complete and consistent picture of guilt, the defense's case will of necessity be more piecemeal and negative—proving an alibi here, undercutting a prosecution claim there. It is easy to see which makes a more readable story, and anyone reading reports of a trial is likely to get a somewhat one-sided picture. Yet since 1948 jurors have not been sequestered (i.e., kept isolated during adjournments) and thereby prevented from reading newspaper accounts. And how many of us can resist reading a review of a play, or an account of a football match, that we have participated in or attended?

The Schizophrenia of Contempt

The fact that there are gaps in the contempt rule demonstrates that English law from time to time makes concessions to the realization that a free press can contribute to the administration of justice. Newspapers are left free to report on the early stages of criminal investigations because somebody sometime realized that the public has a right to be kept informed of the state of law and order in the community, and that publicity can lead to earlier apprehension of the culprit. The rationale underlying the unrestricted reporting of committal proceedings and trials is that maximum visibility of the judicial process will make the public better able to do its part in making that process work. Yet the law fails to follow through with this reasoning. With regard to the periods between charge and committal, and committal and trial, it disregards the values of a free press and single-mindedly concentrates upon the goal of producing a jury unaffected by publicity. Thus, "free press" carries some days, "fair trial" others.

This "schizophrenia" becomes most apparent when we look at the debate raging over the only gap that has ever been recognized as such and given attention: the freedom to report committal proceedings. The spate of publicity accorded the committal hearing in the Bodkin Adams case led to the formation of the Tucker Committee; in 1958 it recommended that although such hearings should continue to be held in public, no reporting of them should be allowed, save for the barest details of the charge, the accused, and the decision. Despite a spirited campaign in opposition, led by the Law Society and the Press Council, the committee's recommendations form a part of the new Criminal Justice Bill.

Not surprisingly, the basic argument advanced by the proponents of the committee's proposal is that which has for years been cited in support of the contempt rule in general: that press reports are bound to incline a jury towards convicting the accused. The arguments *contra* have been stated with equal vigor: that the glare of publicity safeguards the integrity of the committal process, that there has been no showing that press reports in fact incline a jury towards conviction, and that reporting the facts will check the proliferation of unfounded rumors and bring forth witnesses. I obviously do not suggest that these arguments are invalid. They do, however, well point up the double standard inherent in much English thinking about free press and fair trial. For whereas every one of the contra-Tucker arguments cited, carried to its logical conclusion, cuts not only against the committee's proposal but also in favor of a general relaxation of the contempt rule, no one, so far as I know, has used them to support such a complete overhaul. Thus the free press–fair trial debate takes place piecemeal, one stage of the proceeding at a time, and the combatants fail to consider whether their arguments might not have some meaning for the other stages as well.

One possible reaction to this schizophrenia is to say that it demonstrates what a reasonable compromise the English system is. Gaps have been left in the law of contempt so that society can enjoy the benefits of a free press—but at the same time, in order to preserve the right to a fair trial, the press is restricted during most of the process. Comfortably moderate though this may sound, it will not do. The segments of the process that can be reported are not always those most in need of publicity, nor are those events that cannot be publicized the ones that are most likely to influence a jury. For example, reports of committal proceedings probably have more effect on a jury than material reported earlier, right after the arrest, would have. At the same time, the postarrest process of amassing evidence against the accused is in greater need of public surveillance than the committal proceeding, whose only task is to decide whether there is enough evidence to hold the accused and whose errors can therefore be corrected at trial. Yet committal proceedings can be reported. Postarrest investigation cannot. Thus even if a "now you can print it, now you can't" system were desirable, the present compromise is a poor one, because the lines between the reportable and nonreportable segments of the process are not functionally related to the two goals involved.

A more important objection to the "reasonable compromise" view, and indeed to the present state of English law, is that the existence of the gaps makes it difficult to justify the restrictions. If the press, with the blessing of the law, is going to broadcast the prosecution's case (including some data that will not be admitted at the trial) during the committal proceeding in March, how can the fact that in January it tells the public what sort of evidence has been uncovered be thought to prejudice a trial taking place in April? But suppression of freedom can be justified, if at all, only when the benefits thought to derive from such suppression in fact materialize.

Is Improvement Possible?

We have seen that the law of contempt deters newspapers from performing socially valuable functions largely because it is vague. Can it be clarified? The Justice reports took the view that it cannot, since it is impossible to foresee all the ways in which a trial might be prejudiced or the dignity of the judicial system undermined. This seems to me overly pessimistic. Surely some of the problem areas—*e.g.*, at what point proceedings become "imminent," and what sorts of considerations may be advanced while a case is on appeal—could be clarified relatively easily. The reason why these areas, despite the obvious trouble they cause, have not been cleared up is that courts are traditionally limited to deciding the cases that come before them. It is not their function to write guide-books. And cases raising the troublesome issues don't readily come before them because the penalties for contempt are stiff and editors do not take chances. Thus vagueness is self-perpetuating. If clarification is left to the judicial process, it will be a long time in coming.

Parliament, however, need not wait for cases. It could enact a statute providing editors with guidelines more detailed than those that can be gleaned from the present patchwork of cases, and thereby eliminate much of the overkill. Though any effort in this direction is, in my opinion, to be applauded, even a well-drawn statute would not herald the best of all possible worlds. Justice's point is not without some validity. Increased clarity as to what papers can and cannot say would mean an increased possibility that a paper could print something that has a prejudicial effect without running afoul of the law. Only a vague net can catch everything. Of course the chance of escape is a price we always pay for fair warning, and loopholes, once discovered, can be closed. But loopholes ordinarily come to light only after they have been used, which in this context—so long as English courts uphold convictions by juries touched by prejudicial publicity—would in many cases mean after someone convicted by such a jury has gone to prison. Moreover, even a clearly drawn statute is bound to deprive society of some of the benefits deriving from a free press. Such a law would, for example, undoubtedly provide that once a person is charged, the press cannot publish facts that tend to support the inference that he is guilty. But even this relatively limited and specific stricture would discourage press surveillance of the investigative process, eliminate the possibility that someone reading about the evidence would be moved to come to the authorities with information that either buttresses or contradicts it, and (because of the financial loss that arrest would entail) deter newspaper investigation of crimes. Since most sorts of information can be published in a context that will aid the administration of justice, the only wholly satisfactory answer to the free press–fair trial problem is to find a way of leaving the press free to investigate and criticize—and at the same time ensuring that the matter thus published will have no effect on the jury that ultimately tries the case. It is this that the American system—albeit, to date, with a distinct lack of success—tries to do.

A Different Approach

In the United States there are no legal limits (other than the law of libel) upon crime reporting. Three cases decided by the Supreme Court in the 1940s established that newspapers cannot be held in contempt for publicizing or criticizing criminal investigations and trials.[9] The First and Fourteenth Amendments to the U.S. Constitution, which safeguard the freedom of the press, reflect a judgment that the integrity of all governmental processes (the criminal process included) is rendered more secure by the existence of a press willing and free to expose to public view their workings and to comment adversely upon them when they are malfunctioning. Democratic theory presupposes that it is the people who provide the ultimate check on how the government is run; but this theoretical check will be of little avail unless the public is kept informed of what is going on. "The administration of the law is not the problem of the judge or prosecuting attorney alone, but necessitates the cooperation of an enlightened public," the Supreme Court has said.

Nor is the judiciary exempted; judges are neither more nor less susceptible to criticism than other government officials. Of course much criticism will be neither reasoned nor constructive. The men who framed the Constitution evidently felt, however, that to establish a system wherein only "reasonable" complaints are permitted would be to put in someone's hands a dangerous censorial power, and that it is therefore better to let the inherent good sense of the people take care of unjustified and scurrilous attacks. "SAVE OUR REPUBLIC: IMPEACH EARL WARREN!" scream the billboards; yet Chief Justice Warren would be the last to destroy the right to erect them. By refusing to allow the suppression of such abuse, judges do not detract from, but on the contrary enhance, their dignity. As the Supreme Court itself has said:

> The assumption that respect for the judiciary can be won by shielding judges from publicized criticism wrongly appraises the character of American public opinion. For it is a prized American privilege to speak one's mind, although not always with perfect good taste, on all public institutions. And an enforced silence, however limited, solely in the name of preserving the dignity of the bench, would probably engender resentment, suspicion, and contempt much more than it would enhance respect.

To be sure, exposure and criticism of the investigative-legal process will sometimes make it difficult to ensure that a criminal defendant will be tried by a jury untouched by publicity. Unfortunately, however, it is impossible to suppress potentially prejudicial material without at the same time losing some of the benefits of a free press. "Publicity that performs valuable social functions" and "publicity that may prejudice a trial" are not mutually exclusive categories. Two of the most frequently cited examples of American "trial by newspaper" illustrate this point.

Ever since Dr. Samuel Sheppard, a Cleveland osteopath, was convicted in 1954 of murdering his wife, commentators have argued (and the Supreme Court has just agreed) that the publicity given his case was so extensive that it must have influenced the jury that tried him. The contention is convincing. However, much (though by no means all) of the publicity in question took the form of an argument—whose validity I am not in a position to judge—to the following effect: since there is evidence that indicates that Dr. Sheppard is the man responsible for his wife's death, the police should take him into custody, and are failing to do so only because he is influential in the community. A *Cleveland Press* editorial said:

> Who's holding back, and why? What's the difference between a murder in an "ordinary" neighborhood and one in a Lake Road house in suburban Bay Village? Who is afraid of whom? It's just about time that somebody began producing the answers—and producing Sam Sheppard at police headquarters.

The evidence the papers cited in support of this argument probably did incline some of Sheppard's potential future jurors towards finding him guilty. But at the same time, do we not want the press to be able to complain when it feels that the police are failing to move against a person because of his social standing?

Similarly, although it is difficult to disagree with the Warren Commission's conclusion that the disclosure by the Dallas Police of the evidence against Lee Oswald and its consequent publication would have made it extremely difficult to impanel an unbiased jury had Oswald lived, there is also little doubt that the publicity, by indicating the kind of man Oswald was—in particular, that he was a hopeless misfit who apparently had worked alone—helped to alleviate the anxiety of a public that was understandably fearful that the murder of their President had been just the first step taken by a widespread conspiracy bent on subjugating their nation.[10] Thus the fact that publicity makes it more difficult to convene an unbiased jury does not mean that it cannot at the same time perform a valuable social function. The task, and it is not an easy one, is to find a way of preserving the value of publicity while ridding it of its prejudicial impact.

For years American courts failed to face this problem. Just as the English legal system has in large measure struck the balance in favor of insulated trials at the expense of freedom of the press, until recently courts in the U.S.A. focused single-mindedly on the preservation of their free press tradition and paid scant attention to the effect that freedom could have on the fairness of trials.

Within the past decade, however, the system has begun to awaken to the dangers of publicity, and to take the first halting steps towards doing something to guard against them. The answer selected, however, is not the English one of limiting what the press can say. Rather, the effort has been to develop a set of procedural devices (and resuscitate old ones) calculated to ensure a jury that has not been influenced by the publicity. In cases where the pretrial coverage has been intense, the court can use the voir dire (the examination of prospective jurors under oath by both lawyers and sometimes by the judge) to weed out those who have been affected by the publicity. It can delay the trial (grant a continuance) until the uproar has subsided; or it can move the trial (change the venue) to a court outside the area where the case was publicized. In a few states an additional device, the change of venire, is available, whereby jurors can be imported from areas the publicity did not saturate. Should the publicity during the trial become dangerously heavy, the court can sequester the jury, thereby insulating it from the publicity; or, if questioning the jurors indicates that they have already been exposed, it can stop the trial (grant a mistrial) and start over again. What happens if a court fails to invoke the necessary protections, with the result that someone is convicted by a jury that has been exposed to publicity of sufficient intensity to raise the inference that they were influenced by it? Since 1961 it has theoretically been the law that such omission will necessitate a reversal of the defendant's conviction on the ground that he has been denied "due process of law" in violation of the Constitution.[11] On 6 June 1966, the Supreme Court voided Dr. Sheppard's conviction, at least in part on this ground.[12]

In fact the American system has not worked. Many of the state legal systems have hedged the procedural protections in with technicalities that render their invocation difficult; and some, though not all, state courts have shown reluctance to invoke even those that are plainly available. Nor have the federal courts (U.S. courts, which enforce the federal Constitution where the state courts have failed to do so) demonstrated any real determination to upset convictions by juries that have not been adequately insulated. There have been several reversals on publicity grounds, but only in the most egregious cases. Even Dr. Sheppard spent nine years in prison.

However, the system has not been given a real test. Reversal on publicity grounds is a doctrine only five years old—new even in American terms. Moreover, prior to the *Sheppard* decision of eight months ago, the Supreme Court had never explained the doctrinal relation between its two lines of cases—those refusing to restrict the press and those reversing convictions tainted by publicity—with the result that lower courts sometimes failed to appreciate that the two issues are wholly distinct. (Thus, the federal court of appeals that refused to free Sheppard seemed to regard the fact that some of the publicity in dispute was socially useful as a reason for upholding the conviction.) The Supreme Court's opinion in *Sheppard* should go a long way towards eliminating such confusion. Although it reversed the conviction, the Court reiterated its determination not to allow the press to be muzzled:

> A responsible press has always been regarded as the handmaiden of effective judicial administration, especially in the criminal field. Its function in this regard is documented by an impressive record of service over several centuries. The press does not simply publish information about trials but guards against the miscarriage of justice by subjecting the police, prosecutors, and judicial processes to extensive public scrutiny and criticism. This Court has, therefore . . . consistently required that the press have a free hand, even though we sometimes deplored its sensationalism.

Rather, the Court continued, it is up to the trial judge to take steps to insulate the jury:

> The [trial] court's fundamental error is compounded by the holding that it lacked power to control the publicity about the trial. From the very inception of the proceedings the judge announced that neither he nor anyone else could restrict prejudicial news accounts. . . . Since he viewed the news media as his target, the judge never considered other means that are often utilized . . . to protect the jury from outside influence.

Thus for the first time the Supreme Court has made clear that its two lines of cases (no contempt-by-publication, and reversal of tainted convictions) are not, as some law review commentators have myopically suggested, inconsistent. On the contrary, they together constitute an attempt to reap the fruits of publicity while shearing it of its thorns. If the Court's opinion is taken to heart, lower courts will cease to regard the free press–fair trial problem as an unavoidable conflict to be resolved by choosing one value over the other, and begin to view it as a potential conflict to be avoided by the invocation of procedural devices.

Moreover, until 1966, the Supreme Court—though it had indicated that convictions tainted by publicity cannot stand—had not given trial judges very clear hints as to what they could do to avoid the taint. This, too, the *Sheppard* opinion remedied, specifically suggesting continuance, venue change, sequestration, and mistrial.[13]

The implication of the opinion is clear that if trial judges do not take the steps necessary to protect the right to a jury untouched by publicity, the federal courts are to upset the conviction. As this message filters down to state and lower federal courts, we shall have our first real test of whether the American approach can work.[14] At present, all we can say is what G. K. Chesterton said of Christianity: it "has not been tried and found wanting. It has been found difficult, and left untried."

One can certainly argue that to date the English method of dealing with prejudicial publicity—i.e., direct suppression—has produced better results than the American approach. A system that leaves the press wholly free is defensible only if steps are taken sufficient to ensure the integrity of trials; and this we Americans plainly have not done. I can't help believing, however, that the system toward which we are groping—which will, if it works, protect the right to a fair trial without sacrificing freedom of the press—is something a good deal better than what either country now has.

Of course, even if the *Sheppard* decision has the impact I hope it will, and state as well as lower federal courts begin to take the system seriously and make every available effort to insulate juries from publicity, the American system will still have its drawbacks. For one thing, invocation of some of the procedural devices, e.g., postponing the trial or ordering a retrial, can prolong the defendant's undoubted agony. My own feeling, though, is that if such devices constitute the only way both freedom of the press and the right to an unbiased jury can be preserved, their invocation is on balance worth the price.

Once in a while (a very long while, given the availability of continuance and venue change) there may arise a case so sensational that all the procedural devices in the world will not be able to guarantee the defendant a jury that has not been touched by the publicity. In such a case, if the press is to be left free and the right to a fair trial preserved, the only alternative may be to let the defendant go free. The freeing of a person who may well be guilty is not a desirable occurrence.[15] But if it is the only way that two fundamental rights can be preserved, again, is it not worth the price?

Flag Desecration: A Case Study in the Roles of Categorization and Balancing in First Amendment Analysis (1975)[16]

Though it takes off from the problem of nonverbal or "symbolic" expression, the following piece presents a general theory of First Amendment protection.[17]

On three occasions over the past few years the Supreme Court, on one narrow ground or another, has avoided definitively ruling on the constitutionality of convictions for politically inspired destruction or alteration of the American flag.[18] The most recent decision, *Spence v. Washington*, does seem to approach such a ruling, at least if one ignores the various irrelevancies with which the Court hedged its opinion.[19] But logical or not, the qualifications are part of the opinion, and one must assume that the Court finds the issue troubling. At first glance, however, it is hard to see why. Laws prohibiting flag desecration[20] quite obviously inhibit political expression,[21] and the state's interest in doing so—at least when the flag is owned by the person doing the disfiguring, and that is how these cases come up—seems scarcely articulable, let alone strong. The Court's hesitancy, one gathers, stems at least in part from its 1968 decision in *United States v. O'Brien*,[22] upholding a conviction for draft card burning. And indeed the act of burning a flag does look a lot like the act of burning a draft card, which makes it difficult to deny the surface plausibility of the inference that the former can also be proscribed. The plausibility is mostly on the surface, however. Indeed, once certain ambiguities in the test *O'Brien* set forth are resolved—in the only way that is defensible or even remotely consistent with other, virtually contemporaneous decisions—the case will be seen to argue rather strongly *against* the constitutionality of such laws.[23]

I

The "crux of the Court's opinion"[24] in *O'Brien* was that

> a governmental regulation is sufficiently justified . . . [1] if it furthers an important or substantial governmental interest; [2] if the governmental interest is unrelated to the suppression of free expression; and [3] if the incidental restriction on alleged First Amendment freedoms is no greater than is essential to the furtherance of that interest.[25]

Whatever *O'Brien*'s other merits or demerits, the Court is surely to be commended for here attempting something it attempts too seldom, the statement of a coherent and applicable test. The test is not limited to cases involving so-called "symbolic speech."[26] (One conclusion that should emerge from this comment is that that is one of its virtues.) The test is, however, limited in the sense that it is incomplete. The fact that a regulation does not satisfy criterion [2] does not necessarily mean that it is unconstitutional. It means "only" that the case is switched onto another track and an approach other than that indicated in criterion [3] will be employed, a categorizing approach elaborated in other decisions of the late Warren period, which is in fact substantially more demanding than the approach indicated by criterion [3]. Criterion [3] is also incomplete as described in *O'Brien*. In practice its application involves a choice between different conceptions of its standard, a choice made by reference to factors neither *O'Brien* nor any other Supreme Court decision has yet made explicit. This variability in the content of criterion [3] is important: it reduces the reliability of what at first might seem to be the most restrictive element of *O'Brien*'s test, and thus highlights the significance of what is in fact critical—the "switching function" performed by criterion [2]. It is to criterion [3] that we first look.

II

Criterion [3]'s requirement that the inhibition of expression be no greater than is essential to the furtherance of the state's interest strikes a familiar chord: "Less restrictive alternative" analysis is common in constitutional law generally and in First Amendment cases in particular. But there is always a latent ambiguity in the analysis, and *O'Brien* brought it to the surface. Weakly construed, it could require only that there be no less restrictive alternative capable of serving the state's interest *as efficiently as it is served by the regulation under attack.*[27] But as I have noted elsewhere, in virtually every case involving real legislation, a more perfect fit involves some added cost.[28] In effect, therefore, this weak formulation would reach only laws that engage in the gratuitous inhibition of expression, requiring only that a prohibition not outrun the interest it is designed to serve.

Further language in the *O'Brien* opinion,[29] and the holding of the case, indicate that this is the strongest form of less restrictive alternative analysis in which, under the circumstances, the Court was prepared to engage.[30] Coupled with the trivial functional significance the Court attached to criterion [1]'s critical word "substantial,"[31] however, this turned out to be no protection at all:[32] legislatures simply do not enact wholly useless provisions. It is therefore no surprise to discover that earlier cases protecting more traditional forms of expression (such as the distribution of handbills[33]), although they too purported to apply a sort of less restrictive alternative test, gave it a significantly stronger meaning. The point of these cases, in contradistinction to *O'Brien*, was that the absence of gratuitous inhibition is not enough. For in banning the distribution of handbills, municipalities pursue a goal unconnected with the inhibition of expression, the reduction of litter, and they do so without placing any gratuitous limits on expression: the entirety of an anti-handbill ordinance serves the goal of reducing litter. Such cases thus suggest that the existence of possible alternative approaches—such as more trash cans and an anti-littering ordinance—triggers a serious balancing of interests: the question is whether the marginally greater effectiveness of an anti-handbill ordinance relative to alternative means of litter control justifies the greater burden on communication. In order to clear room for effective expression, the Court was saying, cities will simply have to put up with some litter, to be satisfied with less than optimal vindication of the interest they are pursuing, unconnected with expression though it is.

It is not entirely clear what the Court will do, or indeed what it should do, about resolving this apparent discontinuity in its approach to the less restrictive alternative analysis. Bringing the handbill and kindred cases into line with *O'Brien* would go a long way toward eviscerating the First Amendment. Given the state's perfectly legitimate and expression-unconnected interests in keeping thoroughfares clear and controlling crowds, noise, and litter, an approach that rejected only the gratuitous inhibition of expression could effectively close altogether such traditional channels of communication as pamphleteering, picketing, and public speaking. But bringing *O'Brien* into line with the handbill cases' balancing version of the less restrictive alternative analysis has a parade of horribles all its own. Suppose O'Brien had convinced the Court to void his draft card burning conviction on the ground that the government's interest could be fairly well, if not quite as well, served by some alternative means. (The alternative most often suggested by critics of the decision is enforcement of the regulation requiring continued possession of one's draft card.[34]) But then suppose that O'Brien or someone else chose symbolically to flout the possession requirement. (The most dramatic way of doing this would probably be by publicly burning one's draft card.) It is difficult to see why he could not successfully defend this case on the theory of the prior one, namely that his expression is being inhibited for no very good reason, in that the interests served by the possession requirement too can be fairly well, if not quite as well, served by alternative means. (Governmental maintenance of several sets of records and the increased use of mailings and television reminders like those used for alien registration suggest themselves.) That case having been won, someone turning eighteen might make a public point of refusing to register for the draft in the first place, arguing in his defense that the system can get along fairly well (if not quite as well) without his contacting his draft board, as the information the board needs is all readily available without his sending it to them. The point by now is clear, and it is, of course, a point that is not limited to the context of the draft: universalizing the balancing approach of the handbill cases would seem at least potentially[35] to establish the constitutional right symbolically to break any law, or perhaps it is only any "little" law, so long as its purposes can be fairly well served, as of course they almost always can, by alternative means.

Assimilation in either direction thus appearing unlikely, the time will come when a new set of facts will force the Court to acknowledge that indeed a distinction was drawn between the *O'Brien* situation and the handbill and similar early cases, and to turn to the task of giving that distinction determinate content.[36] One approach, and I suspect this in fact was what was unconsciously going on in *O'Brien*, would be to reserve the earlier cases' serious balancing version of less restrictive alternative analysis for relatively familiar or traditional means of expression, such as pamphlets, pickets, public speeches, and rallies—thereby affirmatively obliging the state to free up certain forums, even at some sacrifice of its legitimate expression-unconnected interests—and to relegate other, less orthodox modes of communication to the weak, nay useless, "no gratuitous inhibition" approach that sustained the draft card burning law.[37] The distinction is its own objection, however: only orthodox modes of expression will be protected. There's truth in the old saw that familiarity breeds contempt: nobody goes to Speakers' Corner to listen.

An alternative line of distinction, one that at least on its face would seem to promise a similar avoidance of illimitability without at the same time officially limiting protection to the traditional and therefore relatively humdrum, is suggested by the fact that much of the effectiveness of O'Brien's communication, unlike the others we have been discussing, derived precisely from the fact that it was illegal.[38] Had there been no law prohibiting draft card burning (or requiring the continued possession of one's draft card), he might have attracted no more attention than he would have by swallowing a goldfish. That devious "might" points up the problem with the distinction thus suggested: there will be no bright-line test distinguishing situations where the act's communicative impact results largely from its illegality from those where it does not. But at least the question is intelligible, and it does not seem much harder than others courts answer in this or other contexts. For one prepared to balance reductions in communicative effectiveness against incremental additions to other societal costs—and the approach of the handbill and other early cases has to come to that—this would seem just one of a series of nonquantifiable steps.

But perhaps because of such difficulties of application and probably more because the Court, like most of the rest of us, first learned to think about the First Amendment in more traditional contexts, it seems likely that the Court will continue, either explicitly or implicitly, to distinguish between familiar and unorthodox modes of communication in deciding whether genuinely to balance in evaluating less restrictive alternatives or rather simply to assure itself, as it will always be able to, that no gratuitous inhibition of expression has been effected. In any event, the question of how to accommodate freedom of expression with the state's various expression-unconnected interests is, and will remain, an extremely difficult one. As I hope to demonstrate, however, the question posed by flag desecration laws is not that question, but one a good deal easier.

III

The two sorts of review we have been discussing—the "no gratuitous inhibition" approach that upheld the draft card burning law, and the balancing approach that has been employed in cases involving more familiar forms of expression—do differ significantly. That is not, however, because the latter is especially protective of expression (in fact it is notoriously unreliable) but rather because the former, honestly applied, will invalidate nothing. There was, of course, a time when balancing was sufficient to satisfy a majority of the Court as a general approach to the First Amendment.[39] But that was hardly the attitude of the Warren Court, at least in its later years.[40] During the very period when *O'Brien* was decided, the Court was making clear its dissatisfaction with a general balancing approach, indicating that only expression fairly assignable to one of an increasingly limited set of narrowly defined categories could be denied constitutional protection. Thus in *Brandenburg v. Ohio*, decided a year after *O'Brien*, a unanimous Court, invalidating the Ohio Criminal Syndicalism Act, indicated that

> the constitutional guarantees of free speech and free press do not permit a State to forbid or proscribe advocacy of the use of force or of law violation except where such advocacy is directed to inciting or producing imminent lawless action and is likely to incite or produce such action.[41]

There is in *Brandenburg* no talk of balancing, let alone of a simple prohibition of gratuitous suppression: the expression involved in a given case either does or does not fall within the described category, and if it does not it is protected.[42] (*O'Brien*'s expression, it is hardly necessary to add, did not fall within the described category, and no one claimed it did.) Quite obviously the Court of the late Warren period had two radically different First Amendment approaches for what it saw as two significantly different sets of problems. Something about O'Brien's case caused the Court to adopt an approach much less protective of First Amendment interests than that put forth in *Brandenburg*.

The explanation for this difference is not that Brandenburg was actually talking—moving his mouth and uttering words—whereas O'Brien was expressing himself nonverbally. *Tinker v. Des Moines School District*,[43] decided nine months after *O'Brien*, involved the suspension of school children for wearing black armbands to protest the Vietnam War. The protest's target was very much the same as that in *O'Brien*; the setting, the classroom rather than the post office steps, was if anything more fragile; the penalty was milder; and most important for present purposes, the communication was, again, entirely nonverbal. Yet the Court did not hesitate a moment: this was, it announced—without supporting argument or any attempt to distinguish *O'Brien*—"the type of symbolic act that is within the Free Speech Clause of the First Amendment . . . . It was closely akin to 'pure speech' which, we have repeatedly held, is entitled to comprehensive protection . . . ."[44] Comprehensive protection is certainly what it was given, and the suspensions were reversed. The Court is still unable to account very convincingly for the difference between *O'Brien* and *Tinker*, but the contrast in tone between the two opinions, to say nothing of the results, could hardly be starker.[45] Similarly, in *Cohen v. California*,[46] decided in 1971, the Court reversed the conviction of a young man, obviously a latter day Billy Budd, who found he could adequately convey his feelings only by parading about in a jacket that said "Fuck the Draft." Rejecting the dissenters' claim that "Cohen's absurd and immature antic"—so far one must assume no disagreement—"was mainly conduct and little speech,"[47] the Court employed, and in the process importantly clarified, the categorization approach it had adopted in *Brandenburg*.[48] The dangers of censorship of both emotive and cognitive content, Justice Harlan suggested for the majority, must lead us to reject attempts to punish "offensive language";[49] "fighting words" are unprotected, but that category is no longer to be understood as a euphemism for either controversial or dirty talk but requires instead an unambiguous invitation to a brawl;[50] and anyone who finds Cohen's jacket "obscene" or erotic had better have his valves checked.[51] There is little trace of balancing here, and surely not simply a search for gratuitous inhibition.

IV

The distinction between cases like *O'Brien* on the one hand and cases like *Tinker* and *Cohen* on the other can, in fact, be found in the *O'Brien* opinion itself, but you have to hunt around a bit. The Court gives us at least one false lead[52]—suggesting early on that perhaps O'Brien's act was not "speech" at all and therefore simply not covered by the First Amendment:

> We cannot accept the view that an apparently limitless variety of conduct can be labeled "speech" whenever the person engaging in the conduct intends thereby to express an idea.[53]

Although the Court did not ultimately rely on this distinction, it nonetheless deserves some attention. It has received the endorsement of scholars who must command respect, and the fallacy that underlies it is one that has similarly infected other, apparently more subtle, approaches to the problem of "symbolic speech."

It is, of course, undeniable that O'Brien's burning of his draft card involved conduct as well as expression. As Professor Emerson, the foremost advocate of an "expression-action" distinction, points out:

> To some extent expression and action are always mingled: most conduct includes elements of both. Even the clearest manifestations of expression involve some action, as in the case of holding a meeting, publishing a newspaper, or merely

talking. At the other extreme, a political assassination includes a substantial measure of expression.[54]

He nonetheless maintains that the "predominant element" in a course of conduct can be identified, and First Amendment protection thereby determined. The results of this process can be quite striking. In the first place *O'Brien* was wrongly decided:

> The burning of a draft card is, of course, conduct that involves both communication and physical acts. Yet it seems quite clear that the predominant element in such conduct is expression (opposition to the draft) rather than action (destruction of a piece of cardboard).[55]

The same analysis applies to the turning in of draft cards—"[i]n making this gesture the quality of expression clearly prevails over the element of action"[56]—but not to the consequent condition of being without one's card:

> The separation of expression and action under these circumstances involves some difficulties, but they are not insuperable. The failure to keep a draft card in one's possession would seem to be conduct classifiable as action, not expression. Though the initial destruction or return of the card may have been expression protected by the First Amendment, the consequent failure to carry the draft card is conduct in which the action (or inaction) element predominates.[57]

But burning a draft card to express opposition to the draft is an undifferentiated whole, 100 percent action and 100 percent expression. It involves no conduct that is not at the same time communication, and no communication that does not result from conduct. Attempts to determine which element "predominates" will therefore inevitably degenerate into question-begging judgments about whether the activity should be protected.[58]

The *O'Brien* Court thus quite wisely dropped the "speech-conduct" distinction as quickly as it had picked it up. In *Cohen*, however, Justice Harlan resurrected the distinction, albeit with a somewhat different twist:

> The only "conduct" which the state sought to punish is the fact of communication. Thus, we deal here with a conviction resting solely upon "speech," . . . not upon any separately identifiable conduct . . . . Cf. United States v. O'Brien . . . .[59]

An act like O'Brien's or Cohen's, the Court now seems to be suggesting, is neither entirely speech nor entirely conduct: it has elements of both, and the trick is to look closely and see which element it is the state is regulating. Unfortunately, this is not different enough, for it engages in the same ontological fallacy. Burning a draft card to express one's opposition to the draft is an undifferentiated whole, 100 percent action and 100 percent expression, and to outlaw the act is therefore necessarily to regulate both elements.

V

When the Court in *O'Brien* gets around to what is obviously intended as the definitive statement of its test—specifically in what I have designated criterion [2]—it gives us something substantially more helpful:

> [A] governmental regulation is sufficiently justified . . . if it furthers an important or substantial governmental *interest [that] is unrelated to the suppression of free expression* . . . .[60]

Here the Court shifts from ontology to teleology. It abandons its earlier suggestion that the constitutional answer can be found by examining O'Brien's act—either to determine whether it is really expression or conduct, for of course it is both, or to identify which aspect of the act is being regulated, for of course they both are—and suggests instead an inquiry into whether the governmental interest or interests that support the regulation are related to the suppression of expression.

Obviously this approach is not self-defining: it can, for one thing, be interpreted in a way that will guarantee that its demand can always be satisfied.[61] Restrictions on free expression are rarely defended on the ground that the state simply didn't like what the defendant was saying; reference will generally be made to some danger beyond the message, such as a danger of riot, unlawful action or violent overthrow of the government. Thus in *Brandenburg* the state's defense was not that the speech in question was distasteful, though it surely was, but rather that speeches of that sort were likely to induce people to take the law into their own hands. The reference of *O'Brien*'s second criterion is therefore not to the ultimate interest to which the state is able to point, for that will always be unrelated to expression, but rather to the causal connection the state asserts. If, for example, the state asserts an interest in discouraging riots, the Court will ask why that interest is implicated in the case at bar. If the answer is (as in such cases it will likely have to be) that the danger was created by what the defendant was saying, the state's interest is not unrelated to the suppression of free expression within the meaning of *O'Brien*'s criterion [2]. The categorization approach of cases like *Brandenburg* and *Cohen*, rather than (either variant of) *O'Brien*'s criterion [3] is therefore in order, and the regulation will very likely be invalidated.[62] The critical question would therefore seem to be whether the harm that the state is seeking to avert is one that grows out of the fact that the defendant is communicating, and more particularly out of the way people can be expected to react to his message, or rather would arise even if the defendant's conduct had no communicative significance whatever.[63]

There may be a temptation to conclude that one has seen all this before, or at least its functional equivalent, in the shopworn distinction between "regulation of content" and "regulation of time, place and manner." That would be a mistaken equation, however, and one with severe costs for free expression. For the state obviously can move, and often does, "simply" to control the time, place, or manner of communication out of a concern for the likely effect of the communication on its audience. Thus in *Tinker* the state regulated only the place and manner of expression—no armbands in school—but it did so, or at least this is the account most favorable to the state, because it feared the effect that the message those armbands conveyed would have on the other children.[64] (Had the armbands lacked communicative significance, there would have been no way to defend or even account for the regulation.[65]) The regulation at issue in *Cohen* might well be styled by a resourceful prosecutor as simply a restriction on the manner of expression, or perhaps it can also be regarded as a restriction on content.[66] But this brand of ontology, like the others we have seen, is as irrelevant as it is unintelligible. *O'Brien*'s second criterion is no more concerned with "what sort of regulation it really is" than with "what it is that is really being regulated"; the critical point in *Cohen*, as in *Tinker*, is that the dangers on which the state relied were dangers that flowed entirely from the communicative content of Cohen's behavior. Had his audience been unable to read English, there would have been no occasion for the regulation.

O'Brien was different. The interests upon which the government relied were interests, having mainly to do with the preservation of selective service records, that would have been equally threatened had O'Brien's destruction of his draft card totally lacked communicative significance—had he, for example, used it to start a campfire for a solitary cookout or dropped it in his garbage disposal for a lark. (The law prohibited all knowing destructions, public or private.[67]) Perhaps the Court should have engaged in some serious balancing, but its refusal even to consider the categorization approach appropriate to cases like *Brandenburg* and *Cohen* was quite correct. *O'Brien* is more like *Prince v. Massachusetts*,[68] in which the Court upheld the application of the state's child labor law to a child distributing Jehovah's Witness literature. Obviously the state was thereby regulating expressive activity, but the evil it was trying to avert was one that would have been equally implicated had the child been engaged in work with no communicative component whatever.[69] Similarly, by employing what amounts to a balancing test to permit some municipal regulation of sound-trucks,[70] the Court surely permits some restriction of expression. But again, the values the state seeks to promote by such regulation, values of quiet and repose, would be threatened as much by meaningless moans and static (which is usually how it comes out anyway) as by a political message. And although I am not aware that the Court has ever decided exactly such a case, it seems clear that it would refuse to extend constitutional protection to the right to interrupt a public speaker, even by the most coherent and trenchant of political commentary.[71] For the value the state seeks to protect by forbidding interruption, the right of the originally scheduled speaker to have his say and of his audience to listen, is not geared to the message of the interrupter or even to the fact that he has a message. Interruption that expresses disagreement with the speaker threatens those values, to be sure, but no more than they would be threatened by a chant of "Chocolate Mousse" or a chorus of *South Side Shuffle* on the slide trombone.[72]

Sorting out free speech issues along these lines should have salutary consequences for freedom of expression. The debate on the First Amendment has traditionally proceeded on the assumption that categorization and balancing—and I am using this as a generic term, to encompass all approaches (including "clear and present danger") that consider the likely effect of the communication—are mutually exclusive approaches to the various problems that arise under the First Amendment. The categorizers, or "absolutists,"[73] were surely right that theirs was the approach more likely to protect expression in crisis times.[74] But just as surely, an all-encompassing categorization approach could be made to look awfully silly, indeed to confess error, by demonstrations that there were contexts in which a refusal to admit the possibility of balancing was simply untenable. The sound-truck cases furnished a familiar example: "I understand that you would protect sound-trucks. But what about a hospital zone? What about the middle of the night? Surely you wouldn't let a mayoral candidate aim a bullhorn at your window at three in the morning. Surely you have to balance, or employ a clear and present danger test, at some point."

The argument is convincing—in context. But what the decisions of the late Warren era began to recognize is that categorization and balancing need not be regarded as competing general theories of the First Amendment, but are more helpfully employed in tandem, each with its own legitimate and indispensable role in protecting expression. The fact that one would balance where the evil the state would avert does not grow out of the message being communicated—thereby balancing away the right to use a bullhorn at three in the morning, to shout "Boo!" at a cardiac patient, or to firebomb the induction center in protest against the draft—does not, the Court began to understand, commit him to a balancing approach to the constitutionality of a Criminal Syndicalism Law.

The categorizers were right: where messages are proscribed because they are dangerous, balancing tests inevitably become intertwined with the ideological predispositions of those doing the balancing—or if not that, at least with the relative confidence or paranoia of the age in which they are doing it—and we must build barriers as secure as words are able to make them. That means rigorous definition of the limited categories of expression that are unprotected by the First Amendment. But in order thus to protect what really is in need of and amenable to such protection, we must first set to one side, by determinate principle rather than hunch, those situations to which such a categorization approach will inevitably prove unsuited. The Court has made a clear start in this direction, and it is a good one.

VI

State laws typically extend American flags two separate sorts of protection.[75] One provision, and it is this that is generally referred to as the "desecration" provision,[76] is likely to provide that "[n]o person shall publicly mutilate, deface, defile, defy, trample upon, or by word or act cast contempt upon any such flag."[77] The language outlawing contemptuous words was declared unconstitutional in 1969, in *Street v. New York*,[78] and that prohibiting the casting of contempt was held void for vagueness (even as applied to nonverbal expression) in 1974 in *Smith v. Goguen*.[79] Some of the statutory language that is left ("defile," "defy") is unmistakably limited to hostile treatment of the flag, and even language that in isolation might boldly be characterized as neutral ("mutilate," "deface," "trample upon") would doubtless receive a similar construction, given surrounding language and the obvious legislative intent.[80] Thus such statutes proscribe only ideologically charged acts, and beyond that, only acts charged with a particular set of ideological outlooks. The state's defense, consequently, must be geared to the unusual danger of that set of sentiments; such a defense will of necessity relate to the suppression of expression within the meaning of *O'Brien*'s second criterion.[81] That in turn implies that the categorization approach of *Brandenburg* and *Cohen* is appropriate. Since such laws obviously are not tailored to reach only expressions of incitement to immediate lawless action, or any other presently recognized category of unprotected expression, they must fall.[82]

The other sort of provision typically employed, sometimes called an "improper use" provision,[83] outlaws affixing to the flag any "word, figure, mark, picture, design, drawing or advertisement of any nature," or publicly displaying any flag so embellished.[84] The law is thus ideologically neutral on its face,[85] and would proscribe the superimposition of "Buy Mother Fletcher's Ambulance Paint"[86] or even "It's a Grand Old Flag" as fully as it would the addition of a swastika.[87] Such "improper use" provisions are more complicated constitutionally than the ideologically tilted "desecration" provisions. The difficulty arises not from the suggestion of Justices White[88] and Rehnquist[89] that altering a flag is like painting up a public building (where, it is quite true, even the most patriotic of graffiti are disallowed). For there a governmental interest quite obviously unrelated to the suppression of expression is implicated, namely the cost and trouble of sandblasting. The case the Justices suggest is akin to one involving the alteration of a publicly owned flag, where no one suggests that the state may not protect its own property from defacement.[90] However, the state may assert an interest that justifies control over even privately owned flags similar to that asserted in the case of the interrupting audience. The state's interest in both of these cases might be characterized as an interest in preventing the jamming of signals, an interest not in preventing the defendant from expressing himself but rather in keeping him from interfering with the expression of others. Thus we do not care what the interrupter is saying: all that matters is that he is interrupting another's expression. The flag too is the embodiment of a set of ideas—surely no one defending against a charge of disfigurement is in a position to deny *that*—and our case can therefore be seen in much the same light. The state does not care what message the defendant is conveying by altering the flag: all that matters is that he is interrupting the message conveyed by the flag.[91]

Although the analogy may suggest that improper use provisions—like restrictions on audience interruption—satisfy *O'Brien*'s criterion [2], the analogy seems uneasy under criterion [3], in that the balance looks very different. Acknowledging that the state's interests in the two cases are of similar contour—that each is concerned only with preventing the interruption of a message emanating from another source and not with the content of the interrupter's message—need not commit one to the view that they are of equal weight. In the interrupting audience case, one of the weightiest interests imaginable, namely the First Amendment rights of the speaker, supports the state's intervention. That analysis will not fit the flag disfigurement situation, however. Even granting, as I think we must, the legitimacy of the government's interest in the flag's symbolic value,[92] it plainly is not a First Amendment interest, for the simple reason that the government or polity—and in the case of a flag owned by the disfigurer I don't know who else's rights could be invoked on the prosecution's side—has no First Amendment rights.[93] The cloth, in such a case, is surely the disfigurer's alone. And while the ideas it represents just as surely are not, neither are they the exclusive property of the government.

This distinction, in terms of the relative strength of the governmental interests involved, is less than wholly reassuring, for two reasons. The first is the obvious one, that balancing tests are simply not the stuff on which reassurance can confidently be built. The second is that it is far from clear that the Court would even be prepared to employ the serious balancing version of criterion [3] in either of these cases. Both interrupting and flag disfigurement would, it is true, attract considerable (if lessened) attention even if they were legal. But although I have suggested that this consideration should trigger a serious balance, this seems unlikely, for reasons we have canvassed above, to be the approach the Court will follow in deciding whether such a balance, as opposed to the virtually automatic validation of the "no gratuitous inhibition" approach, is the appropriate specification of *O'Brien*'s criterion [3]. More likely, the Court will extend the stronger brand of protection only to what it is prepared to regard as orthodox modes of expression.[94] And while flag desecration (and interruption of speakers as well) can undoubtedly claim a lengthy historical lineage, the only "tradition" with which the Court is likely to associate them is a tradition of rowdyism. It thus seems highly questionable that a Court proceeding on the assumption that a less restrictive alternative analysis is all that is required would employ a version of that analysis sufficiently serious to invalidate improper use statutes. More likely, it would employ a weak version of criterion [3], akin to that invoked in *O'Brien* itself, and thereby uphold such laws.

If, therefore, the flag alteration and audience interruption cases are to be confidently distinguished, the distinction must be in other than balancing terms. Such a distinction is available. A deeper analysis of "improper use" statutes will reveal that they must after all be regarded as relating to "the suppression of free expression" within the meaning of *O'Brien*'s criterion [2], and that they therefore should be analyzed (and invalidated) under the categorization approach rather than being approached in terms of either version of criterion [3].

What has not yet been sufficiently noted is that although improper use statutes do not single out certain messages for proscription, they do single out one set of messages, namely the set of messages conveyed by the American flag, for *protection*. That, of course, is not true of a law that generally prohibits the interruption of speakers: such a law is neutral not only respecting the content of the interruption but also respecting the content of the message interrupted. The distinction seems a critical one, and suggests that the definition we have thus far given *O'Brien*'s second criterion, as referring to situations where the harm the state seeks to avert is one that arises from the defendant's communication, may have been incomplete. An adjustment of our earlier elaboration of that criterion so as to encompass the case in which the government singles out a specific message or set of messages for protection would fit the cases more comfortably—and in particular, would provide firmer ground for the decision in *Spence*. That it is also required by the sense of the criterion seems clear too, given the functional similarity, in terms of "the free marketplace of ideas," between singling certain messages out for prohibition and singling certain messages out for protection.[95] Orthodoxy of thought can be fostered not simply by placing unusual restrictions on "deviant" expression but also by granting unusual protection to expression that is officially acceptable. An "improper use" statute, neutral respecting the messages it would inhibit though it may be, is not analogous to a law prohibiting the interruption of speeches. It is, at best, analogous to a law prohibiting the interruption of patriotic speeches, and that is a law that is hardly "unrelated to the suppression of free expression."

Two decades later (and quite courageously, given the political circumstances) the Court adopted the analysis of this comment and invalidated flag desecration laws. *Texas v. Johnson, 491 U.S. 397 (1989); United States v. Eichman, 496 U.S. 310 (1990). See also pages 356–57.*

5

Religious Freedom

Memorandum to Chief Justice Warren Concerning
United States v. Seeger (1965)[1]

I seem to have become something of a dinosaur on the subject of what law clerks should reveal about the workings of the courts for which they clerked. (See, e.g., B. Woodward & S. Armstrong, The Brethren [1979].) Thus you'll find nothing of substance here about the interchanges among the justices, or substantive interchanges between me and Chief Justice Warren, concerning the cases decided during the 1964–65 term, which is when I clerked for him. What follows is a short excerpt from a memorandum I wrote to the Chief Justice before the Seeger case was argued; it does not reflect in the slightest his thinking or that of any of the other justices. (Neither does it presage the theory on which the case was ultimately decided: indeed, the Court's opinion embraced the "theory" I derided as irresponsible in the footnote I have reproduced. And, I admit it, the republic has survived.) You will see, however, that the theory of the religious clauses I put forth in this memo is one I have continued to develop: indeed one of the things I have quite consistently found frightening as I have assembled this collection is the extent to which my thinking has remained essentially constant from my student and early career days to the present. Though I don't count that a defect, I'm aware that others will.

Statute Involved

Section 6(j) of the Universal Military Training and Service Act, 50 U.S.C. App. 456(j), provides in pertinent part:

> Nothing contained in this title shall be construed to require any person to be subject to combatant training and service in the armed forces of the United States who, by reason of religious training and belief, is conscientiously opposed to participation in war in any form. Religious training and belief in this connection means an individual's belief in a relation to a Supreme Being involving duties superior to those arising from any human relation, but does not include essentially political, sociological, or philosophical views or a merely personal moral code. . . .

These cases could really turn into a mess. The arguments in the briefs over whether petitioner in No. 29 and respondent in No. 51 are encompassed by the statute demonstrate, better than any argument I could make, that in this area, even if a definition could be agreed upon, concrete fact situations are incapable of rational solution. The reason, of course, is that religion is not and does not purport to be a rational area, as this Court has often wisely realized. . . .

*   *   *

Attempting to review the facts, is not, however, the only way the Court could get into a mess. Just as unwise would be an attempt to define "Supreme Being" and "religion" and see, as the Solicitor General suggests, whether or not the two are coextensive. Philosophers and theologians have tried for years to define those terms; I do not think this Court should try. A fortiori, the definition should not be left to draft boards and the Department of Justice.

In my opinion, the cases can easily be disposed of without either reviewing the facts or trying to define things like "religion," "God," and "Supreme Being." The answer is found in a paragraph in the Court's *Torcaso* [*v. Watkins*] opinion:

> We repeat and again reaffirm that neither a State nor the Federal Government can constitutionally force a person "to profess a belief or disbelief in any religion." Neither can constitutionally pass laws or impose requirements which aid all religions as against non-believers, and neither can aid those religions based on a belief in the existence of God as against those religions founded on different beliefs. [367 U.S. at 495]

The Court should—without attempting to define indefinables—hold:

(1) If "Supreme Being" means "God," the law falls because it establishes some religions as against others.

(2) If "Supreme Being" is broader than "God" but is not broad enough to encompass all religions, it is void because it establishes some religions as against others.

(3) If "Supreme Being" is broader than "God" and *is* broad enough to encompass all religions, it is void because it establishes religion as against nonreligion (by not exempting nonreligious persons who have a good-faith moral objection to serving in the Armed Forces).

Such an alternative rationale is, it seems to me, supported by precedent and avoids the definitional problems.[2] Although Congress perhaps need not grant exemptions to conscientious objectors at all, it cannot either favor some religions over others, or favor religious over nonreligious people, in doing so.

Excerpt from *Legislative and Administrative Motivation in Constitutional Law* (1970)[3]

The Court has often indicated that the religious clauses, read together, counsel governmental neutrality with respect to religion.[4] Stated in these terms, the conclusion is virtually unavoidable. To read the Establishment Clause as anything stronger than a command that the government refrain from favoring one religion over others, or religion generally over non-religion, would be inevitably to invite collision with the Free Exercise Clause. And establishment problems would be created by reading the Free Exercise Clause to require more by way of accommodation of religion than that religion not be disfavored relative to nonreligion, and that no specific religion be disfavored relative to others. Within this broad frame, however, there is room for two distinct approaches. I am persuaded by the view that the whipsaw effect of the two clauses can successfully be avoided only by forbidding governmental bodies or officials to go out of their way in any context to favor or disfavor a religion or religion generally.[5] Others, however, while they agree that courts must never compel the special accommodation or limitation of religion, take the position that there must be "some play in the joints," that some special accommodation or limitation should be constitutionally tolerated.[6]

*   *   *

The ruling rhetoric dates from the school Bible-reading case, *Abington School District v. Schempp*:

> The test may be stated as follows: what are the purpose and the primary effect of the enactment? If either is the advancement or inhibition of religion then the enactment exceeds the scope of legislative power as circumscribed by the Constitution.[7]

This statement falls short in [two] respects. First, it errs in suggesting that impact per se should on some occasions serve to invalidate a governmental choice. Second, it fails to define with sufficient precision the motivation necessary to justify a judicial demand for legitimate justification; what should be required is not simply proof of a desire to help or hinder religion, but proof of a desire comparatively to favor or disfavor religion relative to nonreligion or one religion relative to others.

The Court Should not Intervene on the Basis of Impact Per Se

Were the Court right in asserting that impact alone should trigger judicial intervention under one of the religious clauses, it would be wrong in assert-

ing that motivation is also relevant. For if courts could properly force legislators and administrators affirmatively to accommodate or restrict religious
groups, an assumption necessarily underlying an impact approach, then the
case for the cognizability of motivation could not be made out. A court
would simply have to see whether the law's effects passed muster, and if
they did not, order the state to alter the law accordingly.

But for reasons akin to those adduced . . . in connection with problems
of racial discrimination,[8] impact—though it can often support an inference
of motivation—should not trigger intervention in the absence of such an
inference. Essentially all government spending programs and probably
most regulations aid religion to some extent, and many favor some religions relative to others. They cannot all be unconstitutional, and an attempt
to "equalize" the help or hindrance (or proportion it to membership?)
among all religions, including nonreligion, would obviously be nonsense.
Thus the question of what sort and amount of disproportionate impact
should justify intervention will necessarily arise under an impact theory.
The Court's attempts at quantification have been notably unenlightening.[9]
And even if the necessary quantum of help or hindrance could be defined,
perhaps by some sort of balancing test, an impact test of any variety would
force legislators and administrators to make judgments of just the sort the
framers of the First Amendment sought to discourage by the inclusion of
the religious provisions.

A legislative or administrative practice of pausing to inquire whether a
contemplated action will adversely affect various religious groups—and if
it is determined that it will, making the necessary adjustment—is at least
suspect under the Establishment Clause, and surely should not be required
by a court. Yet that is precisely the kind of behavior an impact approach to
the Free Exercise Clause would necessitate. Likewise, an impact approach
to the Establishment Clause would force decision makers to ask whether a
contemplated action is likely to assist one or more religious groups and, if
it is, to carve out an exception. But that sort of calculation seems exactly
what the Free Exercise Clause was included to prevent; certainly it should
not be compelled either. A motivation approach to the two clauses will
carry neither of these consequences, but instead will withhold judicial intervention pending proof that religious considerations have been taken into
account one way or the other.

A religious motivation will usually[10] be readily inferable where the challenged classification is explicitly religious. The inference would also be
clear were the government to build a church,[11] or outlaw (or, more likely,
require) prayer. *Schempp* is only a short step beyond this: readings from the
Bible without prefatory statements were plainly included in the opening
exercises for purposes of religious indoctrination.

The Court made no inquiry into whether "the primary effect" of the readings was religious, which given its disjunctive rhetoric of "purpose or ef-

fect" is understandable enough, since it had found a religious motivation. But it should not have suggested even in dictum that a religious effect, unaccompanied by a religious motivation, could invalidate a practice. This should have been clear from an observation made later in the opinion:

> It certainly may be said that the Bible is worthy of study for its literary and historic qualities. Nothing we have said here indicates that such study of the Bible or of religion, when presented objectively as part of a secular program of education, may not be effected consistently with the First Amendment.[12]

The distinction is a sensible one. But can the Court seriously be suggesting—as its "purpose or effect" rhetoric would indicate it must—that under these circumstances it would be clear that the "advancement of religion" was not a "primary effect" of the reading? Hopefully students are influenced by the content of what they study "for its literary and historical qualities," and the scriptures can be potent stuff. The more sensible distinguishing factor is the impossibility of inferring a desire to favor a religious viewpoint over others in the context of a general study of literary or historical works. The "primary effect" half of the *Schempp* test is therefore most charitably read as an evidentiary reference, to denote the sort of impact that will support an inference of pro- or antireligious motivation. And if that perchance is not what the Court meant, the reference should be so limited.

Epperson v. Arkansas,[13] decided in 1968, is similar. The Court, invalidating as an establishment of religion a statute prohibiting the teaching in Arkansas public schools and universities of the theory that man evolved from other species of life, explicitly rested its holding upon the conclusion that the law had been passed with the motivation of promoting fundamentalist Christianity. Nor was the reliance upon motivation unnecessary, for the Court's conclusion cannot be justified in terms of the law's impact alone. Surely biology generally, or the study of all theories of man's origins, could under some circumstances be eliminated entirely, even though it would mean that the students would never be exposed to Darwin's theory.[14] There are, moreover, numerous philosophical and scientific theories that would undoubtedly tend to undercut a fundamentalist's faith as much as or even more than evolution. *Epperson* cannot mean that since their omission aids religion, a school is obligated to teach them all.

The way the Court went about demonstrating that the exclusion of evolution from the curriculum was religiously motivated—by quoting newspaper advertisements and letters to the editor from God-fearing citizens, and drawing precious parallels to the Scopes trial—is bound to leave a reader of the opinion feeling somewhat uneasy about the declaration of unconstitutionality. However, a moment's reflection on the significance of evolution to twentieth century assumptions about the origins of man is enough to establish the soundness of the Court's conclusion. The exclusion of evolution and only evolution plainly resulted from more than an arbitrary reaction to the realization that the curriculum had to be closed somewhere. And no other explanation or alternative justification was suggested.[15]

Judicial intervention in "free exercise" cases should also turn on proof of motivation. Laws against polygamy, for example, unquestionably disfavor Mormons relative to others. Yet the Court has upheld them,[16] and properly so. The decision to outlaw multiple marriages is no more susceptible to a "rational" defense than any other decision to make something a crime. But the fact that polygamy was broadly proscribed long before Utah was even a glint in its founders' eyes makes it impossible responsibly to infer an anti-Mormon motivation.

Sherbert v. Verner,[17] decided in 1963, plainly stands for the contrary view, that a regulation's unintended adverse impact upon persons of a particular faith can invalidate it, at least insofar as it is applied to persons of that faith. South Carolina had provided that unemployment benefits would be paid only to persons who made themselves available for employment Monday through Saturday. Mrs. Sherbert, a Seventh Day Adventist, refused to work Saturdays and consequently was unable to find work in any of the local mills. The Court sustained her challenge to the state's refusal to pay her benefits, indicating that under the circumstances[18] the state was obligated to excuse religious objectors from its requirement of availability Monday through Saturday.

The course of action thus suggested by the Court—granting exemptions only to religious persons—is supremely suspect under the Establishment Clause: "neither a State nor the Federal Government . . . can constitutionally pass laws or impose requirements which aid all religions as against non-believers . . . ."[19] That the Court has since *Sherbert* come to the opinion that an exemption solely for religious persons is unconstitutional is strongly indicated by its strained construction of the draft law's conscientious objector provision in *United States v. Seeger*,[20] decided in 1965, and *Welsh v. United States*,[21] decided late last term. The statutory exemption is limited to claims arising from "religious training and belief," which in turn is statutorily defined in terms of the claimant's relation to "a Supreme Being." The Court, nonetheless, has held the statute's exemption to extend to any individual whose refusal to serve is based on a sincerely held moral objection. A construction this strained is defensible only as a response to, and obviously was the product of, a desire to preserve the statute's constitutionality; in *Seeger*, and even more obviously in *Welsh*, the Court plainly (and rightly) was telling Congress that an exemption limited to religious objectors would probably violate the Establishment Clause.[22] A fortiori, such an exemption should not be judicially compelled.

There is, of course, a possible response to *Sherbert* other than the (now rather plainly unconstitutional) one suggested by the Court: allowing an exemption for anyone who has a good faith moral objection to working one of the designated days. Surely a state could, if it wished, voluntarily institute such a system. But a constitutional requirement that such objections be recognized—which requirement *Sherbert* must carry unless it is directly to conflict with the implication of *Seeger* and *Welsh*—would obviously result in substantial disruption of state and federal regulatory programs. (If such exemptions are mandatory in the *Sherbert* context, it is difficult to see why they would not be universally mandatory; at the least, they would be mandatory in a broad range of contexts.) More importantly, despite the surface neutrality of such a requirement, it would in several ways endanger the very values the Establishment Clause exists to protect.

In the first place, since religious training and activity constitute unusually convincing evidence of a good faith moral objection, such a system would in practice inevitably favor religious objectors. (I do not mean to suggest that states for that reason should be barred from instituting such a system, only that courts should hesitate constitutionally to compel it.) Second, in view of the inevitable disruption such a good faith moral objection system would engender, states would institute it only where it appears that someone might raise a religious objection. (The Court obviously would not interfere in the absence of such an objection.) Thus legislatures and administrators would soon fall into a pattern of pausing, after tentative selection of a regulatory course, to inquire whether any religious groups will be offended—and if they would, either creating a "good faith moral objection" exemption or, necessarily in many instances, forgetting the regulation altogether. Such a course of action is obviously at odds with what the Establishment Clause is all about. Third, given the inevitable (indeed, constitutionally mandatory) recognition of religious training and belief as evidence of a good faith moral objection, the state's interest in having as many persons as possible working rather than drawing compensation will inevitably incline state officials toward minimizing exemptions by making sure they select as the day when availability is not required that day—probably but not inevitably Sunday—which is the Sabbath of most of the workers in the industry in question.[23] But to choose a day as the day of rest because it coincides with the Sabbath of the majority is manifestly to violate the spirit of the Establishment Clause. Yet any other response to *Sherbert* (under either a good faith moral objection test or the explicitly religious test the Court suggested) would likely destroy a state's unemployment compensation scheme.

Sherbert was an aberration when it was decided; it and *Braunfield v. Brown*,[24] decided two years earlier, are as irreconcilable as two cases not involving the same parties can be. Whatever authority *Sherbert* ever possessed has been drained by last term's *Welsh* decision. It should not be followed.[25]

The Court Should Intervene Only on the Basis of Proof of an Intention to Favor or Disfavor Religion Relative to Nonreligion, or One Religion Relative to Others.

There is no constitutional bar to helping or hindering religious persons or groups along with otherwise similarly situated persons or groups. Deviation from neutrality occurs only when religion or a religion is singled out for advancement or inhibition. The Court's performance indicates that it understands this perfectly well; my suggestion is only that the language of decision be tailored to this understanding.

In *Board of Education v. Allen*, decided in 1968, the Court upheld a New York law requiring the public school authorities to lend textbooks free of charge to all students in grades seven to twelve, including students attending parochial schools. Speaking through Mr. Justice White, the Court quoted as controlling the "purpose and primary effect" test of *Schempp*, but gave the "purpose" question short shrift indeed:

> The express purpose of 701 was stated by the New York Legislature to be furtherance of the educational opportunities available to the young. Appellants have shown us nothing about the necessary effects of the statute that is contrary to its stated purpose.[26]

If, however, *Schempp*'s undiscriminating reference to "the advancement or inhibition of religion" were to be taken seriously, this dismissal would be cavalier. For the provision obviously aids parochial schools and thereby the Roman Catholic Church among others, and the legislators could hardly have been unaware of this. The point, of course, is that since textbooks were provided to all children, it was impossible to infer a motivation to single out religion or a religion for advancement.

The issues raised by the grant of tax exemptions to religious organizations are similar. Were the government to exempt the property of religious organizations and only religious organizations from real property taxes, there would be an understandable temptation to deal with the case simply by asserting that there has been drawn a distinction for which no legitimate defense can be articulated. This would be an oversimplification, however. For decisions as to what groups or activities to favor and disfavor by the network of distinctions that form a tax code cannot be held up to a test of rationality, and therefore any claim that each distinction of this sort must be backed by a rationally defensible difference is a delusion. When, however, the motivation that generated a taxation distinction is constitutionally impermissible, that distinction is forbidden.[27] And when the exemption is of only religious organizations, the motivation can have been nothing other than the promotion of religion relative to nonreligion, which the Establishment Clause renders illegitimate.

The recently decided *Walz v. Tax Commission of the City of New York*[28] is not this case, however. In *Walz* the Court upheld the constitutionality of a law providing:

> Real property owned by a corporation or association organized exclusively for the moral or mental improvement of men and women, or for religious, bible, tract, charitable, benevolent, missionary, hospital, infirmary, educational, public playground, scientific, literary, bar association, medical society, library, patriotic, historical or cemetery purposes . . . and used exclusively for carrying out thereupon one or more of such purposes . . . shall be exempt from taxation as provided in this section.

It is impossible to find a rationale in Chief Justice Burger's opinion for the Court; its sole uniting theme is that searching for principles is folly. Mr. Justice Harlan's concurring opinion, however, is impressive. Though he doesn't speak explicitly in terms of motivation, the framework he suggests can be fleshed out in no other terms:

> Neutrality in its application requires an equal protection mode of analysis. The Court must survey meticulously the circumstances of governmental categories to eliminate, as it were, religious gerrymanders. In any particular case the critical question is whether the radius of legislation encircles a class so broad that it can fairly be concluded that religious institutions could be thought to fall within the natural perimeter.[29]

The salvation of the *Walz* statute inheres not in some supposed difference of constitutional magnitude between subsidies and tax exemptions. It survives because its terms are considerably more consistent with a desire to exclude from the tax base property generally used for "good works" instead of the economic benefit of its owner, than with a desire to promote religion relative to nonreligion.[30]

Hey, I never said I was influential. In Wisconsin v. Yoder, 406 U.S. 205 (1972), the Court resisted my irresistible analysis and followed Sherbert, granting Amish (and only Amish) people a constitutional right to keep their children home from school. Of late, however—long after my article could have had anything to do with it—the "neutrality" view for which I argued has staged a marked comeback. See, e.g., Employment Division v. Smith, 494 U.S. 872, 881–82 (1990) (Free Exercise Clause does not entitle religiously motivated conduct to judicially created exemption from state criminal laws of general applicability). See also, e.g., Texas Monthly, Inc. v. Bullock, 489 U.S. 1 (1989) (invalidating on Establishment Clause grounds a sales tax exemption for religious periodicals); Church of the Lukumi Babalu Aye, Inc. v. City of Hialeah, 113 S.Ct. 2217 (1993) (invalidating ordinance exempting religious sacrifices from cruelty-to-animals prohibi-

*tion); cf. Lamb's Chapel v. Center Moriches Union Free School Dist.,
113 S.Ct. 2141 (1993) (invalidating the exclusion of religious groups from
public school policy permitting "social, civic, or recreational" uses of
school property by private community groups); Zobrest v. Catalina Foothills School Dist., 113 S.Ct. 2462 (1993) (invalidating the exclusion of
parochial schools from state program otherwise providing sign language
interpreters for hearing impaired public and private school students);
Rosenberger v. Rector and Visitors of the University of Virginia, 115 S.Ct.
2510 (1995) (invalidating the exclusion of a Christian student newspaper
from university funding). Of course the pendulum could swing back in the
other direction at any time, though the Court should bear in mind that under
a "Sherbert" regime, unprincipled backing-and-forthing is virtually inevitable, in that the Constitution can't be interpreted always to provide an
exemption from criminal or other laws on the ground the apparent offender
was acting out of religious conviction.*

Letter to *The New York Times* (1984)[31]

Dean Norman Redlich writes[32] that the Supreme Court's decision in the
Pawtucket, R.I., créche case* "insults American Jews and all others who do
not share what the Court's majority perceives as the country's dominant
belief, Christianity."

That much seems right. But how does Dean Redlich suppose many
Christians feel being told, 5 to 4, that a central symbol of their faith is not
necessarily all that religious—that properly presented, the manger need
connote no more spirituality than a reindeer? The offense is thus not limited to Jews. It extends to everyone who senses an important difference
between Jesus and Santa Clause. That includes some Christians.

*Things I've written have been reprinted lots of places, but I was pleased to
have called to my attention the fact that this letter was reprinted in the
program of the Grace Church in New York (Episcopal)—suggesting that
other Christians were not pleased by the Court's equation. I'm descended
from three centuries of Presbyterian ministers (on both sides, yet) but that
doesn't really give me the right to speak ex cathedra. Thus I was happy to
receive the corroboration.*

* [Lynch v. Donnelly, 465 U.S. 668 (1984), upholding the display of a nativity scene on
public property, so long as it is surrounded by secular symbols of Christmas.]

6

Criminal Procedure

Excerpts from Memoranda to Abe Fortas Concerning
Gideon v. Wainwright (1962)

Between my second and third years of law school, I had the best summer job ever (well, best ever for a law student), helping Abe Fortas—this was obviously before his appointment to the Court—prepare the brief for the petitioner in Gideon v. Wainwright.[1] The circumstances of my employment are briefly described in the speech that follows these excerpts from memoranda I wrote Mr. Fortas.

Prejudice to Gideon's Defense Caused by Lack of Counsel (August 3, 1962)

At first blush, the transcript in *State v. Gideon* seems to present the very model of the myth of *Betts*:[2] a case in which defense counsel is not needed. For the defendant demonstrated remarkable skill in cross-examination and the judge went to great lengths to inform him of his rights. However, an examination of the substantive and evidentiary law of Florida reveals that there were numerous occasions during the trial when counsel would have been of great assistance. Much inadmissible evidence was admitted, and once the judge erroneously excluded an answer to defendant's question. The judge several times misstated the law. The defendant's line of questioning revealed that he was working under misapprehensions as to the law of Florida, and he frequently failed to capitalize on facts brought out by his questions. Further, a motion for a directed verdict was in order at the close of the state's case; yet none was made, nor did the judge suggest to defendant that one was available. Finally, and perhaps most surprisingly, although several facts had been brought out that cast serious doubt upon whether the elements of the offense had been established, the judge gave *no charge whatsoever* on the elements of the crime for which defendant was on trial.

[At this point the foregoing assertions were annotated at length.]

An argument could also be made along the following lines: here is a trial in which the defendant was skillful and the judge made every effort to protect his rights. Yet even here close examination of the law and the facts reveals that defendant was repeatedly hurt by the lack of counsel. If such prejudice occurred in this trial, it would seem that there is *no* trial in which counsel is unnecessary. Thus the rule of *Betts* is based upon a false factual assumption.

This latter form of argument has the advantage of being directed toward overruling *Betts*, rather than simply being an attempt to bring another fact situation within that rule. On the other hand, it puts the "special circumstances" before the Court. Therefore, even if the Court does not choose to overrule *Betts*, it will have available a means of reversing Gideon's conviction.*

Application, Ambiguities, and Weaknesses of the Special Circumstances Rule (July 25, 1962)

* * *

A. *No court is capable of applying the rule.* In theory the *Betts* test is to be applied at the trial level:

> We are not disposed to disagree with the findings and conclusions of the District Court. Its determination was a purely factual one to the effect that Wade was an inexperienced youth incapable of adequately representing himself . . . . This is a judgment which is peculiarly within the province of the trier of facts, based upon personal observation of Wade.

Wade v. Mayo, 334 U.S. 672, 683–84 (1948). It would indeed be desirable if the test could be effectively applied at the outset of the trial, for if a finding that an attorney should have been appointed is made subsequent to trial, a great deal of judicial energy will have been wasted. However, in view of the factors that have been held relevant under *Betts*, the test simply cannot be applied before the trial.

Even such factors as the defendant's age, education, mental health, and court experience may not be brought to the attention of the court. The fact that there is no attorney present to point out the relevant factors to the judge compounds the likelihood that he will fail to consider the long list of rele-

---

* [This was an attempt to resolve an ethical dilemma. In appointing Fortas to represent Gideon, the Court had asked him to address himself to whether *Betts v. Brady* should be overruled. Obviously that was at least the Court's tentative inclination and had to be our principal argument. However, we didn't want to leave Gideon, who was after all our client, without the hedge that he should prevail even under *existing* law. By structuring the argument in the way here suggested—that this is the case that proves that there are *always* "special circumstances"—I felt we could have it both ways.]

vant considerations. But as to the "retrospective" factors the case is even stronger; for it is not even *theoretically* possible that mortal man can discern these before trial. It is quite impossible that a court will be able to predict pretrial that there will be objections that should be but won't be raised, that the defendant will fail to make arguments vital to his defense, that a codefendant will plead guilty in mid-trial, that he (the judge) will neglect to give defendant some crucial advice,[3] that the prosecutor will misbehave, that the trial will be too swiftly conducted or that the sentence prescribed will be lighter than that sought by the prosecutor. Yet the Court has said that all these must be considered. Since any of them may constitute grounds for reversal, the judge who refuses to appoint counsel does so at his peril. It is thus no surprise that one gets the feeling from reading state cases (although, as noted above, validation appears impossible) that trial judges seldom apply the *Betts* test, but instead apply their own automatic rules. For the test has been held to encompass factors that render pretrial application of it impossible.

Although the only widespread attempt to apply the special circumstances rule seems to have taken place at the appellate level, there are factors "relevant" under *Betts* that ensure that *appellate* attempts to apply the rule can be no more successful than trial-level attempts. Essential to a judgment as to the necessity of counsel is a highly personal evaluation of the defendant. An appellate court, armed with no more than a bare record, cannot, barring clairvoyance, make this evaluation:

> There are some individuals who, by reason of age, ignorance or mental capacity are incapable of representing themselves adequately in a prosecution of a relatively simple nature. *This incapacity is purely personal and can be determined only by an examination and observation of the individual.*

Wade v. Mayo, 334 U.S. 672, 684 (1948) (emphasis supplied). Thus the fact that the *Betts* test is, as it must be, an amalgam of personal and retrospective factors ensures lack of success in application at any level. So long as judges are human, a trial court cannot foresee the progress of the trial; nor can an appellate court cull from a record on appeal a reliable picture of a defendant's abilities.

B. *The rule wastes the time and energy of both state and federal appellate courts.* If state trial courts followed the federal rule and appointed counsel for *all* who cannot hire their own, appellate courts would of course hear no more claims of denial of counsel. (Defendants would still be free to argue denial of *effective* counsel. But this claim is infrequently made [and is generally swiftly dispatched].) Under the present rule, however, both state and federal appellate tribunals devote much time to such pleas. (Forty percent of the 1,356 causes presented to the Supreme Court in 1946 were from state convicts. How many of these involved denial of counsel has apparently not been tabulated.)

The cause of this vast array of appeals is not difficult to discern. For the boundaries and weights of the special circumstances rule are so amorphous that there exists no one convicted without counsel who cannot muster a list of reasons why counsel should have been appointed. The waste of energy is more strongly pointed up by the fact that *all* of the eight right-to-counsel cases heard by the Supreme Court since 1959 have resulted in reversal.

Under *Betts*, the trial judge is asked to guess—and it can be no more than a guess—whether the development of the trial will be such as to demand that counsel be at the side of the defendant. Should he guess "no" and guess wrong, not only the trial, but also much appellate litigation, will go for naught. The comparative simplicity of an across-the-board rule is obvious.

C. The Court has said that if it were to discard the *Betts* test, it would be guilty of "an unwarranted federal intrusion into state control of its criminal procedure." Gibbs v. Burke, 337 U.S. 773, 781 (1949). Perhaps the vagueness of the rule can be used to turn this argument against its proponents:

> [T]he unfortunate illusion of "interference" in state proceedings is heightened by the ambiguity of this test and the extreme difficulty of discerning logic or consistency in the cases that have been decided.

W. Beaney, Right to Counsel in American Courts 196 (1955).

D. The language of "illusion" may also be a good way to phrase the argument that the rule is subjectively applied. The *Betts* test has been damned as "natural law at its worst." Green, "The Bill of Rights, the Fourteenth Amendment and the Supreme Court," 46 Mich. L. Rev. 869, 898 (1948). The appellation is difficult to disagree with, but our language should not go so far. For by labeling the test "subjective" we would, by implication, be attacking the foundation of the Court's overall definition of Fourteenth Amendment due process. This attack has been repeatedly rejected. Perhaps the best strategy would be to cite the variety of factors relevant under *Betts* and a few surprising results that have been achieved by balancing them, and let the inference of subjectivity take its own course.

E. Another weakness of the special circumstances rule is that errors in its application stand little chance of being corrected. For it is unlikely that there are many convicts who, like Gideon, have the knowledge, ability, and ambition to institute an appeal from or collateral attack upon their convictions. "The same indigence which resulted in the initial loss of the right to counsel continues to act as a restraint or possible corrective action." Beaney, supra, p. 199. Indeed, it does not seem unfair to conclude that the claims of denial of counsel that the Court hears are made by those who are *best* able to take care of their own interests. Those totally incapable of defending themselves probably serve their terms unaware that they have a remedy, and unable to take advantage of it.

F. The bulk of this memorandum has been devoted to the ways in which the special circumstances rule has proven incapable of administration. There are of course several other sorts of objection that can be made. For example, under House v. Mayo, 324 U.S. 42 (1945), if a defendant can afford to hire an attorney, he has an absolute right to do so. Yet under the rule of *Betts*, there is no such absolute right for indigents. (The line of cases commencing with Griffin v. Illinois, 351 U.S. 12 (1956), which will be explored in a later memorandum, is relevant here.)

Further, there is an absolute right to court-appointed counsel in capital cases. Hamilton v. Alabama, 368 U.S. 52 (1961). All the objections to the capital-noncapital distinction might also be phrased as objections to the special circumstances rule, which operates only with regard to noncapital cases. For example, in a state where rape is a capital crime, a man accused thereof has an absolute right to counsel. But where it is not, the special circumstances rule renders his right to counsel uncertain. (Caveat: if our recommendation is that counsel be mandatory only in *felony* trials, we may not wish to make this argument. For it applies with equal force to the felony-misdemeanor distinction. My own view is that the brief should not comment on misdemeanors; if asked at oral argument, you should say that although that issue is not before the Court, it is doubtful the world would end were misdemeanors covered too.*) This and other objections to the capital-noncapital distinction will be explored in a later memorandum.

Summary

The *Betts* rule has been construed to encompass so many factors that it is easy to understand the accusations of "federal intrusion" and "subjectivity" that have been leveled against it. Lacking any indication from the Supreme Court as to how these diverse factors are to be balanced, state courts have understandably achieved results that border on the unreal. The rule has been indiscriminately applied to three apparently distinct sorts of fact situation, with nary a word from the Court as to *why* one rule should govern all three.

The rule, as presently propounded, is an amalgam of two very different sorts of considerations. This not only has confused state courts (and the supreme tribunal itself) but it also has rendered it impossible that either trial judge or appellate court can have before it all the factors necessary to apply it realistically. Its ambiguity insures that no denial of counsel can be

---

* [This is precisely what Fortas did.]

above suspicion; consequently, many appeals are taken and much appellate energy consumed. The large percentage of reversals bears witness to the fact that many trials have been conducted in vain.

Starting from the questionable assumption that there are on this earth laymen capable of adequately defending themselves against the accusations of the public prosecutor, the special circumstances rule—if it can be called "a rule"—is designed to sort out these fortunate and talented individuals. Twenty years of confusion bear witness to its inadequacy.

Remarks at American University Conference Marking the Thirtieth Anniversary of *Gideon v. Wainwright* (1993)[4]

A lot of nice things have happened here this afternoon, and one of them is that the name of Abe Fortas has been uttered without embarrassment and even with praise. I am delighted that the firm that no longer bears his name saw fit to make the gift in his honor. Whatever mistakes he made—and he plainly made some—he did not deserve the ignominious end he had, as he did some great things. (Of course he didn't do them alone. If I am not mistaken, Abe Krash was also on the *Durham* brief with him. [Krash indicates yes.] And I am sure you would have been on the *Gault* case if you were not a little old to be a law clerk at that point.)

It is not necessary to reminisce about what happened here. That would be superfluous given Tony [Lewis]'s excellent book and the movie based on it. The book is called *Gideon's Trumpet*, of course. I've been a law teacher most of my career, as you heard, and the book has caused me a lot of trouble because endless law students come into my office and say, "I don't want to go the usual route this summer. I want a job like you had."

I say, "Well, that may not be replicable."

Actually, I went to the firm knowing that it had this case, and even had bargained to get to work on it before I went there. Why a firm with lots of associates agreed to let a summer clerk work on this case so centrally I don't know, but I'm sure they knew what they were doing. Or not. Anyway, those guys are all rich now, so who cares? So they didn't get to work on *Gideon*; they could buy and sell me.

Well, anyway, students come in and say, "Let's figure out what's the next *Gideon v. Wainwright*. I am going to angle for this job. We've got to figure this out."

I say, "They paid me $75 a week."

They say, "I'll get back to you on this idea."

I also learned something from the movie. I got, as I guess we all did, a script for my approval. This must have been so we wouldn't sue them. I read through it. It has two sickening scenes that involve me. In one I appear and say, "Oh, Mr. Fortas, congratulations! You are my role model, my hero, you're everything I've ever wanted to be. If I could be like you, I would grow up to be a happy man," or something along those lines, which doesn't sound exactly like the way I usually talk. My other scene was, sitting at the Supreme Court argument, I turn to Abe Krash and whisper, "Now just who is it that's on the other side in this case?" This is after months of working on it.

So there I am, an obsequious and retarded law student.

But in the script there was also this wonderful scene which replicated a memo I sent to Abe Krash and Abe Fortas saying that if Gideon had had a lawyer, here are the various things he could have done. And it had the actor playing me acting out the possible trial, and it was a lengthy and wonderful scene. And I said to myself, okay, I will agree to the package because that scene is in there. I don't like this other stuff, but I'll go for the package.

Well, you can probably figure out what happened. Two of those three scenes are in the movie.

I can't even tell you who played my part. The credits at the end of the movie listed a number of people. They said, "The part of Ralph Temple was played by X; the part of James Fitzpatrick—these were associates in the firm—was played by Y," but nothing about John Ely. So I went up to [director David] Rintels at the screening of the movie at Harvard and I said, "How come it didn't say the part of John Ely was played by so and so? I didn't see my name there."

He responded, "Oh, the guy who played you was up at the beginning without a special billing because you were one of the main characters."

I said, "I had two lines."

He said, "Well, before the cuts were made, you had one of the main parts."

It has become mildly fashionable—we heard the beginnings of it today—to say that this is a case that hasn't panned out. I want to dissent from that, somewhat. I have here a column from the *Washington Post* for January 23 of this year written by Nat Hentoff, called "A Disgrace to the Law." It is about the anniversary of *Gideon v. Wainwright*, and the gravamen is—I use that word for you law students—the gravamen of the column is that *Gideon* hasn't worked. Hentoff's central exhibit is that the percentage of defendants represented by public defenders has gone up markedly over the last ten years. I would like to suggest that that is not an element of proof that anything is going wrong.

You will hear from [D.C. Public Defender Angela] Davis,[5] and I will be interested to hear what she has to say, if she wants to address this. But remember to the extent she is describing her office as bleak, she has a budget that she has to defend and augment. I, however, wish to defend the proposition that by and large public defender's offices (emphatically including hers) are pretty darn good.

As was said in the introduction, after law school and after I clerked and so forth, I went to work as a public defender in San Diego. There were maybe two, three, four, five criminal defense lawyers in town—and this is a city of about a million people—that were better than we were, a handful. Then there were us. Then was everyone else in terms of ability to represent defendants in criminal cases. The "everyone else" subdivided into two categories: people who really needed the work and couldn't get it any other way, who just hung around waiting to be appointed; and corporate lawyers who were smart but didn't know what they were doing in a criminal courtroom.

Now occasionally, it was true, someone that I was appointed to represent would ask for a "real lawyer," and didn't want a public defender. Those scenes are etched in my mind. The judge would get a glint in his eye and say: "Now let me see if I have this straight. I want this on the record. You wish to dismiss Mr. Ely as your counsel? Is that right? I want to be clear that you know what you're doing here. It is your wish that I dismiss Mr. Ely?"—and the judge would proceed to appoint some incompetent in place of me.

I was of course disabled from leaping up and saying, "Idiot, can't you see what's happening? He's about to give you somebody who doesn't know what he's doing!"

There's another interesting thing I noticed. The clients *in jail* never dismissed the public defenders—because they were able to talk to other prisoners and get an idea of who was good and who wasn't. Now, as I say, there were a few people in town who were better than we were, but by and large the best defense came from the public defenders.

I had one guy out on bail I will take just a moment to tell you about. This guy was not so sure. He was thinking about dismissing me. He came to every case I tried and he would sit in the front row to watch me. His case was coming up in a couple of months. He would sit there, and sit there, and usually at a break he would come up and offer to testify as an alibi witness in behalf of the defendant.

Don't worry—I didn't use him more than three or four times.

Now I think it is generally admitted that public defenders are expert and capable lawyers. Several things, however, are true. Number one, they are overburdened. Again quoting from Hentoff, "I have for instance seen enormously overburdened public defenders meeting their clients for the first time only fifteen minutes before a hearing."

That may be true, but you want to know what the hearing is. If the hearing is the arraignment where a plea has to be entered, fifteen minutes is plenty. Unless the prosecution is essentially offering you a dismissal, the plea is "not guilty." You don't need more than fifteen *seconds* to figure that out. Anything else is malpractice.

Of course overburden is a problem, but it is one route to expertise. I don't think anyone who has decided to devote his or her life to this kind of work is going to let it overwhelm them to the point where they are not adequately representing their clients. People who do this kind of work are by nature cantankerous, disagreeable people—I hereby mark myself Exhibit A—and they will speak up and not let it happen.

Second, it is sometimes alleged that there are conflicts of interest because you are representing so many people. It used to be the myth that public defenders would trade so many guilty pleas for so many reductions of pleas. I never saw that happen. It would be flagrantly unethical. Any defense lawyer who did that ought to serve the time for which he had just pleaded his client.

It seems to me a public defender should behave, and this is certainly how I behaved (and I never knew one who didn't), as if he or she were a private lawyer, and make in each case the arguments he or she would make if it were a private client. You don't tailor your arguments in one case because you are thinking about another client, any more than a private lawyer should; and the judge has no more business pointing out in the presence of the jury that you made the opposite argument last week than he would have in a case involving a private lawyer.

Now there are those three or four guys who are better. Either they are more talented—it could happen . . . I guess—or they have more time and money. Okay, we never thought *Gideon* meant that everybody was going to get the best lawyer in town, one who would have a month to think about each case. If you work it through logically, *Gideon can't* mean that. That is a spiral that would have no end.

Of course there are incompetent lawyers. That is one reason I would label atrocious the current Supreme Court's cutback of habeas corpus and postconviction remedies,[6] particularly in capital cases, but in other cases as well. I do not think it is costing us much in terms of either money or erosion of federalism that where there is a serious sentence, we look at criminal convictions again, even repeatedly.

But I don't think incompetent lawyers are any more common than incompetent plumbers, incompetent car mechanics, or incompetent doctors. Many people are not so good at their jobs. I do not think that lawyers are any worse in that regard than others. And I *certainly* do not think that public defenders are less competent at criminal defense than other lawyers. In fact, I think they are substantially more competent. Thus, I think Hentoff is wrong. The increasing percentage of indigent defendants being represented by public defenders seems to me a cause for rejoicing, not a proof that *Gideon* has failed.

There are some decisions of the Warren Court that one can argue have not made much difference. Apparently the school prayer decisions are widely ignored. Even *Brown v. Board of Education* is an arguable case in that respect. It has meant some desegregation; that it has meant increased quality of education for African-Americans or, for that matter, for anybody else, is a highly debatable proposition. [Its symbolic value seems to me great and entirely positive, however.] *Miranda*? I don't think it's done any harm. On the other hand, the incidence of confession doesn't seem to have gone down particularly; the incidence of lawyers actually appearing at station house interrogations is about what it was before *Miranda*—that is, zero. But *Gideon*? I'm sorry, but I have a lot of trouble seeing this as one that has failed. It seems to me that it is one that has succeeded, and in particular I wanted to enter my dissent from the inference from the fact that public defenders may be handling more and more cases to the conclusion that the quality of representation is going down. I rather suspect it is proof that it is going up.

Letter to Anthony Lewis (1990)[7]

Okay, hot shot, you got lucky. Sed sic transit gloria mundi.

Last November, for reasons that are currently obscure, I found myself driving from Key West to New Orleans along the gulf coast, and consequently passed through Panama City. Assuming that the Bay Harbor Poolroom [the object of Gideon's alleged burglary] must have been made a shrine of some sort, I naturally determined to check it out. Pilgrims there, I figured, would probably be anxious to have my autograph.

This proved to be no easy matter. There were no poolrooms, nor any Bay Harbor anythings, in the phone book. My first few inquiries understandably led people to suppose I was looking to shoot a game of pool. It was Sunday morning, and my efforts to explain how my Calvinist upbringing made that thought at this hour grotesque didn't seem to be getting across, so I converted the search into one simply for Bay Harbor. It turned out that there *used* to be a section called Bay Harbor, but various proprietors within what an old map indicated were its environs divided equally between never having heard of it, and thinking it may have been somewhere once but they didn't know where.

What does one do in such a situation—or rather what does a middle class white male do in such a situation? I called the cops. "Why did I want to know?" Clarence Gideon, I explained, perhaps your city's most famous citizen. Hadn't heard of him. Anthony Lewis? Abes Fortas and Krash? Nothing. Ahah—this would work: Henry Fonda? Jose Ferrer? The middle-aged unknown who creatively portrayed establishment pillar Abe Krash as a sort of aluminum siding salesman? The young unknown who played the ingratiating if dull-witted law student "John"? (You may recall his two lines. I know I do. "Congratulations, Mr. Fortas, for being appointed in the *Gideon* case," and, some months later, "Now just who is it that's against us in this case?"). No, the officer hadn't really heard of any of these, though he thought Henry Fonda might be some relation to Jane and once have been an actor himself.

I asked whether there was anyone on duty—it was by now Sunday afternoon—who had been with the force in the early sixties. *Early sixties?* Not even close: if I was under the impression the peace in Panama City was being kept by geezers, I would soon be made to realize my mistake. Well, I ventured, surely he would want to meet me in what used to be Bay Harbor and try to locate the Bay Harbor Poolroom. (Having been a military policeman myself, I know that cops will do almost anything to relieve the boredom.) Obviously by now figuring me for some novel kind of menace, he agreed to join me. Upon his arrival, I explained the deal to him—though I don't think he ever got clear on how I could have had anything to do with this supposed case, given that I wasn't from Panama City and indeed wasn't even admitted in Florida. (Explaining that at the time of the case I wasn't admitted *anywhere* didn't strike me as a sound tactic.)

The building whose picture I enclose, we decided, had to be the place. It had indeed been a poolroom/bar, he now remembered, though it had gone through several name and personality changes and finally been abandoned. It was fast approaching Sunday evening, so I hurriedly took the picture. You can see from the church sign caught by my clever angle that we were indeed in Bay Harbor (which, as I now understand it, never was more than a few square blocks anyhow). So this is great, I said; patience and persev'rance made a bishop of his rev'rence; I'll send this photo off to Tony just as soon as I get the roll developed.

As luck would have it, this was one of the few trips on which I didn't bring along a copy of *Gideon's Trumpet*. Naturally I consulted it on arriving home, but found some distressing details. An alley behind the poolroom! (I suppose it could have been grown over; I wasn't really looking for an alley.) Windows on the alley that were too high to see through from outside! (Well, maybe. Cautious of cave-ins, I didn't spend much time inside or around back.) And finally—this I actually should have remembered, since it's where Gideon lived—there had been a Bay Harbor *Hotel*! My officer friend and I walked all over what he said used to be Bay Harbor, and I certainly didn't see any building a rational person would pay to spend the night in. On the other hand, I reasoned, Bay Harbor never was much even when it existed, so I'm sure (especially judging by its clientele) the Bay

Harbor Hotel never was much either. And of course, the rationalization continued, I hadn't been *looking* for a hotel, or a structure that might once have been passed off as one.

Or . . . was this whole Hitchcockian deal the invention of author Anthony Lewis? Disappearing alleys, disappearing hotels, indeed an entire disappearing community. No one in this burg had even *heard* of Clarence Gideon, and come to think of it I never clapped eyes on the man myself, and I wasn't even sure I knew anybody who had. (I tested my officer friend by asking about Ernesto Miranda, and yes indeed, he'd heard of him. Didn't even try to tie him in with Carmen. Was he supposed to be from Panama City too? No, I said, forget it.) And the officer had a point: I wasn't admitted to practice in Florida, so what *could* I have had to do with this case? And as we both know (as, unfortunately, does everyone who's ever spent more than ten minutes with me) I've never in my life said, "Congratulations, Mr. Fortas, . . ." or anything even close.

I am taking the precaution of addressing a copy of this letter to a Mr. Abe Krash in Washington, D.C., in the hope that such a person in fact exists and might be moved to continue this investigation in the event *I* turn out "never to have existed" after the receipt of the original in Boston.

I know you didn't ask, but I'm going to fill you in on a little chronology here. During my third year in law school (the year following the summer spent helping write the Gideon brief) I was offered (and naturally accepted) Chief Justice Warren's clerkship for the following year. Upon graduation, however, I achieved the dubious honor of becoming the first Supreme Court clerk since World War II to have his draft deferment denied, and ended up as a military policeman. (I put in for this because I knew I was going to be a criminal defense lawyer, at least for a while, and thus wanted to learn to "think like a cop." Besides, it's a job that gives privates a lot of independence [and authority].) There too I suppose I was a constitutional lawyer of sorts, though fortunately there remain no written records of the various "rulings" I made in that capacity—mainly "low-visibility" decisions not to invoke the criminal process—and thus none are included here. Then I did a six-month stint as the junior member of the Warren Commission staff—a bit of that in chapter 9—and then a year as Warren's clerk on the Supreme Court. Next came my Fulbright year in London (see Chapter 4). Then I personally did my bit to help follow up on the promise that was made in Gideon by becoming one of the three founding attorneys of Defenders Inc. in San Diego. People ask why—weren't your clients mainly the scum of the earth? It's true many of them were guilty of the crimes with which they were charged, though some weren't, but essentially all of them were people for whom nobody—surely no member of the establishment—

had ever done anything nice. Even if I lost, as I confess I did sometimes,[8] I think it did my clients some good to see me actually standing up and taking some shots for them. I'm going to stop, as I think this is a point that novelists (though those I'm about to quote are also lawyers) have put better:

> "I always thought I'd become a defense lawyer. But prosecutors have so much power. To do good things, you know—not just bad."
> "Of course. . . . I admire the rectitude for which prosecutors stand."
> "But you wouldn't think of doing it?"
> "I have thoughts. But my view—purely an idiosyncratic one, I stress—is that I would only be doing further damage to what is already smashed and broken. Understand, I truly believe that yours is a job that must be done—but better not by me."
> Scott Turow, *The Burden of Proof* (1990)

> I'm not going to use my skills, such as they are, to force some poor devil into a condemned Victorian slum where he can be banged up with a couple of psychopaths and his own chamberpot.
> John Mortimer, *Rumpole and the Golden Thread* (1983)

Naturally constitutional issues of a sort arise almost daily for a public defender. Nonetheless I have opted not to reproduce here any papers dating from that period, for three reasons. First, most of the argument was oral and largely extemporaneous. Second, like any lawyer concerned more with his clients' welfare than with promoting his own reputation, I typically tailored my arguments so tightly that they were not likely to fit anyone other than the current client: even the legal victory that in context seemed most important to practice in the federal courts of San Diego—the case held that Customs officials* could no longer, simply by calling it a "border search," conduct a rectal probe at the border without a clear indication of the presence of contraband or without securing a search warrant—is of limited

---

* True, these probes were conducted by a doctor. Indeed, they were invariably conducted by the *same* doctor, who lived just a few blocks from the port of entry. A sufficiently specialized practice, I thought, to justify my referring to him in oral argument in the Ninth Circuit as "the long middle finger of the Customs Agency Service"—for which I was immediately reprimanded by one judge, while the other two stifled laughs. You'll not be surprised to learn that as of that moment I was able correctly to predict the vote in the case, though it took them over a year to decide it, conceivably, just conceivably, to give Mr. Huguez some further time in prison to make sure the case would not escape his attention. In some ways he seemed like a nice guy—for years he sent me Christmas cards, and seemed to resemble most of my Mexican smuggling clients in that his crime appeared to have been born of serious economic necessity and was probably performed for a relatively modest fee paid by the actual entrepreneur, who undoubtedly never got even close to a prison. On the other hand Huguez could hardly have been unaware of the presence of the contraband.

general interest as a constitutional holding. Huguez v. United States, 406 F.2d 355 (C.A.9 1968). Besides, it doesn't belong in a family book.

Finally, unlike the other documents contained in this volume, my arguments as a public defender were not objective: subject to an ethical obligation not to mislead the court, they were in each event driven by the goal of minimizing the damage to the client I had been appointed to represent. Of course there is a good deal of advocacy in much that is reprinted herein, but in each event it is advocacy in support of a result that no one had paid or instructed me to reach. (You may recall, if you were noticing, that in connection with Gideon I included only memoranda advising the lawyer for whom I was working, not my [preliminary] version of the brief that was filed with the Court.) However, the following piece, co-authored with Harvard Law Professor (now Frankfurter Professor) Alan Dershowitz was, at least so far as my contribution was concerned, a "last lick" in reaction to a particularly bitter defeat I suffered in the Ninth Circuit. (Martin v. United States, 400 F.2d 149 [C.A.9 1968].)

Harris v. New York: *Some Anxious Observations on the Candor and Logic of the Emerging Nixon Majority (1971)**

Today more and more new and vexing problems reach the courts and they call for the highest order of thoughtful exploration and careful study.
Chief Justice Warren E. Burger, May 18, 1971[9]

When Chief Justice Burger announced the decision in *Harris v. New York*[10]—holding that statements elicited in violation of *Miranda v. Arizona*[11] may be used to impeach—he reportedly characterized it as a matter "of interest mostly to members of the bar" and not worth describing from the bench.[12] On the surface, his opinion for the Court—joined by Justices Blackmun, Harlan, Stewart, and White[13]—does indeed give an impression of little general interest or importance. It is very short—just eleven paragraphs—and is written in the flat, descriptive style typical of simple and uncontroversial cases. The initial six paragraphs set out the facts; the seventh argues that *Miranda* cannot be regarded as controlling; and the remainder of the opinion consists of four arguments—really assertions—in support of the Court's result. There is no indication that important considerations of policy have been weighed or that significant practical results may flow from the decision. Rarely, however, has so short an opinion concealed so much.

* Alan M. Dershowitz co-authored this article (80 Yale L. J. 1198).

We think the result reached in *Harris* was wrong. But that is not the reason why, or the perspective from which, we have chosen to focus on the case. Nor do we wish to use *Harris* as a vehicle for entering the ongoing debate about the proper role of the Supreme Court in the American system of government. In the course of our discussion, we will suggest that the opinion, in its haste to decide a broad and controversial question of constitutional law, ignores a narrower ground of decision that would have compelled a contrary result; and that its brevity and unclarity leave the lower courts without guidance concerning recurrent and related issues. But in the main, our criticisms are not of that order. They are, first, that the majority, in crucial respects, flatly misstates both the record in the case before it and the state of the law at the time the decision was rendered; and second, that each of the arguments set forth by the Court masks a total absence of analysis and provides no support for its result.

If *Harris* were but an isolated instance of these faults, it would still be a source of concern. But, unfortunately, it is not alone. To illustrate this, we have, in the footnotes, made a number of cross-references to Mr. Justice Blackmun's opinion for the Court in *Wyman v. James*,[14] which upheld warrantless "visits" to the homes of nonconsenting welfare recipients. Since the deficiencies of the *James* opinion are apparent on its face and are ably highlighted by Mr. Justice Marshall's dissent, there would be little point in our addressing that case on its merits. But we have found some disturbing similarities of argumentation and striking parallels in the manner in which the Court on the two occasions treated the record and the relevant sources—parallels that suggest that *Harris* may not be an aberration.

Reasonable persons can and do differ about the proper role of the Supreme Court, as they can and do about the balance to be struck between "liberty" and "order." But there is little room for disagreement about the desirability in Supreme Court adjudication of reasoned argument as opposed to arrogant pronunciamento or about the undesirability, indeed the intolerability, of what is, at best, gross negligence concerning the state of the record and the controlling precedents. Because we have chosen to focus on unarguable vices, this comment does not aspire to the sweep and scope of much academic criticism of the Court. Our task, though narrow, is important nonetheless. It is to help keep the Court honest.

*   *   *

The relevant facts in *Harris* can be briefly stated. Petitioner was arrested on January 7, 1966, and taken to police headquarters, where he was questioned about drug transactions that allegedly took place on January 4 and 6. He was given "no warning of a right to appointed counsel"[15] and during the questioning indicated that he would "rather see a lawyer before I keep on."[16] Nevertheless, the questioning continued, and petitioner made certain incriminating statements.

At his trial for two counts of drug sale, petitioner testified in his own behalf and denied committing the alleged crimes. On cross-examination, and over petitioner's objection, some incriminating statements from his pretrial interrogation were read and he was asked whether he remembered them. Petitioner said that he remembered some but not others.[17] The jury was instructed that it could consider the contents of the pretrial statement solely for purposes of evaluating petitioner's "believability."[18] It convicted him on the second count but was unable to agree on the first. The New York appellate courts affirmed the conviction, and the United States Supreme Court granted certiorari.

The Majority's Representation of the Record

Crucial to the Court's conclusion is its assertion that "Petitioner makes no claim that the statements made to the police were coerced or involuntary."[19] The record is clear, however, that petitioner made precisely that claim in the courts below,[20] and reiterated it before the Supreme Court in his briefs and oral argument.[21]

The issue arose at the trial in the following way: at the prosecutor's first reference to the pretrial statements, petitioner's counsel objected on the grounds that the state had failed to "lay a foundation and show that it was voluntarily made, under the law, *and* in conformity with the requirements as set up in the case of *Miranda v. Arizona*."[22] The trial judge overruled the objection, citing *People v. Kulis*, a New York case holding an illegally obtained statement to be "admissible on the question of defendant's credibility as a witness."[23] At the close of cross-examination, the objection was renewed. Petitioner's counsel argued that the interrogation had occurred "prior to any mention of an attorney," and that "[i]n addition" the statement had been "presented to the jury before any examination was had, so that legal voluntariness of this statement" could not be established.[24] The trial judge responded as follows:

> Let the record reflect, Mr. Projansky, for you, that you are taking an exception to the fact that under the Huntley case, it was not offered on a basis of notice required under 831 of the Code of the Criminal Procedure, that you *also* have an exception under the fact that it violates the Miranda against Arizona decision in the United States Supreme Court.[25]

The trial judge thus ruled, in effect, that no hearing was required to establish admissibility under either *Miranda* or the pre-*Miranda* voluntariness tests, since even if the statement were found inadmissible under both tests, it could still be used to impeach under the holding of the *Kulis* case.[26]

In the state appellate proceedings, neither the petitioner nor the state drew any distinction between statements obtained in violation of *Miranda* and those that are involuntary in the pre-*Miranda* sense.[27] The assumption of both parties throughout these proceedings was the same as that of the trial court: that an illegally obtained statement can be used to impeach regardless of whether the illegality was based on a violation of *Miranda* or of pre-*Miranda* standards of voluntariness. As the state's brief in the Appellate Division put it:

> It really makes no difference why the *Kulis* statement was illegal, and it makes no difference why this appellant's statement was illegal. Once it is acknowledged that they are in fact illegal, they have been as tarred as black as they can get.[28]

Nor did petitioner's briefs or oral argument before the Supreme Court in any way abandon or concede his involuntariness claim. In his petition for certiorari, petitioner explicitly argued that *Jackson v. Denno*[29] required a pretrial determination of voluntariness before a statement could be used for any purpose. "Fundamental fairness," he argued, "requires a pre-trial hearing on the question of voluntariness."[30]

During oral argument counsel for petitioner was asked whether there was any "claim here that the statement was coerced. . . ."[31] His answer was as follows:

> [T]he young man who tried this case for legal aid, made such an objection, and he made it by referring to Jackson vs. Denno and to section 813(f) of the Code of Criminal Procedure in New York, which is the statute dealing with a hearing on the question of voluntariness. . . . [W]hen we asked for a hearing on that issue, we were foreclosed by the prosecution's objection that the result of such a voluntariness hearing wouldn't prevent him from using it, and the trial judge . . . agreed with that on the authority of *Kulis* . . . .[32]

One of the justices then summed up petitioner's position in the following exchange:

> Q. Well, then, as to coercion, the involuntariness of this statement, do I understand it to be your submission that because of the attitude the prosecutor took, the ruling of the court was that even assuming it was coerced it could still be used?
> A. Exactly, but I also say—
> Q. We should decide this case therefore on the hypothesis, whatever the facts may be, that this was coerced?
> A. Exactly. . . .[33]

Petitioner's counsel then went on to catalogue the acts pointing toward involuntariness. He described the off-the-record preliminary questioning as "a secret inquisition, something in the nature of a subtle star chamber proceeding. . . ."[34] He told the Court that petitioner was a twenty-three year old addict with a tenth grade education who, at the time he made the statement, "was suffering from withdrawal symptoms."[35] Petitioner also had testified that he could not remember the interrogation because it had occurred at a time when "my joints was down and I needed drugs."[36] He had alleged as well that he may have been suffering from the after-effects of an automobile accident that put him in a hospital for a month, gave him a concussion, and affected his memory,[37] and that he was interrogated off the record prior to the taking of his formal statement in the presence of three assistant district attorneys and two detectives.[38] Finally, petitioner's counsel was asked whether there was a claim that "the contents of the statements are untrue." His answer was, "Yes, Judge."[39]

It is possible, of course, that an evidentiary hearing would not have led to a conclusion that the statement was involuntary in the pre-*Miranda* sense, but that was not the issue before the Court.[40] Nor was that what the Chief Justice said. Joined by four other Justices, he asserted that "Petitioner makes no claim that the statements made to the police were coerced or involuntary." This statement is simply incorrect. In light of the papers and oral argument presented to the Court, it is difficult to understand how it could have been made.[41]

It is also surprising, in light of this record, that the Court reached out to decide the broad constitutional issue of whether a statement obtained in violation of *Miranda* may be used to impeach.[42] During oral argument, counsel for the state was asked the following question by Mr. Justice Stewart: "What if this had been a coerced confession, could you impeach him with that?[43] The answer was as follows:

> If this had been a coerced confession, it is the people's view and the respondent's view that it couldn't have been used for any purpose . . . .[44]

Counsel for the state was then asked what his position would be in a case where petitioner had claimed, at the trial, that the statement was involuntary: "Wouldn't you agree that then you have a hearing outside of the jury?" The state's reply was unequivocal:

> Oh, by all means, Mr. Justice, . . . there has to be some judicial determination of that prior to any concept of throwing this in the man's face. Just simple justice would compel that.[45]

Thus the state explicitly conceded that a hearing would have to be held before a statement alleged to be "coerced or involuntary" could be used for impeachment. Moreover, as previously demonstrated, the record plainly established that petitioner had explicitly requested a hearing to determine whether the statement was involuntary. Accordingly, canons of judicial restraint (to say nothing of "simple justice" to Mr. Harris, who never did get his voluntariness hearing) should have led the Court to remand the case to the state courts for a hearing to determine whether the statement was involuntary in the pre-*Miranda* sense. It could have done this in a short per curiam opinion such as the following:

> The state concedes that a statement that is involuntary or coerced in the pre-*Miranda* sense may not be used for impeachment purposes. It also acknowledges that if a hearing is requested to determine whether a statement was involuntary or coerced, the statement may not be used to impeach unless there has been a judicial determination that it was not involuntary or coerced. At the trial, petitioner requested a hearing to determine whether his statement was involuntary. That request was denied, on the ground that it made no difference for purposes of impeachment whether the statement was involuntary in the pre-*Miranda* sense.
>
> Accordingly, we remand the case for a hearing. If it is determined that the statement was involuntary in the pre-*Miranda* sense, then the conviction must be reversed. If it is determined that it was voluntary in the pre-*Miranda* sense, there will then be occasion for us to decide the issue whether a statement voluntary in the pre-*Miranda* sense but obtained in violation of *Miranda* may be used for impeachment purposes.

The Court did not, however, elect to follow this course of judicial restraint. Instead it reached out to consider an issue about which there was unanimity among the circuits and little conflict among the states, and indeed it decided it *contrary* to the weight of all this authority.[46] It should therefore be instructive to examine the arguments offered by the Court in support of its conclusion.

The Majority's Representation of the Precedents

MIRANDA V. ARIZONA

The most obvious precedential hurdle for the Court in *Harris* was of course, *Miranda* itself, which had held that "the prosecution may not use statements, whether exculpatory or inculpatory . . . unless it demonstrates the use of procedural safeguards effective to secure the privilege against self-incrimination."[47] Prior to *Harris*, that decision had been widely— indeed, almost unanimously—interpreted to preclude the impeachment use of statements obtained in violation of its rules.[48] The opinion in *Harris*, however, disposed of *Miranda* in its first paragraph of argument:

> Some comments in the *Miranda* opinion can indeed be read as indicating a bar to use of an uncounseled statement for any purpose, but discussion of that issue was not at all necessary to the Court's holding and cannot be regarded as controlling.

Miranda barred the prosecution from making its case with statements of an accused made while in custody prior to having or effectively waiving counsel. It does not follow from *Miranda* that evidence inadmissible against an accused in the prosecution's case in chief is barred for all purposes, provided of course that the trustworthiness of the evidence satisfies legal standards.[49]

This summary of *Miranda* is misleading in two respects. First, by stating that "some" comments "can . . . be read" to preclude the *Harris* result, the Chief Justice suggests that that is but one of several possible readings. However, a pervasive and unambiguous aspect of *Miranda* was its explicit rejection of distinctions based on the manner in which a statement is used by the government or the degree to which it is helpful to it:

> The warnings required and the waiver necessary in accordance with our opinion today are, in the absence of a fully effective equivalent, prerequisites to the admissibility of *any statement* made by a defendant. No distinction can be drawn between statements which are direct confessions and statements which amount to 'admissions' of part or all of an offense. The privilege against self-incrimination protects the individual from being compelled to incriminate himself *in any manner*; it does not distinguish degrees of incrimination. Similarly, for precisely the same reason, no distinction may be drawn between inculpatory statements and statements alleged to be merely 'exculpatory.' If a statement made were in fact truly exculpatory it would, of course, never be used by the prosecution. In fact, *statements merely intended to be exculpatory by the defendant are often used to impeach his testimony at trial or to demonstrate untruths in the statement given under interrogation and thus to prove guilt by implication. These statements are incriminating in any meaningful sense of the word and may not be used without the full warnings and effective waiver required for any other statement.*[50]

Miranda's repeated references to "exculpatory" statements[51] were thus intended to cover precisely the kind of statement at issue in *Harris* and the specific use to which it was there put. Nor did these references pass unnoticed. They were the object of explicit and uncomplimentary reference in each of the three dissents filed in *Miranda*.[52] Accordingly, *Miranda* not only "can" be read to require reversal of Harris's conviction, it can be read no other way!

Second, it is of course technically accurate to say that *Miranda*'s discussion of impeachment was not necessary to the Court's holding, because the statements in *Miranda* had been used as part of the prosecution's case in chief. But *Miranda* did not purport to be an opinion limited to its precise facts. Indeed, the stated reason for granting certiorari in that case was because *Escobedo v. Illinois*[53]—which *was* limited to its facts—had been "the subject of judicial interpretation" under which "state and federal courts, in assessing its implications, [had] arrived at varying conclusions." *Miranda* purported to "give concrete constitutional guidelines for law enforcement agencies and courts to follow."[54] Thus, the opinion was deliberately structured so that the constitutional principles that grew out of the experience of many cases were set out before the Court set forth the specific facts of the cases before it.[55] Moreover, the opinion *said* that it was part of its "holding" that an uncounseled "exculpatory" statement could not be used by the prosecution. The Court summarized its sixty-three page opinion as follows:

> Our holding will be spelled out with some specificity in the pages which follow but briefly stated it is this: the prosecution may not use statements, whether exculpatory or inculpatory, stemming from custodial interrogation of the defendant unless it demonstrates the use of procedural safeguards effective to secure the privilege against self-incrimination.[56]

One might wish to criticize the *Miranda* opinion for its far-ranging, "guidebook" format. But, rightly or wrongly, that opinion is what it is, and it does "follow" from it that evidence inadmissible because of a *Miranda* violation "is barred for all purposes." An important part of *Miranda* was squarely overruled in *Harris*; the Court does no service by pretending that it wasn't.

This kind of treatment of a troublesome precedent may not be that unusual. Though more candor was, we think, in order, the Court's behavior with respect to *Miranda* pales beside what it did with *Walder v. United States*.[57] That case, like *Miranda*, squarely faced the *Harris* issue and resolved it in favor of the defendant. But the *Harris* opinion is not content flimsily to "distinguish" *Walder*—instead, by dint of some skillful editing, it represents it as a supporting and controlling precedent!

WALDER V. UNITED STATES

The Court places its principal reliance on *Walder*, suggesting that it is following a general rule laid down in that case and merely extending it slightly to apply to the facts of *Harris*, since there is no "difference in principle" between the two. The Court's entire discussion of *Walder* is as follows:

> In *Walder v. United States*, 374 U.S. 62 (1954), the Court permitted physical evidence, inadmissible in the case in chief, to be used for impeachment purposes.
>
> > "It is one thing to say the Government cannot make an affirmative use of evidence unlawfully obtained. It is quite another to say that the defendant can turn the illegal method by which evidence in the Government's possession was obtained to his own advantage, and provide himself with a shield against con-

tradiction of his untruths. Such an extension of the *Weeks* doctrine would be a perversion of the Fourth Amendment.

"[T]here is hardly justification for letting the defendant affirmatively resort to perjurious testimony in reliance on the Government's disability to challenge his credibility." 347 U.S., at 65.

It is true that Walder was impeached as to collateral matters included in his direct examination, whereas petitioner here was impeached as to testimony bearing more directly on the crimes charged. We are not persuaded that there is a difference in principle that warrants a result different from that reached by the Court in *Walder*.[58]

The actual situation was, however, considerably different from that suggested by the Court. *Walder* did not state the general rule: instead, it stated a rather special exception to the general rule laid down in 1925 by a unanimous Supreme Court in the case of *Agnello v. United States*.[59] In *Agnello*, the Supreme Court had held that a defendant who did not, in his direct examination, testify about an illegally seized item, could not be cross-examined about that item. The *Agnello* Court's analysis was as follows:

And the contention that the evidence of the search and seizure was admissible in rebuttal is without merit. In his direct examination, Agnello was not asked and did not testify concerning the can of cocaine. In cross-examination, in answer to a question permitted over his objection, he said he had never seen it. He did nothing to waive his constitutional protection or to justify cross-examination in respect of the evidence claimed to have been obtained by the search.[60]

The *Walder* case carved out of that general rule a limited exception responsive to the particular and unfair trial tactic of the defendant in that case. The government had unlawfully seized heroin from Walder in 1950 and had indicted him for the possession of it. The evidence had been suppressed and the indictment dismissed. Two years later, the government indicted him for an entirely different drug offense. At his trial for this latter crime, Walder took the witness stand and denied the specific acts with which he stood charged. Then of his own accord he went beyond denying these acts and volunteered testimony that he had never had any narcotics in his possession in his entire life. At that point, the trial court permitted the government to question him about the heroin unlawfully seized from him two years earlier and to introduce the testimony of the officer who had made the seizure. It was in this context that the *Walder* Court held that where the defendant "[o]f his own accord," goes "beyond a mere denial of complicity in the crimes of which he was charged," and makes a "sweeping claim," then the government may "introduce by way of rebuttal evidence illegally secured by it. . . ."[61] The Court in *Walder* explicitly reaffirmed the general rule laid down in *Agnello*:

Of course, the Constitution guarantees a defendant the fullest opportunity to meet the accusation against him. He must be free to deny all the elements of the case against him without thereby giving leave to the Government to introduce by way of rebuttal evidence illegally secured by it, and therefore not available for its case in chief.[62]

Indeed, the *Walder* Court went out of its way to reconcile its limited holding with the general rule of *Agnello*, asserting that *Agnello* had "foreshadowed" the *Walder* result.[63]

Harris, of course, is like *Agnello* rather than *Walder*, and Harris's conviction would clearly have been reversed had the earlier decision been followed. Accordingly, the *Harris* Court did not extend a general rule laid down in *Walder* to the facts in the case before it, as it suggested it was doing; instead, it squarely overruled the unanimous decision in *Agnello* without even citing it.

Nor was the *Harris* Court unaware of the *Agnello* rule it was overturning. For it appears to have gone to some pains to excise from its rendition of *Walder* all reference to *Agnello*. *Harris*'s quotation from *Walder* (reproduced above)[64] begins its second paragraph with a bracketed capital letter, indicating that something has been omitted. That something, it transpires, is *Walder*'s reiteration of the *Agnello* principle. What follows is the original passage from *Walder*. The nonitalicized material is what *Harris* quoted; the italicized material, what it omitted.

> *Take the present situation. Of his own accord, the defendant went beyond a mere denial of complicity in the crimes of which he was charged and made the sweeping claim that he had never dealt in or possessed any narcotics.* Of course, the Constitution guarantees a defendant the fullest opportunity to meet the accusation against him. He must be free to deny all the elements of the case against him without thereby giving leave to the Government to introduce by way of rebuttal evidence illegally secured by it, and therefore not available for its case in chief. *Beyond that, however,* there is hardly justification for letting the defendant affirmatively resort to perjurious testimony in reliance on the Government's disability to challenge his credibility.[65]

It is clear—especially from the (excised) phrase "Beyond that, however"— that the excised material is the general rule, and the (quoted) material "beyond that" the *Walder* exception. The precision of the *Harris* Court's editing of the quotation from *Walder* also suggests that the omission was not inadvertent.[66]

It is important to understand the criticism we are here making. There may be legitimate arguments in favor of overruling the general rule laid down in *Agnello* and reiterated in *Walder*. We do not—at this point— dispute the *conclusion* reached by the Court. But it was misleading for the

Court not to acknowledge that there was a general rule precluding the use of illegally seized evidence to impeach a defendant's testimony denying the crime and that it was squarely overruling a unanimous decision of a prior Supreme Court.

The Court does acknowledge that there is a distinction between *Walder* and the case at bar: "It is true that Walder was impeached as to collateral matters included in his direct examination, whereas petitioner here was impeached as to testimony bearing more directly on the crimes charged."[67] But it immediately proceeds to argue—more precisely, assert—that this is a distinction without a difference: "We are not persuaded that there is a difference in principle that warrants a result different from that reached by the Court in *Walder*."[68] That is all the Court says about the difference between the two cases, leaving unstated the reasons why it was "not persuaded" that a distinction that had been deemed dispositive for nearly a generation was not based on "principle."

There are, in fact, important differences between *Walder* and *Harris*— differences that at the very least should have been faced. *Walder* involved impeachment by means of evidence obtained in violation of the Fourth Amendment—an amendment that does not, in terms, provide for the exclusion of evidence secured in violation of it. Indeed, the Fourth Amendment "exclusionary rule" is a court-created device—of relatively recent vintage—designed to discourage primary violations of the prohibition against "unreasonable searches and seizures."[69] The Fifth Amendment, on the other hand, seems on its face to prohibit the government from using compelled statements "against" the defendant.[70] It *is* an exclusionary rule—and a constitutionally created one. Accordingly, courts would seem less justified in carving exceptions out of the Fifth Amendment's exclusionary rule than out of the Fourth's.

Moreover, the fact that evidence was secured in violation of the Fourth Amendment casts no doubt on its reliability, whereas one of the underlying reasons for excluding evidence obtained in violation of the Fifth Amendment is precisely the possibility that it may be untrustworthy. Although this is somewhat less true of statements obtained in violation of the prophylactic rules of *Miranda*, an important purpose of the *Miranda* rules was "to guarantee that the accused gives a fully accurate statement to the police . . . ."[71]

It was for these reasons, among others,[72] that both before and after *Walder*, the weight of federal and state authority was to the effect that evidence taken in violation of the Fifth—as contrasted with the Fourth— Amendment, could never be used to impeach.[73] The Court in *Harris* fails to acknowledge these distinctions between the Fourth and Fifth Amendments. It simply assumes that in the context of impeachment they are not differences "in principle" deserving even the briefest discussion.

The distinction the Court does allude to—only to dismiss in a conclusory sentence—is also a critical one, in both practical and constitutional terms. There is an important difference between impeaching a defendant's testimony as to collateral matters and impeaching him as to testimony bearing directly on the crime charged. The difference—simply stated—is this: there is a considerable risk that illegally obtained evidence that bears directly on the crime charged will be considered by the jury as direct evidence of the defendant's guilt. This risk is significantly reduced when the illegally obtained evidence does not directly relate to the elements of crime charged. This important difference may be illustrated by contrasting the facts of *Walder* with those of *Harris*. In *Walder*, the illegally obtained evidence related to an event that had occurred two years prior to the alleged crime. In *Harris*, on the other hand, the illegally obtained statements contained admissions of elements of the crime with which the defendant then stood charged. To be sure, the jury—as in *Walder*—was instructed not to consider that evidence as bearing on the elements of the offense, but rather only as bearing on the defendant's credibility. It is possible that the jurors diligently followed this limiting instruction and cleansed their minds of the contents of the statements when they were deliberating about the elements of the crime. But surely the risk of infection is significantly greater in the *Harris*-type case than in the *Walder*-type case.[74]

Indeed, it was this very difference that was explicitly and successfully argued by the government in its brief in *Walder*. The government pointed out that in *Agnello*

> the suppressed evidence was so closely related in point of time to the offense charged that there was a real danger that the suppressed evidence would be considered by the jury as proof of guilt, as of affirmative benefit to the Government. No such danger existed here, since the suppressed evidence related to a point in time remote from the offenses charged.[75]

The government then concluded that

> there was in this case no danger that the supposed evidence would be used as affirmative evidence in behalf of the Government beyond the limited scope for which we contend it was admissible, i.e., merely to neutralize the effect of petitioner's perjury.[76]

A number of recent decisions of the Supreme Court have relied on the principle that the Court in *Harris* found unpersuasive. For example, *Jackson v. Denno*[77] and *Bruton v. United States*[78] both rest on the conclusion that a limiting instruction cannot be relied upon when a confession or admission of the crime at issue is involved. "[T]he risk that the jury will not, or cannot, follow instructions is so great, and the consequences of failure so vital to the defendant, that the practical and human limitations of the jury system cannot be ignored."[79] *Harris*, unfortunately, demonstrates that

Bruton was wrong in at least one respect: these limitations can, in fact, "be ignored."

Finally, there is another—almost self-evident—distinction between *Walder* and *Harris*. It is the distinction that Justice Frankfurter explicitly relied upon in carving the *Walder* exception out of the general rule of *Agnello*. It was this very distinction—as we have previously noted—that the Chief Justice excised from his quotation of *Walder*:

> Of course, the Constitution guarantees a defendant the fullest opportunity to meet the accusation against him. He must be free to deny all the elements of the case against him without thereby giving leave to the Government to introduce by way of rebuttal evidence illegally secured by it, and therefore not available for its case in chief.[80]

There is surely an important difference between using illegally obtained evidence to impeach a defendant who takes the stand only to deny elements of the offense and using it to impeach the defendant who goes beyond that. According to Justice Frankfurter and the Court for which he was writing, it is a difference of constitutional magnitude. And it is a difference that was not unfamiliar to the author of the *Harris* opinion. While a circuit judge he wrote at least one opinion that rested entirely on the very difference that he dismissed as not persuasive in *Harris*. In *Lockley v. United States*[81]—a case that is essentially a carbon copy of *Harris*—Judge Burger, dissenting from the affirmance of a conviction, argued that the defendant "must be permitted to deny the criminal act charged without thereby giving leave to the government to introduce by way of rebuttal evidence otherwise inadmissible."[82] He also recognized "the hazards inherent in letting the full untested written confession in evidence, and then trying to limit the scope and weight which a jury should give to it."[83] Accordingly, he argued that the "proper procedure" was to admit "only that part of the written statement which does not go to the admission of acts which constitute necessary elements of the crime itself, but which at the same time constitute true impeachment . . . ."[84] This distinction was necessary because the "prejudicial impact of the full confession on the jury cannot be eliminated by instruction from the bench, no matter how carefully, pointedly, or precisely phrased."[85]

Judge Burger obviously regarded these distinctions—between impeaching as to the elements of the crime and impeaching as to collateral matters—as distinctions of principle when he wrote his opinion in *Lockley*. He apparently changed his mind when he decided *Harris*. Judges sometimes do that, as they are surely entitled to (perhaps especially when they have been promoted to a higher court in the interim). But even a recently elevated judge is obligated to give his readers some clue as to why distinctions once thought to be constitutionally mandated are no longer differences "in principle."

The Majority's Presentation of the Policy Considerations

THE BENEFITS OF IMPEACHMENT OUTWEIGH THE "SPECULATIVE
POSSIBILITY" THAT IMPERMISSIBLE POLICE CONDUCT WILL
BE ENCOURAGED.

Having distorted the two most important contrary precedents, the Court
briefly suggests three policy arguments. The first is that

> the benefits of [the impeachment] process should not be lost, in our view, because
> of the speculative possibility that impermissible police conduct will be encour-
> aged thereby. Assuming that the exclusionary rule has a deterrent effect on pro-
> scribed police conduct, sufficient deterrence flows when the evidence in question
> is made unavailable to the prosecution in its case in chief.[86]

This unsupported assurance of "sufficient deterrence" masks a failure to
consider the mechanism by which exclusionary rules are supposed to deter
deliberate police misconduct. The assumption underlying such rules is that
if illegally obtained evidence can be used in aid of securing convictions,
then the police will have an incentive to violate the law in instances where
they could not secure the evidence by lawful means.[87] Moreover, it is
widely acknowledged that absent an exclusionary rule there would be nothing to overcome this incentive, since other remedies directed punitively
against individual policemen appear to be unrealistic.[88] Accordingly, there
is no reason to expect an exclusionary rule to deter deliberate violations
unless it has eliminated all significant incentives toward that conduct. If an
exclusionary rule were to eliminate only part of the incentive—say if it
were to require the exclusion of illegally obtained evidence in 50 percent of
the cases randomly selected—it could not be expected to deter anywhere
near that percentage of violations. For in those instances where the police
could not secure the evidence by lawful means, they would still have everything to gain and nothing to lose by obtaining the evidence illegally: they
would have helped secure convictions in half the cases without endanger-
ing the convictions—or anything else of value to them—in the other cases.
Accordingly, they would probably still engage in the prohibited conduct
most of the time even though its fruits could only be used in some of the
cases. This would be especially so in those instances—like the random
percentage exclusion hypothesized above—where the police would not
know at the time they contemplated the unlawful conduct whether its fruits
would or would not be usable at the trial.[89]

That this is precisely the situation with regard to the impeachment use of
statements secured in violation of *Miranda* is easily demonstrated. Consider a situation where the police have lawfully arrested a defendant and
have obtained enough admissible evidence to make a prima facie case. But

their case is not strong, and so an effort is made to elicit a statement by the defendant that would bolster it. The defendant evidences some willingness to talk but when he is asked whether he would like to speak to a lawyer first, he shrugs his shoulders and says, "Why not?" The police know that under *Miranda* he must be given a lawyer before any further questioning; they also realize that as soon as a lawyer arrives there is little chance that any further questioning will be permitted. Under the *Harris* rule, what possible incentive would the police have to comply with *Miranda* by either terminating the interrogation or securing a lawyer? Is it not clear that any reasonable policeman, calculating the advantages and disadvantages of securing a lawyer for the defendant before any further questioning, would always conclude that he should proceed with the questioning in violation of *Miranda*?[90] If the defendant then makes a statement, the net effect of the violation will be that the police will have in their possession an item of evidence they would not have been able to secure had they complied with *Miranda*. And this evidence might very well make the difference between winning and losing the ultimate case. It might well persuade a defendant who would otherwise take the witness stand to "waive" his right to do so. (And it is widely acknowledged that a defendant—at least one without a criminal record—who takes the witness stand and tells his story has a considerably better chance of acquittal than one who stands mute.[91]) Or if the defendant does take the stand, his admission could be used by the government, ostensibly to impeach him, but realistically to shore up its otherwise weak case.

It may be argued that this reflects an overly cynical view of police decisions, that it should not be assumed that policemen will act on the basis of a calculation of advantages rather than out of desire to follow the law. But of course the exclusionary rule itself is based on precisely that assumption. If policemen could be counted on to follow the law without regard to the advantages of violation, there would be little need for an exclusionary rule.

A DEFENDANT'S PRIVILEGE TO TESTIFY IN HIS OWN BEHALF "CANNOT BE CONSTRUED TO INCLUDE THE RIGHT TO COMMIT PERJURY."

Having announced that "sufficient deterrence" is provided by excluding illegally secured statements from the government's case in chief, the Court goes on to respond to an argument no one made:

> Every criminal defendant is privileged to testify in his own defense, or to refuse to do so. But that privilege cannot be construed to include the right to commit perjury.[92]

To the extent the "right to perjury" rhetoric is intended to conjure up the assumption that trial testimony is necessarily less credible than a statement given to the police without the safeguards of *Miranda*, it is of course subject to significant qualification.[93] (In *Harris* itself, the District Attorney acknowledged that the defendant's pretrial, station-house rendition of the events for which he was convicted had been a "false account"![94])

More fundamentally, the entire argument is a straw man. Of course a defendant has no "right to commit perjury." But this was hardly petitioner's argument. Neither does a defendant have the right to commit murder, and yet the government may not prove that crime by means of an illegally obtained statement. Nor, indeed, could it introduce such a statement as part of its case in chief in a perjury prosecution. Whether it should be permitted to use it to prove perjury in the context of a trial for a different crime is the question, and it is not answered by denying that there is a right that no one asserted.

The real issue, never addressed by the Court, is where to strike the balance between the state's interest in challenging the defendant's credibility and the defendant's interest in excluding illegally secured evidence. Of course the value of an exclusionary rule is not absolute, but neither is the value of challenging credibility. Even the Court suggests that not all pretrial statements may be used to impeach: before a statement may be so used, it says, its "trustworthiness [must satisfy] legal standards."[95] This formulation, which seems to indicate that only evidence of uncertain reliability is unavailable for impeachment use, suggests some important questions as to which the Court's opinion gives little guidance. For example, may physical evidence discovered as the result of a coerced statement—as where the defendant is tortured into telling where he hid the murder weapon—now be used to impeach? May an incriminating statement elicited as the result of a grant of "use" immunity be used to discredit a defendant's testimony? (One can imagine the Court paraphrasing the *Harris* opinion as follows: "the shield provided by" the grant of immunity should not "be perverted into a license to use perjury by way of defense, free from the risk of confrontation with prior inconsistent statements.") Thus the absolute manner in which the Court rejects the "right to perjury" provides no limiting principle capable of reasoned application to the range of other cases likely to arise;[96] more importantly, it is not responsive to the real issues presented by the case.

HAD PETITIONER'S STATEMENT BEEN ELICITED BY "SOME THIRD PERSON," IT COULD HAVE BEEN USED TO IMPEACH HIM.

The final argument offered by the Court in support of its conclusion can best be characterized as the first half of a non sequitur:

> Had inconsistent statements been made by the accused to some third person, it could hardly be contended that the conflict could not be laid before the jury by way of cross-examination and impeachment.[97]

It is difficult to understand what conclusion is supposed to be derived from that statement. Of course inconsistent statements made to "some third person" could be introduced for "cross-examination and impeachment." They could be introduced in the government's case in chief as well. For the Fifth Amendment simply does not apply to statements made to private persons, and there is thus no constitutional distinction between the use of such statements in the government's case in chief and its use in cross-examination for impeachment. Is the Court suggesting that all statements made to a third person that would be admissible should also be admissible when elicited by the government? We assume not: for that would—simply put—mark an end to the privilege against self-incrimination (as well as the exclusion of evidence secured in violation of the Fourth Amendment, which also is inapplicable to third persons). Or is the Court expanding the scope of the privilege by applying the rules currently applicable to statements elicited by government agents to statements elicited by private persons? We doubt this as well. But we have been unable to discern any other plausible interpretation of the Court's argument.[98]

Conclusion

Our disagreement with the result reached in *Harris* is not, as we previously noted, the reason we selected it for analysis and criticism. We have no doubt that a respectable opinion affirming the conviction could have been written. But such an opinion would have been obligated to acknowledge that it was working important changes in the law—that it was squarely overruling the general rule of *Agnello* and *Walder*, significantly cutting back on central aspects of *Miranda*, and virtually rejecting the very assumptions on which all exclusionary rules designed to control deliberate police misconduct are built. This is not to say that the Court's prior conclusions respecting these matters should be regarded as sacrosanct. But issues of this moment deserve more substantial treatment than they were here accorded.

A thoughtful opinion acknowledging the value choices at issue and resolving them against the defendant would at least have been candid, though not in our view convincing. This one was neither. It was little more than a vote—a reflection of numerical power. Its intention was apparently not to persuade, but merely to prevail. It has prevailed—for the moment—but, to the credit of the Supreme Court as an institution, decisions that fail to persuade often do not long outlast the justices who wrote them.

The Court's philosophy obviously is changing and doubtless will continue to change as more appointments are made. Ideological ebb and flow is an inherent, though generally more gradual, part of the American judicial system. But failures of logic and candor are neither inherent nor desirable in our highest Court. In that regard, the *Harris* opinion seems to have taken an overdrawn academic caricature of the Warren Court's methodology and used it as a recipe. What is vice in a liberal, however, is not necessarily virtue in a conservative. In light of President Nixon's 1968 campaign attacks on the Warren Court, it is perhaps not surprising that his appointees should seek to reverse many of the holdings of that Court with something more than deliberate speed. The real disappointment is that men of the stuff of Justices Harlan, Stewart, and White would have joined this sort of opinion.

This comment was something of a "gotcha": I am aware of no attempt to answer any of its (often deadly) criticisms. On the other hand Harris has not been overruled or even apparently questioned by the Court. Maybe I should have gone to divinity school after all.

The Proposed "Good Faith" Exception to the Exclusionary Rule (1983)

Police officers don't think in airy theoretical concepts like "probable cause," "clear indication," "mere suspicion," or whatever. Those are hard enough for lawyers to get their minds around, let alone nonlawyers engaged in the grueling, often fatally dangerous, day-to-day work of law enforcement. They think instead—as most of us do most of the time—in checklists, clusters of necessary ingredients. Thus, for example, when a suspect is in custody, you must warn him (a) that he doesn't have to say anything, (b) that he is entitled to a lawyer before answering any questions, and (c) that if he cannot afford a lawyer one will be appointed for him. Actually this one's pretty easy, since an officer can, and most do, carry a card listing these (*Miranda*) warnings.

The question when one can conduct a search or otherwise investigate further is obviously one with many more variations, and thus written lists are impracticable. But it still helps to have lists in your head—lists that in fact are reiterated (and updated) by shift sergeants at police roll calls—this time lists denoting the sort of cluster of observations that is generally necessary and sufficient to justify a search in a given situation. Take the lookout for an airline drug courier: here investigators are likely to be instructed that they can investigate further if an individual has paid for his ticket in cash, not checked any luggage, and is among the last passengers off the plane. Why? Because in such-and-such a case a court of relevant jurisdiction has held that together those factors add up to sufficient cause for a further inquiry or search. Don't do it on anything less, the investigators are likely to be told, or you will lose the bust.

Or another, at a traffic checkpoint: you may subject the suspect to a further search if his pupils are dilated, his speech is slurred, and his behavior upon confronting you was furtive. Together that adds up to probable cause: anything less and you will lose the bust.

Obviously, particularly in this last example—and I must have heard it 100 times when I was a public defender—there is already opportunity for an officer (who in fact has uncovered drugs in his subsequent search) retroactively to "take the edge" a little. As a matter of fact, there is room to take the edge on all three scores: almost any speech can in good faith be remembered as slurred, any behavior as somehow furtive, even any pupils as a little dilated. (Notice that I am not here suggesting that anyone was framed. I do not believe that police ordinarily search people without some basis, however ephemeral, for doing so. My suggestion is only that the factors bearing on probable cause are often so "soft" that an officer can *in all good faith*—after all, the drugs *were* found—conjure up a recollection that fits the legally sufficient profile.)

Many critics of the proposed good faith exception argue that "mistakes" that in fact *weren't* committed in good faith will be passed off in court as innocent. That danger does exist. (Police officers very seldom misrepresent evidence that bears on the defendant's guilt—no more than anybody else are they ordinarily interested in convicting an innocent person—but the temptation to falsify evidence that bears only on the "legal technicalities" surrounding the legality of a search *that in fact uncovered incriminating evidence* must be very great, and we know that they are succumbed to with some frequency.) I want to make a different sort of critique, however: one that assumes no bad faith whatever, that assumes instead (as I take it one adopting the exception would wish to assume) that our various law enforcement officials will tell the truth in court about their states of mind.

Here's how it seems to me it will almost certainly work. Some police officer, somewhere, will forget one item on one of his shopping lists—remember, we are assuming this is all in good faith—and, say, search someone for drugs on the basis of slurred speech and furtive behavior without checking to see if his pupils are dilated. The case comes to court under the new regime. The judge listens to the evidence and says, as I take it the proposed revision requires him to say, "I don't have to reach the question whether slurred speech and furtive behavior alone might have added up to probable cause"—in fact we have hypothesized that they wouldn't— "because I find that the mistake, if in fact it was a mistake, was made in good faith. The officer *thought* he had probable cause, and thus the evidence can be admitted."

So far it follows the prescribed scenario precisely: neither the police officer nor the judge has misbehaved. The problem comes in how this decision, which I assume would be affirmed if it were appealed under the new regime, will be reported to other police at other roll calls. I think I know. (I can almost hear Sergeant Esterhaus of *Hill Street Blues* saying just this.) "Some good news, gentlemen: the court of X has held that slurred speech and furtive behavior alone are enough to justify a search for drugs. By all means look for dilated pupils if you can, but they are no longer necessary. Slurred speech and furtive behavior alone are enough, so let's expect a few more drug bookings, shall we?"

You see what's happened, and it seems to me inexorable. Given the actual dynamics of police behavior and communication, the moment a certain bundle of observations is held to be enough to constitute good faith, that bundle will for practical purposes also become the operational definition of probable cause—and will have done so without bad faith on anyone's part. The clever reader will also understand that the process will not stop at the removal of merely one of the previously required ingredients of probable cause. In the next case, to continue with our example, some rookie cop may act on the basis of a belief that furtive behavior is enough to justify a search; the court, if it is doing its job under the new standard, will hold that he acted in good faith; and the word will go out, if police sergeants are doing *their* job, that furtive behavior alone was held sufficient in the Y case. So the onion will be skinned layer by layer, until there isn't much left at all. In some abstract platonic world, "probable cause" may remain a significant requirement, but on the streets it will, in progressive steps, have been whittled down to a shadow of its former self. And all with nothing but good faith on everybody's part.

Thus far the good faith exception appears generally to have been limited to cases involving defective search warrants. E.g., United States v. Leon, 468 U.S. 897 (1984). However, as of this writing agitation to extend it further persists, perhaps principally in Congress. Cf. Arizona v. Evans, 115 S.Ct. 1185 (1995).

Sure Money Talks, but That's Precisely the Reason We Need the Reasonable Doubt Standard (1995)

Obviously the reasonable doubt standard was the straw that broke the O.J. Simpson prosecution's back. No jury in the world could have supposed it to be *likely* that someone other than Simpson murdered Nicole Brown and Ronald Goldman, or the world's gone mad. The jury simply has to have thought it probable that he did it, but—in light of the defense's vigorous and occasionally telling attacks on the prejudices and procedures of certain of the police officers involved—wasn't convinced beyond a reasonable doubt.

I'm aware that the jury was overwhelmingly African-American, and that is probably part of the explanation for the aquittal. But it was even more overwhelmingly female, largely working-class female, and an acknowledged wife-beater was on trial for his ex-wife's murder. Surely this "gender card," though it received little attention, should have been enough at least partially to neutralize the "race card."

Thus part of the explanation must also reside in the reasonable doubt standard. Because of that standard, a seemingly guilty man has walked free. Is this reason enough to get rid of it? The suggestion's already being made, but it is one of the series of bad ideas that is sure to flow from the Simpson verdict.

Here's why. In the overwhelming majority of criminal cases the defendant is not a rich celebrity, but rather someone who is poor or, worse luck, working-class (because then he won't be entitled to a public defender and will have to take what he can afford, which will probably be worse). The defense in such ordinary cases is outgunned (always) by the superior investigative resources of the prosecution and (usually) by its superior trial experience. The function of the reasonable doubt instruction is to help level this tilted playing field. Getting rid of it would be a terrible mistake, one that would result in the conviction of a significant number of innocent people.

In this case, though, the playing field didn't need to be leveled. If anything, given the defendant's resources, it was tilted in favor of the *defense*, and the instruction served only to make it more so.

Well, should we then think about abolishing or at least weakening the reasonable doubt standard for affluent defendants who can afford fancy lawyers and experts? The temptation may be understandable, but it can't be done. For one thing, it would violate the Sixth Amendment, which heretofore has been interpreted to guarantee everyone's right not simply to counsel of some sort—even if it has to be paid for by the state—but to whatever counsel (and other assistance) he can afford to buy himself. In fact, whether deservedly or not, this latter right is more securely part of the Amendment's original meaning than the former. Attaching to its exercise the penalty of losing the protection of the reasonable doubt instruction would undoubtedly be unconstitutional.

And even if that constitutional constraint is one you'd like to change—though one should always be wary about tampering with the Constitution, particularly on the basis of one unfortunate case—it seems transparently impossible to write a statute (or more to the point, a constitutional provision) that could fairly and effectively separate out those whose defenses have been so costly and effective that they do not need the protection the reasonable doubt instruction provides. (Come to think of it, on this theory an effective defense alone, no matter how much or how little it cost, would seem enough to eliminate the need for an instruction designed to level the field. But now we're verging on the truly perverse.)

Thus despite the unsettling outcome of the trial in Los Angeles, it would be a dreadful idea to use it as the occasion to start weakening the reasonable doubt standard. Sure, here as elsewhere, money talks. It's precisely because it does, however, that we need to keep the standard. O.J.'s walking is the price we pay for giving ordinary defendants even a fighting chance.

Letter to Stanford *Campus Report* (1991)[99]

Though my job is one that has allowed me to write about just about anything on earth I wanted to, my immediate environs during most of my career have been university campuses, which haven't always done so well themselves in complying with the Bill of Rights.

The proposal to abolish the reasonable doubt standard, in order to "make it easier to find students guilty of misconduct" (*Campus Report*, Nov. 13)—substituting something Professor Rhode describes as more on the order of requiring a minimum 70 percent certainty of guilt—continues a disturbing trend on this campus. The argument that no one actually goes to prison as a result of a student disciplinary charge, that no criminal conviction is technically entailed, is eerily reminiscent of arguments common in the 1950s in defense of low burdens of proof "merely," say, costing one her livelihood or ordering her to leave the country. (The latter is actually cited by the charter change's proponents as a supporting precedent.) Disciplinary proceedings are unmistakably punitive in purpose and effect—replicas of criminal proceedings as close as a university has jurisdiction to bring—and sometimes they can shape the entire course of a person's life.

Admittedly "[m]ore than just the interests of the defendant [are] at stake" here, but that is so in every case where society seeks to punish, on campus or off. Of course "[t]here are interests of other individuals" in sexual assault and other cases—but again, every bit as much off campus as on. There are indeed "interests in the [Stanford] honor code in particular," but most communities across the country believe, correctly, they have interests at least as strong in the enforcement of their criminal laws. And while it is true the proposed change will make it easier to convict the guilty—just as it would in any community—it will do so at the same inevitable cost of rendering more likely the punishment of the innocent. (Had the proponents really squared the circle and discovered a standard capable of more readily punishing the guilty without "put[ting] any innocent student at risk," we would all join in insisting that it be immediately imposed not simply at Stanford but everywhere.)

The proposal is part of a broader assault on the Bill of Rights on this campus. Last year this university cut back on the protection of the First

Amendment by permitting the punishment of certain types of inflammatory, insulting, and disgusting speech. The Fifth Amendment is this year's nominee. The general argument underlying this assault is that the campus (at least the Stanford campus) is an usually fragile place, where the interest in law and order must be given extraordinary precedence over the liberties the Constitution guarantees throughout the rest of society. But the upper middle class has been making that claim for its communities since the dawn of the republic, rightly without effect. In fact in most ways a campus is a *less* fragile community than others—vastly less fragile, for example, than racially mixed inner city ghettos, where the Bill of Rights is fully applicable—if anything, a place where liberty should unusually be honored, the lessons of the Constitution communicated to our students.

The First Amendment last year, the Fifth Amendment this. Why not have done with it, and declare at one stroke that Stanford cannot live with the instability that necessarily accompanies *any* of the protections of the Bill of Rights? By our example we might even trigger a nationwide move for a complete abolition of that troublesome document. The arguments in favor of repeal are considerably stronger off campus than on.

The proposal was not adopted.

Memorandum to Other Members of Yale University Police Advisory Board (1971)

Indeed, though Stanford has trouble just staying even, sometimes a university needs to be more *protective of individual liberties than we require the outside world to be. The following arose out of an allegation that a Yale campus police officer had solicited a student to assist with the surreptitious electronic surveillance of his classmates. Since it boiled down to a one-on-one swearing contest without serious corroboration of either version (indeed, as often happens, with a little impeachment of each) we refused officially to find the charges (in this case against the officer) to be true, though we weren't convinced they weren't. On the broader policy issues, I tried, without success, to get my colleagues to adopt the following language.*

Draft Language for "Policy" Section of Report (12/19/71):
Our investigation has stirred large policy issues with respect to which, despite sometime protestations to the contrary on all levels, the university has taken no clear stand. We fear that simply calling attention to these issues without attempting some resolution of them will have the effect of leaving policy undefined—if not forever, at least for a significant period of time—and therefore have decided to state our necessarily somewhat hastily

formed views with respect to the issues raised, with the suggestion that they become university policy until such time as another group gives the issues more careful attention and supersedes this report.

Society's legitimate demands for the exposure and deterrence of conduct harmful to others, and the individual's demand for privacy, are inevitably in a state of tension. We do not pretend that the accommodation of these interests is any easier in a university than it is in any other segment of society. We do, however, start from the assumption that the demands of privacy must be given more heed in a university than they generally are given in other contexts. For universities historically have been, and must continue to be if they are to perform their functions, enclaves where ideological quest and experimentation are not simply tolerated but actively fostered. The beliefs and sympathies of the students and faculty can therefore constitute no proper concern of the university or any of its administrative or police agents. We do not suggest that "privacy" be interpreted, in a university context any more than in any other, so as to deny police officials all opportunity to discover and punish conduct that harms persons other than the actor, nor is it the case that police practices tolerated outside the university necessarily have no place within it. We do, however, reject the assumption made by the police witnesses we heard (a natural enough assumption, as we are not convinced they had ever been told anything different) that any police practice approved by the courts for use outside the university is equally tolerable within it.

Our attempts to reach the proper accommodation between the need for privacy and the legitimate demands of law enforcement are reflected in the following recommended statements of policy.

1. Wiretapping and bugging are permissible outside a university only pursuant to a court order. Because of the unusual need for an atmosphere of privacy in a university, university police officials should under no circumstances seek or assist others in seeking such a court order. In other words, to the extent the university has power to prevent it, wiretapping and bugging should under no circumstances be tolerated at Yale.

2. A student informant is akin to a bug in that he functions as an undisclosed transmitter of information given under the impression the police are not listening. The same policy should therefore obtain, and university officials should neither use nor help others use students as informants. This does not mean that university police are precluded from seeking or accepting help from students who were victims of crimes or percipient witnesses thereto so long as said students did not become witnesses at the behest of the police. It *does* mean that police are not to make students their agents in order that they may, by concealing their relation with the police, gather and report information the police could not themselves gather.

The political views of any member of the university community are no business of the university, and university police are therefore to seek information concerning those views neither from students nor from any other source.

3. University police should never assist the efforts of other law enforcement bodies when they investigate on the campus or with respect to members of the university community, unless they have in advance publicly disclosed their need for and intention to use outside aid in connection with a specified event they feel they cannot handle alone. Should such outside agencies insist on coming on the campus for any purpose, university police should take all possible steps to record their presence and activities and render a full report thereon to the chief, who shall make it available to [the university secretary] and this board.

What Counts as Liberal? Some Observations on French Criminal Procedure and the "Projet Peyrefitte" (1980)

I spent the summer of 1980 in Paris. In addition to what I usually do in Paris—endlessly wander the streets and art museums—I (a) followed the debate in the newspapers over Minister of Justice Alain Peyrefitte's proposed set of criminal law reforms, and (b) sat in on some interrogations conducted by Claude Hanoteau, the *juge d'instruction* then in charge of investigating homicides. The following—which obviously sets our American methods of investigating crimes into longer-range perspective than any of the foregoing—was the result. (Note that like the study appearing at pages 152–73 comparing the British and American approaches to controlling pretrial publicity, this one also concludes that for all its inefficiencies, people not being angels, the American approach is the safer. I'd be tempted to label myself a liberal were that not these days apparently regarded by people of both the left and right as a confession of enormous moral shortcoming; let's just say I'm a Yankee doodle dandy.)

I've never published this before, because although I read French comfortably, I was insufficiently secure of my ability to follow oral French—especially when several people are shouting at each other simultaneously (Hanoteau sometimes, and quite successfully, staged Agatha Christie–type confrontations)—to be sure I'd followed every word of the interrogations. I do so now, however, at the urging of a number of comparativist colleagues who have read the piece and note, correctly, that because of the unusual access I was given the paper is a likely irreplicable resource. Also, even though you're warned that I didn't get every word, I got most of them and certainly got the gist, masterful interrogation whose only client was the *truth. (Though I still end up concluding that any serious move in the direction of attempting to transplant the French system to America would be a mistake.)*

Sometime this fall the French will enact a far-reaching reform, mainly procedural, of their criminal law. (The bill passed the National Assembly in June and thus needs only the approval, all but certain, of the Senate.[100]) This "Projet de Loi Sécurité et Liberté"—or "Projet Peyrefitte," after its sponsor, Minister of Justice Alain Peyrefitte—has been the object of what would count in the United States as incredible public attention. *Le Monde* has a piece on it virtually every day—generally an attack by a staff columnist or a guest attack by a lawyer or law professor—and I have yet to meet an educated French person (of any profession) who is without a quite clear idea of what the bill does and why it is evil.[101]

In general the critics are right: most of the bill is law-and-order-style repression pure and simple.[102] Its central object is to punish more severely acts of violence, and it does so not simply by directly increasing sentences but also by limiting the invocation of attenuating circumstances and the use of the "sursis" (remission or suspension of all or part of a sentence).[103] The provision relating to recidivists—essentially doubling their sentence each time around—is particularly harsh. Early release, work release, and parole are all significantly curtailed, and the authority of the juge d'application des peines, which was significantly weakened in 1978, is now further reduced (or more precisely, subjugated to that of prosecutorial and correctional officials). There are also some new offenses—perhaps most notably one that is aimed at controlling graffiti but whose language goes so far ("la destruction, la dégradation ou la détérioration volontaire d'un bien quelconque") as to render it, appropriately, the object of derision. At the last minute Peyrefitte also added a provision significantly expanding the authority of the police to demand that citizens produce identification papers. (Interestingly, the principal police syndicates quickly criticized this addition, as dangerous to individual liberties and probably ineffective!)[104]

These, however, are not the provisions that have drawn most of the critical attention in the press. To some extent that must be because it's hard to say anything very interesting in opposition to them. ("It's cruel" and "It'll do more harm than good" are both probably right but certainly boring. One point with somewhat more interest has been made a couple of times, that the new "get tough" policy seems to be reserved for "street crimes" and is not even theoretically being extended to the sorts of crimes that might be committed by people like us.) Instead, the features of the project that have drawn the most critical fire are those attempting to reduce the range of penalties for (and thus discretion in sentencing with regard to) a given crime, and those attempting to expedite the process by placing time limits on the instruction and opening the possibility that certain cases involving crimes (punishable by more than five years) will go straight to court without the lengthy delay an instruction entails.

Be very clear about one thing: these are not the attacks of hard-hats, but rather of those with whom an American liberal would most naturally ally himself, those who are also disgusted by the general repressive tenor of the project. Yet to our hypothetical American liberal it must seem initially confusing that these features should be condemned along with the rest, indeed that they should be the ones to evoke the most ink. Unbridled discretion and consequent disparity in sentencing is something we all are (or should be) worried about in the United States: given that French society is observably more class-ridden as ours, the reasons for finding sentencing discretion less frightening there are not apparent. And yet the French liberal literature seems unanimous on this point: "individualization" of sentences is a great and time-honored tradition, and the project must therefore be condemned for threatening it.

Similarly, pretrial delay is an absolute scandal in France. Forty-five percent of those in custody are awaiting trial, delays of two to three years before trial on serious charges are standard—recall that all this is in the context of a system where pretrial release in such cases is very rare—and delays of even five years are not regarded as terribly unusual. Nor is it at all bizarre to expect the elimination of the instruction to generate a court proceeding that is public (as of course the instruction is not) and in which counsel for both sides play a genuine role in bringing out the facts (as they emphatically do not during instruction. Moreover, a French trial now essentially comprises a review of the juge d'instruction's report with essentially no participation by defense counsel and only occasional advice from the prosecutor.) Thus in eliminating the instruction and thereby significantly reducing pretrial delay, the project might be moving France toward something more nearly resembling an Anglo-American adversary proceeding.

Well, all that may be good or bad, but it certainly doesn't seem illiberal, and in this country it would count as quite the opposite. Why, then, is the French left so united in condemning these features along with the rest of the Projet Peyrefitte? A major part of it has to be guilt by association, buoyed by an understandable distrust of the motives of Peyrefitte and his fellows. (The man is a primitive of a species we have happily been spared for a few years: his interviews seem mandatorily to begin with an attack on the honesty of the press and the charge that the opponents of the project are all Communists or fellow-travelers. In fairness it should be noted that hyperbole seems generally more common in France than here: the favorite charge of *opponents* of the project is that it reinstitutes the Vichy government.)

I won't hold out any longer for a surprise ending, though (if only because I know it wouldn't be a real surprise): the "liberal consciousness" in France in 1980 is obviously significantly different from what it is in the United States, and thus quite different institutional inferences are likely to be drawn from a concern for the dignity of the individual. As is common in descriptions of legal/political "consciousness" I shall resort to a comparison that is both oversimplified and helpful, in this case a comparison with the consciousness that dominated American liberalism during the New Deal period (and whose vestiges can be found, of course, in much legal and other theorizing). According to this vision all cases are different and they are thus best handled on their own individual merits—all pros, cons, and intricacies being carefully and fully evaluated—by experts of good will and experience whose business it is to engage in a careful weighing without the procrustean interference of some governing rule that is by definition at least potentially insensitive to nuance. In short, leave important decisions to the experts and don't bind them too closely by some rule that may not have foreseen the situation.

That fundamental difference in consciousness having been identified, I would like nonetheless to look more closely at two issues I've mentioned—discretion in sentencing, and "instruction" versus trial-type determinations of guilt—and ask what, if anything, we can learn from the French or they from us.

Discretion in the Criminal Process

You will have noticed that the subtitle has broadened the inquiry somewhat, so as to include the question of discretion in deciding what charges to lodge. And indeed it is there I want to begin, for two reasons—first, because this topic has for several years dominated American debate about the nature of the French criminal process, and second, to highlight a paradox, which I'm not sure has previously been noted, in the conventional view of the French system, that this system, which at least some commentators suggest has minimized prosecutorial and police discretion in charging, has all the while been quite vociferously congratulating itself on the immense discretion in sentencing it allows. A paradox this stark must at least strongly suggest that half of the description may be wrong. The questions with which I wish to start, therefore, are questions we've grown used to: (1) Do the French prosecutorial authorities have significant effective discretion in deciding what charges to bring? (2) Does the French system have an analogue to the guilty plea (as it claims not to)? (3) Is there plea bargaining in France? The answers are yes, not really, and no (though the French can hardly be proud of the reasons for this last).

I'm not the first to observe that in dealing with French officials one is likely to get formalistic answers—here, that "of course" if a defendant is guilty of a given offense he must be charged with it. "I note," I then say, "that voluntary arson is a capital offense. Aren't you sometimes tempted to omit the allegation of voluntariness in filing your charges?" Well, you see, I have to understand that that's a very old law (to its credit, in fact, the Projet Peyrefitte is changing it) and surely I wouldn't favor *executing* such a person, etc., etc. I'm afraid the fact here is rather clear: there is a good deal of charging discretion in the French system. (Indeed, the practice of "correctionalizing" a crime down to a délit by withholding allegation of provable aggravating circumstances has long been part of standard descriptions of the French system.) Is that discretion bounded by any set of guidelines? Apparently, so far as I've been able to tell, none more precise than the guideline of good sense. (Obviously officials whose hornbook description of their practice is that they charge what the statutes say are not going to issue a guide to altering the statutes.) Professor Goldstein and Mr. Marcus are troubled by the fact that no *judicial* official rides herd effectively on such decisions,[105] but in the context of the French system I'm not quite sure what to make of that: the French prosecutor is a magistrat of identical training and rank with the three magistrats who sit beside him on the bench, acting as judges. Of course his perspective is that of a law enforcement official. But given that the entire French system is one in which law enforcement officials of one sort or another make the effective determinations, and the judiciary simply "checks over the papers," one shouldn't make much of the fact that the prosecutor/magistrat's decision on *this* issue is essentially final. Yes, there is prosecutorial discretion in France, as there is here. It's probably a little less frightening there than here, since the prosecutors are probably a little less adversarial there than here. No, it isn't very effectively supervised by the judiciary there, but then nobody even pretends it is here.

Is there an analogue of the guilty plea? Well, there are lots of confessions and lots of uncontested trials—in fact these are by far the most common— and that has to be largely because the defendants realize what all participants acknowledge to be the case, that in sentencing a court will go significantly easier on a cooperating and "repentant" culprit. So far it's like a guilty plea, but it isn't ultimately, since it doesn't perform the same system-maintaining function of aborting of the trial. Confession or not, the juge d'instruction or the police will quite laboriously check out the facts of the case. Contested or not, the trial judges will ordinarily see their role as one of reviewing the work of the juge d'instruction or the police (albeit very briefly, in both cases). Thus what is functionally a "guilty plea" may get you a lighter sentence, but it doesn't have the same effect it has here, of relieving the state of the obligation to go through the process it would have to go through were there no such plea.

Is there plea bargaining in France? Much as it runs against the prejudice with which I started, there is not. It just doesn't happen. But why not? Professors Langbein and Weinreb are right that "in France plea bargaining is contrary to practice and to professional ethics alike,"[106] but that names symptoms; it does not provide an explanation. Given what has gone before, however, the explanation is not far off. Indeed, Goldstein and Marcus— who are skeptical of the claim that plea bargaining does not exist—should have realized they were on the trail when they noted that trials take about five minutes each.[107] If trials take five minutes, why bargain? What's in it for the prosecutor?

Of course that cheats, since the trial isn't really where the French criminal process is to be found, but the answer lies in the same direction. The trial is really just a look over the shoulder of the juge d'instruction or the police. So there, I guess, is where you would strike your bargain: you'd offer to cooperate early in exchange for a lesser charge later on. In this game, however, the players include the police, the juge d'instruction, the prosecutor, the chambre d'accusation, and either the tribunal correctionnel or the cour d'assize, each with its own set of responsibilities and its own concern for its reputation in its own hierarchy. It is thus not clear whom you would bargain with, and whether they could bind the others. (If you've ever dealt with the French bureaucracy—even, say, at the post office—you'll know this is not a frivolous concern.) Assume that can be worked out, though: again we must ask what "the state" has to gain by a bargain with the defendant. As I already noted, confessions don't close the inquiry (as they essentially do in the United States): every facet of the case is checked out anyway. Since the American debate over French criminal procedure has been marked to a degree by charges that one's adversary doesn't know what he is talking about, perhaps I should explicitly note that at least on this point I do. I spent several days observing the investigations of Claude Hanoteau, one of the most respected juges d'instruction in Paris. The man obviously takes pride in his dossiers and checks *everything*, confession (as there almost invariably is) or no. (When I would ask him why, he would either shrug and say "Perhaps we are too thorough," or tell me the story of some rapist who had confessed to an extra rape or two to help him clear his docket.) One day the pressure of events may force a change, but now, in France, we are dealing within a system where the defendant probably has confessed (because the privilege against self-incrimination appears only in the texts—none of our fetishes about warnings before interrogation, lawyers during the initial police interrogation, or pretending your silence won't be construed against you[108]) and within which the facts will be checked carefully nonetheless (though I'm prepared to assume less carefully when there is not an instruction). There are no bargains because as the system is presently managed the state would gain nothing of significant value by bargaining.

The stage thus set, we can return to the issue raised by the Projet Peyrefitte, that of discretion in sentencing. Of course the issue is fully framed by the debate in the United States, without the necessity of a reference to the French experience, and those who know my other work will not be surprised to learn that I am with those who favor a "narrow window" (the French metaphor is "fouchette," or fork) and thus think the project makes no mistake in turning its back (to a degree) on the French tradition wherein "on juge l'homme, pas les faits." Every case *is* different, but the likelihood that differences that shouldn't be taken into account will be when the opportunity presents itself leads me to want to deny the opportunity. I won't pursue this further: you already know where you stand on this one. It should be noted, though, that virtually all of the objection to speeding up the process (principally the instruction) has been in terms of short-changing the opportunity to gather information on the defendant's background. (The existing procedure of flagrante délit is objected to on the same ground.) I have not seen serious suggestion that the time needed to learn the facts of the charge will not readily be made available. This objection, therefore, is one that seems to stand or fall with one's assessment of the objection to "deindividualizing" sentencing.

This should not be taken as an endorsement of the project's approach to sentencing, however. For Peyrefitte, standardizing sentencing almost invariably means standardizing it upward. (The arson example is one of the few that cuts the other way.) That seems wrong. Also to be reiterated is a point several have made, that this standardization is being prescribed only for "lower class" or blue-collar crime. Thus despite my general sympathy with the cause of standardization, were I French I'd doubtless oppose this as strongly as I would the bulk of the project. Unwrapped, it's a case of "Let's standardize for those guys, upwards."

Administrative Investigation versus Trial-Type Hearing as the Principal Guilt-Finding Mechanism

As French law now stands, instruction is mandatory for crimes and optional (it's essentially up to the prosecutor) in the case of délits. Peyrefitte decided to make scapegoats of the juges d'instruction and ranted and raved about them a good deal. The project ended up not so devastating, however, permitting the prosecutor, when he felt a crime did not need an instruction, to go directly to the chambre d'accusation, which had the option of remanding for an instruction if it thought it appropriate. The commission des lois weakened the bill still further, sending crimes automatically to a juge d'instruction, who has the option of sending them straight to the chambre d'accusation if *he* thinks an instruction is not needed. As Hanoteau pointed out, however, this is not likely to happen except in the clearest of cases: juges d'instruction, like everyone else in the French system, feel they are constantly being "graded" and will dread having sent forth without an instruction a case that turns out to be weak.[109] (That fear, of course, also has a lot to do with why instructions are currently so thorough.) Though little of substance still hangs in the balance, the debate has nonetheless raised issues of interest to an American.

Goldstein and Marcus's horror stories of French trials are, if anything, understated. Defendants are given little opportunity to volunteer anything, but are called upon instead to react to (generally to corroborate) the police reports. Defense counsel are generally appointed (*"Gideon"* was decided in France in 1414, for whatever that turned out to be worth) and appear most often to be young women (which, it was plausibly suggested to me, may suggest the status of this sort of work). In San Diego we used to divide defense counsel into "fighters" and "dancers," the latter term denoting those lawyers who would die before they'd go to trial but gave it a hell of a shot at sentencing time. Whatever their age or gender, French defense attorneys are dancers. No attempt whatever is made to protect one's client from an abusive, face-making judge, in fact at that stage attorney inattention seems the order of the day. When it comes time to sentence, though (and of course this makes eminent good in light of everything that has been said in this paper), defense counsel comes alive and gives what is, usually, a splendid speech—no, oration, complete with the hand-on-chest-center pose one observes in the statues of the great orators in the lobby of the Palais de Justice. Well, they're good speeches, but by American standards they're lousy defenses and even lousier trials. The cour d'assizes puts on a considerably better show than the tribunal correctionnel, and presumably there is some substance beneath, but even there the focus is on the earlier investigation—in this case invariably an instruction—and the burden in fact if not in theory is on the defendant to show that the juge d'instruction should be "reversed."

Thus if you observe what happens in a French courtroom you will be horrified. To look there, however, is not to look at the French criminal process. If you look at the real process in serious cases, though—that is, at the work of the juge d'instruction—you will be dazzled, and find yourself praying that if you're ever unjustly charged with a crime God will loan Claude Hanoteau to the Boston police.[110]

But I've cheated again. The vast majority of délits are not handled by a juge d'instruction but rather are investigated by the police. Goldstein and Marcus thus report that "the overwhelming proportion of *délits* is likely to

proceed to trial with a dossier that is little more than a police report."[111]
Now either Goldstein and Marcus were so caught up in the debate that they
intended to mislead—a hypothesis which, knowing Goldstein, I reject[112]—
or they cannot have studied any significant number of French police dossiers, which bear little resemblance to the "police report" an experienced
American reader's mind will conjure up. They are not the cursory internal
documents we are used to, but rather documents prepared with the knowledge that they will be used in court as the fulcrum of the determination of
the defendant's guilt (and will, like everything else, be at least tacitly
"graded"). Based on what I've seen, they are likely to run about thirty
pages and include primary evidence—signed statements from all concerned, photographs, maps, etc. (The juge d'instruction's dossier is likely
to run volumes.) *Our* "police report," of course, is generally just a police
officer's summary and a rap sheet. (Of course ours are also much easier to
read. As Steve Martin has observed, "Those French have a different word
for *everything*.") Moreover, for the police too, the obtaining of a confession, which is entirely common during the first interrogation, does not
abort the inquiry as it would here.

Nonetheless, cops are cops, and everyone involved in the process with
whom I talked admitted—how could they say otherwise?—that the police are likely to be more biased, more outcome-oriented, than the juges
d'instruction. Obviously the comparative thoroughness of their investigations cannot fully correct for this, and neither, surely, can the defendant's
ultimate court appearance. So at least in the majority of cases, those where
a juge d'instruction does not become involved, the French criminal process is seriously defective in that the critical determinations are effectively made by persons who are likely to be predisposed toward finding
culpability.

Let us not lose our perspective, though. *That statement is true of something like 90 percent of all American criminal cases too.* (I refer, of course,
to the fact that a guilty plea means there will be no trial.) Just as it is myth
to suppose most French cases involve an instruction, it is greater myth to
suppose the ordinary guilt-determining mechanism in the United States is
the trial. (Of course no one *has* to plead guilty, but despite our pretense to
the contrary, we reward people handsomely for doing so.) Now there is a
check on these police determinations in our system that doesn't really exist
in the French system: defense counsel has the option, if he feels the police
investigation has gone seriously awry or that his client otherwise is not
getting a fair shake, of insisting on a real trial of the facts (as opposed to the
sort of appellate proceeding that a French "trial" actually amounts to).
That's a very important safeguard, though obviously its importance varies
with the quality of the defense attorney and everyone else involved in the
process.

If for some reason one were forced to choose between the American and French systems—though in the real world no such clean choice will ever confront a person or a nation—he would do well, I think, to cut through the myths of both systems and recognize that the important fact-finding will inevitably be done by the police. The real question thus is whether one more effectively keeps the police honest by (a) the American approach of extending the defendant the option of a truly independent second look by a court, or (b) the French approach of being more up-front in recognizing that the police determination is the real ball game (subject to only cursory review), thereby attempting to induce the police to realize that precisely *because* they are the crucial decision-makers, they had better try to behave that way rather than as the advocates the American system has made of its police. This is no easy call. Of course the American system would be preferable if the decision to go to trial were one that did not involve great risk for the defendant, but in order to keep the system operational we have been forced to make that option very risky indeed.

A more helpful question from an American's perspective is whether what is preferable about the French system, the somewhat greater sense of responsibility and neutrality entertained by the French police,[113] can somehow be grafted onto the American system. Surely we could do better in this regard were we to stop pretending that our effective guilt-finding process is to be found in the courtroom, but so long as the trial exists as a possible subsequent check on the police it will obviously be impossible to get them to behave with anything resembling genuine neutrality. If you know real judges will genuinely intervene later on, or even if you know they may, it's going to be hard to get *you* to act like a judge.

Preoccupied as my work has been with democracy, I don't think it's a sensible system for determining guilt or innocence[114] and thus might be inclined, stepping all the way back to the original position, to suppose that society might more sensibly assign such decisions to experts rather than to anything resembling "the people." But then one has to stop and recognize that in systems that have done so, the presumption of innocence has seemed to end up at best a verbal formula. Is that coincidence? Anyone who has tried a significant number of criminal cases must suspect that it is not. It surely was my impression, one I believe is shared by others, that a "new" jury is better from the defendant's perspective than an "old" one (i.e., one whose members had sat on other trials) and in most cases either was better than a judge. For cases fall into patterns—barring bizarre circumstances the *only* defense in a car theft case is that someone lent you the car, just as the *only* defense in a smuggling case that you were unaware the contraband was there. Those who have heard the defense several times before are much less inclined to believe it—even on the rare occasion when it's true. It is thus entirely understandable that more expertise has seemed to mean more convictions. That's not an unalloyed evil: the number of guilty people who get off in our system exceeds the number of innocent people who are convicted, and I'm as pleased as the next man to be able with a totally clear conscience to put a female friend on the Métro at midnight. But our system has not made this choice and for reasons that need not be rehearsed, I think we have been right in refusing to do so: a convicted innocent and an acquitted culprit are not even close to fungible.

At all events the idea of *substituting* all or even part of the French system for our own is unrealistic: our institutions have grown in a way that would make such a substitution impossible. Thus, here, we have so accustomed our police to the notion that they are not to be neutral (because someone else will supply the neutrality later on) that it would be reckless to move even part way to a model that depended for its fairness on their so acting. Indeed, the mirror image of this realization is what is animating so much of the French opposition to the Projet Peyrefitte: French concerned with individual liberties know that their attorneys and their courts aren't really equipped suddenly to behave like their Anglo-American counterparts, and thus quite rightly turn deaf ears to the claim that one really needn't worry about, say, a reduction in the incidence of instruction because, after all, there will be a public, adversary trial to take its place. The French are no more able to imitate us than we are to imitate them, or so at least we (both) should assume when someone suggests that we borrow an institution and substitute it for some liberty-protecting mechanism we have in place.

As I said, however, that needn't mean we shouldn't borrow what appear to be useful institutions or attitudes and *superimpose* them on those we have, in an effort further to safeguard the liberty of the individual. And here, it seems, there *is* something in French practice that could sensibly be borrowed without weakening any of our existing institutions. We should stop pretending that "in America we decide guilt or innocence by a trial," though we certainly should keep that institution as the check it now is. Rather, we should recognize candidly that in most cases guilt is determined by a police investigation, involving in many cases little more than the obtaining of a confession, in most a negotiated guilty plea. Once we recognize that *that* is really our criminal process, we should begin to take steps to render it more responsible, not simply by attempting to change police attitudes but also (and much more easily and realistically) by having the trial judge make a genuine inquiry into the facts, and the bargain, at the time of the guilty plea. I know there is some development along this line, but it should be accelerated and it should be more thoroughgoing. For the guilty plea is the core of our criminal process, a core we are not justified in ignoring simply because we have such impressive peripheries. Goldstein and

Marcus claim that in France "[p]rosecutors and examining judges generally do little more than confirm what the police have already done."[115] I think that's seriously overstated, at least in the case of the juge d'instruction, but even assuming it isn't, it represents a good deal more than our judges do in the vast majority of our cases.

7

Racial Discrimination

Excerpts from *Legislative and Administrative Motivation in Constitutional Law* (1970)[1]

Some of the chapters of this book, even on important topics, are short for the obvious reason that I haven't written much about them. This one's relatively short for a different reason, however: that racial discrimination is much discussed in Democracy and Distrust. Nonetheless, there's a whole lot here that isn't there. I begin my discussion here with excerpts from my "tenure piece," a 136-page tome I wrote during the first two years I taught. This was an important article, of which I remain proud, really the first to argue against what was then the conventional wisdom, that laws could not be constitutionally invalidated because of the motivations with which they had been enacted. As such it helped spearhead a modest "paradigm shift" in constitutional theory, from a "victim perspective" (one that invariably decides constitutional questions by looking at who is being harmed by the government action in issue, and how) to a "perpetrator perspective" (which holds that it will often be necessary and proper to inquire into who was responsible for the deprivation in issue, and with what apparent motivations).

Despite its originality and influence, however, I omit most of the article from this book,[2] for two reasons. The first is that it is very long.[3] I was a young man in a hurry, who couldn't take the time to write a shorter (or for that matter less jargon-laden) piece. I hadn't yet learned what much of the profession generally has, frankly, yet to learn, that people are more likely to read articles that are shorter, simpler, and written in English as opposed to legalese. The second reason I don't reprint the whole piece (or anything approaching it) is related to the first, that a number of more recent articles, written by others, have stated something not very different from my thesis much more economically.

Disproportionate racial impact is usually the best evidence that race has been employed as the criterion of selection. This frequent conjunction between impact and motivation is doubtless one reason courts generally have failed to indicate clearly which factor triggers the judicial response. The choice between the two is of more than theoretical interest, however. There are laws that fall most heavily on one racial group from which it would be difficult to infer racial motivation; in such situations the question whether impact or motivation triggers judicial review is obviously crucial. Moreover, the decision makers' statements of intention, the law's terms, and the historical context in which it was passed—while they can on occasion constitute persuasive evidence of motivation—would constitute irrelevant referents were an impact model to control. Finally, there is on a motivation theory the possibility that the inference of motivation that arises from the statistical impact can be rebutted. It is of course difficult to imagine that anything could have served as a rebuttal in *Gomillion* [v. *Lightfoot*[4]]. Given the delicacy with which the new [city] line wove its way through the old city [so as to exclude all but a handful of the city's four hundred previously resident black voters], it would have taken authenticated motion pictures of the coins being flipped or the computer running amok; surely no amount of legislative history, no matter how carefully doctored, could have served. But the statistics are not always so overwhelming, and convincing proof that the selection was in fact made at random would, on a motivation but not an impact theory, serve as a rebuttal.

Affirmative Duties of Accommodation

Where a regulation is challenged on the ground that it impermissibly disadvantages a group whose interests the Court is willing to compel government officials to go out of their way to protect, there can be no occasion to refer to the officials' motivation. In such situations the Court need only ask whether the group's interests have been disadvantaged to an intolerable extent and, if they have, order the state to eliminate the disadvantage it should have taken pains to avoid in the first place.

Such an affirmative duty of accommodation has been developed in the recent spate of "equal protection-poverty" cases.[5] The Court has determined that there are some disadvantages that the state simply cannot visit upon poor people, even if it takes a deviation from some broader policy in no sense designed to injure the poor to avoid doing so. The state is expected to consider the likelihood of its laws' unusually disadvantaging the poor in certain ways and, if necessary, to take intentional steps to avoid their doing so. Thus, when a law is challenged on the ground that it impermissibly disadvantages the poor, the Court has no occasion to refer to the motivation that produced it. It need only inquire whether the law has in fact unusually disadvantaged the poor to an extent under the circumstances impermissible and, if it has, order the state to take the steps necessary to eliminate the disadvantage.

The Duty to Be Neutral with Respect to Race: An Affirmative Duty to Seek a "Balanced" Impact, or a Duty Not to Use Race as a Criterion of Selection?

A number of commentators have asserted that government officials may, if they wish, go out of their way to favor the members of minority races without violating the Constitution. But none of whom I am aware, and certainly not the Court, has argued that such favoritism is constitutionally *required*: the Fourteenth Amendment is read only to require "neutrality" toward such groups. The difficult question is what neutrality ought to mean in this context. The guarantee of "the equal protection of the laws" might be construed to require that laws shall not in fact disproportionately disadvantage racial minorities; or it might mean simply that race shall not (at least outside of "affirmative action" situations[6]) be employed as a criterion of selection for benefit or deprivation. On the choice between these propositions turns the relevance of governmental motivation to problems of racial discrimination. If the achievement of a racially "balanced" impact is affirmatively required, the Court need not inquire into the motivation with which a given selection was made or a given law passed; a simple look at the statistics will determine whether invalidation, or a demand for justification, is in order.

Of course, the suggestion that a showing of disproportionate racial impact, whether intended or not, should trigger judicial review has extremely far-reaching implications. There are many towns and voting districts throughout the United States whose residents are predominantly or exclusively white (not to mention those whose residents are largely Protestant, Catholic, conservative, liberal, Republican, or Democratic), and a number of them are abutted by largely Negro (or whatever) communities. The implications for laws which concern subjects other than districting are probably even more far-reaching.[7]

One who favors an impact approach might, by way of partial though far from total avoidance of such implications, assert that invalidation or review should not be triggered by just any disproportionate impact, but only a substantial one. In response to this, one is surely entitled to ask "disproportionate as compared to what"—the racial distribution in the nation, the state, or the surrounding area, however that might be defined? And assuming that question can be answered, how disproportionate is disproportionate enough?

However, the observation that a constitutional doctrine will have far-reaching implications cannot count as a refutation; whatever else we may or may not know about the adoption of the Fourteenth Amendment, it plainly was intended to make a difference. The fact that no standards push themselves forward for determining the degree of disproportion which should be required to trigger intervention cannot be a determinative answer either. Were the Court to conclude that an affirmative requirement of "balanced" impact would best serve the values underlying the guarantee of equal protection, the chain of reasoning by which that conclusion was established presumably would suggest guidelines that could be given specific content on a case-by-case basis. Courts have proceeded thus in other legal contexts; there is no reason to think they could not do so here. There are, however, more fundamental reasons why the Court has been unwilling to find in the Fourteenth Amendment an affirmative command of racial balance. Since the case for imposing such an affirmative duty can be made most strongly with respect to jury selection, it is in that context that I shall explore the reasons underlying the Court's hesitation to do so.

The "disadvantageous distinction model" is inapplicable to choices made in jury selection [that is, the state is not obligated, as it is in many other contexts, to justify the choice of one person as a juror rather than another simply because a choice has been made] because we realize that the state inevitably will have to distinguish among persons who are indistinguishable in terms of the characteristics relevant to an ability to hear and decide cases.[8] That realization does not, however, answer one way or another the question whether states should be affirmatively obligated to include on each panel a percentage of minority group members equivalent to the percentage of the entire population they constitute.[9] And if the imposition of such an affirmative obligation is ever appropriate, it is surely in the jury selection context. The harm that accrues to a litigant from the underrepresentation of his race on the jury that sits in judgment on him is exactly the same whether the underrepresentation was achieved intentionally or unintentionally.[10] No argument can be made, as it can in the [voting district] situation, that a degree of racial imbalance serves a desirable political function. And a standard for policing the obligation to seek a balance readily suggests itself: the state could be obligated to make the racial composition of the panel conform as closely as possible to the most recent census figures for the area from which the jury is drawn.

Yet no member of the Court has ever suggested imposing such an obligation in the jury context. As Mr. Justice Douglas observed last term:

> We have often said that no jury need represent proportionally a cross-section of the community. . . . Jury selection is largely by chance; and no matter the race of the defendant, he bears the risk that no racial component, presumably favorable to him, will appear on the jury that tries him. The law only requires that the panel not be purposefully unrepresentative.[11]

Indeed, the Court has gone further, and has indicated that it would be constitutionally *impermissible* for a state intentionally to achieve a racial cross-section.[12]

The reasons thought to support this prohibition were stated in 1950 in *Cassell v. Texas*:

> Obviously the number of races and nationalities appearing in the ancestry of our citizens would make it impossible to meet a requirement of proportional representation. Similarly, since there can be no exclusion of Negroes as a race and no discrimination because of color, proportional limitation is not permissible.[13]

The Court's first point here is that perfect proportionality would be impossible to achieve. And indeed it would. The state's duty of neutrality in the jury selection context must, as the Court indicates by mentioning nationality, extend beyond race—certainly to religion and politics, indeed, to any factor that is irrelevant to one's ability to observe the proceedings and draw inferences therefrom but nonetheless likely to affect his sympathy with one side or the other.[14] Such factors are too numerous, and they overlap in too many combinations, to permit perfectly proportional representation. But this is not a sufficient objection. Although a purposefully proportional method of jury selection would not work perfectly, there is every reason to think that in the long run it could do at least as good a job as random selection in achieving a cross-section.[15] And on a day-to-day basis, which is what matters to individual defendants, it would certainly do a better job.

The Court's second stated objection to a purposefully proportional system of selection—although awkwardly stated—is more telling. It is that race is simply not something jury commissioners should be allowed to take into account in making their selections, even for the purpose of achieving racial balance. This objection rests in the main on two considerations.[16] The first is the difficulty of constructing a system of review capable of ensuring that the consideration of race and other personal characteristics is not turned to improper ends. If, for example, the jury commissioner can take into account the fact that a prospective juror is a Negro, it might be hard to prevent him from taking into account the fact that he is a militant Negro. Moreover, if consideration of race (or religion or politics) is permitted in the jury context, it would be difficult logically to bar its consideration in numerous other contexts where the problems of control might be even more aggravated. Perhaps the safest long-run course is to demand that officials be entirely "colorblind," no matter how neutral or benevolent they claim they wish to be. The second consideration is that the government's intentional and explicit use of race as a criterion of choice is bound—no matter how careful the explanation that this is a "good" use of race—to weaken the educative force of its concurrent instruction that a person is to be judged as a person, that his race has nothing to do with his merit. Citizens, thus besieged by what will understandably be taken to represent two conflicting government-endorsed principles, are likely to listen to the voice they wish to hear.[17]

Although the Court has quoted the passage from *Cassell* with approval as recently as 1965, it is difficult to believe—in light of the widespread undertaking and judicial legitimization of affirmative attempts to achieve racial balance in public schools—that it necessarily represents its last word on the permissibility of such attempts in the jury context. But one thing does seem quite clear: the Court is a long way from *requiring* states to seek racial balance on juries by taking race into account. And this, indeed, would be a significantly different matter. The difficulty of designing a selection system capable of ensuring proportional representation is properly taken into account at this level. If a state wishes to take on the task and does it tolerably well, that is one thing. It would be quite another for the Court to *order* the performance of a difficult task where an apparently acceptable alternative (random selection) exists. The difficulty of ensuring effective judicial surveillance of governmental consideration of race would, moreover, obviously be compounded were the Court to insist upon such consideration. And since the Supreme Court is preeminently entrusted with the care of the nation's principles, it most of all should hesitate to issue a pronouncement which can be read to mean that Negroes are different from white persons. The success of the Court's work always depends in large part on the moral clarity and force of its pronouncements: the success of its greatest work to date may depend in particular upon acceptance of the proposition that a person's race is an irrelevance. Colorblindness may in time turn out, here as elsewhere, to be a less-than-absolute constitutional command. But for the foreseeable future it is constitutionally satisfactory.

So long as the Court remains unwilling to order states to take race into account in selecting their jury panels, judicial review must await proof of racial motivation and cannot be triggered by disproportion per se. To undertake automatically to invalidate panels because of racial disproportion would obviously be to order that balance be intentionally achieved. And so would holding that disproportion per se triggers a duty of either rational or compelling justification. For as we have seen, there will almost certainly be no difference between those who are on the panel and those who are not which is rationally—let alone "compellingly"—relatable to their ability to hear and decide cases. To call for a legitimately defensible difference on the basis of an unintended racial disproportion would therefore be tantamount to invalidating all panels exhibiting such a disproportion—which would, in turn, amount to ordering the intentional achievement of racial balance.[18]

In discussing *Gomillion*, the Court [in *United States v. O'Brien*,[19] which generally denied the constitutional relevance of motivation and thus attempted to pass *Gomillion* off as strictly an impact case] would have been well advised to refer to the jury discrimination cases, for the considerations that there imply that judicial review must await proof of the intentional use of race as a criterion of selection counsel the employment of a motivation model with respect to the bounding of political units as well. In 1964, in *Wright v. Rockefeller*, the Court hinted that there might be constitutional problems with the intentional achievement of racially balanced voting districts.[20] I doubt, again because of the analogy to what is happening with respect to pupil assignment, that the Court would be moved to invalidate a districting plan on such a ground. However, the reasons that counsel against *forcing* states to consider race in selecting jury panels apply to the drawing of district lines. And a judicial declaration that racially lopsided cities or districts are per se unconstitutional (or what, again, would be functionally equivalent, that racial disproportionality triggers a demand for a rational or compelling defense) would amount to a command that state legislatures consider race in drawing district lines.

* * *

What Proof of Motivation Should Trigger Review?

RANDOM CHOICE SITUATIONS

In jury and districting situations, review is triggered by a showing that selection was not random. [That is,] review should be triggered as to any exclusion from a jury panel that can be shown to have resulted from the employment of a criterion of selection not random with respect to those characteristics that are likely to influence the way one will hear evidence and decide cases; review of a districting selection should be triggered by proof that it was not random with respect to characteristics likely to influence voting or other political behavior.

To agree with the Court that review should, in racial contexts as in others, await proof of motivation is by no means necessarily to approve its view of what constitutes proof that race was taken into account during the selection process. A resolution not to force states to consider race in making their selections, and a consequent toleration of colorblind choice, is plainly indefensible absent an equally strong resolution to prevent the intentional underrepresentation of minority groups. Yet the Court's definition of what counts as prima facie proof of such intentional underrepresentation has at times been insupportably demanding. Doubly dangerous are statements like the following, from the insufficiently notorious *Swain v.*

Alabama:[21] "We cannot say that purposeful discrimination based on race alone is satisfactorily proved by showing that an identifiable group in a community is underrepresented by as much as 10%."[22] Of course a 10 percent underrepresentation might on occasion be rebuttable by convincing proof that the selection was in fact made at random or on the basis of criteria legitimately related to fitness to serve. But to announce that a 10 percent disparity is not sufficient to call for such a rebuttal is practically to guarantee all the evils of a disproportionate impact model of review without its accompanying benefits: race very likely will be considered, but minorities very likely will be underrepresented—by about 10 percent.

At the least, any nonnegligible variation over a period of time from what we would expect totally random selection to produce should shift to the state the burden of proving that the selection was in fact generated by a combination of exclusion on the basis of legitimately defensible characteristics and random selection. The facts, after all, are far more accessible to the state than the defendant. It does not seem too demanding to ask that a credible witness be present when the names are drawn from the hat. Indeed, the approach best designed to avoid the consideration of impermissible factors would be to place that burden on the state the moment the defendant puts the matter in issue.

Nor is there anything in the reasoning that counsels the choice of motivation over disproportionate impact per se as the factor triggering judicial review that should prevent the Court from invalidating, as a prophylactic measure, methods of jury selection that invite intentional racial discrimination. Systems whereby the jury commissioner selects from among his acquaintances, without obligation to refer to a city directory or some other broad and racially neutral list, should be disapproved.[23] So should statutory standards of the sort approved last term in *Carter v. Jury Commission of Greene County*[24] ("generally reputed to be honest and intelligent . . . and . . . esteemed in the community for . . . integrity, good character and sound judgment") and *Turner v. Fouche*[25] ("discreet," "upright," and "intelligent"). The Court has, correctly in my view, opted for a motivation model. It should seriously employ it.

* * *

Pupil Assignment and Some Other Problems of Racial Discrimination

In *United States v. Montgomery County Board of Education*,[26] decided in 1969, the Supreme Court reinstated Judge Johnson's timetable for gradually making the ratio of white to Negro teachers in each of Montgomery's schools substantially the same as it was throughout the school system. The

Court stressed that the Court of Appeals, in modifying Johnson's order, had erred in reading it as "rigid and inflexible." But its opinion must nonetheless be read as approving in some circumstances court orders of a sort we have not seen with regard to jury selection or voting districts: those requiring local authorities intentionally to achieve racial balance. It is important, however, to read *Montgomery County* and lower federal court decisions issuing similar orders in context. Judge Johnson's order was made in response to a long history of racially motivated teacher assignment, and the United States argued for its reinstatement on that basis alone. Its brief, in a passage significantly quoted by the Court, asserted:

> [The order] is designed as a remedy for past racial assignment. . . . We do not, in other words, argue here that racially balanced faculties are constitutionally or legally required.[27]

In the circumstances that confronted Judge Johnson, an order setting forth statistical requirements is understandable, and entirely proper. A series of dodges designed to avoid desegregation orders must at some point move even the most patient judge to respond in effect, "So long as I know there is no chance of your choosing without taking race into account, the best I can do—even granting the general undesirability of such orders—is to order you to take it into account in a way that will produce roughly the same results that not taking it into account would produce." Moreover, the objections that apply generally to orders requiring racial balance are somewhat diluted in situations like this. The difficult question of how disproportionate the impact must be to call for such an order need not be asked here, because the order is rendered in response not to disproportion per se but rather to a history of racially motivated choices. The dangers of unreviewable misuse of the criterion of race are mitigated by the court's setting of the figures and its already inevitably close surveillance of the situation. And experience shows that orders issued in contexts like this are not taken by legal scholars, government officials, or the popular press[28] as expressions of a principle, which would run counter to so much of the Court's work, that race constitutes an acceptable, indeed mandatory, criterion for sorting people out. They are understood for what they are, virtually unavoidable responses to officials who have shown themselves unable to *avoid* using race as such a criterion.

Of course the situation is in flux, and these limited remedial orders may in time turn out to have been the first steps in the development of a general judicial command of racially balanced schools. Should this transpire, there will be no place for reference to motivation: a look at the statistics will suffice. But we are not there, and for the moment such a development seems improbable.[29] It is quite clearly established that states can if they wish affirmatively seek racial balance in their schools, but the Court has scrupulously refrained from saying that they must. Thus the theoretical

framework controlling review of voting district decisions should obtain
with regard to school attendance zones as well: courts should not intervene
by automatic invalidation or imposition of an extraordinary burden of justification on the basis of imbalance per se, but should await proof of an
intentional racial gerrymander.

In seeking to identify unconstitutional motivation in this context or
others, courts should not consider themselves bound by any rigid action-
inaction distinction. A racially motivated decision not to alter attendance
zone lines should trigger a judicial demand for an explanation as readily as
a racially motivated decision to redraw them, though the . . . problems [of
proving motivation] are likely to be more substantial. Moreover, where a
pattern of segregated housing can confidently be attributed to racially motivated government action and the racial imbalance in the schools is attributable to that residential segregation, a court should not hesitate to find the
segregation of the schools the product of racially motivated government
action. The realization that these two conclusions follow from the considerations properly controlling review in this area should make the courts more
willing to infer unconstitutional motivation than they have been in the
past.[30]

However, neither a motivation approach to review nor any other is likely
to produce anything resembling total integration, except in the rural South,
if "community," in the sense of an area whose residents are united by ethnic
and economic ties, is credited as a legitimate criterion of choice. The confusion of several questions and definitions makes it difficult to determine the
extent to which such choice is condoned. It is widely accepted that school
districts—a district being an area whose schools are controlled by a common governing authority—can legitimately be constructed along such
"community" lines. I am not aware, however, of widespread acceptance of
the view that within such districts the various attendance zones can properly be drawn along community lines of an ethnic or economic nature. The
obvious problem with this combination of positions is that if effective racial segregation can be justified under the guise of "community" distinction
at the level of constructing school districts, a hesitancy to permit the use of
such criteria of choice in subdividing the districts into attendance zones
may be largely meaningless. This realization might suggest that the acceptance of "community" as a legitimate criterion of choice even at the district
level ought to be reexamined. Certainly those who charge the courts with
thwarting integration by their refusal to embrace a pure impact test by declaring "de facto segregation" of attendance zones unconstitutional would
do well to consider not only the costs of instructing local officials to take
into account the races of the persons they are sorting out, but also whether
such a broad pronouncement would actually achieve integration in view of
the recognition of "community" as a legitimate criterion of choice at the
district level.

The review of official decisions regarding teacher placement and the location of new schools has been approached by the courts in terms of motivation, and properly so. Each could constitutionally be done at random, but once such a decision is shown to be the product of a desire to promote the separation of the races, a (rarely satisfiable) judicial demand for a legitimate defense is appropriate.

In *Griffin v. County School Board of Prince Edward County*,[31] decided in 1964, the Supreme Court, speaking the language of motivation, invalidated Virginia's closing of Prince Edward County's public schools, which had been ordered integrated. One way of dealing with such a case, which was employed as an alternative ground by a three judge district court in the earlier and similar case of *Hall v. St. Helena Parish School Board*,[32] would have been to hold such geographical discriminations subject to the disadvantageous distinction model and thus demand ab initio a legitimate defense of a decision to provide a public service in one county but not another. The Supreme Court has declined to do so, however, holding that geographical discriminations need not generally be defended. Against that somewhat questionable background, the reference to motivation was quite in order. A decision to close the schools in only that county where integration has been ordered can fairly be taken, in the absence of rebuttal evidence, to have been motivated by a desire to continue segregation. And that motivation should, in turn, trigger a demand for a rational and nonracial defense of the choice of that county—a defense which almost certainly would not be, and in the event was not, forthcoming. Indeed, should a state close *all* its schools under circumstances clearly revealing that it has done so in order to preserve segregation, the same theory would apply.[33] Ordinarily a state need provide no legitimate defense of a decision to terminate one public service rather than another, but when the choice has been made for an unconstitutional reason, such a defense should be required. (It would almost certainly not be available. Of course closing all schools—or, indeed, closing one school—saves the state money, but what requires a legitimate defense is the choice, the decision to save money this way rather than some other.)

The theory proposed herein also applies to problems of racial discrimination raised by residential zoning and by the choice of sites for public housing projects.[34] Similar problems are raised by *Deerfield Park District v. Progress Development Corporation*,[35] which one commentary described and analyzed as follows:

> Upon learning that a private developer was about to construct an integrated housing development, the Deerfield Park District, a municipal corporation governed by a board of five elected members, immediately condemned the developer's land for use as a public park. The conflict between motive and purpose was thus sharply drawn; the condemned land was to be used for a park (the purpose of the

action), but the reason that the land was condemned was allegedly to prevent residential integration (the board's motive). The Supreme Court of Illinois declined to examine the board's motives and upheld the condemnation. The court treated the board's members as "legislators" and therefore found inquiry into their motives improper. This conclusion would seem correct. Although the board of five members was not as numerous as a state legislature, it was a popularly elected and politically responsive body performing a legislative function—determining what land was to be condemned—within its area of power. It would, therefore, seem sufficiently legislative to bar examination of its members' motives.[36]

This passage graphically illustrates the difficulties which flow from (a) the assumption that the controlling principles differ as between "legislative" and "administrative" action, and that a sensible line between the two can be drawn for purposes of determining the relevance of motivation;[37] (b) the assumption that "motive" and "purpose" refer to separate species of legislative aims;[38] and (c) the failure to distinguish two separate questions— whether to have a park, and where to put it. Of course the city fathers can have a park, and ordinarily they would not be obligated to provide a rational defense of their decision to place it at point X rather than somewhere else. But it follows from neither the realization that a park may be created, nor the realization that random selection of the location would be constitutionally tolerable, that the selection of point X may be made on any basis whatsoever.

School Desegregation: A Sense of Déjà Vu (1977)[39]

In 1975–76 I served as the General Counsel (the third-ranking official) of the Ford administration's Department of Transportation. Most of the issues I dealt with at DOT were not constitutional issues, at least not directly, though there can be little doubt that a number of administrative decisions were reached in the shadow of constitutional values (such as our decision to admit women to the Coast Guard Academy). Two remnants of this service appear in this book nonetheless: (1) my letter to Attorney General Levi urging the administration to be completely open with Congress and the public about prior negotiations with France and Great Britain respecting the admission to United States service of the Concorde SST—this one, which appears in chapter 9, succeeded, in fact the entire Concorde matter was one whose handling might serve more often than it appears to as a model for administrative procedures generally—and (2) the following explosion a year after I left the administration (again on the pages of The New York Times) about one thing I think the Ford administration did not do right, namely its Justice Department's handling of the busing issue.

I was saddened when I read, in *The New York Times*, remarks on school desegregation by Assistant Attorney General Drew S. Days, who heads the Justice Department's Civil Rights Division. But it took me a while to figure out why. I surely had no right to be surprised: Mr. Days' bosses had made no secret of their general attitude on the subject, and it's a little early in the [Carter] administration to hope for insubordination. No, the reaction wasn't one of surprise; it was one of déjà vu.

Attorney General Edward H. Levi and others in the Ford administration's Justice Department devoted some effort last summer to seeking a way to reverse the federal courts' historical response to school desegregation suits, which has been to assume that a proved segregatory intent on the part of a school board probably infected all of that board's decisions affecting which students would attend what schools.

Consequently, the courts have typically moved to mitigate whatever racial imbalance exists in the entire school district that a board controls. (Often this will require only the realignment of the attendance zone boundaries; sometimes, unfortunately for everyone concerned, it necessarily involves busing children some distance from their homes.)

Henceforth, the Ford Justice Department's idea went, a combined showing of a racially motivated school board and racially imbalanced schools throughout the district that self-same board controlled was not to be enough. The plaintiff was also to be required, somehow, to demonstrate exactly which sets of schools the board's motive had infected, and the remedy was to run only that far.

I was General Counsel of the Department of Transportation in the Ford administration, and spent part of my last few weeks—I left last summer— helping Secretary William T. Coleman Jr. combat these efforts.

You may wonder—others did—what business our department had sounding off about busing. The answer—that buses are, after all, means of transportation—had to be accompanied by a wink, and the truth is that we were simply unwilling to compartmentalize our feelings on this issue and didn't want the administration of which we were a part to take what we regarded as an unfeeling if salable position on the rights of black and other minority children.

It's hard enough to prove that a school board intended to segregate. To go further, we argued, and require the plaintiff to prove which among the many racially imbalanced attendance zones within the board's jurisdiction were the causal product of the proved intent is obviously to require the impossible. This point had not been lost on the Supreme Court.

In *Keyes v. School District No. 1* (1973), it explicitly held that proof of intentional segregation in one section of Denver was sufficient to support a citywide remedy. "Common sense," the Court observed, dictates the conclusion that officials who intentionally segregate in one part of the district they control are very likely similarly motivated as regards their actions in other parts, even though the plaintiffs may not be able directly to prove it elsewhere. In seeking to reverse the Supreme Court, we felt, the Justice Department's approach denied that obvious common sense.

Moreover, in other legal areas federal courts have historically imposed remedies that go beyond the provable scope of the violation involved. It is settled, for example, that an antitrust remedy can require the divestiture of parts of the erring business that were acquired lawfully, in ways that did not violate the antitrust laws. We felt a double standard—one that disadvantaged the constitutional rights of minority children—was being urged.

One battle was won and another was lost. The Ford administration decided not to file in support of a reversal of the Boston desegregation order (and the Supreme Court refused to review it). But the administration sent to Congress the proposed "School Desegregation Standards and Assistance Act of 1976," which indicated, among other things, that remedies in school cases were to be limited to the restricted area where the racial imbalance could be shown to have been causally generated by the school board's segregative intent.

It upset me that the administration in which I served would make such a gesture, but I found refuge in a sense of confidence that the bill wouldn't pass, and that nothing further would be heard of the idea. . . . [O]n this, I believed, the Democrats could be trusted.

Thus, my reaction to Mr. Days' reported position that courts should not order citywide school desegregation to remedy limited instances of illegal school segregation and his consequent announcement that he will not press for wide-ranging desegregation measures unless there was proof of intentional segregation throughout a school system.

For what this obviously suggests is that the present administration's policy on the critical question of system-wide relief will be essentially that contained in the Ford administration's bill.

Of course it's early in the Carter administration and actions sometimes do speak louder than words. But words can constrict the possible sphere of action, and the words we hear are troubling. I only hope that Mr. Days, whose civil rights record is very good indeed, understands and will continue to understand that outside the administration (and doubtless within it as well) there are those who would count it tragic were the hard-won victory of the *Keyes* case squandered.

Eleven years after I wrote this, as I was leaving the Stanford Law School deanship, I was reminded by Secretary Coleman's tribute of details of the episode I had long since forgotten:

When the President's cabinet was debating the Ford Administration's position on school busing as a remedy in school desegregation cases, . . . John felt so *strongly about the civil rights policies at stake that he submitted to me, with no threat of publicity, a letter of resignation that would be effective if the President were to side with the busing opponents. I needed little shoring up on this issue,[40] and ultimately John and I prevailed in persuading the Attorney General that busing was an appropriate remedy in the government's civil rights enforcement arsenal.*

Coleman, *"John Hart Ely: Counsel for the Situation," 40 Stan. L. Rev. 357, 358 (1988).*

Having thus defended busing as an entirely justifiable legal remedy—it would have been a scandal had the Ford administration filed a brief undercutting the heroic efforts of so many federal judges—I cannot deny, as Anthony Lucas's sensitive book *Common Ground* (1985) demonstrated, that it is a remedy that took an enormous toll on those (of all races) directly affected, while most of us in the upper middle class sat on the sidelines relatively unaffected. (Sure my kids went to public schools, but public schools so safely ensconced in the suburbs that although busing provided them a token number of black friends, it never presented the kind of perceived threat experienced by both black and white inner city children.) All in all a tragic situation.

I trust it also doesn't need explicit note that the criticism of Drew Days was entirely friendly; beyond cavil he had then and has since done a good deal more for the cause of civil rights than most of the rest of us.

Excerpt from *Professor Dworkin's External/Personal Preference Distinction* (1983)[41]

We turn now to another wrenching issue, that of racially specific affirmative action. I suppose the standard academic take is that it is constitutional, but the standard argument to that effect is blather, distinguishing discrimination against racial minorities from discrimination in their favor essentially on the ground that the former is bad, the latter good. Professor Dworkin's defense is more sophisticated, though in the excerpt that follows I argue that it doesn't work either.

Professor Ronald Dworkin has made several important contributions to contemporary constitutional theory. A phrase that I have quite openly purloined, because it so evocatively summarizes so much of what I have argued for, is the "right to equal concern and respect in the design and administration of the political institutions that govern" us.[42] There are other suggestive distinctions—that between constitutional concepts and conceptions for one, that between equal treatment and treatment as an equal for another. Strangely, however, the distinction Dworkin may most often insist

upon as constitutionally useful—indeed his theory of rights rests on it—
namely the distinction between personal and external preferences, is the
one that on analysis turns out to be least useful.

The distinction was presented in *Taking Rights Seriously* as capable of
coping with two of the classic constitutional conundrums—that of equality
and that of personal autonomy. It was there invoked, in particular, to demonstrate (a) why laws favoring members of minority races are constitutional whereas those favoring whites are not, and (b) why laws outlawing
homosexual sex, contraception, and pornography should be declared invalid.

Affirmative Action

Dworkin sets up the affirmative action problem by contrasting *Sweatt v.
Painter*,[43] involving the exclusion of blacks from the University of Texas
Law School, with *DeFunis v. Odegaard*,[44] involving the favoring of blacks
by the admissions committee of the University of Washington Law School.
Dworkin asserts—and with this much I agree, even if the United States
Supreme Court appears not to[45]—that the latter practice should be upheld
whereas the former should not.

To arrive at his conclusion Dworkin first distinguishes two general types
of argument for the proposition that a given law makes a community better
off. *Utilitarian* arguments are those that assert that "the average or collective level of welfare in the community is improved." *Ideal* arguments are to
the effect that the law in question makes the society "more just, or in some
other way closer to an ideal society, whether or not average welfare is
improved."[46] According to Dworkin, the University of Washington Law
School might properly "use either utilitarian or ideal arguments to justify
its racial classification."

> It might argue, for example, that increasing the number of black lawyers reduces
> racial tensions, which improves the welfare of almost everyone in the commu-
> nity. That is a utilitarian argument. Or it might argue that, whatever effect minor-
> ity preference will have on average welfare, it will make the community more
> equal and therefore more just. That is an ideal, not a utilitarian, argument.[47]

Dworkin then turns to *Sweatt v. Painter*. "The University of Texas, on
the other hand, cannot make an ideal argument for segregation. It cannot
claim that segregation makes the community more just whether it improves
the average welfare or not."[48] Dworkin's wording here is infelicitous, almost inevitably generating the question *why* the University of Texas can't
make an ideal argument for segregation. In fact, wasn't segregation most
often defended precisely on the ground that it represented the natural order,

and was "closer to an ideal society" than one in which the races mix? What Dworkin must mean here, therefore, is that the University of Texas cannot make an ideal argument for segregation *that does not offend the United States Constitution*. That the world would be a better place if all Presbyterians were killed is an ideal argument, but it is an ideal argument that violates the Constitution.

There is a temptation at this point to respond that the overall structure Dworkin thus implicitly introduces is just a gigantic mechanism for begging questions. Why doesn't he simply come out and argue that racial segregation violates the Constitution, drawing on the materials that every other constitutional lawyer draws on, without gussying it up with all this talk of ideal versus utilitarian arguments? This too is unfair. Although the line between the two types of argument is certainly not crystal clear,[49] the distinction does make rough sense. Sometimes state attorneys general will defend laws in terms of their consequences, arguing that they will help more people than they hurt, but sometimes they will mount a different sort of defense, one pitched to the simple rightness of what the state has done. (Actually it is to Dworkin's credit that he appreciates that such "ideal" arguments are constitutionally appropriate. Too often result-oriented constitutional commentary will try in particular contexts to slip by on the notion that such arguments do not count, that the state must argue tangible benefit and cannot rest on rightness or morality.) And when the state does rely on such an "ideal" argument, of course the court must judge it by constitutional standards: how else would we cope with our Presbyterian-killing example?

Texas's "ideal" argument for segregation thus dispatched, Dworkin asserts, the "arguments it makes to defend segregation must therefore be utilitarian arguments."[50] Indeed, he notes, it is quite plausible to suppose, at least in postwar Texas, that "the preferences of the people were overall in favor of the consequences of segregation in law schools, even if the intensity of the competing preference for integration, and not simply the number of those holding that preference, is taken into account."[51] To cope with this realization Dworkin draws the distinction that is the subject of this article, that between personal and external preferences.

> Preference utilitarianism asks officials to attempt to satisfy people's preferences so far as this is possible. But the preferences of an individual for the consequences of a particular policy may be seen to reflect, on further analysis, either a personal preference for his own enjoyment of some goods or opportunities, or an external preference for the assignment of goods and opportunities to others, or both.[52]

Dworkin's claim is that utilitarianism is "corrupted" when external preferences are registered by the utilitarian calculus. This is surely true, he maintains, of an external preference to the effect that members of a certain group be deprived of certain goods or opportunities:

> Suppose many citizens, who are not themselves sick, are racists in political theory, and therefore prefer that scarce medicine be given to a white man who needs it rather than a black man who needs it more. If utilitarianism counts these political preferences at face value, then it will be, from the standpoint of personal preferences, self-defeating, because the distribution of medicine will then not be, from that standpoint, utilitarian at all.[53]

There is a similar corruption, he claims, when the external preferences that are counted are altruistic:

> Suppose many citizens, who themselves do not swim, prefer [that their city build a pool rather than a theater] because they approve of sports and admire athletes. . . . If the altruistic preferences are counted, so as to reinforce the personal preferences of swimmers, the result will be a form of double counting; each swimmer will have the benefit not only of his own preference, but also of the preference of someone else who takes pleasure in his success.[54]

Dworkin's bottom line on *Sweatt* is that Texas's utilitarian argument for segregation must fail because it is based on external preferences. *What* external preferences exactly? To describe them as "the preferences of the community at large for racial separation"[55] doesn't help much, as it obviously is racial separation whose constitutionality is at issue. At another point Dworkin appears to get more specific, characterizing as an external preference a desire for segregation growing out of the fact that one "has contempt for blacks and disapproves social situations in which the races mix."[56] But an expression of preference "for racial separation," or a disapproval of the "mixing of the races," unelaborated, seems very clearly an expression of a (misguided) vision of an ideal society. It is therefore necessary to revert to Dworkin's definition of an external preference to understand more precisely what he has in mind.

An external preference, remember, is a preference "for the assignment of goods and opportunities to others," which suggests that Dworkin means to assimilate the school segregation situation to the medical hypothetical he used to define the distinction. Just as the racist in that case wanted blacks to gain fewer "goods and opportunities" (specifically medicine) than whites (because he thought "a black man [was] to count for less and a white man therefore to count for more than one"[57]), so the ultimate idea in *Sweatt* must be that the racist wishes fewer opportunities for blacks, in this case fewer opportunities to become lawyers. He may dress it up as an ideal argument for the justice of racial segregation or the unnatural nature of racial mixture, but what he *really* wants—or at least what he has to want if he is to comply with Dworkin's definition of an external preference—

is that blacks should suffer comparatively, that they should count for "less than one" and therefore be assigned fewer goods and opportunities than whites.

But were the preferences of whites for segregation, even in postwar Texas, "external" in this sense? Dworkin considers "the associational preference of a white law student for white classmates." He grants that this can be considered as a "personal preference" for an immediate environment that one finds less alien or threatening. But, says Dworkin, this "is a personal preference that is parasitic upon external preferences: except in very rare cases a white student prefers the company of other whites because he has racist social and political convictions, or because he has contempt for blacks as a group."[58] (And, in turn, such "racism" must wish for blacks fewer goods and opportunities than are available to whites, if it is to fit Dworkin's definition of an external preference.) Thus, according to Dworkin, preferences like the white law student's, however "personal" on the surface, are "external" down deep, and utilitarian balances affected by them must be disallowed.

Let us return to *DeFunis*. Dworkin asserts that "[t]he arguments for an admissions program that discriminates in favor of blacks are both utilitarian and ideal."[59] Unlike the *Sweatt* situation in which both sorts of argument were invalid, both are valid regarding affirmative action. Dworkin grants that "[s]ome of the utilitarian arguments do rely, at least indirectly, on external preferences, such as the preference of certain blacks for lawyers of their own race."[60] (He must be given points for consistency here. Just as the preferences of white law students for white classmates must, if Dworkin's argument is to be internally consistent, be translated into a deeply held desire that whites be given opportunities that blacks are denied, so too, Dworkin seems here to be assuring us, a preference of a black client for a black lawyer must similarly screen a deep desire that blacks be given opportunities that are denied to whites.) However, "the utilitarian arguments that do not rely on such preferences are strong and may be sufficient."[61]

Recall Dworkin's example of such a utilitarian argument for affirmative action, quoted above, "that increasing the number of black lawyers reduces racial tension, which improves the welfare of almost everyone in the community. That is a utilitarian argument."[62] It's a utilitarian argument all right, but doesn't it follow from what Dworkin has just said that it is a utilitarian argument polluted by external preferences, namely the preferences of blacks that blacks be given more opportunities to become lawyers? In arguing earlier against the constitutionality of segregation, Dworkin addressed a comparable argument: "if the argument [for segregation] notices, for example, that because of prejudice industry will run more efficiently if factories are segregated, then the argument has the consequence that the black man's personal preferences are defeated by what others think of him," and is invalid by virtue of saturation by external preference.[63] But if arguments for segregation on the ground that it will reduce racial tension are invalid, it is difficult to see why arguments for integration on the ground that *it* will reduce racial tension are not also invalid on Dworkin's premises. Each of these tension-reduction arguments relies on an assumed desire on people's part (whites in one case, blacks in the other) for more lawyers of their own race. In both cases, according to Dworkin, that preference amounts to an external preference.

It is thus past time we looked to the "ideal argument" for affirmative action, if we are to have any hope of distinguishing *DeFunis* from *Sweatt* in Dworkin's terms. The ideal argument for affirmative action "[does] not rely upon preferences at all"; it is instead "the independent argument that a more equal society is a better society even if its citizens prefer inequality."[64] We granted above, as any constitutional lawyer must grant, that the overall structure Dworkin draws upon here is legitimate: some entirely respectable arguments are entirely nonutilitarian, relying instead on the simple justice or rightness of what the state has done, and such arguments should be judged valid or invalid depending on their comportment with constitutional principles.

So there is nothing wrong with the structure here: it's the application that's troubling—troubling not, as it happens, in its outcome, but rather because the argument is entirely question-begging. Whether affirmative action of a sort that involves weighing certain people's race positively in law school admissions decisions (which necessarily means that certain other people will be denied admission because of their race) in fact inures to a juster (or for that matter more egalitarian) society is an excruciatingly difficult question, which cannot be answered by simply asserting that it does. Begging the question that the ideal argument for segregation is unconstitutional is one thing; begging the question that the ideal argument for racially specific affirmative action is constitutional is another.

In fact I agree with Dworkin's conclusion that *Sweatt* and *DeFunis* can be distinguished, though not on his terms.[65] Nothing in either the distinction between ideal and utilitarian arguments, or the distinction between personal and external preferences, has given us any reason to suppose that the utilitarian arguments for segregation and affirmative action, and for that matter the ideal arguments for both, are other than wholly symmetrical.

My own defense of affirmative action follows immediately. We will return to Professor Dworkin's personal/external preference distinction (this time in the contexts of homosexuality, contraception, and pornography) at pages 311–27.

The Constitutionality of Reverse Racial Discrimination (1974)[66]

"You really had to be there" for this one—the Conference on Equality and Discrimination in American Law, held at the University of Chicago Law School on May 3–4, 1974, and sponsored jointly by the law school and the Anti-Defamation League of B'nai B'rith. Others present have speculated that this conference, and in particular the slack-jawed hush that greeted the presentation of this paper, marked the birth of neoconservatism. I've got a lot to answer for.

The problems were so intractable that this time it really looked like Fred and Ginger might not get together. But then Fred sang "I Used to be Color Blind,"[67] and suddenly we knew that everything would turn out all right. Unfortunately, life is not an Astaire-Rogers musical—let alone one called, as this one was, *Carefree*—and though not being colorblind may begin to solve some of our problems, it raises serious new ones. If we are to have even a chance of curing our society of the sickness of racism, we will need a lot more black professionals.* And whatever the complex of reasons, it seems we will not get them in the foreseeable future unless we take blackness into account and weigh it positively when we allocate opportunities. But that must mean denying opportunities to some people solely because they were born white. Either way, it's no musical, and I confess I have trouble understanding the place of righteous indignation on either side of this wrenching moral issue.[68]

On the surface at least, the constitutional issue is also quite troubling. We would not allow a state university to favor applicants because they are white, not even an iota, whether it called the adjustment a quota, affirmative action, or anything else. To allow one to favor applicants because they are black seems to be countenancing the most flagrant of double standards.[69]

There is some authority, however, for the permissibility of "benign" racial classification. Closest to the mark, perhaps, is the Supreme Court's

---

* [And professionals of other minority ethnicities, for example Latinos (and Latinas) and Native Americans. The argument made herein supports the constitutionality of any affirmative action program running in favor of any group that does not constitute a majority of the legislature enacting the program. For simplicity's sake the article (like Dworkin's discussion and for that matter virtually every other early defense of affirmative action) centrally phrased its discussion in terms of discrimination for and against blacks, though the principle argued for would extend to other ethnic minorities as well. But sometimes simplifications are not that sensitive, and fortunately in the past two decades most of us have learned to word our discussions of the issue more broadly.]

dictum in *Swann v. Charlotte-Mecklenburg Board of Education*,[70] making explicit its view that a local community may bus children according to race, if it wishes, to remedy school segregation caused by residential patterns. No obvious distinctions come to mind by which voluntary busing plans can be distinguished from other "benign" discrimination. First, although the contrary claim is voiced all too frequently, it is incorrect to say that no one is hurt by busing. Children can be hurt by busing, not simply by the inconvenience of the transportation process itself, but also by the transition from a school environment in which they have grown secure to strange surroundings in which they are likely to find themselves in a racial minority for the first time. Second, the argument that busing hurts neither race more than the other—which may or may not be true, depending on the particular plan—is foreclosed, and rightly so, by cases like *McLaughlin v. Florida*[71] and *Loving v. Virginia*.[72] The constitutionally relevant fact is that busing hurts certain people precisely because of their color.[73] Third, it might be contended that, busing or no busing, every child will go to some school, whereas a preferential admissions program for a given law school will mean, after its effects have trickled down the entire law school hierarchy, that someone will be completely denied the opportunity to go to law school because he is white. But even assuming this is so,[74] it points to a difference in degree that probably should not go to the constitutional point. Places in desirable public schools are also scarce resources: an opportunity to attend some school is not the equivalent of an opportunity to attend the most desirable school in the area.[75]

The problem in relying on precedent here is that the Court has never told us what the constitutional point is. Voluntary busing plans may, for all we know, be approved by the Court for any of four reasons: (1) the state's goal, racial integration, is a "compelling" one; (2) the use of a racial classification serves that goal perfectly and not approximately; (3) such plans are benignly motivated and therefore not "suspect" in the first place; or (4) the Court believes that even the most apparently "de facto" residential segregation has a bit of state action in its family tree, and that since busing has been imposed as a remedy for de jure segregation there would be no point in forbidding school boards to adopt similar methods. Or it may be—and the delayed dodge of *DeFunis v. Odegaard*[76] strongly suggests this possibility—that the Court simply cannot agree about the significance of its constitutional precedents.[77]

The standard constitutional defense of preferential treatment for blacks accepts the principle that racial classifications are suspect and therefore subject to unusually demanding scrutiny. But that does not mean, the argument continues, that racial classifications are necessarily illegal: they can be justified, but only on the basis of a compelling state interest. It is true that the imposition of a compelling state interest requirement has generally been a prelude to invalidation. But surely, the argument concludes, the promotion of racial integration must be compelling enough. The words certainly flow in logical sequence, but simple assertions of relative importance can never wholly satisfy; one might again respond "double standard," were "no standard" not more obviously appropriate.

I shall argue that reverse racial discrimination can be constitutional, but for reasons quite different from those in the conventional account. Rather than asserting that the demands of "strict scrutiny" can be met—an assertion neither the Court nor anyone else has given us criteria for evaluating— I shall suggest that "strict scrutiny" is not appropriate when white people have decided to favor black people at the expense of white people. On one level there is a double standard here too: whites can do things to whites they could not do to blacks. But on another, the principle I propose is a neutral one: regardless of whether it is wise or unwise, it is not "suspect" in a constitutional sense for a majority, any majority, to discriminate against itself.[78]

I

The unconstitutionality of all racial discrimination, malign and benign alike, is sometimes urged on the ground that the Fourteenth Amendment, although it does not mention race, was enacted largely to outlaw racial discrimination. But the express preoccupation of the framers of the amendment was with discrimination against blacks, that is, with making sure that whites would not, despite the Thirteenth Amendment, continue to confine blacks to an inferior position.[79] That this is the amendment's history surely cannot conclude the matter; given the historical context, discrimination against blacks is about all the framers would have been concerned about, and the Equal Protection Clause has rightly been construed to protect other minorities. But at the same time, the amendment cannot be applied without a sense of its historical meaning and function. Responsible inquiry must seek to determine the reasons why courts give unusually demanding scrutiny to classifications by which the dominant white majority has advantaged itself at the expense of blacks, and to what extent those reasons apply where that majority chooses to disadvantage itself in favor of blacks.

As a prelude, it may be useful to examine the manner and rationale of the ordinary ("rational relationship") review accorded ordinary ("nonsuspect") classifications under the Equal Protection Clause.[80] Let's take a familiar example, a state statute that permits optometrists, but not opticians, to duplicate lenses.[81] Consider further the plea of an optician who wishes to demonstrate that, although it may be true that most optometrists are better qualified to duplicate lenses than most opticians, *he* is as well or better qualified to duplicate lenses than a number of optometrists. The proffered proof would be rejected, on the theory that legislative classification on the basis of admittedly imperfect comparative generalizations—stereotypes, if you will—must be tolerated: unbearable cost would result if the government were obligated to create procedures for deciding each and every case on its individual merits.

Our optician's next argument would be that although classifications rooted in comparative generalization are sometimes permissible, the unfairness that results to a number of individuals, himself included, from *this* classification is so great that it cannot be justified by the savings it effects. If the fit between classification and goal could be made tighter at no cost whatever, the court might label the classification "irrational" and demand that it be made more discerning.[82] But where, as in virtually every case involving real legislation, a more perfect fit would involve some added cost—either the cost to society of permitting some unqualified people to practice or the cost to the government of creating a case-by-case test of qualification—the court would refuse to second-guess the legislative cost-benefit balance. There is no reason to suppose, at least in an "ordinary" case like this, that legislatures are any more likely than courts either to undervalue the unfairness of a rough or undiscerning classification or to overvalue the cost of reducing the incidence of unfairness.

The usual point of departure from the realm of ordinary review is Justice Stone's "*Carolene Products* footnote," which may indeed point the way toward an acceptable mean between crabbed literalism in constitutional interpretation and a roving commission to correct social ills. For present purposes I refer to the suggestion that

> prejudice against discrete and insular minorities may be a special condition, which tends seriously to curtail the operation of those political processes ordinarily to be relied upon to protect minorities, and which may call for a correspondingly more searching judicial inquiry.[83]

The passage is a vague one, as Justice Rehnquist has recently reminded us: "It would hardly take extraordinary ingenuity for a lawyer to find 'insular and discrete' minorities at every turn in the road."[84] Indeed, in a sense the complainant in every equal protection case speaks for such a group: he would not be in court if the class in which the legislature had placed him were not, on at least one occasion, a political minority (they lost), both discrete (they're on the disfavored side of the statutory line) and insular (they couldn't gather enough allies to defeat the legislation). Such tautologies demonstrate the perils of an excessively narrow frame of reference: in seeking criteria that identify the appropriate occasions for distrust, we must look beyond the state activity in the specific case at bar.

Two factors often mentioned to account for the special scrutiny accorded racial classifications[85] are that racial minorities have been subjected to legal disadvantage throughout our history,[86] and that race is "generally . . . irrelevant to any legitimate public purpose."[87] Neither factor alone can adequately account for extraordinary scrutiny. Some minorities (extortionists, for example) have been repeatedly disadvantaged by the law with good reason. And the fact that a characteristic is irrelevant in almost all legal contexts (as most characteristics are) need not imply that there is anything wrong in seizing upon it in the rare context where it isn't.[88] Still, these two factors in combination add up to something significant. The fact that a group has repeatedly been disadvantaged in ways that no one could rationally defend should make us suspicious of any legislation that singles out that group for disadvantage. There is reason to suspect that the prejudices that generated the plainly irrational legislation of past eras are also partly responsible for the facially more palatable classifications of the present day. That suspicion in turn would seem to support the Court's disinclination to credit the usually sufficient imperfect-but-plausible statistical generalization in such contexts. For the usual mode of review assumes that legislatures can generally be trusted to appreciate the unfairness of a loose-fitting classification and objectively balance that unfairness against the savings it effects. Where there is unusual reason to suspect a legislative desire generally and irrationally to subjugate the group disadvantaged by the classification, however, this usual assumption seems an inappropriate basis for a system of review.

Of course, it cannot be said with assurance that all classifications by race that disadvantage minorities were intended to do so.[89] The word, however, is "suspect." The soundness of the Court's decision to treat these classifications with suspicion, irrespective of what can actually be proven about the legislature's underlying motivation, is corroborated by another point of distinction from the usual classification (to which the "rational relationship" standard is applied). Racial classifications that disadvantage minorities are rooted in "we-they" generalizations and balances as opposed to "they-they" generalizations and balances. Few legislators are opticians; but few are optometrists either. Thus, although a decision to distinguish opticians from optometrists incorporates a stereotypical comparison of two classes of people, it is a comparison of two "they" stereotypes, viz., "*They* [opticians] generally differ from *them* [optometrists] in certain respects that we find sufficient on balance to justify the decision to classify on this basis." Legislators, however, have traditionally not only not been black; they have been white. A decision to distinguish blacks from whites therefore has its roots in a comparison between a "we" stereotype and a "they" stereotype, viz., "*They* [blacks] differ from *us* [whites] in certain respects that we find sufficient on balance to justify the decision to classify on this basis."[90]

The choice between classifying on the basis of a comparative generalization and attempting to come up with a more discriminating formula always involves balancing the increase in fairness that greater individualization will produce against the added costs it will entail. But in we-they situations two dangers inherent in this balancing process are significantly intensified. The first is that legislators will overestimate the costs of bringing "them" into a position of equality with "us." But the balance is also likely to be skewed in another, though related, way—through an undervaluation of the countervailing interest in fairness. It is no startling psychological insight that most of us are delighted to hear and prone to accept characterizations of ethnic or other groups that suggest that the groups to which we belong are superior to others.[91] The second danger is therefore one of overestimating the fit of the proposed stereotypical classification. By seizing upon the positive myths about our own class and the negative myths about theirs, or for that matter the realities respecting some or most members of the two classes, legislators may too readily assume that not many of "them" will be unfairly deprived, nor many of "us" unfairly benefited, by the proposed classification.[92]

II

An understanding of why the Court has approached racial classifications that disadvantage minorities with suspicion unfortunately generates no bright line test to determine whether other, nonracial minorities should receive similar protection.[93] The implication of that understanding for the present discussion, however, seems obvious. When the group that controls the decision making process classifies so as to advantage a minority and disadvantage itself, the reasons for being unusually suspicious, and, consequently, employing a stringent brand of review, are lacking. A white majority is unlikely to disadvantage itself for reasons of racial prejudice; nor is it likely to be tempted either to underestimate the needs and deserts of whites relative to those of others, or to overestimate the costs of devising an alternative classification that would extend to certain whites the advantages generally extended to blacks.[94] The conclusion is corroborated by the realization, given eloquent voice in Justice Jackson's *Railway Express* opinion,[95] that the function of the Equal Protection Clause is in large measure to protect against substantive outrages by requiring that those who would harm others must at the same time harm themselves—or at least widespread elements of the constituency on which they depend for reelection. But the argument does not work the other way around: similar reasoning supports no insistence that one cannot hurt himself, or the majority on whose support he depends, without at the same time hurting others as well.

Of course, there will be cases in which it will not be clear whether the legislative majority or the allegedly benefited minority has ended up, on balance, with the comparative advantage—or, more to the point, whether the decision makers intended a greater benefit to the "we"s or the "they"s. In these cases we should be suspicious.[96] Furthermore, preoccupation with a majority-minority analytic framework should not obscure the fundamental premise that racial and related prejudices can properly give rise to suspicion. Such prejudice could obviously generate a "they-they" classification, and for that matter a classification that facially disadvantages the legislative majority but was intended, and will function, as a de facto they-they classification. Thus, there might be reason to believe that a law that apparently favors blacks over whites was specifically intended to disadvantage a subset of whites that is both inadequately represented in the decision making body and the object of unusual prejudice. But where there is no reason to suspect that the comparative disadvantage will not be distributed evenly throughout the "we" class, a we-they classification that favors the "they"s does not merit "strict scrutiny"—though obviously the court should take a careful look to make sure that the case presented fits this description. Whether or not it is more blessed to give than to receive, it is surely less suspicious.[97]

III

*   *   *

Some of us used to worry that any employment by the government of racial classifications for "benign" purposes—particularly with the Supreme Court's legitimation—would retard public acceptance and enforcement of decisions like *Brown v. Board of Education*.[98] The concern might have carried the day so long as there was reason to hope that simply removing racial access barriers would result in genuine integration of society's various institutions. Although the barriers have not yet been entirely removed—heated debate on "benign" discrimination must not fool us into believing that malign discrimination is a thing of the past—we have enough experience to suggest that an "open door" is not sufficient, that if we are to have any hope of defeating racial prejudice we will, at least for a time, have to take race into account for some purposes. And if that is the course we are to take, then that is the message we will have to project, difficult though it may be to expose the "contradiction" as only apparent.

> Governmental use of benign racial classifications may destroy blinding myths by teaching people that race is indeed a factor of great importance in our society and that many people are now disadvantaged because of past and continuing racial

discrimination. These measures may illustrate that in appraising individuals for many purposes race cannot be ignored if the appraisal is to bear a realistic relation to the person's circumstances. . . .[99]

The question is whether the negative educative effects of using racial criteria to overcome centuries of discrimination are so inevitable, and so threatening, as to outweigh the good that such programs may accomplish. It is a difficult question, but the basis for an affirmative answer can hardly be secure enough to support an absolute declaration of constitutional impermissibility.

A credible explanation of why "benign" racial classifications are not suspect, however, would require the Court to expose some of the considerations that have made malign racial classifications suspect, and that exposure poses arguable risks for the judicial process. Explaining that the Court has accorded special review to most racial classifications because they are often the product of irrational prejudice might prompt a charge that the Court builds its constitutional judgments on "sociology, not law."[100] Even if the Court could sidestep that charge with an explanation phrased more in terms of the relative nonsuspiciousness of a group's decision to disadvantage itself in favor of another, it would still find itself in sensitive territory. The justices might feel awkward about publicly taking into account the racial or other composition of the decision-making body, or perhaps of its constituency,[101] even assuming that the pertinent facts are obvious.[102] As far back as 1879 the Court, in a passage that indeed begins to hint at the analysis suggested in this paper, indicated that it saw no particular impropriety in such a reference:

> If in those States where the colored people constitute a majority of the entire population a law should be enacted excluding all white men from jury service, thus denying to them the privilege of participating equally with the blacks in the administration of justice, we apprehend no one would be heard to claim that it would not be a denial to white men of the equal protection of the laws.[103]

Perhaps there is more unseemliness here than met the Court's eye, but it seems insufficient to justify a broad "prophylactic" rule that would deny the states the power to pursue a vision of racial equality with positive action.

Those who are troubled would be better advised to consider another alternative, eloquently elaborated in the earlier writings of Professor Bickel (indeed, "benevolent quotas" were one of his chief examples): denial of review. Powerful attacks have been mounted on the use of the "passive virtues" to avoid the invalidation of practices that are wrong on constitutional principle.[104] The use suggested here is different, however, and is addressed to anyone who takes the (debatable) view that although the practice in question is not unconstitutional on principle, explaining why it is not would carry serious costs for the nation generally and the Court in particular.

By virtually inviting another *DeFunis* case, the Court seems to have indicated that it sees no great costs in writing the opinion, and I am inclined to agree. But that decision—and not the decision on the constitutional merits—is the hard one. Measures that favor racial minorities pose a difficult moral question that should, by one method or the other, be left to the states. There is nothing suspicious about a majority's discriminating against itself, though we must never relent in our vigilance lest something masquerading as that should in fact be something else.

Into the 1990s the Supreme Court pursued a policy of cagey compromise concerning racially specific affirmative action, e.g., Regents of the University of California v. Bakke, 438 U.S. 265 (1978), adding in the early part of that decade the novel twist that at least with respect to affirmative action, equal protection doctrine places more stringent demands on the states than on the federal government. Compare City of Richmond v. J.A. Croson Co., 488 U.S. 469 (1989) with Metro Broadcasting, Inc. v. FCC, 497 U.S. 547 (1990). In Adarand Constructors, Inc. v. Peña, 115 S.Ct. 2097 (1995), however, the situation was seemingly clarified somewhat. The good news is that the federal and state standards were apparently restored to their previous unitary condition. The bad news is that the assimilation was in the wrong direction, toward the standard applicable to old-fashioned antiminority racial discrimination ("strict scrutiny") and beyond that the goal of combatting racism was (at least in the absence of a provable history of malign racial discrimination in the particular context involved) disallowed as an invocable governmental goal. Peña was a 5–4 decision, however— the two Clinton appointees numbering among the four dissenters—so presumably the chaos will continue, a prediction that in this case must reluctantly also be placed in the good news column.

Excerpt from *Legislative and Administrative Motivation in Constitutional Law* (1970)[105]

Governmental Encouragement of Private Discrimination

In *Reitman v. Mulkey*,[106] decided in 1967, the Court invalidated an amendment to the California constitution that repealed existing fair housing legislation by recognizing an absolute right to sell or rent to whomever one pleases. In *Hunter v. Erickson*,[107] a 1969 decision, it struck down an amendment to the Akron city charter that provided:

> Any ordinance enacted by the Council of the City of Akron which regulates the use, sale, advertisement, lease, sub-lease or financing of real property of any kind or of any interest therein on the basis of race, color, religion, national origin or ancestry must first be approved by a majority of the electors voting on the question at a regular or general election before such ordinance shall be effective. Any such ordinance in effect at the time of the adoption of this section shall cease to be effective until approved by the electors as provided herein.

The Court's rationale in *Reitman* is less than coherent, but the opinions in *Hunter* begin to delineate the possible grounds of decision. Writing for the Court, Mr. Justice White at one point suggests that the invalidity of such amendments stems from the realization that they will in fact unusually disadvantage racial minorities.[108] The difficulties with this impact approach have been canvassed at length above.[109] At another point he suggests that the amendments are invalid because they cannot legitimately be distinguished from various other amendments that might have been, but were not, passed.[110] This line of argument assumes that a decision constitutionally to enshrine one right rather than another—or otherwise to render it relatively immune to the democratic process—is subject from the outset to a demand for (at least) a rational defense. That position cannot be maintained, however, for such choices cannot be held up to a standard of rationality. If asked to justify their decision to protect a right of privacy but not a right to indictment by a grand jury, or vice versa, the drafters and enactors of a state constitution can really say no more than that they thought it more important or more fundamental; courts can apply a "rationality-irrationality" calculus here no more than they can with respect to a criminal code.

The fact that such a "disadvantageous distinction model"[111] cannot intelligibly be imposed on such choices suggests the applicability of the analysis proposed by this article. A decision to render a particular right relatively immune to the democratic process is not subject ab initio to the demand for a legitimate defense, but proof of a motivation that violates the federal Constitution should trigger such a demand. Since it is ultimately impossible to analyze or support a decision thus to enshrine a particular right in terms of anything *but* a value judgment, proof of an unconstitutional motivation would inevitably ensure the invalidation of such a choice.[112] Though he gets there by a different route, this is essentially the position Mr. Justice Harlan takes in his concurrence in *Hunter*, which suggests that *Reitman* was wrongly decided and attempts to distinguish the two cases.

If states are not affirmatively obligated to combat private acts of racial discrimination, Mr. Justice Harlan's conclusion that no unconstitutional motivation was proven in *Reitman* seems well founded. It is difficult to infer that a majority of those voting for the California amendment were moved by a desire to impose a special disadvantage upon racial minorities attempting to gain passage of fair housing legislation, rather than by the broader and nonracial motivation reflected on the face of the provision on which they were asked to pass judgment—a desire to place *all* restrictions on vendors' and renters' freedom of choice beyond the reach of the ordinary political processes.

> Neither the State nor any subdivision or agency thereof shall deny, limit or abridge, directly or indirectly, the right of any person, who is willing or desires to sell, lease or rent any part or all of his real property, to decline to sell, lease or rent such property to such person or persons as he, in his absolute discretion, chooses.

Although one must suspect that a number of voters had racial or religious discrimination in mind when they voted for this provision, its language is more consistent with a desire to safeguard the seller's or landlord's right to refuse to deal with anyone who for any reason that displeases him—be it because of his race, his age, the length of his hair, or the cut of his jib—than it is with a desire to place unusual obstacles in the path of racial or religious groups seeking legislative protection from discrimination.[113] And if we are to take seriously the Court's assertions that states are under no affirmative obligation to discourage [private] racial and religious discrimination—that in taking or refraining from various actions,[114] they need simply maintain a position of neutrality with respect to the likely or actual practice of such discrimination[115]—the former motivation cannot be counted unconstitutional.

The *Hunter* amendment, Mr. Justice Harlan correctly asserts, cannot be regarded as neutral in this sense: because it is directed in terms at legislation respecting racial and religious groups, it plainly was enacted with the motivation of rendering unusually difficult the efforts of such groups to secure protection via the political process.

Mr. Justice Harlan's employment of a motivation approach in this context is sound only if neutrality is sufficient in the sense that states are not affirmatively obligated to combat racial discrimination in the sale and rental of housing and other transactions which the law historically has regulated. If however, as Professor Black has forcefully argued,[116] the state's duty to ensure "the equal protection of the laws" incorporates such an obligation, reference to motivation is out of place; the Court need only survey the steps the state has taken and determine whether they constitute adequate fulfillment of the constitutional obligation. Doubtless some, perhaps for historical reasons, will not agree that the Fourteenth Amendment can responsibly be given this expansive a reading. But one objection which clearly should not be heeded is that this position shares the dangers that inhere in requiring states affirmatively to seek racial balance in various areas by quota systems or other methods that take race into account. A resolution not to force states to take race into account in making choices, and a consequent requirement only that they not take race into account, coexists quite comfortably with a resolution to require states to require their citizens, similarly, *not* to take race into account. Since *Reitman* is defensible on no other basis,[117] we might do well to regard it (admittedly tendentiously) as having established this affirmative obligation.

Despite the fact that the Fourteenth Amendment forbids states to "deny to any person within [their] jurisdiction the equal protection of the laws," there seems not a chance in hell that during our lifetimes the Supreme Court will buy my last suggestion, that states are affirmatively obligated to enact and enforce laws forbidding their citizens to discriminate on the basis of race. That being so, I remain convinced that the only coherent approach to the so-called "state action" problem is to hold that whenever the state has helped to enforce an act of discrimination there is sufficient "state action" to activate the Constitution, but then go on to ask—as did the foregoing excerpt—whether in doing so the relevant state body or official was motivated by an intention to facilitate discrimination or simply pursuing a general policy of vindicating private choices. The question, in other words—again supposing we remain unwilling to impose on the state an affirmative duty to prevent discrimination—is whether the discriminatory motive was the state's or that of some private party acting pursuant to the state's permission. If the former, or if both, the law in question should fall even under this more conservative reading of the Fourteenth Amendment.

8

"Substantive Due Process"[1]

Memorandum for Chief Justice Warren Concerning
Griswold v. Connecticut (1965)[2]

Appellant Buxton is a physician and professor at Yale Medical School.
Appellant Griswold is executive director of the Connecticut Planned Parenthood League. After this Court's decision in *Poe v. Ullman*, 367 U.S.
497, the Planned Parenthood Center of New Haven was opened. Buxton
was its medical director, Mrs. Griswold its acting director. The center's
purpose was to provide information, instruction, and medical advice to
married persons about the ways of preventing conception. It did so during
the period it was open, November 1 to November 10, 1961. The general
procedure with regard to a woman who came seeking advice was to "take
her case history" and explain to her the various methods of contraception.
She was then examined by a staff doctor, who prescribed for her the sort of
device she selected, unless he saw reasons why it would be inappropriate
for her. The patient was furnished with the device, and a doctor or nurse
explained its use. Fees were charged according to family income, ranging
from nothing to $15.

Appellants were arrested on informations alleging violations of 53–32
and 54–196 of the Connecticut General Statutes.

Section 53–32 provides:

> *Use of drugs or instruments to prevent conception.* Any person who uses any
> drug, medicinal article or instrument for the purpose of preventing conception
> shall be fined not less than fifty dollars or imprisoned not less than sixty days nor
> more than one year or be both fined and imprisoned.

Section 54–196 provides:

> *Accessories.* Any person who assists, abets, counsels, causes, hires or com-
> mands another to commit any offense may be prosecuted and punished as if he
> were the principal offender.

Appellants demurred on the grounds, inter alia, that the statutes denied due
process under the Fourteenth Amendment, and denied freedom of speech
under the First and Fourteenth Amendments. The demurrers were overruled. Appellants were tried before the court without a jury, convicted, and

given $100 fines. The Appellate Division affirmed, despite a challenge on the constitutional grounds mentioned above, as did the Connecticut Supreme Court of Errors.

* * *

I think the conviction should be reversed, but that the Court should carefully choose its ground of decision, for some of those urged by appellants have dangerous implications.

* * *

Just as I think the Court should vigorously enforce every clause in the Constitution, I do not think the Court should enforce clauses that are not there, no matter how strong one's dislike for the piece of legislation in question may be. Despite Justice Brandeis's lifelong crusade for a [tort of invasion] of privacy, and despite the desirability of having such a right form the basis of a tort action, the Constitution says nothing about any such right. It is true that privacy is protected by the Constitution in many ways. The First Amendment protects freedom of religion, which is a form of privacy if one wishes to call it that, but it is limited to religion; it suggests no general right of privacy. And so it is with the Third, Fourth, and Fifth Amendments: each protects a certain aspect of privacy. But it by no means follows that because several parts of the Constitution protect aspects of what might be called privacy, the Constitution therefore contains a general right of privacy, with a content over and above the content of the various specific provisions.[3] Simply to announce that the Ninth Amendment protects privacy . . . is of course to beg the question.

Even if it be assumed that the Constitution does protect some general right of privacy, appellants have not shown that the instant case would be covered by such a right. . . . I can see how one could say that eavesdropping, spying, midnight raids, and searches are invasions of privacy. But how is a law prohibiting the use of contraceptives such? Admittedly, the subject matter of the law touches a very intimate area. But it is a long step from that admission to the conclusion that the constitutional right of privacy, assuming such exists, has been invaded. With all respect, it seems to me that Mr. Justice Harlan's opinion in *Poe* [*v. Ullman*[4]] boils down to a statement that he does not like the Connecticut law. This vague, "outrage" approach to the Fourteenth Amendment constitutes, in my opinion, the most dangerous sort of "activism."

* * *

Nonetheless, I think the case should be reversed. It seems to me that the real vice of the birth control statute lies in the way it works in practice. The prohibition on sale and use, and the prohibition on advice given by private physicians, are not enforced. Thus the rich and well-informed, who can go to private doctors, or who know enough about contraception to go to the drugstore and purchase the appropriate devices, are not bothered by the law. It is the poor and ill-informed who most need contraception and advice on family planning. Clinics are of course the answer. Yet it is only against the clinics that the law is enforced, as it was in the *Nelson* case and has been in this case. Thus those who need birth control most are the only ones who are denied it. Ordinarily, [given the lack of probative statistics,] it would be difficult for this Court to go off on disparities in enforcement. However, here the disparity is not simply among the classes of persons against whom the law is enforced, but among the different *provisions* of the law. This sort of disparity is easier to pin down. Indeed, the Court could take note of its statement in *Poe* if it needed authority for the proposition that the law is enforced only against clinics. In *Yick Wo v. Hopkins*, 118 U.S. 356, 375 (1885), this Court held:

> Though the law itself be fair on its face and impartial in appearance, yet, if it is applied and administered by public authority with an evil eye and an unequal hand, so as practically to make unjust and illegal discriminations between persons in similar circumstances, material to their rights, the denial of equal justice is still within the prohibition of the Constitution.

* * *

The case should thus be reversed . . . on the ground that the law is administered so as to hurt only the poor and ill-informed. To reverse it either on the ground that some sort of right to privacy has been violated, or on the ground that a moral judgment also espoused by the Roman Catholic church is one that cannot permissibly be accepted by a state legislature, would, in my opinion, have very dangerous implications.

Once again, it appears my habits of thought were formed at an age some might find distressingly early. (I confess I don't.) The self-assured tone of the language also suggests a young man who doesn't quite know his place—conceivably another continuing theme (without the "young" part). However all that may be, Chief Justice Warren didn't buy a word of this (aside from the recommendation that the Court reverse the conviction) and went along with the Court's right to privacy line.

The Wages of Crying Wolf: A Comment on Roe v. Wade (1973)[5]

> The interests of the mother and the fetus are opposed. On which side should the State throw its weight? The issue is volatile; and it is resolved by the moral code which an individual has.[6]

In *Roe v. Wade*,[7] decided January 22, 1973, the Supreme Court—Justice Blackmun speaking for everyone but Justices White and Rehnquist[8]—held unconstitutional Texas's (and virtually every other state's[9]) criminal abortion statute. The broad outlines of its argument are not difficult to make out:

1. The right to privacy, though not mentioned in the Constitution, is protected by the Due Process Clause of the Fourteenth Amendment.[10]

2. This right "is broad enough to encompass a woman's decision whether or not to terminate her pregnancy."[11]

3. This right to an abortion is "fundamental" and can therefore be regulated only on the basis of a "compelling" state interest.[12]

4. The state does have two "important and legitimate" interests here,[13] the first in protecting maternal health, the second in protecting the life (or potential life[14]) of the fetus. But neither can be counted "compelling" throughout the entire pregnancy: Each matures with the unborn child.

> These interests are separate and distinct. Each grows in substantiality as the woman approaches term and, at a point during pregnancy, each becomes "compelling."[15]

5. During the first trimester of pregnancy, neither interest is sufficiently compelling to justify any interference with the decision of the woman and her physician. Appellants have referred the Court to medical data indicating that mortality rates for women undergoing early abortions, where abortion is legal, "appear to be as low as or lower than the rates for normal childbirth."[16] Thus the state's interest in protecting maternal health is not compelling during the first trimester. Since the interest in protecting the fetus is not yet compelling either,[17] during the first trimester the state can neither prohibit an abortion nor regulate the conditions under which one is performed.[18]

6. As we move into the second trimester, the interest in protecting the fetus remains less than compelling, and the decision to have an abortion thus continues to control. However, at this point the health risks of abortion begin to exceed those of childbirth. "It follows that, from and after this point, a State may regulate the abortion procedure to the extent that the regulation reasonably relates to the preservation and protection of maternal health."[19] Abortion may not be prohibited during the second trimester, however.[20]

7. At the point at which the fetus becomes viable[21] the interest in protecting it becomes compelling, and therefore from that point on the state can prohibit abortions *except*—and this limitation is also apparently a constitutional command, though it receives no justification in the opinion—when they are necessary to protect maternal life or health.[22]

I

A number of fairly standard criticisms can be made of *Roe*. A plausible narrower basis of decision, that of vagueness, is brushed aside in the rush toward broader ground.[23] The opinion strikes the reader initially as a sort of guidebook, addressing questions not before the Court and drawing lines with an apparent precision one generally associates with a commissioner's regulations. On closer examination, however, the precision proves largely illusory. Confusing signals are emitted, particularly with respect to the nature of the doctor's responsibilities[24] and the permissible scope of health regulations after the first trimester.[25] The Court seems, moreover, to get carried away on the subject of remedies: even assuming the case can be made for an unusually protected constitutional right to an abortion, it hardly seems necessary to have banned during the first trimester *all* state regulation of the conditions under which abortions can be performed.[26]

By terming such criticisms "standard," I do not mean to suggest they are unimportant, for they are not. But if they were all that was wrong with *Roe*, it would not merit special comment.[27]

II

Let us not underestimate what is at stake: having an unwanted child can go a long way toward ruining a woman's life.[28] And at bottom *Roe* signals the Court's judgment that this result cannot be justified by any good that anti-abortion legislation accomplishes. This surely is an understandable conclusion—indeed it is one with which I agree—but ordinarily the Court claims no mandate to second-guess legislative balances, at least not when the Constitution has designated neither of the values in conflict as entitled to special protection. But even assuming it would be a good idea for the Court to assume this function, *Roe* seems a curious place to have begun. Laws prohibiting the use of "soft" drugs or, even more obviously, homosexual acts between consenting adults can stunt "the preferred life styles"[29] of those against whom enforcement is threatened in very serious ways. It is clear such acts harm no one besides the participants, and indeed the case that the participants are harmed is a rather shaky one.[30] Yet such laws survive, on the theory that there exists a societal consensus that the behavior involved is revolting or at any rate immoral.[31] Of course the consensus is not universal but it is sufficient, and this is what is counted crucial, to get the laws passed and keep them on the books. Whether anti-abortion legislation cramps the life style of an unwilling mother more significantly than anti-homosexuality legislation cramps the life style of a homosexual may be a close question. But even granting that it does, the other side of the balance looks very different. For there is more than simple societal revulsion to support legislation restricting abortion: abortion ends (or if it makes a difference, prevents) the life of a human being other than the one making the choice.

The Court's response here is simply not adequate. It agrees, indeed it holds, that after the point of viability (a concept it fails to note will become even less clear than it is now as the technology of birth continues to develop[32]) the interest in protecting the fetus is compelling.[33] Exactly why that is the magic moment is not made clear: viability, as the Court defines it,[34] is achieved some six to twelve weeks after quickening.[35] (Quickening is the point at which the fetus begins discernibly to move independently of the mother and the point that has historically been deemed crucial—to the extent *any* point between conception and birth has been focused on.[36]) But no, it is *viability* that is constitutionally critical: the Court's defense seems to mistake a definition for a syllogism.

> With respect to the State's important and legitimate interest in potential life, the "compelling" point is at viability. This is so because the fetus then presumably has the capacity of meaningful life outside the mother's womb.[37]

With regard to why the state cannot consider this "important and legitimate interest" prior to viability, the opinion is even less satisfactory. The discussion begins sensibly enough: the interest asserted is not necessarily tied to the question whether the fetus is "alive," for whether or not one calls it a living being, it is an entity with the potential for (and indeed the likelihood of) life.[38] But all of arguable relevance that follows[39] are arguments that fetuses (a) are not recognized as "persons in the whole sense" by legal doctrine generally and (b) are not "persons" protected by the Fourteenth Amendment.

To the extent they are not entirely inconclusive, the bodies of doctrine to which the Court adverts respecting the protection of fetuses under general legal doctrine tend to undercut rather than support its conclusion.[40] And the argument that fetuses (unlike, say, corporations) are not "persons" under the Fourteenth Amendment fares little better. The Court notes that most constitutional clauses using the word "persons"—such as the one outlining the qualifications for the presidency—appear to have been drafted with postnatal beings in mind. (It might have added that most of them were plainly drafted with *adults* in mind, but I suppose that wouldn't have helped.) In addition, "the appellee conceded on reargument that no case can be cited that holds that a fetus is a person within the meaning of the Fourteenth Amendment."[41] (The other legal contexts in which the question could have arisen are not enumerated.)

The canons of construction employed here are perhaps most intriguing when they are contrasted with those invoked to derive the constitutional right to an abortion.[42] But in any event, the argument that fetuses lack constitutional rights is simply irrelevant. For it has never been held or even asserted that the state interest needed to justify forcing a person to refrain from an activity, whether or not that activity is constitutionally protected, must implicate either the life or the constitutional rights of another person.[43] Dogs are not "persons in the whole sense" nor have they constitutional rights, but that does not mean the state cannot prohibit killing them: it does not even mean the state cannot prohibit killing them in the exercise of the First Amendment right of political protest. Come to think of it, draft cards aren't persons either.[44]

Thus even assuming the Court ought generally to get into the business of second-guessing legislative balances, it has picked a strange case with which to begin. Its purported evaluation of the balance that produced anti-abortion legislation simply does not meet the issue: that the life plans of the mother must, not simply may, prevail over the state's desire to protect the fetus simply does not follow from the judgment that the fetus is not a person. Beyond all that, however, the Court has no business getting into that business.

III

Were I a legislator I would vote for a statute very much like the one the Court ends up drafting.[45] I hope this reaction reflects more than the psychological phenomenon that keeps bombardiers sane—the fact that it is somehow easier to "terminate" those you cannot see—and am inclined to think it does: that the mother, unlike the unborn child, has begun to imagine a future for herself strikes me as morally quite significant. But God knows I'm not *happy* with that resolution. Abortion is too much like infanticide on the one hand, and too much like contraception on the other, to leave one comfortable with any answer; and the moral issue it poses is as fiendish as any philosopher's hypothetical.[46]

Of course, the Court often resolves difficult moral questions, and difficult questions yield controversial answers. I doubt, for example, that most people would agree that letting a drug peddler go unapprehended is morally preferable to letting the police kick down his door without probable cause. The difference, of course, is that the Constitution, which legitimates and theoretically controls judicial intervention, has some rather pointed things to say about this choice. There will of course be difficult questions about the applicability of its language to specific facts, but at least the document's special concern with one of the values in conflict is manifest. It simply says nothing, clear or fuzzy, about abortion.

*   *   *

[The Court asserts] that there is a general right of privacy granted special protection—that is, protection above and beyond the baseline requirement of "rationality"—by the Fourteenth Amendment,[47] and that that right "is broad enough to encompass" the right to an abortion. The general right of privacy is inferred, as it was in *Griswold v. Connecticut*,[48] from various provisions of the Bill of Rights manifesting a concern with privacy, notably the Fourth Amendment's guarantee against unreasonable searches, the Fifth Amendment's privilege against self-incrimination, and the right, inferred from the First Amendment, to keep one's political associations secret.

One possible response is that all this proves is that the things explicitly mentioned are forbidden, if indeed it does not actually demonstrate a disposition not to enshrine anything that might be called a general right of privacy.[49] In fact the Court takes this view when it suits its purposes. (On the *same day* it decided *Roe*, the Court held that a showing of reasonableness was not needed to force someone to provide a grand jury with a voice exemplar, reasoning that the Fifth Amendment was not implicated because the evidence was not "testimonial" and that the Fourth Amendment did not apply because there was no "seizure."[50]) But this approach is unduly crabbed. Surely the Court is entitled, indeed I think it is obligated, to seek out the sorts of evils the framers meant to combat and to move against their twentieth-century counterparts.

Thus it seems to me entirely proper to infer a general right of privacy, *so long as some care is taken in defining the sort of right the inference will support*. Those aspects of the First, Fourth, and Fifth Amendments to which the Court refers all limit the ways in which, and the circumstances under which, the government can go about gathering information about a person he would rather it did not have.[51] *Katz v. United States*,[52] limiting governmental tapping of telephones, may not involve what the framers would have called a "search," but it plainly involves this general concern with privacy. *Griswold* is a long step, even a leap, beyond this, but at least the connection is discernible. Had it been a case that purported to discover in the Constitution a "right to contraception," it would have been *Roe*'s strongest precedent. But the Court in *Roe* gives no evidence of so regarding it,[53] and rightly not. Commentators tend to forget, though the Court plainly has not,[54] that the Court in *Griswold* stressed that it was invalidating a portion of Connecticut law that proscribed the use, as opposed to the manufacture, sale, or other distribution of contraceptives. That distinction (which would be silly were the right to contraception being constitutionally enshrined) makes sense if the case is rationalized on the ground that the section of the law whose constitutionality was in issue was such that *its enforcement would have been virtually impossible without* the most outrageous sort of governmental prying into the privacy of the home. And this, indeed is the theory on which the Court appeared to settle:

> The present case, then, concerns a relationship lying within the zone of privacy created by several fundamental constitutional guarantees. And it concerns a law which, in forbidding the *use* of contraceptives rather than regulating their manu-

facture or sale, seeks to achieve its goals by means having a maximum destructive impact upon that relationship. Such a law cannot stand in light of the familiar principle, so often applied by this Court, that "a governmental purpose to control or prevent activities constitutionally subject to state regulation may not be achieved by means which sweep unnecessarily broadly and thereby invade the area of protected freedoms." *NAACP v. Alabama*, 377 U.S. 288, 307. Would we allow the police to search the sacred precincts of marital bedrooms for telltale signs of the use of contraceptives? The very idea is repulsive to the notions of privacy surrounding the marriage relationship.[55]

Thus even assuming (as the Court surely seemed to) that a state can constitutionally seek to minimize or eliminate the circulation and use of contraceptives, Connecticut had acted unconstitutionally by selecting a means, that is a direct ban on use, that would generate intolerably intrusive modes of data-gathering.[56] No such rationalization is attempted by the Court in *Roe*—and understandably not, for whatever else may be involved, it is not a case about governmental snooping.[57]

The Court reports that some amici curiae argued for an unlimited right to do as one wishes with one's body. This theory holds, for me at any rate, much philosophical appeal. However, there would have been serious problems with its invocation in this case. In the first place, more than the mother's own body is involved in a decision to have an abortion; a fetus may not be a "person in the whole sense," but it is certainly not nothing. Second, it is difficult to find a basis for thinking that the theory was meant to be given constitutional sanction: surely it is no part of the "privacy" interest the Bill of Rights suggests:[58]

[I]t is not clear to us that the claim . . . that one has an unlimited right to do with one's body as one pleases bears a close relationship to the right of privacy . . . .[59]

Unfortunately, having thus rejected amici's attempt to define the bounds of the general constitutional right of which the right to an abortion is a part, on the theory that the general right described has little to do with privacy, the Court provides neither an alternative definition[60] nor an account of why it thinks privacy is involved. It simply announces that the right to privacy "is broad enough to encompass a woman's decision whether or not to terminate her pregnancy." Apparently this conclusion is thought to derive from the passage that immediately follows it:

The detriment that the State would impose upon the pregnant woman by denying this choice altogether is apparent. Specific and direct harm medically diagnosable even in early pregnancy may be involved. Maternity, or additional offspring, may force upon the woman a distressful life and future. Psychological harm may be imminent. Mental and physical health may be taxed by child care. There is also the distress, for all concerned, associated with the unwanted child, and there is the problem of bringing a child into a family already unable, psychologically and otherwise, to care for it. In other cases, as in this one, the additional difficulties and continuing stigma of unwed motherhood may be involved.[61]

All of this is true and ought to be taken very seriously. But it has nothing to do with privacy in the Bill of Rights sense or any other the Constitution suggests.[62] I suppose there is nothing to prevent one from using the word "privacy" to mean the freedom to live one's life without governmental interference. But the Court obviously does not so use the term. Nor could it, for such a right is at stake in *every* case. Our life styles are constantly limited, often seriously, by governmental regulation; and while many of us would prefer less direction, granting that desire the status of a preferred constitutional right would yield a system of "government" virtually unrecognizable to us and only slightly more recognizable to our forebears. The Court's observations concerning the serious, life-shaping costs of having a child prove what might to the thoughtless have seemed unprovable: that even though a human life, or a potential human life, hangs in the balance, the moral dilemma abortion poses is so difficult as to be heartbreaking. What they fail to do is even begin to resolve that dilemma so far as our governmental system is concerned by associating either side of the balance with a value inferable from the Constitution.

But perhaps the inquiry should not end even there. In his famous *Carolene Products* footnote, Justice Stone suggested that the interests to which the Court can responsibly give extraordinary constitutional protection include not only those expressed in the Constitution but also those that are unlikely to receive adequate consideration in the political process, specifically the interests of "discrete and insular minorities" unable to form effective political alliances.[63] There can be little doubt that such considerations have influenced the direction, if only occasionally the rhetoric, of the recent Courts. My repeated efforts to convince my students that gender should be treated as a "suspect classification" have convinced me it is no easy matter to state such considerations in a "principled" way. But passing that problem, *Roe* is not an appropriate case for their invocation.

Compared with men, very few women sit in our legislatures, a fact I believe should bear some relevance—even without an Equal Rights Amendment—to the appropriate standard of review for legislation that favors men over women. But *no* fetuses sit in our legislatures. Of course they have their champions, but so have women. The two interests have clashed repeatedly in the political arena, and had continued to do so up to the date of the opinion, generating quite a wide variety of accommodations. By the Court's lights virtually all of the legislative accommodations had unduly favored fetuses; by its definition of victory, women had lost. Yet in every legislative balance one of the competing interests loses to some extent; indeed usually, as here, they both do. On some occasions the Constitution throws its weight on the side of one of them, indicating the balance must be restruck. And on others—and this is Justice Stone's suggestion—it is at least arguable that, constitutional directive or not, the Court should throw its weight on the side of a minority demanding in court more than it was able to achieve politically. But even assuming this suggestion can be given principled content, it was clearly intended and should be reserved for those interests which, *as compared with the interests to which they have been subordinated*, constitute minorities unusually incapable of protecting themselves.[64] Compared with men, women may constitute such a "minority"; compared with the unborn, they do not.[65] I'm not sure I'd know a discrete and insular minority if I saw one, but confronted with a multiple choice question requiring me to designate (a) women or (b) fetuses as one, I'd expect no credit for the former answer.[66]

Of course a woman's freedom to choose an abortion is part of the "liberty" the Fourteenth Amendment says shall not be denied without due process of law, as indeed is anyone's freedom to do what he or she wants. But "due process" generally guarantees only that the inhibition be procedurally fair and that it have some "rational" connection—though plausible is probably a better word[67]—with a permissible governmental goal. What is unusual about *Roe* is that the liberty involved is accorded a far more stringent protection, so stringent that a desire to preserve the fetus's existence is unable to overcome it—a protection more stringent, I think it fair to say, than that the present Court accords the freedom of the press explicitly guaranteed by the First Amendment.[68] What is frightening about *Roe* is that this superprotected right is not inferable from the language of the Constitution, the framers' thinking respecting the specific problem in issue, any general value derivable from the provisions they included, or the nation's governmental structure. Nor is it explainable in terms of the unusual political impotence of the group judicially protected vis-à-vis the interest that legislatively prevailed over it.[69] And that, I believe—the predictable early reaction to *Roe* notwithstanding ("more of the same Warren-type activism") is a charge that can responsibly be leveled at no other decision of the past twenty years.[70] At times the inferences the Court has drawn from the values the Constitution marks for special protection have been controversial, even shaky, but never before has its sense of an obligation to draw one been so obviously lacking.

IV

Not in the last thirty-five years at any rate. For, as the received learning has it, this sort of thing did happen before, repeatedly. From its 1905 decision in *Lochner v. New York*[71] into the 1930s the Court, frequently though not always under the rubric of "liberty of contract," employed the Due Process

Clauses of the Fourteenth and Fifth Amendments to invalidate a good deal of legislation. According to the dissenters at the time and virtually all the commentators since, the Court had simply manufactured a constitutional right out of whole cloth and used it to superimpose its own view of wise social policy on those of the legislatures. So indeed the Court itself came to see the matter, and its reaction was complete:

> There was a time when the Due Process Clause was used by this Court to strike down laws which were thought unreasonable, that is, unwise or incompatible with some particular economic or social philosophy. In this manner the Due Process Clause was used, for example, to nullify laws prescribing maximum hours for work in bakeries, *Lochner v. New York*, 198 U.S. 45 (1905), outlawing "yellow dog" contracts, *Coppage v. Kansas*, 236 U.S. 1 (1915), setting minimum wages for women, *Adkins v. Children's Hospital*, 261 U.S. 525 (1923), and fixing the weight of loaves of bread, *Jay Burns Baking Co. v. Bryan*, 264 U.S. 504 (1924). This intrusion by the judiciary into the realm of legislative value judgments was strongly objected to at the time . . . . Mr. Justice Holmes said,
>
> > "I think the proper course is to recognize that a state legislature can do whatever it sees fit to do unless it is restrained by some express prohibition in the Constitution of the United States or of the State, and that Courts should be careful not to extend such prohibitions beyond their obvious meaning by reading into them conceptions of public policy that the particular Court may happen to entertain."
>
> . . . The doctrine that prevailed in *Lochner, Coppage, Adkins, Burns*, and like cases—that due process authorizes courts to hold laws unconstitutional when they believe the legislature has acted unwisely—has long since been discarded. We have returned to the original constitutional proposition that courts do not substitute their social and economic beliefs for the judgment of legislative bodies, who are elected to pass laws.[72]

It may be objected that *Lochner* et al. protected the "economic rights" of businessmen whereas *Roe* protects a "human right." It should be noted, however, that not all of the *Lochner* series involved economic regulation;[73] that even those that did resist the "big business" stereotype with which the commentators tend to associate them; and that in some of them the employer's "liberty of contract" claim was joined by the employee, who knew that if he had to be employed on the terms set by the law in question, he could not be employed at all.[74] This is a predicament that is economic to be sure, but is not without its "human" dimension. Similarly "human" seems the predicament of the appellees in the 1970 case of *Dandridge v. Williams*,[75] who challenged the Maryland Welfare Department's practice of limiting AFDC grants to $250 regardless of family size or need. Yet in language that remains among its favored points of reference, the Court, speaking through Justice Stewart,[76] dismissed the complaint as "social and economic" and therefore essentially Lochneresque.

> [W]e deal with state regulation in the social and economic field, not affecting freedoms guaranteed by the Bill of Rights. . . . For this Court to approve the invalidation of state economic or social regulation as "overreaching" would be far too reminiscent of an era when the Court thought the Fourteenth Amendment gave it power to strike down state laws "because they may be unwise, improvident, or out of harmony with a particular school of thought." . . . That era long ago passed into history. . . .

> To be sure, the cases cited . . . have in the main involved state regulation of business or industry. The administration of public welfare assistance, by contrast, involves the most basic economic needs of impoverished human beings. We recognize the dramatically real factual difference between the cited cases and this one, but we can find no basis for applying a different constitutional standard. . . . It is a standard . . . that is true to the principle that the Fourteenth Amendment gives the federal courts no power to impose upon the States their views of wise economic or social policy.[77]

It may be, however—at least it is not the sort of claim one can disprove—that the "right to an abortion," or noneconomic rights generally, accord more closely with "this generation's idealization of America"[78] than the "rights" asserted in either *Lochner* or *Dandridge*. But that attitude, of course, is precisely the point of the *Lochner* philosophy, which would grant unusual protection to those "rights" that somehow *seem* most pressing, regardless of whether the Constitution suggests any special solicitude for them. The Constitution has little to say about contract, less about abortion, and those who would speculate about which the framers would have been more likely to protect may not be pleased with the answer.[79] The Court continues to disavow the philosophy of *Lochner*. Yet as Justice Stewart's concurrence admits, it is impossible candidly to regard *Roe* as the product of anything else.[80]

That alone should be enough to damn it. Criticism of the *Lochner* philosophy has been virtually universal and will not be rehearsed here. I would, however, like to suggest briefly that although *Lochner* and *Roe* are twins to be sure, they are not identical. While I would hesitate to argue that one is more defensible than the other in terms of judicial style, there are differences in that regard that suggest that *Roe* may turn out to be the more dangerous precedent.

All the "superimposition of the Court's own value choices" talk is, of course, the characterization of others and not the language of *Lochner* or its progeny. Indeed, those cases did not argue that "liberty of contract" was a preferred constitutional freedom, but rather represented it as merely one among the numerous aspects of "liberty" the Fourteenth Amendment protects, therefore requiring of its inhibitors a "rational" defense.

> In our opinion that section . . . is an invasion of the personal liberty, as well as of the right of property, guaranteed by that Amendment. Such liberty and right

embraces the right to make contracts for the purchase of the labor of others and equally the right to make contracts for the sale of one's own labor; each right, however, being subject to the fundamental condition that no contract, whatever its subject matter, can be sustained which the law, upon reasonable grounds, forbids as inconsistent with the public interests or as hurtful to the public order or as detrimental to the common good.[81]

Undoubtedly, the police power of the State may be exerted to protect purchasers from imposition by sale of short weight loaves. . . . Constitutional protection having been invoked, it is the duty of the court to determine whether the challenged provision has reasonable relation to the protection of purchasers of bread against fraud by short weights and really tends to accomplish the purpose for which it was enacted.[82]

Thus the test *Lochner* and its progeny purported to apply is that which would theoretically control the same questions today: whether a plausible argument can be made that the legislative action furthers some permissible governmental goal. The trouble, of course, is that they misapplied it. *Roe*, on the other hand, is quite explicit that the right to an abortion is a "fundamental" one, requiring not merely a "rational" defense for its inhibition but rather a "compelling" one.

A second difference between *Lochner* et al. and *Roe* has to do with the nature of the legislative judgments being second-guessed. In the main, the "refutations" tendered by the *Lochner* series were of two sorts. The first took the form of declarations that the goals in terms of which the legislatures' actions were defended were impermissible. Thus, for example, the equalization of unequal bargaining power and the strengthening of the labor movement were declared ends the legislature had no business pursuing; thus, its actions could not thereby be justified.[83] The second form of "refutation" took the form not of denying the legitimacy of the goal relied on but rather of denying the plausibility of the legislature's empirical judgment that its action would promote that goal.

In our judgment it is not possible in fact to discover the connection between the number of hours a baker may work in the bakery and the healthful quality of the bread made by the workman.[84]

There is no evidence in support of the thought that purchasers have been or are likely to be induced to take a nine and a half or a ten ounce loaf for a pound (16 ounce) loaf, or an eighteen and a half or a 19 ounce loaf for a pound and a half (24 ounce) loaf; and it is contrary to common experience and unreasonable to assume that there could be any danger of such deception.[85]

The *Roe* opinion's "refutation" of the legislative judgment that anti-abortion statutes can be justified in terms of the protection of the fetus takes neither of these forms. The Court grants that protecting the fetus is an "important and legitimate" governmental goal,[86] and of course it does not deny that restricting abortion promotes it. What it does, instead, is simply announce that that goal is not important enough to sustain the restriction. There is little doubt that judgments of this sort were involved in *Lochner* et al., but what the Court *said* in those cases was not that the legislature had incorrectly balanced two legitimate but competing goals, but rather that the goal it had favored was impermissible or that the legislation involved did not really promote it.

Perhaps this is merely a rhetorical difference, but it could prove to be important. *Lochner* et al. were thoroughly disreputable decisions; but at least they did us the favor of sowing the seeds of their own destruction. To say that the equalization of bargaining power or the fostering of the labor movement is a goal outside the ambit of a "police power" broad enough to forbid all contracts the state legislature can reasonably regard "as inconsistent with the public interests or as hurtful to the public order or as detrimental to the common good"[87] is to say something that is, in a word, wrong.[88] And it is just as obviously wrong to declare, for example, that restrictions on long working hours cannot reasonably be said to promote health and safety.[89] *Roe*'s "refutation" of the legislative judgment, on the other, is not obviously wrong, for the substitution of one nonrational judgment for another concerning the relative importance of a mother's opportunity to live the life she has planned, and a fetus's opportunity to live at all, can be labeled neither wrong nor right. The problem with *Roe* is not so much that it bungles the question it sets itself, but rather that it sets itself a question the Constitution has not made the Court's business. It *looks* different from *Lochner*—it has the shape if not the substance of a judgment that is very much the Court's business, one vindicating an interest the Constitution marks as special—and it is for that reason perhaps more dangerous. Of course in a sense it is more candid than *Lochner*.[90] But the employment of a higher standard of judicial review, no matter how candid the recognition that it is indeed higher, loses some of its admirability when it is accompanied by neither a coherent account of why such a standard is appropriate nor any indication of why it has not been satisfied.

V

I do wish "Wolf!" hadn't been cried so often. When I suggest to my students that *Roe* lacks even colorable support in the constitutional text, history, or any other appropriate source of constitutional doctrine, they tell me they've heard all that before. When I point out they haven't heard it before from *me*, I can't really blame them for smiling.

But at least crying "Wolf!" doesn't influence the wolves; crying "Lochner!" may. Of course the Warren Court was aggressive in enforcing its ideals of liberty and equality. *But by and large, it attempted to defend its decisions in terms of inferences from values the Constitution marks as special.*[91] Its inferences were often controversial, but just as often our profession's prominent criticism deigned not to address them on their terms and contented itself with assertions that the Court was indulging in sheer acts of will, ramming its personal preferences down the country's throat—that it was, in a word, Lochnering. One possible judicial response to this style of criticism would be to conclude that one might as well be hanged for a sheep as a goat: so long as you're going to be told, no matter what you say, that all you do is Lochner, you might as well Lochner. Another, perhaps more likely in a new appointee, might be to reason that since Lochnering has so long been standard procedure, "just one more" (in a good cause, of course) can hardly matter. Actual reactions, of course, are not likely to be this self-conscious, but the critical style of offhand dismissal may have taken its toll nonetheless.

Of course the Court has been aware that criticism of much that it has done has been widespread in academic as well as popular circles. But when it looks to the past decade's most prominent academic criticism, it will often find little there to distinguish it from the popular. Disagreements with the chain of inference by which the Court got from the Constitution to its result, if mentioned at all, have tended to be announced in the most conclusory terms, and the impression has often been left that the real quarrel of the academy, like that of the laity, is with the results the Court has been reaching and perhaps with judicial "activism" in general.[92] Naturally the Court is sensitive to criticism of this sort, but these are issues on which it will, when push comes to shove, trust its own judgment. (And it has no reason not to: law professors do not agree on what results are "good," and even if they did, there is no reason to assume their judgment is any better on that issue than the Court's.) And academic criticism of the sort that might (because it should) have some effect—criticism suggesting misperceptions in the Court's reading of the value structure set forth in the document from which it derives its authority, or unjustifiable inferences it has drawn from that value structure—has seemed for a time somehow out of fashion, the voguish course being simply to dismiss the process by which a disfavored result was reached as Lochnering pure and simple. But if the critics cannot trouble themselves with such details, it is difficult to expect the Court to worry much about them either.

This tendency of commentators to substitute snappy dismissal for careful evaluation of the Court's constitutional inferences—and of course it is simply a tendency, never universally shared and hopefully on the wane— may include among its causes simple laziness, boredom, and a natural reluctance to get out of step with the high-steppers. But in part it has also reflected a considered rejection of the view of constitutional adjudication from which my remarks have proceeded. There is a powerful body of opinion that would dismiss the call for substantive criticism, and its underlying assumption that some constitutional inferences are responsible while others are not, as naive. For, the theory goes, except as to the most trivial and least controversial questions (such as the length of a senator's term), the Constitution speaks in the vaguest and most general terms:[93] the most its clauses can provide are "more or less suitable pegs on which judicial policy choices are hung."[94] Thus anyone who suggests the Constitution can provide significant guidance for today's difficult questions either deludes himself or seeks to delude the Court. Essentially all the Court *can* do is honor the value preferences it sees fit, and it should be graded according to the judgment and skill with which it does so.[95]

One version of this view appears to be held by President Nixon. It is true that in announcing the appointment of Justices Powell and Rehnquist, he described a "judicial conservative"—his kind of justice—as one who does not "twist or bend the Constitution in order to perpetuate his personal political and social views."[96] But the example he then gave bore witness that he was not so "naive" after all.

> As a judicial conservative, I believe some court decisions have gone too far in the past in weakening the peace forces as against the criminal forces in our society. . . . [T]he peace forces must not be denied the legal tools they need to protect the innocent from criminal elements.[97]

That this sort of invitation, to get in there and Lochner for the right goals, can contribute to opinions like *Roe* is obvious. In terms of process, it is just what the President ordered.

The academic version of this general view is more subtle. It agrees that the Court will find little help in the Constitution and therefore has no real choice other than to decide for itself which value preferences to honor, but denies that it should necessarily opt for the preferences favored by the justices themselves or the president who appointed them. To the extent "progress" is to concern the justices at all, it should be defined not in terms of what they would like it to be but rather in terms of their best estimate of what over time the American people will make it[98]—that is, they should seek "durable" decisions.[99] This, however, is no easy task, and the goals that receive practically all the critics' attention, and presumably are supposed to receive practically all the Court's, are its own institutional survival and effectiveness.[100]

Whatever the other merits or demerits of this sort of criticism, it plainly is not what it is meant to be—an effective argument for judicial self-restraint. For a Governor Warren or a Senator Black will rightly see no reason to defer to law professors on the probable direction of progress; even less do they need the academy's advice on what is politically feasible; and they know that despite the Court's history of frequent immersion in hot water,[101] its "institutional position" has been getting stronger for two hundred years.

Roe is a case in point. Certainly, many will view it as social progress. (Surely that is the Court's view, and indeed the legislatures had been moving perceptibly, albeit too slowly for many of us, toward relaxing their anti-abortion legislation.) And it is difficult to see how it will weaken the Court's position. Fears of official disobedience are obviously groundless when it is a criminal statute that has been invalidated. To the public the *Roe* decision must look very much like the New York Legislature's recent liberalization of its abortion law. Even in the unlikely event someone should catch the public's ear long enough to charge that the wrong institution did the repealing, the public has heard that "legalism" before without taking to the streets. Nor are the political branches, and this of course is what really counts, likely to take up the cry very strenuously: the sighs of relief as this particular albatross was cut from the legislative and executive necks seemed to me audible. Perhaps I heard wrong—I live in the Northeast, indeed not so very far from Hyannis Port. It is even possible that a constitutional amendment will emerge, though that too has happened before without serious impairment of the Position of the Institution. But I doubt one will: *Roe v. Wade* seems like a durable decision.

It is, nevertheless, a very bad decision. Not because it will perceptibly weaken the Court—it won't; and not because it conflicts with either my idea of progress[102] or what the evidence suggests is society's—it doesn't. It is bad because it is bad constitutional law, or rather because it is *not* constitutional law and gives almost no sense of an obligation to try to be.[103]

I am aware the Court cannot simply "lay the Article of the Constitution which is invoked beside the statute which is challenged and ... decide whether the latter squares with the former."[104] That is precisely the reason commentators are needed. . . .

> No matter how imprecise in application to specific modern fact situations, the constitutional guarantees do provide a direction, a goal, an ideal citizen-government relationship. They rule out many alternative directions, goals, and ideals.[105]

Of course that only begins the inquiry. Identification and definition of the values with which the Constitution is concerned will often fall short of indicating with anything resembling clarity the deference to be given those values when they conflict with others society finds important. (Though even here the process is sometimes more helpful than the commentators would allow.) Nor is it often likely to generate, full-blown, the "neutral" principle that will avoid embarrassment in future cases. But though the identification of a constitutional connection is only the beginning of analysis, it is a necessary beginning. The point that often gets lost in the commentary, and obviously got lost in *Roe*, is that *before* the Court can get to the "balancing" stage, *before* it can worry about the next case and the case after that (or even about its institutional position) it is under an obligation to trace its premises to the charter from which it derives its authority. A neutral and durable principle may be a thing of beauty and a joy forever. But if it lacks connection with any value the Constitution marks as special, it is not a constitutional principle and the Court has no business imposing it. I hope that will seem obvious to the point of banality. Yet those of us to whom it does seem obvious have seldom troubled to say so. And because we have not, we must share in the blame for this decision.

I often find myself in the course of analyzing a rule in another context—say in teaching criminal law—concluding that because either of two views might plausibly be maintained, they both must be "all right." That of course misses the point, which is to find out which view seems best, and I think the reason is that I began as a constitutional lawyer (in which context, absent a constitutional prohibition, the fact that a view is plausible generally means it's permissible). This helps put in context the opposite phenomenon: commentators who started (as most do) in areas other than constitutional law who make the opposite inference, that their job is to decide what is right and then to impose that solution as the only one the Constitution allows.

Excerpts from Testimony on S. J. Res. 119 and 130 before the Senate Judiciary Committee, Subcommittee on Constitutional Amendments (1974)

I am of course aware that the Constitution contains some clauses so open-ended as to suggest that their content was meant to be worked out over time. But surely they are not carte blanche for courts, or we might as well stop pretending we are in any significant respect a democracy. The question, therefore, is how the Court should give them content. It might respond by reading the vaguer charters to incorporate conventional morality, or as Professor [Philip] Heymann [who had testified on the same panel] puts it, "deeply prized and widely shared" societal values. I am not at all sure that *Roe* comes out his way under this test, but more importantly it seems to me a test most inappropriate for judicial application. I doubt that we can ever confidently discover the "true moral principles of the people," but I am clear that legislatures are more likely to reflect them than courts. The more appropriate general approach, it seems to me, is to assign to the courts a role lawyers are specially trained to fulfill, that of ensuring purity of process. There are some interests that are unlikely to be adequately represented in elected bodies, namely the interests of what Chief Justice Stone called "discrete and insular minorities," and it is at least arguable that the Court should assume a special role in protecting them. There are difficulties in this approach, to be sure, having mainly to do with expressing it in adequately principled terms. But however expressed, it seems inappropriate to the abortion situation. [A]s between the interests of women and the interests of fetuses, it is difficult to conclude that the former cannot get a fair hearing in the political arena.

Professor [Laurence] Tribe [another panelist] defends *Roe* in somewhat different terms. I have no difficulty with rephrasing the question, as he does, as one of "role allocation": all constitutional questions are that. (The First Amendment, for example, doesn't tell you what to say or what not to say, but rather leaves you the decision free from government interference.) I simply do not find that it helps support Justice Blackmun's conclusion. Professor Tribe argues that the goal of protecting the "life" of a nonviable fetus cannot be invoked in defense of anti-abortion legislation, since the question whether a fetus is alive is one fraught with religious overtones. I am troubled by the argument: to disallow defenses embraced by sizable religious groups—or what is its functional equivalent, to disallow legislation when such defenses are rife—seems to require a sort of secularization at war with the spirit of the Free Exercise Clause. The religious clauses, read together, counsel neutrality with respect to religion: to remove a subject from public debate because religiously inspired views are found to be competing with others does not strike me as neutrality. But passing that, there is another defense of anti-abortion legislation to contend with, one geared not to the proposition that the fetus is alive but rather to the proposition, and it is undeniable, that whether or not a nonviable fetus is alive, it will likely become so unless it is aborted. And that, I would argue, is enough to permit the state to protect it. Professor Tribe grants that this is not an inherently religious defense, but dismisses it as "hardly compelling." (87 Harv. L. Rev. at 26.) The first question is why the defense has to be "compelling" in the first place: it is, admittedly, a religiously neutral defense, and Professor Tribe quite wisely does not join Justice Blackmun's claim that the right to an abortion is somehow enshrined by the Constitution. The second question, of course, is why the "potential life" defense *isn't* compelling, a question that is further focused by Professor Tribe's later assertion that the protection of a viable (third trimester) fetus *is* a compelling interest. "[A] state wishing to prevent the killing of infants simply has *no way* to distinguish the deliberate destruction of the latter from what is involved in postviability abortions." (Id. at 28, emphasis added.) After six months, the argument based on the realization that the

fetus will if unaborted proceed to full personhood is apparently so compelling as to be undeniable: prior thereto, for reasons I do not understand, it is
so unconvincing as to disallow state reliance on it. The analysis is a good
deal more sophisticated than Justice Blackmun's, but ultimately it has to
beg the same questions, since that is the only way to get to the same result.

Some General Observations on Constitutional Amendment in Response to Supreme Court Decisions

If I am an expert on anything, it is constitutional law, not abortion, and I
therefore assume the subcommittee has little interest in my views on the
merits of the latter subject. (My outrage was directed at what had been done
with the existing Constitution, and had nothing to do with my feelings
respecting what the Constitution *ought* to say on the subject of abortion.)
I might add some remarks on the amending process, however.

One who feels that the abortion decision was constitutionally indefensible, but nonetheless arrived at an appropriate moral and political conclusion, is faced with a not entirely obvious choice. On the one hand, the
Constitution has, in a functional sense, been "amended" to read as it
should. The problem is that the wrong tribunal did the amending, and there
may exist some danger—particularly after debate on the possibility of a
constitutional amendment—that a failure to amend will reassure the Court
in the view of constitutional adjudication the opinion evidences. The ideal
response, given such a set of views, might therefore be a constitutional
amendment *confirming* what was done in *Roe*, and thereby suggesting at
the same time (a) that the Court arrived at the politically preferable result but (b) that it should not have done so under the existing Constitution.
Such an exercise is plainly implausible, though—obviously more burdensome and possibly more dangerous than it is worth—and someone holding the set of views described probably should let well enough alone. The
likelihood that the Court will view *Roe* as an experiment whose success
recommends a general loosening of the previously accepted criteria of constitutional judgment is at least somewhat mitigated by the widespread condemnation of the decision by lawyers and law professors.

But suppose one is of the opinion that *Roe* did not arrive at a politically
and morally desirable result: is it clear that he should therefore support a
constitutional amendment calculated to reverse the decision? I think the
answer comes out yes, though I would reject the broader view that amendment is always appropriate under such circumstances. One who disagrees
with a particular decision should hesitate to move against it by constitutional amendment if it can reasonably be thought that doing so would
threaten the integrity of an entire constitutional fabric. For example, one

might strongly disagree with a particular First Amendment holding but
still, quite wisely, hesitate to attempt a reversal of that holding: any attempt
to tinker with the First Amendment would at least have the potential of
upsetting, in a host of unforeseeable ways, the whole body of doctrine,
generally successful doctrine, that has been developed under that amendment.[106] It is hard to view this problem in that way, however. The abortion
decision, by comparison, seems a rather isolated episode*—indeed, the
only clear excursion into substantive due process we have witnessed since
the 1930s—and it seems to me it could be reversed without threatening an
entire fabric of doctrine.[107]

S. J. Res. 119 and 130

I find neither resolution[108] clearly calculated to reverse the decision in *Roe*,
which I assume is what they are meant to do. There is, in the first place, a
"state action" problem. *Roe*, as Professor Tribe's article makes clear, remanded "the abortion decision" to the pregnant woman and her doctor. It
could at least be argued that because the termination of the fetus's life is the
act of those two persons, permitted but not required by the state, the direct
or indirect placement of the due process and equal protection limits on the
state respecting abortions simply does not reach the question. This would
be a strained construction, but it is at least possible.

More importantly—passing the state action problem—the substantive
provisions of the resolutions are not clearly calculated to reverse *Roe*. De-
nominating the fetus a person for purposes of the Fourteenth Amendment
simply does not, if *Roe* is carried to what we might loosely call its logical
conclusion, settle the question that case posed. As I said in my article:

> [I]n fact all that would be established [by concluding that the fetus is a person] is
> that one right granted special protection by the Fourteenth Amendment was in
> conflict with what the Court felt was another; it would not tell us which must
> prevail.

Nor does explicitly providing the fetus with due process and equal protection necessarily settle the matter. The Supreme Court in *Roe* obviously
thought there was a "reasonable basis" (and that is what the two clauses
typically require) for permitting the abortion of nonviable fetuses: indeed it found the arguments so compelling it forbade the states to take a
contrary view.

That leads to my final objection, and it is a fundamental one, to the two

---

* [This was so in 1974 (one year after *Roe*), when this testimony was given. I would say it
isn't today, which in my opinion argues strongly for not overruling *Roe*. See page 305.]

proposed amendments, as least as I understand their intendment. And that is that they share with Justice Blackmun and his brethren a crucial assumption that I reject—that the matter is one appropriate to a uniform federal solution. I understand that section 3 of each resolution will leave some room for local variation, but unless I misunderstand the general thrust it is that abortions generally are not to be permitted (except, perhaps, in the extraordinary situation mentioned in section 2 of Resolution 119.[109]) Thus, in general terms, the Court permitted abortions, and the proposed amendments seek to forbid them. I have trouble, however, understanding— whichever way the issue is resolved—what it is that makes this an issue appropriate to solution by the central government. It does not seem a peculiarly "federal" issue, and it involves a difficult moral issue on which compassionate people (and state legislatures) can differ. If there is a disposition to react to *Roe* by way of constitutional amendment, I would think an amendment clearly calculated to return to the status quo ante *Roe*—that is, to leave a good deal of discretion with the several states—would be the more appropriate response.

Let There Be Life (1981)*

Sometimes it's hard to keep up. First it was life created in a test tube. Then patented life forms. And now we're told that all Congress has to do is pass a statute redefining "life"—by declaring fetuses to be "persons" from the moment of conception—and, presto, *Roe v. Wade*, the United States Supreme Court's 1973 decision preventing legislative interference with abortions until late pregnancy will disappear. No muss, no fuss, and, most important, no struggle for all the votes it would take to amend the Constitution the old-fashioned way.

The two of us have been on opposite sides of the debate over the constitutional legitimacy of *Roe* since it was decided. But we have no trouble at all agreeing that this formula for overturning it is badly misguided. It won't work, and it's a good thing it won't.

Even if it were offered in the form of a constitutional amendment, it would be at best an unpredictable vehicle for overruling *Roe*. If fetuses really are to be regarded as persons from the moment of conception, that would seem to require states to punish rape victims who get abortions as murderers and the druggists who provide them morning-after pills as

* Laurence H. Tribe co-authored this article (New York Times, March 17, 1981 [written in response to S. 158, 97th Cong., 1st Sess., a Bill "To provide that human life shall be deemed to exist from conception," introduced by Senator Helms of North Carolina.] Professor Tribe, like me, was then a professor at Harvard Law School, where he now holds the Tyler Professorship of Constitutional Law, a chair I occupied briefly prior to becoming Dean at Stanford]).

accomplices to murder. If, on the other hand (as certainly seems likely) the statute's proponents assure us that they don't mean *that*—that some distinctions between the extinction of fetal life and the extinction of other life can still be drawn—it could then become at least arguable that the goal of overruling *Roe* had not in fact been realized.

Let's suppose, though, that the Supreme Court would uphold a ban on abortion on the strength of a "fetal life" amendment to the Constitution. It doesn't follow that a mere act of Congress could accomplish the same result. The point of *Roe v. Wade* was not that the Supreme Court had too little "scientific" information about when life began or what a fetus was, but rather that the government, merely "by adopting one theory of life," could not "override the rights of the pregnant woman." For Congress to proclaim the theory that a fetus is a person from the very beginning would leave this constitutional calculus unchanged. It was a question of rights, not an issue of biology or a matter of definition, that *Roe* resolved.

Congressional power to rescue an otherwise unconstitutional law by the expedient of redefining the terms of the Fourteenth Amendment would have dizzying implications well beyond the abortion controversy.

Should we make it as easy for government officials to sue for libel as it was before *The New York Times v. Sullivan*, which barred damages for defamation of public officials in the absence of deliberate or reckless falsehood? That's simple enough: Congress need only announce that one's "liberty" of reputation demands that any publisher of libelous matter about an official be strictly liable for every falsehood. How about bringing back the racially restrictive covenants that were common before the Supreme Court in 1948 held them to be unenforceable? No problem. Just have Congress define judicial refusal to enforce racial restrictions on real-estate sales as a "deprivation of property." Yearn for the halcyon days when coerced confessions were admissible as evidence? Easy. Congress proclaims that from here on releasing any defendant on the ground that his rights were violated will be deemed to deprive all members of the public of their "liberty" from fear.

Indeed, why not skip all the bother and just let Congress redefine "due process of law" to include "any law Congress or a state legislature approves." It hardly matters—once Congress can defeat liberty by definitional fiat. Reducing the Constitution to whatever those in power want it to mean is an awfully high price to pay for making *Roe* disappear. We're all lucky—supporters and opponents of *Roe* alike—that such a gambit won't work.

Of course Senator Helms wasn't conceived yesterday, and his constitutional advisers undoubtedly have explained to him why an attempt to overrule *Roe v. Wade* by statute must fail. Obviously, the idea is to score points with the "pro-life" constituency at the expense of the courts, which as the Senator well knows will have no choice but to strike the statute down. When *Roe* was decided, many screamed—including one of us (Mr. Ely)—that the Court was playing politics. With treatment like this at the hands of the Congress, what else can we really expect?

Abortion for the Rich (1977)

When the Supreme Court decided in 1973 that there was a constitutional right to a nontherapeutic abortion throughout the first six months of pregnancy, I wrote a strong attack on the decision. It was reprinted and circulated by anti-abortion forces, which was a little ironic because I've always favored the right to an abortion as a nonconstitutional policy matter. I stick by my constitutional criticism, though: there's nothing in the Constitution that remotely supports the right to an abortion, and the decision cannot be defended as one protecting a politically powerless minority.

I suppose when it decided last week that states need not fund nontherapeutic abortions with Medicaid payments,[110] the Court may have thought it would assuage some of us the original decision had outraged. My own reaction, and I hope that of others, is outrage squared. It is no answer to the charge that the Court has created a constitutional right out of whole cloth (or its own political predilections) subsequently to limit that right to those who least need it. It is the poor who can least afford unwanted children, and it is the unwanted children of the poor who will face the most miserable lives. In fact, the only theory on which the original decision had even a slight hope of making sense was a wealth discrimination theory, focusing on the way general prohibitions on abortion discriminated against the poor.[111] Rich women, we all knew, could afford the fare to some jurisdiction here or abroad where abortions were legal; poor women were relegated to a life with an unwanted child or the vicissitudes of some back-alley butcher. By last week's decision they are again.

The Burger Court's one-two punch reveals a disturbing constitutional philosophy. In the first third of this century, we had a Supreme Court that did not hesitate to impose its values on the contrary values of the legislature in the name of the Constitution—though it represented them as, and probably thought they were, the "fundamental values of our society." That Court's particular favorite value was something called liberty of contract—in application, the "liberty" of an employer and an employee to contract for work at less than the minimum wage or longer than the maximum hours. As a society we came to understand that wasn't legitimate constitutionalism, and for a time the Court was rather uniformly quiescent. Then came the Warren Court, also interventionist, but in a different and substantially more legitimate way. Rather than impose on the elected branches its own substantive values, it concentrated more on questions of process and distribution—seeking to ensure, first, that everyone had a vote on and a chance freely to debate issues of public policy, and second, that whatever values the legislature chose after such debate to protect would be protected equally for all alike—black and white, poor and rich. Woman and man should be added to any such list, and to its credit the Burger Court has in some contexts begun to do so.

In other ways, however, the current Court has signaled a reversion to the jurisprudence of earlier, value-imposing Courts. Surely the first abortion decision was this—one concerned neither with process nor with distribution but rather with whether the legislature had protected those values that to the Court seem truly fundamental. Of similar ilk would be a decision, which many are predicting, outlawing racially preferential admissions practices. Such a holding is mandated by neither the language nor the legislative history of the Equal Protection Clause. (A number of laws passed by the Reconstruction Congress that passed the Fourteenth Amendment specifically granted benefits to blacks.) Nor can it be defended in terms of the unusual political impotence of the group being discriminated against: we all like to feel put upon, but we have not yet reached the point where whites as a group cannot protect themselves politically. Last week's abortion decision is further evidence of a withdrawal from the Warren Court's concern with discrimination against the powerless, and together with the 1973 abortion decision begins to suggest a general attitude that is exactly upside down: that imposing its own notion of what values are fundamental is the business of the Supreme Court and preventing discrimination against the powerless is not. In the context of such a general attitude the mix of results the Court has come up with in its two abortion decisions comes into understandable relief. If value imposition is the business of the Court, we shouldn't be surprised to see the interests of the middle class getting priority.

Letter to Justices Kennedy, O'Connor, and Souter Concerning *Planned Parenthood v. Casey*,[112] (1992)[113]

Despite my serious misgivings about Roe, I've thought for some years it would be a mistake to overrule it. Though my views to this effect were reported in Lincoln Caplan's book The Tenth Justice 126 (1987), I haven't previously said this in print. Since I obviously hate to leave any thought unexpressed, and even more obviously am not running for a judicial appointment—it's kind of hard to envision the president who would appoint someone who (a) is pro-choice but (b) was a conspicuous critic of Roe, and by the way (c) doesn't think it should be overruled*—I do so now.

I'm not much of a fan letter writer, but it seemed to me an exception was in order here, since I know you'll receive a lot of grief from true believers on both sides of this one.

Your joint opinion is excellent—I guess law professors are allowed to say that occasionally—not only reaching what seem to me entirely sensible results, but defending the refusal to overrule Roe v. Wade splendidly.

As you're aware, I thought (and think) Roe was constitutionally indefensible, but overruling it now would have been a terrible mistake as well. Our society has indeed built up expectations on the basis of it, particularly as regards the aspirations of women. And falling into a pattern whereby presidents appoint justices with the essential promise that they will overrule particular cases, and then having them dutifully proceed to do so, would weaken the Court's authority immeasurably.

The nation is in your debt.

Yes, I am aware that saying nice things about Casey is politically incorrect. That's why I sent them the letter, because I knew few others would.[114]

I don't have a well-developed theory of stare decisis, that is, of when courts should defer to precedent rather than reconsider it afresh; I'm actually not sure anyone does. My fear, of course, is that I don't think Roe should be overruled because I approve of it politically if not constitutionally, and there may indeed be something there. I also think, as the letter suggests, that Roe has contributed greatly to the more general move toward equality for women, which seems to me not only good but also in line with the central themes of our Constitution. I don't think a principled opinion along those lines could have been written at the time—"We don't know exactly how, but somehow this holding will importantly help undergird a more general movement toward women's equality, which movement is mandated by the Constitution" obviously doesn't make it—but I am clear that overruling it now would wreak havoc on that constitutionally legitimate movement.

---

* See also page 478n27 (Professor Tushnet's description of the quintessentially unappointable person, which may fit the private thoughts of others but conspicuously—though I'm sure this wasn't his intention—matches my public pronouncements and I'm not sure who else's). Actually it gets worse. While the "litmus test" of the 1980 and 1984 Republican platforms required that judicial nominees not be pro-choice (which I am), candidate Clinton indicated during the 1992 campaign that his litmus test required them to be "strong supporters of Roe" (which I'm not). Good thing the job I've got is better.

Actually there's a serious point to be made here. A longing for judicial appointment has either inhibited or warped the intellectual product of many a constitutional law scholar, and I will be eternally grateful for the moment I realized this was not a price worth paying.

So far as my constitutional approval of *Casey's* upholding of certain
laws affecting abortion is concerned, requiring a woman to reflect for
twenty-four hours before getting an abortion or informing her of the costs
(along with the benefits) of a abortion may reduce the likelihood that she
will get one, but that strikes me as an entirely appropriate outcome, unless
"pro-choice" is to become mere code for "pro-abortion." Of course, should
such waiting periods be abused by pro-lifers (by either side for that matter)
and become simple windows for overreaching propaganda, they will in fact
not conduce to choice and thus would properly be invalidated. The extent
to which they are so used seems an appropriate question for serious empirical study.

Democracy and the Right to Be Different (1981)[115]

Most of what I have to say about "Constitutional Adjudication and Democratic Theory"[116] I said in *Democracy and Distrust*.* Most of the criticisms
that have appeared so far—at least those that address arguments I actually
made—were anticipated in the book, and I won't bore the reader by restat-
ing the debate from my perspective.

I do want to spend a moment, however, on one particular style of response because it has been so recurrent, appearing in the reactions of commentators as diverse as Robert Bork, Paul Brest, Archibald Cox, and Mark
Tushnet.[117] The general form of the response is this: "Ely's theory is indeterminate to the point of virtual uselessness because *Carolene Products*
premises could be used, in a way I am about to demonstrate, to generate
conclusion *X* (which conclusion is either absurd or one that on other
grounds we know or assume Ely would reject)."

In fact I was aware that the *Carolene Products* premises I defended in
chapter 4 could be elaborated in various ways: that's why I wrote chapters
5 and 6. I was also aware that the general case the critics variously pose, the
law that does not classify but nonetheless by prohibiting a defined act bears
most harshly on a particular minority, is related in some ways to those
covered by the theory I elaborated. However, for reasons indicated in the
book, I was unable in the abstract to make constitutional sense of the notion
that discrete and insular minorities deserve special protection and therefore
was forced to restrict my theory (in the absence of unconstitutional motivation) to laws that classify, specifically those that do so on the basis of the
self-aggrandizing, other-denigrating generalizations of politically dominant classes.[118]

---

* Clouded crystal ball. This book's about twice as long as that one.

It would certainly be fair to counter my argument by attempting to demonstrate that the three paragraphs of the *Carolene Products* footnote in fact do not exhaust the set of appropriate constitutional premises for our courts: indeed, the possibility of this sort of argument is the main subject of this paper. It would also be fair to criticize the particular ways in which I elaborated those premises in chapters 5 and 6, if possible by suggesting an alternative elaboration that remains principled—by which I mean that it stops short of proving everything—but nonetheless generates results more to the critic's liking. What seem beside any point I made are demonstrations that the premises with which I began, *Carolene Products* premises, might be elaborated in unprincipled ways.

I share a certain frustration with the book, however, one I suspect may be fueling much of the criticism. A *Carolene Products* approach *is* well designed to protect minorities from discriminatory treatment, but it makes no move whatever in the direction of protecting—except to the extent specific provisions of the Constitution (and therefore paragraph one of the *Carolene Products* footnote) protect various aspects of it—the right not to conform, that is, the right to be different.

In fact, outside the areas of political and religious freedom, the various specific provisions of the Constitution evince little concern with this sort of interest. On the other hand, James Fleming is surely right in noting that the syntax of the Privileges or Immunities Clause and the Ninth Amendment is most naturally that of substantive entitlement.[119] In the end I don't think this observation fatal—it does no violence to these provisions to read them as I believe they ultimately must be read, as protecting rights of participation in the processes and outputs of representative government—but at least in combination with the libertarian instincts many of us share it makes the effort seem worth a try.

Of course every case involves a potential "liberty" claim, and thus some limiting strategy is needed, some way of telling which constitutionally unstated "liberties" are to receive constitutional protection and which are not. In his review of *Democracy and Distrust*, James O'Fallon sketches the beginnings of a strategy that he correctly indicates was not among those criticized in the book, one that takes off from Ronald Dworkin's distinction between "'personal preferences,' regarding the assignment of goods or opportunities to oneself, and 'external preferences,' one's views as to how such advantages ought to be granted or denied to others."[120] Dworkin admits that this distinction will be of limited practical significance: "democracy cannot discriminate, within the overall preferences imperfectly revealed by voting, distinct personal and external components, so as to provide a method of enforcing the former while ignoring the latter."[121] This would not be true, however, of a case in which the regulation in question was necessarily instituted on the basis of *wholly* external preferences,[122] that is, a case involving the regulation of what John Stuart Mill called self-regarding conduct.[123]

Mill defended his liberty principle—that "the only purpose for which power can be rightfully exercised over any member of a civilized community, against his will, is to prevent harm to others"[124]—on the utilitarian ground that adoption of the principle would promote the general good.[125] Even assuming that argument to be correct, however, it is one whose adoption as constitutional law would be susceptible to the criticisms of judicial imposition of "fundamental values" advanced in chapter 3 of *Democracy and Distrust*—every bit as susceptible as any other argument of a you-must-do-this-because-it's-good form. Thus Paul Brest asks rhetorically, "If the Constitution does not enact Herbert Spencer's *Social Statics*, does it enact John Stuart Mill's *On Liberty*?"[126]

But although Mill may have defended it that way, his liberty principle does not seem to be simply another philosophical vision of what is good. It can also be defended—more convincingly in my opinion—in constitutive terms, in a way that plugs into the account of democracy as "applied utilitarianism."[127] If people are given votes in order to ensure that their interests will be counted in their community's "greatest happiness" calculus, it would seem to follow rather directly that those whose happiness is not affected one way or the other by whether a given event takes place should not have a vote about whether it does.

There even are documentary pegs on which one could attempt to hang the conclusion that this theory is legitimately attributable to our Constitution. Perhaps the most obvious is the Obligation of Contracts Clause, particularly if one concludes that the Court misread the original understanding when it held that clause to be strictly an antiretroactivity provision, applicable only to contracts in existence at the time the statute in issue was passed. For if the framers did not mean that, and thus meant constitutionally to provide that decisions affecting only the contracting parties were their business alone and not that of the government, it seems likely they would also have wanted an individual's wholly self-regarding act to be immune to state regulation.[128]

A less obvious reference, admittedly, would be the Tenth Amendment: "The powers not delegated to the United States by the Constitution, nor prohibited by it to the States, are reserved to the States respectively, or to the People." In isolation the last four words say nothing we wouldn't know from the Ninth Amendment and the Privileges or Immunities Clause, that people retain some unenumerated immunities to government regulation, and in that sense they simply restate the problem. By their placement they may suggest a little more, however. It is familiar history that the Tenth Amendment is a reminder, in particular a reminder that just as decisions with national consequences are to be made by the national government, decisions whose consequences are more local are to be made by more local governments. What may not be so familiar is that the amendment adverts to a tripartite division of decision "power"—national, local, *and individual*. And although that in turn by no means compels the conclusion that decisions with merely individual consequences are to be made individually, that conclusion certainly fits.

The position does seem to entail conclusions many would find troubling. Presumably it would invalidate, and indeed Mill used examples along these lines,[129] laws prohibiting the distribution (with adequate notices, of course) of impure foods and quack medical remedies and those setting minimum standards for housing and the safety of workplaces. And ironically— though it was obvious from my allusion to a "nonretroactive" Contracts Clause—it would legitimate the case which after *Plessy v. Ferguson*[130] it is most imperative for liberals to distinguish, *Lochner v. New York*.[131] That case and its progeny obviously can be rationalized, and some of them were, on the libertarian ground that what two or more adults contract to do with or to another is nobody's business but their own, and it is certainly not the government's.[132] *Lochner* too can be found in Mill if one troubles to read him:[133] many of his examples involved contract,[134] and he understood that once one starts regulating the agreements of adults either to keep them "conscionable" or on the theory that bargaining power is unequal, there will soon be nothing left of his theory.[135]

Well, what does that prove? Only that if everyone sat down and reread *On Liberty*, some of those now disposed to constitutionalize it might decide not to, and some of those instinctively opposed might become enthusiasts. Interesting perhaps, but it hardly cuts one way or the other on the legitimacy of the constitutive argument sketched above. Redemption of the devious "seem" in the sentence leading off the preceding paragraph will generate a more telling objection, however. It is in fact the rarest of regulations that will not on analysis be understood as furthering the interests of persons beyond the actor or cooperating actors. Rescue parties may have to risk their lives searching for some not-so-rugged individualist; clean-up crews may have to collect what is left of another. And beyond that, times have changed since Mill wrote: today any person's death or illness diminishes us all, because we are involved in insurance and taxes.[136]

Well, what does *that* prove? Only that the constitutionalization of *On Liberty* would on full analysis turn out to be trivial in its practical consequences. Interesting perhaps, if only because it shows that constitutionalizing Mill's theory is not likely to satisfy many people's craving for liberty, but it certainly isn't a reason *not* to constitutionalize it. The point goes further, though: if it truly were the case that the conduct in question was not affecting the happiness of someone other than the actor(s), the government wouldn't be intervening to prevent it. If no one else cared, there wouldn't be a law against it, and if there were a law, it wouldn't be enforced. And if that is so this entire discussion has been about a set of cases that is not simply trivial but empty, the set of cases in which the law is invoked to control activity that concerns no one but the actor(s).

That may seem like a play on the word "concerns." For another's act may "concern" you by affecting your tangible interests, or it may "concern" you simply because you think it's wrong for the actor to be doing what he's doing. That brings us back to Dworkin's distinction, of course, but that is a distinction one cannot draw, pace O'Fallon, without running smack into the rebuttal arguments of chapter 3. Even granting arguendo that a truly self-regarding act should be immune to regulation, the moment the law intervenes we know the act in question wasn't that. And as for sorting among the reasons persons other than the actor are moved to intervene, in particular distinguishing between "tangible" injury and moral distress as bases for intervention, a couple of points should be made. Revulsion in the absence of tangible harm to oneself is by no means inevitably the reaction of an intermeddling Comstockian. Even ignoring all the tangible costs a suicide inflicts on a community, news of a suicide—it is simply impossible not to evoke John Donne in this context—diminishes us all.[137] I agree that such reactions of moral "diminution" should not often become the occasion for state regulation, but that is a debatable and (more importantly for present purposes) nonconstitutive choice of one vision of the way members of a community should interact over another. The moment the actor's behavior adversely affects others—no matter what it is about the receptor that occasions his upset—the two are interacting and become (at least as concerns that act) part of the same community, and the constitutive argument from democracy as utilitarianism becomes inapplicable.

There are therefore no acts that affect only the actor—at least none against which state officials will be tempted to intervene—only some that do so less than others. The recurrent problem of regulation is when the effects become great (and "legitimate") enough to justify government response: unless there is unusual reason to distrust our elected representatives on a certain such issue, there can be no justification in our system for taking it away from them. That attempt having failed, it seems to me there is no principle for deciding which varieties of nonpolitical and nonreligious liberty to protect constitutionally that is not on the one hand so fatuously vague as to be useless or on the other easy prey for the sorts of arguments advanced in chapter 3 of *Democracy and Distrust*.

How much ought that to upset us? I indicated that I too find it frustrating, but I'm not sure a much stronger reaction is in order. The range of political thought and behavior has historically been quite narrow in the United States, and that narrowness has all too often been reinforced by law. And needless to say our treatment of minorities has oftentimes been scandalous. The right not to conform in fashions other than political, however, does not seem to have been a particular problem in this country, at least not in the sense that conformity outside the political arena has habitually been compelled by law.

I hope you will have noted that although it is true that the theory advanced in my book provides no constitutional remedy for this last problem, which I am suggesting has not in fact been much of a problem historically, it is centrally directed to the first two problems—affording minorities protection from discriminatory treatment and protecting rights of political expression—and if taken seriously would go a long way toward correcting them. Is that because I set out to write a book designed to correct those evils I had identified as most egregious? Anyone who has read it will recognize that that was hardly the methodology. But at the same time it is no coincidence that it works out that way. The "right to be different" is fundamentally, though obviously not inevitably, an upper middle class right: it is, if you will, the right of my son to wear his hair as long as he pleases. Our nation's underclass—the poor, the black, the Hispanic—by and large could not care less about the "right" to wear tattered clothes and let their grooming go: with the help of the law we've kept them in a state of difference so long they'd like at least the option of becoming, in some important respects, more the same. That aspiration is one that will continue to need protecting, but for reasons elaborated at length in the book the aspirations of "people like us" do not need particular protection from the political process.

Excerpt from *Professor Dworkin's External/Personal Preference Distinction* (1983)[138]

Personal Autonomy

Dworkin's larger use of the external/personal preference distinction[139] is to support his theory of rights. He correctly notes that it will often be impossible to unpack an election to determine how many votes were grounded in personal preferences and how many in external: indeed it will often be impossible to untangle a single voter's mixed motivations. This leads him to propose a prophylactic theory:

> I wish now to propose the following general theory of rights. The concept of an individual political right . . . is a response to the philosophical defects of a utilitarianism that counts external preferences and the practical impossibility of a utilitarianism that does not. It allows us to enjoy the institutions of political

democracy, which enforce overall or unrefined utilitarianism, and yet protect the fundamental right of citizens to equal concern and respect by prohibiting decisions that seem, antecedently, likely to have been reached by virtue of the external components of the preferences democracy reveals.[140]

Dworkin cites laws such as those prohibiting homosexual acts, contraception, and pornography as "antecedently likely" to have been passed "by virtue of" external preferences.[141] In contrast, Dworkin asserts, no such antecedent likelihood of pollution by external preference existed regarding the statute challenged in *Lochner v. New York*:[142]

> What can be said, on the general theory of rights I offer, for any particular right of property? What can be said, for example, in favor of the right to liberty of contract sustained by the Supreme Court in the famous *Lochner* case, and later regretted, not only by the court, but by liberals generally? I cannot think of any argument that a political decision to limit such a right, in the way in which minimum wage laws limited it, is antecedently likely to give effect to external preferences . . . . If, as I think, no such argument can be made out, then the alleged right does not exist; in any case there can be no inconsistency in denying that it exists while warmly defending a right to other liberties.[143]

But this surely is doubtful. As Lawrence Sager has observed:

> If ever there was a decision-making environment polluted by external preferences, it is that which must have surrounded the enactment of New York's labor law, which regulated the hours and working conditions of bakery employees. It was surely the humanitarian instinct on the part of large segments of the public and their elected representatives to improve the conditions of other persons which induced the enactment of such labor-protective legislation. Under Dworkin's analysis, the *Lochner* Court would appear to have been correct in recognizing a constitutional right to resist legislation stemming from such external, altruistic preferences and to contract free from government interference.[144]

Since there can hardly be doubt that such humanitarian "external" preferences did play a role in generating the law involved in *Lochner*, Dworkin's overall strategy in response would have to involve some sort of appeal to an "ideal" argument to the effect that worker-protective legislation simply conduces to a juster world.[145] Within this overall strategy there are two possible substrategies. The first is to take the view that the ability to articulate an "ideal" argument that does not offend the Constitution simply ends the matter: the law is constitutional whether or not its passage was significantly affected by external preferences. In defending against certain criticisms Dworkin does indeed sometimes seem to take this first position.[146] It is, however, one that is hard to square with the general statement of his theory of rights, which, recall, indicated that rights against government action are to be recognized respecting decisions that seem, antecedently, "likely to have been reached by virtue of" external preferences.

The second possible substrategy is closely related, but differs sufficiently to make it consistent with Dworkin's statement of his general theory of rights. It is to take the view that although the existence of a plausible and not impermissible ideal argument in favor of the challenged legislation does not automatically function (as in the first substrategy) as a legislation-saving "trump," nonetheless the ability to articulate such an ideal argument should cause one to hesitate long and hard before drawing the inference that the decision is "likely to have been reached" on the basis of external preferences.[147] On this second reading of Dworkin, the *Lochner* legislation must owe its constitutionality to a strong presumption that where a given law appears to have been the product of a mixture of ideal arguments (in this case for a juster world) and external preferences (in this case based on sympathetic identification with overworked bakery employees), it was in fact the ideal argument that predominated, thus rescuing the legislation from the fatal charge of having been generated by external preferences.

This reading becomes troubled, however, when one returns to Dworkin's examples of laws that should be invalidated under the "rights" branch of his theory—laws against homosexual acts, contraception, and pornography. He asserts repeatedly that these laws are polluted by external preferences and should for that reason fall, but is somewhat less clear on the subject of just what sort of external preferences are supposed to have been involved. He notes that laws such as these are rooted in a belief "that a community that permits rather than prohibits these acts is inherently a worse community" and goes on immediately to label that an external preference.[148] Thus stated, however, it isn't, but instead fits precisely his definition of an ideal argument (to the effect that the law in question makes the society "more just, or in some other way closer to an ideal society"). Arguments of "inherent worseness" are ideal arguments.

So far this sounds dangerously parallel to Dworkin's rendition of *Lochner*. But we should proceed slowly and examine in this context the implications of the two possible substrategies we examined there. If it is in fact Dworkin's position that the mere ability to articulate an ideal argument that does not offend the United States Constitution is enough to save a law whether or not external preferences actually generated it, then Dworkin simply is wrong about homosexuality et al. (Of course, many people have tried to articulate theories of "privacy" or "personhood" to support the proposition that an ideal argument suggesting the moral preferability of a world without homosexuality or contraception is one that offends properly understood constitutional principles, but, to his credit, Dworkin has not endorsed any of them.[149] His claim, instead, is that such laws are unconstitutional on the basis of the theory as sketched thus far. It would require an entirely separate effort, which Dworkin has neither made nor endorsed, to demonstrate that the ideal argument against homosexuality, contraception, or pornography is one that violates the Constitution.[150]) If, therefore, Dworkin is to have even a chance of succeeding in his argument that these laws are unconstitutional, he must pursue a version of the second possible substrategy, and maintain that although an ideal argument in support of such laws can be articulated, that argument is a rationalization, and the laws in question were actually generated by external preferences.

What further does Dworkin have to say about the likely motivation for such laws? Some light is shed by the "pool versus theater" example alluded to earlier.[151] In fact the first time around I edited some language out of the quotation. This time I shall restore that language and italicize it:

> There is a similar corruption when the external preferences that are counted are altruistic or moralistic. Suppose many citizens, who themselves do not swim, prefer the pool to the theater because they approve of sports and admire athletes, or because they think that the theater is immoral and ought to be repressed. If the altruistic preferences are counted, so as to reinforce the personal preferences of swimmers, the result will be a form of double counting: each swimmer will have the benefit not only of his own preference, but also the preference of someone else who takes pleasure in his success. *If the moralistic preferences are counted the effect will be the same: actors and audiences will suffer because their preferences are held in lower respect by citizens whose personal preferences are not themselves engaged.*[152]

So it isn't simply a case of the "inherent worseness" of a world containing homosexuality, contraception, or pornography. It is rather that the preferences of people who engage in such pursuits "are held in lower respect" by their fellow citizens than are other preferences. And this lessened respect for a particular view of what is proper behavior is assimilated, repeatedly, to a lessened respect for the person who holds it, a general desire that in utilitarian calculations his interest be counted at less than one.

> Utilitarianism claims that people are treated as equals when the preferences of each, weighted only for intensity, are balanced in the same scales, with no distinctions for persons or merit. The corrupt version of utilitarianism just described, which gives less weight to some persons than to others, *or discounts some preferences because these are ignoble*, forfeits that claim.[153]

The problem is that the two things here assimilated—generally counting a person's welfare as less important than the welfare of others, and specifically regarding his (or anybody's) desire to engage in a particular antisocial or immoral act as blameworthy (and in that sense less worthy than other *preferences*)—are not the same at all. H. L. A. Hart has put this point well:

What is fundamentally wrong is the suggested interpretation of denials of freedom as denials of equal concern or respect. This surely is mistaken. . . . The
majority . . . may regard the minority's views as mistaken or sinful; but over-
riding them, for those reasons (however objectionable on other grounds), seems
quite compatible with recognizing the equal worth of the holders of such views
and may even be inspired by concern for them. In any event both the liberal
prescription for governments, "impose no scheme of values on any one," and its
opposite, "impose this particular conception of the good life on all," though they
are universal prescriptions, seem to have nothing specifically to do with equality
or the value of equal concern and respect any more than have the prescriptions
"kill no one" and "kill everyone," though of course conformity with such universal prescriptions will involve treating all alike in the relevant respect.[154]

Or (heady company) as I once put it:

Attempting to preclude the entire population from acting in ways that are perceived as immoral is not assimilable to comparatively disadvantaging a given
group out of simple hostility to its members. . . . In raising my children not to act
in ways I think are immoral, even punishing them when they do, I may incur the
condemnation of some, but the sin is paternalism or some such, hardly that of
leaving my children's interests out of account or valuing them negatively.[155]

In answering this, Professor Dworkin grants that I am right "in supposing that a utilitarian justification of laws against homosexuals does not
leave their interests out of account or value them negatively":

It counts the damage to homosexuals at full value, but finds it outweighed by the
interests of those who do not want to associate with practicing homosexuals or
who find them and their culture and lives inferior. But a utilitarian justification of
racial discrimination does not ignore the interests of blacks or the damage discrimination does to them. It counts these at full value, and finds them outweighed
by the interests of others who do not want to associate with blacks, or who find
them and their culture and habits inferior or distasteful. The two utilitarian justifications are formally similar.[156]

Reading this in light of Dworkin's earlier discussion of racial discrimination, we can see that his claim has shifted markedly. It turns out, apparently, that a "moralistic" objection to homosexual acts is not ipso facto an
external preference. Instead, the situation is "formally similar" to that of
racial discrimination, and a purported moral or ideal objection to homosexual sex is now seen as masking a more general distaste for homosexuals
generally (which we now understand, in light of the racial discrimination
comparison—and indeed this move is necessary to fit the homosexual case
to Dworkin's definition of external preference—must be understood as a

general desire to see that homosexuals as a class receive fewer of life's "goods and opportunities" than the rest of us). In short, those who vote to outlaw sodomy do so because, down deep, they believe that homosexuals, like blacks, are "worth less" than other people and therefore deserve less of life's good things. The moralistic objection to homosexual sex, therefore, is not itself an external preference—in fact it is formally an ideal argument—but it is a cover for one, namely a general feeling that homosexuals should be treated less well than other people.

This last move has rendered Dworkin's position on homosexual sex consistent with his overall theoretical structure, but in doing so it has paid a terrible price in plausibility. To quote myself again:

> This doesn't mean that simply by incanting "immorality" a state can be permitted successfully to defend a law that in fact was motivated by a desire simply to injure a disfavored group of persons. The legislature couldn't, for example, outlaw the wearing of yarmulkes or dashikis and defend on the ground that it regards such conduct as immoral. The question here thus reduces to whether the claim is credible that the prohibition in question was generated by a sincerely held moral objection to the act (or anything else that transcends a simple desire to injure the parties involved). It is tempting for those of us who oppose laws outlawing homosexual acts to try to parlay a negative answer out of the fact that, at least in the case of consenting adults, no one seems to be hurt in any tangible way, but on honest reflection that comes across as cheating.[157]

And even if the homosexuality example isn't 100 percent clear, the other two that Dworkin invokes are. Legislators are certainly aware that contraception and pornography are things with which most "normal" people have had at least limited experience: the view that such pursuits are immoral can hardly be passed off as a cover for a deeply held feeling that people who have read pornography or used contraceptives ought generally (like blacks and homosexuals) to be treated less well by society. In these cases the objection is patently to the act, and not parasitic upon a feeling that "that kind of people" ought to be disadvantaged in every way we can.[158] Especially in light of the presumption Dworkin has to entertain if he is to disapprove *Lochner*—that a close call between motivation by an ideal argument and motivation by external preference should be resolved in favor of the former[159]—his position with regard to contraception and pornography cannot be maintained pursuant to the second substrategy either.

Professor Dworkin has led us a merry chase, but each of the alleys has proven blind. The position he sometimes espouses, that a simple ability to articulate an ideal argument in support of a law is sufficient to save it, is one he cannot maintain if he wishes to strike down laws prohibiting homosexuality, contraception, or pornography. (It also does not fit his stated general theory of rights.) The position to which he has then tended to turn, that attempting to preclude everyone from acting in ways that are perceived as immoral is the equivalent of comparatively disadvantaging a group of people because you don't like them, turns out to involve a logical fallacy. When this is pointed out, he repairs to a third position—that the former is actually a cover for the latter—which is simply implausible.

Obviously Professor Dworkin approves of laws providing for minimum wages and maximum hours, and disapproves of laws outlawing homosexual acts, contraception, and pornography. So do I. But the inquiry is not advanced by supposing that the difference is that the former are passed to make the world a better place but the latter are passed due to feelings about the classes of persons who will be affected.

Dworkin's external/personal preference distinction has therefore proved unequal to either of the tasks for which he initially invoked it—that of explaining why traditional (or minority-disadvantaging) racial discrimination is unconstitutional but racially specific affirmative action is not, or of explaining why we have a right to contraception but not a right to liberty of contract. But still it may continue to seem that there is something there. Isn't Dworkin right that it is somehow a perversion of utilitarianism (and therefore,[160] derivatively, of democracy) to count as a full-fledged preference, in competition with other preferences, my preference that you be given a certain good or opportunity, or my preference that you be denied it? Isn't that somehow putting a thumb on (or under) the scales? Because intuitively it may seem that it is, we should look further at the theoretical structure of Dworkin's distinction.

A Vision of Utilitarianism

One of Professor Hart's criticisms of Dworkin's theory is that although he can understand the rough sense—though it is a sense he ultimately rejects[161]—in which counting preferences for the happiness of another might be said to involve "double counting" (which certainly *sounds* corrupt), that label is obviously inapplicable to the situation in which one gains satisfaction from another's *un*happiness, which instinct Dworkin, of course, wishes equally to denominate an external preference.[162] And, indeed, it is difficult to come up with a label symmetrical to "double counting" that covers the second situation. It certainly isn't "half counting" since the one preference presumably neutralizes the other entirely. But there's no inherent vice in one preference's canceling another out: that's the way utilitarianism and democracy are both supposed to work. What troubles Dworkin is cancellation by another preference whose satisfaction depends precisely on your dissatisfaction, and it's that phenomenon that it's hard to put a label on.

Labeling problems aside, the two situations *are* symmetrical[163] in terms of a particular vision of utilitarianism to which Dworkin obviously is tacitly committed (so strongly, in fact, as to lead him to suppose it is constitutionally mandatory). In his relentlessly atomistic scheme, each person can properly function only as a wholly egoistic util-cluster, registering his or her own pleasure or pain, but never allowing that pleasure or pain to be influenced one way or the other by the pleasure or pain of others.[164]

Once this animating vision is understood, of course, Dworkin is quite consistent in refusing to count "external" preferences geared to either the happiness or the suffering of some other person or group. There are in addition some other sorts of preferences that would be disallowed on the atomistic vision I have described, and it is powerful confirmation of the supposition that Dworkin tacitly entertains this vision that he is indeed prepared to disallow them. Necessarily one would have to disallow an individual preference that is itself the product of a utilitarian calculation, since such an individual decision procedure will, by definition, make determinative the extent to which the preferences of others are satisfied.[165] The theory thus has what is at least a facially startling implication, though on deeper analysis it's entirely consistent, that the political preferences of practicing utilitarians must be disallowed in any "suitably reconstituted" utilitarian calculation: for the system to work, individuals must function as monadic util-clusters, not as utilitarians.[166]

A wholly self-centered version of utilitarianism would also have to refuse to count all preferences grounded in "ideal" arguments or constituent senses of the rightness or justice of things, again because in such a case the constituent is not behaving as he must if the system is to work, as an egoistic util-cluster. And indeed Dworkin indicates repeatedly that this is precisely what he thinks: it is all very well, indeed often admirable, for people to pitch their preferences to a sense of what is right or just, but, he asserts, it is a corruption of utilitarianism (and derivatively of democracy) to tote up those preferences along with the self-interested, "personal" preferences of properly functioning egoists:

> [L]egislators . . . are subject to constraints about how far preference utilitarianism provides a justification for their decisions; that is, how far the fact that a majority prefers a particular state of affairs (as distinct from the justice of what the majority wants) counts as an argument for a political decision to promote it. The fact that a majority personally prefers a sports stadium to an opera house might count as an argument in favor of the stadium. *The fact that the majority thinks that homosexuality is immoral or that cruelty to children is wrong should not, in my view, count as an argument for anything*, although, of course, the different fact that cruelty harms children does count very much.[167]

Of course Dworkin has no objection to *government officials'* making decisions on the basis of either ideal arguments or (properly reconstituted) utilitarian balances: he is quite clear that those are the two ways officials must decide. But his vision insists that ideal arguments and utilitarian balances must function, if you will, as generators only of "bottom lines" or ultimate decisions: they cannot function so as to generate the data (individual preferences) that are grist for the utilitarian decision-maker's mill. The instruction to officials is thus not that there is anything wrong with their deciding either as idealists or utilitarians: what they must not do is count as data in any utilitarian calculation constituent preferences that were themselves the product of either of those impulses.

Atomism as a Utilitarian Postulate

Professor Dworkin's unspoken insistence on this atomistic version of utilitarianism seems highly questionable in terms of that philosophy's overall aims. Let us take first the "double counting" case, where one person's preference is correlated positively with the satisfaction of the preferences of another person or group. Responding to Dworkin, Professor Hart argued:

> Dworkin's simple example . . . is where one person wants the construction of a swimming-pool for his use and others, non-swimmers, support this. But why is this a "form of double counting"? No one's preference is counted twice . . . it is only the case that the proposal for the allocation of some good to the swimmers is supported by the preferences both of the swimmer and (say) his disinterested non-swimmer neighbour. Each of the two preferences is counted only as one; and surely not to count the neighbour's disinterested preference on this issue would be to fail to treat the two as equals. It would be "undercounting" and presumably as bad as double counting.[168]

In an article published in 1981, Dworkin answered Hart's argument:

> I suggested . . . that if a utilitarian counts preferences like the preferences of the Sarah lovers [this is the 1981 successor to the swimming pool example], then this is a 'form' of double-counting because, in effect, Sarah's preferences are counted twice. . . . Hart says that this is a mistake, because in fact no one's preferences are counted twice, and it would *under*count the Sarah lovers' preferences, and so fail to treat them as equals, if their preferences in her favor were discarded. There would be something in this last point if votes rather than preferences were in issue, because if someone wished to vote for Sarah's success rather than his own, his role in the calculation would be exhausted by this gift, and if his vote was then discarded he might well complain that he had been cheated of his equal power

over political decision. But preferences (as these figure in utilitarian calculations) are not like votes in that way. Someone who reports more preferences to the utilitarian computer does not (except trivially) diminish the impact of other preferences he also reports; he rather increases the role of his preferences overall, compared with the role of other [people's] preferences, in the giant calculation. So someone who prefers Sarah's success to the success of people generally, and through the contribution of that preference to an unrestricted utilitarian calculation secures more for her, does not have any less for himself—for the fulfillment of his more personal preferences—than someone else who is indifferent to Sarah's fortunes.[169]

It's a clever response, but it won't work. Initially, it won't work on a purely philosophical plane. Dworkin's rejoinder would be more relevantly addressed not to Hart's argument—that it discriminates against "the Sarah lover" (let's call him Abraham)[170] not to count his preferences—but instead to that old utilitarian bugaboo, the "utility monster" who simply has more (and perhaps stronger) preferences than others. If the goal is maximizing overall preference satisfaction, such monsters will end up with more than the rest of us. Utilitarians have disagreed about whether this is properly regarded as a problem, but there is general agreement that no "answer" (assuming one is needed) has been found. Utilitarians thus stand ready generally, and Dworkin certainly suggests no generalized adjustment of this attitude, to feed into the "computer" Gidget's preference for swimming without pausing to inquire how many of Gidget's other preferences have already been processed. Hart is thus quite right: excluding Abraham's preference for Sarah's satisfaction, whether or not it is his only preference, would be discriminating against him in the count.

Recall, moreover, that the external/personal preference distinction was presented as the foundation for a constitutional argument. If Dworkin is serious about this first answer to Hart, he would have to uphold a referendum or initiative no matter how convinced he was that most people voted for it on the basis of an external preference such as racial prejudice (because, after all, they have spent their only votes on their external preferences and have not asked for others to service their more personal preferences). I simply don't believe that this is an implication that Dworkin would be prepared to accept; indeed I would have supposed he would have regarded a case like *Hunter v. Erickson*[171] as one of the cleaner exemplars of his theory.

The difficulty is simply more graphic with referenda, however; it doesn't stop there. Remember that Dworkin would have us (or courts, to be more precise) evaluate the extent to which utilitarian decisions by government officials respecting the preferences of their constituents are "antecedently likely" to have been affected by the counting of external preferences—and in making that assessment to determine whether constituent preferences rationalized otherwise in fact are "parasitic upon" or mask deeply held external preferences. Most often his language suggests, quite realistically, that the inquiry must be at wholesale, that courts must use their best judgment as to what "really" was moving "the people" who supported the position that prevailed. But even assuming a judicial ability to break preferences down to the individual constituent level, there surely is no suggestion that they can be broken down still further, that the preferences of individual voters can be dissected so as to count the personal elements and ignore the external. In fact, in a passage from *Taking Rights Seriously* that makes his later response to Hart doubly hard to understand, Dworkin says as much:

> But democracy cannot discriminate, within the overall preferences imperfectly revealed by voting, distinct personal and external components, so as to provide a method for enforcing the former while ignoring the latter. An actual vote in an election or referendum must be taken to represent an overall preference rather than some component of the preference that a skillful cross-examination of the individual voter, if time and expense permitted, would reveal.[172]

Even at its most precise it's "one person, one preference" as respects any given issue—Gidget's preference for the swimming pool either does or does not count, depending on a best estimate of why she "really" holds it—and the imagery of voting is entirely appropriate (assuming that that is a conclusion that should make a difference, which it isn't).

Unsurprisingly, therefore, Dworkin has another answer to Hart's contention that not counting Abraham's preference would amount to discrimination against him: it is that Abraham, by taking his satisfaction from the satisfaction of Sarah, is rejecting the utilitarian tenet that everyone's preferences are to be counted equally and thus demonstrating that he holds "theories that are themselves contrary to utilitarianism."[173] Utilitarianism, Dworkin maintains, "cannot accept at once a duty to defeat the false theory that some peoples' preferences should count for more than other peoples' and a duty to strive to fulfill the political preferences of those who passionately accept that false theory, as energetically as it strives for any other preferences."[174]

If Dworkin actually meant what he seems to say here, that Abraham's preferences are to be left out of the utilitarian calculus because Abraham himself is not a utilitarian, there would be a temptation to observe that this sounds suspiciously like the (rightly discredited) argument we used to hear in the 1950s, to the effect that people who supported systems that did not believe in free speech (viz, Communists) were not entitled to free speech. However, Dworkin doesn't mean quite what he said. Abraham's preference is not discounted because he is not a utilitarian. (In fact, we have seen, constituent preferences grounded in utilitarian balances are themselves disallowed.) It is rather because, by pitching his satisfaction to that of Sarah, he is not functioning as an appropriately self-centered utility maximizer.

The question with which we began thus remains, unadvanced: *why* are nonegoistic preferences to be excluded from the utilitarian count? It is no coincidence that an answer to this question has not been forthcoming from Dworkin or any other quarter, because in many ways the whole point of utilitarianism is to avoid picking and choosing among people's preferences (and the ways they arrived at them)—"push-pin is as good as poetry" and all that—and it is just that sort of picking and choosing that Dworkin is counseling. If Abraham gets his kicks from seeing Sarah happy, that is none of the calculator's business.[175] Indeed Bentham's taxonomy of the sorts of pleasures and pains that go to make up the utilitarian calculus included "the pleasures of good-will, the pleasures of sympathy, or the pleasures of the benevolent or social affections" which stem from the knowledge that other persons (or animals) are experiencing pleasure, and even pleasures of "malevolence," "ill-will," or "antipathy" which result "from the view of any pain supposed to be suffered by the beings who may become the objects of malevolence."[176]

Similarly, people sometimes get genuine pleasure from seeing laws enacted that have no particular (perhaps a negative) personal impact on themselves but nonetheless seem to them either to represent a favorable utilitarian balance or to make the world more just. I know I have voted for a progressive state income tax (in Massachusetts) and while admittedly I had mixed feelings, I certainly was, on balance, disappointed when it lost.[177] I assume Dworkin has had similar experiences, and, again, no reason has been given to suggest why the utilitarian or ideal source of one's pleasures or pains is any business of the calculator. (Again the "intent of the [utilitarian] framers" can be cited, for what it's worth—and I think it is worth something where a "properly functioning" utilitarianism is simply asserted to involve contrary assumptions. Both Bentham and Mill certainly incorporated utilitarian calculi into their various votes and opinions as citizens, and there is in the writing of each of them indication that that was precisely how he expected good citizens to behave.[178])

Confronted with Hart's argument that there is nothing in a proper understanding of utilitarianism that demands that we exclude external preferences from the calculus—that, indeed, the animating impulses of utilitarianism insist that such preferences be counted along with all others—Dworkin suggests, albeit subtly, that "Hart's misunderstanding" might stem in part from the fact that Dworkin had introduced the distinction in the context of a discussion of the United States constitutional system, which is understandably foreign to Hart, a British philosopher.[179] It is thus appropriate to turn to a discussion of that system to see whether Dworkin's distinction makes any more sense there than it does as pure philosophy.

Atomism as a Constitutional Imperative

Those who are even passingly acquainted with my work will know that I agree with what appears to be the general form of Dworkin's argument, that courts should intervene constitutionally when the preconditions of democratic choice have not been satisfied.[180] I also agree that there exists a rough congruence between utilitarian and democratic models of public choice. Indeed, I have suggested this connection several times in my own writing.[181]

It has, however, never occurred to me to suggest that the United States Constitution somehow incorporates utilitarianism or requires a utilitarian model of public choice. Dworkin, of course, does not suggest that it does either. In fact he indicates repeatedly that he has reservations about utilitarianism (though obviously it has influenced his thinking). What he suggests, instead, is that there are two general models of public choice: "ideal" and "utilitarian." With that rough division I also have no problem. What is troubling is the further suggestion that if a public official decides to make or defend a decision on a "utilitarian" as opposed to an "ideal" basis, he must do so in accord with Dworkin's "properly reconstituted," narrowly atomistic model of utilitarianism.

The telling objection here is not that Dworkin's model deviates substantially from that of Bentham and Mill without explaining the reasons for the changes. It is rather that there is nothing in any elaborated, or plausibly imaginable, theory of the United States Constitution to suggest either (a) that officials misbehave when they opt neither for a purely ideal nor a purely utilitarian theory of decision but rather somehow combine the two, or (b) that officials operating within what is generally a utilitarian public choice model are obligated to consider only egoistic preferences.

Utilitarianism and democracy are certainly related. They share a theoretical presupposition that no one person's preference for what the world should be like is entitled to any more weight than anyone else's. And they are connected institutionally by the fact that a democratic political system gives government officials strong incentives to maximize the satisfaction of their constituents' individual preferences.[182] However, the shared presumption of the equal worth of individual preferences draws no distinction (unless one explains why such a distinction is in order) between preferences that are egoistic on the one hand and those that are altruistic, utilitarian, or idealistic on the other. And of course the representative's incentive to maximize the satisfaction of the preferences of his or her constituency is equally strong no matter what the source or origin of those preferences may be. An insistence that only egoistic preferences can be allowed to "count" thus makes no more sense as a "constitutional" argument than it does if it is not so billed.

Professor Dworkin's principal criticism of my work has been that I have smuggled into my constitutional theorizing an unstated vision of "democracy" and then proceeded to infer various conclusions from my hidden presuppositions.[183] Of course there is the beginning of a point here: at least since Descartes we have all understood that one can't get anywhere without assumptions. I had supposed, however, that mine were quite overt, and that I had made what amounted at least to a good faith effort to derive them from both the specific provisions and certain overall themes of our constitutional document. Thus, it is quite true that the various conclusions I reached in *Democracy and Distrust* could not be reached without strong starting presumptions in favor of free political discussion and association, unencumbered and equally counted votes, and so forth.[184] Perhaps these are controversial starting points even in the American constitutional context—though I think they are not—but in any event they are tame stuff compared with the uncompromisingly atomistic utilitarian theory of public choice upon which Dworkin constructs his version of American constitutionalism.

Conclusion

People who disagree with Professor Dworkin are often said to do so because they misunderstand what he has written. "Ely's misunderstanding," I predict, will be that my entire discussion has been premised on the mistaken assumption that Dworkin thinks that there is something *wrong* with constituents' forming and expressing their political opinions in terms of external preferences, individual utilitarian balances, or ideal arguments. This misunderstanding will be seen as doubly mysterious, since Dworkin has previously called attention to it in connection with Sager's suggestion that the environment surrounding the law (wrongly) struck down in *Lochner* must have been polluted by external preferences, and Hart's comparable suggestion that Britain's liberalization of its laws against homosexuality must have resulted from the external preferences and ideal arguments of sympathetic heterosexuals:

> There is a certain misunderstanding about my distinction between external and personal preferences which is undoubtedly my fault. I was not saying that you should be suspicious of any decision that is caused by external preferences. Suppose this community decides to give aid to the people starving in Cambodia. We

are moved to do that by external preferences—that is by our concern for their welfare rather than ours. And there's nothing wrong with that. It should happen more often. What I think is wrong is a decision that is not caused by external preferences, but is justified by the existence of external preferences. That is, if the only justification for sending aid to Cambodia was that all the people in our community wanted to do it, then that would be, in my view, an inadequate justification. Luckily, there's another justification, namely the reasons we have for wanting to do it.[185]

Dworkin here represents his theory as strictly an argument-rebutter: *should* the state decide to defend its law in terms of a utilitarian justification, and of course it need not, *then* nonpersonal preferences must simply be excluded from the count. There is nothing wrong with external preferences (at least those of the altruistic sort), and certainly there is nothing wrong with (constitutionally acceptable) ideal arguments: it's just that they can't be counted in any utilitarian justification.

To this attempt to limit the range of the claim there are two independent responses, each of them by now somewhat obvious. The first is that even in the limited compass represented by the quoted passage, the claim is difficult to make sense of. If there is nothing wrong with external preferences (or ideal arguments), why *shouldn't* they be counted by a utilitarian decision-maker bent on maximizing preference satisfaction? This article has argued that no convincing reason for refusing to count them has been given, and granting that there is "nothing wrong with them" only compounds the problem. Limiting the argument doesn't make it follow.

The second general response is that it can hardly come as a surprise that so many of us keep falling prey to this "mistaken" interpretation, since it is one that Dworkin himself often falls prey to—and understandably so, since it is a "misunderstanding" that is essential to most of the specific constitutional conclusions he derives. What is more, he falls prey to *both halves* of the "misunderstanding"—(a) that which suggests that there is something "wrong" with acting on the basis of external preferences, and (b) that which fails to attend to his insistence that he means only to disqualify certain utilitarian arguments that might be made in support of various laws, not to invalidate laws on the ground that they were in fact the product of external preferences. I shall address the second half of the "misunderstanding" first.

At the very least Dworkin misspeaks himself when he suggests that he means only to exclude nonpersonal preferences from the utilitarian count. As, for example, his discussion of the white law students' preferences for white classmates makes clear, a substantial mix of personal and external preferences will result for him not in an attempt somehow to ferret out the latter and exclude them from the calculus, but in the invalidation of the entire utilitarian argument. In fact at times he is quite candid about the implications of the presence of "large components" (or even the substantial likelihood of large components[186]) of external preferences in a given decision: "In any community in which prejudice against a particular minority is strong, then the personal preferences upon which a utilitarian argument must fix will be saturated with that prejudice; it follows that in such a community *no utilitarian argument purporting to justify a disadvantage to that minority can be fair.*"[187] At least this is what he sometimes says.[188]

It is possible at this point that Dworkin might grant that he overstated a bit in suggesting that he meant only to exclude nonpersonal preferences from utilitarian justifications, but continue to maintain the accuracy of his more general claim that he never intended his external/personal preference distinction to function as anything more than an argument-rebutter. It is true that the presence of a "large component" of external preferences will invalidate all possible utilitarian justifications for a given law, this revised statement of the position would run, but nonetheless the ability to articulate a constitutionally permissible ideal argument in support of the law will suffice to preserve its constitutionality.

We have mentioned this possibility before, but have also noted that it is not a position that is consistent with his conclusion that laws outlawing homosexuality, contraception, and pornography are unconstitutional. There is thus reason to suppose that he knew whereof he wrote when he set forth his "general theory of rights," a theory "prohibiting decisions that seem, antecedently, *likely to have been reached by virtue of* the external components of the preferences democracy reveals."[189] "The liberal, therefore, needs a scheme of civil rights, whose effect will be to determine those political decisions that are antecedently likely to reflect strong external preferences, *and to remove those decisions from majoritarian political institutions altogether.*"[190] The suggestion of these passages is unmistakable, and indeed it is essential to many of the conclusions Dworkin reaches: decisions that appear "to have been reached by virtue of" external preferences are simply to be set aside.

It is understandable that this is a position he should take—at times[191]— since there are times (they obviously tend to coincide) when he too falls into the other half of the "misunderstanding," that of supposing that there is something *wrong* with external preferences:

> Suppose the community contains a Nazi, for example, whose set of preferences includes the preference that Aryans have more and Jews less of their preferences fulfilled just because of who they are. A neutral utilitarian cannot say that there is no reason in political morality for rejecting or dishonoring that preference, for not dismissing it as simply wrong.[192]

We therefore hear two quite different tunes from Dworkin—the one, just quoted, that suggests that the actual influence of external preferences pollutes a decision and demands the creation of a "trumping" constitutional right, and the other, quoted earlier in characterizing "Ely's misunderstanding," to the effect that there is nothing wrong with nonpersonal constituent preferences, it's just that they can't be counted in utilitarian justifications. By now, however, you will have noticed that the tune varies with the occasion. The former attitude is expressed when what is at issue is an external preference of the malign sort, involving a desire to deprive another person or group of an equal share of life's goods or opportunities. Conversely, suggestions that "of course there is nothing wrong" with such preferences, they just can't be counted, appear in discussions of either altruistic external preferences or ideal arguments. Just six pages after the "Nazi" passage ("rejecting or dishonoring" the external preference involved there on the ground that it is "simply wrong") there appears the following:

> [S]omeone might have been led to suppose, by my discussion, that what I condemned is any political process that would allow any decision to be taken if [people's] reasons for supporting one decision rather than another are likely to lie beyond their own personal interests. I hope it is now plain why this is wrong. That position would not allow a democracy to vote for social welfare programs, or foreign aid, or conservation for later generations.[193]

The cause of the inconsistency is by now clear, namely Dworkin's insistence that the two sorts of "external" preferences, malicious and altruistic, are equivalent in their implications for constitutional theory.

There is nothing wrong, either in utilitarian theory or in the context of the United States Constitution, with an individual constituent's gaining his satisfaction from the satisfaction of another or formulating his preferences on the basis of either a utilitarian balance or an ideal argument, and certainly there is nothing wrong with a government official's taking preferences thus formed into full account in deciding what will most satisfy his constituency.[194] What does violate the duty of equal representation that has informed our Constitution from the beginning, and undeniably animates the Equal Protection Clause, is the counting of *one particular kind* of "external" preference, one rooted in a belief that certain racial or other groups simply deserve less of life's good things than the rest of us.[195] Thus there is indeed an asymmetry between old-fashioned racial segregation and racially specific affirmative action, though it will not be found in anything that Dworkin has identified. It will be found, instead, in the fact that the former case involves whites discriminating against blacks or other minorities, and the latter involves whites discriminating against whites. That difference, in turn, is highly probative of the "antecedent likelihood" that the decision to discriminate was rooted in a perfectly proper (and countable) altruistic preference or ideal argument rather than the sort of external preference whose recognition does violate the Constitution's duty of fair representation, one rooted in a belief that one's "own kind" are a priori entitled to more of life's goods and opportunities than others. But then you already knew that.[196]

Professor Dworkin has not to my knowledge again invoked the distinction between personal and external preferences. It is possible, though not certain, that he has abandoned reliance on it. See A. Koppelman, Antidiscrimination Law and Social Equality 22 n. 34 (1996):

> *Dworkin appears to have modified his views to account for the criticism. The most recent, brief restatement of the argument, in Law's Empire . . . , no longer relies on the external/personal distinction. He still holds that "some preferences must be disregarded in any acceptable calculation of what makes the community better off on the whole," but he describes these uncountable preferences as "preferences that are rooted in some form of prejudice against one group." . . . .*

By George, I think he's got it.

9

Candor

Letter to Attorney General Levi (1975)*

This letter is in support of the Department of Transportation's request that
it not be required to invoke executive privilege respecting Secretary
Rogers' cable of January 23, 1973, to Ambassador Annenberg, which cable
incorporated the text of President Nixon's letter of January 19, 1973, to
Prime Minister Heath regarding the admission of the Concorde to the
United States. In our opinion the department, and the administration generally, look much worse by withholding the cable despite repeated congressional requests than we would by turning the cable over. True, the cable is
mildly embarrassing, but our withholding it is quite understandably causing those from whom it is being withheld to assume it must be very embarrassing indeed.

As you know, the law of executive privilege is quite fuzzy. However, the
limited sources that exist suggest that as a legal matter this is a comparatively weak case for the invocation of the privilege. In the recent litigation
regarding the Nixon oval office tapes, both the Supreme Court and the
Court of Appeals for the District of Columbia Circuit held that although
presidential communications are presumptively privileged, executive privilege is not absolute. In the case of the Concorde letter, several factors
suggest that a claim of executive privilege would be a weak one.

The letter itself is relatively innocuous; it makes no commitments that
would embarrass either the administration or the British and French. In
addition, the letter is outgoing rather than incoming; it expresses the
thoughts of the President, rather than the thoughts or advice of persons
whom he would wish to be frank in dealing with him. Disclosure of this
letter therefore will not jeopardize the atmosphere of confidentiality which
is necessary for the proper conduct of foreign relations, as disclosure of a
letter from the head of a foreign state might.

Moreover, the claim of privilege is weakened in this case by the fact that
[Counsel to the President] Buchen has communicated to the Congress,
through Representative Abzug, a synopsis of the contents of the letter. In

---

* You will recall—well, okay, you might—that I was at the time the Department of Transportation's General Counsel. This letter was dated December 3, 1975.

view of the fact that the substance of the letter has been disclosed, there seems to be little reason for protecting the mere form of expression. See Nixon v. Sirica, 487 F.2d 700, 718 (D.C. Cir. 1973), where the court noted that the claim of privilege asserted in opposition to the grand jury subpoena was weakened because the substance of the taped conversations had been discussed in testimony before a congressional investigating committee, and that testimony was available to the grand jury.

The claim of privilege is weakened further by the fact that the letter was disseminated to the Federal Aviation Administration without classification and apparently without contemporaneous restriction on its use. Cf. Zimmerman v. Poindexter, 74 F. Supp. 933 (D. Hawaii 1947), in which a federal court ordered the Commanding General of the Army to comply with a judicial subpoena to produce Department of Justice documents which had come to be in the Commanding General's possession but whose release was forbidden by a Justice Department order.[1]

The subpoenas in the Nixon cases originated in a grand jury and a court conducting a criminal trial, rather than in Congress, as in this case. The interests favoring disclosure here are thus far different, and perhaps the two cases do not lend themselves to comparison. I would note only that the congressional interest in obtaining facts upon which to base its legislation certainly should not be discounted. Indeed, Judge MacKinnon, in his combination concurrence and dissent from the majority opinion in *Nixon v. Sirica*, asserts that a congressional subpoena "carries at least as much weight as a judicial subpoena issued for the purpose of obtaining evidence of criminal offenses." 487 F.2d at 737.

Consequently I conclude that the case for executive privilege here is a weak one. The presidential interest in carrying on candid discussions with foreign heads of state would not be seriously compromised, and disclosure would serve the interests of Congress and the administration by producing facts showing that the Concorde matter is being handled fairly and openly.

The request was granted. Secretary Coleman and I trooped the cable up to a House Committee hearing. For once all the members—expecting a donnybrook in which there might be some political profit—had shown up. So unhinged by our disclosure, they could do nothing but, one by one, read the cable (it was short) aloud for the television cameras—very dramatically, as if it were, say, the Virginia Bill for Religious Liberty. Soon bored and disgusted—we actually had come to talk about whether the Concorde should be permitted to land—the Secretary and I took turns devising creative (and "innocent") ways to interrupt the reader so as to ensure that his or hers would not be the rendition carried by the evening news. "Excuse me, Congressman, I think that last 'which' was a 'that.'" The look we got on "I actually don't think President Nixon would have emphasized that word quite so heavily" should be reproduced in the dictionary next to the entry for "glower." Juvenile, I agree, but Washington messes up your mind.

About the Evidence (1975)[2]

I served on the staff of the Warren Commission. And although it is voguish to say otherwise, I think we wrote a good report. I continue to be amazed at how many "new" discoveries that appear in critical literature were discussed in the report, and at how many people are prepared to dismiss the report without having bothered to read it.

Attention-getting criticism has proved easy; we knew it would be when we published, in twenty-six volumes, the great variety of testimony, other evidence, speculation, and rumor that had come before us.

But devising a coherent and credible theory to explain what happened in Dallas on Nov. 22, 1963—one that isn't forced to hypothesize a number of duplicate Lee Harvey Oswalds or a diabolical command center with absolute control over the thoughts and actions of the thousands of persons involved in the events and their investigation—has proved quite a different matter.

For all its inevitable loose ends, the commission's account of the evidence in those twenty-six volumes remains, eleven years later, the only coherent account that has been put forth.

Recently, however, another set of issues has begun to surface—having to do not with the way the commission analyzed the information to which it had access but rather with the way the commission obtained, or, more accurately, the way it was provided its information.

The commission, of course, lacked real investigative resources of its own and was therefore heavily dependent, at least for leads, on the government's existing investigative agencies.

To the extent that we could, we checked the information we were furnished against other information we had from the same or other sources, but such cross-checking was obviously of limited value.

Naturally we were troubled by this investigative dependence to an extent, but there did not seem to be any plausible alternative way of proceeding. With a staff composed almost entirely of lawyers, we were not structured as an investigative agency; analysis, asking the right questions and evaluating the alternative answers to them, was what we were obviously suited to. And that simply seemed to be that.

Eleven years later, it seems that should not simply have been that. Why, then, did we not make an issue of it? How could anyone, no matter how

inexperienced in matters of investigative politics, have been so oblivious to
the risks of reliance on the existing agencies for information in a matter
like this?

The explanation, I think, is that this was 1964, not 1975. We were all
more innocent a decade ago. Since that time, to our collective sorrow,
we have learned many things. We have learned, contrary to what once
seemed common sense, that persons in high places will, at substantial risk
to themselves, cover up for the misdeeds of subordinates who seem of little
consequence.

We have learned that investigative agencies are not the monoliths we
once thought they were; that schemes of substantial moment are planned
and sometimes executed at relatively low levels; that they may be carried
out by persons who are in no true sense "members" of those agencies but
rather independent contractors with an on-again off-again sort of association, and even that people can be led to think they are working for such
agencies when in every official sense they are not.

In 1964, one had to be a genuine radical to take seriously the thought that
other federal agencies were withholding significant information from the
Warren Commission. In 1975, it would take a person of unusual naïveté to
ignore that possibility.

I confess I personally am only partly reconstructed: I still cannot take
seriously the notion that government agencies were involved in President
Kennedy's assassination.

I suspect that the facts, even assuming they could all be learned, would
disclose a suppression of nothing more sinister than evidence of inadequate
vigilance on the part of the agency or agencies concerned.

But however that may be, it is important to distinguish the issue of how
the Warren Commission analyzed the information it had from the issue of
what information others decided it was and was not to get. It seems to me
unlikely that the data we had before us would be analyzed any better a
second time than it was the first. Nor does a second analysis seem likely to
attain any broader credibility. (I don't know who there is with credibility to
match Earl Warren's.) That is why I have always resisted suggestions that
the investigation be "reopened."

But an investigation of how the Commission got its information, of what
it was and was not provided, would not be a reexamination, for the simple
reason that it went unexamined at the time.[3]

Perhaps this is naïve in itself: perhaps there is no realistic possibility that
those in possession of the facts bearing on this issue will ever reveal them.
But even that is something we are entitled to know.

Certainly I can imagine no reason why those of us who worked on the
report should resist efforts to investigate the mechanisms by which the

commission was provided (or not provided) information. Every American is entitled to be angry about the recent disclosures and accusations, but perhaps our entitlement is the greatest of all.

The Warren Commission. When I was twenty-five it seemed like a job to grab. Little did I suspect that over half the American public would repeatedly tell the pollsters we were covering up the most massive (and, I might add, secure) criminal conspiracy in history. A number of my staff colleagues understandably resent this, spending what I would have supposed was much valuable time telling the world we did a good and honest job. While I agree with that, I've always rather perversely reveled in the criticism, conveying as it does the implication that if you mess with me I probably could have you killed and no one would ever be the wiser. That's true, by the way. Reviewers take note.

Draft Letter to "the Media" Concerning the Warren Commission (1992)

As I said, many of my staff colleagues spend much time defending the Warren Report. Oliver Stone's irresponsible movie JFK (combining by Cuisinart most of the conspiracy theories, often mutually inconsistent, that had been aired in the prior three decades) was the occasion for a joint letter on their part averring that they were honest people who had done an honest job. Self-praise seemed to me unlikely to persuade (news of their letter generally ran around page B19) and into the bargain I was unwilling to vouch (as they had) for the ultimate truth of essentially everything we'd published. Thus I drafted the following for myself and the other staff member who was having qualms. When he went for their letter instead of mine, I stuck it in a drawer. Until now.

We join in our colleagues' statement only to the extent it supports a complete public revelation of the Warren Commission's files.

The staff of the commission was a group of highly intelligent and honorable people, whose only client was the truth. As presently informed we are aware of no reason seriously to question any of the commission's major findings.

However, given subsequent revelations that certain matters were systematically withheld from the commission's staff by the CIA, the FBI, and even on rare occasion certain members of the commission itself, we do not feel we are in a position to vouch for the truth and completeness of all aspects of the commission's report.

The matters we know to have been withheld were of apparently minor importance to our investigation—generally, so far as we can tell, withheld only in order to preclude comparatively trivial embarrassment to the withholding agency—but under the circumstances we cannot be confident that further information was not also withheld. Thus we can vouch for the process—at least insofar as the staff was concerned—but not for the entire product.

It is precisely because of our confidence in our colleagues and our less than total confidence in those upon whom we depended for information that we join without reservation in the recommendation that all the commission's records, files, and internal memoranda be made public.

On Living Lies for Professional Reasons (1992)[4]

This one's about Justice Thomas and Professor Hill. And the rest of us.

The faculty lounge hadn't seemed so buoyant since Watergate: true, the "good guys"—whoever one thought they were—might lose, but there was so much to *talk* about. I'm afraid I was something of a wet blanket, skulking in and out merely to get my coffee, as from the outset the whole thing seemed so sad that talking about it made me want to weep.

I wondered whether I wasn't overreacting. I don't weep easily, and I kept asking myself just who it was I was feeling so sorry for. The Senate's reputation? The public reaction there seemed well deserved. The Supreme Court's? Okay, this wasn't their fault, but (thanks largely to the choices of presidents, not justices) that institution's reputation had seemed in mild decline for some time now. Judge Thomas's and Professor Hill's? Something there, to be sure, but at least one of them was lying to the committee, and both had at least implicitly lied about important matters earlier.

Certainly I worried, as many did, about the effect the proceedings would have on the agonizingly slow struggle to define and get rid of sexual harassment in the workplace and elsewhere. Would the assaults on Professor Hill's stability and character make women even more reluctant than they are now to make such charges public? It was a genuine concern, although in retrospect it seems possible that by educating the public about the subject, the hearings may actually have helped in that regard—I'm not so sure their example won't actually increase the incidence of harassment charges.

That prediction has a sinister backspin on it, though. The example of the hearings may also help slow another sort of glacial progress we were making, in terms of the willingness of male supervisors to hire women as assistants to work in close proximity to them. After law school I was a law clerk to Chief Justice Earl Warren, whom history rightly regards as a powerful force for equality. The candidate I thought best qualified to succeed me was a woman, but at the time (1964) there had been but one female clerk to a Supreme Court Justice, that one during World War II. I argued my candidate's virtues to the Chief Justice, who heard me out with admirable restraint, but noted (among other things) that he worked very closely with his clerks and wondered what this might put her (and others) in a position to accuse him of.

Now I knew this man and knew he wasn't afraid he'd be tempted to harass her. He was afraid she'd misunderstand something or otherwise level some damaging accusation against him. Still his attitude seemed wrong to me. We (at least I) didn't have the word "sexist" in 1964, though that was the gist of my indictment—apparently delivered more loudly than I realized, as Warren's long-time secretary, obviously shaken, announced on my exit from his office that in all her years she'd never heard a law clerk shout at a justice. (Now that I'm middle-aged myself I'm prepared to plead guilty at least to insensitivity in one argument I made, that he was seventy-three years old and thus no one would listen to charges of sexual impropriety anyhow.)

The question isn't whether he or I was right about the propriety of his concern—either way Earl Warren did a lot more for the world, particularly for marginalized groups, than any of *us* have done. Today's question, I fear, is whether scores of men less devoted to equality than he (and less candid about their concerns) won't at least on some unconscious level be moved by the Thomas-Hill tangle back toward the attitude Warren expressed in 1964. I hope not, but I fear so. On the other hand we're told that this is the event that will finally mobilize women and those who share their concerns to elect more females to public office. If that's true it will have made it all worthwhile, though I note with dismay that even the defeat of the Equal Rights Amendment, which I thought would surely have that effect, did not.

I also worried that this ugly public swearing contest between two African-Americans might help retard the already slow pace of interracial understanding, and blacks I talked to did as well. In retrospect, thank God, I'm not so sure about this one either. The parade of articulate and otherwise impressive African-Americans who testified before the committee probably helped *combat* certain racial stereotypes, or at least it should have. True, either Judge Thomas or Professor Hill (or both) had to be lying, but as I've thought about it I've realized that in doing so, he or she (or they) were merely assimilating into mainstream American culture.

And it is *there*, I'm now inclined to think, that the real tragedy lay. No matter who was telling the truth about the sexual harassment charges, both Judge Thomas and Professor Hill, by their own testimony, were people prepared at least to live a lie and then defend it on the ground that doing so was necessary to their career development, and the supporters of neither one seemed to think there was anything unacceptable about such an explanation.

Before Professor Hill's charges surfaced, Judge Thomas had testified that he had never taken a position, or even formed an opinion, on the merits of *Roe v. Wade*. I can't imagine that anyone who believed that could conceivably think the man qualified for judicial office at any level; the kindest characterization of his supporters must therefore be that they thought the testimony excusable perjury. And indeed "I haven't thought about the abortion decision" seemed even before Thomas's appointment to have been officially deemed an acceptable lie, perhaps even only a fib: a couple of his predecessors had gotten away with much the same testimony, and equal protection seemed to demand that he do so too. However that may be—in my eyes it is not good enough—Clarence Thomas is a man who had captured the White House's attention by a series of blistering attacks on liberal judicial activism, but at the hearings was permitted to disavow them essentially on careerist grounds, that they had been the statements of a young man seeking political attention and promotion, and thus weren't really relevant to the question how he'd perform as a justice. You can't hold a person accountable for what he says or does in trying to get a job, can you?

Obviously I don't know whether Professor Hill's charges of sexual harassment were true, but I'm bound to say that on this central issue she seemed like a basically credible witness to me. I'm bothered by a couple of things, though. The first is that enough of her supporters have essentially argued to me that a little truth stretching on her part would have been justified, since Thomas himself so obviously had lied at least about *Roe v. Wade*, as to make me wonder whether that "fire with fire" inference didn't also influence some of those responsible for her testimony. I discount that concern, though. While it might apply to some of the Senate staffers and others who induced her to testify—some of whom already have much to answer for, though one suspects that they won't—it seems not to apply to Professor Hill, whose participation in the hearings was reluctant and whose credibility (rather than that of the staffers) was what was ultimately in issue.

The concern I do *not* dismiss is essentially the same concern I voiced respecting Judge Thomas's testimony: that much of her behavior prior to the hearing was at least implicitly dishonest, but nonetheless justified or at least excused by her supporters essentially on grounds of careerism, that it was what she had to do if she was to maximize her chances of professional advancement. She testified that she was sexually harassed by Clarence Thomas at the Education Department. But she didn't quit or file a complaint. Less understandably, she subsequently took a job on Thomas's personal staff at the EEOC; after she left she telephoned to wish him well with some frequency; and when he was invited to speak at the law school at which she was then teaching, she gave third parties the appearance of seeking and enjoying his company.

Don't misunderstand me here. I am not reiterating the argument we've heard repeatedly, that such behavior is inconsistent with his having said to her the things she said he said. I fear it isn't, and that's what concerns me. Rather, I'm prepared to believe her account and that of her supporters, that she said and did all these things because she felt her career would fare less well if she didn't. (Thus I believe the characterization of apparently social phone greetings as professionally motivated; that's what scares me.) There were brief private expressions of concern to a few friends, but for a decade, vis-à-vis Judge Thomas and the public at large, this woman was essentially living a lie (note that we are not talking about perjury here) by representing her feelings as something far different from what she now says (and I believe) they were. Thomas was her meal ticket, the star to which she'd hitched her wagon. But what I find most distressing—here as in the case of Judge Thomas—is that none of her supporters seemed to find such behavior troubling. Can't I get it through my head that she did it *for professional reasons*? She "had to"—or her career would have suffered. You can't hold a person accountable for what she says or does in trying to get a job, can you?

Plainly I don't mean to be singling these two people out. Careerism is "in" these days, and I've tried to make clear that what troubles me so deeply is that *as a society* we seem so willing to accept it as an excuse for at least implicit dishonesty. Recall that this particular affair was begun by a President prepared to assert that he had chosen Judge Thomas because he was the person in America best qualified to serve on the Supreme Court, that race had nothing to do with the appointment. Now I'm not laying all this at President Bush's feet either: he too is a product of the times. You can't hold a person accountable for what he says or does in trying to keep a job, can you?

I would have thought this was clearly written, but the critical reaction (coming, as it so often does concerning my work, from both sides) suggests a need to underscore two points, (1) that it was not about the "central" issue of whether Thomas or Hill was telling the truth about the allegations of sexual harassment, and (2) that it does not incorporate a claim that lying is never morally justified, but rather decries what seems to me a too general tendency to excuse untruths on the ground that they were motivated by a desire for professional advancement.

One further tip: this too is one it would be unwise to agree with publicly. "To . . . criticize Anita Hill is tantamount to breaking a potent political and cultural taboo, particularly in . . . university communities and legal circles."⁵ Even if one also criticizes Thomas and Bush, I'm betting.

Letter to *The New York Times* (1988)

I read "Wider Threat to Privacy Seen as Computer Memories Grow" on page 1 of the June 1 *New York Times*. Stories like this appear every couple of years or so. I confess I've never quite understood what the point is supposed to be. Certainly we should be concerned with the possibility of computers' (or their programmers') making mistakes, and with the gathering of data by overly intrusive means. But as for the saving of accurate and properly gathered data, what's the objection?

The answer has to be that we Americans recognize a right to reconstruct the past—to deny the reports that you were once a political radical, or posed nude, or whatever. Extensive and accurate computer memories can interfere with this right.

At the same time we are unforgiving about past events. If you once were a Communist (or posed nude), it is likely to follow you for the rest of your life. Although it was never clear to me how recent or recurrent was the marijuana use Ms. Totenburg's informants were talking about, the reaction of many to Douglas Ginsburg's revelation—that it really didn't matter how recent or recurrent—is another case in point.

This all adds up to a distressingly sporting approach to our pasts: if you did something stupid twenty years ago, that is likely forever to disqualify you from many of the good things of life. *However*, you can avoid this disqualification by reconstructing your past, and it is cheating for society to check on you too effectively. The game, in short, goes to those prepared to lie about their pasts. Why can't we have a world in which accurate pictures of people are permissible, but making mistakes is too?

No, I never did either one. I'm actually pretty dull.

Letter to *The New York Times* (1989)

Nominations sometimes get in trouble—John Tower's is only the latest example—because of the "appearance of impropriety." This could mean either of two things, neither of which is acceptable.

It could mean that there has been no wrongdoing that anyone can substantiate, but that nonetheless people keep spreading rumors about the nominee. However, this is an outrageous basis on which to block a nomination. If someone has charges to make, let him bring his evidence forward: he should not be permitted to succeed by whispering, or even by publicly making accusations he cannot back up.

Or it could mean, as I suspect it often does, that in fact the charges *can* be substantiated, but for reasons of compassion or clubbiness those in control of the facts are unprepared to make them public, choosing instead to rationalize their rejection of the nominee in terms of an "appearance" of impropriety.

That may be merciful to the individual nominee involved, but it disserves the process. It leaves the notion, that mere appearances can appropriately disqualify someone, lying around like a loaded weapon—there to be picked up and employed in a case where the charges *can't* be substantiated and rumor in fact is all there is.

It's an insidious phrase, one we should get rid of. Those who have behaved with disqualifying impropriety shouldn't serve in high positions, and that should be the ground stated. Those there is no credible reason to suppose have so behaved should not be barred (assuming they are otherwise qualified). "The appearance of impropriety"—as either innuendo or sugarcoating—has no proper role in the process.

10

In Conclusion

Another Such Victory: Constitutional Theory and Practice in a World Where Courts Are No Different from Legislatures (1991)[1]

I'm pleased to reproduce this one here, as I frankly don't think it's received the attention it deserves. (Before you convict me of insufferable arrogance, let me add that I'm fully aware that overall my work has acquired ample attention: indeed, this piece appeared in an issue of the Virginia Law Review devoted entirely to Democracy and Distrust a decade after its publication. Can't ask for a lot more than that.)

> There is nothing worse than an idea whose time has come.
> Linda Hunt[2]

Recess Period for the Legal Process School

> Modern constitutional scholarship is generally characterized by a desire to take up the question . . . what politics should judges pursue, and on the basis of what conception of the good should they act?
> Robin West[3]

> [I]nstead of chastising courts for their imperial presumption, commentators celebrate them as the preferred forum for democratic deliberation.
> Allan C. Hutchinson[4]

I never took the course on Legal Process. Indeed the idea that appointed and life-tenured judges should behave differently from elected officials had always seemed so evidently correct that it took me a long time to understand that it even had a label, let alone an entire "school" named after it.[5] You can therefore imagine my befuddlement at what is going on today. The academic left is telling us there is no reason courts should feel an obligation to behave differently from elected officials. The large liberal academic center, always first to be second, is generally going along. And in what the naive might deem an ironic twist—though it is not likely greatly to surprise those radicals who understand their project—our recent Republican presidents have adopted the idea with a vengeance,[6] and so to a substantial extent has Congress. Just about everybody is climbing aboard.

Naturally, the conviction that judges interpreting the Constitution are supposed to be doing something other than enforcing their own values survives in certain segments of the legal culture—albeit mainly among people educated in an earlier era. Nor am I suggesting (what is almost always an error) that the present is an entirely unique time. The attitude in ascendance has conspicuous precursors, notably the legal realist movement of the early twentieth century.[7] In fact the legal realists were less likely than the legal culture is today to draw the fallacious inference from (a) the observation that judges in fact allow their politics to affect their constitutional interpretations to (b) the prescription that that's what judges *should* do:[8] in that regard, today's development is new.[9] It's basically a cycle, though, and as of 1991, the neo-realists (which turns out to include your local critical legal scholar, and Ronald Reagan, and just about everybody in between) seem almost certainly to have won the day, which is to say about the next twenty years (about as long as anyone should ever try to predict anything anyhow).

TEACHERS AND STUDENTS

This is a legacy of the sixties—the old conviction that if any private sentiment is strong enough it's entitled to carry the day.
Bart Giamatti

Dr. Spock was indicted for the wrong crime.
Vern Countryman

The generation coming of age in legal academia—we might as well admit it, the generation doing its most creative work[10]—received its legal education in the late 1960s or later. During this period, largely thanks to the disgraceful duo of Indochina and Watergate, impatience with institutional deference, impatience in particular with deference to the "democratic" branches, reached what may be an all-time high in this country. This impatience has reflected itself, with a vengeance, in legal scholarship.

It is articulated most clearly among those who identify themselves as critical legal scholars. Here one finds a general skepticism of traditional notions of judicial craft, as exhibited in the following from Mark Tushnet:[11]

[C]onsider the craft of "writing novels." Its practice includes Trollope writing *The Eustace Diamonds*, Joyce writing *Finnegans Wake*, and Mailer writing *The Executioner's Song*. We might think of Justice Blackmun's opinion in *Roe* as an innovation akin to Joyce's or Mailer's. It is the totally unreasoned judicial opinion. To say that it does not look like Justice Powell's decision in some other case is like saying that a Cubist "portrait" does not portray its subject in the manner that a member of the academy would paint it. The observation is true but irrelevant to the enterprise in which the artist or judge was engaged and to our ultimate assessment of his or her product.*

In particular, the legal process school's core methodological assumption is scornfully cast aside, here by Duncan Kennedy:

> I will have nothing to say about the impact of "institutional competence" considerations on the motives for lawmaking I discuss. I assume that the only grounds for distinguishing between courts, legislatures and administrative agencies as lawmakers are (i) that the false consciousness of the public requires it or (ii) that the decisionmaker has a quite specific theory about how his or her particular institutional situation should modify his or her pursuit of political objectives.[12]

Critical scholars are not a fringe group in contemporary legal scholarship; in time it will be understood that their influence on the profession has approached that of their legal realist forebears, which is to say it will have

---

* *On the Constitution as a Lead Sheet.* Over the years I've thought about trying to elaborate the metaphor between constitutional interpretation and jazz improvisation. It "works" on the gimmicky level that various approaches to interpreting the Constitution can validly be compared to various jazz styles. One might point to: approaches that embellish but never entirely lose the original melody; those that gradually abandon the original melody entirely but insist that each phrase relate to its predecessor; so-called horizontal approaches that abandon the melody but maintain a relation to the chord progression of the entire song; horizontal approaches geared to the chord progression of the particular line; "vertical" approaches that insist only on compatibility with the particular chord being played at the time, and so forth. (Having written that, I understand why music lecture rooms are equipped with pianos.) It should be no trick for readers of this article to attach the names of various constitutional scholars to these brief descriptions. If you have trouble placing a clause-bound "originalism," that's because it is essentially a rejection of any sort of "jazz" in this context. (The problem with this view is that the Constitution quite often—and quite intentionally, I think, though for present purposes that doesn't matter—gives us nothing but chords.) The sort of legal realism that is the subject of this article also seems to me not to fit, as it totally rejects the relevance of the "chart" except, perhaps, as a device for inducing false consciousness.

The reason I haven't written this up is that it was never clear what anyone was supposed to learn from it about either constitutional theory or jazz—aside from something thoroughly trivial about the one she knew less about. (I do find it interesting that the way I play—basically a mix of the first, third, and fourth approaches mentioned—corresponds pretty well to the way I write about constitutional law, though I hasten to add that I am not so demented as to have sought this integration consciously.) The metaphor turns out not to be of much use in positioning us to say "this is just pounding—it doesn't count as constitutional law." For every time there develops what appears to be a consensus among musicians (and their listeners), to the effect that a certain interval is unacceptable noise, someone who can't be dismissed on any principled basis as "not a real musician" starts using it, and often others follow. Minor seconds and major sevenths weren't really accepted in jazz until the 1930s (classical music was often several decades ahead), and the raised fourth or tritone—originally if loosely, the "flatted fifth"—was controversial as recently as the 1940s, but today is accepted as commonplace, if

been major. The large liberal center of legal academia, characteristically fearful of getting out of step with the latest trend, has been importantly affected by the anti-legal process message here.

It wasn't a hard sell. Most law teachers went to law school to become lawyers: if we'd wanted to be theorists we would have gone to graduate school. But we got high grades in law school (on examinations rarely designed to measure scholarly skills) and learned we could get this unconscionably cushy job: teaching yes—but with shorter hours, higher pay, and slimmer tenure requirements than other sorts of teaching—and almost an open invitation, at some schools a virtual obligation, to pass oneself off not simply as a lawyer but also as an expert on any subject on which he or she took two or more courses in college. Who among this group are the most likely to be drawn to constitutional law specifically? Generally those interested in public policy analysis, in figuring out what changes, on balance, would be good for society. And what gets in the way of simply doing that analysis and calling it constitutional law? The assumption that courts aren't supposed to behave exactly like legislatures. Thus it becomes a liberating day indeed when headliners like Kennedy announce that there is nothing improper in courts' imposing their own policy preferences in the name of constitutional law, indeed that there may even be something vaguely fascist about supposing they should be doing anything else.

Thus, no less a luminary than Laurence Tribe—the Tyler Professor of Constitutional Law at Harvard, needless to say no "crit," and himself a formidable influence on the profession—has resolutely refused to let himself get sidetracked worrying about the differences among various legal institutions,[13] but has forthrightly defined the constitutional task of courts as that of making "difficult substantive choices" among "inevitably controverted political, social, and moral conceptions."[14] And indeed, the legal literature generally analyzes constitutional issues in terms of wise social policy—which, felt strongly, is likely to be labeled "principle"—before

---

not indeed a trifle tired. (While I suppose this too will pass, an unadorned minor or flatted ninth—one that is neither wrapped within a "bigger" chord nor formed by a fleeting, or "passing," note in the melody—still strikes my ear, as I believe it does most people's, as uncivilized. Indeed, I hereby propose the unadorned minor ninth as the artistic equivalent of *Roe v. Wade*, in place of Tushnet's blasphemous nomination of Joyce.)

This isn't to say that certain forms of constitutional interpretation aren't illegitimate for specific institutions in specific societies with specific constitutional charters: they are. All that can be inferred from this excursion is what Tushnet infers from the literary context, that those who assert the possibility of differentiating valid from invalid constitutional interpretation on the basis of "craft limits" of a sort they assert are recognized in the arts are likely to be badly disappointed when they get around to a close examination of the alleged analogues. There are, however, more valid ways of testing constitutional theories than by the educated "feel" of those in the "interpretive community."

proceeding to the inevitable demonstration that, properly understood, the precedents do not preclude the proffered outcome.[15] The really fancy thinkers appear to understand (albeit tacitly) that such an approach is unacceptably reductionist, or perhaps what they understand is that it isn't a very interesting way to spend their time. In any event, they are drawn increasingly to the development and embroidery of "constitutional theories" that may borrow from other disciplines in new ways (new at least to lawyers), but whose relevance to any issue affecting how courts are supposed to act—or for that matter how any nonacademic segment of the profession or state is supposed to act—is elusive.[16]

Some of the people I've described, however, are getting a little long in the tooth themselves. Could this just be a rapidly passing fancy? I don't think so. Teachers are important forces in shaping future thinking. Sometimes societal forces can render a generation of students resistant to what their teachers are trying to get across: it happened in the late 1960s and early 1970s and produced the people I've been talking about, which is to say the generation of teachers most likely to influence the students of today. Might not today's students stage a similar rebellion against those very (realist) teachers? In time, of course; as I said, it's a cycle. What law school deans say on opening day is true: our students really are getting smarter all the time, and they don't come close to accepting everything their teachers say. On some issues the current student generation's rebellion against its teachers is likely to be felt quite swiftly. On the issue of whether courts should be trying to do something other than enforce their own political preferences, however, I'm afraid it will be a while.

In the first place, if "realism" is an attractive haven for young law teachers, it is even more so for law students. Meta-analysis, asking questions about questions rather than asking the questions themselves, is unfamiliar and frustrating, particularly for already flummoxed students who were hoping to find in the constitutional law course an outlet for the sort of political and moral debate they had enjoyed in college (and which may even have led them to suppose, however benightedly, that they'd like to be lawyers). "Getting to the point"—well, is abortion murder or isn't it?—is more familiar and comfortable. In years past constitutional law professors battled to domesticate this impulse out of their students. But today, many teachers (by now it's probably most) agree with the student impulse, and direct their efforts toward bringing around the politically unenlightened—as of course one would if one thought it to be the unvarnished role of constitutional courts to find and do the politically correct thing. And many of them are very popular, I have no doubt also very gifted, teachers.

The stereotype has it, though, that today's law students are more conservative politically than their professors. Like most stereotypes this one has its counterexamples; it also contains a good deal of truth. Doesn't that suggest a quicker turnaround than I have predicted? Again, not on the legal process/legal realism dispute. In the first place, our conservative students aren't stupid. Given who's making the judicial appointments these days, why shouldn't judges enforce their vision of the good society in the name of the Constitution?[17] Awesome—er, I mean, Right On, Professor. Second, and on a less calculating level, today's students are unusually fertile ground for the realist message. Yuppies (and yuppie wanna-bes) don't need to be sold on instant gratification. The drugs of choice may have changed, but they still want their Maypo and they want it *now*,[18] an impulse that is incompatible with the notion that in certain areas courts should await political decision. Thus, the victory over that archaic idea seems assured for some time to come: on the left and on the right, in the classroom and in the writings of emerging constitutional scholars,[19] the "false consciousness" that judges should behave differently from other politicians is on the run.

THE JUDICIAL APPOINTMENT PROCESS

> One can imagine that people could have views on the merits of political issues . . . that contradict their views of the constitutional aspects of the same question. But the people who position themselves to be nominated for federal judgeships are not part of that imagined group.
> Mark Tushnet[20]

Over the past decade there have been important changes in the way federal judges are selected.[21] First, a good deal more attention than before seems to be devoted to the question of how prospective nominees are likely to vote on the issues that can be anticipated.[22] Previously, thanks in part to the then prevailing "myth" that judges are not just another set of politicians,[23] the tendency was to appoint "first-rate lawyers,"[24] the "lions of the bar," without much attention to how exactly they were likely to vote on particular issues.[25] Second, judicial philosophy and political predilection have been conflated more explicitly than before, and the appointments process has achieved a degree of "realism" that should put even the "crits" to shame. Recall that Reagan's judicial "litmus test," which actually made it into the Republican platforms in 1980 and 1984, was not "What does the candidate think about *Roe v. Wade*?" but rather "What does the candidate think about *abortion*?"[26] Should the answers to those questions run in opposite directions, the assumption is evidently that the latter is the more reliable datum. Better not to face that choice, though, as people for whom the answers differ are people to avoid, if not indeed dangerous schizophrenics.[27] Thus, although the nomination of Robert Bork to the Supreme Court was accompanied by the usual smoke about his being a judge who would follow the law instead of making it, few were fooled: Bork was named because he had spent a career essentially promising to reverse certain outcomes the Reagan administration found politically distasteful.[28] The popular support for Bork, of course, was thus rooted as well.[29]

The reasons for the Senate's rejection of Bork may be more complicated.[30] The account most favorable to the senators is that they were convinced that Bork's purported allegiance to the legal process ideal was bogus, a cover for a remarkably consistent tendency to reach the politically conservative result, and rejected him for that reason. There is little doubt that genuine feelings along this line moved some of Bork's critics.[31] The notion that such suspicions are what account for the majority vote against him in the Senate, however, is one that strains credulity past the breaking point.

The more believable explanation is basically the exact opposite, that during the hearings Bork resolutely refused to conflate law and politics, or at least to conflate them in a way that would promise delivery of certain outcomes the senators were prepared to make their own litmus tests. Thus, the best existing study of the Bork affair (and a studiously "balanced" work) characterizes Senator Kennedy's opening salvo, the day the nomination was announced, in terms that seem only mildly overdramatic:

> The speech was a landmark for judicial nominations. Kennedy was saying that no longer should the Senate content itself with examining a nominee's personal integrity and legal qualifications, as had been the custom—at least publicly—for half a century. . . . In fulfilling its constitutional duty of "advice and consent" on judicial appointments, [Kennedy suggested] the upper house should take politics and ideology fully into account.[32]

In his opening statement at the Judiciary Committee's hearings, Chairman Biden, describing what he would be looking for in a Supreme Court justice, made the point in quieter terms: "I believe all Americans are born with certain inalienable rights. As a child of God, my rights are not derived from . . . the Constitution . . . but . . . were given to me and to each of our fellow citizens by the Creator and represent the essence of human dignity."[33] Such "natural rights" rhetoric dates back in our own history to the Declaration of Independence, but it wasn't presented there the way Biden was presenting it, as a recipe on whose basis federal judges are supposed to overturn legislation enacted by the elected branches of our government. The natural rights rhetoric must have flowed smoothly for Senator Biden, who was raised a Roman Catholic, as the Catholic church is essentially the only institution in twentieth century America that clings to the faith that that concept can provide humankind with a knowable and determinate set of moral commands. But in support of what rights is the concept here being adduced? Most conspicuously, as the hearings attest throughout, the rights to practice birth control and secure abortions, "natural rights" calculated to convert the most composed convent into Our Lady of Perpetual Commotion. Thus, no matter how trippingly the rhetoric rolled off his tongue, Biden was saying only what Senator Kennedy had said before him: there were certain political outcomes that he (or important elements of his constituency) simply had to have—no matter what.[34]

Surely the popular campaign against Bork (like the popular campaign in his favor) was waged in these terms.[35] This seems the inevitable result of making such disputes matters of general controversy, as the public can't be expected genuinely to understand and debate theories of constitutional interpretation. It also seems likely that such decisions will continue to be regarded by the general populace as politics as usual, at least for a considerable period: "Law has evolved in the public's mind from a technical specialty, such as engineering or medicine, to a terrain for the struggle over public policy."[36] And it would be most surprising if the terms in which constituents were reacting did not become in large measure the terms on whose basis the senators made their decision.[37]

Robert Bork died by the sword that almost got him to the top. He was nominated because he bid fair to restrict abortion, enhance presidential power, get tough with criminals, and so forth—and he was rejected for the same reasons. Judicial philosophy, as opposed to the raw political desirability of the outcomes, had little to do with it either way. One might hope that the Senate's overtly political reaction could be limited to cases like Bork's, where (whatever the candidate's own beliefs[38]) the nomination was made for transparently political reasons.[39] There can be no question that that was an aggravating factor, but it seems likely that it will not be a limiting one. There is much in the Senate's performance to suggest that, like the emerging academic consensus, and like Ronald Reagan as well, the Senate sees the political desirability of the outcomes reached as the sole appropriate test of judicial performance.[40]

Writing in *The New York Review of Books* after the Senate's rejection of Bork, Ronald Dworkin opined that the judge's demurrer to Biden regarding the right to "privacy" had been "so thoroughly discredited in the hearings, and proved so generally unpopular, that [he] doubt[ed] that [it] will any longer be advanced even by lawyers and judges who found [it] congenial before."[41] If Dworkin means to include law professors in this legion of the intimidated, I have to disappoint him: since when are we supposed to tailor our constitutional theories to either popular opinion or the theoretical insights of the Senate Judiciary Committee? Dworkin may have a valid narrower point, however: the contrary view is not likely to be articulated very clearly *by those trying to position themselves for appointment to, or promotion within, the federal judiciary*—at least not until control of the Judiciary Committee changes hands.

Perhaps you're beginning to wonder whether I am acquainted with the name David Souter, whose confirmation for the Supreme Court was both recent and smooth.[42] I am. Indeed, I hereby mark Souter's Judiciary Committee hearings and Senate vote as exhibits to be introduced in support of my upcoming claim that Senate muscle-flexings in this area are likely to be episodic and ultimately unavailing. But one should not try to make too much one way or the other of Souter himself at this point, for even by the end of the hearings we hadn't learned very much about him. Of course we learned some things. Judge Souter's answers were certainly fluent (the man speaks in paragraphs) and he assimilated well his advisers' admonitions not to come across as "another Bork" (either by stating his opinions in terms so sharp that someone might be moved to disagree, or by asking the various panel members to clarify their still more impenetrable "questions"). He also stated often enough that he is a "good listener" that the senators believed it (a surprising number indicating that this was qualification enough for them).

We learned one other thing that is more to the present point: whatever else he may or may not be, Justice Souter is not a strong devotee of the notion that constitutional adjudication is supposed to differ in kind from the decisions of elected politicians. When pressed for his judicial philosophy, he regularly invoked the adjectives "practical" and "pragmatic,"[43] words that conjure up a habit of thoughtful moderation but do not signal any attitude toward his judicial role that differs from what a responsible moderate would hope for in a candidate for Congress or the local board of selectmen. The judge's defense of various prior Supreme Court decisions on the ground that they were responses to "problems to be solved that the states [or Congress[44]] simply would not address and the people wanted addressed"[45] is, similarly, not a theory of judicial review that even hints at role differentiation. "There are many things legislatures 'haven't done anything about' that should be left in precisely that condition,"[46] and attempting to sort among various pieces of "unfinished business" on the basis of which among them "the people really want" is a task so plainly ill-suited to appointed and life-tenured judges that one can be confident that any such purported performance would entirely reflect the judges' own notions of what needs doing.[47]

The game thus quickly and understandably became an attempt to ferret out Souter's politics.[48] This proved a fool's errand, however, partly because Souter was cagier than his pursuers, and perhaps partly because, not being an overly passionate fellow generally, Souter seems not to invest deeply in whatever political views he happens to entertain either. But though the evidence was circumstantial, most observers thought they detected in some of Souter's answers a man considerably less conservative than they had been led to expect on the basis of reports that Souter had been "vouched for" by former Governor Sununu and Senator Rudman, and Judge Bork's prehearings op-ed paean to Souter.[49]

What happened? There are at least four possibilities. First, Souter in fact may be another Bork—okay, another Anthony Kennedy—and just did a very good job of hiding it. Souter was nothing if not clever, and the passages in his testimony that gave some of us hope would hardly require a Houdini to get out of. Second, the White House may simply have screwed up. Rudman is no arch-conservative, Sununu no lawyer, and I doubt that Bork's conspicuous endorsement was even unambiguously welcomed, let alone the product of crucial inside information the rest of us lack.[50] Third, even if David Souter doesn't turn out to be an exact clone of, say, Antonin Scalia, there is no strong reason to suppose George Bush is any more an exact clone of Ronald Reagan when it comes to judicial appointments than he is otherwise. Fourth, the appointment was not to just any seat, but to that of Justice William J. Brennan, Jr. True, there was much liberal claptrap when moderate Justice Lewis Powell retired, about how it would be sacrilege to fill *his* seat with a conservative, but this time the point[51] was valid: Brennan had anchored the Court's liberal wing for four decades. It is possible that this fact influenced Bush and his advisers. Indeed, replacing a moderate justice with a conservative and, later, a liberal with a moderate, seems exactly the course one might reasonably expect from a moderately conservative president with even a modicum of respect for judicial continuity.

However true that all may be, the Souter proceedings did not signal a return to the legal process ideal and indeed probably helped solidify the new wisdom that it is futile to pretend that one can judge potential nominees on anything other than their politics. What's more, though the specific incentives are likely to vary over time with changes in the control of the executive branch and the Senate, the general incentive system now in place seems unlikely to change for some time. Action breeds reaction, and the next liberal Democrat elected president is not likely to worry too much about judicial philosophy per se—we have seen that the Democrats in Congress are hardly sticklers for legal process—but rather to seek to redress what he will see as the political imbalance wrought by his predecessors.

This alteration of the reward system is likely to have unfortunate feedback effects on academia. The dream of high judicial appointment has probably always warped the work of constitutional law professors to a degree. Back in the "lions of the bar" days, one suspects it led mostly to the trimming of sails, thereby costing us some scholarly creativity. Two things are different now. First, the appointments of Justices Scalia and Kennedy and the attempted elevation of Judges Bork and [Douglas] Ginsburg, the first academics nominated for the Supreme Court since 1943,[52] may have rekindled similar dreams in the bosoms of many law teachers. It's easy to see why presidents interested in radical reform through the courts would be drawn to professors: unaccustomed to the need for compromise and coming from a profession that puts a premium on personal consistency, academics are likely to be more doctrinaire and thus more "reliable."[53] The "Schwab's Drugstore effect"[54] on scholarly writing for the next few decades is not likely to be salutary, though.[55]

The second difference is that, because of the changes in appointments criteria, the pressure is no longer toward maintaining a balanced, common law judge's image—"I'm no ideologue; I'd decide every case on its individual merits"—or even a consistent *judicial* philosophy, but rather toward pleasing one of the standard political constituencies. If you believe that the Court should not constitutionally invalidate state laws mandating affirmative action, you had better take the position that it *should* strike down state laws restricting abortion. Contrariwise, if you are prepared to uphold anti-abortion laws, you had better be prepared at the same time to *invalidate* affirmative action laws—even though neither combination is easily reconcilable with any coherent philosophy of judicial review that is not heavily dependent on its purveyor's political preferences.[56] The pressure now, in other words, is to make no enemies on, pick one, the political left or the political right. (President Reagan appointed a remarkable percentage of the nation's conservative law teachers to the federal bench, many of them quite young. Discovering you were a conservative in 1980 was like buying stock in Apple Computer the same year.)

Thus, the entire gang appears to be on board. "Overrule the flag burning case," "Appoint Bork," and for that matter "Dump Bork," are all united in their message that the role of judges is no different from that of other politicians.[57] I doubt that the unity of left and right on this level surprises true believers on either side. The right must be confident it can prevail for the foreseeable future, and for the far left, it may be part of the long-term recipe for revolution. I can't help but wonder, though, if liberals along for the ride really understood what they were getting into.

Maybe a "Legislative Judiciary" Is Our Best Hope for a Viable Separation of Powers, Given Congress's Vanishing Role as a Policy-Making Force

We are simply afraid to make any difficult decisions. We're afraid we'll make someone mad at us.
Congressman Ed Jenkins[58]

You just don't see much good legislation anymore.
Former Governor Lester Maddox

In recent decades there has developed something approaching a consensus among political scientists and other observers that Congress has essentially lost the ability to function as a policymaking alternative to the executive. One important factor has been the breakdown of party discipline. In the late twentieth century members of Congress appear to regard the preferences of their party platform or leaders as a sort of tie-breaker, to be consulted only when the representative's particular constituent and other parochial interests do not dictate a course of action.[59] When this development is coupled with the fact that in a complex institution like Congress it is considerably easier to block initiatives than to push them through,[60] the results can be dramatic.[61]

Much of the fault lies in the related development, since the New Deal, of a sort of congressional reelection assurance plan.[62] Modern congressmen follow a fairly standard recipe for survival[63]—a maximum of "casework," or particularized services for constituents[64] (and other interest groups seen as critical to reelection[65]) and a minimum of "programmatic" or legislative activity.[66]

> Congressmen know that the specific impact of broad national policies on their districts is difficult to see, that effects are hidden, so to speak. . . . Thus, in order to attain reelection, congressmen focus on things that are both more recognizable in their impact and more credible indicators of the individual congressman's power—federal projects and individual favors for constituents.[67]

As the mix has shifted, the reelection rate has gone up enormously.[68]

Things titled statutes do still get passed, but what do they generally comprise? Sometimes just more of the same, pork barrel and other constituent service measures.[69] Legislation of broader import also sometimes emerges,[70] though it is likely to consist of an appropriation[71] for a new or existing bureaucracy, "controlled" by what amounts to no more than an admonition to "take care of" this or that problem.[72] This combination in turn helps secure the framework for the reelection assurance plan. "The existence of the Washington system locks us into the New Deal way of doing things: pass a law, appropriate a lot of money, and establish a new federal bureaucracy. No reasoned analysis underlies that method of operation. The electoral interest of incumbent congressmen does."[73]

How so? Most obviously, such a "law," by saying next to nothing, provides little by way of substantive content against which an incumbent's fitness for continuation in office can be measured. A statutory injunction to "do something" risks few votes. Second, such open-ended delegations leave maximum range for congressional scolding. Once they see (or purport to see) how such a formless mandate is being interpreted by those to whom they entrusted it, members are free to retort—each in accord with what he takes to be the preferences of his constituency—"That's not what we wanted you to do; indeed it's nothing short of a betrayal of the American people."[74] Finally, such unrestricted delegations give congressional committee chairpersons (and their staffs), and to a lesser degree other members of Congress who happen to be interested, significant informal influence over various executive branch interpretations[75]—influence that can be heavily arrayed in support of the interests of one's geographical or other "constituents" (but, again, does not entail negative accountability).[76]

However, influence exercised in either of these ways—by unofficial intervention into the enforcement process, or post facto allegation that the legislative will immanent in the statute has been thwarted—cannot be passed off as representing the judgment of "Congress"; rather, it will reflect the judgment and influence of a limited number of well-placed individuals. Nor, of course, is it calculated to add up to anything approaching a coherent policy judgment. Instead, it represents a series of ad hoc interventions by widely disparate persons, sometimes in the service of perceptions of the public interest, often quite flagrantly in the interests of their individual constituents. At our luckiest, "[p]ublic policy emerges from the system almost as an afterthought."[77]

Sometimes the situation will be so sensitive politically that Congress will be leery of delegating the power of effective decision to the executive bureaucracy. What to do in such a case? An innocent might expect that Congress would be moved to make the troublesome decision or decisions itself—by passing some old-fashioned legislation, complete with standards and everything. Congressional decision entails congressional accountability, however, and thus an increasingly popular gimmick has been created for this kind of case, whereby the problem is passed off for effective decision by some third party. The 1988 creation of the military base-closing commission[78] is a recent textbook example of this, though it certainly was not without precedent.[79] The Salary Act of 1967[80] operates the same way, and Congress's repeated refusals to make the Federal Reserve more accountable politically are conventionally attributed to the fact that the Fed spares Congress "the responsibility of making painful choices about the economy."[81] The Gramm-Rudman-Hollings Act[82] was similar, though perhaps a little sneakier, in that the effective decision there was passed to the Comptroller General, whom Congress had reason to believe was in some sense "their guy," but at the same time wasn't so closely identified with them that they would have to take the heat when he axed some of their constituents' favorite programs.[83]

The third party may also be the courts.[84] Walter Murphy and Joseph Tanenhaus have suggested that the Senate's "apparently illogical behavior" in rejecting judicial nominees (like Bork) who think courts should generally defer to legislatures may be explainable in these terms:

> One explanation is that some senators were loath to accept such power because it would have increased their responsibility—and accountability—to constituents. It can be comforting to elected officials who face divisive issues like prayer in public schools, federal aid to parochial schools, and abortion to wash their

hands of the problems by mournfully proclaiming that the Supreme Court has spoken, wrongfully perhaps, but authoritatively. Thus, legislators can express sympathy with individual constituents of all persuasions without incurring heavy costs at the next election.[85]

It briefly baffled me that everyone (advocates, critics, media alike) treated the Supreme Court as the final authority on the content of federal civil rights statutes. An observer who took the paper system seriously would respond that such a view is unfair, as Congress can always overrule an interpretation of a statute by amending it—it's not as if the Constitution were implicated. The answer, of course, is that by now we all know perfectly well that, whichever way the Court holds, the odds are extremely low that Congress is going to overrule it.[86] Thus, although the matter is "statutory," the Court is likely to have the last word. The last legally effective word, I should say: there will be plenty of scolding by individual members, generally with the television cameras rolling.

Occasionally Congress will summon the courage to assign to *itself* the effective decision authority regarding problems it knows it has been ducking, and to seek to build in procedural safeguards to prevent its continuing to do so. The War Powers Resolution of 1973[87] has been its most notable effort along these lines, in my opinion an admirable one. Unfortunately, the experience under the resolution has been that when push has come to shove, Congress has lacked the hardihood to hang in there and take the heat.[88]

I am not arguing that Congress has lost the ability to make life miserable for the president. It still knows how to get in the way; the Senate's refusal to confirm Justice-designate Bork and both houses' refusal to enact a constitutional flag burning amendment are conspicuous recent examples. A willingness thus to obstruct might well on occasion prove a useful bulwark against tyranny.[89] It should be noted, though, that in each of the cited instances, Congress's affirmative approval of the executive's plan was inescapably required. Such occasions are rare, however, given the existence of so many broad delegations to the executive, whether actually granted by Congress or simply acquiesced in. And Congress's willingness to become involved where there exists an even vaguely articulable option not to has been highly restricted of late. The contribution it is able to make toward insuring that the policy judgments enforced for and against the American people represent the combined judgment of a group of persons (some of whom are not beholden to the president), has thus become very questionable.[90] "[Congress] can act negatively, to disrupt the policy the President pursues, but it cannot act affirmatively to carry out a comprehensive substitute policy of its own, even if through structural reform it could develop the capacity to create it."[91]

Of course the disappearance of Congress even here, as an independent

influence on federal policy, has not been complete. There's enough of a
trend, however, to suggest that we have a problem with respect to the separation of powers. Hence the further suggestion of this Part's title: perhaps
it is a good thing that the federal courts generally, and the Supreme Court
in particular, are being urged on all sides to drop the pretense that they
shouldn't behave like legislators. Given Congress's vanishing act,[92] this
development may represent our best hope of providing an effective policy
counterbalance to the president for the foreseeable future.[93] (In particular,
liberal supporters of the development might be moved by the fact that at
least for the time being our presidents are coming from the right half of the
political spectrum.) Might what's happening not make sense as a way of
providing a liberal counterweight, perhaps indeed our best contemporary
hope of approximating the sort of balanced system the framers envisioned?

Fat Chance

There are two objections to this suggestion, one theoretical and debatable,
the other practical and dispositive.

OBJECTION ONE: THE SUGGESTION IS WRONG IN PRINCIPLE, AS THE
ALTERNATIVE POLICY-MAKING CENTER SHOULD BE
DEMOCRATICALLY SELECTED

First Rejoinder: Says Who?

In my opinion an entirely convincing argument can be made that it would
be inconsistent with the overall theory of our Constitution, particularly as
it has evolved by amendment over the past 150 years, for one of our principal policymaking organs to be unelected.[94] It is obvious, however, that
most contemporary commentators are not convinced, as they argue either
openly for an appointed judiciary that enforces its own values in the name
of the Constitution, or for what will amount to the same thing, judicial
enforcement of the values held by "society" (albeit, mysteriously, not by its
elected representatives).

It is true that this disagreement with Objection One is never made explicit. The commentators do not, for example, admit (let alone proclaim)
that what they are actually proposing is a version of the old idea of "mixed
government," a combination of democracy and oligarchy, as developed in
the writings of such theorists as Locke and Montesquieu. Given that these
two men are conventionally recognized as important influences on the
framers, one might wonder why not,[95] but of course the answer is obvious:
"undemocratic" has become a dirty word in this country, to the point where

even its approximate invocation would be rhetorical suicide. "In essence, there are two choices: abandon the term democracy as the major premise in analysis or redefine it to portray accurately the nature of government embodied in the Constitution. Because the former is improbable, the latter is essential."[96] Thus, the position is wrapped in gobbledygook—generally stressing how democratic it is to have an unelected judiciary superimposing "our" values on the decisions of our elected representatives[97]—but it prevails nonetheless. Down deep most commentators simply do not agree that our principal policymaking organs must be democratically selected.

*Second Rejoinder: Given the Changes in the Appointments Process,
the Suggested Model Is a Good Deal More "Democratic" than It
Used to Be*

Federal judges have always been appointed by one elected official and confirmed by a bunch of other elected officials (since 1913, directly elected officials). During periods when the judge's job was widely conceived as involving something other than the ordinary political skills, however, it would have been difficult to maintain that this method of selection rendered federal judges "democratic officials." Indeed, again precisely because of the then-prevailing assumption that judges weren't just another set of politicians, even state judges who were actually elected (and reelected) by the people were not regarded until recently as democratic officials in the usual sense. Only rarely, for example, were they turned out of office for unpopular decisions:[98] Rose Bird had to stand for reelection in a way that Roger Traynor never did.[99]

What it was about Felix Frankfurter that supposedly "fooled" Franklin Roosevelt was the "legal process" joker, the assumption that there are times when one may strongly disapprove of a law without being prepared to declare it unconstitutional.[100] Once that joker is expelled from the deck, however, as both recent presidents and the Senate Judiciary Committee have indicated they intend to do, the deal is changed somewhat. Candidates whose political views have been thoroughly checked, and who then have been all but required to pledge that they will enforce those political views in the name of the Constitution, can be said—in an admittedly limited sense, but one that would not have rung true before—to have been "democratically" selected. (The Secretary of Labor isn't elected either, but she is certainly a "political" official, and we fully expect her to behave like one.) On the other hand, federal judges still do not have to stand for reelection— nor, unlike the Secretary of Labor, do they have a boss who must—a fact that renders them significantly less "accountable to the people" than they otherwise would be.[101] So this second rejoinder also is attenuated, but it cannot be dismissed entirely: given the changes in the selection system, judges are now closer to "ordinary politicians" than they used to be. The

"argument from democracy" against the evolving "new separation of powers" thus may be one that I find convincing, but admittedly under present
conditions it is debatable.

OBJECTION TWO: THE COURT WON'T PROVIDE AN EFFECTIVE
COUNTERBALANCE TO THE POWER OF THE PRESIDENT

The Supreme Court has certainly held its own over the past two hundred
years; indeed, its influence has for the most part grown quite steadily.[102]
That does not mean, however, that it is realistic to suppose that it can fill the
vacuum left by the disappearance of Congress as an effective policy counterbalance to the executive. The more serious the Court becomes about
presenting itself as a policymaking alternative to the president, or for that
matter the more it is seen as playing that role, the more the president will
be induced (and to a degree has already been induced) to apply the
screws.[103] And, because of his vastly larger staff (this is what we call an
understatement), his singular access to the media—and, if I may be permitted to mention it, the fact that he is an elected official—he will inevitably
dominate.

Control by Overrule?

Though overrule by constitutional amendment may be the most obvious
method of controlling the Supreme Court, we can say quite confidently as
of 1991 that it is not an effective one. In 1980 I wrote: "Our recent experience with the Equal Rights Amendment, endorsed by both major parties
and hardly advancing a radical proposition, corroborates the difficulty of
amending the Constitution. In all our history only four decisions of the
Supreme Court have been reversed by constitutional amendment."[104] Just
one in this century[105] (and that one essentially invited by the Court[106]), I
might have added. I thought for sure I was going to have to eat these
words—in fact the first draft of this article did so—in light of the recent flag
burning brouhaha. President Bush's swift rhetorical onslaught on *Texas v.
Johnson*[107] had quite effectively forced almost every member of Congress
to choose between (a) agreeing with him that the First Amendment should
be amended, and (b) taking the courageous "opposing" position (which
"prevailed" over Bush's token disagreement) that before we amend the
Constitution we should pass a new and slightly different statute outlawing
flag burning, in the hope that the Supreme Court would also be intimidated
and change its mind. As of the passage of the Flag Protection Act of 1989,
I would have given approximately even odds that the Supreme Court
would engineer a "switch in time," and about nine-to-one that if it didn't,
Congress would cave in and vote to amend the Constitution in the way the

President wanted. Well, neither of them caved,[108] God bless 'em.[109] Wrapping himself in the flag may have helped President Bush defeat Governor Dukakis, but it wasn't enough to pull off a constitutional amendment. And if Old Glory can't do it, what can?

Control by Appointments?

Though on the surface one might expect the appointments power to be a relatively effective control mechanism, historically its utility also has proved to be limited: "It has . . . proved hard to predict how someone in another line of work will function as a justice and one sometimes wonders whether the appointee who turns out differently from the way the President who appointed him expected is not the rule rather than the exception."[110] The possibility of surprise can never be entirely eliminated. I suspect, however, that the recent changes in the appointments process we have noted have done much to alter this assessment (which was published the year Ronald Reagan was first elected President). As indicated, there seems to be more concentration now than before on how the candidate is likely to vote on various issues.[111] Moreover, candidates now are much less frequently involved in any functional sense "in another line of work." All five of the post-Nixon appointees to the Supreme Court (plus the two Reagan nominees who didn't make it) were, at the time, members of Federal Circuit Courts of Appeal.[112] This represents quite a dramatic shift.[113] History strongly supports what common sense would have suggested, that persons who have already served as judges make vastly more predictable justices.[114] (Also, as I indicated above, even for lower court appointments, President Reagan favored academics[115]—who for the reasons cited tend to be more predictable than practitioners or politicians.) Finally, the apparent elimination of the legal process "joker" has enormously enhanced predictability. The behavior of candidates who have been induced to assure the administration (and the Judiciary Committee) that they will make no nice distinctions between their political views and their judicial philosophy is much easier to anticipate.

Of course the Senate may not just roll over. On two occasions since 1930—specifically in 1970 and 1987—it has voted not to confirm the president's first choice.[116] Each of these cases was, however, in some sense special. Judge Bork had devoted a career to becoming the most confrontational conservative on the block (a distinction that both made and unmade him). The rejection of Judge Haynsworth is more complicated, but much of the opposition had little to do with Haynsworth himself, resulting instead from a combination of liberal frustration that Abe Fortas had not become Chief Justice two years earlier[117] and displaced opposition to Nixon's appointee to that position, Warren Burger, who had been regarded as somewhat Borkian himself.[118] (Burger had been Nixon's first appointment and may for that reason have received some extra deference.[119])

The easy confirmation of Judge Souter—despite the combination of administration assurances that he was all that conservative Republicans could hope for, and Democratic control of the Senate and its Judiciary Committee—corroborates the proposition that the Senate has no taste for frequent opposition. Indeed, the idea was originally floated that although it was entirely appropriate to ask nominees (like Bork) to explain discussions of current legal issues they had published in law reviews and elsewhere, it would somehow be improper to ask nominees (like Souter) who hadn't published what they thought about the very same issues. (The notion was thus to transpose the existence of a "paper trail" from an evidentiary liability, a repository of possible prior inconsistent statements, to a prerequisite to asking any questions at all about live legal issues.[120]) This is, if anything, upside down, in that nominees who have not commented publicly are precisely those the Senate needs to question if it is to learn anything. And while I certainly am not suggesting we should make publication a necessary qualification for judicial office, God save us if we should make it a disqualification.

Thus, that ground rule, while bruited early, faded soon, but was quickly replaced by another that was every bit as nonsensical, though more limited in scope. Although it was never phrased in precisely these terms, this committee acceded to what amounted to the issuance of a "free pass" to the nominee to pick one issue respecting which it would be "improper to comment" because it was likely to come before the Court. As is well known, Souter picked abortion. He shared with the Committee his views on affirmative action,[121] capital punishment,[122] the *Miranda* rule,[123] and the authority of federal courts to order states to raise their taxes in order to fund the enforcement of federal rights.[124] These issues, like abortion, all come before the Court year after year for clarification of a controversial principle it has previously established; lurking perpetually in each of their backgrounds is the question of whether the principle itself should be reconsidered. However, Souter was "sure the senators would understand" that it would be improper for him to comment on abortion, at which point the senators would nod sagely and agree that they certainly didn't want to be a party to anything improper.[125] Certain senators went so far as to praise Souter for his courage in taking this stand. Arlen Specter, often lauded for having bested Bork by acute cross-examination,[126] indicated early on that it was "a tribute to Judge Souter's character that he took the position that he would not come to Washington to be interviewed for this position if he was going to be asked" his views on *Roe v. Wade*.[127] Chairman Biden, also admiringly, may have come closer in assessing to what Souter's position was a tribute:

Senator Biden suggested that Judge Souter, who at every turn portrayed himself as a pragmatist, was simply taking the pragmatic course.

"If he said he was for it, Biden would be satisfied, and [Senator Charles] Grassley would go into orbit . . . . If he said he wasn't, it would be the opposite. A nomination that was not in trouble would then be in trouble no matter what he said."[128]

Whatever lay behind it, this "one-issue-pass" approach worked:[129] Souter was confirmed, ninety to nine. Since the grant of such a "pass" so evidently makes no principled sense whatever,[130] we should ask why the Democratic-controlled Judiciary Committee and Senate went along with it. Sure, Souter looked better than the Democrats had expected, but it may be—the point is we don't know—that he looked that way because he was permitted to pick the one issue they had advertised as critical going in and, by fiat, to shield his views on it. The more convincing explanation thus seems to be that the Bork affair was not yet three years past, and the Senate simply lacked the stomach for another donnybrook so soon.[131] In order to protect their incumbency, though, it apparently seemed wiser not to push Souter very hard on *Roe* than to run the risk that he would come out against it and thus turn up the political heat. If you're planning to roll over, you don't want to ask too many questions: better to spend your allotted time suggesting that the nominee visit an Indian reservation.[132]

Of course, the Senate is not likely always to be so docile as it proved in Souter's case; it will recurrently decide to "get tough" with a nominee. But even that isn't likely to matter much (except to the ritual victims), as the Senate's idea of getting tough these days is to pester, and the president can be pretty sure that he will ultimately be able to appoint someone whose predicted performance is not importantly different from that of his first choice.[133] The Senate, and anti-administration interest groups, are unlikely to have the energy to gear up for many concerted oppositions in a row[134]—and beyond the occasional ritual slaughter, the likely political returns diminish. Thus, there has been little indication (pre- or post-appointment) that Justice Kennedy is philosophically much different from Bork,[135] and while subsequent developments have moved Justice Blackmun significantly to the left,[136] at the time of his appointment he was not regarded as importantly different in terms of predicted performance from Haynsworth.[137]

It is possible that the Senate could truly toughen up and attempt to do more than harass, that is, to demonstrate a determination to hold out until it gets somebody who fits its agenda. Possible, yes, but two things should be noted. First, no matter how tough it gets, the best the Senate will be able to hope for is compromise. It can hold out till hell freezes over, and it still won't acquire the ability to send a nomination up.[138] Second, you shouldn't hold your breath. Habits of deference die hard, especially for a body whose members' principal priorities seem to be keeping (a) out of the line of fire, and (b) their jobs.

An obvious objection to the suggestion that presidents will be able by virtue of their appointment power to exercise relatively effective control over the Supreme Court is that justices outlast presidents. Thus, the argument would run, the "other branch" in our reconfigured separation of powers will comprise people generally appointed not by the president but by his predecessors. There are two answers to this. First, one shouldn't be misled by recent conspicuous cases of justices who vow to die on the bench and then decide not to die at all. In the 122 years since we finally settled on a nine-person Supreme Court, presidents have made sixty-seven (confirmed) appointments to it. That's one appointment every 1.82 years,[139] which means that a president serving eight years gets to make, on average, 4.39 appointments—a president serving a four-year term half that many. Consequently, by the end of a president's term, several of the justices *are* likely to be his appointees.[140]

Beyond that, so long as we remain in a pattern of Republican presidents, which many pundits are predicting will be quite a while, the objection becomes even more attenuated: if they were all appointed by Republicans (and checked for dangerous tendencies to let their notions of constitutional compulsion stray from their political preferences) it won't matter greatly to, say, a President Quayle that he didn't personally put them there. Naturally we won't have Republican presidents forever. Over the course of our history, however, presidents have run in streaks—a run of Democrats, a run of Republicans, a run of Somebody Elses. If this continues, and I know no reason to suppose it won't, the general point will remain valid. For every president except the comparatively rare one who has interrupted a long reign by the other party, most of the sitting justices—given the expulsion of the legal process joker (and the consequent reduction of surprise)—are likely to be quite simpatico.

Concluding Constructive Postscript

Our best hope for a viable counterbalance to the president thus remains with Congress. It would certainly be a good thing, as many well-meaning commentaries have suggested, if Congress would pull up its socks and get back into the policymaking business. Some glimmers of hope are cited here, among which are the beginnings of a restrengthening of the political parties[141] and some moves away from "subcommittee government"[142] toward a more "floor-centered" Congress.[143] But they certainly are no more than glimmers, and even if Congress were serious it would be years before either showed real effects. Given the incentive system we have described, it is difficult to imagine Congress ever enthusiastically reinserting itself into the policymaking (and heat-taking) arena without significant outside prodding, and equally difficult to imagine the voting public's ever insisting that it do so.[144]

There are other potential prodders, however: the courts can play a useful role in forcing Congress to perform its constitutionally contemplated functions.[145] Helping devise such judicial Congress-prodding doctrines thus seems to me the most productive use that can currently be made of a constitutional scholar's time; at any rate it's how I've been spending mine lately.[146] The attentive reader will discern in such efforts an attempt to resolve what might have been taken to be the paradox in my work between the call for deference to the considered products of legislatures and the observation that legislative products are frequently unconsidered. You also will not have missed the unsurprising fact that what is suggested is yet another "legal process" technique. It is, however—as most of my earlier work has been as well—an "activist" use of legal process, one I am suggesting will ultimately be more useful in reinvigorating our separation of powers than the more common contemporary impulse toward having the courts do the legislating themselves.

Author's Comment on Legislative and Administrative Motivation in Constitutional Law *and* The Wages of Crying Wolf: A Comment on *Roe v. Wade* (1991)[147]

This was part of one of Yale's many self-celebratory ceremonies, featuring comments by the (living) authors of the twenty-five most cited articles in its Law Journal's history. (Mine finished third and fifth.) The tone of my comment turned to be not exactly that of the others.

There's a chance you missed the 1969 movie *A Walk in the Spring Rain.* Most of the details have mercifully faded from memory, but the general plot line was that Ingrid Bergman, temporarily resident in a pastoral mountain locale and driven up the wall by her wearisome husband, resisted but finally succumbed to an affair with a virile local man-child—if he wasn't actually a gamekeeper, he should have been—played by Anthony Quinn.

In order to keep the audience from simply dismissing Ms. Bergman as an unsympathetic trollop, the husband, played by Fritz Weaver, had to be portrayed as one pretty desiccated prune, and he was: they made him a professor. Not just any professor would do, though—Indiana Jones is a professor—so they made Fritz a professor of constitutional law. I always figured that that had tedium pretty well cornered—until I received the fateful letter from Mr. Shapiro telling me my place in the scheme of things. Third. Maybe fifth. Something in that general range. Not something you're exactly tempted to put on your résumé, but enough to rob you of the rationalization that your work is so brilliant or controversial that others are afraid to cite it. Sentenced to a sabbatical with me, Ms. Bergman would probably take up with the Hell's Angels.

Of the two articles, *Motivation* is by far the more important contribution. Unfortunately, no evidence exists that anyone has read it. (True, it gets mentioned, but generally in string citations supporting the proposition that questions of motivation are complicated and have spawned some literature.) There are at least three reasons for this. The first is that the title doesn't begin to reveal what the article is about. True, it's about the constitutional relevance of official motivation. But it makes other general theoretical points as well, including the insight that, the usual rhetoric notwithstanding, it is not the case that we either do or should enforce a background requirement that government choices be rational. And it was an important first step toward a modest paradigm shift in the analysis of constitutional suspiciousness to which my later work has also contributed, from a victim perspective (who's getting screwed, and how) to a perpetrator perspective (who made this allocation, and with what incentives).

Since it purports to explore the relevance of motive in essentially all areas of constitutional law, *Motivation* necessarily attempts, albeit often briskly, to identify the sorts of evils to which the document's various clauses are addressed, before attempting to say how motivation should fit into the analysis. Thus it discusses not simply a wide range of equal protection problems, but, among other things, the state action doctrine, the range of federal power, congressional control of the jurisdiction of federal courts, congressional investigations, and a host of First Amendment problems as well. The discussion of the religion clauses, for example, is an important one, yet it is seldom even mentioned in the voluminous subsequent literature on that subject. The reason seems obvious: there isn't a hint of religion in the article's title, any more than there is of the other topics I have mentioned.

There are at least two other reasons *Motivation*, while often cited—well, fifth—is seldom read. One is that it is much too long (136 pages); the other is that it is not very well written (especially the off-putting introductory summary I added during the editing process). I wrote it my second year in teaching. ("Hey, why wait? I'm a teacher now, and teachers write, and if you have to clean up all of constitutional law before you can make your point, I guess that's what you do. Does the school furnish a Dictaphone?") Had I realized that Yale was about to embark on a siege of not promoting anybody for a decade or so I wouldn't have been so cocky. In fact I suppose I'd have developed a block of my own. Some would say the profession would be better off for that, but I continue to believe that, despite its lack of discipline, *Motivation* is an important piece. Fewer people should cite it; more people should read it.

Wages may have been more conspicuous politically—how many law review articles get mentioned in presidential speeches?—but it is substantially less important theoretically. I haven't yielded an inch on my criticism of *Roe* (which isn't, as I have explained elsewhere, necessarily to say that the case should now be overruled). However, writing a convincing criticism of *Roe v. Wade* was hardly an assignment requiring a rocket scientist. Merely a kamikaze pilot. (*Wages* would surely rank first on any list of articles with which other academics have expressed agreement privately but never gotten around to doing so publicly. Such a study is thus far lacking.)

Yet *Wages* gets cited a lot—well, third—and there is some evidence it actually gets read as well. I'd learned some lessons in the intervening three years. *Wages* is short. It is better written than *Motivation* (not that it was written any more deliberately, but diatribe is an easier milieu). And since it isn't about very much, the title was able comfortably to capture the subject. Finally, of course, abortion is a hot topic—or at any rate the Supreme Court made it one.

If three and five were unsettling numbers, however, 1970 and 1973 were more so, even causing me briefly to wonder whether I'd somehow missed my own obituary. I quickly consulted my bibliography to make sure I'd published some things since these two, and was relieved to learn that I had, albeit in other forums.* In the context of this celebration, however—Dean Calabresi's various communications to the alumni are calculated to instill the same doubts—one is compelled to wonder whether, in the overall scheme of things, publication anywhere other than in the *Yale Law Journal* really . . . well, counts.

I leave you with one final thought: Cite *this* piece! I've still got an outside shot at a low straight.

Fritz Weaver's kind of hand.[148]

Excerpt from *On Constitutional Nihilism* (1980)[149]

If the test of success is whether one's theories will gain general acceptance over time—most competent work will gain *some* acceptance—then of course the odds are almost certain that each of us will fail. But does it follow that we should abandon the effort? I don't think so, for several

* A mistake I'm not likely to make again. In introducing the review-specific citation study, Mr. Shapiro has created the academic equivalent of the frequent flier club.

reasons. First, it is a mistake to suppose that genuine theoretical and, some-times, social progress is not made by the intercommunication of liberal legal scholars. I think, for example, of the continuing and heroic work of Frank Michelman on the constitutionalization of welfare rights,[150] and re-call that when I began scholarly work in the equal protection area—eleven years ago, not so terribly long—the word "rationality" was often bandied about but no one had a remotely precise idea of what its components might be, and calls for "more than rationality" were if anything even more likely to degenerate into hopeless confusion: the admittedly troubled concepts of fit, weight, fundamental interest, suspect classification, etc., that are now second nature to those working in the field had not yet even been separated out. People were still saying in all apparent innocence that so long as it was permissible to infer a government official's motivation from what he or she had done, there obviously wasn't any difference between invalidating an action because of its motivation and invalidating it because of its effects—a confusion that replicated a broader failure to distinguish end state review from process review. I assume the situation must be the same elsewhere, but I *know* that in the areas in which I work we have come a long way in the past eleven years.

It is possible to *say* that the issues haven't changed over that period or even in 100 years, but only by stating "the issues" in terms so broad and fatuous that the conclusion could hardly be otherwise—as, for example, by posing the choice as one between judicial activism and judicial self-restraint, or between individual rights and collective choice. Stated in terms such that they are recognizable as real issues, however, progress has been made. It's been slow, and thanks to the personnel of the Supreme Court it has been almost entirely theoretical in the past few years, but it has been observable. Where, on the other hand, can reiterating that "nothing can work" possibly lead?[151]

In fact it is a message that seems bound to generate undesirable results all along the line. It caters to just those instincts in our students that are least in need of reinforcement. Complaining is always fun, and certainly it is easier than constructing theories—especially when one is not expected to have a citadel of his own against which the barrage he fires off today may be turned tomorrow. Moreover, if it is an article of faith that no successful theory is possible, it will quite understandably become less important to get the theories one is criticizing down too precisely—a rough approximation will do. Best of all, perhaps, this style of analysis tells the student the courts can do whatever they want and thus permits constitutional discussion to degenerate to the more comfortable mode of ordinary policy analysis.

Of course the appropriate inference from the conclusion that no theory will work might be that judicial review shouldn't exist, but we know that won't be the message for many. The message, rather, will be that courts needn't hang themselves up on niceties like principled decision-making. Perhaps the new realists find reassurance in that sea of idealistic young faces peering back over the student benches. I find less in a truly realistic appraisal of the ideology that is likely to issue from those faces when they've grown old enough to peer over judicial benches.

And as for those of us who are their teachers, what could possibly be the joy in a life devoted to reiterating that nothing will work? If that's what you think—as you might well—go build a boat in a bottle or lead a revolution. But a life instructing law students and cautioning colleagues that of course none of it will work? Where do I apply for medical school?

Perhaps we never will get the boulder to the top of the mountain. But the struggle itself is enough to fill a person's heart. One must imagine Sisyphus happy.[152]

Notes _____

Notes (or portions thereof) that were added after the publication of the original of the text to which they are appended appear in brackets. A number of notes appearing in the original have been deleted. For humanitarian reasons.

Chapter 1

1. 88 Harv. L. Rev. 11.
2. The rest of the article appears at pages 340–61.

3. 77 Va. L. Rev. 833, 834 n. 4.
4. Democracy and Distrust 103.

5. 17 Stanford Lawyer 3. This paper was delivered as the Rocco J. Tresolini Lecture at Lehigh University on March 8, 1982.
6. 56 N.Y.U. L. Rev. 547 (1981).
7. Jean Jacques Rousseau, The Social Contract, bk. 1, ch. 8 (1762). See also, e.g., Carl Cohen, Democracy 268–73 (1971); Ramon Lemos, "A Moral Argument for Democracy," 4 Social Theory & Practice 57 (1956).
8. Two Hundred Million Americans in Search of a Government 54 (1969).
9. "Philosophy and Democracy," 9 Political Theory 379 (1981).
10. [I had long wondered why Ron Ely hadn't changed his name—Ely is not a particularly euphonious appellation, and a lifelong empirical study indicates that it is mispronounced approximately half the time—and was thus shocked to learn from a film encyclopedia that he *had* changed his name . . . from Ron Pierce *to* Ron Ely! I suspect this helps account for his not having been heard of since his kamikaze gig as Bert Parks' first replacement at the Miss America Pageant. Of course Tarzan wasn't supposed to be real smart.]
11. E.g., Robert Dahl & Charles Lindblom, Politics, Economics, and Welfare 41–45 (rev. ed. 1976); Carl Cohen, Democracy 241–67 (1971). Cf. Joseph Schumpeter, Capitalism, Socialism, and Democracy 264–65 (2d ed. 1947).
12. At least in law schools, where moral philosophy is currently in vogue, one gathers points by denying that he is a utilitarian and affirming just as loudly that he is a "Kantian." The latter term is used so broadly (and so often under conditions that must raise a doubt whether the user has ever actually read Kant) that it is probably safest to translate the adjective "Kantian" as "moral." Even more surprisingly in light of the historical antecedents, "utilitarian" seems for these people to connote something like "ruthless."
13. See, e.g., Carl Becker, The Declaration of Independence 236–37 (Vintage ed. 1958; Alexis de Tocqueville, Democracy in America 233 (Anchor ed. 1950); Jack Lively, Democracy 111, 19 (1975).
14. See Bernard Williams, "A Critique of Utilitarianism," in J. J. C. Smart & Bernard Williams, Utilitarianism: For and Against 93–100 (1973).
15. Charles Fried, Right and Wrong 13–14, 169–70 (1978).

16. Cf. Charles Fried, Contract as Promise 16 (1981) (rule-utilitarian/act-utilitarian dispute irrelevant to legislative choices).

17. N.Y. Times, Book Review Section, July 16, 1972, p. 1.

18. E.g., Bruce Ackerman, Social Justice in the Liberal State 45–49 (1980).

19. E.g., Germain Grisez, "Against Consequentialism," 23 American Journal of Jurisprudence 21, 26–41 (1978); John Finnis, Natural Law and Natural Rights 111–18 (1980). But see James Griffin, "Are There Incommensurable Values?" 7 Philosophy & Public Affairs 39 (1977).

20. E.g., Ronald Dworkin, Taking Rights Seriously 276 (1977).

21. 424 U.S. 1 (1976).

22. In a direct democracy, one might argue, the fact that every affected person can vote on every issue assures individuals and minorities all the representation to which they are rightfully entitled (even when the majority outvoting them is taking pleasure from inflicting suffering upon them). Cf. 56 N.Y.U. L. Rev. 543 (1981) (commentary of Lawrence Sager). Whatever persuasive power that assertion might have in a direct democracy vanishes, however, when we switch to the representative democracy situation. In that context it is nonsense to suppose that minorities on whose support the representative does not count for reelection—in fact, it may behoove her to mistreat them—are in any plausible sense "actually represented" in the process, and thus we must insist upon a kind of "virtual representation" by insisting that the representatives not value the welfare of such persons either negatively or at zero.

23. See Frank Goodman, "De Facto School Segregation: A Constitutional and Empirical Analysis," 60 Calif. L. Rev. 275, 313 (1972).

24. J. Mill, "Utilitarianism," ch. 5 in 10 Collected Works of John Stuart Mill 157 (1969). See also J. Bentham, "Constitutional Code," in 9 Works of Jeremy Bentham 107 (J. Bowring ed. 1843); H. Sidgwick, The Methods of Ethics 416–17 (1930).

25. See also Ely, "Constitutional Interpretivism: Its Allure and Impossibility," 53 Ind. L. J. 399, 405–8 (1978).

26. Speech to the Canadian Institute for Advanced Legal Studies, Palo Alto, Calif., July 29, 1986.

27. L. Tribe, American Constitutional Law 944–46 (1978).

28. [Democracy and Distrust 173–76 argues for the unconstitutionality of capital punishment on other grounds.]

29. Keynote Address at Northwestern University Symposium Celebrating the Hundredth Anniversary of James Bradley Thayer's "The Origin and Scope of the American Doctrine of Constitutional Law," 7 Harv. L. Rev. 129 (1893).

30. E.g., Fleming, "Constructing the Substantive Constitution," 72 Tex. L. Rev. 211, 240 (1993). Professor Fleming is generally one of the more thoughtful commentators on my work, so the possibility has to be taken seriously that there is more to the point than I realize.

31. 7 Harv. L. Rev. at 144.

32. Id.

33. Id. at 149.

34. A. Bickel, The Least Dangerous Branch 40 (1962).

35. Id. at 41.
36. 7 Harv. L. Rev. at 149.
37. Id. at 141.
38. INS v. Chadha, 462 U.S. 919 (1983).

Chapter 2

1. Modern Uses of Logic in Law 117, 121–23 (September 1963).
2. [". . . but all Duties, Imposts and Excises shall be uniform throughout the United States . . . ."].
3. 3 Writings of Thomas Jefferson 147–49 (Lib. ed. 1904) (emphasis deleted).
4. United States v. Gettysburg Electric Railway Co., 160 U.S. 668, 681 (1896).
5. The General Welfare Clause (1926).
6. But cf. United States v. Lopez, 115 S.Ct. 1624 (1995).

7. 87 Harv. L. R. 693, 701–2. [The remainder of the article appears at pages 39–61.]

8.
We are not now required to ascertain the scope of the phrase "general welfare of the United States" or to determine whether an appropriation in aid of agriculture falls within it. *Wholly apart from that question, another principle embedded in our Constitution* prohibits the enforcement of the Agricultural Adjustment Act. The act invades the reserved rights of the states.

United States v. Butler, 297 U.S. 1, 68 (1936) (emphasis supplied).
9. Hammer v. Dagenhart, 247 U.S. 251, 276 (1918) (emphasis supplied). See also, e.g., United States v. Constantine, 296 U.S. 287, 295–96 (1935).
10. Though the Constitution does not use the term, states are often said to have a general "police power." The term refers simply to a general governmental power, and its use means only that nothing in the United States Constitution requires that *state* governments possess only "few and defined powers." . . . Thus ["the police power" does not denote] an enclave of exclusively local affairs—if it did, the federal government would be virtually powerless.
11. See, e.g., NLRB v. Jones & Laughlin Steel Corp., 301 U.S. 1, 97 (1937) (McReynolds, J., dissenting):

The Constitution still recognizes the existence of states with indestructible powers; the Tenth Amendment was supposed to put them beyond controversy.

12. See also 9 Writings of James Madison 199–200 (G. Hunt ed. 1910).
13. See NLRB v. Jones & Laughlin Steel Corp., 301 U.S. 1, 31–32 (1937).

14. 79 Yale L. J. 1205, 1302–6
15. Other excerpts from this article appear at pages 136–37, 190–96, 247–58, 275–78.
16. [Gomillion v. Lightfoot, 364 U.S. 339 (1960). See pages 248, 253.]
17. 195 U.S. 27 (1904).
18. But cf. United States v. Lopez, 115 S.Ct. 1624 (1995).
19. E.g., Katzenbach v. McClung, 379 U.S. 294 (1964); Heart of Atlanta Motel v. United States, 379 U.S. 241 (1964).

20. E.g., Champion v. Ames, 188 U.S. 321 (1903); Caminetti v. United States, 242 U.S, 470 (1917); United States v. Sullivan, 332 U.S. 689 (1948).

21. 87 Harv. L. R. 693. In order to enable the reader to discount for possible bias, be warned that I was Chief Justice Warren's law clerk the Term *Hanna v. Plumer* was decided.

22. Morley, "What the President Reads," 9 Saturday Rev. of Literature 117 (1932).

23. See Hearings on Proposed Rules of Evidence before the Special Subcomm. on Reform of Federal Criminal Laws of the House Comm. on the Judiciary, 93d Cong., 1st Sess., ser. 2, at 169 (1973).

24. 304 U.S. 64 (1938).

25. 28 U.S.C. § 1652 (1970).

26. 28 U.S.C. § 2072 (1970).

27. See Bernhardt v. Polygraphic Co. of America, 350 U.S. 198 (1956).

28. See Guaranty Trust Co. v. York, 326 U.S. 99 (1945). It was during the reign of this outcome determination test that the Court made explicit the magnitude of Erie's influence, indicating that Erie is every bit as relevant to the choice between state and federal law when there is a Federal Rule of Civil Procedure covering the point as when there is none, and, indeed, that its clout is sufficient to invalidate an Act of Congress defining the applicable law.

29. 356 U.S. 525 (1958).

30. 380 U.S. 460 (1965).

31. This Article will use "Federal Rule" to mean a Federal Rule of Civil Procedure or other Rule promulgated pursuant to the Rules Enabling Act for use in all federal district courts, and "federal rule" to mean a rule followed in one or more federal courts but not promulgated under the Enabling Act.

32. 312 U.S. 1 (1941).

33. See Ragan v. Merchants Transfer & Warehouse Co., 337 U.S. 530 (1949); cf. Woods v. Interstate Realty Co., 337 U.S. 535 (1949); Cohen v. Beneficial Indus. Loan Corp., 337 U.S. 541 (1949).

34. See Bernhardt v. Polygraphic Co. of America, 350 U.S. 198 (1956).

35. 380 U.S. at 475 n.2, citing H. Hart & H. Wechsler, The Federal Courts and the Federal System 678 (1953).

36. 380 U.S. at 475 (footnote omitted). See also id. at 474–75:

> [T]he scheme of our Constitution envisions an allocation of law-making functions between state and federal legislative processes which is undercut if the federal judiciary can make substantive law affecting state affairs beyond the bounds of congressional legislative powers in this regard. Thus, in diversity cases *Erie* commands that it be the state law governing primary private activity which prevails.

With the first sentence, of course, the majority would have no quarrel. It is the equation implied by the word "Thus"—which Justice Harlan's subsequent discussion of the cases, and his rejection of the majority's constitutional test, indicate he meant—that is critical.

37. [This paragraph also appear at pages 35–36 of this book. It is reproduced

both places because it is needed both places, and asking you here to look there seemed sadistic. However, the notes are not reproduced again; you can look back for them if you're interested.]

38. *Erie* was decided a year after NLRB v. Jones & Laughlin Steel Corp., 301 U.S. 1 (1937), and three years before United States v. Darby, 312 U.S. 100 (1941).

39. 41 U.S. (16 Pet.) 1 (1842).

40. C. Wright, Law of Federal Courts 229 (2d ed. 1970).

41. It was fashionable for a time to refer to *Erie*'s constitutional discussion as dictum. See, e.g., Sampson v. Channell, 110 F.2d 754, 756–57 n. 4 (1st Cir.), *cert. denied*, 310 U.S. 650 (1940). In fact the constitutional argument was the most telling the Court advanced in support of its revised construction of the Rules of Decision Act. The distinctions the Court had developed under *Swift* did indeed pose hard questions of application, see 304 U.S. at 74, but so do many legal tests; in any event, *Erie* was not the only road to simplification. Forum shopping of the sort practiced in Black & White Taxicab Co. v. Brown & Yellow Taxicab Co., 276 U.S. 518 (1928), see 304 U.S. at 73, could have been dealt with by foreclosing jurisdiction in such aggravated cases. Cf. Sheldon v. Sill, 49 U.S. (8 How.) 441 (1850). Nor is it necessary to believe in a "transcendental body of law outside of any particular State"—Black & White Taxicab Co. v. Brown & Yellow Taxicab Co., supra, at 533 (Holmes, J., dissenting); see 304 U.S. at 79—to approve *Swift*; one might just prefer to have federal judges making law. It does seem true that "the benefits expected to flow from" *Swift* to which the Court in *Erie* (though not, incidentally, the Court in *Swift*) alluded, 304 U.S. at 74, had not in fact materialized; and surely the "fairness" rationale underlying the Rules of Decision Act, see page 49, applies as forcefully to common as to statutory law. It was, however, a *statute* the Court was expounding. Charles Warren's researches, "New Light on the History of the Federal Judiciary Act of 1789," 37 Harv. L. Rev. 49, 81–88 (1923), had not in fact "established" that *Swift*'s construction was not the one intended by the Act's authors. 304 U.S. at 72. See 2 W. Crosskey, Politics and the Constitution in the History of the United States 866–71 (1953); Friendly, "In Praise of *Erie*—and of the New Federal Common Law," 39 N.Y.U. L. Rev. 383, 389–90 (1964). And in any event Congress had not, despite much criticism, 304 U.S. at 72 nn. 3 & 4, altered it for ninety-six years; it had, indeed, reenacted it. Friendly, supra, at 390 n. 37.

42. Congressional legislation based upon the Commerce Clause certainly could have covered the specific question at issue in *Erie* and probably even that involved in *Swift*. The *Erie* opinion's point was that there was no constitutional basis for the sort of general lawmaking authority exercised under the *Swift* doctrine; that Congress therefore could not have delegated such general authority to the courts; and that the Act consequently should not be construed to have done so.

The decision in Katzenbach v. Morgan, 384 U.S. 641 (1966), might have suggested that congressional power could be found in § 5 of the Fourteenth Amendment to combat state court discrimination against out-of-staters by giving them access to a neutrally developed body of substantive law unavailable in suits between cocitizens. Any such inference seems to have been intercepted by Oregon v. Mitchell, 400 U.S. 112 (1970). Should *Morgan* be resurrected in a way that would support the inference suggested—or, indeed, should the Court arrive at the point where it is prepared to recognize the fact of diversity of citizenship as alone sufficient under the Commerce Clause—that would serve only to strengthen the conclusion, suggested in *Hanna* and pressed in this article, that meaningful protection against federal overreaching in the context of the diversity jurisdiction must be found in the controlling statutes rather than in the Constitution.

43. 304 U.S. at 78.

44. See note 42 supra.

45. That is, not to apply in "simple" diversity actions, involving neither a maritime transaction nor foreign or interstate commerce as defined by the Act.

46. 350 U.S. at 202. Nor was this by any means a throwaway: the Court's opinion reported that certiorari had been granted "because of the doubtful application by the Court of Appeals of *Erie R. Co. v. Tompkins* . . . ." Id. at 200. Concurring, Justice Frankfurter opined that the contrary construction "would raise a serious question of constitutional law . . . ." Id. at 208. Justice Douglas's formulation for the Court—"If respondent's contention is correct, a constitutional question might be presented," id. at 202—seems milder, until one reads on: "Our view . . . is that § 3, so read, would invade the local law field. We therefore read narrowly to avoid that issue." Id.

47. In fact, the Court's presentation of a rather complete list of the ways in which arbitration differs from trial demonstrated, albeit unwittingly, that the reasons one would be likely to opt for arbitration are procedural reasons—reasons concerned with the process by which cases are resolved, in particular with making that process less formal, generally less cumbersome, and, by dispensing with the rules of evidence, more likely to uncover all the facts. See 350 U.S. at 203, 203–4 n. 4. Of course, if a feature of a system of arbitration could not find justification in process terms—such as a liability-creating or liability-limiting rule that arbitrators but not courts were entitled to follow—its application in a diversity case would be unconstitutional unless the rule could be given some independent justification, such as under the Commerce Clause. But *Bernhardt* was not such a case, a least not as the Court described it.

48. 380 U.S. at 471–72 (footnote omitted and emphasis supplied).

49. 28 U.S.C. § 1652 (1970).

50. The Court did note that "Congress has no power to declare substantive rules of common law applicable in a State . . . ." 304 U.S. at 78. But that was by way of demonstrating the unconstitutionality of excluding the entire species "general common law" from the coverage of the Act, and not by way of suggesting a test for deciding which state rules were "rules of decision." This is the opinion's only use of the word "substantive"; the word "procedural" does not appear. But cf. 304 U.S. at 92 (Reed, J., concurring).

51. 312 U.S. 1, 10–11 (1941).

52. See pages 58–59 .

53. 326 U.S. 99, 109 (1945).

54. 380 U.S. at 468–69.

55. 356 U.S. 525 (1958).

56. 372 U.S. 221, 222 (1963).

57. See also P. Bator, P. Mishkin, D. Shapiro & H. Wechsler, Hart & Wechsler's The Federal Courts and the Federal System 697–98 (2d ed. 1973); Hart, "The Relations between State and Federal Law," 54 Colum. L. Rev. 489, 505, 513 (1954);

McCoid, "*Hanna v. Plumer*: The *Erie* Doctrine Changes Shape," 51 Va. L. Rev. 884, 907–09 (1965).

58. See pages 61–86.

59. Hart, supra note 57, at 489.

60. 380 U.S. at 474 n. 1.

61. 304 U.S. at 74–75.

62. 380 U.S. at 467–69.

63. The *Erie* opinion's reference to "discrimination by non-citizens against citizens," 304 U.S. at 74, has been criticized as misleading, since citizen plaintiffs also have access to federal courts [in diversity cases]. P. Bator, P. Mishkin, D. Shapiro & H. Wechsler, supra note 57, at 707. See also id. at 747 (criticizing *Hanna*, 380 U.S. at 468 n. 9, on the same ground). But the Court did not simply close one eye. What it obviously had in mind on both occasions was that although either a resident plaintiff or a nonresident defendant can get into federal court against the other's will, the situation is not so symmetrical when a nonresident sues a resident. A resident defendant has no right to removal, see 28 U.S.C. § 1441 (1970), and is stuck with the nonresident plaintiff's choice of either forum. Thus in terms of ability to select the court, noncitizens are favored over citizens.

To permit resident defendants to remove would give citizens of a state the same right of access to federal courts as noncitizens. Such a removal rule, like the present rule giving resident plaintiffs access to federal court, would deviate from the rationale of the diversity jurisdiction, which was to protect litigants from the biases of foreign courts. In general, the more one equalizes the ability to choose the forum, the further one deviates from the rationale of the diversity jurisdiction. In any event, the present compromise—giving resident plaintiffs but not resident defendants access to federal court—is defensible in terms of neither goal.

64. Unless there is some jurisdictional basis other than diversity, one involved in litigation with a cocitizen can never be forced into federal court; but one involved in litigation with a noncocitizen can—save only where he is the plaintiff and the suit is brought in the defendant's home state. Of course the resident plaintiff—though not the resident defendant—has the same right his adversary has: he too can get the case into federal court if he wants to. But the point is that he may not want to; he may prefer state law, and he can be deprived of it in a way that someone suing a cocitizen cannot. (The fact that you can hurt your adversary as much as he can hurt you does not imply that you are not being treated unfairly vis-à-vis your cocitizens.) This sort of discrimination cannot be cured by tinkering with the removal provisions, but must be approached by attending to the differences between federal and state law. We might well decide to take away the resident plaintiff's right of access to federal court, but so long as we neither take that right from his nonresident adversary nor grant it to his resident adversary—and obviously we will do neither so long as we retain the diversity jurisdiction at all—discrimination among cocitizens along lines of adversary residence will remain.

65. 304 U.S. at 75.

66. For one thing, the construction of a federal statute was in issue, and Bolling v. Sharpe, 347 U.S. 497 (1954) (reading an equal protection command into the Fifth Amendment) had not yet been decided.

67. I do not have in mind a body of law loaded in favor of nonresidents, but

rather one developed by federal courts and therefore presumptively devoid of any systematic bias.

68. Pursuing its rationale of material unfairness, the Court indicated that the relative difficulty of complying with the two rules is ordinarily to be assessed at a time when compliance with both is still possible, not when the time limit on one but not the other has run. 380 U.S. at 468–69. (In the unusual event that one of the time limits was sufficiently shorter than the other to render compliance on the part of a diligent litigant or attorney substantially more burdensome, the Court presumably would require that the state rule be followed.)

69. It is fashionable to regard Klaxon Co. v. Stentor Elec. Mfg. Co., 313 U.S. 487 (1941)—which held that diversity courts must follow state choice of law rules—as presenting a markedly different sort of question from other cases arising under the Rules of Decision Act, and to argue that *Klaxon is* inconsistent with *Erie* since it destroys the predictability sought by the earlier decision. See H. Hart & H. Wechsler, supra note 35, at 634–35; Hart, supra note 57, at 513–15. Admittedly, whenever there is the possibility of being sued in more than one state, there will be uncertainty under *Klaxon* as to what state's choice of law rules will be applied. But even accepting Hart's questionable assumption that federal courts freed of *Klaxon* would develop uniform, clear, and predictable choice of law rules, there would remain uncertainty under his system too, over whether state or "general federal" choice of law rules will be applied. Of course there are only two possible choice of law rules to which one can be subjected against his will under Hart's system, given that a defendant can remove to federal court if sued in any state but his own, whereas under *Klaxon* there are theoretically as many as there are states where he can be served. But it is not clear in how many states the typical potential defendant is amenable to suit. And, human energy and imagination—and the proclivity of lawyers to hang onto lawsuits—being what they are, the possibility of forum shopping "across the street" may well be more likely than forum shopping across state lines. Cf. D. Cavers, The Choice-of-Law Process 222 (1965). Thus, the predictability question is a knotty empirical one, and it is wrong to characterize the debate over *Klaxon* as one about the desirability or importance of predictability. Each answer creates its own brand of unpredictability, and it is not clear which is the more serious.

Of course *Erie* did not purport to be a decision about predictability, and claims that that is the key to understanding it have been overdone. The concern it discussed was discrimination among classes of litigants. But discrimination, like predictability, is a function of disuniformity, and since the *Klaxon* issue poses a choice of disuniformities, it is no surprise that analyzing it in terms of discrimination will also yield a choice of evils. With respect to the plaintiff's advantage over a noncocitizen defendant, see note 63 supra, the situation is precisely the same. Under *Klaxon* the plaintiff cannot shop for a favorable result within the defendant's home state, but he may be able to shop across state lines if the defendant is amenable to suit elsewhere; under Hart's system it would be the other way around. With respect to discrimination among cocitizen litigants, see note 64 supra, *Klaxon* would seem to come out ahead. Under *Klaxon*, everyone's case, regardless of the residence of his adversary, will be decided by the whole law of the state in which suit is brought. Under Hart's system, the fact that one's adversary is a noncocitizen will give him the opportunity, with one exception, to opt out of the state legal system and take advantage of the federal. The exception is the defendant sued at home. But far from improving the situation for Hart's system, that means that a plaintiff suing a noncocitizen would have a double advantage over a plaintiff suing a cocitizen: he would be able to lock his adversary into either of two legal systems, "general federal" or defendant's state, against his will. Eliminating that exception by granting resident defendants a right of removal would eliminate this double advantage, but would not erase the general discrimination Hart's system would create.

Thus, once again the problem reduces itself to a choice of uniformities, specifically a choice between horizontal uniformity among all federal courts and vertical uniformity between the federal and state courts of a given state. But that choice was at the heart of the disagreement between *Swift* and *Erie*, and *Erie* signaled a recognition that although the promotion of one kind of uniformity inevitably sacrifices the other, the Rules of Decision Act had made a choice, and had chosen vertical uniformity. Quarreling over which kind of disuniformity is worse may be great fun, but the controlling statute says that "the laws of the several states" shall be the rules of decision.

70. The *Hanna* Court pointedly indicated, however, that state statutes of limitation are to be followed. 380 U.S. at 469. The Court may have distinguished the two situations on the basis of a difference in difficulty of compliance. (The citation of Woods v. Interstate Realty Co., 337 U.S. 535 [1949], and Cohen v. Beneficial Indus. Loan Corp., 337 U.S. 541 [1949], in the same footnote in which the Court distinguished Guaranty Trust Co. v. York, 326 U.S. 99 [1945], and Ragan v. Merchants Transfer & Warehouse Co., 337 U.S. 530 [1949]—both cases the Court had treated as raising statute of limitations problems—supports this reading. Both *Woods* and *Cohen* were cases in which compliance with the state requirement was apparently still possible at the time suit was brought but required substantially more effort, and in the latter case money, than compliance with its federal counterpart.) The idea would be that in many cases, given that the fact and extent of injury and other developments implying the necessity of a suit or even of consulting a lawyer are not always immediately apparent, compliance with a short statute of limitations may be substantially more difficult than compliance with a long one—whereas variations in time limits on responsive pleadings will ordinarily affect only a lawyer's ordering of his business. (This would be an unfair characterization were one time limit sufficiently shorter than the other substantially to affect the ability to comply without serious burden, but presumably the Court did not mean to cover that case.)

That, however, is a debatable line of distinction, at least in the factual context of *Ragan*. See page 56. But whatever reason the *Hanna* Court had in mind, its indication that in the absence of a Federal Rule federal courts should follow state statutes of limitation generally, and the sort of state rule involved in *Ragan* in particular, seems amply justified. For as we shall note later on, such state rules establish rights that must be counted substantive. That implicates what surely was one concern that gave rise to the Rules of Decision Act, a concern with undercutting state policies relating to subjects other than the management of litigation. That this concern must be retained in any sensible interpretation of the Rules of Decision Act is corroborated by the consideration that if it were not, the theoretical possibility would exist that even though a Federal Rule had been declared invalid under the second sentence of the Enabling Act for abridging substantive rights created by a given state rule, local federal courts could turn around and on their own motion impose the same federal rule in the teeth of the same state rule. Whatever else we may or may not know about the intent of the two statutes, we know they do not mean to countenance that. One of *Hanna*'s main points was that the Rules of Decision Act is more protective of state prerogatives than the Enabling Act. A number of commentators appear to disagree and think the two are equally protective, but no one has suggested that it is, or even that it ever is, the other way around.

71. But cf. note 68 supra.

72. It is important here as elsewhere not to let a law's rationale outrun the plausible limits of its language. Differences in judges and juries may indeed cause forum shopping, see 380 U.S. 460, 475 (1965) (Harlan, J., concurring); they may also be outcome determinative even in *Hanna*'s refined sense. But whatever else they may be, judges and juries are not rules of decision, though the rules demarcating their respective jurisdictions may be. Indeed, of the thirteen factors cited in one survey as reasons for choosing between state and federal court, only two—broader federal discovery procedures and the availability of federal interpleader—could be characterized as involving a choice of "rules" of any kind. Summers, "Analysis of Factors that Influence Choice of Forum in Diversity Cases," 47 Iowa L. Rev. 933, 937–38 (1962).

73. When the Rules of Decision Act is interpreted in light of its fairness rationale—or, for that matter, in light of a desire either to minimize forum shopping or to avoid "uncertainty in the planning of everyday affairs"—it becomes clear that there is no place in the analysis for the sort of balancing of federal and state interests contemplated by the *Byrd* opinion. (Of course, if the "federal interest" involved is one whose recognition is required by the United States Constitution, it should be honored regardless of what the Rules of Decision Act might otherwise imply.)

74. See, e.g., Bernhardt v. Polygraphic Co. of America, 350 U.S. 198, 203 (1956) ("[T]he federal court enforcing a state-created right in a diversity case is . . . in substance 'only another court of the State.' ")

75. 28 U.S.C. § 2072 (1970).

76. 28 U.S.C. § 2072 (1970).

77. 312 U.S. 1, 14 (1941).

78. Id. at 11.

79.
> Hence we conclude that the Act of June 19, 1934, was purposely restricted in its operation to matters of pleading and court practice and procedure. Its two provisos or caveats *emphasize this restriction*. The first is that the court shall not "abridge, enlarge, nor modify substantive rights," *in the guise of* regulating procedure.

Id. at 10 (emphasis supplied). See also, e.g., Miller, "Federal Rule 44.1 and the 'Fact' Approach to Determining Foreign Law: Death Knell for Die-Hard Doctrine," 65 Mich. L. Rev. 613, 740–41 (1967):

> The jugular issue in determining the validity of a Federal Rule under the act's rule-making delegation is whether the rule relates to "practice and procedure" or affects "substantive rights."

80. 312 U.S. at 14 (emphasis supplied).

81. 380 U.S. at 462–63 n. 1.

82. Id. at 471.

83. There is essentially no legislative history. See 78 Cong. Rec. 9362–63, 10866 (1934).

84. The Enabling Act is applicable even in nondiversity cases.

85. See generally Clark & Moore, "A New Federal Civil Procedure," 44 Yale L. J. 387, 1291 (1935).

86. See Fed. R. Civ. P. 26–31, 33–34, 36.

87. See Fed. R. Civ. P. 8(f), 15(a). It is, of course, in theory always *possible* to comply with pleading requirements. But a number of state requirements, particularly those prevailing around the time the Rules were promulgated, were sufficiently serpentine as to render compliance substantially more difficult than it is under the Rules.

88. See, e.g., Clark, "Federal Procedural Reform and States' Rights; to a More Perfect Union," 40 Tex. L. Rev. 211, 214 (1961). Both innovations were mentioned by those pushing the passage of the Enabling Act. See Clark & Moore, supra note 85, at 1300–1303; Taft, "Possible and Needed Reforms in Administration of Justice in Federal Courts," 8 A.B.A. J. 601, 606 (1922).

89. The *breadth* of discovery provided by Fed. R. Civ. P. 26(b)(1) might well be subject, however, to an Enabling Act challenge in a state whose narrower provision could be shown to be rooted in a concern for privacy respecting those effects and matters that cannot be brought out at trial. (But cf. Fed. R. Civ. P. 26(c), 30(d), which are rooted in, and at least on some occasions can adequately serve, the same concerns.) A disagreement over the timing of disclosure reflects only a procedural difference of opinion over whether truth arises more naturally from forewarning or surprise, but a disagreement over its scope may reflect a different ordering of competing procedural and substantive goals.

90. But cf. note 70 supra.

91. Were such a presumption expressed not in the abstract but rather in a particular substantive context, the likelihood that it too was designed to serve a substantive end would have to be carefully explored. Where the state presumption is designed to serve some substantive policy, not even a Federal Rule should be permitted to displace it. Since most presumptions are substantively intended, and in any event the cost of sifting out the few that are not would be high, the Advisory Committee, despite the confusion with which it defended the move, did well to defer to state presumptions in diversity cases.

92. A similar analysis would seem appropriate to most disputes respecting whether certain out-of-court statements are to be excluded as hearsay. The disputes generally have to do with the best way to get at the truth, but the differences are nonetheless material in the Rules of Decision Act sense.

93. The Rules of Decision Act does not, and neither did the test suggested at page 49.

94. The test suggested is geared to the purposes underlying the state rule and not to whether the rule "in fact" serves substantive or procedural ends. This focus reflects an assumption that it was the subversion of state *policies* concerned with subjects other than the sensible management of litigation that the framers of the Enabling Act wished to avoid. Moreover, it would seem that any rule can be said to have both "procedural effects," affecting the way in which litigation is conducted,

and "substantive effects," affecting society's distribution of risks and rewards. Thus, an "effects test" would seem destined either to unintelligibility or to the invalidation of every Federal Rule, thereby rendering the Enabling Act entirely self-defeating.

95. The test suggested is therefore not geared, at least not directly, to how "important" the right may seem to the court. Thus, for example, the fact that the right to counsel is so important that it is included in the Constitution does not make it any the less a procedural right, provided in order to ensure the adequacy of the hearing.

Of course state legislative history is frequently not recorded, and even if it were it would not necessarily reflect every purpose underlying a given rule. Thus, whether a substantive account of the origins of the rule in question seems plausible in light of the statutory complex in which it appears will become important. Since the plausibility of such an account will inevitably be in part, though only in part, a function of the importance or triviality of the substantive interest around which it revolves, there is a sense in which the importance of the asserted state interest will become relevant. That the points are thus interconnected might lead some directly to embrace a balancing approach to the Enabling Act. Interestingly, whereas such an approach has been suggested, as in *Byrd*, for the Rules of Decision Act—in which context it patently should have no place, see note 73 supra—it has not to my knowledge been suggested for the Enabling Act. But it would be a good deal more defensible in the Enabling Act context, given that that law's concern is not with the emulation of state law in all material respects but rather, quite overtly, with *both* sides of the uneasy tension between federal procedural reform and state nonprocedural policies. But while a balancing approach is not the one here recommended— over and above the usual objections to balancing, I would note that the statutory language provides no semblance of basis for any such interpretation—even a balancing test would represent an advance, since it would at least begin to take the Enabling Act's second sentence seriously. That is a start the Court has yet to make.

96. Note that this is a definition by exclusion only in the sense that a substantive purpose is defined as a nonprocedural purpose. The possibility that a rule can be both procedural and substantive, when it is informed by both procedural and nonprocedural purposes, is left open and will indeed become important.

97. E.g., H. Hart & H. Wechsler, supra note 35, at 678; Hanna v. Plumer, 380 U.S. 460, 475, 477 (1965) (Harlan, J., concurring).

98. Cf. Grant v. McAuliffe, 41 Cal. 2d 859, 264 P. 2d 944 (1953).

99. Cf. Milliken v. Pratt, 125 Mass. 374 (1878). [Obviously I'm passing the question whether such laws are constitutional, which they seem clearly not to be.]

100. Cf. Lilienthal v. Kaufman, 239 Ore. 1, 395 P. 2d 543 (1964).

101. The same analysis applies to damage ceilings, although the immunization there is partial.

102. Whether a dismissal pursuant to a federal limitations period *shorter* than the state period would be "on the merits" is not entirely clear. Compare Venner v. Great N. Ry., 209 U.S. 24, 34–35 (1908), with Fed. R. Civ. P. 41(b). If not, and suit in state court remained possible, it could be argued that such a dismissal would not "abridge, enlarge or modify" any substantive right.

103. Cohen v. Beneficial Indus. Loan Corp., 337 U.S. 541, 559 (1949) (Rutledge, J., dissenting).

104. 337 U.S. 585 (1949).

NOTES TO PAGES 55–57

105. See note 70 supra. The dissenters questioned whether the state legislature intended to close federal as well as state courts. 337 U.S. at 538–40 (Jackson, J., dissenting); cf. Angel v. Bullington, 330 U.S. 183, 193 (1947) (Reed, J., dissenting). In all likelihood, of course, the point was not considered by the legislature, at least not specifically: its "intent" respecting the matter, were it relevant, would have to be inferred from the more general purposes of the statute. And no one questioned that the purposes of the statute involved in *Woods* included not simply the reduction of the docket but also the encouragement of corporate qualification. I suppose it is conceivable that one might think it appropriate to encourage qualification by closing state courts but leaving federal courts open. But given that diversity is virtually automatic when one party is an out-of-state corporation, the implication of such a self-defeating intent would require an unusually clear legislative history, and certainly more than the fact that the statute is couched in "jurisdictional" terms. More importantly, however—and this is one reason state legislatures do not think about such things—the question whether there was an intention on the part of the Mississippi legislature to close federal courts is simply not relevant to the question whether they should be closed. State legislatures lack power to control the jurisdiction of federal courts, no matter how much they might want to. The question in cases like *Woods* and *Angel* is whether *federal law*, specifically the Rules of Decision Act, requires federal courts to emulate state practice and deny jurisdiction. And the preferable interpretation of that Act renders the intent underlying the state law in question irrelevant.

106. "The capacity of a corporation to sue . . . shall be determined by the law under which it was organized." Fed. R. Civ. P. 17(b). Respondent in *Woods* was a Tennessee corporation.

107. Of course any denial of jurisdiction will help reduce the size of the docket. But here there were reasons unconcerned with the management of litigation as well.

108. 337 U.S. 541 (1949).

109. Id. at 556. This made the case a Rules of Decision Act case, and as such it was correctly decided. See note 70 supra.

110. So did the *Hanna* majority. 380 U.S. at 470 n. 12.

111. Id. at 477–78.

112. 337 U.S. at 547–50.

113. 337 U.S. 530 (1949).

114. Id. at 533.

115. Id. See also id. at 534.

116. 380 U.S. at 477; see note 121 infra.

117. See 380 U.S. at 463 n. 1, 469 n. 10, 470 n. 12. Despite this, some courts and commentators have concluded that *Hanna* overruled *Ragan*. See, e.g., J. Moore, A. Vestal & P. Kurland, Moore's Manual: Federal Practice and Procedure 174 (1963); sources cited C. Wright, *supra* note 40, at 246 n. 38. But see id. at 246:

> [W]hen the Court has not overruled Ragan, and has gone to great lengths to indicate why Hanna is not inconsistent with Ragan, it seems the safer course to assume that the Ragan decision is still authoritative.

118. In addition, the issue was not before the Court, and whether or not *Ragan* was correct under the Enabling Act—in terms of which it had not been analyzed, surely not by the *Ragan* Court itself nor even by Justice Harlan in *Hanna*—does not

seem so clear as to justify a conclusion one way or the other in a case raising a very different issue.

119. One's heart must surely go out to Mr. Ragan, who did all that Rule 3 seemed on its face to require—and at the time there was no authoritative case law to advise him otherwise—only to learn that it was not enough to get him into court. It is not clear what one does about this, however. A strictly prospective invalidation of the Rule, even assuming it would otherwise be defensible, would seem to flout the Act's instructions; by hypothesis enforcement of a plaintiff-favoring Rule that violates the Act's second sentence will deny the defendant a substantive right. And solomonic compromises are not the general stuff of our legal system. In any event, the question Justice Harlan invited the Court to consider had nothing to do with reparations for Mr. Ragan but rather was whether the rule of his case should be reconsidered sixteen years later.

120. The Advisory Committee on the Federal Rules of Civil Procedure foresaw *Ragan* quite clearly in Note 4 to Rule 3 (28 U.S.C. foll. Rule 3 [1970]):

> When a federal or state statute of limitations is pleaded as a defense, a question may arise under this rule whether the mere filing of the complaint stops the running of the statute, or whether any further step is required, such as, service of the summons and complaint or their delivery to the marshal for service. The answer to this question may depend on whether it is competent for the Supreme Court, exercising the power to make rules of procedure without affecting substantive rights, to vary the operation of statutes of limitations.

121. On this account of the Kansas law, the state and federal tolling provisions were not, as Justice Harlan suggested they were, fungible in terms of the state statute's purpose. They would have been fungible if, for example, Rule 3 had tied tolling to the service of the complaint rather than the filing of it. But it did not; the difference between the actual provisions was a difference between notice and no notice, and that goes to the essence of the right the state legislature seems to have been trying to create. Justice Harlan put the case cleverly: "At most, application of the Federal Rule would have meant that potential Kansas tort defendants would have to defer for a few days the satisfaction of knowing that they had not been sued within the limitations period." 380 U.S. at 377. But while potential tort defendants may not be a group deserving of accolades, it is the group the statute was unmistakably designed to protect. The relief of knowing that you are not to be sued hardly belongs in the Bill of Rights, but the question the Enabling Act makes relevant is whether the state right involved is substantive. And a few days is not a few years, but the whole point of a statute of limitations is to identify a day on which susceptibility to suit ceases and one can stop walking on tiptoe.

122. See page 55.

123. Act of Mar. 12, 1909, ch. 182, § 58, [1909] Kan. Session Laws 338 (repealed 1963). Kansas cases had stressed the distinction between tolling by service and "commencement" for other purposes. See, e.g., Green v. McCracken, 64 Kan. 330, 67 P. 857 (1902); Webster v. Long, 63 Kan. 876, 66 P. 1032 (1901); Dunlap v. McFarland, 25 Kan. 488, 490–91 (1881).

124. Cf. C. Wright, supra note 40, at 246 (footnote omitted) ("There are matters other than those involving the statute of limitations for which it is important to know how and when an action is commenced.").

125. *Hanna*'s characterization of *Ragan* also had the effect of diminishing its value as precedent for the view that Federal Rules are limited by the Rules of Decision Act, without at the same time involving the Court in a full-scale discussion of the Enabling Act.

126. 380 U.S. at 462–63 n. 1. There is, of course, a sense in which one will "breathe easier" simply by virtue of the assurance that the state is making a special effort to ensure that notice of suit will not get lost. But presumably every rule, substantive or procedural, will contribute to the peace of mind of at least one party, and again we must look to the nature of the underlying mandate, to what it is the party is encouraged to rest easy about. Thus, the fact that one is reassured by the knowledge that in the event he is sued, exceptions to the hearsay rule will be narrowly limited, thereby enabling him to confront most of those whose declarations would harm him, does not make the right to narrow hearsay exceptions substantive. Similarly, the peace of mind that one may derive from comparatively fastidious notice requirements—unlike the feeling of release from the possibility of any further trauma respecting a past event that the state seeks to create by a statute of limitations—is a feeling that derives from a strictly procedural assurance, to the effect that steps are being taken to manage the trial process in a way that will allow him to relate his side of the story and otherwise to pursue the truth.

127.
Actual notice is of course also the goal of Rule 4(d) (1); however, the Federal Rule reflects a determination that this goal can be achieved by a method less cumbersome than that prescribed in § 9. In this case the goal seems to have been achieved; although the affidavit filed by respondent in the District Court asserts that he had not been served in hand nor had he accepted service, it does not allege lack of actual notice.

380 U.S. at 463 n.1.

128. There were undoubtedly several factors at work. One may have been a simple desire to save the Rules, though it can be noted, at least with the benefit of hindsight, that taking the Enabling Act seriously in the early 1940s would probably have precluded the subsequent, and vastly more threatening, application of the Rules of Decision Act's standard to the Rules. Another may have resulted from petitioner's ill-advised attempt to read "substantive" as "important," and the Court's understandable reluctance to get into the sort of balancing that that equation would entail. See 312 U.S. at 14. That, however, is not the only possible, nor is it even the most natural, definition of "substantive."

129. 312 U.S. at 13.

130. The Court did indicate that if Rule 35 were *held invalid*, the law of Indiana would become applicable. Having indicated that if Rule 35 were procedural it would control, it continued:

> On the other hand if the right to be exempt from such an order is one of substantive law, the Rules of Decision Act required the District Court, though sitting in Illinois, to apply the law of Indiana, the state where the cause of action arose, and to order the examination.

Id. at 10–11 (footnote omitted); *cf.* Hanna v. Plumer, 380 U.S. 460, 472 n. 15 (1965). Thus, the remark was part of a pincer movement on Mrs. Sibbach—substantive or procedural, you get examined either way—a movement that entailed two

questionable assumptions. The first was that the definitions of substance and procedure appropriate to the Enabling Act were equally appropriate to interstate
conflicts analysis. (Whether its suggestion that under the Rules of Decision Act
Indiana law would be applicable reflected an anticipation of *Klaxon* and an assumption about Illinois conflicts law, or rather the direct application of its own
ideas about conflicts, is not altogether clear. Given the lack of citation to Illinois
conflicts authorities, the latter may be the more natural reading.) The second assumption was that, for purposes of the Rules of Decision Act too, the world of legal
problems was divided into wholly separate categories of substance and procedure. See also 312 U.S. at 10. But cf. id. at 17 (Frankfurter, J., dissenting). Had the
Court recognized the possibility, contemplated by the Act, that a Rule could be
procedural but nonetheless invalid for abridging substantive rights, the analysis
might have been quite different. An invalidation of that sort would have meant—
if we hold constant the Court's assumption of monolithic definitions of substance
and procedure—that if the law of any state were to become applicable, that state
would have been the forum state, Illinois. An invalidation of that sort, however,
would have required a determination that a substantive right had been abridged, and
that in turn would have required an answer to the question the Court never got
around to asking—what law would have been applicable had Rule 35 never been
promulgated?

131. See note 69 supra.

132. See also Sampson v. Channell, 110 F.2d 754 (1st Cir.), cert. denied, 310
U.S. 650 (1940). Moreover, even assuming the relevance of state law, the *Klaxon*
issue might well have been avoided on the ground that the choice between Indiana
and Illinois was without significance. Indiana courts permitted physical examinations. 312 U.S. at 7. The courts of Illinois did not, id., but in terms that gave little
evidence of substantive concern. Most often it had simply been announced that
power to order such an examination was lacking. See, e.g., Chicago v. McNally, 227
Ill. 14, 20, 81 N.E. 23, 25 (1907); Parker v. Enslow, 102 Ill. 272, 279 (1882). What
rationale there had been seems either irrelevant to the sort of examination contemplated by Rule 35, see Illinois v. Scott, 326 Ill. 327, 346–47, 157 N.E. 247, 256
(1927), or rooted wholly in a procedural concern for the most likely way to find the
truth:

> Medical experts are not infallible, and however conscientiously and carefully the
> examination is made there is a possibility that an erroneous conclusion may be
> reached. There is no law under which the court could direct or control such an
> examination . . . .

Mattice v. Klawans, 312 Ill. 299, 307, 143 N.E. 866, 869–70 (1924). See also Peo-
ria, D. & E. Ry. v. Rice, 144 Ill. 227, 232 (1893). As we shall see, however, the main
reason the *Sibbach* Court felt no obligation to decide the *Klaxon* issue was that
given its thinking in 1941 about the Rules of Decision and Conformity Acts, state
law simply was not relevant.

133. Thus, given the state of the Rules of Decision Act in 1941, the place to look
to see whether application of Rule 35 would abridge a substantive right would have
been to preexisting federal law (and in the event of a division, to the law applied in
Illinois federal courts). The majority never acknowledged this—its construction of

the Enabling Act dispensed with the necessity of identifying the otherwise applicable law—but it did for one reason or another feel obligated to dismiss its own prior decisions denying federal courts the power to order physical examinations as rooted in procedural concerns. 312 U.S. at 11–13. There is, however, rather strong language in one of them, Union Pac. Ry. v. Botsford, 141 U.S. 250, 251–52 (1891), to the effect that the rule precluding examination was rooted in a concern for bodily privacy and not simply in a general approach to procedure hostile to discovery. (*Botsford* has had a checkered career. Held in *Sibbach* not even to establish a substantive right, it was characterized in Roe v. Wade, 410 U.S. 113, 152 (1973), as quite possibly the wellspring of the constitutional right of privacy.) And Camden & Suburban Ry. Co. v. Stetson, 177 U.S. 172 (1900), holding that notwithstanding *Botsford* the Rules of Decision Act required a diversity court to follow a state statute permitting examinations, was pretty clear evidence that nine years later the Court did not view *Botsford* as settling a purely procedural matter. (The *Sibbach* Court explained that *Stetson* must have confused the Rules of Decision and Conformity Acts. 312 U.S. at 12–13.) Thus, a strong argument can be made that in historical context *Sibbach* was wrongly decided. Given that the Court's interpretation of the Rules of Decision Act would have permitted it to overrule *Botsford* and allow federal courts to order physical examinations without the sanction of a Federal Rule, however, its reluctance to press the point is understandable. (Today, of course, the validity of Rule 35 would properly be determined in the context of the state rule rendered applicable by the choice of law rules of the forum state. Klaxon Co. v. Stentor Elec. Mfg. Co., 313 U.S. 487 (1941).)

134. The Conformity Act, 17 Stat. 196 (1872), which generally required federal courts to follow state procedure (though the Court so riddled it with exceptions as to leave little standing, see P. Bator, P. Mishkin, D. Shapiro & H. Wechsler, supra note 57, at 671–72) was not officially repealed until 1948. But although there were isolated lower court decisions in the late 1930s and early 1940s taking the view that the Conformity Act had been rendered inoperative only where the matter in issue was covered by a Federal Rule, see 4 C. Wright & A. Miller, Federal Practice and Procedure §1030, at 135 (1969), the weight of authority in the circuits was to the effect that the combination of the Enabling Act and the promulgation of the Rules had implicitly repealed the Conformity Act in toto. See, e.g., Griffith v. Bank of New York, 147 F.2d 899 (2d Cir.), cert. denied, 325 U.S. 874 (1945); Continental Collieries v. Shober, 130 F.2d 631 (3d Cir. 1942); Carnegie Nat'l Bank v. City of Wolf Point, 110 F.2d 569 (9th Cir. 1940); Dallas Ry. & Terminal Co. v. Sullivan, 108 F.2d 581 (5th Cir. 1940). See generally Schram v. Holmes, 4 F.R.D. 119 (E.D. Mich. 1943). See also Fed. R. Civ. P. 83. *Sibbach*'s language respecting this point is somewhat ambiguous, but seems to accord with the majority position: "Whatever may be said as to the effect of the Conformity Act while it remained in force, the rules, if they are within the authority granted by Congress, repeal that statute . . . ." 312 U.S. at 10 (footnote omitted). In any event, the Court's analysis in other cases decided between 1938 and 1948 makes clear its assumption that the Conformity Act had ceased to be a factor. See Palmer v. Hoffman, 318 U.S. 109, 117 (1943); Cities Serv. Oil Co. v. Dunlap, 308 U.S. 208, 212 (1939).

135. In *Sibbach* the state would have been Indiana, whose rule was the same as Rule 35. See note 132 supra. In other cases, however, a conclusion that the Federal

Rule in question was nonprocedural would have led to the application of a contrary state rule.

136. The Enabling Act, in limiting Federal Rules promulgated for civil actions, indicates no distinction between diversity and federal question cases. See 28 U.S.C. § 2072 (1970); cf. Perry v. Allen, 239 F.2d 107 (5th Cir. 1956). However, the Rules of Decision Act is not applicable in nondiversity cases, Holmberg v. Armbrecht, 327 U.S. 392 (1946), and while the otherwise applicable law in federal question cases will sometimes be state law, it will probably more often be federal. See generally Hill, "State Procedural Law in Federal Nondiversity Litigation," 69 Harv. L. Rev. 66 (1955).

137. At that point *Sibbach* was the only Enabling Act precedent, and it could have been distinguished on the grounds just outlined.

138. 326 U.S. 438 (1946) (upholding the validity of Rule 4[f]).

139. 379 U.S. 104 (1964) (upholding the validity of Rule 35 as applied against defendants).

140. 56 F.R.D. at 232–33. By way of contrast, the Committee generally deferred to state law with respect to presumptions in diversity cases, and took the position that the deference was compelled:

A series of Supreme Court decisions in diversity cases leaves no doubt of the relevance of Erie Railroad Co. v. Tompkins . . . to questions of burden of proof . . . . [The cases cited are all pre-*Hanna*.] In each instance the state rule was held to be applicable.

56 F.R.D. at 211. The two passages quoted from the Committee's Report are inconsistent with regard to whether *Hanna* so transformed *Erie* that the old precedents can be disregarded. But they are of a piece in their general view that all choices between federal and state law in diversity actions are governed by a single doctrine, whose influence is the same whether or not the point is covered by a Federal Rule.

141. The section of the opinion from which the "choice rather than necessity" notion must have been derived was that concerned with the Constitution, in particular with demonstrating its functional insignificance in light of the stronger protection extended by the relevant statutes.

142. Admittedly it would have been difficult to style *Sibbach* a new development, given that it was decided twenty-four years before *Hanna* and only three years after *Erie*, but there really was no need to come up with a new development, since the privilege cases the Committee was seeking to discredit were irrelevant.

143. Wright, "Procedural Reform: Its Limitations and Its Future," 1 Ga. L. R. 563, 572 (1967). (It should be noted that Professor Wright goes on to draw a conclusion different from mine respecting the command of the Enabling Act.) Attention might also be called to §(b) of Rule 35—only §(a) was involved in *Sibbach*—which seems similarly at war with state doctor-patient privilege rules.

144. Act of Mar. 30, 1973, Pub. L. No. 93–12, 87 Stat 9.

145. At the moment it appears most unlikely that it will. [It didn't.]

146. [If you haven't already overdosed on Erie, you might want to look at Chayes, "Some Further Last Words on Erie—The Bead Game," 87 Harv. L. Rev. 741 (1974); Ely, "Some Further Last Words on Erie—The Necklace," 87 Harv. L. Rev. 753 (1974); and/or Mishkin, "Some Further Last Words on Erie—The

Thread," 87 Harv. L. Rev. 1682 (1974). Chayes quarrels mainly with some of the ways I apply my framework to the cases; Mishkin's emendation, though also friendly, is slightly more fundamental.]

147. 23 William & Mary L. Rev. 173. This article was delivered as the Cutler Lecture at William & Mary on October 1, 1981.

148. Professor Currie never did get around to sorting out whether he meant to be talking about residence, domicile, citizenship, or "the state to which one belongs." See, e.g., B. Currie, Selected Essays on the Conflict of Laws 83, 86, 103, 141 n. 53 (1963). I don't mean to either: my critical comments apply to the entire enterprise. Concerning the approach I would think appropriate on those rare occasions when invocation of such a concept seems justified, see note 205 infra.

149. *See* Neumeier v. Kuehner, 31 N.Y.2d 121, 132–33, 286 N.E.2d 454, 460–61, 335 N.Y.S.2d 64, 73–75 (1972) (Bergan, J., dissenting); Tooker v. Lopez, 24 N.Y.2d 569, 597, 249 N.E.2d 394, 411–12, 301 N.Y.S.2d 519, 543 (1969) (Breitel, J., dissenting); Brilmayer, "Interest Analysis and the Myth of Legislative Intent," 78 Mich. L. Rev. 392 (1980); Twerski, "Neumeier v. Kuehner: Where Are the Emperor's Clothes?" 1 Hofstra L. Rev. 104 (1973).

150. There were important precursors, including my colleagues David Cavers and Paul Freund, but Currie's was certainly a more complete system of interest analysis: his work is among the most formidable corpora in all of legal theory. (As we shall be noting, Cavers' thought has evolved considerably since his early work. Freund, of course, has migrated to another field, albeit one he could hardly have supposed to be free of landmines of its own.)

151. 125 Mass. 374 (1878).

152. B. Currie, supra note 148, at 85–86.

153. 341 U.S. 609 (1951).

154. B. Currie, supra note 148, at 292.

155. 9 N.Y.2d 34, 172 N.E.2d 526, 211 N.Y.S.2d 133 (1961).

156. B. Currie, supra note 148, at 705 (footnotes omitted). Cf. D. Cavers, The Choice-of-Law Process 151 (1965) ("New York has a measure of damages for wrongful death which is designed to give full financial protection to the dependents of New Yorkers wrongfully killed." [footnote omitted]). See also B. Currie, supra note 148, at 270:

> So far as appears, Minnesota had no interest in the application of its nonforfeiture policy in the *Walsh* case. That policy was for the protection of purchasers, and the purchaser, being a resident of North Dakota, was not within the ambit of Minnesota's governmental concern.

See also, e.g., id. at 228 ("In the *Head* case the Court held, quite properly, that the state had no legitimate interest in the application of its policy to nonresidents"); id. at 417, 724 ("The guest statute expresses a policy for the protection of defendants. The defendant here, however, is not a citizen or resident of Ontario. . . .").

157. E.g., Currie, "The Disinterested Third State," 28 Law & Contemp. Prob. 754, 756 (1963); Baade, "Counter-Revolution or Alliance for Process? Reflections on Reading Cavers: The Choice-of-Law Process," 46 Tex. L. Rev. 141, 144 (1967); Kay, "Conflict of Laws: Foreign Law as Datum," 53 Cal. L. Rev. 47, 63 (1965);

Von Mehren, Book Review, 17 J. Legal Educ. 91, 92 (1964); M. Traynor, "Conflict of Laws: Professor Currie's Restrained and Enlightened Forum," 49 Cal. L. Rev. 845, 847 (1961).

158. See, e.g., von Mehren, "Special Substantive Rules for Multistate Problems: Their Role and Significance in Contemporary Choice of Law Methodology," 88 Harv. L. Rev. 347, 366 (1974).

159. See note 205 infra.

160. E.g., R. Cramton, D. Currie & H. Kay, Conflict of Laws 216–17 (3d ed. 1981) (statement of B. Currie); A. Von Mehren & D. Trautman, The Law of Multistate Problems 76–77 (1965).

161. Sedler, "Rules of Choice of Law Versus Choice-of-Law Rules: Judicial Method in Conflicts Torts Cases," 44 Tenn. L. Rev. 975, 1036 (1977).

162. Freund, "Chief Justice Stone and the Conflict of Laws," 59 Harv. L. Rev. 1210, 1216–17 (1946).

163. Baxter, "Choice of Law and the Federal System," 16 Stan. L. Rev. 1, 7–8 (1963). See also, e.g., id. at 14 ("involvement of an X borrower of the protected class is a necessary condition to the application of X law . . .").

164. Trautman, "Rule or Reason in Choice of Law: A Comment on Neumeier," 1 Vt. L. Rev. 1, 6–7 (1976). See also note 213 infra.

165. Baade, supra note 157, at 144 (footnote omitted). See also J. Martin, Conflict of Laws 256 (1978) ("Most, but not all, current commentators accept Currie's concept of and resolution of false conflict cases"). For further examples, see Kay, "Comments on Reich v. Purcell," 15 U.C.L.A. L. Rev. 584, 592 (1968) ("[T]he defendant is not a member of the class of local domiciliaries whom Missouri sought to protect by limiting damages. . . ."); D. Currie, "Comments on Reich v. Purcell," 15 U.C.L.A. L. Rev. 595, 597 (1968) (footnote omitted) ("[A]n Arizona law whose purpose, if any, was the protection of Arizona estates was simply not applicable to a dead Californian."); Ratner, "Choice of Law: Interest Analysis and Cost Contribution," 47 S. Cal. L. Rev. 817, 820–21 (1974):

> [T]he purpose of the Missouri rule, to avoid the imposition of excessive financial burdens on Missouri defendants, would not be implemented by applying the rule on behalf of a defendant not from Missouri, while the purpose of the Ohio rule, to accord full recovery to its injured residents, would be implemented by applying the rule on behalf of the Ohio plaintiffs.

See also sources cited notes 207, 208, 209 infra.

166. B. Currie, supra note 148, ch. 5.

167. Allstate Ins. Co. v. Hague, 101 S. Ct. 633 (1981); Clay v. Sun Ins. Office, Ltd., 377 U.S. 179 (1964); Richards v. United States, 369 U.S. 1, 12–13, 15 (1962); Watson v. Employers Liab. Assur. Corp., 348 U.S. 66, 70–73 (1954). See also Day & Zimmerman, Inc. v. Challoner, 423 U.S. 3 (1975) (explicated in Brilmayer, "Legitimate Interests in Multistate Problems: As Between State and Federal Law," 79 Mich. L. Rev. 201, 233 n. 127 [1981]).

168. Compare B. Currie, supra note 148, at 162 n. 99, 225–27, 485, 496, 510, 540, 612, with New York Life Ins. Co. v. Head, 234 U.S. 149, 160–62 (1914). Compare also B. Currie, supra note 148, at 232–33, with Home Ins. Co. v. Dick, 281

U.S. 397, 407–8 (1930). See also, e.g., John Hancock Ins. Co. v. Yates, 299 U.S. 178 (1936); New York Life Ins. Co. v. Dodge, 246 U.S. 357 (1918).

169. There is an initial if little noticed question whether the Equal Protection Clause—whose protection, unlike that of its sister Due Process and Privileges or Immunities Clauses, is limited to persons "within [the state's] jurisdiction"—was meant to protect out-of-staters at all. In 1898 the Court ruled that a Virginia corporation (a person for equal protection purposes) not doing sufficient business in Tennessee to be subject to process there, did not, simply by suing in Tennessee, bring itself within that state's jurisdiction sufficiently to enable it to raise an equal protection objection to a Tennessee law. Blake v McClung, 172 U.S. 239, 260–61 (1898). This holding has obviously been eroded by expanding notions of suability, and it appears to have been quietly overruled in Kentucky Fin. Corp. v. Paramount Auto Exch. Corp., 262 U.S. 544 (1923).

170. For good reason. See page 71.

171. Toomer v. Witsell, 334 U.S. 385, 395 (1948). The distribution of state largess generally has been assumed to constitute an exception to the general command of the clause. The exception is obviously troubled, if apparently necessary: in any event it does not touch the subject matter of this article.

172. Id. at 396–99.

173. 410 U.S. 179, 200 (1973).

174. Cf. Corfield v. Coryell, 6 F. Cas. 546 (C.C.E.D. Pa. 1823). But cf. J. Ely, Democracy and Distrust 198 n. 64 (1980); Simson, "Discrimination Against Nonresidents and the Privileges and Immunities Clause of Article IV," 128 U. Pa. L. Rev. 379 (1979).

175. 436 U.S. 371 (1978).

176. Id. at 388–89.

177. 437 U.S. 518 (1978).

178. B. Currie, supra note 148, at 185.

179. But cf. R. Cramton, D. Currie & H. Kay, supra note 160, at 502–7.

180. B. Currie, supra note 148, chs. 10 & 11. The latter is technically about equal protection, but the authors did not significantly distinguish the two attacks: both articles are about the constitutionality of defining protective interests as running only in favor of locals.

181. See, e.g., id. at 504–5. See also D. Cavers, supra note 156, at 200.

182. See, e.g., B. Currie, supra note 148, at 495, 498, 508.

183. Id. at 568 n.174, 572.

184. See Currie, supra note 157.

185. Despite its rather flagrant "locals-first" attitude, this does not seem to raise any (large c) *constitutional* problems that more "balanced" brands of interest analysis do not. When the forum resolves a true conflict by applying its own law, the foreign party loses, but he obviously would have lost even if he had been local: he therefore is not being discriminated against because he is an out-of-stater. Now it is true that if his opponent had been from the same state he was from, the conflict would probably have been denominated false and he would have won (under his home state's law): the basis on which he is being discriminated against can thus he characterized as the residence of his *opponent*, specifically the fact that his opponent

does not come from the same state he does. Whether that should count as a denial of equal protection—it obviously would have to trigger special scrutiny to do so— drives us straight to the general question under discussion, one with equal implications for non-Currian brands of interest analysis, whether it is permissible to make choice-of-law determinations turn on the residences of the parties.

186. [As of 1996, several states have pitched the welfare benefits of new residents to what they were receiving in the state from which they moved. Such statutes seem inconsistent with Shapiro v. Thompson, 394 U.S. 618 (1969), and as of this writing no court to my knowledge has upheld one. At all events such statutes involve a discrimination between old residents and new residents (which receives strict scrutiny under the Equal Protection Clause because it burdens the right to relocate)—the theory of these new statutes seems to be that because *some* welfare benefits are provided new residents there is not the required "penalty"—not the sort of discrimination between residents and nonresidents that is the subject of, and is generally absolutely barred by, the Privileges and Immunities Clause. (Although, to complicate matters still further, we have noted that state "largess," such as welfare, generally is not held subject to the latter clause, note 171 supra. As noted the cases under discussion in this piece do not involve such largess.)]

187. 420 U.S. 656 (1975).

188. At first blush it might seem that a choice-of-law rule geared to the parties' *common* domicile would be immune to *Austin*. That is obviously a possible outcome, but not, I think, the most logical. Assume that the rule in question is one I rather like, see page 85, that the damage ceiling rule of the common domicile should apply, and assume further that the plaintiff is a resident of the forum, which has a damage ceiling so low that any defendant would like to take advantage of it. A local defendant obviously will be able to under my proposed rule. A defendant from a state without a damage ceiling *probably* won't be, depending on what the rest of our choice-of-law rules look like (and on some facts I haven't specified). Assume in any event he won't be: obviously there will be some such cases. This defendant plainly is in a position to complain that he is being denied the benefit of a local protection because he isn't local: someone exactly like him in every respect except that he was local would be protected. If, as *Austin* seems to hold, it is no answer to his claim to note that his home state does not protect him, it appears that he has been treated unconstitutionally even though the choice-of-law rule that victimized him was geared to common domicile.

189. Cf. Pennsylvania v. New Jersey, 426 U.S. 660 (1976). [It still hasn't.]

190. 101 S.Ct. 633 (1981).

191. The plurality mentioned three contacts supporting the application of Minnesota law: that the deceased worked there, that the defendant insurance company does business there, and that the plaintiff widow now lives there. It "expressed no view" on whether the first two contacts without the third would have been sufficient, id. at 644 n. 29, and noted as well that "respondent's bona fide residence in Minnesota was not the sole contact Minnesota had with this litigation." Id. at 643. This latter statement might suggest a doubt about the sufficiency of the third contact standing alone, were it not for the fact that it was made in the context of, and seems to be limited by, an argument over whether residency acquired after the accident (as the widow's was) should be sufficient.

In context, therefore, I take the plurality to have implied that residency predating the accident and continuing to the present would have been sufficient to support the application of favorable local law. See also note 193 infra. Actually, that conclusion is not ultimately critical: if it is unconstitutional to favor residents over nonresidents it should be equally unconstitutional to make local residence "one of the reasons" for favoring someone. For it is in the nature of a balance that any one factor can tip it: if local residence can be considered positively, some out-of-staters will lose who would have won had they been locals. (This is one reason the frequently articulated position on affirmative action that one "doesn't mind blackness being a factor just so it isn't the only factor" is gibberish: try substituting "whiteness" for "blackness." [See also page 267.]) But see A. von Mehren & D. Trautman, supra note 160, at 162–63 n. 66 ("Recognition of this kind of community concern [because 'one of the members of its community is involved'] might be superficially seem analogous or in some way related to Professor Currie's view . . . . It may be true . . . that the kind of concern we are discussing can tip the scales in a case of true conflict, but this fact should not in any way be confused with Professor Currie's analysis.")

192. *See* Watson v. Employers Liab. Assur. Corp., 348 U.S. 66, 72 (1954); Home Ins. Co. v. Dick, 281 U.S. 397, 408 (1930). Neither of these says that local residence on the part of the party to be benefited is *sufficient* either. "No court has squarely held that the sole factor of plaintiff's domicile . . . is enough to support application of forum law for the purpose of imposing liability upon a nonresident defendant not otherwise liable." Kay, "The Use of Comparative Impairment to Resolve True Conflicts: An Evaluation of the California Experience," 68 Cal. L. Rev. 577, 597 (1980) (footnote omitted). In fact it is *Hague* (decided after the publication of Professor Kay's article) that comes closest to enunciating such a proposition. (Interestingly, Professor Brilmayer's recent article on *Hague* seems to assume that the local residence of the party to be benefited is a contact that is sufficient constitutionally to support the application of local law, Brilmayer, supra note 167, at 231, even though, at least on my understanding of her theory, it probably shouldn't be. The consistency of such an assumption, which I agree the Court does seem to make, with its recent decisions respecting adjudicatory jurisdiction also seems problematic. See Silberman, "Can the State of Minnesota Bind the Nation? Federal Choice of Law Constraints After Allstate Insurance Co. v. Hague," 10 Hofstra L. Rev. 103 [1981].)

193. 101 S. Ct. at 643–44. The plurality and the dissenters disagreed over whether it was proper to take this into account given that the plaintiff had moved to the state after the accident. But seven of the eight justices participating agreed that her local residence would have been a relevant (and constitutionally legitimate) contact had she lived there all along. (The eighth was Justice Stevens, who concurred in upholding Minnesota's application of local law but whose precise position on the issue under discussion seems unclear.)

194. J. Ely, supra note 174, at 83.

195. The connection is made at 436 U.S. at 383.

196. See, e.g., Nadelmann, "Some Historical Notes on the Doctrinal Sources of American Conflicts Law," in Ius et Lex—Festgabe zum 70. Geburtstag von Max Gutzwiller 263 (1959), cf. Emory v. Grenough, 3 U.S. (3 Dall.) 369, 370 (1797); note 242 infra.

197. The "right to travel" cases certainly contain no suggestion that what would otherwise be violations of that right can be cured by giving new residents whatever benefits they were receiving in the state they just moved from. [But cf. note 186 supra.] And indeed that is as it should be, as the case is entirely different. The local political process is the only one to which the new resident, having moved, can turn. The Court's point, I guess, was that new residents—or at least (and this helps justify the Court's recent twists more powerfully than its ill-fitting talk of "penalties") new residents of the economic class that needs welfare benefits—are a "group" that seems unusually unable to influence that process. In any event new residents, unlike visitors, do not have another recourse even in theory. Of course it is true that while the recent cases have concerned new residents and thus what is essentially a right to relocate, older cases establish that [the right to travel] is also a right to pass through, to traverse. E.g., Crandall v. Nevada, 73 U.S. (6 Wall.) 35 (1868). See also J. Ely, supra note 174, at 177–79. It is difficult to suppose, however, that the Court would find *that* right unduly burdened by a choice-of-law rule giving the traveler the benefit of his or her home state's law.

198. Note, "Products Liability and the Choice of Law," 78 Harv. L. Rev. 1452, 1465–66 (1965) (footnote omitted). See also, e.g., D. Cavers, supra note 156, at 135–36; Kahn-Freund, Book Review, 76 Harv. L. Rev. 223, 227–28 (1962).

199. Indeed, those not so hopelessly mired in legal positivism as I am often accused of being would do well to consult their Bibles, in particular Leviticus 24:22: "Ye shall have one manner of law, as well for the stranger, as for one of your own country: for I *am* the LORD your God."

200. E.g., McDougal, "Comprehensive Interest Analysis Versus Reformulated Governmental Interest Analysis: An Appraisal in the Context of Choice-of-Law Problems Concerning Contributory and Comparative Negligence," 26 U.C.L.A. L. Rev. 439, 468 n. 142 (1979), and passages from B. Currie, supra note 148, quoted therein; Kay, supra note 165, at 592; Babcock v. Jackson, 12 N.Y.2d 473, 483, 191 N.E.2d 279, 284, 240 N.Y.S.2d 743, 750–51 (1963).

201. Brilmayer, supra note 149. Borrowing statutes do sometimes make the statute of limitations longer for local plaintiffs. However, Professor Brilmayer's distinguishing explanation, in terms of the avoidance of interstate forum shopping, seems valid. Id. at 427.

202. In fact, to prefigure somewhat the ensuing discussion, I can see no reason to suppose that to the extent legislators *are* focusing particularly on the fortunes of local people, they must be thinking solely in terms of vindicating the litigative efforts of such people—ensuring them recoveries on the one hand, protecting them from unjustifiable liability on the other. Why is it not sensible to assume that legislators are just as concerned with the "flip sides" of these interests, with ensuring on the one hand that the people they have in mind (by hypothesis, locals) make recompense when they have wronged others, and on the other hand that they not be afforded recoveries they do not deserve?

203. E.g., B. Currie, supra note 148, at 228, 420, 621.

204. E.g., id. at 210 n. 84, 294 n. 51, 488 n. 148, 495 n. 172.

205. It has long been recognized in the literature, as it was to a degree by Currie himself, that his devices of "rational altruism" and "restraint and enlightenment in the definition of interests" provided ways of ignoring or submerging potentially

competing state interests and thereby alchemizing true conflicts into "false" ones. E.g., D. Cavers, supra note 156, at 75; B. Currie, supra note 148, at 604–05; Currie, supra note 157, at 763. For a graphic demonstration, compare B. Currie, supra note 148, at 167, with Currie, supra note 157, at 759.

Currie also was not above simply dismissing apparent interests as either too attenuated to merit consideration—see, e.g., B. Currie, supra note 148, at 277, 343, 497–98, 540 n. 63, 701–2; see also Tooker v. Lopez, 24 N.Y.2d 569, 575, 249 N.E.2d 394, 397–98, 301 N.Y.S.2d 519, 523–24 (1969)—or "illegitimate" (though not among the set of interests that have been declared constitutionally impermissible). E.g., B. Currie, supra note 148, at 322. See also D. Currie, "Suitcase Divorce in the Conflict of Laws: Simons, Rosensteil, and Borax," 34 U. Chi. L. Rev. 26, 45–46 (1966); Kay, supra note 165, at 587–89; Trautman, supra note 164, at 7–8 (policy discounted because not "wise and just").

Currie also sometimes quite candidly resorted to "fictions," see B. Currie, supra note 148, at 590—such as the fiction that all the deceased's dependent relatives live where he lived at the time of his death, id. at 145–46, 292–93; see also, e.g., D. Currie, supra note 165, at 600, and the fiction that the insurance company (and thus its states of incorporation and/or principal business) have no interest in the application of a liability-limiting rule. B. Currie, supra note 148, at 143 n. 61. (Obviously insurance companies are not able to pass all the costs on, as they lobby very hard for such rules.) In each case, however, it should be noted that Currie (and on his premises this only compounds the sin) effectively retained discretion to look behind the fiction to the actual interests when it seemed desirable to do so. Id. at 160, 210, 292–93.

Somewhat more subtle devices for accomplishing the same result, i.e., making interests disappear, were (and sometimes are) invoked, however. For example, and this relates closely to the uses of "fiction" just alluded to, there is always a question whether to "conventionalize" a case—that is, to analyze it in terms of the interests that might, or might ordinarily, be implicated by the sort of situation at bar—or rather to look at the particular facts more closely and ask whether the interest in question in fact is implicated in this very case. Compare Carroll v. Lanza, 349 U.S. 408, 413 (1955) (Douglas, J., for the Court) with id. at 420 (Frankfurter, J., dissenting). The former course is obviously preferable in terms of administrability, but the latter can sometimes turn an apparent conflict "false." Professor Currie appears to have left himself discretion to go either way. B. Currie, supra note 148, at 371. But see Brilmayer, supra note 149, at 412–14.

Apparent interests also can be eliminated by the questionable premise that no more than one jurisdiction can have a "homelike" interest in the welfare of a given litigant. Compare B. Currie, supra note 148, at 232, with Record at 10, Home Ins. Co. v. Dick, 281 U.S. 397 (1930). For other examples, see Reich v. Purcell, 67 Cal. 2d 551, 555–56, 432 P.2d 727, 730–31, 63 Cal. Rptr. 31, 34–35 (1967); M. Traynor, "Conflict of Laws: Professor Currie's Restrained and Enlightened Forum," 49 Cal. L. Rev. 845, 850–51 (1961). Cf. Brilmayer, supra note 167, at 231. But see Cavers, "Habitual Residence: A Useful Concept?" 21 Am.U. L. Rev. 475, 482–84 (1972). (In my opinion any rule geared to the parties' common domicile, see, e.g., page 86, should be applied with a constant recognition that domicile, residence, and home are neither clear nor necessarily unitary concepts, and that consequently where a plausible argument can be mounted that more than one jurisdiction has a "homelike" interest in one or both of the parties—and the laws of the "homelike" jurisdictions differ on the question at issue—recourse should probably be had to another rule, not geared to domicile.)

Currie yielded himself further discretion by condemning "unprincipled eclecticism," by which condemnation he meant that interest analysis should not be employed issue-by-issue in a way that ended up generating a result that would not be generated by the domestic law of at least one of the states involved. He didn't quite mean this, though, as is evidenced by his approval of Scheer v. Rockne Motors Corp., 68 F.2d 942 (2d Cir. 1934), insulating from liability a New York bailor whose automobile was taken to Ontario, where by virtue of the bailee's negligence it injured the plaintiff under circumstances where the bailor would have been liable had the case been wholly domestic to either New York or Ontario. D. Cavers, supra note 156, at 39 (written by Currie, id. at 17). The reasons he distinguished *Scheer* seem opaque to me, as they did to Professor Cavers. Id. at 40–43.

Still further play in the true faith seems to have been created by Professor Kay's recent declaration that "California's desire to compensate [resident] tort victims is limited by its recognition that liability should be imposed only upon those whom it regards as tortfeasors"—which may mean, she goes on to suggest, that it may not extend to cases where the defendant is from elsewhere and the tort took place outside California! Kay supra note 192, at 597. That sounds suspiciously territorial.

206. Pages 62, 64–65.

207. B. Currie, supra note 148, at 63. "Such a state would not be expected to apply its law to any case in which the creditor is a local resident and the married woman a foreigner . . . ." *Id.* at 89.

So far as appears, Minnesota had no interest in the application of its nonforfeiture policy in the Walsh case. That policy was for the protection of purchasers, and the purchaser, being a resident of North Dakota [though the vendor was from Minnesota], was not within the ambit of Minnesota's governmental concern.

Id. at 270.

208. Weintraub, "A Method for Solving Conflict Problems—Torts," 48 Cornell L. Q. 215, 231 (1963).

209. Cavers, "The Conditional Seller's Remedies and the Choice-of-Law Process—Some Notes on Shanahan," 35 N.Y.U. L. Rev. 1126, 1140 (1960). (But cf. D. Cavers, supra note 156, at 144, suggesting a change in view.) See also, e.g., Hurtado v. Superior Court, 11 Cal. 3d 574, 581, 522 P.2d 666, 670, 114 Cal. Rptr. 106, 110 (1974) ("Since it is the plaintiffs and not the defendants who are the Mexican residents in this case, Mexico has no interest in applying its limitation of damages—Mexico has no defendant residents to protect and has no interest in denying full recovery to its residents injured by non-Mexican defendants."); von Mehren, "Choice of Law and the Problem of Justice," 41 Law & Contemp. Prob. 27, 35 (1977) ("From New York's perspective, the New York defendant's claim is stronger than that of the Ontario plaintiff as no New York interest in compensating a resident or his estate [under its host liability rule] is present"); Ratner, supra note 165, at 830 (emphasis deleted) ("Because the . . . Mexican plaintiffs are not members of the [class that the] California [unlimited] recovery rules are designed to

benefit (i.e., injured residents) . . . California has [no] interest in the application of its recovery rule to resolve the case [against a California defendant]"); Sedler, "The Contracts Provisions of the Restatement (Second): An Analysis and a Critique," 72 Colum. L. Rev. 279, 305 (1972) ("New Jersey, in contrast, had no interest in denying protection to a New Jersey corporation against a New Yorker broker").

210. See, e.g., Gordon v. Parker, 83 F. Supp. 40, 42 (D. Mass. 1949); Alaska Packers Ass'n v. Industrial Accident Comm'n, 1 Cal. 2d 250, 258, 34 P.2d 716, 724 (1934), aff'd, 294 U.S. 532 (1935); Williams, "The Aims of the Law of Tort," 4 Current Legal Prob. 137, 140 (1951).

211. Professor Currie was unusually myopic regarding such "flip side" interests. For example, having noted that wrongful-death statutes generally are modeled on Lord Campbell's Act, whose preamble had recited that "it is oftentimes right and expedient that the Wrongdoer in such Case should be answerable in Damages for the Injury so caused by him," Currie went on to opine that the application of such a statute should be reserved for situations where the *plaintiff* is a local resident. B. Currie, supra note 148, at 292. He was equally blind to flip side interests (this time in denying certain classes of plaintiffs recovery) where defenses were concerned. For a graphic example, compare id. at 399, 405, with id. at 506.

212. Indeed, the Supreme Court has come close to indicating that the local residence of the defendant is enough to give a state jurisdiction to prosecute him or her for an act committed elsewhere. Skiriotes v. Florida, 313 U.S. 69, 76–77 (1941). Of course this proposition does not have to be right for the point in the text to be.

213. This sort of determination in my opinion can validly be made only categorically, not state by state. I therefore think Professors von Mehren and Trautman are engaging in wishful thinking (again in the direction of alchemizing genuine conflicts into false ones) when they posit that where a given rule can plausibly be supported by two or more separate rationales, it will be possible, if a court will only think about it hard enough, to determine that whereas state *A* passed the rule for two entirely compatible reasons, *m* and *n*, state *B* passed the selfsame rule only for reason *m* and not for reason *n*. Von Mehren, supra note 158, at 369; Trautman, supra note 164, at 6–7. See also Brilmayer, supra note 149, at 399–400. But see Ely, "Legislative and Administrative Motivation in Constitutional Law," 79 Yale L. J. 1205, 1213–14 (1970).

214. The definitions are indifferent to the number of states whose law is potentially applicable. (The set of all possible two-party cases will be exhausted, no matter how many states are involved, by the subsets of cases (a) where the laws of the parties' home states are identical, and (b) where they are not. Subset (a) is the "common domicile" category. Subset (b) will be exhausted by the "head-on" and "criss-cross" categories.) It also seems clear that the addition of further parties would complicate the analysis but not affect the conclusions. Of course the likely presence of "interests" geared not to which party wins or loses, but rather to more general behavior-shaping or process-protecting concerns, significantly multiplies the number of possible configurations of interests. However, that realization only serves to underscore my ultimate point, that interest analysis will not on full and candid application be able to fulfill its crucial boast by identifying significant numbers of false or inconsequential conflicts.

215. Twerski, supra note 149, at 108 (footnote omitted).

216. 31 N.Y.2d 121, 286 N.E.2d 454, 335 N.Y.S.2d 64 (1972).

217. Sedler, "Interstate Accidents and the Unprovided for Case: Reflections on Neumeier v. Kuehner," 1 Hofstra L. Rev. 125, 137–38 (1973) (footnotes omitted). See also, e.g., B. Currie, supra note 148, at 90–91.

218. See also Twerski, supra note 149, at 109; cf. D. Cavers, supra note 156, at 39 ("Judge" Currie, labeling a state's policy of deterrence "non-existent" in cases where state law provides an exemption); B. Currie, supra note 148, at 152 (similar reaction). Rare defenses may fit the account of spendthrift statutes suggested at page 75 (that there may be an "interest" in shielding the defendant but none in thwarting the plaintiff.) But that surely isn't *Neumeier*—the thwarting of ungrateful guests was a rationale too often articulated during the era guest statutes were being enacted to be wished away in order to simplify our conflicts analyses—and in fact it is very few cases indeed. The "shared policy" notion thus cannot constitute a general or even frequent answer to the criss-cross case, though on rare occasions it might make sense. At all events, the burden must surely lie heavily on one who asserts that a given state in enacting a given defense was interested only in shielding defendants and not in thwarting plaintiffs.

219. See also R. Weintraub, Commentary on the Conflict of Laws 320 (2d ed. 1980).

220. Cf. note 218 supra. He rejected three other possible solutions. See generally B. Currie, supra note 148, at 152–56.

221. Id. at 156, 189 n. 3.

222. Id. at 120–21. See also id. at 609, 721.

223. E.g., id. at 488–89; D. Cavers, supra note 156, at 33 ("Judge" Currie).

224. To the extent the assumption is unrealistic, and I think it is, that serves more forcefully to underscore my broader point that there will be few real cases in which the locals-only premise will make a difference. Hurtado v. Superior Court, 11 Cal. 3d 574, 522 P.2d 666, 114 Cal. Rptr. 106 (1974), is a case the court described as involving much the configuration I am describing here, though the behavior-shaping interest in that case seems if anything more questionable than that in our hypothetical.

225. E.g., R. Weintraub, supra note 219, at 352; Comment, "False Conflicts," 55 Cal. L. Rev. 74, 77 (1967).

226. See page 79.

227. Of course guest statutes are in decreasing favor, which may unconsciously disincline an observer to suppose any state is ever interested in applying one.

228. At least if "conventionalizing" is permitted. See note 205. (The encouragement of carpooling cuts both ways: to the extent there is any effect at all, a guest statute will encourage hosts but discourage guests from entering into such arrangements.)

229. It is, however, much of the point of this article that this redefinition will not render interest analysis any more useful than it now is respecting head-ons and criss-crosses. See page 84.

230. The latter may be subject to a rare exception for situations of the "spendthrift statute" configuration. See page 75.

231. I am obviously no longer assuming arguendo that a rule of host liability contributes significantly to the level of driving safety within a state.

232. Where the parties are from two states, each with a host liability rule, one will be interested in "its" guest's recovery, the other in "its" host's paying his fair way.

233. The parenthetical expression, of course, is one of the usual canons of interest analysis, but it turns out it may be without great functional significance. See note 242 infra.

234. This, at least, has been the hypothesis for some pages. If *Austin v. New Hampshire* is accepted as written, *neither* of the approaches indicated is constitutional. See note 188 supra.

235. See Neumeier v. Kuehner, 31 N.Y.2d 121, 132, 286 N.E.2d 454, 460, 335 N.Y.2d 64, 73 (1972) (Bergan, J., dissenting); Twerski, "Enlightened Territorialism and Professor Cavers—The Pennsylvania Method," 9 Duq. L. Rev. 373, 384–85 (1972).

236. Criss-crosses where one (and only one) of the states has a litigant-independent interest *are* rendered more manageable by the locals-only premise, though I have argued that the premise is particularly unattractive in that context. See pages 79–80.

237. Reese, "Choice of Law: Rules or Approach," 57 Cornell L. Q. 315, 322 (1972). See also B. Cardozo, The Paradoxes of Legal Science 67 (1928). Thus even the "purest" of interest analysts has smuggled some rules into his system, as for example by simply indicating the system's inapplicability to certain problems or by the question-begging concept of foreign law as "datum." For examples of the former technique, see Currie, "Comment on Babcock v. Jackson," 63 Colum. L. Rev. 1233, 1241–42 (1963); Currie, Book Review, 1964 Duke L. J. 424, 427 (real property problems exempted from interest analysis). On the latter, see B. Currie, supra note 148, at 58–74.

238. Rheinstein, "How to Review a Festschrift," 11 Am. J. Comp. L. 632, 660 (1962).

239. Reese, supra note 237, at 326–27 (footnote omitted).

240. The case where the situs has a host liability rule and a third party defendant is attempting to implead the host probably should be distinguished, however. Cf. Weintraub, "Comments on Reich v. Purcell," 15 U.C.L.A. L. Rev. 556, 560 (1968).

241. Here too there is a process-protecting interest (in minimizing appellate review and retrial occasioned by excessive jury verdicts), which to me at least seems somewhat stronger than that present in the guest statute situation.

In cases where the law of the parties' home states differs and all that is at stake is the amount of recovery—as it would be in a damage ceiling dispute—the suggestion that the difference be split, e.g., M. Traynor, supra note 157, at 866; von Mehren, supra note 158, at 366–67, becomes tempting. I confess I have trouble rendering the suggestion even coherent in the more common situation, where the disagreement is over whether there should be recovery at all. Unfortunately, even cases that are "simply" about the amount of recovery also resist holding still for splitting. What does one do, for example, when the laws of the parties' home states differ and the forum (which may or may not be one of the two residences) has a/the comparatively low damage ceiling? Or where the situs has a/the comparatively high one, or none? I end up thinking that even where "all" that is in issue is the amount, the only workable (and legitimate) alternatives where the law of the parties' homes differs are references to either the law of the forum or that of the situs.

242. A common rule is that referring intestate distribution of movables to the law of the decedent's domicile at the time of his death. This one is different, of course, not simply in that it seeks to approximate the decedent's likely intent or expectation, but also in that it is not geared to the residence of any of the *parties*: it thus does not offend as "personal law."

The rule has still another feature—that it takes the law referred to "either way" and not simply if it favors one or another party, as do the standard canons of interest analysis. It is tempting to generalize this feature and hold that there is nothing wrong with gearing a choice-of-law rule to the residence of a particular party (perhaps "the party whose capacity is in issue," perhaps even "the plaintiff") so long as one takes the law "either way." I didn't pick either of those parenthetical examples at random: it has been a quite frequent suggestion that contractual capacity be determined by the law of the residence of the party in question, and though it may be wrapped in mythical talk of "marital" domicile, realistically the widespread choice-of-law rule regarding divorce is that the law of the plaintiff's domicile governs. But cf. Alton v. Alton, 207 F.2d 667, 684–85 (3d Cir. 1953) (Hastie, J., dissenting), vacated as moot, 347 U.S. 610 (1954).

In 1960 Professors Currie and Kay observed of choice-of-law rules geared to the law of the domicile of one party that "it has apparently never occurred to anyone to suggest seriously that it is invidious thus to treat persons differently because they have their homes in different states." B. Currie, supra note 148, at 445 (footnote omitted). They were right: the omission was an odd one for critics of their system. It is an omission I would like now to remedy.

We have for some pages been operating on assumptions that imply that such rules do not violate the judicially enforceable or "large c" Constitution. In the divorce situation, for example, all plaintiffs will be accorded the benefits or burdens of their home states' law. Thus on our present assumptions there is no discrimination among plaintiffs on the basis of residence that offends the Privileges and Immunities Clause. See pages 71–72. Of course defendants as a class are not accorded such treatment. But even leaving aside the fact that the "treatment" will sometimes be a benefit and sometimes be a burden—and I think it is well to leave it aside, since as a practical matter at least divorce plaintiffs have substantial control over their "residences" for purpose of divorce suits and thus over what law will govern—there is nothing of which I am aware that makes it unconstitutional to discriminate quite systematically in favor of plaintiffs and against defendants. Many statutes and common law rules are adopted with precisely that goal; choice-of-law rules should not be subject to more stringent equal protection requirements in this regard. If, however, *Austin* is right as written, it is hard to see how such rules can survive, that is, how a forum with a particular protective rule can be permitted to deny its benefit to any out-of-stater who notes that if he were a local he would be entitled to it.

I don't in general think such rules are advisable, since they so flagrantly ignore the interest of the home state of the *other* party—the party contracting with the person now claiming incapacity in the one case, the defendant in the divorce case—and very likely of other states as well. Obviously not everyone is convinced on that score, however, so the in-between question must be faced, whether such rules violate our "small c" constitution, or at least common sense, in ways analogous to those I have suggested the usual canons of interest analysis do. I fear it's a mixed and confusing bag. From a "macro" perspective choice-of-law rules of this sort *do* recognize "flip side" interests: that is, they recognize not only the interests of states with one sort of rule in promoting litigative victories for their residents, but also the interests of states with the opposite sort of rule in holding their residents to account.

Perhaps that should settle the matter: I confess I have swings of mood on the subject. Perhaps, however, this system-wide perspective is not the appropriate one from which to evaluate the sorts of discrimination in which various states should be permitted to engage. The *attitude* of ordinary interest analysis canons may be different, in that states are held to be interested only in advantaging their own and not in holding them to account. *In practice*, however, the results will probably—there are too many versions of interest analysis to be more definitive—not come out very differently system-wide. On an interest analysis approach, if the party in question is from a state whose rule protects him, that state at the very least will be held to be interested and he may very well win (though he may not, if another state's interest is found to predominate). If on the other hand he's from a state whose rule doesn't protect him, that state won't be interested (at least not on that score) and he may well lose (though he may not). Cf. B. Currie, supra note 148, at 113.

Assume a state has a choice-of-law rule of the sort under discussion, specifically that it decides questions of contractual capacity by the law of the state of residence of the party whose capacity is in issue. Assume further—it will work the same the other way around—that it has what is in context the defendant-protecting rule of contractual capacity. On what occasions will this state apply its defendant-favoring rule? The answer is a familiar one: whenever the defendant is local (or comes, and here the parallel to interest analysis is extended, from another state with the same rule).

From this "micro" perspective we can see clearly this state's failure to recognize "flip side" interests: in being instructed by its choice-of-law rule to apply its domestic law only when the party whose capacity is in issue is local, this state is in effect instructed to vindicate only its interest in protecting local defendants, and to renounce any interest in thwarting those local plaintiffs who are seeking to collect from (nonlocal) persons in the class its domestic lawmaking authorities have judged incompetent to contract. (Of course *other* states, with less restrictive capacity rules, are granted by such a choice-of-law rule an interest in *dis*advantaging some of their own—specifically, defendants. But by reasoning symmetrical to that just traversed, those other states are granted no interest in vindicating the interests of those among their own locked in litigation with out-of-staters hiding behind capacity rules their lawmakers have judged too protective.)

Our first state has what amounts to a "protect locals only" policy, or, more accurately, a "protect only those whose local law protects them" policy. If that is a sort of discrimination our "small c" constitution, or at least common sense, ought to prohibit, and I have argued it is, it does not seem like an answer to note that other states have a "thwart locals only" policy. Indeed, as I suggested in the last parenthetical, that may only compound the difficulty. Cf. Shelley v. Kraemer, 334 U.S. 1, 22 (1948) ["Equal protection of the laws is not achieved through the indiscriminate imposition of inequalities"].

243. Twerski, supra note 149, at 118 (commenting on Neumeier v. Kuehner, 31 N.Y.2d 121, 286 N.13.2d 464, 335 N.Y.S.2d 64 [1972]).

244. See generally D. Cavers, supra note 156, ch. VI. Professor Cavers would not apply the law of the common domicile when the relation between the parties is "seated" elsewhere. For a particularly attractive example from Cavers' perspective, see id. at 309. Naturally such authority must exert a pull, but for now at least I'm inclined to stick to my guns. The seat of the relationship seems to speak most directly to the parties' expectations, which have little relevance to choice of law in tort, and however little actual input into their home state's political processes the parties in fact have had, they lack even that theoretical influence in other states. Whether or not one actually ends up adopting choice-of-law rules geared to the parties' common domicile—and I've actually only suggested a couple—is not the main point of this article, however. What I have wished primarily to demonstrate is that such rules are legitimate in ways an approach geared to the protection of the local party is not.

245. 107 U.C.L.A. L. Rev. 107.

246. See Cohen, "State Law in Equality Clothing: A Comment on Allegheny Pittsburgh Coal Company v. County Commission," 38 U.C.L.A. L. Rev. 87 (1990).

247. Allegheny Pittsburgh Coal Co. v. County Comm'n, 488 U.S. 336 (1989).

248. 316 U.S. 535 (1942).

249. J. Ely, Democracy and Distrust: A Theory of Judicial Review 245–46 n. 38 (1980); see also, e.g., Zobel v. Williams, 457 U.S. 55, 61–63 (1982); Shapiro v. Thompson, 394 U.S. 618, 632–33 (1969); J. Ely, supra, at 246 n. 38:

> Considered in the context of the Court's earlier decision in Roe v. Wade, 410 U.S. 113 (1973), the case of Maher v. Roe, 432 U.S. 464 (1977), upholding the exclusion of abortions from the class of operations [for] which poor people are statutorily entitled to funding, is susceptible to a similar analysis. The goal in terms of which the Court upheld this legislative choice, that of discouraging abortions, is one that it had resoundingly declared unconstitutional four years earlier in *Roe*. That left only the goal of saving the taxpayers' money, to which discouraging abortions among poor people arguably does not relate even rationally. (Of course, under *Roe*, the law should have been subjected to scrutiny even stricter than this.) Cf . . . United States v. Brown, 381 U.S. 437 (1965) (direct or "tautological" defense uninvocable due to unconstitutionality under First Amendment; indirect or "empirical" defense to which government thus forced to resort held bill of attainder).

250. Cf. Linde, "Due Process of Lawmaking," 55 Neb. L. Rev. 197, 229 (1976). Considerations of this sort may account for Justice Douglas's otherwise mysterious failure in his Court opinion in Railway Express Agency, Inc. v. New York, 336 U.S. 106 (1949), even to discuss Justice Jackson's "doing for hire may have a different moral status from doing for free" rationale, id. at 115–17, and to strain instead for an unintelligible safety rationale to uphold the distinction in issue. Id. at 109–10. (That is, he may have felt that as a matter of New York law, the pursuit of Jackson's moral theory would have been ultra vires for the New York City police commissioner, who promulgated the regulation in issue.) Sometimes, of course, the Court

gives neither of these justifications for excluding certain goals from the calculus, but achieves that result instead by main force, simply announcing that "in this context all distinctions must be justified by reference to goal x." See, e.g., City of Richmond v. J. A. Croson Co., 488 U.S. 469 (1989) (assuming, without a pretense of justification, that the only goal in terms of which state affirmative action programs can be justified is the remedying of past discrimination); Harper v. Virginia Bd. of Elections, 383 U.S. 663, 668 (1966) ("[w]ealth . . . is not relevant to one's ability to participate intelligently in the electoral process").

251. These two goals can operate in tandem. I live, for example, in a hilly, "rural" community just minutes from more conventional upscale suburbs. Forty years ago people could easily buy houses there for less than $20,000. (And, as is evident from the odd Studebaker rusting away in the front yard and the packs of marauding mangehounds, a number of this generation of purchasers still live there.) Today it costs about a half million dollars to buy a house in the neighborhood. Were the long-term residents forced to pay taxes geared to current market value, they might not be able to afford them, and thus could be forced to sell and move to a less desirable neighborhood, where they could afford both the purchase price of a house and the taxes on it. (I am aware that in theory, and probably sometimes in practice as well, such people could borrow against the increased asset value and invest the money thus derived in an account from which they could pay their taxes. But such transactions are far from costless, either psychologically— perhaps particularly for the class of people we are talking about here—or for that matter even financially.) As Professor Cohen points out, the fairness of forcing this result is at least debatable. (The Studebakers argue one way for me, the fact that my own dog seems to have assumed command of one of the more swashbuckling local gangs, the other.) [More than one reader—two, actually—have inquired whether this is the same dog that nearly became Secretary of Agriculture in *Democracy and Distrust*. It isn't, which may have it somewhat backwards, as the cabinet candidate (Buffo) was much bigger, the juvenile delinquent (Portland) a good deal smarter. Or maybe . . .]

252. But see Glennon, "Taxation and Equal Protection," 58 Geo. Wash. L. Rev. 261, 262 (1990) ("The implications [of *Allegheny*] are ominous indeed."); Cohen, supra note 246.

253. In re 1975 Tax Assessments Against Oneida Coal Co., 360 S.E.2d 560, 564–65 (1987), rev'd sub nom. Allegheny Pittsburgh Coal Co. v. County Comm'n, 109 S. Ct. 633 (1989).

254. In fact, this had been the West Virginia trial court's holding and was reversed by the state supreme court. Id. at 563.

255. I actually agree with Professor Cohen's recommendation that the rationality test be abandoned. In *Democracy and Distrust* I argued that it is not justifiable either in constitutional theory ("unless there is special reason to distrust the democratic process in a given case, substantive review of its output, no matter how 'weak,' is not justified,") or as a means of smoking out unconstitutional motives ("[w]here there exists no licit purpose to which the classification in issue relates even rationally . . . a direct inference of unconstitutional motivation will probably be virtually inevitable . . ."). J. Ely, supra note 249, at 251 n. 69. Thus, I concluded, the rationality test is likely to remain a dangerous loaded weapon ("to arm the judiciary with a

universal warrant to review for 'rationality' . . . is unavoidably to tempt judges to exercise a general and illegitimate substantive review authority"). Id.

However, I retain the feeling that "there is little chance that the rationality test in fact will be abandoned . . . ." Id. at 252 n. 69. Thus this article has assumed the validity of the rationality test, indeed granted that within the logic of that test, *Allegheny*'s finding of an equal protection violation makes perfectly good sense, but has argued nonetheless that the Supreme Court's reversal was without justification, and indeed that the Court should not review any similarly configured case in the future. I have not missed the fact that this makes the conclusion that the Equal Protection Clause is violated in such a case Pickwickian; that seems to me just as it should be.

256. Of course the Supreme Court would have jurisdiction to correct a lower *federal* court's reading of state law. However, for reasons identical to those I have suggested apply to Supreme Court review of a state decision, a federal district court confronted with an *Allegheny*-type claim—for example a section 1983 action claiming a violation of equal protection based entirely on an assertion that state law has been violated—should grant a remedy neither more nor less drastic than that which the state courts would grant. (If state law is unclear as to what the remedy should be, it would be quite sensible for courts at all levels to start from a presumption that state law tracks the federal courts' ordinary and quite sensible approach.)

257. Nor should the Court grant review to a *state* that has lost an *Allegheny*-type case below. The state court's finding of a violation of state law is binding on the Supreme Court, and surely there is nothing to *forbid* a state's granting the standard equal protection remedy placing the burden of gap-closing on the state.

Chapter 3

1. 10 Harv. Civil Rights–Civil Liberties L. Rev. 1.

2. [One thing that has not been sufficiently remarked is what a great man Telford Taylor is. Thus I do so here.]

3. Ch. 218, 57 Stat. 431, 450 (1943).

4. 328 U.S. 303 (1946).

5. R. Lovett, All Our Years 298 (1948).

6. 307 U.S. 325 (1939).

7. Indeed, Miguel v. McCarl, 291 U.S. 442, 451 (1934), had raised doubts about a district court's power to order a government official to pay salaries where the ambiguous legitimacy of the salary claim required resolution through administrative interpretation.

8. Any argument by Lovett, Watson, and Dodd that they were not sufficiently high level to count as "officers" within the meaning of this provision would undercut part of their substantive argument—that section 304 had worked an unconstitutional removal of officers of the United States. Salary suits by officers are no longer excluded from the district court's concurrent jurisdiction. See 28 U.S.C. § 1346(a)(2) (1970).

9. But see 28 U.S.C. § 347 (1940), superseded by 28 U.S.C. §§ 1254(1), 2101(e) (1970), providing for certiorari before a decision of a court of appeals. If the district court issued a declaratory judgment *against* the constitutionality of section 304, the

United States could take a direct appeal to the Supreme Court pursuant to 28 U.S.C § 349a (1940), superseded by 28 U.S.C. § 1252 (1970), inter alia.

10. See 28 U.S.C. § 380a (1940), superseded by 28 U.S.C § 2282 (1970), inter alia. [The requirement that requests to enjoin the operation of federal and state statutes be heard by a district court comprising three judges was abolished in August of 1976.]

11. See cases cited in Lovett v. United States, 66 F. Supp. 142, 146 (Ct. Cl. 1945).

12. See United States v. Vulte, 233 U.S. 509 (1914); United States v. Langston, 118 U.S. 389 (1886).

13. The Court of Claims was initially set up in 1855 as an advisory body to Congress to evaluate money claims against the United States. Over the decades it came to look more like a court. Its judgments were routinely paid out of a fund that Congress regularly appropriated for such payment. Nevertheless, each judgment to be paid was specifically set out in the yearly appropriations bill. At the time of the Lovett litigation, Congress had refused to pay perhaps twenty Court of Claims judgments. See Note, "The Court of Claims: Judicial Power and Congressional Review," 46 Harv. L. Rev. 677, 685–86 n. 63 (1933). See generally H. Hart & H. Wechsler, The Federal Courts and the Federal System 108–11, 340–51, 1140–44 (1953). The status of the Court of Claims as a full-fledged constitutional court was subsequently solidified by legislation and Glidden Co. v. Zdanok, 370 U.S. 530 (1962). See P. Bator, P. Mishkin, D. Shapiro, & H. Wechsler, The Federal Courts and the Federal System 98–102, 375–418 (rev. ed. 1973).

14. See Williams v. United States, 289 U.S. 553 (1933); District of Columbia v. Eslin, 183 U.S. 62 (1901).

15. Compare Gordon v. United States, 69 U.S. (2 Wall.) 561 (1865) (refusing to take jurisdiction over appeals from Court of Claims decisions where payment reviewable by Secretary of Treasury), with United States v. Jones, 119 U.S. 477 (1886); In re Sanborn, 148 U.S. 222 (1893) (acceptance of review of Court of Claims judgments, but not in executive department reference cases).

16. See Williams v. United States, 289 U.S. 553, 564 (1933).

17. Recall also that 28 U.S.C. § 41(20) (1940) eliminated from the general concurrent jurisdiction of the district courts "cases brought to recover fees, salary, or compensation for official services of Officers of the United States." It is at least arguable that Congress limited such jurisdiction to the Court of Claims, a body over which it had a long history of supervision, precisely for the purpose of permitting congressional review of such judgments.

18. As it turned out, in the crucial vote on the appropriation to pay the Lovett judgment, the House voted 99 to 98 to pay. 93 Cong. Rec. 2973–75, 2977, 2987–91 (1947).

19. The three men were in identical positions, with two exceptions: (1) Their jobs were of different levels of responsibility in the federal hierarchy. This point might have been relevant to the argument over the executive power of removal. (2) Dodd had not been informed of the charges against him before he went before the Kerr Committee, even though he had requested them. He therefore had a stronger claim with regard to procedural due process. Apparently neither of these differences was viewed as significant, for the three cases were argued as one.

20. 118 U.S. 389 (1886).

21. 328 U.S. at 307.

22. 347 U.S. 497 (1954).

23. [But compare City of Richmond v. J.A. Croson Co., 488 U.S. 469 (1989), with Metro Broadcasting, Inc. v. FCC, 497 U.S. 547 (1990), together suggesting that at least (and probably only) as regards affirmative action programs, the equality constraints the Constitution places on the federal government are weaker than those it places on the states. Adarand Constructors, Inc. v. Peña, 115 S.Ct. 2097 (1995), apparently restored us to a unitary (and stringent) standard.]

24. See e.g., Hirabayashi v. United States, 320 U.S. 81, 100 (1943); Hurtado v. California, 110 U.S. 516, 535 (1884) (speaking of both the Fourteenth and Fifth amendments).

25. 71 U.S. (4 Wall.) 277 (1866).

26. 71 U.S. (4 Wall.) 333 (1866).

27. Pierce v. Carskadon, 83 U.S. (16 Wall.) 234 (1872).

28. 272 U.S. 52 (1926).

29. Record at 5–6, 10–11. 15–16, United States v. Lovett, 328 U.S. 303 (1946).

30. In oral argument Justice Rutledge forced the concession from Mr. Gall that the logic of his position required the conclusion that a congressional provision that "no Negro shall be paid a government salary" would be unreviewable by the courts. 14 U.S.L.W. 3379, 3380 (U.S. May 7, 1946).

31. Moreover, even if the Court awarded back pay, it could deny that it was "appropriating." Congress had the final authority to make or reject appropriations to pay Court of Claims judgments. See pages 94–95.

Congress also seems to have hinted that section 304 was not severable from the rest of the Urgent Deficiency Appropriation Act. It is not clear what Mr. Gall was trying to accomplish here; perhaps he was trying to scare the Court of Claims away from the constitutional issues. The argument was not strong, since section 304 was one of the most obvious "riders" in history. The Court of Claims therefore dismissed it out of hand, and it was not again raised.

32. 295 U.S. 602 (1935).

33. As we have seen, the due process and equal protection arguments were not weighty on their own terms, but were clever indirect ways of reintroducing the bill of attainder theme.

34. See Petition for Writs of Certiorari to the Court or Claims at 7.

35. 66 F. Supp. 142 (Ct. Cl. 1945).

36. I have in mind an opinion like Judge Edgerton's brilliant dissent in Bailey v. Richardson, 182 F.2d 46, 66 (D.C. Cir. 1950), aff'd ex necessitate, 341 U.S. 918 (1951).

37. Congress apparently found the opinions of the Court or Claims so inauthoritative that it hesitated to make good the judgment. See Petition for Writs of Certiorari at 15; Brief for the Congress of the United States in Support or Petition for Writs of Certiorari at 6. The documents do not make clear the nature of this hesitation; they do imply, though, that a clear and authoritative adjudication would trigger the appropriations.

38. Petition for Writs of Certiorari at 2.

39. Brief for the Congress of the United States at 24.

40. Though of course the justiciability argument was an indirect way of arguing that section 304 was only an exercise of the appropriations power.

41. This section included a great deal of historical material (much of it irrelevant) supporting the breadth of the appropriations power. The weakest link in this chain of reasoning was the claim that salary appropriations may be withheld by name, which was supported by no relevant statutes and no cases at all. Brief for the Congress of the United States at 97–101.

42. 328 U.S. at 322–23.

43. Brief for the Petitioner at 71–72.

44. Id. at 10–11.

45. Id. at 69.

46. Brief for Respondent at 41. See also id. at 36–39.

47. Letter from Charles A. Horsky to author, April 11, 1963.

48. The argument before the Supreme Court is reported in 14 U.S.L.W. 3379 (U.S. May 7, 1943).

49. See, e.g., Watkins v. United States, 354 U.S. 178 (1957); Pennsylvania v. Nelson, 350 U.S. 497 (1955).

50. Myers v. United States, 272 U.S. 52 (1926), whose expansive view of the President's removal power had required nearly three years' contemplation and a reargument, was greatly limited just nine years later in Humphrey's Executor v. United States, 295 U.S. 602 (1935). Justice Frankfurter commented at the oral argument of *Lovett*: "For 125 years this Court avoided passing on the removal power, and when it did, the result was not very felicitous." 14 U.S.L.W. at 3381.

51. Id. at 326. Although the requirement of a declaration of guilt was never adopted by a majority of the Court, for a time Justice Frankfurter's strict historical approach was. See pages 114–17. It has been since laid to rest. United States v. Brown, 381 U.S. 437 (1965).

52. It seems fairly obvious that Frankfurter should have recused himself in Lovett's case, as both of their autobiographies (without mentioning the case) report that they were friends. See Felix Frankfurter Reminisces 282–84 (H. Phillips ed. 1960); R. Lovett, All Our Years 184, 192–93 (1948).

53. Actually, the House initially once again balked at appropriating funds for the three men but eventually surrendered, 99–98. The Senate and President of course concurred, and the plaintiffs were paid.

54. But see, e.g., Barenblatt v. United States, 360 U.S. 109 (1959). [See also page 136.]

55. 72 Yale L. J. 330.

56. See, e.g., the Act for the Attainder of Thomas Fitzgerald, Earl of Kildare 1534, 26 Hen 8, c. 6 (priv.):

... And Further be it enacted by the auctorite aforesaid, that all suche persons whiche be or hereafter have ben conffortours abbetours partakers confederates or adherents unto the said Erle in his said false and trayterous acts and purpos shall in lyke wise stonde and be atteynted adjugged and convycted of High Treason ... And be it further enacted ... that the same atteynder juggement and convyccion ageynst the said conffortours abettours ... confederates and adherents shalbe as astronge and effectuall in the lawe ageynst them and every of them as though they and every of them had be specially singulerly and particulerly named by their propre names and surnames in this said Acte.

See also An Act to attaint persons concerned in the late horrid conspiracy . . ., 1696, 8 Will. 3, c 5 (pub.).

57. See statutes cited supra note 56; see also 25 Hen. 8, c. 12 (pub.) (1533); An act for the attainder of divers offenders in the late most barbarous, monstrous, detestable and damnable treasons, 1605, 3 Jac. 1, c. 2 (pub.); an Act for the attainder of several persons guilty of the horrid murder of his late sacred Majesty King Charles the First, 1660, 12 Car. 2, c. 30 (pub.); 19 Geo. 2, c 26 (pub.) (1746); An act to incapacitate . . . [69 names] from voting at elections of members to serve in parliament. . . . 1770, 11 Geo. 3, c. 55 (pub.).

58. Corruption of blood was separately outlawed by the United States Constitution, at least as a penalty for treason. U.S. Const., art. III, § 3.

59. See, e.g., 29 Hen. 6, c. 1 (pub.) (1450); 13 Eliz., c. 16 (pub.) (1570); An act for the attainder of divers offenders in the late most barbarous, monstrous, detestable and damnable Treasons, 1605, 3 Jac. 1, c. 2 (pub.); An Act for continuing the imprisonment . . . for the late horrid conspiracy to assassinate the person of his sacred Majesty, 1699; 10 & 11 Will. 3, c. 13 (pub.); An Act for the Attainder of the pretended Prince of Wales of High Treason, 1701, 13 Will. 3, c. 3 (pub.); An Act to inflict pains and penalties on John Plunket, 1722, 9, Geo. 1, c. 15 (pub.).

60. See pages 116–17.

61. See, e.g., Attainder Act of Oct. 22, 1779, 1 Laws of New York, third session, c. XXV; Attainder Act of May 12, 1784, 1 Laws of New York, seventh session, c. LXIV; James's Claim, 1 U.S. (1 Dall.) 47 (1780); Respublica v. Gordon, 1 U.S. (1 Dall.) 232 (1788); Inglis v. Sailor's Snug Harbour, 28 U.S. (3 Pet.) 99 (1830).

62. See, e.g., Act of Disenfranchisement of May 12, 1784, 1, Laws of New York, Seventh Session, c. LXVI; Cooper v. Telfair, 4 U.S. (4 Dall.) 14 (1800).

63. U.S. Const. art. I. § 9.

64. U.S. Const. art. I. § 10.

65. Congress has declared the Communist Party to be unentitled to "any of the rights, privileges, and immunities attendant upon legal bodies created under the jurisdiction of the laws of the United States," and there are on the books specific provisions restricting the party's use of the nation's mails and air waves, and denying it certain income tax deductions. Communist Control Act § 3, 68 Stat. 776 (1954), 50 U.S.C. § 842 (1958); Subversive Activities Control Act §§10, ll(a), 64 Stat. 996 (1950), 50 U.S.C. §§ 789–90 (1958).

The individual members of the party cannot hold any nonelective government office, work in defense facilities or for a labor union, represent either employer or employee in National Labor Relations Act proceedings, or get a passport. Subversive Activities Control Act §§ 5(a)(l)(B), 5(a)(l)(D), 64 Stat. 992 (1950), 50 U.S.C. §§ 784(a)(1)(B), 784(a) (1) (D) (1958); Communist Control Act §§ 6, 13A(h), 68 Stat. 777, 779 (1954), 50 U.S.C. §§ 784(a) (1) (E), 792a(h) (1958); Subversive Activities Control Act § 6(a), 64 Stat. 993 (1950), 50 U.S.C. § 785(a) (1958).

Further, an alien who is a member of the party is automatically ineligible for admission (or naturalization) and, even if already admitted, is subject to deportation, at which time his social security benefits will be terminated. Immigration and

Nationality Act § 212(a) (28) (c), 66 Stat. 184 (1952), 8 U.S.C. §1182(28) (c) (1958); Immigration and Nationality Act § 313(a) (2), 66 Stat. 240 (1952), 8 U.S.C. § 1424(a) (2) (1958); Immigration and Nationality Act § 241(a) (6) (C), 66 Stat. 205 (1952), 8 U.S.C. § 1251(a) (6) (C) (1958); Social Security Act Amendments of 1954 §107, 68 Stat. 1083, 42 U.S.C. § 402(n) (1958).

66. 328 U.S. 303 (1946).

67. The view that in order to be a bill of attainder, a statute must inflict "punishment," is criticized below. See pages 127–28. However, since all the case law speaks in these terms, this comment, in describing the contrasting approaches to the constitutional provision, will, for the time being, also speak in terms of "punishment."

68. 339 U.S. 382 (1950).

69. Cummings v. Missouri, 71 U.S. (4 Wall.) 277, 325 (1866).

70. 10 U.S. (6 Cranch.) 87, 138 (1810).

71. 71 U.S. (4 Wall.) 277 (1866).

72. 71 U.S. (4 Wall.) 333 (1866).

73. Id. at 323.

74. United States v. Lovett, 328 U.S. 303, 322–23 (1946).

75. Pierce v. Carskadon, 83 U.S. (16 Wall.) 234 (1872). See also Drehman v. Stifle, 75 U.S. (8 Wall.) 595 (1869); Minor v. Happersett, 88 U.S (21 Wall.) 162 (1874); Presser v. Illinois, 116 U.S. 252 (1886).

76. 129 U.S. 114 (1889).

77. 170 U.S. 189 (1898).

78. Green v. Shumway, 39 N.Y. 418, 430–31 (1868) (Mason, J., dissenting).

79. 71 U.S. at 386–90.

80. See National Maritime Union v. Herzog, 78 F. Supp. 146, 164 (D.D.C. 1948), aff'd, 334 U.S. 854 (1948).

81.
> All bills of attainder specify the offense for which the attainted person was deemed guilty. . . . There was always a declaration of guilt. . . . § 304 lack[s] the essential declaration of guilt.

328 U.S. at 322–23.

> Congress omitted from § 304 any condemnation for which the presumed punishment was a sanction. Thereby it negatived *the essential notion* of a bill of attainder.

Id. at 326 (emphasis supplied).

82. The requirement is of course out of line with the functional approach taken by the early decisions. There is also explicit language in the *Cummings* opinion that strongly suggests that the absence of a declaration of guilt is a mere formal technicality and should not be dispositive. 71 U.S. at 324–25.

83. See an Act for the Attainder of Thomas Earl of Strafford of High Treason, 1640, 16 Car. 1, c.i. (priv.); 12 Car. 1, c. 1 (1641); 2 Wooddeson, Vinerian Lectures 629–33 (1792).

84. 328 U.S. at 322–25.

85. 339 U.S. 382, 413–14 (1950).

86. 367 U.S. 1, 86–87 (1961).

87. An Act for the Attainder of several Persons guilty of the horrid Murder of his late Sacred Majesty King Charles the First, 1600, 12 Car. 2, c 30 (pub.).

88. The postmortem attainder was more than an empty gesture, as it added the deprivation of corruption of blood.

89. 13 Will. 3, c. 3 (pub.).

90. Statute quoted note 167 infra. See also Professor Chafee's account of the attainder of Thomas Haxley. Z. Chafee, Three Human Rights in the Constitution 102–3 (1956).

> If the ousted adviser were left at liberty, he could readily turn his resentment into coercion or rebellion and make a magnificent comeback to the utter ruin of those who had driven him from his high place.

Id. at 103–4.

91. The prophylactic purpose of much of this legislation is aptly summed up by the title of a 1777 Maryland act: "An Act to punish certain crimes and misdemeanors, and to prevent the growth of toryism." 1 Laws of Maryland 453 (Kilty 1799). The fact that many of the statutes were repealed as soon as the war and therefore the Tory danger was ended lends credence to the view that their purpose was not primarily retribution for past misdeeds.

92. See page 115.

93. This requirement too was originally suggested in Frankfurter's *Lovett* concurrence. 328 U.S. at 327.

94. 339 U.S. at 414.

95. 367 U.S. at 82.

96. Id. at 88.

97. 31 Ky. (1 Dana) 481, 510 (1833) (separate opinion, two judges participating).

98. 1746, 19 Geo. 2, c. 26 (pub.). Also of this form are, e.g., An Act of Banishing and Disenabling the Earl of Clarendon, 1667, 19 Car. 2, c. 10 (pub.); An act to attaint such of the persons concerned in the late horrid conspiracy to assassinate his Majesty's royal person, 1696, 8 Will. 3, c. 5 (pub.); An Act for the Attainder of Henry Viscount Bolingbroke, 1714, 1 Geo. 1 Stat. 2, c. 16 (pub.); An Act for the attainder of James Duke of Ormonde, 1714, 1 Geo. 1 Stat. 2, c. 17 (pub.); An Act for the attainder of George Earl of Marischall, 1715, 1 Geo. 1 Stat. 2, c. 42 (pub.).

99. An Act for banishing and disenabling the Earl of Clarendon, 1667, 19 Car. 2, c. 10 (pub.), printed in 6 Howell's State Trials, p. 391.

100. See, e.g., An Act to Attaint Josiah Philips, 1778, 9 Laws of Virginia 463 (Hening 1821); Pemberton's Lessee v. Hicks, 3 U.S. (3 Dall.) 479 (1798).

101. 71 U.S. at 324.

102. 328 U.S. at 321. See also Rochin v. California, 342 U.S. 165, 169–70 (1952).

103. For example, the word "writings," as it appears in the Copyright Clause, seems on its face as inflexible as any that appears in the Constitution. U.S. Const. Art. I § 8. Yet "writings" has been construed to cover, inter alia, maps (Amsterdam v. Triangle Publications, Inc., 189 F.2d 104 [3d Cir. 1951] [dictum]), paintings (Leigh v. Gerber, 86 F. Supp. 320 [S.D.N.Y. 1949]), photographs (Burrow-Giles Lithographic Co. v. Sarony, 111 U.S. 53 [1884]), and lamp bases shaped like "male and female dancing figures" (Mazer v. Stein, 347 U.S. 201, 202 [1954]). There are

sound policy considerations underlying this broad interpretation, but the fact remains that the Copyright Clause provides a beautiful example of the flexible interpretation of a facially inflexible constitutional term.

Further, the copyright provision deals with rights as between private parties, whereas the Bill of Attainder Clause protects the rights of the individual against the state; it thus might be argued that the broader interpretation should be accorded the *latter.* For in this age of extremely broad interpretation of those constitutional provisions permissive of government action, the tethering of constitutional restrictions on government action to allegedly historical requirements will badly deform the original constitutional balance.

104. Frankfurter joined in the opinion of the Court in Mazer v. Stein, note 103 supra.

105. 328 U.S. at 321.

106. Id. at 323–24.

107. Note 56 supra.

108. Note 83 supra.

109. See, e.g., An Act to inflict pains and penalties on Francis Lord Bishop of Rochester, 1722, 9 Geo. 1, c. 17 (pub.); Proceedings Against Hugh and Hugh Le Despencer, 1 State Trials 23 (1320).

110. See, e.g., An Act to incapacitate John Burnett, et al., from voting at elections of members to serve in parliament . . ., 1770, 11 Geo. 3, c. 55 (pub.).

111. See The Sons of the persons before attainted excluded from Parliament, 1397, 21 Rich 2, c. 6 (pub.).

112. Montesquieu, The Spirit of Laws 154 (6th ed. 1792) (Nugent translation). See generally Sharp, "The Classical American Doctrine of 'The Separation of Powers,'" 2 U. Chi. L. Rev. 385 (1935).

113. See T. Cooley, Constitutional Limitations 316 (6th ed. 1890).

114. The Federalist No. 47, at 373–74 (Hamilton ed. 1880) (Madison).

115. Id., No. 48, at 383–84.

116. Id., No. 44, at 351 (Madison).

117. J. Story, Commentaries on the Constitution of the United States 210 (4th ed. 1873). See also 2 Wooddeson, supra note 83, at 621–22.

118. Some hundreds of gentlemen, every one of whom had much more than half made up his mind before the case was opened, performed the functions both of judge and jury. They were not restrained, as a judge is restrained, by the sense of responsibility. . . . They were not selected, as a jury is selected, in a manner which enables the culprit to exclude his personal and political enemies.

The arbiters of his fate came in and went out as they chose. They heard a fragment here and there. . . . During the progress of the bill they were exposed to every species of influence. One member was threatened by the electors of his borough with the loss of his seat; another might obtain a frigate for his brother. . . . In the debates arts were practised and passions excited which are unknown to well constituted tribunals, but from which no great popular assembly divided into parties ever was or ever will be free.

T. Macaulay, History of England ch. 22 (1st ed. 1855), quoted in Z. Chafee, supra note 90, at 135. See also Pound, "Justice According to Law II," 14 Colum. L. Rev. 1, 7–12 (1914).

119. See Professor Chafee's description of how Parliament enacted attainders. Z. Chafee, supra note 90, at 112, 132.

120. T. Cooley, Constitutional Limitations 314 (6th ed. 1890).

Historically, the "bill of attainder" and the "impeachment" were regarded as two alternative ways of accomplishing the same results. See, e.g., Z. Chafee, supra note 90, at 98–144; Adams, Constitutional History of England 228 (rev. ed. 1934). To insure that the Bill of Attainder Clause's prohibition of legislative adjudication would not be evaded by the device of calling the proscribed action an "impeachment," the legislature's traditional impeachment power was severely narrowed. Congress was forbidden to impeach anyone other than a government official; and even then the sanction was limited to removal and disqualification from office. U.S. Const. art. I § 3. This clause may therefore be viewed as a grant to Congress of the power to pass one highly restricted kind of bill of attainder.

121. [My student editor, Alan Dershowitz, helped a lot with this entire comment, but particularly with this analogy to Article III, which as I recall was his idea, and remains one of the best things in the piece.]

122. T. Jefferson, Notes on the State of Virginia 195 (1784) [emphasis in original].

123. 10 U.S. (6 Cranch.) 87, 136 (1810).

124. 339 U.S. at 389.

Substantial amounts of evidence were presented to various committees of Congress . . . that Communist leaders of labor unions had in the past and would continue in the future to subordinate legitimate trade union objectives to obstructive strikes when dictated by party leaders, often in support of the policies of a foreign government.

Id. at 388.

125. Id. at 418 (emphasis added).

126. Id. at 424.

127. See, e.g., K. Davis, Administrative Law Treatise § 5.03 (1958).

128. E.g., Hannah v. Larche, 363 U.S. 420, 442 (1960). See Administrative Procedure Act § 5 (Adjudication), 60 Stat. 239 (1946), 5 U.S.C. § 1005 (1958). Compare id. § 4 (Rule Making), 60 Stat. 238 (1946), 5 U.S.C. § 1004 (1958).

In absence of statutory requirement of hearing, and in absence of a dispute of adjudicative facts, the case law ordinarily does not require either a speech-making hearing or a trial-type hearing for rule making.

K. Davis, supra note 127, § 6.12.

129. As to the claim that government employment is a "privilege" and that therefore its deprivation cannot constitute a bill of attainder, see pages 129–30.

130. The problem of distinguishing such statutes from bills of attainder has rarely been faced in either the case law or the literature. However, two possible distinctions have been suggested. Professor Wormuth has argued that the epileptic statute is not a bill of attainder because it does not involve a "censorial judgment" on the part of the legislature. That is, the legislature has not inquired into the "character," "culpability," or "guilt" of the epileptics. Wormuth, "Legislative Disqualifications as Bills of Attainder," 4 Vand. L. Rev. 603, 608–10 (1951). See

also E. Freund, Administrative Powers over Persons and Property 100 (1928). The "censorial judgment" test would appear to be but a variant of the traditional "punitive intent" test and subject to the same difficulties. See pages 127–28. The statute "John Jones, because he is an epileptic, shall not drive," is a bill of attainder, despite the lack of any normative judgment as to Jones. A second possible ground of distinction that has been suggested by the cases and the literature is that the epileptic statute is not a bill of attainder because it enacts a "reasonable qualification" for driving. See, e.g., Dent v. West Virginia, 129 U.S. 114 (1889); Hawker v. New York, 170 U.S. 189 (1898); Garner v. Board of Public Works of Los Angeles, 341 U.S. 716, 720–24 (1951); Linehan v. Waterfront Comm'n of New York Harbor, 347 U.S. 439 (1954). See generally Comment, 63 Yale L. J. 844, 850–55 (1954). But this attempted distinction also fails, for it does not greatly strain the Ku Klux Klan statute to couch it in terms of a "qualification." Just as an epileptic is not qualified to be on the roads because of the likelihood of his causing an accident, so, it can be argued, a member of the Klan is not qualified to work for the Civil Rights Division (or a given rebel is not qualified to live in England) because of *his* propensities.

131. Quaere: Is there a definite line between "tautological" and "judicially noticeable" judgments? Or does repeated empirical experience lead us to incorporate additional elements into our "definitions" of various terms? "Bachelors are not married" is clearly a nonempirical observation. "Grand mal epileptics are likely to have seizures" begins to look more like "syphilitics are likely to bear diseased children." This comment proposes, however, that the "epileptics" statement is tautological in the sense that the term "grand mal epileptics" was created to refer to persons subject to certain kinds of seizures, whereas "syphilitics" was clearly not created to refer to persons likely to bear syphilitic children. In any case the line is not a clear one. This fact can, however, make little difference to the analysis presented in this comment, for it is proposed that both definitional and judicially noticeable propositions are permissible legislative inferences.

132. See, e.g., C. McCormick, Evidence § 325, at 691–92 (1954):

[W]e have here an important extension of judicial notice to the new field of facts "capable of accurate and ready demonstration," . . . In this realm fall most of the facts, theories, and conclusions which have come to be established and accepted by the specialists in the areas of natural science.

Also judicially noticeable are facts "so certainly known as to make [them] indisputable among reasonable men." Id., § 324. Under the test proposed by this comment, these facts too would be "legislatively noticeable."

To the extent that the proposition that the children of syphilitics are likely to have syphilis is controversial and not judicially noticeable, reliance upon it by a legislature would be inappropriate, and reliance upon it here is misplaced. [This caveat should obviously also be applied to the discussion of epilepsy.]

133. There would seem to be no theoretical objection to having such focused adjudication performed by an administrative agency, provided that the agency is set up in such a way that (1) it must respect the safeguards put upon judicial trials, and (2) it is isolated from the pressures that render the legislature incapable of fairly deciding to whom the rule is to apply. Such a scheme would both avoid the danger

of overconcentration of power in the hands of the legislature and force the legislature clearly to define the objects of its legislation.

134. But cf. Matter of Albertson (Lubin), 8 N.Y.2d 77, 84–85, 168 N.E.2d 242 (1960), rev'd sub. nom. Communist Party v. Catherwood, 367 U.S. 389 (1961), apparently judicially noticing facts about the Communist Party because Congress had stated them in the form of legislation! (Needless to say, this holding does not imply that the facts are judicially noticeable in the sense that it is permissible for Congress to use them in narrowing the ambit of its rules.)

135. See, e.g., Flemming v. Nestor, 363 U.S. 603, 613 (1960).

136. See, e.g., Cummings v. Missouri, 71 U.S. (4 Wall.) 277, 323 (1866); Communist Party of the United States v. Subversive Activities Control Bd., 367 U.S. 1, 146 (1961) (Black J., dissenting); W. Douglas, An Almanac of Liberty 103 (1954). But see Flemming v. Nestor, 363 U.S. 603, 626 (1960) (Black, J. dissenting).

137. E.g., Wormuth, "Legislative Disqualifications as Bills of Attainder," 4 Vand. L. Rev. 603, 610 n. 37 (1951).

138. E.g., Fong Yue Ting v. United States, 149 U.S. 698, 730 (1893); Bugajewitz v. Adams, 228 U.S. 585, 591 (1913); Mahler v. Eby, 264 U.S. 32, 39 (1924); Harisiades v. Shaughnessy, 342 U.S. 580, 594–95 (1952); Quattrone v. Nicolls, 210 F.2d 513, 518 (1st Cir. 1954), cert. denied, 347 U.S. 976 (1954).

139. See page 118.

140. See, e.g., Proceedings Against Hugh and Hugh Le Despencer, 1 State Trials 23 (1320); An act to inflict pains and penalties on Francis lord bishop of Rochester, 1722, 9 Geo. 1, c. 17 (Pub.); An act for banishing and disenabling the earl of Clarendon, 1667, 19 Car. 2, c. 10 (Pub.).

141. 71 U.S. (4 Wall) 277, 320 (1866). But cf. Brown v. Wilemon, 139 F.2d 730, 732 (5th Cir. 1944).

142. E.g., Anderson v. Baker, 23 Md. 531 (1865); Blair v. Ridgely, 41 Mo. 63 (1867); Randolph v. Good, 3 W.Va. 551 (1869); Wooley v. Watkins, 2 Idaho 590, 22 Pac. 102 (1889); Shepherd v. Grimmett, 3 Idaho 403, 31 Pac. 793 (1892); cf. Boyd v. Mills, 53 Kan. 594, 37 Pac. 16 (1894).

143. E.g., State ex rel. Wingate v. Woodson, 41 Mo. 227 (1867); Crampton v. O'Mara, 193 Ind. 551, 139 N.E. 360 (1923), appeal dismissed, 267 U.S. 575 (1925); cf. City of Detroit v. AASER, 332 Mich. 237, 51 N.W.2d 228, appeal dismissed, 344 U.S. 805 (1952).

144. 71 U.S. (4 Wall.) 277, 320 (1866).

145. Id. at 321–22.

146. 339 U.S. at 389–90.

147. Id. at 390.

148. 363 U.S. 603, 617 (1960). It is not suggested that this was the sole ground of decision, as the case also discussed "punitive intent" at length. See id. at 612–21.

149. Thompson v. Whittier, 185 F. Supp. 306, 310–12 (D.D.C. 1960). But see Steinberg v. United States, 163 F. Supp. 590, 592 (Ct. Cl. 1958).

150. See page 118; An Act for the preventing of bribery and corruption in the election of members to serve in parliament for the borough of Cricklade, in the county of Wilts, 1782, 22 Geo. 3, c. 31 (Pub.); An Act to exclude the Bourough of Grampound, in the County of Cornwall, from sending Burgesses to serve in Parliament . . . , 1821, 1 & 2 Geo. 4, c 47 (Pub.).

151. See note 111 supra.

152. E.g, an Act to inflict pains and penalties on John Plunkett, 1722, 9 Geo. 1, c. 15 (Pub.); an Act for the further limitation of the crown, and better securing the rights and liberties of the subject, 1700, 12 & 13 Will. 3, c 3; an Act for restraining popish recusants to some certain places of abode, 1593, 35 Eliz., c. 2 (Pub.). For an interesting parallel, see Professor Chafee's description of the "Popish Plot." Z. Chafee, supra note 90, at 122–23.

153. 9 J. Adams, The Life and Works of John Adams 408 (1854).

154. 66 Stat. 205 (1952), 8 U.S.C. § 1251(a)(6)(C) (1958).

155. 68 Stat. 775–80 (1954), as amended, 50 U.S.C. §§ 781–857 (1958).

156. Communist Control Act § 3, 68 Stat. 776 (1954), 50 U.S.C. § 842 (1958).

157. Id., § 2, 68 Stat. 775–76 (1954), 50 U.S.C. § 841 (1958).

158. 367 U.S. 389 (1961).

159. Text accompanying note 157 supra.

160. 4 Annals of Congress 934 (1794). . . .

161. Smith Act § 2(a) (3), 54 Stat. 671 (1940), as amended, 18 U.S.C. § 2385 (1958).

162. See Scales v. United States, 367 U.S. 203 (1961). [The Smith Act should have been invalidated under the Fist Amendment, however.]

163. 64 Stat. 987 (1950); 50 U.S.C. §§ 781–98 (1958).

164. Subversive Activities Control Act § 3, 64 Stat. 989 (1950), 50 U.S.C. § 782 (1958).

165. Id. § 7, 64 Stat. at 994 (1950), 50 U.S.C. § 786 (1958).

166. Id. § 12(e), 64 Stat. at 997 (1950), 50 U.S.C. § 791(e) (1958).

167. Members of an organization designated a "Communist-action organization" are deprived of certain income tax exemptions. Subversive Activities Control Act § ll(a), 64 Stat. 996 (1950), 50 U.S.C. § 790(a) (1958). Further, such persons and organizations are denied access to the National Labor Relations Board either as an employer or as the representative of any employee. Communist Control Act §§ 6, 13A(h), 68 Stat. 777, 779–80 (1954), 50 U.S.C. §§ 784(a)(1)(E), 792a(h) (1958). Also, "Communist-action organizations" cannot send mail or broadcast over radio or television without announcing that the information is being "disseminated by a Communist organization." Subversive Activities Control Act § 10, 64 Stat. 996 (1950), 50 U.S.C. § 789 (1958). The use of restrictions upon the opportunity to communicate, as a means of containing a threat to the national security, is far from novel; in its attainder of the Prince of Wales, Parliament decreed:

> And for preventing traiterous correspondence between your Majesty's subjects and the said pretended prince of Wales, or his adherents; be it further enacted . . . That if any of the Subjects of the Crown of England . . . shall . . . hold, entertain, or keep any intelligence or correspondence in person, or by letters, messages, or otherwise, with the said pretended prince of Wales, or with any person or persons employed by him, knowing such person to be so employed . . . such person so offending, being lawfully convicted, shall be taken, deemed, and adjudged to be guilty of high treason, and shall suffer and forfeit as in cases of high treason.

An act for the Attainder of the pretended Prince of Wales of High Treason, 1701, 13 Will. 3, c. 3 (pub.). (Of course this section of the act is not a bill of attainder.)

Registration under § 7 of the Subversive Activities Control Act also inflicts deprivations directly upon the individual members of a Communist-action organization. They are forbidden to "hold any non-elective office or employment under the United States," "engage in any employment in any defense facility," or "hold office or employment with any labor organization . . . or to represent any employer in any matter or proceeding arising or pending" under the National Labor Relations Act. Subversive Activities Control Act §§ 5(a)(1)(B), 5(a)(1)(D), 64 Stat. 992 (1950), 50 U.S.C. § 784(a)(1)(B), 784(a)(l)(d) (1958); Communist Control Act § 6, 68 Stat. 777 (1954), 50 U.S.C. § 784(a)(l)(E) (1958). Members are also ineligible for passports. Subversive Activities Control Act § 6(a), 64 Stat. 993 (1950), 50 U.S.C. § 785 (1958).

Further, the list of members' names is to be kept open for public inspection. Subversive Activities Control Act § 9(b), 54 Stat. 996 (1950), 50 U.S.C. § 788(b) (1958). Thus the chances of additional deprivations, inflicted by the community, are increased. For example, Communist lawyers and doctors are faced with the possibility of exclusion from their professions, while teachers and actors who are past or present members of the party are confronted with serious problems in obtaining employment. See Konigsberg v. State Bar of California, 366 U.S. 36 (1961); Barsky v. Board of Regents, 347 U.S. 442 (1954); Adler v. Board of Educ. 342 U.S. 485 (1952); Horowitz, "Loyalty Tests for Employment in the Motion Picture Industry," 6 Stan. L. Rev. 438 (1954).

168. The argument that the full panoply of statutes, read together, permits of no conclusion other than that the Communist Party comes within the language of § 3 has been rejected by the Court. Communist Party v. Subversive Activities Control Bd., 367 U.S. 1, 110–15 (1961).

169. The ultimate inquiry must be: were the empirical underpinnings of the narrowing of the rule certain enough considering the specificity of the application? A more "absolute" test would no doubt be easier to apply to the difficult middle areas between pure rulemaking and pure adjudication. Cf. Black, "Mr. Justice Black, the Supreme Court, and the Bill of Rights," Harper's Magazine, Feb. 1961. However, it is probably the case that the continuum here proposed cannot be translated into "absolute" terms. Because there is no sharp distinction between "broad rules" and "specifications thereof," a rule like "a legislature can never specify the persons who are to be subject to its broad rule, unless it does so by means of definitions or judicially noticeable propositions," cannot be utilized without degenerating into the sort of inquiry set forth at the beginning of this footnote. The continuum, as the text demonstrates, is not difficult to apply to most legislation; as to the middle areas, it can do no more than suggest the approach.

170. Communist Control Act § 4(a), 68 Stat. 776 (1954), 50 U.S.C. § 843 (1958).

171. See pages 131–32.

172. Communist Party v. Subversive Activities Control Bd., 367 U.S. 1, 115 (1961).

173. It has been suggested by certain adherents of the literalist approach that an attempt to determine the meaning and scope of the Bill of Attainder Clause is something of a waste of time, because the more general standard of "due process" affords sufficient protection against the evils to which the Bill of Attainder Clause is directed.

Congress omitted from § 304 any condemnation for which the presumed punishment was a sanction. Thereby it negatived the essential notion of a bill of attainder. It may be said that such a view of a bill of attainder offers Congress too easy a mode of evading the prohibition of the Constitution. Congress need merely omit its ground of condemnation and legislate the penalty! But the prohibition against a "Bill of Attainder" is only one of the safeguards of liberty in the arsenal of the Constitution. There are other provisions in the Constitution, specific and comprehensive, effectively designed to assure the liberties of our citizens.

United States v. Lovett, 328 U.S. 303, 326 (1946) (Frankfurter, J., concurring).

This sort of attack can be answered simply by pointing out that although it is arguable that the concept of "due process" should encompass a prohibition of legislative adjudication (but caveat: the separation of powers as we know it is primarily an American phenomenon), the recent cases demonstrate that the Court's definition does not extend that far. For such flagrant instances of legislative adjudication as § 9(h) of the Taft-Hartley Act have been upheld not only against the charge that they are bills of attainder, but also against attacks grounded in the Due Process Clause. To suggest that one constitutional provision is superfluous because another provision, *if its present interpretation were altered*, might perform the same function is nothing short of absurd.

Bills of attainder are often at the same time ex post facto laws; this no doubt is one reason the two prohibitions were united in one constitutional clause. But the proscription of ex post facto laws does not, as has at times been suggested, render the bill of attainder prohibition superfluous, for frequently bills of attainder were—and are—not ex post facto laws. For one thing, parliamentary bills of attainder often were findings that the person attainted was guilty of a crime previously defined by the statutes. Second, bills of attainder were sometimes passed not primarily to punish past acts at all, but rather to prevent future conduct. The classes of "bills of attainder" and "ex post facto laws" are thus overlapping but not coextensive; the framers were fully justified in treating the two prohibitions separately. It is also worth noting that while there is in the case law authority for the proposition that the prohibition of ex post facto laws is limited to criminal statutes, the authority concerning the bill of attainder clause explicitly rejects such limitation. Compare Calder v. Bull, 3 U.S. (3 Dall.) 386 (1798), and Mahler v. Eby, 264 U.S. 32, 39 (1924), with Cummings v. Missouri, 71 U.S. (4 Wall.) 277 (1867), and United States v. Lovett, 328 U.S.303 (1946).

So long as the bill of attainder clause is regarded as a proscription of a specific form of parliamentary statute, it can be convincingly argued that it is a safeguard of little independent value in today's world. However, once it is realized that the term "bill of attainder" has no specific historical referent, and that the constitutional provision is a prohibition of legislative adjudication in any guise, it becomes clear that it is a safeguard that is, especially today, independently vital. If the courts are led to read the Bill of Attainder Clause out of the Constitution as anachronistic surplusage, we shall have lost the right to be judged by persons other than those who enact the law.

174. J. Story, supra note 117, at 210–11.

175. The Federalist No. 47, supra note 114, at 373–74 (Madison).

176. My other favorite encounter over *Brown* involved a dissenting justice, Tom Clark, who met me in the hall while the case was pending and wondered in his Texas drawl: "A bill of attainder! What the on *earth* is a bill of attainder?" I responded that he ought to know what a bill of attainder was, as he had probably written more opinions than any other sitting justice rejecting bill of attainder claims. He responded, "Yes, but remember what my opinions said: 'It is also argued that this is a bill of attainder. It is not.'" (If you're going to be a judge, the United States Supreme Court has its advantages.)

177. 79 Yale L. J. 1205, 1306–8.

178. Hart, "The Power of Congress to Limit the Jurisdiction of Federal Courts: An Exercise in Dialectic," 66 Harv. L. Rev. 1362 (1953).

179. The existence of an administrative remedy equal to the task of vindicating the federal right might serve to rebut the charge of unconstitutional motivation. (I put to one side the question whether Article III may not demand that such questions be decided by judges with fixed salaries and lifetime tenure.) So on some occasions might a history of effective state court protection of the right in issue. But this should not be overdone: the existence of the state courts obviously cannot rebut the inference that must be drawn concerning the motivation underlying the Tuck Amendment, H.R. 11926, 88th Cong., 2d Sess. (1964):

> § 1259. The Supreme Court shall not have the right to review the action of a Federal court of a State court of last resort concerning any action taken upon a petition or complaint seeking to apportion any legislature of any State of the Union or any branch thereof.
>
> § 1331(c). The district courts shall not have jurisdiction to entertain any petition or complaint seeking to apportion or reapportion the legislature of any State of the union or any branch thereof, nor shall any order of decree of any district or circuit court now pending and not finally disposed of by actual reapportionment be hereafter enforced.

The coin has another side, which is that portion of the Norris-LaGuardia Act which rendered yellow dog contracts unenforceable in federal courts was just as clearly motivated by a desire to deny employers constitutional rights which had been recognized in Adair v. United States, 208 U.S. 161 (1908), and Coppage v. Kansas, 236 U.S. 1 (1915). Lest the Court be so swept away by my argument as to begin looking for a case in which to invalidate that provision, I should note that time, and the passing of *Adair* and *Coppage*, have rendered the motivation no longer unconstitutional.

180. Of course any diminution of jurisdiction will save money, but what needs justification here—and I say it often because the distinction is often neglected—is the decision to save money this way.

181. May 31, 1973.

182. Of some relevance is Charles Pinckney's remark:

> Let us inquire, why the Constitution should have been so attentive to each branch of Congress, so jealous of their privileges [he had previously mentioned privilege from arrest], and have shewn so little to the President of the United States in this

respect. . . . No privilege of this kind was intended for your Executive, nor any except that which I have mentioned for your Legislature. The Convention which , formed the Constitution well knew that this was an important point, and no subject had been more abused than privilege. They therefore determined to set the example, in merely limiting privilege to what was necessary, and no more.

3 Farrand, The Records of the Federal Convention of 1787, at 385 (1966).

183. [The relevance of even this narrowest claim of presidential susceptibility to process is of obvious relevance to Paula Jones's lawsuit against President Clinton, in limbo as I write, for sexual harassment (a term of admittedly frightening vagueness, albeit not as applied to this case, if Ms. Jones's allegations are even close to true). And for reasons we need not rehearse, the old saw is true: justice delayed often *is* justice denied. We've come far enough toward the sort of regal presidency the framers abhorred without effectively immunizing behavior of the sort alleged: if Ms. Jones is lying, the President's lawyers will make short shrift of her claims without serious inconvenience to the man himself, let alone the country. See further note 185 infra.]

184. In holding as it did, the Court reasoned that either the president would disobey its order, in which case it really had no further weapons at its disposal, or he would obey, in which case there would be an executive-legislative "collision." The latter consideration is inapplicable here, and the former is one the Court has indicated in cases like *Powell v. McCormack* it will not countenance.

185. The same footnote also quotes Jeremy Bentham:

Are men of the first rank and consideration, are men high in office, men whose time is not less valuable to the public than to themselves, are such men to be forced to quit their business, their functions, and what is more than all, their pleasure, at the beck of every idle or malicious adversary, to dance attendance upon every petty cause? Yes, as far as it is necessary,—they and everybody! . . . Were the Prince of Wales, the Archbishop of Canterbury, and the Lord High Chancellor, to be passing by in the same coach while a chimney-sweeper and a barrow-woman were in dispute about a halfpennyworth of apples, and the chimney-sweeper or the barrow-woman were to think proper to call upon them for their evidence, could they refuse it? No, most certainly.

4 The Works of Jeremy Bentham 320 (J. Bowring ed. 1843).

186. At this point the argument will run into boundary problems: is it, for example, a violation of the constitutional plan for prosecutorial authorities to *gather evidence* of criminal involvement on the part of the president prior to impeachment?

187. E.g., Federalists 65 & 69 (both Hamilton); 3 Elliot's Debates 240 (George Nicholas). Cf. 4 Elliot's Debates 109 (Iredell): "If the President . . . commits any misdemeanor in office, he is impeachable, removable from office . . . If he commits any crime, he is punishable by the laws of his country." There may be room for an inference here that in case of a felony, prosecution can be immediately pursued, but the quotation is also consistent with the contrary view.

188. It is with trepidation that I note the obvious tie-in with the Bill of Attainder Clause here. [As Solicitor General, Cox had argued *United States v. Brown* for the government. See pages 135–36.]

189. So, of course, would an impeachment proceeding.

190. In addition, the "station" and "disruption" objections to the general view that criminal prosecution can precede impeachment apply to at least some applications of the hybrid view.

191. October 25, 1973. Unsent, for the reasons outlined in the letter to Mr. Bork that follows this one.

192. January 24, 1994.

193. New Republic, May 23, 1988.

194. Los Angeles Times, December 23, 1990.

195. New York Times, October 23, 1993.

Chapter 4

1. Encounter, March 1967, pp. 80–92.

2. Anthony Lewis of *The New York Times* quotes the conclusion of one English newspaper lawyer's memorandum to the editorial staff of his paper: "If there is any doubt, don't publish. Let some other editor go to jail."

3. "Press investigations have sometimes helped considerably in bringing criminals to justice, notably in the Rouse case, the 'Brides in the Bath' case, and in the Messina Brothers case." The Lawyer, "The Press and the Law II," vol. 7, no. 2, p. 11 (Trinity 1964).

4. The hesitation engendered by the statute's ambiguity is compounded by the fact that it is the law in Scotland that once the police start investigating, which usually means as soon as the crime is committed, the press cannot conduct an independent probe. A number of English newspaper lawyers are fearful that an English court might one of these days adopt the Scottish rule. This fear cannot help but color the advice they give their editors.

5. In view of the disclosure that the *News of the World* was making payments to the star prosecution witness in the Moors murder case, it may not be out of order explicitly to note that freedom to report need not carry with it a right to pay witnesses, and surely implies no right to condition the amount of the payment on the outcome of the trial.

6. The contempt rule can discourage even posttrial appeals for witnesses. The 1965 Report on the Law and Press (issued by a joint working party of Justice and the International Press Institute) reported that on at least one occasion, fear of a contempt citation had prevented a newspaper from acceding to a request, made in behalf of a man who had just been convicted, that it run an item requesting anyone who was in a position to corroborate his alibi to come forward.

7. Even Mr. Kennedy, for one reason or another, repeatedly made the point that the trial judge may have been unaware of the effect his remarks were having.

8. At the other extreme, one magistrate announced that he would refuse to hear charges against drivers exceeding the new 70 m.p.h. speed limit. "I am making my stand in defence of a basic freedom," he declared. "If we accept this rule, it is going to make us into a nation of milk-sops. . . ."

9. The Court's language left open the possibility that a paper might be held in

contempt for printing a story presenting a "clear and present danger" to the administration of justice. The way the Court interpreted those words, however, left little doubt that it would be practically impossible for a contempt citation to escape reversal, and in fact since the three decisions no state court system has permitted a newspaper to be held in contempt, nor has Congress or any state legislature passed a statute restricting the coverage newspapers can give the criminal process.

10. To recognise this, of course, is neither to sanction the fact that reporters, television cameras and lights, etc., were permitted to crowd the interior of police headquarters—a condition that ultimately contributed to Oswald's death—nor to suggest that all the remarks made by the authorities, which included detailed and at times inaccurate characterisations of the evidence as well as assurances that the case against Oswald was "cinched," were in the public interest. [Neither—I write this sentence in the midst of the O. J. Simpson trial—does it seem to me that anything in this article requires the televising of trials, and certainly not extensive editorial comment on them by counsel for either side.]

11. Reversal on this ground does not prevent the state from trying the defendant again, for the reversal implies only that he was not given a fair chance to counter the state's case, and not necessarily that he is innocent. (On re-trial, Dr. Sheppard was acquitted by a jury, and is now a free man.) In England convictions are not reversed on publicity grounds. If they were, however, there could be no further trial, since reversal on any ground bars retrial.

12. The Court was moved also by the fact that the judge had permitted reporters such freedom of action inside the courtroom that they disrupted the trial. This sort of thing could, of course, never happen in a British courtroom. I hope it is unnecessary to point out that nothing I have said implies that it should.

13. The Court additionally suggested that state legal systems give some thought to limiting what police officers, lawyers, and witnesses can say to the press. Although there probably is a constitutional difference between muzzling the press and cutting off its sources of information (though I do not find the point so obvious as to justify the Court's total failure to discuss it), it would, I think, be unwise as a matter of policy for a state abruptly to outlaw all such press releases. Drying up the sources of information would carry with it some of the costs of the contempt rule. It would, for example, render difficult press surveillance of the investigative process and minimize the possibility that potential witnesses would hear about the case and come forward. Moreover, silencing those directly involved in a case might well have the effect of forcing the press to turn to others whose information is less reliable and possibly more damaging. (Remember the two cleaning ladies at Vassall's Dolphin Square flat, of whom the Vassall Tribunal's *White Paper* concluded: ". . . after their connection with Vassall had become known to the Press, they had been susceptible to the excitements and temptation of publicity and had made or at any rate encouraged certain statements about Vassall and his relations with Mr. Galbraith about which they had no real knowledge or even the means of it.")

14. The Supreme Court hinted that it, too, regards the next few years as a testing period: "We conclude that these [procedural protections] would have been sufficient to guarantee Sheppard a fair trial *and so do not consider what sanctions might be available against a recalcitrant press . . . .*" (Emphasis supplied.)

15. The specter of occasionally freeing a guilty person becomes less frightening if it is viewed against the fact that the perpetrators of most crimes are never apprehended in the first place. In England in 1964, of 1,066,467 offenses known to the police (which is somewhat less than all the offenses committed), only 39.6 percent were cleared up. (*The Times*, 21 July 1965, p. 6.) The rate of apprehension is probably higher with respect to the more serious offenses.

16. 88 Harv. L. Rev. 1482.

17. The theory was summarized briefly in *Democracy and Distrust*; its fuller development is presented here.

18. See Spence v. Washington, 418 U.S. 405 (1974) (per curiam); Smith v. Goguen, 415 U.S. 566 (1974); Street v. New York, 394 U.S. 576 (1969).

19. See 418 U.S. at 413–15 (relying on facts that Spence's disfigurement was temporary and unlikely to lead viewers to conclude that the government agreed with his views). One also hopes that the Court is not prepared to distinguish among future cases on the basis of its characterization of Spence's behavior as "a pointed expression of anguish" rather than "an act of mindless nihilism." Id. at 410. See also id. at 414–15 n. 10. It could happen, though. Cf. Wisconsin v. Yoder, 406 U.S. 205, 216–17, 222–23 n.11, 235–36 (1972) (distinguishing Amish, who are nice people not on welfare, from other groups who might seek to keep their children out of school).

20. "Desecration" and "improper use" statutes are commonly distinguished. See page 184. Until we reach section VI of this comment, at which point the distinction will become relevant, I shall use "desecration" to encompass all alterations.

21. Property rights would also seem to be involved. Believers in substantive due process—and I do not so count myself—might well question whether the state can constitutionally prohibit the destruction of one's own personal property unless it is unique (a Rembrandt) or scarce (uranium). The point is not pursued, however, since a governmental justification that would answer the First Amendment objection would seem a fortiori to dispose of this one.

22. 391 U.S. 367 (1968).

23. This comment makes no attempt to synthesize or even to describe the First Amendment thinking of the present Supreme Court. It suggests, rather, that there was a period of several years, spanning the end of Earl Warren's Chief Justiceship and the beginning of Warren Burger's, when the Court (with important, though by no means exclusive, input from Justice Harlan) began to describe a general theory of the First Amendment that assigned distinct and quite sensible roles to the two general techniques of evaluation—categorization and balancing—that had theretofore been regarded as mutually exclusive approaches to all free expression problems. The record of the Court more recently is by no means uniformly negative: much that was good in the period I have mentioned has been preserved. But the effort at explicit systematization seems to have been suspended, and the more recent decisions therefore do not figure importantly in this discussion.

24. This is Justice Harlan's characterization. 391 US. at 388 (Harlan, J., concurring).

25. Id. at 377 (bracketed numbers added). The requirement that the regulation be "within the constitutional power of the Government," id., is omitted on the ground

that it is superfluous in light of the most natural reading of what is designated criterion [1]. (Accepted notions of what is within the constitutional power of government have, in any event, become extremely broad.)

26. Earlier in the paragraph in which the Court stated its test, there is reference to cases in which "'speech' and 'nonspeech' elements are combined in the same course of conduct." Id. at 376. But the decisions cited in connection with that passage concern forms of expression that transcend narrowly defined "symbolic speech." See id. at 376–77 & nn. 22–27.

27. See, e.g., Struve, "The Less-Restrictive-Alternative Principle and Economic Due Process," 80 Harv. L. Rev. 1463, 1463 (1967) (footnotes omitted):

> The principle [endorsed by the author] is this: an economic regulation violates due process if the government . . . can achieve the purposes of the challenged regulation equally effectively by one or more narrower regulations. The term "equally effective" is meant literally: a regulation should not be invalidated because of an alternative that is "nearly as effective" or "tolerably effective."

28. See page 270. See also note 30 infra.

29. The 1965 Amendment prohibits such conduct and does nothing more. In other words, both the governmental interest and the operation of the 1965 Amendment are limited to the noncommunicative aspect of O'Brien's conduct. The governmental interest and the scope of the 1965 Amendment are limited to preventing harm to the smooth and efficient functioning of the Selective Service System.

391 U.S. at 381–82.

> In conclusion, we find that . . . because amended § 462(b) is an appropriately narrow means of protecting this interest and condemns only the independent noncommunicative impact of conduct within its reach . . . a sufficient governmental interest has been shown to justify O'Brien's conviction.

Id. at 382.

30. See also Ely, 'Legislative and Administrative Motivation in Constitutional Law,' 79 Yale L. J. 1205, 1340 (1910). In his opinion for the Court in United States v. Robel, 389 U.S. 258 (1967), decided a year before O'Brien, Chief Justice Warren had insisted in a footnote that less drastic means analysis involves no balancing of interests whatever, but rather an almost mechanical pruning of superfluous restraints:

> It has been suggested that this case should be decided by "balancing" the governmental interests expressed in the statute against the First Amendment rights asserted by the appellee. This we decline to do. . . . We have ruled only that the Constitution requires that the conflict between congressional power and individual rights be accommodated by legislation drawn more narrowly to avoid the conflict.

Id. at 268 n. 20. That is good propaganda, but it does not accurately reflect what was going on in Robel and similar cases. Of course the balancing is "at the margin," comparing the incremental promotion of the interest on which the government relies with the incremental threat to free expression. See Note, "Less Drastic Means and the First Amendment," 78 Yale L. J. 464, 467–48 (1969); see also United States v. Robel, 389 U.S. 258, 266 (1967) (stressing the nonsensitive nature of many of the positions from which Communists were barred). Thus a more manageable, indeed more intelligible, sort of balancing is involved, but it remains balancing nonetheless. But although *Robel*'s footnote did not accurately describe what was happening in *Robel*, it seems to have been taken seriously in *O'Brien*.

31. The interests served by protecting draft cards from destruction are listed by the Court, 391 U.S. at 378–80: they are plausible but little more. Should it be answered that that is the wrong level at which to view the government's interests— that the interests really involved are the draft, thus the armed forces and the very security of the nation—one can only respond that that move is always available. (An antihandbill ordinance, for example, does not simply reduce littering, it guards against urban deterioration and preserves the ecological balance, thereby safeguarding the very quality of life and even the survival of the planet.) There is, to repeat, nothing in *O'Brien*'s response to its requirement of "substantiality" that suggests that the requirement will not always be satisfiable.

32. In fact, the protection *O'Brien* ended up extending to the expression there involved is the precise equivalent of the protection that has been extended, since the mid-1930s, to economic activity by the so-called "minimum rationality" test. The question is whether there is any restriction that does not to some extent serve the state's goals, and the answer, provided the test is candidly applied, must inevitably be no.

33. See, e.g., Schneider v. State, 308 U.S. 147, 162 (1939).

34. See, e.g., T. Emerson, The System of Freedom of Expression 84–85 (1970). See also O'Brien v. United States, 376 F.2d 538, 540 & n. 6 (1st Cir. 1967), vacated, 391 U.S. 367 (1968). It is difficult to understand the respect in which this regulation is "narrower" or "less drastic." (The penalties for violation are precisely the same.) It seems, if anything, broader, in that it would cover all persons who had destroyed their draft cards and all other nonpossessors as well.

35. The qualification is necessitated by the inherent unpredictability of balancing tests.

36. I refer here to the two distinct approaches the Court has taken to the issue covered by *O'Brien*'s criterion [3]. A more important distinction, which is the major concern of this comment, was drawn by criterion [2]. See pages 181–83, 186–87.

37. This distinction between familiar and unfamiliar modes of expression rose to the surface in Justice Blackmun's plurality opinion in Lehman v. City of Shaker Heights, 418 U.S. 298 (1974):

> These situations [involving political advertising on public transit vehicles] are different from the traditional settings where First Amendment values inalterably prevail. . . . Here, we have no open space, no meeting hall, park, street corner, or other public thoroughfare. . . . No First Amendment forum is here to be found.

Id. at 302–4. Cf. United States v. O'Brien, 391 US. 367, 388–89 (1968) (Harlan, J., concurring) (availability of familiar forms of communication cited as reason for denying protection to unfamiliar).

38. This suggests another sort of reductio of O'Brien's argument. Since the expressive impact of the act derives largely from its illegality, that suggests that someone burning his draft card after O'Brien had won his case should lose. For the fact that O'Brien had won would probably mean that draft card burning would attract less attention, and that would make the First Amendment balance, necessarily at the heart of every burner's case, look very different. (O'Brien's challenge, of course, was only to the statute as applied. 391 US. at 376.) But that would seem to imply that the third burner—draft card burning again apparently being illegal—should win: he is back in O'Brien's position so far as the First Amendment balance is concerned. This would seem to generate a pattern of alternating constitutionality, with only the even-numbered burners—O'Brien being burner #1—going to jail. But people might soon catch on to the pattern, and start paying attention only to the even-numbered burners, since they are the only ones that are in any real sense risking imprisonment. That would imply that the even-numbered burners *shouldn't* go to jail, since burning greatly enhances their expressive ability and tips the First Amendment balance in their favor. So maybe it is the odd-numbered burners who should go to jail after all, since people will anticipate their winning and thus pay no attention. Or maybe only the burner immediately succeeding (a victorious) O'Brien should be punished, since he is the only one people will assume (albeit wrongly) is taking no risk and therefore ignore in sufficient numbers to blunt his First Amendment claim. You may have detected an element of frivolity in all this, but it does underscore the oddity of extending First Amendment protection to an act whose effectiveness as expression derives largely from its illegality.

39. See, e.g., Communist Party v. Subversive Activities Control Bd., 367 U.S. 1, 91 (1961); Barenblatt v. United States, 360 U.S. 109, 126 (1959). See also Dennis v. United States, 341 US. 494, 510 (1951).

40. The recent restriction of the overbreadth doctrine—see Parker v. Levy, 417 U.S. 733, 760–61 (1974); Broadrick v. Oklahoma, 413 U.S. 601, 615 (1973)—to the contrary notwithstanding, the Burger Court has kept alive many of the protections devised by the Warren Court to safeguard First Amendment values. *Brandenburg*, in particular, survives. See Hess v. Indiana, 414 U.S. 105, 108 (1973) (per curiam).

41. 395 U.S. 444, 447 (1969) (per curiam).

42. By indicating that a speech, to be punishable, must not only advocate immediate lawless action but also be likely to produce it, the Court supplements its categorization test with a reference to likely effect. The two elements are not stated in the alternative; both are plainly required. Thus in *Brandenburg* the danger question never had to be reached, because the speech itself did not fit within the category described by the Court. See also Cohen v. California, 403 U.S. 15, discussed at page 179; Yates v. United States, 354 U.S. 298, 325–25 (1957). Cf. Street v. New York, 394 U.S. 576, 591–93 (1969). On the difference between categorization on the one hand, and "clear and present danger," balancing and other approaches that are geared to the effects of the speech on the other, see also Gunther, "Learned Hand and the Origins of Modern First Amendment Doctrine: Some Fragments of History," 27 Stan. L. Rev. 719, 722, 754 (1975); Linde, "'Clear and Present Danger' Reexamined: Dissonance in the Brandenburg Concerto," 22 Stan. L. Rev. 1163, 1168–69 (1970); note 50 infra.

43. 393 U.S. 503 (1969).

44. Id. at 505–6.

45. *Tinker*, like *O'Brien*, does not employ a categorization approach. However, quite unlike *O'Brien*, it starts with an unmistakable presumption that the regulation involved is unconstitutional and sticks with it despite some far-from-trivial arguments on the other side. Nor is the difference attributable to a "swing vote" or two. Only Justices Black and Harlan dissented in *Tinker*, only Justice Douglas in *O'Brien*.

46. 403 U.S. 15 (1971).

47. Id. at 27 (Blackmun, J., dissenting). But see page 180.

48.

> [T]his case cannot be said to fall within those relatively few categories of instances where prior decisions have established the power of government to deal more comprehensively with certain forms of individual expression simply upon a showing that such a form was employed.

403 U.S. at 19–20.

> [W]e cannot overemphasize that . . . most situations where the State has a justifiable interest in regulating speech will fall within one or more of the various established exceptions, discussed above but not applicable here, to the usual rule that governmental bodies may not prescribe the form or content of individual expression.

Id. at 24.

49. Id. at 23–26.

50. Id. at 20, 23. But see Feiner v. New York, 340 U.S. 315 (1951).

As Justice Harlan suggests, the context in which a message is communicated may have to be considered in determining its meaning and thereby whether it falls within one of the unprotected categories of speech. 403 U.S. at 20, 23. (The less verbal the communication, the more necessary such a reference will be: an armband, for example, might convey a variety of messages or even no message at all.) What distinguishes a categorization approach from "clear and present danger" and similar tests is that context is considered only to determine the message the defendant was transmitting and not to estimate the danger that the audience would react to the message by antisocial conduct. Of course such considerations figure in the initial definition of the unprotected categories. See, e g., Chaplinsky v. New Hampshire, 315 U.S. 568, 571–72 (1942). But once they are defined, a categorization approach, in determining the constitutionality of a given restriction of expression, asks only "What was he saying?"—though admittedly a reference to context may be needed to answer that question. A clear and present danger or ad hoc balancing approach, in contrast, would regard that question as nondispositive: a given message will be sometimes protected and sometimes not, depending on the actual or projected behavior of the audience in response to it. See also Linde, supra note 42, at 1169.

Of course, the two kinds of reference to context will on occasion, particularly when nonverbal communication is involved, come so close to converging that it will be difficult to argue that the two general approaches in which they figure are importantly different. And none of us is so naive as to be unaware that any verbal formula is subject to conscious or unconscious manipulation. Perhaps, therefore, the wisest course is that recommended at various times (though not in precisely these terms) by Justices Black and Douglas: a total refusal to allow the inhibition of expression for reasons having to do with the actual or expected audience reaction to the message communicated. Although that is in fact my inclination (subject to a limited exception for demonstrable falsehoods regarding people or products), a majority of the Court has never endorsed such a view. And within the range of realistic alternatives, a categorization approach, which looks only to the message conveyed, does seem to me significantly preferable to one that would guess about dangers case by case. It cannot guarantee fair warning, nor is it a sure barrier against judicial capitulation in times of national hysteria. But in both regards it seems the best we are likely to be able to do: words may let us down from time to time, but they are all we have to work with.

51. See 403 U.S. at 20.

52. Thus Professor Henkin cites only this passage and proceeds to criticize the Court on that basis. See Henkin, "The Supreme Court, 1967 Term—Foreword: On Drawing Lines," 82 Harv. L. Rev. 63, 77–80 (1968).

53. 391 U.S. at 376.

54. T. Emerson, supra note 34, at 80.

55. Id. at 84.

56. Id. at 86.

57. Id.

58. See also Scanlon, "A Theory of Freedom of Expression," 1 Phil. & Pub. Aff. 204, 207–8 (1972). The expression-action distinction is by no means all there is to Professor Emerson's theory of the First Amendment. His sensitive explication of the values underlying that amendment cannot be ignored by anyone who would try to understand it. The impulse to define clear categories, and thus better to safeguard freedom of expression in times of national panic, is one I obviously share. I simply do not think this distinction can be made to work.

Nor will the cases be helpfully distinguished by asking whether the act involved is intended as political expression and/or likely to be perceived as such; see, e.g., Spence v. Washington, 418 U.S. 405, 410–11 (1974) (per curiam); Cohen v. California, 403 U.S. 15, 18 (1971); Note, "Symbolic Conduct," 68 Colum. L. Rev. 1091, 1109 (1968). The firebombing of an induction center or the assassination of a president can obviously be both.

59. 403 U.S. at 18 (citation omitted).

60. 391 U.S. at 377 (emphasis added).

61. See, e.g., Feiner v. New York, 340 U.S. 315, 319–20 (1951) ("Petitioner was thus neither arrested nor convicted for the making or the content of his speech. Rather, it was the reaction which it actually engendered."). See also Tinker v. Des Moines Indep. Community School District, 393 U.S. 503, 526 (1969) (Harlan, J., dissenting).

62. Conceivably, the government might assert that two interests justify its action, one related to expression, the other not. For example, a municipality might attempt to enjoin the operations of a new drive-in theater both because the theater plans to specialize in racy films and because public showing of films at the theater will create a traffic hazard. (The theory here would be that any configuration of shapes on the screen, communicative or not, would distract drivers.) On review, the

first justification would "fail" criterion [2] and would be invalid unless the films were obscene under the prevailing standard. However, the second justification would "pass" criterion [2] and its validity would be judged under criterion [3]. At this point, the outcome would depend upon the particular less restrictive alternative test used by the court. See pages 175–77. If the second justification satisfies criterion [3], the regulation would be valid even if the first justification failed to survive the categorization analysis.

63. The *O'Brien* opinion itself suggests this definition of its test, in distinguishing the earlier—and in terms of the conduct regulated, disturbingly similar—case of Stromberg v. California, 283 US. 359 (1931):

> The case at bar is therefore unlike one where the alleged governmental interest in regulating conduct arises in some measure because the communication allegedly integral to the conduct is itself thought to be harmful. In *Stromberg v. California* . . . , for example, this Court struck down a statutory phrase which punished people who expressed their "opposition to organized government" by displaying "any flag, badge, banner, or device."

391 U.S. at 382. I shall suggest later that this specification of *O'Brien*'s criterion [2], though correct and helpful as far as it goes, is incomplete.

64. Had armbands been banned simply because the school board favored the war, the case would have been still easier. See Tinker v. Des Moines Indep. Community School District, 393 U.S. 503, 526 (1969) (Harlan, J., dissenting). However, given that the state's alternative account—a fear of disruption and distraction—plausibly fit the regulation, the Court was quite correct in refusing to assume the less admirable motivation. But that turns out not to matter greatly, because the state's account too was geared to the communicative nature of the armbands.

65. *Tinker* would have been a quite different case had it arisen, for example, in the context of a school regulation banning armbands in woodworking class along with all other sartorial embellishments liable to become safety hazards.

66. See 403 U.S. at 26 ("words are often chosen as much for their emotive as their cognitive force").

67. See 50 U.S.C. § 462(b)(3) (Appendix) (1970).

68. 321 U.S. 158 (1944).

69. I am disregarding for purposes of this analysis the fact that religious literature was involved. In fact I would argue that it should be disregarded even for purposes of a "free exercise" analysis, since the regulation did not single out religious expression for inhibition. See pages 191–96. The Court has not always agreed, however. Compare Martin v. City of Struthers, 319 U.S. 141 (1943), with Breard v. Alexandria, 341 U.S. 622 (1951).

70. See Kovacs v. Cooper, 336 U.S. 77 (1949).

71. Cf. Reynolds v. Tennessee, 414 U.S. 1163 (1974) (refusing to review conviction, under statute prohibiting disturbance of religious assemblies, for chanting during President Nixon's speech at the Reverend Billy Graham's East Tennessee Crusade, held in a football stadium in Knoxville). Of course, it may prove difficult to frame such a statute in language not vulnerable to charges of vagueness, particularly if one does not wish to outlaw applause.

72. The Court's reaction to disorderly conduct convictions would also quite ob-

viously vary significantly according to whether or not the theory of the arrest and conviction was that the disorder arose in response to what the defendant was saying. A loud and incoherent drunk is one thing, a "provocative" speaker another.

73. "Absolutism" is a term that has been used inconsistently by both friend and foe. The only clear core meaning it carries is that *something* is "absolutely" required, forbidden or protected, regardless of context: thus certain restrictions may be absolutely proscribed, certain categories of speech absolutely sheltered. Any categorization approach, therefore, can quite properly be labeled absolutist. The term has often been identified, usually by foes, with the view that all expression is to be absolutely protected. However, I am aware of no one who has been seriously prepared so to define it and at the same time endorse it. See, e.g., pages 179–80 (views of Professor Emerson). But cf. Linde, supra note 42, at 1183 (arguing that "any law directed in terms against some communicative content of speech" should be declared unconstitutional, provided that "the proscribed content is of a kind which falls under any circumstances within the meaning of the first amendment"). Professor Linde's approach has obvious similarities to that suggested in the text of this comment—surely the animating instincts are related—but there is at least one clear and important difference. I do not refer to my recognition that some categories of speech can be proscribed because of their content, for Linde's proviso has precisely the same effect. (Indeed, it appears he may be willing to exclude from the coverage of his principle certain *modes* of communication on the ground that they are not protected "speech." See id. at 1183 n. 66 [flagging the possibility that cases like *Tinker* and *Street* may fall outside his principle].) The important difference, and perhaps this is the ground on which Professor Linde would prefer to distinguish *Tinker* and *Street*, is that I would treat as properly subject to the stronger categorization approach any restriction that is justified by reference to the message the defendant is communicating, irrespective of whether the law authorizing the restriction is in terms directed to the restriction of expression. Where the authorizing law is not so directed on its face, Linde is prepared to test the restriction by clear and present danger or another approach that considers the likely effect of the communication. See id. at 1174, 1185.

74. It is true that even the clearest principle can be manipulated—but only up to a point. Thus while such principles cannot guarantee liberty—nothing can—they are the surest hedge against judicial capitulation that is available:

> [E]ven their Ineffabilities, the Nine Elder Statesmen, have not shown themselves wholly immune from the "herd instinct" . . . . I own I should prefer a qualitative formula, hard, conventional, difficult to evade. If it could become sacred by the incrustations of time and precedent it might be made to serve just a little to withhold the torrents of passion to which . . . democracies [are] subject . . . .

Letter from Learned Hand to Zechariah Chafee, Jr., Jan. 2, 1921, quoted in Gunther, supra note 42, at 749–50. (Hand's views obviously changed as he grew older. See generally L. Hand, The Bill of Rights [1958].)

75. See generally Rosenblatt, "Flag Desecration Statutes: History and Analysis," 1972 Wash. U. L. Q. 193, 195–98 & nn. 17, 22. One might wonder whether the protection of the American flag is not a matter of exclusively federal concern. This argument was rejected in Halter v. Nebraska, 205 U.S. 34 (1907). The Court rested

its decision in part upon the questionable conclusion that no federal statute then enacted was relevant. Id. at 41–42. But see id. at 39. There is one now, however, see 18 U.S.C. § 700(a) (1970), quoted note 80 infra, but Congress has expressly provided that the statute not be construed to preempt state laws, see 18 U.S.C. § 700(c) (1970).

76. See Spence v. Washington, 418 U.S. 405, 406 (1974) (per curiam). However, the Uniform Flag Act, 9B Uniform Laws Ann. 48 (1966), which has been adopted in a number of states, see Rosenblatt, supra note 75, at 196–97, entitles this the "mutilation" provision, reserving "desecration" for another purpose. See Uniform Flag Act §§ 2, 3, supra.

77. Uniform Flag Act § 3, supra note 76.

78. 394 US 576 (1969). Actually the holding was that the law's application to verbal expression was unconstitutional in all but the most unusual circumstances— as where the defendant incited immediate lawless action or directly invited physical retaliation. See id. at 591–92. Since Street did neither, the Court was not confronted with, and did not comment on, the question whether the preponderance of possible unconstitutional applications rendered the provision relating to words void for overbreadth. We shall see, however, that the provision is unconstitutional on its face for reasons other than overbreadth, in that its application is limited to "unpatriotic" expression. Thus even if its overinclusiveness is not fatal, its underinclusiveness is.

79. 415 US. 566 (1974). The language actually at issue—"treat contemptuously" rather than "cast contempt upon"—was obviously so close that distinction is impossible.

80. Were these words to be construed otherwise, they would raise the problem discussed at pages 184–87. The federal statute, 18 U.S.C. § 700(a) (1970), leaves no doubt about its lack of neutrality:

> Whoever knowingly casts contempt upon any flag of the United States by publicly mutilating, defacing, defiling, burning, or trampling upon it shall be fined not more than $1,000 or imprisoned for not more than one year, or both.

81. Justice Fortas's suggestion that because the state can generally prohibit burning on public thoroughfares it necessarily can prohibit the contemptuous burning of flags there, see Street v. New York, 394 U.S. 576, 616 (1969) (Fortas, J., dissenting), is a classic example of the "greater includes the lesser" fallacy. The old saw that the government can "deal with one part of a problem at a time" surely has no application in First Amendment cases. See, e.g., Police Dep't v. Mosley, 408 U.S. 92 (1972). Had Street in fact been charged under a general no-burning ordinance, his prosecution would have raised the sort of problem considered at pages 175–77.

82. Virtually all prosecutions authorized by such laws would be unconstitutional under *Brandenburg* and *Cohen*. The likelihood that the laws would be invalid on their face as overbroad has been diminishing in recent years. See, e.g., Broadrick v. Oklahoma, 413 U.S. 601 (1973). But even if such statutes were judicially or legislatively limited to the categories approved by *Brandenburg* and *Cohen*—and thus outlawed only those hostile alterations or destructions of the flag that (as by a prearranged signal) either directly incited immediate lawless action or explicitly invited retaliation—they would still be invalid on their face for limiting their coverage to contemptuous treatment of the flag. See Smith v. Goguen, 415 US. 566, 588

(1974) (White, J., concurring in the judgment); cf. Police Dep't v. Mosley, 408 U.S. 92, 96 (1972) (law allowing labor picketers but not others to demonstrate in front of schools unconstitutional); Schacht v. United States, 398 U.S. 58, 62–63 (1970) (law denying actors use of military uniforms if their theatrical production would "tend to discredit" the military unconstitutional). See also Stromberg v. California, 283 U.S. 359, 369–70 (1931).

83. See Spence v. Washington, 418 U.S. 405, 406–7 (1974) (per curiam). Somewhat perversely, the Uniform Flag Act entitles this the "desecration" provision.

84. Uniform Flag Act § 2, supra note 76.

85. Neutral, that is, as respects the message the defendant is conveying. But cf. pages 186–87.

86. The constitutionality of banning this sort of embellishment might be thought to depend on the question whether "commercial speech" will remain an unprotected category of expression. [It has not.]

87. A similar approach of ideological neutrality might be employed in an attempt to save certain aspects of the "desecration" provisions discussed above. For example, a state might without qualification simply outlaw intentionally stepping on the flag. It seems unlikely that any such "neutral" approach to flag burning would be practicable, however, at least so long as the Boy Scouts continue to insist that that is the only appropriate way to dispose of one.

88. Smith v. Goguen, 415 U.S. 566, 587 (1974) (White, J., concurring in the judgment).

89. Spence v. Washington, 418 U.S. 405, 417 (1974) (Rehnquist, J., dissenting).

90. See id. at 409 ("We have no doubt that the state or national governments constitutionally may forbid anyone from mishandling in any manner a flag that is public property").

91. The fact that such laws typically prohibit the public display of altered flags does not, of course, imply that the state is concerned only with censoring the alterer's expression: it is entirely consistent with an intention only to prevent interference with the ideas the flag conveys.

In a footnote in *Spence* the Court stated:

If this interest [prevention of interference] is valid, we note that it is directly related to expression in the context of activity like that undertaken by appellant. For that reason and because no other governmental interest unrelated to expression has been advanced or can be supported on this record, the . . . analysis of United States v. O'Brien . . . is inapplicable.

418 U.S. at 414 n. 8. Of course expression is involved, namely the expression of the ideas the flag conveys; what the Court apparently fails to take into account is the fact that the state interest is one that is unconcerned with what ideas, if any, the defendant is expressing. However, there may have been more analysis in the Court's footnote than meets the eye. I shall argue later that the Court's conclusion was correct, that indeed this should be regarded as an interest that is related to the suppression of expression within the meaning of *O'Brien*'s second criterion. See pages 186–87.

92. Otherwise, the official endorsement of the flag as a national symbol would seem to be unconstitutional. West Virginia Bd. of Educ. v. Barnette, 319 U.S. 624

(1943), is not authority to the contrary: a declaration that people cannot be compelled to affirm their patriotism by saluting the flag is not the same as a declaration that the government has no interest whatever in encouraging patriotism by such a symbol. *Barnette* is, however, a precedent most relevant to the problem posed by improper use statutes. See note 95 infra.

93. An individual can obviously employ his flag in the exercise of his First Amendment freedoms; indeed he does so every time he flies it. By interfering with that expression, whether or not I actually destroy his physical property, I would be subjecting myself to quite justifiable punishment by the state: *that* seems the case that is analogous to the interrupting audience.

94. See pages 176–77.

95. Cf. West Virginia Bd. of Educ. v. Barnette, 319 U.S. 624 (1943) (mandatory flag salutes held unconstitutional).

Chapter 5

1. 380 U.S. 163.

2. The holding must be on constitutional grounds, as it would be a gross perversion of congressional intent to hold that the Supreme Being Clause is broad enough to encompass *all* conscientious objections. [This, however, is basically what the Court (obviously moved by constitutional considerations) did. See pages 193–94.] Striking down the Supreme Being Clause would not entail striking down the entire conscientious objector provision, as it seems to me the Supreme Being Clause is severable; if this Court affirms No. 50, the result will be—until Congress acts—that any good-faith conscientious objector will be entitled to exemption.

3. 79 Yale L. J. 1205, 1313–27.

4.

> Government in our democracy, state and national, must be neutral in matters of religious theory, doctrine, and practice. It may not be hostile to any religion or to the advocacy of no-religion; and it may not aid, foster, or promote one religion or religious theory against another or even against the militant opposite. The First Amendment mandates governmental neutrality between religion and religion, and between religion and nonreligion.

Epperson v. Arkansas, 393 U.S. 97, 103–4 (1968).

5. See Welsh v. United States, 398 U.S. 333, 357–62 (1970) (Harlan, J., concurring); Kurland, "Of Church and State and the Supreme Court," 29 U. Chi. L. Rev. 1 (1961); Weiss, "Privilege, Posture and Protection: 'Religion' in the Law," 73 Yale L. J. 593 (1964).

6. See Walz v. Tax Commission of the City of New York, 397 U.S. 664, 668–72 (1970); cf. A. Bickel, The Supreme Court and the Idea of Progress 67–68 (1970). This was Mr. Justice Harlan's view. Sherbert v. Verner, 374 U.S. 398, 422–23 (1963) (Harlan, J., dissenting). It is no longer. Welsh v. United States, 398 U.S. 333, 359 n. 9 (1970) (Harlan, J., concurring).

Conceivable, of course, is a third view, albeit one difficult to reconcile with the notion of neutrality: that the Court should force government officials sometimes to make special accommodations for, and sometimes to impose special limitations upon, religions. Though I have not surveyed all the literature, I have not seen this advocated as a general approach, though—as we shall see—the *Sherbert* case can be defended in no other terms.

7. 374 U.S. 203, 222 (1963).

8. [See pages 247–53.]

9. *Schempp*, for example, indicates that if "the primary effect" is religious, a law must fall, but that if a "a primary effect" is secular, it must stand. 374 U.S. at 222.

10. The exceptional case is exemplified by Everson v. Board of Education, 330 U.S. 1 (1947). The regulation under attack did, it is true, specify that bus transportation would be furnished to students at public and Roman Catholic schools. Id. at 4 n. 2. It is therefore understandable that Justice Jackson, dissenting, framed the question for decision thus: "Is it constitutional to tax this complainant to pay the costs of carrying pupils to Church schools *of one specified denomination?*" Id. at 21 (emphasis supplied). However, when it is taken into account that all children in the township attended either a public or Roman Catholic school, id. at 4 n. 2, the Court's formulation seems more apt: "Its legislation, as applied, does no more than provide a general program to help parents get their children, regardless of their religion, safely and expeditiously to and from accredited schools." Id. at 18. The terms in which a law classifies are indeed important, as they are immensely probative of a desire specially to advance or limit religion, and ninety-nine times out of a hundred, a religious classification will prove a religious motivation. But analyses geared solely to "classification" inevitably will boggle over *Everson*. See Kurland, supra note 5, at 67–72. For *Everson* is the hundredth case.

11. Restoring a Roman Catholic mission as part of a general program of preserving historic monuments would probably present a difference case. But cf. Frohliger v. Richardson, 63 Cal. App. 209, 218 P. 497 (1923).

12. 374 U.S. at 225.

13. 393 U.S. 97 (1968).

14. There might be circumstances under which an illegitimate motivation could be found to underlie the elimination of all study of man's origins and perhaps even the elimination of biology altogether. The most obvious example would be an action taken by Arkansas in response to the *Epperson* decision.

15. The state did urge that Darwin's theory is unusually controversial. This is a defense the Court is [rightly] unwilling to credit as legitimate, however.

16. Reynolds v. United States, 98 U.S. 145 (1878). See also Cleveland v. United States, 329 U.S. 14 (1946); cf. Prince v. Massachusetts, 321 U.S. 158 (1944).

17. 374 U.S. 398 (1963).

18. See note 23 infra.

19. Torcaso v. Watkins, 367 U.S. 488 (1961).

20. 380 U.S. 163, 166, 173 (1965).

21. 398 U.S. 333 (1970).

22. The *Seeger* construction is widely assumed to have resulted from constitutional pressure—a conclusion with which it is impossible to quarrel, since it is so plainly indefensible on any other basis. See Clark, "Guidelines for the Free Exercise Clause," 83 Harv. L. Rev. 327, 341 (1969); [pages 188–90].

23. On the other hand, the Court suggested that one of the reasons it was prepared to honor Mrs. Sherbert's claim was that there were few Seventh Day Advent-

ists in the county involved, and that most of them had been able to find suitable employment. 374 U.S. at 399 n. 2, 409–10. This suggestion could incline officials toward requiring work on a day that constitutes the Sabbath of a sizeable minority; for if we are to take the Court seriously, the existence of a large number of religious objectors might serve to defeat all their claims. I am with Justice Harlan in hoping the Court did not here mean what it said:

> The Court does suggest, in a rather startling disclaimer . . . that its holding is limited in applicability to those whole religious convictions do not make them "non-productive" members of society, noting that most of the Seventh-day Adventists in the Spartanburg area are employed. But surely this disclaimer cannot be taken seriously, for the Court cannot mean that the case would have come out differently if none of the Seventh-day Adventists in Spartanburg had been gainfully employed, or if the appellant's religion had prevented her from working on Tuesdays instead of Saturdays. Nor can the Court be suggesting that it will make a value judgment in each case as to whether a particular individual's religious convictions prevent him from being "productive." I can think of no more inappropriate function for this Court to perform.

374 U.S. at 420–21 n. 2. (Harlan, J., dissenting).

24. 366 U.S. 599 (1961).

25. The second flag salute decision, West Virginia State Board of Education v. Barnette, 319 U.S. 624 (1943), is occasionally said to stand for the proposition that the state is sometimes obligated to carve religious exemptions out of valid across-the-board requirements. See, e.g., Braunfield v. Brown, 366 U.S. 599, 603 (1961). The Court in *Barnette*, however, stated that the presence or absence of religious objections on the part of the complainants was entirely beside the point, 319 U.S. at 634–35. What *Barnette* holds is that the state simply cannot compel an affirmation of patriotic loyalty.

26. 392 U.S. 236, 243 (1968).

27. [See 79 Yale L. J. at 1272–73.]

28. 397 U.S. 664 (1970).

29. Id. at 697. The reference to gerrymanders is particularly suggestive, since whether something is a "gerrymander" is a question of motivation. See page 253.

30. The statute's list of organizations might well turn out to be underinclusive with respect to any general goal one could formulate. But that is beside the point, which is that the list fits some broader aim with precision sufficient to negate the suggestion of a desire to single out religion for advancement. See 397 U.S. 696–99 (Harlan, J., concurring).

31. April 13, 1984.

32. ["Nativity Ruling Insults Jews," New York Times, March 26, 1984.]

Chapter 6

1. 372 U.S. 335. Actually, at the time I was working on it the case was *Gideon v. Cochran*, but before it was decided Cochran was replaced by Wainwright as director of the Florida Division of Corrections.

2. [Betts v. Brady, 316 U.S. 455 (1942), holding that states are constitutionally obligated to appoint counsel for indigent defendants in felony trials only where there are "special circumstances" unusually requiring the assistance of a lawyer.]

3. At least I *hope* he won't be able to predict that one.

4. 43 Am. U. L. Rev. 28 (1993). The talk was delivered March 18, 1993.

5. [Different one.]

6. [And now, at least potentially, Congress's.]

7. June 25, 1990.

8. Less than you might imagine, as San Diego had long been a city where guilty verdicts were essentially automatic. The sight of an appointed lawyer actually fighting for his client so shocked local juries that a number of them actually acquitted. (Of course some other lawyers also fought as well, and our example increased the incidence of such behavior, and to this day—obviously thanks as much to our successors as to us founding fathers—at least the federal defender program in San Diego remains one of the models nationwide.)

9. New York Times, May 19, 1971, at 28, col. 1.

10. 401 U.S. 222 (1971).

11. 384 U.S. 436 (1966).

12. Washington Post, Feb. 25, 1971, at A-1, col. 7.

13. Mr. Justice Brennan wrote a dissenting opinion for himself and Justices Douglas and Marshall. Mr. Justice Black dissented without opinion.

14. 400 U.S. 309 (1971); see notes 41, 42. 66, 96, 97 infra.

15. 401 U.S. at 224. The questioning took place before the Court's decision in Miranda v. Arizona, 384 U.S. 436 (1966), but the trial was held after it. Thus under Johnson v. New Jersey, 384 U.S. 719 (1966), the *Miranda* rules were applicable.

16. Appendix in the Supreme Court at 74, Harris v. New York, 401 U.S. 222 (1971). He subsequently indicated he would be satisfied to see a lawyer "tomorrow." Id.

17. Id. at 58–63. Concerning the transaction for which he was convicted, petitioner testified at trial that the bags that had been sold contained baking powder rather than heroin. Id. at 30–31. He was then asked on cross-examination whether he recalled having admitted to the police that he had bought "two five-dollar bags of heroin for Bermudez," and that he had "handed the narcotics to Bermudez who had given him twelve dollars and half of the heroin in one of the envelopes." See Brief of District Attorney of New York County at 12, Harris v. New York, 401 U.S. 222 (1971). There can be no doubt, therefore—as indeed the Chief Justice acknowledged—that the impeachment was direct rather than collateral.

18. Appendix at 95.

19. 401 U.S. at 224. The Court's assertion is crucial because it later states that an inadmissible statement can be used to impeach "provided of course that the trustworthiness of the evidence satisfies legal standards." Id. The reference to "legal standards" apparently relates to the "voluntariness of the confession." Id. at 229 n. 2.

20. Appendix at 57, 69.

21. Petition for Certiorari at 10, Brief for Petitioner at 11, 19, 24, Transcript of Oral Argument at 12, 18, Harris v. New York, 401 U.S. 222 (1971).

22. Appendix at 57 (emphasis supplied).

23. 18 N.Y.2d 318, 322–23, 221 N.E.2d 541–42, 274 N.Y.S. 873, 875 (1966).

24. Appendix at 69. Counsel was cut off by the trial judge before he could complete the sentence, but the meaning is clear.

25. Id. at 70 (emphasis supplied).

26. *Kulis* involved a statement whose admissibility was not governed by *Miranda*. The court found it inadmissible under Escobedo v. Illinois, 378 U.S. 478 (1964), and People v. Donovan, 13 N.Y.2d 148, 193 N.E.2d 628, 243 N.Y.S.2d 841 (1963). No distinction was drawn in *Kulis* between statements secured in violation of *Escobedo* and those that would be deemed involuntary in the more traditional sense of that term.

27. See, e.g., Appellee's Brief at 4, Harris v. People, 31 App. Div. 2d 828, 298 N.Y.S.2d 245 (1969). In referring to statements that are involuntary in the pre-*Miranda* sense, we mean to include those statements that would be deemed involuntary or coerced under Johnson v. New Jersey, 384 U.S. 719 (1966).

28. Appellee's Brief at 4. In its brief in opposition to certiorari, the state took the position that there was no need for a hearing on the issue of voluntariness, since

> without doubt, the statement would have been ruled involuntary and hence inadmissible at the trial, because, as we have already pointed out, it was deficient in terms of *Miranda*. . . . [T]he District Attorney's Office, because the defect is a glaring one, came to precisely the same conclusion, that it was involuntary and inadmissible . . . .

Respondent's Brief in Opposition to Certiorari at 9–10, Harris v. New York, 401 U.S. 222 (1971). The state did not, in its brief in opposition, distinguish between a statement taken in violation of *Miranda* and a statement that would have been deemed involuntary in the pre-*Miranda* sense. "It is our submission to the Court that *Miranda* represents simply a new and heightened gauge of voluntariness." Id. at 4. In refusing to draw such a distinction, the state was following New York law, which likewise drew no such distinction for impeachment purposes. See People v. Kulis, 18 N.Y.2d 318, 221 N.E.2d 541, 274 N.Y.S.2d 873 (1966).

In its brief on the merits, the state shifted its position, arguing that "on its face there is surely no flaw in the voluntariness of this statement." Brief for Respondent at 35, Harris v. New York, 401 U.S. 222 (1971). The state also said that "the question of voluntariness was never raised at the trial . . . ." Id. (The record, however, clearly establishes that it was. See page 213.) Indeed, the state conceded that "[i]f the question of voluntariness is decided adversely to the prosecutor, he may not use the statement to impeach. . . ." (It is not clear whether this purported to be a statement of New York law or federal constitutional law.)

Thus, in its first brief before the Court, the state apparently conceded that the statement was involuntary, but argued that even involuntary statements may be used to impeach; whereas in its second brief, it apparently conceded that if the statement was involuntary it could not be used to impeach, but argued that the statement was voluntary. This confusion was somewhat cleared up during the oral argument, where the latter position was taken.

29. 378 U.S. 368 (1964). *Jackson* involved a claim of involuntariness in the pre-*Miranda* sense.

30. Petition for Certiorari at 10.

It is respectfully submitted that such an illegally obtained statement cannot be used unless and until the requirements of a pretrial determination of voluntariness have been fulfilled in accordance with *Jackson*.

Id.

31. Transcript of Oral Argument at 10.

32. Id. at 10–11.

33. Id. at 12. Petitioner's counsel then went on to restate his position in the following terms:

I think it was clearly illegally obtained and I point out respectfully that that was conceded all the way through the New York courts. It was treated as such. It was not conceded to be involuntary in the classic sense, but by our foreclosure from it, by the trial judge's reading of Kulis as allowing this in an involuntary case, I think this is the posture in which this case comes before this Court.

Id. at 13–14. Petitioner's claim that the statement was involuntary in the pre-*Miranda* sense was asserted in another relevant context. Justice Blackmun asked whether petitioner would "be here today" if Johnson v. New Jersey, 384 U.S. 719 (1966), had held "that retroactivity was directed to the time of the taking of the statement rather than to the time of the beginning of the trial." Transcript of Oral Argument at 19. (The trial in this case postdated *Miranda*, but the statement was taken before that decision.) Petitioner's counsel answered: "Yes, because in that posture could they possibly have denied us a hearing on voluntariness?" Id. at 20. In other words, petitioner asserted that even if *Miranda* had not been applicable, he would have "been here" on the voluntariness claim.

34. Id. at 12.

35. Id. at 4.

36. Appendix at 59.

37. Id. at 64; Brief for Petitioner at 5.

38. Id.; Appendix at 72, 74.

39. Transcript of Oral Argument at 7. Indeed, the New York County District Attorney's brief acknowledged that the relevant portion of the pretrial statement was a "false account." Note 94 infra.

40. Nor did the Court purport to be determining for itself—as it could not properly do on this record—that the statement was voluntary in the pre-*Miranda* sense. See, e.g., Machibroda v. United States, 368 U.S. 487 (1962).

41. Mr. Justice Blackmun's opinion for the Court in Wyman v. James, 400 U.S. 309 (1971), at one point uses a somewhat similar approach, albeit with respect to a much less crucial point. In arguing that most welfare home "visits" are reasonable (an irrelevant argument, since the claim of respondent accepted by the court below was that a warrant should have been obtained), the Court notes that Mrs. James received advanced written notice of the visit she refused (with the consequence that her assistance was terminated). 400 U.S. at 320. And so she did. But *James* was a class action, and all twelve of the affidavits other than Mrs. James's filed by the

plaintiffs recited that the case worker "most often" comes without warning! The Court simply notes this troublesome fact in a footnote and makes no comment whatsoever in response. 400 U.S. at 320 n. 8. This is, we suppose, preferable to not mentioning it at all but still seems less than adequate.

42. Wyman v. James, 400 U.S. 309 (1971), in several ways provides another textbook example of reaching out prematurely to decide a broad and novel issue of constitutional law. (And, like *Harris*, it disregards at least one narrow ground that would have compelled the contrary decision.) The record was so inadequate with respect to some details of home visits—for example, whether advance notice is typically given, see note 41 supra—that even counsel for the state conceded in oral argument that a hearing might be appropriate to clarify the situation. Transcript of Oral Argument at 3, Wyman v. James, 400 U.S. 309 (1971). The state further argued that Mrs. James had failed to exhaust her state remedies, that the Court should withhold decision for the moment to let the state system grapple with the issue and perhaps build in safeguards that would blunt Mrs. James's claim of unreasonableness. It is quite clearly settled that the exhaustion requirement as such does not apply in Section 1983 actions, which *James* was. See Damico v. California, 389 U.S. 416 (1967). But the Court of late has shown a renewed enthusiasm for having district courts, in 1983 actions as well as others, "abstain" while the state system clarifies and has the first constitutional crack at the practice under attack. See, e.g., Dyson v. Stein, 401 U.S. 200 (1971). (On the admittedly fine distinction between the exhaustion and abstention doctrines in 1983 actions, see, e.g., C. Wright, Law of Federal Courts 197 [2d ed. 1970]).

If such abstention is proper in First Amendment areas, where the very rights in issue will be "chilled" while the state system operates, it would surely seem proper in the *James* context as well, particularly in light of representations made in the state's brief concerning the sort of safeguards that might be built in by the state authorities.

> [T]he appellee here began but did not complete the administrative hearing process. She had a prior termination hearing but did not proceed to a state fair hearing. . . . Complete exhaustion of administrative remedies was particularly important here because of the vague nature of the complaint and the essentially administrative nature of the relief sought. Appellee was complaining about being asked unspecified questions. The twelve recipients supporting her position complained of the timing of the visits and the circumstances under which interviews are conducted. . . .
>
> [A] state forum, judicial or administrative, might have been able to alter substantially the nature of the questions involved . . . by its interpretation of Section 134-a of the New York Social Services Law which requires investigation of an application and personal contacts but does not mandate a home visit. This would apparently be a case of first impression for the State agency which could promulgate a flexible rule or adhere to a strict one. . . . At the least, they might require a showing of individual necessity for a home as opposed to an office visit before termination of aid if such a course were deemed wise.

Brief for Appellant at 43–44, Wyman v. James, 400 U.S. 309 (1971). Of course the optimism expressed in the quoted passage is somewhat self-serving, but one thing is clear: a court genuinely committed to avoiding the decision of issues whose contours cannot clearly be discerned could have somehow—by remand or a sort of abstention—found a way to educate itself concerning the precise nature of the visits under attack before permanently placing on them the imprimatur of constitutional legitimacy.

Additionally, the Court in *James* made no attempt whatever to counter Justice Marshall's argument that unconsented-to visits (as Mrs. James's certainly were) have been forbidden by the supervising federal authorities. Marshall's suggested nonconstitutional disposition not only would have had the effect of "remanding" the question to the political processes, but also seems soundly grounded in the language of the federal handbook of Public Assistance Administration:

> The [state welfare] agency especially guards against violation of legal rights and common decencies in such areas as entering a home by force, *or without permission*, or under false pretenses; making home visits outside of working hours, and particularly making such visits during sleeping hours.

Dep't of HEW, Handbook of Public Assistance Administration, Pt. IV § 2200(a) (emphasis supplied). A federal regulation, so long as it is within the authority delegated by a valid federal statute, generally takes precedence over state law. Whether the handbook's provision should count as such a regulation seems to us somewhat unclear. The Court did not address that issue, however, and indeed used the word "forbidden" in relying on other phrases of the very same regulation to buttress its claim that home visits generally are reasonable. 401 U.S. at 321.

Even granting the Court's desire to break with the tradition that only an emergency can justify invading a citizen's privacy without a warrant, it did so precipitously, without really knowing what the searches in issue looked like, without letting the state system operate so as to inform it and perhaps to deal with the searches' more objectionable features, and without acceding to the apparent federal command that such searches take place only with the consent of the searched. But just as questionable practices should not be invalidated in ignorance, they should not be legitimated in ignorance.

43. Transcript of Oral Argument at 25.

44. Id. This issue was pressed further in the following exchange among Justice Stewart, Chief Justice Burger, and counsel for the state:

> Q. I didn't mean an untrue confession, I meant simply an involuntary confession, could you use that to impeach him?
> A. No, Mr. Justice Stewart, I don't think we could, for this reason: The point I am trying to make is a voluntary confession, if it is voluntary in the traditional sense, can be relied upon to express the truth, whereas an involuntary confession is subject, to take the obvious example, a man will say anything to keep from being beaten and all we have to do is go to some of the countries beyond the Iron Curtain to demonstrate that. There is a point beyond which human endurance can't continue. . . .
> Q. . . . And let's assume further that it is wholly true. Could you have used that to impeach him?
> A. I don't think so, Mr. Justice Stewart, because the thought is that we must define

a class of confessions which may be used for these purposes, and I think once you define the class as being a true confession rather than a voluntary confession, then you're getting into extraneous matters that perhaps aren't properly explored in the context of this.

Q. What you are saying then is that it can't be given any use because it is inherently unreliable as being involuntary?

A. As being involuntary, yes, Mr. Chief Justice.

Id. at 26–27.

45. Id. at 27–28. The oral argument then proceeded in the following way:

Q. Now your brother on the other side has told us that because of the posture in which this question arose in the trial court, we must proceed upon the hypothesis that this was an involuntary confession.

A. Mr. Justice Stewart, I think perhaps Mr. Aurnou may have expressed himself somewhat more enthusiastically than was his intention. I don't think you have to make such a presumption because when you read the record and when you see what it was that was sought to be brought into context here, it was not the voluntariness of the confession as to voluntariness alone. The only point that was brought into context was whether it was admissible in terms of Miranda, a question on which all of us agree, there was never any doubt about that. We had come to that conclusion months and months and months before this trial.

Q. When the prosecution sought to use it for impeachment purposes, was there any request for hearing on the involuntariness of the confession?

A. I would have to get these minutes to refresh my recollection before I could give you an absolutely definitive answer, Mr. Chief Justice. My recollection is that there was a hearing for the purpose of discovering whether—there was a hearing requested for the purpose of discovering whether or not this was admissible, and we all know it wasn't.

Id. at 28. As demonstrated above, however, a check of the "minutes" would have plainly established that a hearing to determine the voluntariness of the statement—in addition to its admissibility under *Miranda*—had been requested.

46. As Justice Brennan's dissenting opinion noted, with supporting authority, six federal courts of appeals and the appellate courts of fourteen states had reached a result contrary to that reached by the *Harris* majority, while only three state appellate courts had agreed with it. 401 U.S. at 231 n. 4.

47. Miranda v. Arizona, 384 U.S. 436, 444 (1966).

48. See note 46 supra.

49. 401 U.S. at 224.

50. 384 U.S. at 476–77 (emphasis supplied).

51. See also id. at 444.

52. Id. at 502 (Clark, J., dissenting and concurring); id. at 505 (Harlan, J., dissenting); id. at 535 (White, J., dissenting).

53. 378 U.S. 478 (1964).

54. 384 U.S. 436, 440–42 (1966).

55. Because of the nature of the problem and because of its recurrent significance in numerous cases, we have to this point discussed the relationship of the Fifth

Amendment privilege to police interrogation without specific concentration on the facts of the cases before us. We turn now to these facts to consider the application to these cases of the constitutional principles discussed above.

Id. at 491. The only previous allusion to the facts in the cases at bar had, significantly, not specified whether the statements at issue were used as part of the prosecution's case in chief or by way of impeachment. Id. at 445.

56. Id. at 144.

57. 347 U.S. 62 (1954).

58. 401 U.S. at 224–25.

59. 269 U.S. 20 (1925). *Agnello*, in turn, relied on Justice Holmes's opinion for the Court in Silverthorne v. United States, 251 U.S. 385 (1920).

60. Agnello v. United States, 269 U.S. 20, 35 (1925).

61. Walder v. United States, 347 U.S. 62, 65 (1954).

62. Id.

63. Id. at 66.

64. See text at note 58 supra.

65. Walder v. United States, 347 U.S. 62, 65 (1954) (emphasis supplied).

66. Again, Wyman v. James, 400 U.S. 309 (1971), is disturbingly similar. In support of its irrelevant claim, see note 41 supra, that most home visits are reasonable, the Court observes:

Forcible entry or entry under false pretenses or visitation outside working hours or snooping in the home are forbidden.

400 U.S. at 321. What the Court omits to mention is that the provision in question, Part IV, § 2300(a) of the HEW Handbook of Public Assistance Administration, refers to

entering a home by force, *or without permission*, or under false pretenses; making visits outside of working hours. . . .

Dep't of HEW, Handbook of Public Assistance Administration, Pt. IV, § 2300(a), quoted 400 U.S. at 346 (Marshall, J., dissenting) (emphasis supplied). Nowhere does the Court mention the reference to entry without permission, though it draws support from the phrases on either side of it. As in *Harris*, the device of convenient omission (by paraphrase rather than ellipsis this time) has saved the Court the bother of facing a passage which, if taken seriously, might have defeated the government's claim.

67. 401 U.S. at 225.

68. Id.

69. See Weeks v. United States, 232 U.S. 383 (1914); Mapp v. Ohio, 367 U.S. 643 (1961).

70. The relevant portion of the Fifth Amendment reads as follows: "nor shall be compelled in any criminal case to be a witness against himself."

71. Miranda v. Arizona, 384 U.S. 436, 470 (1966); cf. Johnson v. New Jersey, 384 U.S. 719 (1966).

72. Permitting impeachment by means of illegally seized evidence is more likely to induce violations of the Fifth than the Fourth Amendment. For physical evidence

is often, perhaps most often, contraband, and if it is suppressed as to the government's case in chief, the case will frequently have to be dropped. Confessions and statements, however, are practically always nothing more than buttressing evidence: suppression of a confession or other statement will seldom cause the prosecution to drop its case. With respect to a statement, therefore, it would be worthwhile (in a way it would not be with respect to contraband) for the police to press on and get it illegally when it has become clear it cannot be obtained legally. For despite the illegality the case will likely go forward, and if the statement can be used for impeachment, it will likely keep the defendant off the stand or at any rate discredit his testimony. With respect to contraband, however, no such incentive will exist. For once the search is declared illegal, the case will probably be dropped. And *Walder* situations—where the defendant is later indicted for a similar crime and on the stand denies ever having transgressed—are obviously rare, surely not so common as to figure into a policeman's calculus.

73. See generally Annot., 89 A.L.R.2d 478 (1963), and cases cited. Several cases involving the *Mallory* rule (Mallory v. United States, 354 U.S. 449 [1957]) have gone the other way. See, e.g., Bailey v. United States, 328 F.2d 542 (D.C. Cir. 1964), cert. denied, 377 U.S. 972.

74. To be sure, there is always a risk of the jury's inferring that liars are more likely to be criminals than truth-tellers, and—where the impeachment evidence relates to a prior similar crime—of the jury's inferring from that that the defendant is guilty of the crime charged. These risks, which are fairly common to impeachment evidence, are, however, considerably easier to guard against than an improper "truth of the matter asserted" inference from a statement admitting guilt of the crime charged.

75. Brief for the United States at 32–33, Walder v. United States, 347 U.S. 62 (1954).

76. Id. at 33.

77. 378 U.S. 368 (1964).

78. 391 U.S. 123 (1968).

79. Bruton v. United States, 391 U.S. 123, 135 (1968). But cf. Dutton v. Evans, 400 U.S. 74 (1970).

80. Walder v. United States, 347 U.S. 62, 65 (1954).

81. 270 F.2d 915 (D.C. Cir. 1959). In *Lockley*, the statement at issue was not in Judge Burger's view coerced. It was alleged to have been obtained in violation of the *Mallory* rule. Judge Burger explained the difference as follows:

> A coerced confession is rejected because it is not a true statement but one exacted by duress or force and thus inherently unreliable. A confession rejected under Rule 5(a) for "unnecessary delay" is not discredited as inherently untrustworthy; it is rejected as a means of enforcing Rule 5(a)—a prophylactic suppression.

270 F.2d at 921 n. 1 (Burger, J., dissenting).

82. 270 F.2d at 921.

83. Id.

84. Id. at 920.

85. Id. Judge Burger went on to make another argument that he implicitly rejected in *Harris*:

Any other course, it seems to me, would permit the use of proscribed confessions in rebuttal even in the case where the trial court had taken testimony and held it inadmissible by virtue of physical or mental coercion, actual or inherent. Can it be possible to say that a court could on Monday, hold a confession obtained by force and duress inadmissible, and on Wednesday allow it to impeach the defendant's veracity?

270 F.2d at 921 n. 2.
   86. 401 U.S. at 225.
   87. See generally Mapp v. Ohio, 367 U.S. 643 (1961). See also Kaufman v. United States, 394 U.S. 217 (1969), where the Court—holding search claims to be cognizable in § 2255 proceedings—rejected the following argument:

This deterrent function, the Government argues, is adequately served by the opportunities afforded a federal defendant to enforce the exclusionary rule before or at trial, so that the relatively minimal additional deterrence afforded by a post-conviction remedy would not seem to justify, except in special circumstances, the collateral release of guilty persons who did not raise the search and seizure issue at trial or on direct appeal.

Id. at 224–25. *Kaufman* thus implicitly accepts the theory advanced by this comment, that deterrence will be ineffective so long as any significant incentive for disobedience remains. See id. at 225.
   88. Mapp v. Ohio, 367 U.S. 643, 651–52 (1961).
   89. The elimination of all significant incentives is necessary in cases of deliberate misconduct, where the police know that the only way of securing the evidence at issue is to violate the rules. It may well be that in the case of the "blundering constable" (see People v. Defore, 242 N.Y. 13, 21, 150 N.E. 585, 587 [1926])—where the police could have obtained the evidence lawfully, but simply "blundered" or took the "easy" way—sufficient deterrence would be provided by exclusion of some, but not all, of the unlawfully obtained evidence. Professor Amsterdam, in concluding that a random percentage exclusion in search and seizure cases would provide sufficient deterrence, neglects to distinguish these different categories of violation. Amsterdam, "Search, Seizure and Section 2255," 112 U. Pa. L. Rev. 378, 388–91 (1964). Moreover, Amsterdam was concerning himself exclusively with violations of the Fourth Amendment, which will probably involve calculated violations less frequently than *Miranda*. See note 90 infra.
   90. The *Miranda* situation is unlike the typical search situation in that it is tailor-made for a sequential "try it legally—if you fail, try it illegally" approach. That is, the police can attempt to obtain a statement admissible in the case in chief by giving the required warnings. If, however, the suspect requests a lawyer, they can then (instead of honoring the request and thereby losing the statement) go on—given *Harris*—to try for an uncounselled statement to use for impeachment. There is thus no moment at which the police must irrevocably decide whether to follow the Constitution or not; given *Harris*, a legal-illegal sequence is the most rational course.
   91. See. e.g., A. Amsterdam, B. Segal & M. Miller, Trial Manual for the Defense of Criminal Cases 2–298 (1967); Handbook on Criminal Procedure in the United States District Court (Federal Defenders Program of San Diego, Inc.) 218 (1967).

92. 401 U.S. at 225. The Court at one point in the opinion varies this theme as follows: "The shield provided by *Miranda* cannot be perverted into a license to use perjury by way of a defense, free from the risk of confrontation with prior inconsistent utterances." 401 U.S. at 226. The reference to perjury derives from Justice Frankfurter's opinion in *Walder*, where he said, inter alia, "[T]here is hardly justification for letting the defendant affirmatively resort to perjurious testimony in reliance on the Government's disability to challenge his credibility." Walder v. United States, 347 U.S. 62, 65 (1954). But in *Walder*, of course, the defendant's trial testimony was contradicted by physical evidence whose trustworthiness was not disputed. In cases involving violation of the Fifth Amendment—as in this case—there is some question whether the statements elicited by the police were the accurate ones. See note 93 infra.

93. It may well be, of course, that the pretrial statement will be true and the trial statement false, especially where the former is inculpatory and the latter exculpatory. The trial testimony, which is further in time from the events at issue, may well reflect a more calculated "story" than the earlier, perhaps more spontaneous, statement. There are, however, other considerations that suggest that the trial testimony will sometimes be more accurate than the statement elicited by the police. Trial testimony is taken under oath with the sanction of a perjury prosecution available, whereas the police statement is unsworn. Trial testimony is also prepared and elicited by an attorney who is bound not to countenance perjury in his witnesses (an obligation taken quite seriously by most lawyers), whereas the police statement is by hypothesis given without consultation with counsel. Most fundamentally, of course, the pretrial statement will, by definition, have been given without the safeguards of *Miranda*, safeguards designed, at least in part, to ensure that the inherently coercive atmosphere of an in-custody police interrogation will not elicit an untrue statement. As the Court said in *Miranda*: the presence of counsel may help "to guarantee that the accused gives a fully accurate statement to the police and that the statement is rightly reported by the prosecution at trial." 384 U.S. at 470.

94. Brief for District Attorney of New York County at 12. The brief alleged that the account of the events of January 4 was "a truthful" one, but the jury was deadlocked over whether petitioner was guilty on account of these events. The brief said that the account of the events of January 6—for which the jury convicted—was "false." Petitioner's lawyer made the following relevant point in his oral argument:

> Very often when a young and inexperienced person is before the police, and that is what happened here and that is the only case that makes a difference, because your professional criminal just doesn't get involved in this. He may give a false exculpatory statement whereas the truth were to acquit him, but he doesn't know that, and he is afraid to tell the police what happened. He thinks he had better talk to his lawyer first. So he makes up a false exculpatory statement. He can be torn to shreds at the trial by an experienced prosecutor. That is just what happened here. But it doesn't prove that the statements that he makes in his testimony at the trial is false, because it may well be that the statement unconstitutionally obtained was false.

Transcript of Oral Argument at 17.
95. 401 U.S. at 224.

96. Another unanswered question is how *Harris* relates to California v. Green, 399 U.S. 149 (1970), holding that states may constitutionally use prior inconsistent statements against a defendant who has taken the stand not simply to impeach his testimony but also to prove the truth of the matter earlier asserted. It is true that the trial judge in *Harris* instructed the jury to consider the earlier statement only as to credibility, but the Court does not indicate that its decision is limited by that fact. If it is not, the one-two punch of *Harris* and *Green* could be potent indeed.

The bounds of the "principle" of *Wyman v. James*, permitting warrantless and unconsented-to "visits" to the homes of welfare recipients to make sure the grants are not being misused or fraudulently claimed, are similarly unclear. Can the government engage in an unconsented-to and warrantless search of a taxpayer's home to see whether the claimed dependents really exist? Can it similarly search the homes and places of business of all those who receive any sort of governmental benefit, as most of us today do in one form or another, in order to determine eligibility?

There is reason to think not. Perhaps the most regrettable feature of the Court's opinion in *James* is the double standard it apparently applies to the claims of the poor and the claims of the rest of us, a double standard disfavoring the former.

In relying on the state's interests in uncovering child abuse and welfare fraud to uphold its suspension of the warrant requirement for welfare recipients, the Court provides a textbook example of a sort of discrimination it has repeatedly told legislatures and administrators they are not to indulge in, namely assuming that poor people are morally inferior to others and consequently applying a different set of rules to them. Anyone may mistreat his child; yet, the Court surely would not uphold warrantless "visits" of the homes of the more affluent to check for such mistreatment. And any of us may misrepresent his eligibility for a particular form of governmental benefit, be it a farm subsidy or a tax deduction; but with respect to the claims of the non-poor, government officials have always had to be content with whatever sort of convincing validation the claimant is able and willing to come up with—they have never had a mandate to "visit" his home over his protests unless they get a warrant.

That the Court intends to retain this comparative immunity for the affluent is indicated by a fallacious analogy:

> It seems to us that the situation is akin to that where an Internal Revenue Service agent, in making a routine civil audit of a taxpayer's income tax return, asks that the taxpayer produce for the agent's review some proof of a deduction the taxpayer has asserted to his benefit in the computation of his tax. If the taxpayer refuses, there is, absent fraud, only a disallowance of the claimed deduction and a consequent additional tax.

Wyman v. James, 401 U.S. 309, 324 (1971). Mr. Justice Marshall's answer, here as often, is decisive:

> [T]he analogy is seriously flawed. The record shows that Mrs. James has offered to be interviewed anywhere other than her home, to answer any questions and to provide any documentation which the welfare agency desires. The agency curtly refused all these offers and insisted on its "right" to pry into appellee's home. Tax

exemptions are also governmental "bounty." A true analogy would be an Internal Revenue Service requirement that in order to claim a dependency exemption, a taxpayer must allow a specially trained IRS agent to invade the home for the purpose of questioning the occupants and looking for evidence that the exemption is being properly utilized for the benefit of the dependent. If such a system were even proposed, the cries of constitutional outrage would be unanimous.

Id. at 343 (Marshall, J., dissenting).

97. 401 U.S. at 225–26. This "argument" is a popular one with the emerging majority. Mr. Justice Blackmun's opinion for the Court in *Wyman v. James* argues, inter alia, that:

> The home visit is not a criminal investigation, does not equate with a criminal investigation, and despite the announced fears of Mrs. James and those who would join her, is not in aid of a criminal proceeding.

400 U.S. at 323. The relevance of this assertion is questionable at best. The state defended its rejection of Mrs. James's offer, to meet anywhere but in her home and there to provide all relevant information, on the ground that it needed to visit the home in order to ferret out possible welfare fraud and child abuse. Leaving aside for the moment the possibility of criminal sanctions, it should be noted that a finding of fraud can lead to a termination of benefits, a finding of child abuse to loss of custody. Camara v. Municipal Court, 387 U.S. 523 (1967), a case *Wyman* purports not to disturb, is crystal clear that the Fourth Amendment, and in particular its warrant requirement, apply to inspections that can result only in civil sanctions. See also See v. City of Seattle, 387 U.S. 541 (1967). But in any event, pursuing its (irrelevant) argument that a welfare visit is not "in aid of a criminal proceeding," the Court continues:

> And if the visit should, by chance, lead to the discovery of fraud and a criminal prosecution should follow,[12] then, even assuming that the evidence discovered upon the home visitation is admissible, an issue upon which we express no opinion, that is a routine and expected fact of life and a consequence no greater than that which necessarily ensues upon any other discovery by a citizen of criminal conduct.

400 U.S. at 323. This passage is in several ways misleading. The statute whose citation appears in the Court's note 12, § 145 of the New York Social Welfare Law, defines the crime of welfare fraud *and* obligates welfare officials to turn over "to the appropriate district attorney or other prosecuting official" any evidence of such fraud they uncover. The Court is of course technically correct in its claim that it is not deciding that evidence uncovered during a home visit is admissible in a criminal proceeding. For that issue is not before it. But the issue has been settled for years: it has always been the law that evidence uncovered during a lawful search, no matter what the purpose of the search was, is admissible in a criminal proceeding. See, e.g., Terry v. Ohio, 392 U.S. 1, 20 (1968). And evidence uncovered during home visits is of course routinely admitted in state welfare fraud prosecutions. The Court can hardly be unaware of all this, and demonstrates it is not by going on to "explain" that even if such evidence is admitted, that, after all, would be no different from admit-

ting evidence of the observations of a layman. Thus as in *Harris* the Court attempts to legitimate the admission of evidence gathered by government officials by noting that the same evidence would be admissible if discovered by a private citizen. Since constitutional limitations do not bind private citizens, this recurrent "logic" has the potency to carry the emerging majority virtually any place it wishes to go.

98. There is one sentence in the opinion that exceeds all others in confusion:

> The conflict between petitioner's testimony in his own behalf concerning the events of January 7 contrasted sharply with what he told the police shortly after his arrest.

401 U.S. at 225. In the first place, it is unclear what the "events of January 7" were. The two-count indictment charged sales on January 4 and January 6, not on January 7. The only relevant events of January 7 were petitioner's arrest and interrogation. And there was no conflict whatever between petitioner's trial testimony "in his own behalf" concerning his arrest and what he told the police. Indeed he barely mentioned January 7 and his arrest in his trial testimony, and he did not mention it at all in his statement to the police. Nor did he testify "in his own behalf" about the interrogation of January 7. He was of course asked about it on cross-examination. but merely replied that he remembered some of the questions but not others. How then can it be said that the "conflict between petitioner's testimony in his own behalf concerning the events of January 7 contrasted sharply with what he told the police . . ."? (The syntax of the sentence confuses things even more: how can a "conflict between" one statement "contrast sharply" with another statement?)

Perhaps the Chief Justice merely got his dates confused. He may have meant to say "the events of January 4 or 6," in which case he would be speaking of the circumstances giving rise to the two count indictment. But at an earlier point in the opinion he had said, more accurately, that petitioner's statement to the police "partially contradicted" his direct testimony concerning those events (not that it "contrasted sharply" with it). Id. at 223.

99. November 20, 1991.

100. [It got it.]

101. One thing the episode may demonstrate is the relative impotence of professional elites in France, or at least of the legal profession. All the important lawyers' organizations have come out against the bill, as have the magistrats (judges and prosecutors) and juges d'instruction (investigating magistrates). Yet all concede that passage is virtually certain. I know that the study of law is more of a catchall in France than in the U.S.; I have witnessed at length the somnambulism that passes for advocacy in French courts; and I've had more than my fill of the sort of formalism that often counts as academic legal commentary in France. Nonetheless I am at a loss to understand why the French legal profession cannot stop this bill. (Public opinion polls, to the extent one can get anything straight out of them, seem pro but not overwhelmingly so.)

102. I would suppose the entire performance to be preelection theater (which obviously doesn't exclude a desire for passage) were it not for the facts that the government has (1) put the screws to its own people to vote for this one; (2) expedited the matter by officially labeling it "urgent" (although it was the product of a

five-year study); and (3) invoked the antifilibuster rule. Plainly passage before the election is important to the government. Gauchiste friends suggest the government fears an "uprising" among the lower classes and thus want to put this instrument of repression in place. I'm skeptical about this, since sophisticated observers (which may not include Peyrefitte but surely does others of his party) have to recognize that this law will not make all that much difference in terms of controlling the masses. Also, France does not exude the aura of a nation poised for revolution: the same commentators grant that Giscard will probably be reelected. [He wasn't, but at least from afar that seems not to have made a tremendous difference.] Like the matter traversed in the prior footnote, this one is beyond my competence.

103. This last is quite important. The sursis apparently had become quite routine, a trend Peyrefitte wishes to stop. His original project forbade its use in cases where the sentence prescribed by law exceeds two years in prison. The National Assembly's commission des lois—perhaps most analogous to our Senate Judiciary Committee—raised the figure to three years, which is important, in that sursis will now be available for crimes passionels (due to jealousy) and euthanasia.

104. There are other provisions that purport to enhance individual liberty. That purporting to introduce "habeas corpus" into the French system is so narrow and cynical as not to merit discussion. That protecting the rights of those being held for deportation seems enlightened on the surface, until one learns that it is actually a retrenchment from what the conseil constitutionnel had earlier required!

The project lists among its major goals the protection/indemnification of victims, and surely that is hard to object to. The way it originally read, however, a defendant's sentence was automatically cut in half if he made recompense. The objection to this is obvious and was made by commentators: that it favors affluent defendants. As the draft now stands, whether the defendant has made recompense is a factor to be taken into account in possible extenuation, and the ability of the defendant to pay is to be considered. The provisions protecting those psychiatrically hospitalized seem laudable (a conclusion that is corroborated by the psychiatric syndicates' protests that there is nothing to protect against).

One move that should also be noted is the severance of necessary connection between instruction and custody beyond the "garde à vue"period (48 hours). (There has also been general criticism of the attempt to reduce the number of instructions. This we will discuss. What I'm concerned with here is only the connection between custody and instruction.) As the law now stands there are three options with respect to a délit (an offense punishable by between two months and five years)—(1) instruction (a full inquiry by an investigating magistrate); (2) citation direct, or release and later trial without instruction (despite the lack of attention in the American literature, this is the way most délits are handled); and (3) flagrante délit, whereby the defendant is kept in custody and given an expedited trial. A gap is created by the facts that citation direct requires release, but flagrante délit requires that the defendant essentially be caught in the act: thus to keep the defendant in custody, except in cases of flagrante délit, an instruction is required. Since instruction consumes a great deal of time and other resources, that seems undesirable. The project deals with it by expanding the notion of flagrante délit (though it deletes that label in an obvious attempt to appear liberal) to include any case in which guilt is clear (say, possession of contraband plus confession) and not just those where apprehension was essentially part of the res gestae.

I confess to not finding this too terrifying. Obviously one would want to be very tough about whether guilt really is clear. Just as obviously, release should be an option (as it is, theoretically, and will continue to be) during an instruction, and prompt recourse to a judicial officer on the subject of custody should always be available. (In fact juges d'instruction are very chary about granting release during instruction. That is a very serious defect in the French system. It is not, however, a problem the Projet Peyrefitte will aggravate; in fact, to the extent it will reduce the number of instructions and enhance the number of expedited trials, it is one it will alleviate [though at a cost, to be sure].) At all events, the instinct to sever custody from instruction seems healthy; having awakened to the possibility of custody (albeit brief) without instruction, let us now hope the French system will become capable of genuinely contemplating instruction without custody.

105. Goldstein & Marcus, "The Myth of Judicial Supervision in Three 'Inquisitorial' Systems: France, Italy, and Germany," 87 Yale L. J. 240 (1977).

106. Langbein & Weinreb, "Continental Criminal Procedure: 'Myth' and Reality," 87 Yale L. J. 1549, 1557 (1978).

107. 87 Yale L. J. at 268.

108. Thus Hanoteau assured me that defendant's refusal to answer—which is very rare—is not held against him (since "he has that right") but went on to say, "We simply assume he agrees with our questions." This is, indeed, the way a person of common sense would ordinarily proceed, though of course in this instance, as in others, we have, quite correctly, construed our Constitution to preclude what "common sense" might otherwise require.

109. Hanoteau agrees the current delays are scandalous and suggests what could be at least a partial alternative answer, namely removing the chambre d'accusation (between the juge d'instruction and the trial court) from the process. Its intervention consumes about five weeks with respect to a délit and eight months with regard to a crime. Its main function is to make sure the juge d'instruction complied with all relevant legal requirements. It would seem that that is a function the trial court could perform.

110. I should say, for the benefit of anyone interested in doing work in this area, that I have the feeling permission to sit in on instructions is not ordinarily granted to outsiders. (At least so everyone assured me before I asked.)

111. 87 Yale L. J. at 255.

112. To avoid leaving a possible negative implication dangling: I don't know Marcus.

113. Coupled (I am aware I have not stressed this enough) with what is all too often excessive brutality. One can postulate a connection—brutality *is* one way of getting the facts—but I am not convinced the conjunction is necessary.

114. See pages 111–35. But cf. Léauté, Nouvel Observateur, May 18, 1980: "De quel droit un legislateur poussé par le pouvoir exécutif se permettrait-il d'empêcher le jury d'être le reflet du sentiment du peuple, alors que la raison d'être du jury, c'est justement de représenter le peuple!"

115. 87 Yale L. J. at 248–49.

Chapter 7

1. 79 Yale L. J. 1205, 1254–61, 1263–65, 1289–98.

2. You've already been exposed to three (shorter) chunks of it, at pages 37–38, 136–37 and 190–96. See also pages 257–78.

3. In 1970 much contemporary constitutional doctrine *not* directly related to motivation—in particular the many levels of equal protection analysis—was yet to be developed. Thus much underbrush had to be cleared before I could get to the point of discussing where motivation ought to fit in. As of 1996, however—thanks in part to this piece but in addition to the work of many others—the underbrush would seem so exotic you would wonder why I was bothering to talk about it.

4. [364 U.S. 339 (1960).]

5. See, e.g., Griffin v. Illinois, 351 U.S. 12 (1956). See generally Michelman, "Foreword: On Protecting the Poor through the Fourteenth Amendment," 83 Harv. L. Rev. 7 (1969).

6. [See pages 261–75.]

7. See Kaplan, "Segregation Litigation and the Schools—Part II: The General Northern Problem," 58 Nw. U. L. Rev. 157, 177 (1963). Consider also tax breaks for farmers and oilmen, sales taxes, graduated income taxes, literacy tests, and various criminal statutes in various sorts of communities.

8. [This point is elaborated at 79 Yale L. J. at 1231–33.]

9. The disadvantageous distinction model will be inapplicable even if a quota system is substituted for random selection. Even if each panel is made, say, 12 percent Negro, there still will be no difference that distinguishes those Negroes who are on the panel from those who are not, those white persons on the panel from those who are not, or the total class of persons on the panel from the total class excluded.

10. There has been dispute in the literature over whether Negro children suffer harm of the sort described in *Brown* when school segregation by race results from factors other than the obvious design of the white majority. But the harm accruing to a Negro defendant *surely* is the same regardless of whether the underrepresentation of Negroes on the jury which tries him was achieved intentionally or unintentionally.

11. Carter v. Jury Comm'n of Green County, 396 U.S. 320, 343 (1970) (Douglas, J., dissenting in part). [With the quoted passage the majority emphatically agreed.]

12. Swain v. Alabama, 380 U.S. 202, 208 (1965).

13. 339 U.S. 282, 286–87 (plurality opinion of Reed, J.).

14. Sex and educational background should be included. [See J.E.B. v. Alabama ex rel. T.B., 114 S.Ct. 1419 (1994); but cf.] Fay v. New York, 332 U.S. 261 (1947).

15. In a districting situation, selection without regard to personal characteristics is even less likely to produce a cross-section, since persons of similar races, etc., often live in the same areas.

16. Requiring proportional representation might also involve courts in the difficult and unpleasant business of litigating a person's race. See Bittker, "The Case of the Checker-Board Ordinance: An Experiment in Race Relations," 71 Yale L. J. 1387, 1420–22 (1962); Kaplan, supra note 7, at 180–81.

17. Id. at 379–80.

18. Of course, statistical disparity is often suggestive of illicit motivation. The "danger" that this realization will coerce a commissioner to consider race and attempt to achieve a respectable balance should be mitigated, however, by the realization that under a motivation test, the suggestion of the statistics can be rebutted by the convincing proof that he in fact chose at random. And even if the mitigation is less than total, the Court's judgment that states should not be forced to take race into account is obviously served better by a motivation test than by an impact test. Indeed, a motivation test is the best we can do in this regard.

19. [391 U.S. 367 (1968).]

20. 376 U.S. 52, 57–58 (1964).

21. 380 U.S. 202 (1965) [overruled in part—actually not this part—in Batson v. Kentucky, 476 U.S. 79 (1986). *Swain* is discussed in more detail at 79 Yale L. J. 1264 n. 173.]

22. 380 U.S. at 208–9.

23. But cf., e.g., Smith v. Texas, 311 U.S. 128, 130–31 (1940).

24. 396 U.S. 320 (1970).

25. 396 U.S. 346 (1970).

26. 395 U.S. 225 (1969).

27. 395 U.S. at 236 (emphasis omitted).

28. See e.g., "Civil Rights: Desegregation Yes, Integration No," Time, April 6, 1970, at 11, relating and commenting on President Nixon's statement on school desegregation.

29. [It seems even more improbable as of 1996.]

30. Professor Bickel has recently observed, A. Bickel, The Supreme Court and the Idea of Progress 134 (1970):

> All too many federal judges have been induced to view themselves as holding roving commissions as problem solvers, and as charged with a duty to act when majoritarian institutions do not. Not all of them have so far resisted, and not all will resist invitations to take charge, whether by being more skeptical of the *bona fides* of local school administrators, or by directly confronting the *de facto* problem.

The suggestion of this article is that there is, despite the similarity of the results which specific cases may generate, a substantial difference between the two attitudes Bickel assimilates—assuming an attitude of skepticism with regard to the bona fides of government officials, and affirmatively commanding racial balance.

While I do not mean to suggest that courts be cavalier in their inferences—which course of action would soon be recognized for what it is and thus involve the same costs as an impact test—there need be no overly strong resolution to err on the side of refusing to find the alleged motivation. For so long as it can convincingly phrase its opinion in terms of a finding of motivation, the court will be able at the same time to require the reformulation of a districting plan that has produced substantial racial imbalance, and to avoid instructing other districters that they must take race into account.

31. 377 U.S. 218 (1964).

32. 197 F. Supp. 649 (E.D. La. 1961), aff'd 368 U.S. 515 (1962).

33. This probably is closer to *Prince Edward County*, as the decision to close the schools was made at the county level.

34. See Gautreaux v. Chicago Housing Authority, 296 F. Supp. 907 (N.D. Ill. 1969).

35. 22 Ill.2d 132, 174 N.E.2d 850 (1961), cert. denied, 372 U.S. 968 (1962).

36. "Developments in the Law—Equal Protection," 82 Harv. L. Rev. 1887, 1100–1101 (1969) (footnotes omitted).

37. [See 79 Yale L. J. at 1284–89.]

38. [See id. at 1217–21.]

39. New York Times, April 13, 1977.

40. [Secretary Coleman has of course long been active in the civil rights movement—having served, for example, on Thurgood Marshall's litigation team in *Brown v. Board of Education*, and more recently as chairman of the board of the NAACP Legal Defense and Educational Fund.]

41. 1983 Duke L. J. 959–65.

42. R. Dworkin, Taking Rights Seriously 180 (rev. ed. 1978), quoted in Democracy and Distrust 82.

43. 339 U.S. 629 (1950).

44. 82 Wash.2d 11, 507 P.2d 1169 (1973), vacated and remanded as moot, 416 U.S. 312 (1974).

45. See pages 267–75.

46. R. Dworkin, supra note 42, at 232.

47. Id.

48. Id.

49. See, e.g., Baker, "Counting Preferences in Collective Choice Situations," 25 U.C.L.A. L. Rev. 381 (1978).

50. R. Dworkin, supra note 42, at 232.

51. Id. at 233.

52. Id. at 234; see also id. at 275.

53. Id. at 235.

54. Id.; see also page 314.

55. R. Dworkin, supra note 42, at 237.

56. Id. at 235.

57. Id. at 275; see also page 326.

58. R. Dworkin, supra note 42, at 236.

59. Id. at 239.

60. Id.

61. Id.

62. See page 262; see also R. Dworkin, supra note 42, at 228.

63. Id. at 237; cf. id. at 230 (similar arguments applied in law school admissions context).

64. Id. at 239.

65. [See pages 267–75.]

66. 41 U. of Chi. L. Rev. 723. [*Democracy and Distrust*, 170–72, comprises a two-page "Aside on Affirmative Action," which summarizes the conclusions reached in this earlier and fuller discussion.]

67. Irving Berlin, 1938 (ASCAP).

68. See also W. Kaufmann, Without Guilt and Justice 74 (1973).

69. The debate on preferential admissions has been clouded by an inference that because a strictly "meritocratic" system of selection for law school or other places is best, it must also somehow be a constitutional requirement. The premise is respectable, but the conclusion is not. Surely there is nothing uniquely "just" about distributing desirable lives to persons who were fortunate enough to be born smart (or tall, agile, or whatever). . . . A meritocratic system is efficient—it picks the people thought to be most likely to perform the tasks in question well—but the Constitution, which indeed sometimes mandates inefficiency, certainly conveys no general message that inefficient systems are unjust.

70. 402 U.S. 1, 16 (1971).

71. 379 U.S. 184 (1964).

72. 388 U.S. 1 (1967). See also note 90 infra.

73. Moreover, like the DeFunises, children in busing programs are singled out to bear disproportionately large shares of the costs of the social policy the state has decided to pursue. While this result is by no means unprecedented in the law, it must surely be an object of concern.

74. The argument assumes (1) that all places at all law schools are filled; (2) (and this too seems most unlikely) that "the" black applicant who (would have) displaced DeFunis at the University of Washington Law School would not have been admitted "on the merits" at any law school; and finally (3) that the rejected applicant (after the trickle down effect) at the bottom of the law school hierarchy is white.

75. I hope I will pick up as many friends as I lose by suggesting that the difference may sometimes be as great as the difference DeFunis perceived between the University of Washington Law School and, say, the University of Oregon Law School [where he was admitted]. His preference was doubtless partially attributable to a desire to stay near home, but that only extends the parallel to busing.

76. 82 Wash.2d 11, 507 P.2d 1169 (1973), vacated and remanded as moot, 416 U.S. 312 (1974).

77. If the Court's apparent hope for an easier preferential admissions case is pinned on Justice Douglas's call in his dissent for a record that demonstrates that the Law School Admissions Test and other standard predictors predict less well for blacks than for whites, it may be in for a disappointment. No such simple salvation seems imminent, for this is not a simple problem.

Existing evidence suggests that, to the extent there is a difference at all (and there seems to be little), the standard predictors work better for blacks than whites, and moreover that white students earn somewhat higher law school grades relative to their predictor scores than black students. Schrader & Pitcher, Predicting Law School Grades for Black American Law Students (Educational Testing Service Rep. 1973). (And if the answer is that law school requirements are culturally biased—as they, and for that matter the requirements of the profession, undoubtedly are—one is surely entitled to ask what the ultimate remedy can be.) The cited study acknowledges certain limitations on its methodology, but for the moment we have nothing better.

The real hope lies, I think, in the fact that parents seem to make a difference. . . . If we underwrite a generation of black professionals, even a generation that does not do quite as well in professional school as their white classmates, their children and their children's children may grow up with interests, motivations and aptitudes that are not dissimilar from those the rest of us grew up with, and, consequently, are likely to do as well in school as whites from similar backgrounds. The case for "reparations" or payments for two hundred years of oppression may be an uneasy one, but those two hundred years have to have made a difference. No matter how plausible this reasoning sounds, however, it remains a speculation, and the question must be reached whether it can sustain what is, after all, a racial classification.

78. Nonetheless, all racial classifications should be carefully examined to make sure they fall within the rather limited subset to which the more demanding standard of review is inappropriate. There are some racial classifications that do not merit "strict scrutiny," but I cannot imagine one that does not merit a careful and skeptical look.

79. See, e.g. Strauder v. West Virginia, 100 U.S. 303, 307–8 (1880); Slaughter House Cases, 83 U.S. (16 Wall.) 36, 81 (1873). See generally Frank & Munro, "The Original Understanding of 'Equal Protection of the Laws,' " 50 Colum. L. Rev. 131 (1950); Graham, "Our 'Declaratory' Fourteenth Amendment," 7 Stan. L. Rev. 3 (1954).

80. [Much from the next two paragraphs was substantially replicated in Democracy and Distrust 155–56. However, this discussion would suffer were they deleted here. But cf. note 97 infra. Had I know in 1980 I'd be publishing this collection, I'd have resorted to the paraphrasing skills that served us all so well in doing our high school history homework. But I didn't, so I didn't.]

81. See Williamson v. Lee Optical Co., 348 U.S. 483 (1955).

82. But cf. id. at 487 (1955): "The . . . law may exact a needless, wasteful requirement in many cases. But it is for the legislature, not the courts, to balance the advantages and disadvantages of the new requirement."

83. 304 U.S. 144, 152 n. 4 (1938). See also Hobson v. Hansen, 269 F. Supp. 401, 507–8 (D.D.C. 1967).

84. Sugarman v. Dougall, 413 U.S. 634, 657 (1973) (dissenting opinion).

85. [*Democracy and Distrust* criticizes other common accounts of why racial classifications are accorded special scrutiny—in particular those keyed to the immutability of the classifying trait (p. 150) and the assertion that racial classifications are unusually stigmatizing (pp. 150–51). It goes on to explain, however, how each of these factors—while it cannot be the point-in-chief—can serve as an appropriate buttress to what *is* the appropriate point-in-chief, the tendency of dominant groups to overcredit the positive stereotypes about themselves and, correlatively, the negative stereotypes about others. (Pp. 154–55, 160.)]

86. E.g., Frontiero v. Richardson, 411 U.S. 677, 684 (1973) (plurality opinion); Note, "The Legality of Homosexual Marriage," 82 Yale L. J. 573, 577–78 (1973).

87. See Frontiero v. Richardson, 411 U.S. 677, 686 (1973) (plurality opinion).

88. See Tussman & tenBroek, "The Equal Protection of the Laws," 37 Calif. L. Rev. 342, 355–56 (1949).

89. Who is to say that the majority of a legislature which enacts a statute segregating the schools is actuated by a conscious desire to suppress and humiliate the Negro? Who is to say that for many members more decent feelings are not decisive—the feeling, for example, that under existing circumstances Negro children are better off and can be more effectively educated in schools reserved exclusively for them, and that this is the most hopeful road to the goal of the equality of the races under law?

A. Bickel, The Least Dangerous Branch 61–62 (1962). Or, perhaps more plausibly, racial segregation may have been based on a feeling that blacks were "different," and therefore had a different "place" in the proper scheme of things—coupled with an unfeeling assumption that because *we* aren't bothered by segregation, they won't be either. In asserting that segregation will hurt only if blacks choose to let it hurt, the majority in Plessy v. Ferguson, 163 U.S. 537, 551 (1896), convicted itself not so much of racial prejudice as of the lesser included offense of gross insensitivity.

90. The statutes invalidated in McLaughlin v. Florida, 379 U.S. 184 (1964), and Loving v. Virginia, 388 U.S. I (1967), treated blacks no worse than whites. In addition to having obvious roots in racial prejudice, however, the statutes did discriminate against (a) racially mixed couples and (b) persons wishing to marry outside their race—both of which are they-groups.

91. The analysis suggested in the text probably should be limited to situations where most of the "we"s have always been "we"s, and will therefore have difficulty being objective about precisely what the difference entails. Cf. Ferguson v. Skrupa, 372 U.S. 726 (1963). Classification based on youth should therefore probably be excluded from the suspicious category. [Classification based on "old age" is a tougher case: most of us haven't been there, but probably hope to be.] Classifications disadvantaging aliens, on the other hand, might properly be regarded with suspicion. For even though alienage is an alterable status, most legislators are, and consequently have always been, native-born citizens.

92. By speaking in we-they terms, I am not suggesting the existence of permanent "have" and "have not" classes with respect to legislative power. The majority with respect to a given issue comprises an amalgam of various interest groups, which may array themselves quite differently on other issues. My suggestion is rather that there will be occasions on which a majority of the decision-making body belongs to the class that is comparatively advantaged (or, as in the *DeFunis* situation, disadvantaged) by the distinction it has drawn. It makes no sense in terms of the analysis here proposed to talk of "we"s and "they"s without reference to the classification in issue.

There is, of course, a danger of a sort of distortion when the lobby for an interest group is unusually strong. Cf. R. Posner, Economic Analysis of Law 271 (1973). Although the laws that emerge from such situations may be somewhat suspicious, it is difficult to see how the Court could react other than as it has, by refusing to undertake the investigation invited by the complainant. See, e.g., Daniel v. Family Sec. Life Ins. Co., 336 U.S. 220 (1949). There is probably some psychological difference here. Political support may induce a legislator to swallow his scruples and draw an optometrist-optician line in circumstances where he knows substantial unfairness will accrue to a number of opticians; but where the line is we-they, he is less likely even to *see* the unfairness. The more important distinction, however, is an institutional one. Courts usually cannot know (and probably should not announce when they do know) the extent to which various members of the legislature are under the thumbs of various lobbies—cf. Fletcher v. Peck, 10 U.S. (6 Cranch) 87, 130 (1810); United States v. Des Moines Nav. & Ry. Co., 142 U.S. 510, 544–45 (1892)—but they can tell when a legislature is predominantly white. (And if the makeup of the legislature is less certain they should apply special scrutiny to the racial classification. See page 274.) Arguably it is more appropriate for *state* courts to take local political pressures into consideration. See W. Lockhart, Y. Kamisar & J. Choper, Constitutional Law 481 (3d ed. 1970), and sources cited.

93. [The theory is developed further in Democracy and Distrust 145–61, its application to discrimination against aliens, the poor, gays and lesbians, and women considered at pp. 161–70 thereof.]

94. Of course, the legislative goal may be defined in a way that would render extension of the advantage to any whites at all senseless—as where the goal is not aiding the culturally disadvantaged generally, but rather curing the underrepresentation of blacks in the legal profession. In that instance the point would be that there is no special reason to be suspicious of a white legislature's decision to pursue that goal.

95. Railway Express Agency, Inc. v. New York, 336 U.S. 106, 111–13 (1949) (Jackson, J., concurring). See also Buel, "Democracy and the American Revolution: A Frame of Reference," 21 Wm. & Mary Q. 165, 182–85 (1964).

96. But see Otero v. New York City Housing Auth., 484 F.2d 1122 (2d Cir. 1973). Of course, a practice like that involved in *DeFunis* may well hurt blacks in some ways: it may insult them or serve to undercut the value of their degrees. But where it is clear, as I think it is here, that the package as a whole advantages blacks relative to whites, and that everyone assumed it would, the danger that the majority is simply legislating in its own self-interest is largely absent.

Some might claim that busing plans whose participants are selected by race are not suspect, by arguing that we can easily tell from the statistics which race is being injured more, or perhaps that the hurt, though real, is comparatively trivial. But the problems with busing cannot be so easily waved away. The more candid approach is to admit that these classifications are suspect, because they do not fall within the relatively small subset of racial classifications as to which it is clear that the majority is comparatively disadvantaging itself in favor of a minority. It can then be argued, however, that special scrutiny is satisfied, because (1) the goal—integration in the sense of homogenization and not, say, increasing the percentage of blacks in a given profession—would be nonsuspicious no matter who fixed upon it (and was specifically approved in *Brown*), and (2) the racial classification employed fits that goal perfectly, not approximately. Every white bused into a predominantly black school, and every black bused into a predominantly white school, promotes racial integration irrespective of his other characteristics.

97. [At this point the article discussed the danger of affirmative action's disadvantaging particular white subgroups. (The point is most often made respecting Jews.) Since that discussion appears in fuller form at pages 171–72 and 258–60 of *Democracy and Distrust*, it is omitted here.]

98. See pages 251–52, pushing the point only to the extent of arguing that the Court should not force states to consider race in drawing various lines; but it might be pushed further, to the conclusion that states should not be allowed to do so. E.g., Kaplan, "Equal Justice in an Unequal World: Equality for the Negro—The Problem of Special Treatment," 61 Nw. U. L. Rev. 363 (1966).

99. "Developments in the Law—Equal Protection," 82 Harv. L. Rev. 1065, 1113 (1969).

100. Of course, the development of constitutional doctrine has often, and properly, taken societal interests and attitudes into account, and there is nothing unusually controversial here. The Court's tactical error in *Brown* seems to have been the citing of books. But the experience there suggests the possibility of the reaction.

101. I would have thought the point too obvious to warrant mention, but it has so often been put to me as an "embarrassing question" that perhaps I had better answer it. Of course it works both ways: a law that favors blacks over whites would be suspect if it were enacted by a predominantly black legislature. [One should be careful with his "of course"s: it has become clear to me in retrospect that this language was overdrawn. Certainly a law favoring blacks would be suspect were it passed by a predominantly black legislature in a predominantly black state. The Supreme Court said so in so many words in 1879: see page 274. A law favoring blacks passed by a city council, a majority of whose members are black, in a state whose majority, and a majority of whose state legislators, are white, seems a more difficult case: in such a case I would argue that blacks are not the relevant controlling majority. Compare Democracy and Distrust 165–66 with City of Richmond v. J.A. Croson Co., 488 U.S. 469, 495–96 (1989), quoting the first two sentences of this footnote against the position I had taken in an amicus brief filed for the A.C.L.U. supporting the affirmative action plan in issue in *Croson*.]

There is a problem when the decision-making body is predominantly composed of the class advantaged by the legislation, but its constituency is not. This presents no difficulty in a case like *DeFunis*: the Washington legislature is heavily white and so is the state as a whole. (And so, as Chief Justice Hale needled in dissent—not realizing he was walking into my little trap—is the faculty of the University of Washington Law School: "This policy of ethnic minority selection apparently was not to apply to faculty positions." 82 Wash. 2d at 51, 507 P.2d at 1192.) The question obviously arises in connection with discrimination against women: all our legislatures are overwhelmingly male, but women constitute a majority of the voting population. Should we be suspicious nonetheless of the unconscious biases of male legislators when they enact legislation on the assumption that women are in certain ways less qualified than men, or rather conclude that women should simply vote the rascals out if they don't like what is being done to them? I would reject the latter response. (Voters typically are not confronted with single issue referendums but rather with packages of views that we call candidates. Cf. Tullock, "Problems of Majority Voting," 67 J. Pol. Econ. 571 (1959). Most women are not injured in an obvious way by laws that classify on the basis of sex, and the fact that they elect representatives who are unprepared to repeal these laws means only that there are other issues about which they feel more strongly.) But the issue is by no means trivial [and thus was revisited in *Democracy and Distrust*].

102. If the facts about the legislature's composition are not obvious, a racial or similar classification should be regarded as suspicious. Evidentiary hearings on the issue would appear inappropriate. It is obvious, however, that as of 1974 the legislature of every American state is overwhelmingly white, male, native born, and comfortably above the poverty line. The predominantly Protestant cast of most state legislatures seems beside any constitutional point, given that the combination of the Establishment and Free Exercise Clauses, read responsibly, precludes the comparative favoring or disfavoring of any religion.

103. Strauder v. West Virginia, 100 U.S. 303, 308 (1879). The passage is cited for its hint that equal protection might be a function of who is doing the discriminating, and not for its specific point. For the jury situation seems special in that the litigant's interest in procedural due process requires a jury from which members of his own race have not been systematically excluded, irrespective of whether his race is a majority in the community at large. (It is entirely possible, of course, that the Court alluded to a black majority only because it assumed there were no other circumstances under which a law comparatively disadvantaging whites would be enacted.)

104. See Gunther, "The Subtle Vices of the 'Passive Virtues': A Comment on Principle and Expediency Judicial Review," 64 Colum. L. Rev. 1 (1964).

105. 79 Yale L. J. 1205, 1299–1302.

106. 387 U.S. 369 (1967).

107. 393 U.S. 385 (1969).

108. Id. at 391.

109. [Pages 249–53.]

110. 393 U.S. at 390. Cf. Black, "Foreword: 'State Action,' Equal Protection, and California's Proposition 14," 81 Harv. L. Rev. 69, 74–83 (1967); A. Cox, The Warren Court 47 (1969).

111. [See page 250.]

112. [*See* 79 Yale L. J. at 1272–73.]

113. [Recall that the amendment was adopted by a majority of the California electorate—many of whom undoubtedly confronted it for the first time in the polling booth—as opposed to a legislature or city council.]

114. In *Reitman* the Court characterized the amendment there invalidated as different in constitutional significance from either a state's decision to repeal a fair housing law or a decision not to enact such a law. But surely either of the latter two courses of action can "encourage" private discrimination—as indeed, can essentially any governmental act (the provision of a postal system; a charitable contribution deduction; the enforcement of bequests by name). Sooner or later the Court must follow logic one way or the other. Either the state can act without regard to how its actions or inactions are going to affect the likelihood or private discrimination, in which case judicial intervention should await proof of an intention to foster such discrimination, or the state is obligated to combat such discrimination by taking some actions and refraining from others.

115. But cf., eg., Shelley v. Kraemer, 334 U.S. 1 (1948).

116. Black, supra note 110.

117. See note 114 supra.

Chapter 8

1. The term is an oxymoron, but the issues it raises (whether and how to protect rights that are neither mentioned nor plainly implied by the constitutional document) might fairly have arisen under other clauses, such as the Ninth Amendment and the Fourteenth Amendment's Privileges or Immunities Clause. See Democracy and Distrust 14–41.

2. 381 U.S. 479.

3. [I later changed my mind about the propriety of inferring a general constitutional right of "privacy," though I continued to have qualms about whether it would apply in cases like *Griswold* and *Roe*. See pages 285–88.]

4. [367 U.S. 497 (1961).]

5. 82 Yale L. J. 920.

6. United States v. Vuitch, 402 U.S. 62, 80 (1971) (Douglas, J., dissenting in part).

7. 410 U.S. 113 (1973).

8. Were the dissents adequate to the occasion, this comment would be unnecessary. But each is so brief as to signal no particular conviction that *Roe* represents an important, or unusually dangerous, constitutional development.

9. See 410 U.S. at 118 n. 2. See also Doe v. Bolton, 410 U.S. 179, 182 (1973).

10. 410 U.S. at 153–54. But cf. note 47 infra.

11. 410 U.S. at 153.

12. Id. at 155.

13. Id. at 162.

14. The Court indicates that the constitutional issue is not to be solved by attempting to answer "the difficult question of when life begins." Id. at 159. See also id. at 150. But see pages 284–85.

15. 410 U.S. at 162–63.

16. Id. at 149.

17. See pages 284–85.

18. See 410 U.S. at 163.

19. Id.

20. Id. at 163–65.

21. This, the Court tells us, is somewhere between the twenty-fourth and twenty-eighth weeks. Id. at 160. But cf. page 283–84.

22. 410 U.S. at 164–65. (Thus the statutes of most states must be unconstitutional even as applied to the final trimester, as they permit abortion only for the purpose of saving the mother's life. See id. at 117–18.) This holding—that even after viability the mother's life or health (which presumably is to be defined very broadly indeed, so as to include what many might regard as the mother's convenience, see 410 U.S. at 207–08 [Burger, C. J., concurring]); United States v. Vuitch, 402 U.S. 62 [1971]) must, as a matter of constitutional law, take precedence over what the Court seems prepared to grant at this point has become the fetus's life, see page 284—seems to me at least as controversial as its holding respecting the period prior to viability. (Typically, of course, one is not privileged even statutorily, let alone constitutionally, to take another's life in order to save his own life, much less

his health.) Since, however, the Court does not see fit to defend this aspect of its decision at all, there is not a great deal that can be said by way of criticism.

23. The Court's unusual theory seems to be that narrow grounds need not be considered when there is a broad one that will do the trick: "This conclusion makes it unnecessary for us to consider the additional challenge to the Texas statute asserted on grounds of vagueness." 410 U.S. at 164.

24. Apparently doctors are expected, or at least can be required despite the decisions, to exercise their best "medical" or "clinical" judgment (and presumably can be prosecuted if they perform abortions conflicting with that judgment). Id. at 192, 199. But if it is unconstitutional to limit the justifications for an abortion to considerations of maternal life and health, what kind of "medical" judgment does the Court have in mind? See Stone, "Abortion and the Supreme Court: What Now?" 41 Modern Medicine 32, 36 (1973): "[T]here are no clear medical indications for abortion in the vast majority of cases. Where there are no indications, there is no room for clinical judgment."

25. Compare 410 U.S. at 163–65 with id. at 193–200. An additional element of confusion may have been injected by Justice Douglas's indication in his concurrence that "quickening" is the point at which the interest in protecting the fetus becomes compelling. Id. at 215. But see id. at 160, where the Court distinguishes quickening from viability and holds the latter to be the crucial point. See also id. at 163; page 284.

26. The state can require that the abortion be performed by a doctor, but that is all. Even after the first trimester, the limits on state regulation of the conditions under which an abortion can be performed are extremely stringent. See Doe v. Bolton, 410 U.S. 204 (1973).

27. With respect to the capital punishment litigation too, the Court rejected a narrow ground of invalidation one term, only to come back with a coup de main the next. Compare McGautha v. California, 402 U.S. 183 (1971) with Furman v. Georgia, 408 U.S. 238 (1972). Miranda v. Arizona, 384 U.S. 436 (1966), has something of a "guidebook" quality about it. United States v. Wade, 388 U.S. 218 (1967), to take but one example, has always struck me as a case where the Court, starting from the entirely valid realization that trials cannot be fair if lineups are not, went a bit far in limiting the appropriate remedies. And of course many opinions have emitted confusing signals respecting what is henceforth permissible.

28. The child may not fare so well either. Of course the Court requires of the mother neither sort of showing, though it may be hoping the doctors will do so.

It is also probably the case, although this is the sort of issue where reliable statistics and comparisons are largely unobtainable, that a number of women have died from illegal abortions who would have lived had they been able to secure legal abortions. It is a strange argument for the unconstitutionality of a law that those who evade it suffer, but it is one that must nevertheless be weighed in the balance as a cost of anti-abortion legislation. The Court does not mention it, however; and given the severe restrictions it places on state regulation of the conditions under which an abortion can be performed, it apparently did not appreciably inform its judgment.

29. 410 U.S. at 214 (Douglas, J., concurring).

30. The claim that the participants are injuring their health seems at least as

plausible respecting abortion. To the extent that the use of soft drugs and homosexual activities interfere with the lives of those other than the participants, those interferences can generally be dealt with discretely.

31. Cf. Poe v. Ullman, 367 U.S. 497, 551–53 (1961) (Harlan, J., dissenting), quoted in part in Griswold v. Connecticut, 381 U.S. 479, 499 (1965) (Goldberg, J., concurring), distinguishing laws proscribing homosexual acts (even those performed in the home) as not involving the "right" at stake in those cases. [See also Bowers v. Hardwick, 478 U.S. 186 (1986).]

32. It defines viability so as not to exclude the possibility of artificial support, 410 U.S. at 160, and later indicates its awareness of the continuing development of artificial wombs. Id. at 161. It gives no sign of having considered the implications of that combination for the trimester program the Constitution is held to mandate, however.

33. Albeit not so compelling that a state is permitted to honor it at the expense of the mother's health. See note 22 supra.

34. Note 21 supra.

35. See 410 U.S. at 132.

36. Id. at 132–39.

37. Id. at 163. See also id. at 160:

Physicians and their scientific colleagues have regarded [quickening] with less interest and have tended to focus either upon conception or upon live birth or upon the interim point at which the fetus becomes "viable," . . .

The relevance of this observation is not explained. It is, moreover, of questionable validity:

The court has drawn its line beyond quickening, beyond the point where any religion has assumed that life begins, beyond the time when abortion is a simple procedure, and beyond the point when most physicians and nurses will feel the procedure is victimless. It is also beyond the point which would have satisfied many like myself who were long-term supporters of the right to abortion.

Stone, supra note 24, at 35.

38. Logically, of course, a legitimate state interest in this area need not stand or fall on acceptance of the belief that life begins at conception or at some other point prior to live birth. In assessing the State's interest, recognition may be given to the less rigid claim that as long as at least potential life is involved, the State may assert interests beyond the protection of the pregnant woman alone.

410 U.S. at 150. See also id. at 159:

We need not resolve the difficult question of when life begins. When those trained in the respective disciplines of medicine, philosophy, and theology are unable to arrive at any consensus, the judiciary, at this point [sic] in the development of man's knowledge, is not in a position to speculate as to the answer.

The Texas statute, like those of many states, had declared fetuses to be living beings. See id. at 117 n. 1, 119 n. 3; cf. id. at 141–42, 146–47 n. 40, 151 n. 55.

39. The opinion does contain a lengthy survey of "historical attitudes" toward abortion, culminating in a discussion of the positions of the American Medical Association, the American Public Health Association, and the American Bar Association. Id. at 129–47. (The discussion's high point is probably reached where the Court explains away the Hippocratic Oath's prohibition of abortion on the grounds that Hippocrates was a Pythagorean, and Pythagoreans were a minority. Id. at 130–32.) The Court does not seem entirely clear on what this discussion has to do with the legal argument, id. at 117, 129, and the reader is left in much the same quandary. It surely does not seem to support the Court's position, unless a record of serious historical and contemporary dispute is somehow thought to generate a constitutional mandate.

40.
[T]he traditional rule of tort law had denied recovery for prenatal injuries even though the child was born alive. That rule has been changed in almost every jurisdiction. In most States recovery is said to be permitted only if the fetus was viable, or at least quick, when the injuries were sustained, though few courts have squarely so held. In a recent development, generally opposed by the commentators, some States permit the parents of a stillborn child to maintain an action for wrongful death because of prenatal injuries. Such an action, however, would appear to be one to vindicate the parents' interest and is thus consistent with the view that the fetus, at most, represents only the potentiality of life. Similarly, unborn children have been recognized as acquiring rights or interests by way of inheritance or other devolution of property, and have been represented by guardians ad litem. Perfection of the interests involved, again, has generally been contingent upon live birth. In short, the unborn have never been recognized in the law as persons in the whole sense.

Id. at 161–62 (footnotes omitted). See also, e.g., W. Prosser, Handbook of the Law of Torts 355 (3d ed. 1964).

41. 410 U.S. at 157 (footnote omitted).

42. See pages 285–89.

43. Indeed it is difficult to think of a single instance where the justification given for upholding a governmental limitation of a protected right has involved the constitutional rights of others. A "free press–fair trial" situation might provide the basis for such an order, but thus far the Court has refused to approve one. See pages 152–73.

In the Court's "defense" it should be noted that it errs in the other direction as well, by suggesting that if a fetus were a person protected by the Fourteenth Amendment, it would necessarily follow that appellants would lose. 410 U.S. at 156–57. Yet in fact all that would thereby be established is that one right granted special protection by the Fourteenth Amendment was in conflict with what the Court felt was another; it would not tell us which must prevail.

44. See United States v. O'Brien, 391 U.S. 367, 376–77 (1968). And if you don't like that example, substitute post offices for draft cards.

45. I would, however, omit the serious restrictions the Court puts on state health regulation of the conditions under which an abortion can be performed, and give serious thought—though the practical difference here is not likely to be great—to placing the critical line at quickening rather than viability.

46. Some of us who fought for the right to abortion did so with a divided spirit. We have always felt that the decision to abort was a human tragedy to be accepted only because an unwanted pregnancy was even more tragic.

Stone, supra note 24, at 37.

47. The Court does not seem entirely certain about which provision protects the right to privacy and its included right to an abortion.

Appellant would discover this right in the concept of personal "liberty" embodied in the Fourteenth Amendment's Due Process Clause; or in personal, marital, familial, and sexual privacy said to be protected by the Bill to Rights or its penumbras . . . or among those rights reserved to the people by the Ninth Amendment. . . .

410 U.S. at 129.

This right of privacy, whether it be founded in the Fourteenth Amendment's concept of personal liberty and restrictions upon state action, as we feel it is, or, as the District Court determined, in the Ninth Amendment's reservation of rights to the people, is broad enough to encompass a woman's decision whether or not to terminate her pregnancy.

Id. at 153. This inability confidently to pigeonhole the right involved is not important in and of itself. It might, however, have alerted the Court to what *is* an important question: whether the Constitution speaks to the matter at all.

48. 381 U.S. 479 (1965).

49. See Katz v. United States, 389 U.S. 347, 364 (1967) (Black, J., dissenting); Griswold v. Connecticut, 381 U.S. 479, 529 (Stewart, J., dissenting).

50. United States v. Dionisio, 410 U.S. 1 (1973). See also United States v. Mara, 410 U.S. 19 (1973) (handwriting exemplars), also decided the same day as *Roe*, and Couch v. United States, 409 U.S. 322 (1973) (finding no privacy interest in records a taxpayer had turned over to her accountant) decided thirteen days earlier.

51. Cf. Fried, "Privacy," 77 Yale L. J. 475 (1968). The Third Amendment, mentioned in *Griswold* though not in *Roe*, surely has this aspect to it as well, though it probably grew in even larger measure out of a general concern with the pervasiveness of military power.

52. 389 U.S. 347 (1967).

53. The *Roe* opinion does not rely on the obvious contraception-abortion comparison and indeed gives no sign that it finds *Griswold* stronger precedent than a number of other cases. See 410 U.S. at 152–53; note 60 infra. In fact it seems to go out of its way to characterize *Griswold* and Eisenstadt v. Baird, 405 U.S. 438 (1972), as cases concerned with the privacy of the bedroom. See 410 U.S. at 159; note 60 infra. It is true that in *Eisenstadt* the Court had at one point characterized *Griswold* as protecting the "decision whether to bear and beget a child," 405 U.S. at 453, but, mysteriously in light of that characterization, it had also pointedly refused to decide whether the earlier case extended beyond use, to the distribution of contraceptives. Id. at 452–53. Nor is there any possibility that the refusal to extend *Griswold* in this way was ill-considered; such an extension would have obviated the *Eisenstadt* Court's obviously strained use of the Equal Protection Clause.

54. See Eisenstadt v. Baird, 405 U.S. 438, 443 (1972). Cf. 410 U.S. at 159; note 60 infra.

55. 381 U.S. at 485–86 (emphasis in original).

56. That the Court in *Griswold* saw fit to quote Boyd v. United States, 116 U.S. 616, 630 (1886), also seems significant. See 381 U.S. at 484–85 n. *.

57. Of course in individual cases the government might seek to enforce legislation restricting abortion, as indeed it might seek to enforce any law, in ways that violate the Fourth Amendment or otherwise intrude upon the general privacy interest the Bill of Rights suggests. The Court rightly does not suggest, however, that the laws at issue in *Roe* are in any sense unusually calculated to generate such intrusions.

The theory suggested in Poe v. Ullman, 367 U.S. 497, 551–52 (1961) (Harlan, J., dissenting), extending heightened protection to activities—though it turns out to be *some* activities, note 31 supra—customarily performed in the home, is also inapplicable to *Roe*.

58. See pages 286–87.

59. 410 U.S. at 154.

60. The Court does assert that

only personal rights that can be deemed "fundamental" or "implicit in the concept of ordered liberty," Palko v. Connecticut, 302 U.S. 319, 325 (1937), are included in this guarantee of personal privacy. They also make it clear that the right has some extension to activities relating to marriage. Loving v. Virginia, 388 U.S. 1, 12 (1967), procreation, Skinner v. Oklahoma, 3156 U.S. 535, 541–42 (1942), contraception, Eisenstadt v. Baird, 405 U.S. 438, 453–54 (1972); id. at 460, 463–65 (White, J., concurring), family relationships, Prince v. Massachusetts, 321 U.S. 158, 166 (1944), and child rearing and education, Pierce v. Society of Sisters, 268 U.S. 510, 535 (1925), Meyer v. Nebraska, [262 U.S. 390, 399 (1923)].

410 U.S. at 152–53. The *Palko* test was stated and has heretofore been taken as a definition (of questionable contemporary vitality) of due process generally, not of privacy. *Loving* was a case involving explicit racial discrimination and therefore decidable (and decided) by a rather straightforward application of the Equal Protection Clause. . . . And while the *Loving* Court did, inexplicably, append a reference to due process, it did not mention privacy. *Skinner* invalidated the Oklahoma criminal sterilization act's distinction between larcenists and embezzlers. Although it too did not allude to privacy, it did suggest it was applying a higher equal protection standard than usual. Why it did so is unclear. "Faced with the possibility of a finding of cruel and unusual punishment and the virtual certainty of invalidation under the clause proscribing ex post facto laws, the state declined to argue the case on the theory that the . . . Act was a penal statute, and therefore tried to justify the distinction in 'regulatory' terms." Ely, "Legislative and Administrative Motivation in Constitutional Law," 79 Yale L. J. 1205, 1235 n. 101 (1970). That being so, the state was unable to come up with even a plausible justification for the distinction. *Eisenstadt* was a case purporting to apply "traditional" equal protection standards, albeit in a less than satisfactory way. See Note, "Legislative Purpose, Rationality, and Equal Protection," 82 Yale L. J. 123 (1972). The passage cited by the Court in *Roe* reiterated *Griswold*'s conclusion that privacy interests are threatened by a ban on

the use of contraceptives, but declined to decide whether its rationale should be extended to restrictions on distribution. *Prince* upheld the application of a child labor law to Jehovah's Witness children distributing religious literature. It did, however, reiterate the conclusion of *Pierce* and *Meyer* that family relationships are entitled to special protection. Those two cases are products of "the *Lochner* era," see pages 289–93. The vitality of the theory on which they rested has been questioned, Epperson v. Arkansas, 393 U.S. 97, 105–6 (1968), and the Court has attempted to recast them as First Amendment cases. Griswold v. Connecticut, 381 U.S. 479, 482 (1965); cf. Poe v. Ullman, 367 U.S. 497, 533–34 (1961) (Harlan, J. dissenting). Even reading the cases cited "for all they are worth," it is difficult to isolate the "privacy" factor (or any other factor that seems constitutionally relevant) that unites them with each other and with *Roe*. So the Court seems to admit by indicating that privacy has "some extension" to the activities involved, and so it seems later to grant even more explicitly.

> The pregnant woman cannot be isolated in her privacy. She carries an embryo and, later, a fetus. . . . The situation therefore is inherently different from marital intimacy, or bedroom possession of obscene material, or marriage, or procreation, or education, with which *Eisenstadt, Griswold, Stanley, Loving, Skinner, Pierce,* and *Meyer* were respectively concerned.

410 U.S. at 159.

61. Id. at 153.

62. It might be noted that most of the factors enumerated also apply to the inconvenience of having an unwanted two-year-old or a senile parent around. Would the Court find the constitutional right of privacy invaded in those situations too? I find it hard to believe it would; even if it did, of course, it would not find a constitutional right to "terminate" the annoyance—presumably because "real" persons are now involved. But cf. pages 284–85 & note 43 supra. But what about ways of removing the annoyance that do not involve "termination"? Can they really be matters of constitutional entitlement?

63. United States v. Carolene Products Co., 304 U.S. 144, 152 n.4 (1938).

64. If the mere fact that the classification in issue disadvantages a minority whose viewpoint was not appreciated by a majority of the legislature that enacted it were sufficient to render it suspect, all classifications would be suspect.

65. Even if the case could be made that abortion is an issue that pits the interests of men against those of women, that alone would not bring it within a theory that renders suspect classifications based on generalizations about the characteristics of men and women. And even if there were some way to expand the theory (and it is difficult to see what judicial remedy would be appropriate were the theory so expanded) to cover all "interests of men versus interests of women" situations, it will take some proving to establish this is one:

> [D]ecisions in society are made by those who have power and not by those who have rights. Husbands and boy friends may in the end wield the power and make the abortion decision. Many women may be forced to have abortions not because it is their right, but because they are forced by egocentric men to submit to this procedure to avoid an unwanted inconvenience to men.

Stone, supra note 24, at 37. [See also MacKinnon, *"Roe v. Wade*: A Study in Male Ideology," in Abortion: Moral and Legal Perspectives 45, 49, 51 (J. Garfield ed. 1985).]

66. It might be suggested that legislation restricting abortion had been kept on the books by the efforts of an intense minority and did not represent the will of most legislative majorities. Though I am aware of no basis for inferring that this is any truer here than it is with respect to other sorts of legislation, it is the sort of claim that is hard to disprove. . . . In any event it is not the Court's job to repeal such legislation. In the first place there is nothing unusual, and I was not aware there was anything wrong, with an intense minority's compromising on issues about which it feels less strongly in order to garner support on those it cares most about. Moreover, precisely because the claims involved are difficult to evaluate, I would not want to entrust to the judiciary authority to guess about them—certainly not under the guise of enforcing the Constitution.

67. The claimed connection is often empirical, causal, or normative. About all that does not seem to become involved is formal logic.

68. See Branzburg v. Hayes, 408 U.S. 665 (1972).

69. The thing about permitting disparity among state laws regulating abortion that I find most troubling is not mentioned by the Court, and that is that some people can afford the fare to a neighboring state and others cannot. Of course this situation prevails with respect to divorce and a host of other sorts of laws as well. I wish someone could develop a theory that would enable the Court to take account of this concern without implying a complete obliteration of the federal system that is so obviously at the heart of the Constitution's plan. I have not been able to do so.

70. Of course one can disagree with the lengths to which the inferences have been taken; my point is that the prior decisions, including those that have drawn the most fire, at least started from a value singled out by, or fairly inferable from, the Constitution as entitled to special protection. Whatever one may think of the code of conduct laid down in Miranda v. Arizona, 384 U.S. 436 (1966), the Constitution does talk about the right to counsel and the privilege against self-incrimination. Whatever one may think of the strictness of the scrutiny exercised in Furman v. Georgia, 408 U.S. 238 (1972), the Eighth Amendment surely does indicate in a general way that punishments are to be scrutinized for erratic imposition ("unusual") and severity disproportionate to any good they can be expected to accomplish ("cruel").

Note that the claim in the text has to do with the capacity of the earlier decisions to be rationalized in terms of some value highlighted by the Constitution, not with the skill with which they were in fact rendered. It is now pretty generally recognized, for example, that the various "wealth discrimination" cases could better have been defended in terms of the constitutional attention paid explicitly or implicitly to the "goods" whose distribution was in issue—the right to vote and the assurance of fair judicial procedures. See, e.g., Michelman, "Foreword: On Protecting the Poor Through the Fourteenth Amendment," 83 Harv. L. Rev. 7 (1969). Reynolds v. Sims, 377 U.S. 533 (1964), is a badly articulated opinion. [However, it is defensible in terms of process values the Constitution marks as special. See Democracy and Distrust 120–25.] [T]he fight in *Reynolds*, like that in *Miranda*, turns out to be not so much over the [presence of a constitutional mandate] as over the need for a clean prophylactic rule that will keep the courts out of messy factual disputes.

In his concurrence in *Roe*, Justice Stewart lists ten cases to prove that "the Due Process Clause of the Fourteenth Amendment covers more than those freedoms explicitly named in the Bill of Rights." 410 U.S. at 168. His point is obviously that the freedoms involved were given protection above and beyond the ordinary demand for a "rational" defense and therefore *Roe* is just more of the same. It is not. Schware v. Bd. of Bar Examiners, 353 U.S. 232 (1957): Aptheker v. Secretary of State, 378 U.S. 50 (1964); and Kent v. Dulles, 357 U.S. 116 (1958), are all obviously rationalizable as First Amendment cases and indeed have since been so rationalized. . . . Concerning *Pierce v. Society of Sisters* and *Meyer v. Nebraska*, see note 60 supra. As to Shapiro v. Thompson, 394 U.S. 618 (1969), and United States v. Guest, 383 U.S. 745 (1966), see Democracy and Distrust 177–79. With respect to Carrington v. Rash. 380 U.S. 89 (1965), see Democracy and Distrust 142 and C. Black, Structure and Relationship in Constitutional Law (1969).

71. 198 U.S. 45 (1905).

72. Ferguson v. Skrupa, 372 U.S. 726, 729–30 (1963) (footnotes omitted).

73. See Pierce v. Society of Sisters, 268 U.S. 510 (1925); Meyer v. Nebraska, 262 U.S. 390 (1923).

74. E.g., Adkins v. Children's Hospital, 261 U.S. 525, 542–43 (1923). See also Adair v. United States, 208 U.S. 161, 172–73 (1908). Cf. Hammer v. Dagenhart, 247 U.S. 251 (1918).

75. 397 U.S. 471 (1970).

76. But cf. note 80 infra.

77. 397 U.S. at 484–86.

78. Karst & Horowitz, "*Reitman v. Mulkey*: A Telophase of Substantive Equal Protection," 1967 Sup. Ct. Rev. 39, 57–58, cf. 2 L. Pollak, The Constitution and the Supreme Court: A Documentary History 266–67 (1966).

79. See U.S. Const. Art. I, § 10; Calder v. Bull, 3 U.S. (3 Dall.) 386 (1798).

80. 410 U.S. at 168. The only "*Lochner* era" cases Justice Stewart cites are *Meyer* and *Pierce*. It therefore may be that he intends to pursue some sort of "economic-noneconomic" line in selecting rights entitled to special protection. But see text at note 77 supra. The general philosophy of constitutional adjudication, however, is the same.

81. Adair v. United States, 208 U.S. 161, 172 (1908). See also id. at 174.

82. Jay Burns Baking Co. v. Bryan, 264 U.S. 504, 513 (1924). See also id. at 517; Meyer v. Nebraska, 262 U.S. 390, 399–400, 403 (1923); Adkins v. Children's Hospital, 261 U.S. 525, 529 (1923); Coppage v. Kansas, 236 U.S. 1, 14 (1915), Lochner v. New York 198 U.S. 45, 53, 54, 56, 5, (1905); id. at 68 (Harlan, J., dissenting).

83. Coppage v. Kansas, 236 U.S. 1, 16–17, 17–18 (1915). See also Meyer v. Nebraska, 262 US. 390, 403 (1923); Adair v. United States, 208 U.S. 161, 174 75 (1908); Lochner v. New York, 198 U.S. 45, 57–58 (1905).

84. Id., at 62. See also id. at 57, 58, 59, 64.

85. Jay Burns Baking Co. v. Bryan, 264 U.S. 504, 517 (1924). See also Coppage v. Kansas, 236 U.S. 1, 15–16 (1915).

86. Note 13 supra.

87. Adair v. United States, 208 U.S. 161, 172 (1908), quoted more fully at pages 291–92. See also, e.g., Lochner v. New York, 198 U.S. 45, 54 (1905).

88. Wrong, that is, if one assigns to the words anything resembling their ordinary meanings. One can of course argue that states should also have governments of few and defined powers, that they should not be vested with broad authority to go after whatever they regard as evils. But the Federal Constitution imposes no such restraint, and according to the test accepted even at the time of *Lochner*, such authority, at least as a matter of federal constitutional law, does exist.

89. It is possible, of course, that I am here time-bound, and that the wrongness of *Lochner* et al. is obvious only because a half century of commentary has made it so. While I cannot rebut this, I am inclined to doubt it. In those decisions the Court stated the applicable tests in language much the same as would be used today— language the dissents cogently demonstrated could not be reconciled with the results. That views with which one disagrees can be reasonable nonetheless was a concept hardly new to lawyers even in 1900.

90. With respect to the Equal Protection Clause, by way of contrast, the Court has taken to claiming it is simply applying the traditional rationality standard, whether it is or not. For a more optimistic view of the development, see Gunther, "Foreword: In Search of Evolving Doctrine on a Changing Court: A Model for a Newer Equal Protection," 86 Harv. L. Rev. 1 (1972).

91. See note 70 supra.

92. See, e.g., Kurland, "Foreword: Equal in Origin and Equal in Title to the Legislative and Executive Branches of Government," 78 Harv. L. Rev. 143, 144– 45, 149, 163, 175 (1964).

93. See e.g, A. Bickel, The Least Dangerous Branch, at 84–92 (1962); A. Bickel, The Supreme Court and the Idea of Progress 177 (1970); Mendelson, "On the Meaning of the First Amendment: Absolutes in the Balance," 50 Calif. L. Rev. 821 (1962).

94. Linde, "Judges, Critics, and the Realist Tradition," 82 Yale L.J. 227, 254 (1972) (characterizing, not endorsing, the view under discussion).

95. E.g., Kurland, supra note 92, at 175.

96. 7 Weekly Comp. of Presidential Documents 1431 (Oct. 25, 1971).

97. Id. at 1432.

98. See generally A. Bickel, The Supreme Court and the Idea of Progress (1970).

99. See Hart, "Foreword: The Time Chart of the Justices," 73 Harv. L. Rev. 84, 99 (1959). See also A. Bickel, supra note 98, at 99; Kurland, "Earl Warren, the 'Warren Court,' and the Warren Myths," 67 Mich. L. Rev. 353, 357 (1968). Cf. Karst, "Invidious Discrimination: Justice Douglas and the Return of the 'Natural-Law-Due-Process' Formula," 16 U.C.L.A. L. Rev. 716, 746–48 (1969); Karst & Horowitz, supra note 78, at 79.

100. E.g., A. Bickel, supra note 98, at 95; Kurland, "Toward a Political Supreme Court," 32 U. Chi. L. Rev. 19, 20, 22 (1969).

101. See generally W. Murphy, Congress and the Court (1962); C. Warren, The Supreme Court in United States History (rev. ed. 1932).

102. See page 285. Of course there are some possible uses of the decision that

scare me, particularly when it is considered in conjunction (a) with some of this Court's notions relating to a mother's "waiver" of AFDC assistance, see Wyman v. James, 400 U.S. 309 (1971) [discussed at pages 433–35, 437, 441–43], and (b) with Buck v. Bell, 274 U.S. 200 (1927), which was indeed relied on by the Court in *Roe*, 410 U.S. at 154, and cited without apparent disapproval in Justice Douglas's concurrence, id. at 215. But those are quite different cases I'm conjuring up.

103. In judicial review, the line between the "juridical" and the "legislative" mode does not run between "strict constructionists" and competing theorists of constitutional interpretation. Rather, it divides constructionists and non-constructionists, those who do and those who do not see judicial review as a task of construing the living meaning of past political decisions . . . .

Linde, supra note 94, at 254–55 (footnote omitted).

104. United States v. Butler. 297 U.S. 1, 62 (1936).

105. Wright, "Professor Bickel, the Scholarly Tradition, and the Supreme Court," 84 Harv. L. Rev. 769, 785 (1971) (footnote omitted).

106. [Apparently Congress appreciated this in connection with the attempt to overrule 1989's flag-burning decision. See pages 356–57.]

107. There is, of course, a danger that I am here merely reiterating my estimate of the decision's validity. One who approved it would be more likely, or at least so I hope, to see it as part of the warp and woof of American constitutional law.

108. [S. J. Res. 119, introduced by Senator Buckley, and S. J. 130, introduced by Senator Helms, were both proposed amendments to the Constitution and thus not to be confused with the *statute* introduced by Helms that is the subject of the piece co-authored with Professor Tribe and reproduced next. In different words both resolutions essentially declared that for constitutional purposes fetuses were to be regarded as persons from the moment of conception.]

109. [Where the mother will die unless an abortion is performed.]

110. [Maher v. Roe, 432 U.S. 464 (1977).]

111. What stops the theory from ultimately working is the realization that it would mean all states would have to have the same laws on all subjects that importantly affect people. That the Constitution doesn't mean.

112. 112 S.Ct. 2791 (1992).

113. July 1, 1992.

114. [Yes, they all answered. No, I won't tell you what they said, though two seemed genuinely touched, the third politely grateful.]

115. 56 N.Y.U. L. Rev. 397

116. [This was the title of the symposium of which this paper was a part.]

117. See, e.g., Bork, "The Impossibility of Finding Welfare Rights in the Constitution," 1979 Wash. U. L. Q. 695, 700 ("Representation-reinforcement could take us back to *Lochner*"); Tushnet, "Darkness on the Edge of Town: The Contributions of John Hart Ely to Constitutional Theory," 89 Yale L. J. 1037, 1055 n. 74 (1980) (same suggestion); Brest, "The Substance of Process," 42 Ohio St. L. J. 130, 137–38 (1981) (laws prohibiting sodomy and marijuana use and prescribing school dress

codes are indistinguishable in principle from suspect "we-they" classifications); Cox, Book Review, 94 Harv. L. Rev. 700, 710–11 (1981), sketches an "Ely-ish attack upon the Hyde Amendment." (I'm not sure I get to choose, but I much prefer "Elysian." See Leedes, Book Review, 59 N.C. L. Rev. 628 [1981]). Cox's rendition seems somewhat beside the point, since I had in the book (and previously) excoriated *Harris v. McCrae*'s predecessor, *Maher v. Roe*. See Democracy and Distrust 162, 246 n. 38, 248–49 n. 53. He goes on to suggest, however, that *Carolene Products* premises might be used to defend even *Roe v. Wade*, of which, he correctly notes, I was quite critical. . . . For another answer to Cox's argument, see Lupu, Book Review, 15 Harv. C.R.-C.L.L. Rev. 779, 794 (1981).

118. The temptation to apply my approach to laws that do not classify but rather, say, simply prohibit a defined act, seems related to another confusion, that I think the world is divided into "we"s and "they"s, from which metaphysical view I suppose it might follow that courts should specially scrutinize any law of any shape that bears harshly on (a high percentage of?) "they"s. See Tushnet, supra note 117, at 1053 n. 69; Tribe, "The Puzzling Persistence of Process-Based Constitutional Theories," 89 Yale L. J. 1063, 1074 (1980). In fact I confess utter inability to tell a "we" from a "they" outside the context of a particular classification: the abstract question "Which am I?" would strike me as utterly baffling no matter who asked it. See also page 451, n. 92.

119. Fleming, "A Critique of John Hart Ely's Quest for the Ultimate Constitutional Interpretivism of Representative Democracy" (Nov. 21, 1980) (paper delivered at Annual Meeting of Northeast Political Science Ass'n).

120. O'Fallon, Book Review, 68 Calif. L. Rev. 1070, 1089 (1980); see R. Dworkin, Taking Rights Seriously 234–36, 262, 275–76 (1977); cf. J. Mill, On Liberty 102 (C. Shields ed. 1956).

121. R. Dworkin, supra note 120, at 276. [See also pages 261–66, 311–28.)

122. A regulation that necessarily was motivated entirely by personal preferences is something I have trouble even imagining.

123. J. Mill, supra note 120, at 96; cf. O'Fallon, supra note 120, at 1091–92. I shall be arguing later that although such conduct is imaginable at least in theory, the notion of governmental intervention to prevent it is self-contradictory.

124. J. Mill, supra note 120, at 13; see also id. at 92, 114.

125. See id. at 14, 77. At one point Mill appears to have come close to making the constitutive argument, but on analysis the argument is utilitarian: it ran that people would be inexpert at estimating the happiness of others and thus if they were permitted to do so (as they necessarily must be in the case of controlling self-regarding conduct) the utilitarian calculus would be inaccurate. Id. at 102.

126. P. Brest, Processes of Constitutional Decisionmaking 798 (1975).

127. See pages 6–17; Ely, "Constitutional Interpretivism: Its Allure and Impossibility," 53 Ind. L. J. 399, 407–8 (1975); O'Fallon, supra note 120, at 1089.

128. Of course there are conflicting currents—such as the late-eighteenth century "Commonwealth's" perceived responsibility for the spiritual life of its citizens—but there surely is no need to get mired in a debate over either the original understanding or its relevance if, as I shall argue, the idea is not one that can be made to pan out in theory.

129. J. Mill, supra note 120, at 116–18.

130. 163 U.S. 537 (1896).

131. 198 U.S. 539 (1905).

132. See Coppage v. Kansas, 236 U.S. 1, 18–19 (1915); Adair v. United States, 208 U.S 161 174–75 (1908).

133. J. Mill, supra note 120, at 107. [Thus Professor Brest's "two questions" turn out to be the same.]

134. "[T]he liberty of the individual, in things wherein the individual is alone concerned, implies a corresponding liberty in any number of individuals to regulate by mutual agreement such things as regard them jointly, and regard no persons but themselves." Id. at 124; see also id. at 16.

135. Id. at 112; cf. id. at 100, 107; Coppage v. Kansas, 236 U.S. 1, 17 (1915).

136. See also L. Tribe, American Constitutional Law 889–90 (1978).

137. Cf. J. Mill, supra note 120, at 97 ("No person is an entirely isolated being . . .").

138. 1983 Duke L. J. 959, 965–86.

139. [See pages 261–66.]

140. R. Dworkin, Taking Rights Seriously 277 (1977).

141. See id. at 275–76; see also Dworkin, "Is There a Right to Pornography?" 1 Oxford J. Leg. Stud. 177 (1981).

142. 198 U.S. 45 (1905).

143. R. Dworkin, supra note 140, at 278.

144. Sager, "Rights Skepticism and Process-Based Responses," 56 N.Y.U. L. Rev. 417, 434 (1981) (footnote omitted); see also Regan, "Glosses on Dworkin: Rights, Principles, and Policies," 76 Mich. L. Rev. 1213, 1221 n. 18 (1978).

145. See also Sager, supra note 144, at 434.

146. See pages 324–25.

147. Compare Democracy and Distrust 138 ("it will be next to impossible for a court responsibly to conclude that a decision was affected by an unconstitutional motivation whenever it is possible to articulate a plausible legitimate explanation for the action taken") (footnote omitted) with id. at 243 n. 15 ("I overextended this point in 1970 by indicating that the possibility of alternative explanation rendered proof of illicit motivation completely irrelevant").

148. R. Dworkin, supra note 140, at 276.

149. Neither does Dworkin rely on a claim that such phenomena have no effect on anyone but the perpetrator, which claim is of debatable constitutional relevance and in any event plainly false where the state or another party is proceeding legally against the perpetrator. See pages 306–11.

150. See also Sager, supra note 144, at 434.

151. Page 264.

152. R. Dworkin, supra note 140, at 235.

153. Dworkin, supra note 141, at 202 (emphasis supplied); see also id. at 194, 205, 207–9; R. Dworkin, supra note 140, at 273; Dworkin, "The Forum of Principle," 56 N.Y.U. L. Rev. 469, 513 (1981).

154. Hart, "Between Utility and Rights," 79 Colum. L. Rev. 828, 843–44 (1979). A year earlier, Dworkin had essentially granted Hart's point—that "impose no scheme of values on any one" may be a tenet of liberalism but is not implied by the

concept of equality—when he wrote that neutrality on the question of what constitutes the good life is a component of a "liberal theory of equality" but not a component of a "second (or non-liberal) theory of equality." Dworkin, "Liberalism," in Public and Private Morality 127–28 (S. Hampshire ed. 1978). That he no longer is prepared even to come close to conceding the point is suggested by his failure to do so in his response to Hart, see Dworkin, supra note 141, at 206–12; the quite contrary view expressed in his response to me, see infra text accompanying note 156; and, of course, the fact that he is currently engaged in a multifronted effort to derive his entire political and constitutional philosophy from the single value of equality. See generally Dworkin, "What is Equality?" 10 Phil. & Pub. Aff. 185, 283 (1981); Dworkin, "What Liberalism Isn't," N.Y. Rev. Books, January 20, 1983, at 47; Dworkin, "Why Liberals Should Believe in Equality," N.Y. Rev. Books, February 3, 1983, at 32.

155. Democracy and Distrust 256 n. 92.

156. Dworkin, supra note 153, at 514.

157. Democracy and Distrust 256 n. 92. This seems as inconspicuous a place as I am likely to find to confess that Dean Sandalow appears to have nailed me on my attempt to distinguish laws denying homosexuals employment opportunities from laws criminalizing acts of homosexual sex—or at least he has nailed me insofar as (a) the employment disqualification does in fact require (and I am not sure he is right that this is typically the case) actual proof of homosexual sex, and (b) the disability in question is imposed prospectively only, thus avoiding ex post facto problems. See Sandalow, "The Distrust of Politics," 56 N.Y.U. L. Rev. 446, 465–66 (1981).

Professor Brest has also criticized the passage quoted in the text, suggesting that antimiscegenation laws can equally be defended on the basis of a "bona fide feeling that [miscegenation] is immoral." Brest, "The Substance of Process," 42 Ohio St. L. J. 131, 135 (1981). This too is a troubling criticism, but one that can be answered. As the Supreme Court has recognized, antimiscegenation laws were born of a desire to maintain white supremacy by keeping those of other races "in their place"—that is, away from the rest of us. Loving v. Virginia, 388 U.S. 1, 7, 11 & n. 11 (1967). Whatever objection one may have to laws proscribing homosexual acts, they cannot be responsibly thus characterized. I agree that such laws are stupid and cruel, but the claim that they respond to genuine revulsion with the act rather than constituting part of a general attempt to isolate a minority is vastly more credible in the homosexual case. Indeed, as Professor Fickle has pointed out, laws against homosexuality—dramatically unlike laws against miscegenation—are assimilationist, designed to "encourage people to join the majoritarian community." Fickle, "The Dawn's Early Light: The Contributions of John Hart Ely to Constitutional Theory," 56 Ind. L. J. 637, 653 (1981). One need hardly be a blinkered interpretivist to suppose that the difference between a law that assimilates and a law that segregates is one that is constitutionally relevant.

158. Perhaps I am a little optimistic about people's self-perceptions in the case of pornography. It may be that in voting to ban pornography, even legislators who have looked at it themselves—and who hasn't?—tend to censor that fact out of their consciousness and instead to conjure up visions of a class of "dirty old men in raincoats" whose interests should generally be counted for less than the interests of

"people like us." Even [bending over backward to grant arguendo] the partial validity of that point in the pornography context, however, it is difficult even to imagine a legislative supposition that "contraceptive users" constitute a minority who are "not like us" and whose interests should therefore be generally devalued.

159. Cf. infra note 188.

160. But see page 323.

161. See infra text accompanying note 168.

162. Hart, supra note 154, at 842.

163. The situation that is symmetrical to the "double counting" situation is that in which someone derives pleasure from depriving another person or group of life's goods. Obviously I do not mean to grant Dworkin's further assumption that the universal proscription of behavior perceived as immoral is assimilable to the latter. See pages 314–15.

164. Cf. J. Plamenatz, Democracy and Illusion 153–55 (1973) (discussing Anthony Downs' "self-interest axiom").

165. See also R. Wolff, The Poverty of Liberalism 35 n. * (1968); cf. Kuflik, "Majority Rule Procedure," in Nomos XVIII: Due Process 296, 303–4 (J. Pennock & J. Chapman eds. 1977).

166. Cf. pages 321–22.

167. R. Dworkin, supra note 140, at 358 (emphasis supplied); see also B. Barry, Political Argument 64 (1965); Dworkin, supra note 141, at 208:

> Utilitarianism holds that . . . we should work to achieve the maximum possible satisfaction of the preferences we find distributed in our community. If we accept this test in an unrestricted way, then we would count the attractive political convictions of the 60's liberals simply as data, to be balanced against the less attractive convictions of others, to see which carries the day in the contest of number and intensity. . . .
>
> But I have been arguing that this is a false test, which in fact undermines the case for utilitarianism, if political preferences of either the liberals or their opponents are counted and balanced to determine what justice requires. . . . [T]he liberals who campaigned in the interests of homosexuals in England in the 60's most certainly did not embrace the test I reject. They of course expressed their own political preferences in their votes and arguments, but they did not appeal to the popularity of these preferences as providing an argument in itself for what they wanted, as the unrestricted utilitarian argument I oppose would have encouraged them to do. . . . [T]he case for reform would have been just as strong in political theory even if there had been very few or no heterosexuals who wanted reform.

168. Hart, supra note 154, at 842 (footnote omitted); see also Baker, "Counting Preferences in Collective Choice Situations," 25 U.C.L.A. L. Rev. 381, 386 (1978); Ely, "Constitutional Interpretivism: Its Allure and Impossibility," 53 Ind. L. J. 399, 407 n.32 (1978) ("[T]here is nothing unworthy of moral recognition in getting one's happiness from what one perceives as beneficial impacts on persons other than himself. [I suppose it is a form of double-counting but it's a justifiable form. If A's immediate happiness makes both A and B happy, A's immediate happiness *should* be counted both times].").

169. Dworkin, supra note 141, at 206–7.

170. "Sarahocrat," id. at 204, is hardly an improvement on "Sarah lover."

171. 393 U.S. 385 (1969) [described at page 276].

172. R. Dworkin, supra note 140, at 276.

173. Id. at 235.

174. Dworkin, supra note 141, at 204; see also id. at 202–3.

175. But cf. infra note 194.

176. Bentham, "Principles of Morals and Legislation," in 1 Works of Jeremy Bentham 18 (J. Bowring ed. 1962).

177. [Okay, the secret's out: professors make enough to be disadvantaged by a progressive income tax. I hope the guild doesn't expel me for revealing this.]

178. J. Mill, "Representative Government," in Utilitarianism, Liberty and Representative Government 217 (Everyman ed. 1951); J. Lively, Democracy 120 (1975) (Bentham). Neither has there been any discernible shift in the thinking of our leading contemporary utilitarian theorists on this issue. See, e.g., P. Singer, Practical Ethics (1979); Smart, "An Outline of a System of Utilitarian Ethics," in J. Smart & B. Williams, Utilitarianism: For and Against 30–42 (1973); Hare, "Ethical Theory and Utilitarianism," in Utilitarianism and Beyond 23 (A. Sen & B. Williams eds. 1982).

179. Dworkin, supra note 141, at 209.

180. I therefore do not agree, at least on the level of constitutional theory, with Hart's [view that it counts as a criticism of] Dworkin's theory [that it] creates rights only for a democratic context and that it makes their content vary with what prejudices are current in a given society at a given time. Hart, supra note 154, at 840.

181. See Ely, supra note 168, at 405–8; pages 6–16; see also R. Dworkin, supra note 140, at 276, 364.

182. See further page 11.

183. Dworkin, supra note 156.

184. See also infra note 195.

185. Dworkin, Commentary, 56 N.Y.U. L. Rev. 525, 544 (1981); see also Dworkin, supra note 141, at 208–9; R. Dworkin, supra note 140, at 357–58:

> I have also been interpreted—even less plausibly—as arguing that external preferences are in themselves bad, and that people should strive not to have them and should vote ignoring the ones they do have. . . . Nothing could be further from what I suppose. . . . I argue only against counting external preferences, whether malevolent or altruistic, good or bad, in some utilitarian justification for a political decision.

186. R. Dworkin, supra note 140, at 277.

187. Id. at 236–37 (footnote omitted; emphasis supplied); cf. Dworkin, supra note 141, at 197 ("We therefore encounter, in peoples' motives for objecting to the advertising or display of pornography, at least a mix and interaction of attitudes, beliefs and tastes that rule out any confident assertion that regulation justified by appeal to these motives would not violate the right to moral independence"). But cf. infra note 188.

188. But cf. pages 312–13, 316. (Of course these situations involved benign external preferences, but that will be my point exactly. See page 327. Dworkin, supra

note 141, at 205–6, proposes a more "neutral" standard for deciding which cases are "appropriate . . . for a prophylactic refusal to count any motive whenever we cannot be sure that the motive is unmixed with" external preferences. (So far as I know, this is the only time that Dworkin has recognized that he has two practices regarding the subject.) The question under consideration is the public display of pornography (as opposed to its private enjoyment) and Dworkin's suggestion is "that restriction may be justified even though we cannot be sure that the preferences people have for restriction are untinged by the kind of preferences we should exclude" because "[t]his is a situation in which the egalitarian cast of utilitarianism is threatened from not one but two directions." That is, were the censorial preferences discarded entirely on the ground that they are polluted by external preferences, then "the neutrality of utilitarianism" would be "compromised in the other direction" since the *personal* preferences that people have for censorship of public pornography (preferences, according to Dworkin, concerning the sexual experience they want for themselves) would not be counted. This plainly will not work as a distinction, however—ignoring a mixed bundle of personal and external preferences will by definition have the effect of refusing to count some personal preferences—and one has to suspect that again the decision is being made on a ground that is not finding full expression. (And, indeed, the public display of pornography *is* more offensive than its private enjoyment.)

189. Taken from quotation on pages 311–12 (emphasis now supplied).

190. Dworkin, Liberalism, in Public and Private Morality 134 (S. Hampshire ed. 1978) (emphasis supplied).

191. But cf. supra note 188, infra note 193.

192. Dworkin, supra note 141, at 203.

193. Id. at 209; see also R. Dworkin, supra note 140, at 358 (laws helping disabled persons can be upheld on basis of ideal argument though generated by altruistic external preference); Dworkin, supra note 141, at 208 (similar conclusion concerning Britain's liberalization of its antihomosexuality laws); page 266 (affirmative action); pages 312–13 (*Lochner* law); pages 323–24 (aid to Cambodia).

194. Of course such preferences may well be felt less intensely than purely selfish ones, in which case (a common bromide to the contrary notwithstanding) they are likely effectively to be counted for less by a system of representative democracy such as ours. See pages 13–14; Ely, supra note 168, at 407–8. Of course they may *not* be felt less intensely, in which case they are not likely to be effectively discounted by a representative system, a result that I am suggesting, contrary to Dworkin, is entirely correct.

195. See Ely, Commentary, 56 N.Y.U. L. Rev. 525, 543–44 (1981) (suggesting that *Democracy and Distrust* effectively adopts something resembling half, but only half, of the external preference notion). For the representative to act on the basis of a naked desire—either his own or that of his constituents—that some minority simply be denied an equal share of life's goods and opportunities (Dworkin's terminology) is surely tantamount to valuing the welfare of that minority negatively (my terminology), and that, I argue at length, is a violation of the constitutionally imposed duty to "represent" the entirety of one's constituency. See also id. at 539–40; see generally Democracy and Distrust, especially chs. 4 & 6; cf. Aristotle, "Nicomachean Ethics" ii.7.1108b in The Basic Works of Aristotle 961 (R. McKeon ed.

1941) (defining spite as taking pleasure from the undeserved pain of others); accord, J. Rawls, A Theory of Justice 533 (1971).

If you were watching carefully, you saw the rabbit go into the hat with the words "or that of his constituents." That *is* tantamount to discounting malign constituent external preferences. And contrary to my detractors' sometime renditions of what I must have supposed I was doing, I am fully aware that it is a move that is not compelled by pure logic (uniformed by any theory of the Constitution) and, further, that it is a move with consequences. It is, however, a move that seems to me to follow from the duty imposed by the Fourteenth Amendment to review legislative and other governmental output for equality. Without such a discount (however expressed) the 88 percent nonblack majority could, for example, legislate that our 12 percent black population shall henceforth be consigned to menial labor at best.

Commentators on my work have felt it necessary to observe that this move does not follow from an unmodified utilitarianism that seeks simply to maximize satisfaction of constituent preferences, however destructive of other constituents. See, e.g., Sager, supra note 144, at 429 ("Unrefined utilitarianism can offer no solace to Ely"); Dworkin, supra note 156, at 512 n. 101 ("The pure utilitarian account would not support Ely's own argument that minority interests constitutionally are guaranteed 'virtual representation' in the political process . . . and that political decisions based on prejudice [unconstitutionally] deny such representation"). In fact I was aware of this. Ely, supra note 168 (published three years before these two observations) had stated, at 406 (footnotes omitted):

> And even if that impulse to qualify utilitarianism [by rights] is of arguable legitimacy, there is another that seems rather plainly not to be: inherent in utilitarianism is a problem of equity that simply cannot be ignored. An ethical system that was serious in demanding only the greatest happiness of the greatest number would have to count as moral a world in which 75 percent of the people systematically promoted their own happiness at the expense of the other 25 percent under circumstances where no one could say there was a relevant difference between the two classes. Now this is more than a little troubling, in fact if uncorrected it is fatal, and philosophers and societies have been forced, with varying degrees of success, to find mechanisms for correcting it.

The unsurprising fact of the matter is that the United States Constitution does not incorporate unmodified preference utilitarianism: in fact I have argued earlier in this article, contrary to Dworkin's sometime hints, that it does not incorporate utilitarianism of any sort, however reconstituted. And I defy anyone to give the Equal Protection Clause any meaning whatever without incorporating, by one mechanism or another, a willingness to discount the malign (e.g., racist) external preferences of constituents.

196. See pages 267–75. See generally Democracy and Distrust.

Chapter 9

1. [It strikes me as a good idea whenever possible to cite, ever so gently, a prior case in which the court or other office to which you are appealing was reversed by higher authority, even where, as here, the reversed official was not the person you are addressing but rather his predecessor. A fast ball high and tight: gives them

something to think about. Actually I think that unless I'd submitted total gibberish Levi would have called this one our way, but somehow I just can't stop teaching.]

2. New York Times, October 30, 1975.

3. [Just in case you're wondering: *of course* I realized the two inquiries could not be neatly separated. That was not a prospect that frightened me.]

4. 9 Constitutional Commentary 1.

5. D. Brock, The Real Anita Hill viii (1993).

Chapter 10

1. 77 Va. L. Rev. 833. An earlier version of this was presented as the Sibley Lecture at the University of Georgia Law School on October 31, 1989. [Halloween was fitting, as the lights went out about a third of the way into the lecture, completely darkening the auditorium. This induced (a) the dean to conclude it must be some kind of protest—that's how deanships get you to thinking—and (b) me (once I'd been supplied with a flashlight) to alternate between spooky half-lit faces of the sort we used to make at camp, and a low-rent light show ("Welcome to the crypt . . . No, let's disco!"). Lord knows I aspire to be a serious person, but you see, it was weird speaking in the dark, and besides I figured everyone must have left. However, when the lights came back on (with about five minutes to go) it seemed, if anything, there were *more* people there than at the beginning. Maybe southerners really are more polite than the rest of us. Or maybe it was too dark to find one's way out. The protest turned out to have been some hapless squirrel deciding a dive into the generator might be refreshing.]

2. Quoted in Zarin, "A Part in the Play," New Yorker, July 30, 1990, at 39.

3. West, "Progressive and Conservative Constitutionalism," 88 Mich. L. Rev. 641, 644 (1990).

4. Hutchinson, "The Three 'Rs': Reading/Rorty/Radically" (Book Review), 103 Harv. L. Rev. 555, 555 (1989) (citing Dworkin and Tribe).

5. My own methodology for determining what issues are appropriately assigned to courts—and in this respect I am conventionally described as a member of the legal process school, e.g., M. Kelman, A Guide to Critical Legal Studies 189–90 (1987)—is one rooted not in any supposed difference in reasoning capacity or political predilection between judges and other officials, but rather primarily in the fact that judges (at least federal judges) need not stand for reelection. [The remainder of this footnote appears at pages 5–6.]

6. See West, supra note 3, at 641 (footnote omitted):

American constitutional law . . . is in a state of profound transformation. The "liberal-legalist" and purportedly politically neutral understanding of constitutional guarantees that dominated constitutional law and theory during the fifties, sixties, and seventies, is waning, both in the courts and in the academy. What is beginning to replace liberal legalism in the academy, and what has clearly replaced it on the Supreme Court, is a very different conception—a new paradigm—of the role of constitutionalism . . . in a democratic state. Unlike the liberal-legal paradigm it is replacing, the new paradigm is overtly political—and overtly conservative—in its orientation and aspiration.

Professor West is not one to see only what scares her, and she does not commit that error here. She is quite clear that the legal process school is under serious attack from both ends of the political spectrum: "Both the progressives and conservatives seem increasingly willing to grant to the critics of liberal theory their main point . . . that constitutional adjudication is . . . necessarily political." Id. at 644.

7. The legal process movement is conventionally referred to as part of a post-realist reconstruction.

8. Indeed, the very point of early realists like Holmes and Brandeis was that judges should understand that what they are doing is not essentially different from legislating, and approach their jobs with appropriate restraint.

9. Of course the refrain that one's opponents are "reading their personal political views into the Constitution" is as old as the republic, and most of the time it has probably had some foundation. It takes an unusually strong or apolitical judge to avoid being discernibly affected by her assessment of the politically desirable outcome. What is new is the evolving consensus on most fronts that that is the way judges are supposed to behave.

10. As they approach middle age, law professors tend to deny their dwindling creativity by becoming deans, media personalities, advisers to politicians, or some other form of jackanapes.

11. M. Tushnet, Red, White, and Blue: A Critical Analysis of Constitutional Law 54 (1988) (footnote omitted).

12. Kennedy, "Distributive and Paternalist Motives in Contract and Tort Law, with Special Reference to Compulsory Terms and Unequal Bargaining Power," 41 Md. L. Rev. 563, 564–65 (1982). Mark Kelman confirms my instinct that Kennedy's position is atypical of critical scholars only in its candor. M. Kelman, supra note 5, at 192.

13. See, e.g., L. Tribe, American Constitutional Law § 1–9, at 15–17 (2d ed. 1988); cf. L. Tribe, Constitutional Choices 6 (1985) ("For me, such questions [of how judicial review is legitimated] seem basically unanswerable; theories that offer or presuppose answers to them—any answers—seem not worth pursuing with passion or even worth criticizing in great detail.").

14. L. Tribe, American Constitutional Law, supra note 13, § 8–7, at 584; see also, e.g., id. § 1–8, at 13–14; L. Tribe, God Save this Honorable Court ix (1985). To the same general effect, see, e.g., Dworkin, "The Forum of Principle," 56 N.Y.U. L. Rev. 469, 470–71 (1981); Brest, "The Fundamental Rights Controversy: The Essential Contradictions of Normative Constitutional Scholarship," 90 Yale L. J. 1063 (1981); Tushnet, "The Dilemmas of Liberal Constitutionalism," 42 Ohio St. L. J. 411, 424 (1981).

15. Under this approach every question of public policy is a constitutional question. Many do not regard this implication as an occasion for rethinking. Those who do are probably most likely to respond that not all questions of public policy are constitutional questions, only those that involve *rights*. Any constitutional attack, however, can be framed in terms of rights; see, e.g., Coppage v. Kansas, 236 U.S. 1, 18–19 (1915); Adair v. United States, 208 U.S. 161, 172–75 (1908); the "right to choose"/"right to life" debate, "right to work" laws, "victims' rights," and so forth should also be consulted. The position that the only rights that count are those alluded to in the Constitution having been foresworn, the response that the dis-

favored cases don't "really" involve rights is likely to translate into the position that they don't involve rights the commentator thinks deserve recognition.

There are two standard strategies for "sophisticating" this approach (and, incidentally, drawing it out into a full-semester course). First, one can admit that where the judiciary is not in as good a position as other governmental actors to get a reliable grip on the facts bearing on the wisdom of the action in question, it should proceed cautiously. This might be styled a sensitivity to considerations of justiciability. Second, one might hold that in order to declare a legislative action unconstitutional, a court (or commentator) must conclude that it is not simply a bad idea, but a *really* bad idea. This introduces a second layer of unvarnished subjectivity.

The fact that so much legal writing today boils down so quickly to the expression of political preferences has contributed massively to the notorious lack of recent consensus within legal academia about what counts as good scholarship. (In turn, the inevitable playout of that lack of consensus, in increasingly political hiring decisions, has understandably induced the literature to get still more political.) I suspect this description has always fit law more than other disciplines. (At no point have law teachers generally been anything other than lawyers who knew a good thing when they saw it, and there have for many years been an embarrassingly large number of professional journals in our business, most of whose publication decisions are made by persons with substantially less academic training and experience than even we have[—that is, law students.]) But the description seems to fit particularly well now.

16. In particular, I have in mind here the now-common discussions of techniques of literary criticism, cf. pages 341–42, and the rediscovery of "the republican tradition," which a number of commentators find of significant intellectual interest but whose social and political assumptions seem substantially irrelevant to twentieth-century America.

[The second paragraph of this note, further discussing "republicanism" and "pluralism," appears at pages 17–18.]

The increasing call in the legal literature for "different voices" denotes a worthy goal of judicial and academic appointments, and of a "legal process" approach to the allocation of political power. Presented as a first order theory of judicial review, however, it constitutes only another version of the reductionist view that judges should do what, based on their experience, seems right to them.

[I'm bound to think that the legal literature's increasingly common references to "pragmatism" (in terms suggesting that at least to the author the reference amounts to something beyond a nod in the direction of moderation and common sense) belong on this list as well. As a theory of scientific truth "pragmatism" at least appears to *mean* something, however unexciting: thus "there's a door over there" is true in this core pragmatic way if I can walk through the segment of the wall to which I'm pointing without breaking my nose. But, transparently, one cannot judge whether a proposition of law "works" without a separately stated (and, dare we hope, defended) theory of what law should accomplish. (On deeper analysis I believe this to be true of the scientific examples as well, but as respects law it seems obvious on the surface.) Thus "pragmatism" may currently serve for legal moderates a function analogous to that served by "critical theory" for legal leftists, as a capacious and cooling beach umbrella under which to spread one's towel, but not much more. Of course I confess to being a moderate myself, and thus suppose I would deny no more than I affirm that I am a pragmatist, were it not for the fact that the latter term is used in the legal literature (interestingly, again like "critical theory") to deride even the possibility of successful "grand theory," and I'm nothing if not a grand theorist. It was, of course, Franz Bibfeldt who opined that "pragmatism is all right, as long as it works." It goes without saying, but bears remarking, that on this I stand with Bibfeldt. And with his critics.]

17. How do the teachers miss this, you may ask? I expect true believers don't: presumably it's all part of the recipe for revolution. For liberals I suspect the myopia results from their general and unrealistic optimism about the power of reason to "enlighten" (get others to see things their way).

18. See N.Y. Times, July 21, 1989, at C1-C2 (reporting on "Beyond the Deficit Problem: 'Now-Now-ism' and 'The New Balance,'" a speech by Richard Darman to the National Press Club on July 20, 1989).

19. See, e.g., E. Chemerinsky, Interpreting the Constitution xi (1987) (recommending open-ended modernism on the part of the judiciary, an "indeterminate, open-ended process"). "The core characteristic of open-ended modernism is its explicit premise that justices have, and should have, discretion in deciding constitutional cases, and that their decisions are inevitably based on their personal values." Id. at 109. Lest you suppose I have chosen some obscure eccentric to make my point, I hasten to point out that Chemerinsky is the author of the Foreword to the Harvard Law Review's 1989 Supreme Court issue, and thus presumptively the second "hottest" constitutional theorist in the country. See Chemerinsky, "The Supreme Court, 1988 Term—Foreword: The Vanishing Constitution," 103 Harv. L. Rev. 43 (1989) (an extended exposition of the same thesis; see especially id. at 47–49). (Nor am I pulling a fast one by dragging you back to the historic recesses of 1989. By the same rough measure, *the* hottest constitutional theorist is Robin West, quoted above, supra note 3. See West, "The Supreme Court, 1989 Term—Foreword: Taking Freedom Seriously," 104 Harv. L. Rev. 43 (1990); see also, e.g., infra note 27.)

20. Tushnet, "Does Constitutional Theory Matter? A Comment," 65 Tex. L. Rev. 777, 780 (1987).

21. I necessarily am talking mainly about former President Reagan here. It seems likely, however, that President Bush will behave in much the same way. See Lewis, "Bush Picking the Kind of Judges Reagan Favored," N.Y. Times, April 10, 1990, at A1, col. 2; see also pages 348–49 (discussing appointment of Justice Souter). In significant degree this began with former President Carter, who did a fairly good job of stacking the lower federal courts with liberals. Carter had no strong philosophy of appropriate judicial behavior; this therefore appears in large measure to have been a by-product of his program of appointing larger numbers of minorities and women. The intrusiveness of Senate confirmation hearings has also greatly increased over the past few years. E.g., Totenberg, "The Confirmation Process and the Public: To Know or Not to Know," 101 Harv. L. Rev. 1213 (1988).

22. See also infra note 103 (suggesting that more attention is now paid to appointments process because it is perceived as more important).

23. Indeed this was the model Ronald Reagan followed when he was Governor of California.

24. Hart, "The Supreme Court, 1978 Term—Foreword: The Time Chart of the

Justices," 73 Harv. L. Rev. 84, 101 (1959). (It's not my ideal either, as it tends to perpetuate uniformity of outlook. Democracy and Distrust 59. However, there are ways of dealing with that problem that are more responsible than discarding the idea that judges are supposed to behave differently from legislators.)

25. President Ford made one appointment to the Supreme Court, that of John Paul Stevens, who appeared at the time, and indeed has turned out, to be somewhere between moderate and liberal. President Nixon got the opportunity to appoint four people, only two of whom could be comfortably classified as conservatives. President Johnson, it is true, made two liberal appointments, though one was an extremely close friend and the other was probably picked in part because Johnson discerned, correctly, that it was high time there was a black person on the Court. President Kennedy made two appointments, one of a liberal who didn't stay very long, the other of a man who did not appear to be much of a liberal at the time and has indeed proved not to be. President Eisenhower's appointments included two of the Court's most liberal and activist recent members (Warren and Brennan); on the other hand, of President Truman's four appointments three were quite conservative, one a moderate. Thus, to find a precedent for Reagan's approach one has to go back to Franklin Roosevelt, who was quite single-minded about appointing justices who could be counted on to side with the New Deal on issues of federal power. (It's true that Felix Frankfurter and Stanley Reed are not remembered as "liberal" Justices, but that's because they stuck around long enough for the issues to change, not because Roosevelt's investigation was faulty.)

Of course presidents have always taken cognizance of the nominal political party (if any) of a prospective nominee, but historically—though this too is changing—to know that was not to know much. Moreover, appointments of members of "the other" party were not all that rare.

26. See N.Y. Times, July 13, 1980, at 14, col. 1 ("We will work for the appointment of judges at all levels of the judiciary who respect traditional family values and the sanctity of innocent human life."); N.Y. Times, Aug. 22, 1984, at A18, col. 1 ("reaffirming support" for such appointments). This works both ways. See, e.g., Senator Kennedy's attempts to get Judge Souter to share with the Judiciary Committee his moral views on abortion (though admittedly Kennedy and the rest of the Committee had been thwarted in attempting to discern Souter's legal views on the subject). N.Y. Times, Sept. 15, 1990, at 10, col. 5. (Actually this turned into a pretty neat whipsaw for Souter: having refused to share his legal views about abortion on the ground that that would be improper, see page 358, he then refused to share his moral views on the subject on the ground that they wouldn't properly affect his legal judgment. Id.)

27. Thus in the writing of emerging academics, the position that judges should not invariably enforce their policy choices in the name of the Constitution has become not simply wrongheaded but essentially inconceivable. See, e.g., Estrich, "Controlling the Language, Winning the Debate," 41 Harv. L. Bull. 33 (1989): "We could debate endlessly the question whether *Roe v. Wade* was rightly decided. . . . I think it is; and every pro-choice person I know agrees. Every anti-abortion person I know thinks it isn't." See also Hirshman, "Bronte, Bloom, and Bork: An Essay on the Moral Education of Judges," 137 U. Pa. L. Rev. 177, 202 n. 158 (1988) (suggesting that I misdescribed my position when I indicated during my criticism of *Roe* that

I am opposed to laws restricting abortion). I suppose I should be thankful that unlike my erstwhile colleague Estrich, Hirshman is at least aware of my discussion of *Roe*: having one's credibility questioned is recognition of a sort. However, given Professor Tushnet's obviously correct description of the incentive system, page 345, I have some trouble imagining what my motive is supposed to have been. Indeed the first example Tushnet gives of the sort of politically suicidal position he has in mind is precisely the one Hirshman suspects I am feigning, that "it is a terrifically important thing for women to have the right to choose abortion . . . , [but there is no] constitutional warrant for the displacement of legislative decisions to restrict the availability of abortions." Tushnet, supra note 20, at 779.

28. For example, Mario Cuomo observed:

> Bork was selected not for his objectivity but because the President believes Bork will give him the results the President desires politically—for example, cut back of affirmative action. The evidence that that's what the President wants and expects is in the statements by lobbyists on behalf of Bork, who are talking to conservatives and telling them that if Bork is selected, you'll get a change in abortion, you'll get a change in criminal justice. That's the proof positive.

Quoted in N.Y. Times, Sept. 13, 1987, at 37, col. 1. Governor Cuomo's characterization receives at least indirect corroboration from Bruce Fein, who spent the first Reagan term working on judicial selection in the Justice Department: "It became evident after the first term that there was no way to make legislative gains in many areas of social and civil rights. The President has to do it by changing the jurisprudence." "Judging the Judges," Newsweek, Oct. 14, 1985, at 73. (This may not represent Judge Bork's own thinking, see infra note 31; my suggestion is only that it is why he was nominated.) For further remarks on the subject of attempting to achieve judicially what one cannot achieve legislatively, albeit this time from the left, see infra note 34 (quotation from Hodding Carter).

29. See generally E. Bronner, Battle for Justice: How the Bork Nomination Shook America (1989); P. McGuigan & D. Weyrich, Ninth Justice: The Fight for Bork (1990).

30. One thing can be said with certainty: many of the tactics employed against Bork were disgusting—such as the use of Oil, Chemical and Atomic Workers International Union v. American Cyanamid, 741 F.2d 444 (D.C. Cir. 1984), to suggest that he approved of mandatory sterilization, the charge that he favored the "separate but equal" doctrine, allegations that he was an agnostic, and the argument that although he had spent almost all of his career in teaching and government service, he had never functioned as a public interest lawyer. See E. Bronner, supra note 29, at 177–80, 261–63. Also disappointing (at least to one generally inclined to regard Senator Simon as relatively straightforward) was Simon's statement at the hearings that he had recently read Dred Scott v. Sandford, 60 U.S. (19 How.) 393 (1857), and "[i]t sounded an awful lot like Robert Bork." 1 The Nomination of Robert H. Bork to be Associate Justice of the Supreme Court of the United States: Hearings Before the Senate Judiciary Committee, 100th Cong., 1st Sess. 314 (1987) [hereinafter Bork Hearings]. In fact, since his early and repudiated flirtation with *Lochner*, Judge Bork has been a tireless critic of the "substantive due process" theory of *Dred Scott*.

To the extent Simon meant "only" to imply that Bork is a racist, the charge is without foundation.

31. See, e.g., Posner, "Bork and Beethoven," 42 Stan. L. Rev. 1365 (1990); Ackerman, "Robert Bork's Grand Inquisition" (Book Review), 99 Yale L. J. 1419 (1990) (much the same argument, albeit from a more liberal perspective). Critics have cited Bork's early endorsement of *Lochner*-style substantive due process in Bork, "The Supreme Court Needs a New Philosophy," Fortune, December 1968, at 138, to which one might add his more recent habit of inferring from the fact that two commentators approve a line of cases that they must share a political agenda. E.g., Bork, "Styles in Constitutional Theory," 26 S. Tex. L. J. 383, 393–94 (1985). (The latter point makes sense, of course, only if one is prepared to define constitutional theories strictly in terms of the outcomes they achieve, and is no fairer than suggesting that because Bork and the Grand Wizard of the Ku Klux Klan both disapprove of Shelley v. Kraemer, 334 U.S. 1 (1948), and Bolling v. Sharpe, 347 U.S. 497 (1954), they must have the same agenda.) It is possible to make too much of these data. Bork's affair with *Lochner* was long since forthrightly faced and forcefully abandoned. Most of his commentary on constitutional law between 1971 and his hearings was quick and polemical, mainly speeches to sympathetic audiences, a style that particularly lends itself to oversimple pigeonholing. His postrejection book, R. Bork, The Tempting of America: The Political Seduction of the Law (1990), is a vastly more discriminating work. (To pick a not entirely random example, its criticism of my work, however convincing or unconvincing, is among the fairest that has appeared, which unfortunately is no small sample.) But even here Bork can't resist the same revealing fallacy:

> There is a remarkable consistency about these theorists. No matter the base from which they start, they all wind up in the same place, prescribing a new constitutional law that is much more egalitarian and socially permissive than either the actual Constitution or the legislative opinion of the American public. *That, surely, is the point of their efforts.*

Id. at 6 (emphasis supplied). . . .

Moreover, on at least some occasions when political desire or necessity has conflicted with Bork's reiterated theory of judicial review, a jurisprudence of original intent, it has been the latter that seems to have given way. Repeatedly *The Tempting of America* forecloses issues by a simple citation of judicial precedents that are at least contestable as a matter of original intent. (Bork's impatience with such precedent under other circumstances is notorious.) See, e.g., R. Bork, supra, at 37 (eviscerating "construction" of Privileges or Immunities Clause by Slaughter-House Cases, 83 U.S. [16 Wall.] 36 [1873]), at 63 (same opinion's indication that despite general language serious review under Equal Protection Clause to be limited to racial discrimination), at 150 (imposition of a "reasonableness" test on all classifications), at 43 (limitation of Obligation of Contracts Clause to preexisting contracts), and at 48 (Justice Black's position that Fourteenth Amendment incorporates the Bill of Rights). It is true that the last two of these positions would be political anathema to an extreme right-winger, but each of them is legally settled beyond reasonable possibility of overrule—Black's with exceptions (indictment, civil

juries) that there seems little question Bork would endorse. A virtue thus may have
been made of necessity, endorsement of the precedents serving to save the discussion from consignment to what most readers would regard as the lunatic fringe. An
understandable course, but not one open to an originalist. Perhaps more disturbing
has been the fact that Bork has been a consistent champion of expansive executive
power vis-à-vis Congress. While there are grounds on which one might defend this
attitude, the constitutional text and framers' intent are not among them. (Executive
power understandably escapes discussion in *The Tempting of America*.)

On the other hand, no one is or can be completely devoid of tendencies to let his
politics influence his constitutional theorizing, and Bork is better than many in this
regard. There certainly have been occasions when Bork's constitutional outcomes
have not been in accord with what appear to be his political predilections. E.g.,
Finzer v. Barry, 798 F.2d 1450 (D.C. Cir. 1986) (Bork, J., constitutionally protecting right to protest outside embassy). Noting that the case involved an Episcopal
priest wishing to demonstrate outside the Soviet and Nicaraguan embassies seems
to be slicing it a little thin; in any event it is difficult thus to "explain" Lebron v.
Washington Metro. Area Transit Auth., 749 F.2d 893 (D.C. Cir. 1984) (Bork, J.,
protecting constitutional right to display in subway posters sharply critical of President Reagan). Of course one can argue, if somewhat desperately, that both of those
were judicial opinions subject to Supreme Court review. But one cannot thus dismiss Professor Bork's 1981 testimony against the Human Life Bill, on the ground
that it unconstitutionally sought to overrule *Roe v. Wade* by statute. See R. Bork,
supra, at 289–90, 325; [cf. pages 301–3]. That testimony seems impossible to regard
as signaling anything other than a genuine commitment to the legal process ideal.
(To these exhibits can now be added the fact that despite what he understandably
regards as the Senate's stupid and unfair denial of his dream of serving on the
Supreme Court, he continues—ironically unlike the very senators who did him in,
see infra note 34—to articulate the position that society's fundamental value
choices are to be made by the elected branches rather than the judiciary.)

32. E. Bronner, supra note 29, at 99.

33. 1 Bork Hearings, supra note 30, at 101.

34. Note also the unspoken premise that the very body in which Biden and Kennedy sit, the United States Congress, cannot be counted on to deliver the desired
outcomes. (That's what makes it necessary for them to insist on justices who will do
so whatever the inclination of the elected branches.) See 1 Bork Hearings, supra
note 30, at 37 (Sen. Hatch quoting Hodding Carter):

> The nomination of Judge Bork forces liberals like me to confront a reality we
> don't want to confront, which is that we are depending in large part on the least
> democratic institution, with a small "d," in government to defend what it is we no
> longer are able to win out there in the electorate.

35. M. Pertschuk & W. Schaetzel, The People Rising: The Campaign against the
Bork Nomination (1989); sources cited supra note 29.

36. E. Bronner, supra note 29, at 349. (Actually it seems doubtful that law ever
seemed as arcane to the public as medicine.)

37. Conversely, the terms of the Senate debate are likely to powerfully influence
the way the public thinks about issues of judicial qualification, and to an extent the

way the Court conceives its own role. See Friedman, "Tribal Myths: Ideology and the Confirmation of Supreme Court Nominations" (Review Essay), 95 Yale L. J. 1283, 1317 (1986).

38. Bork's postrejection book, *The Tempting of America*, supra note 31, seriously presents a theory of judicial review, one he had been developing for some time. But that isn't why he was nominated.

39. See Moran, "Biden Taps Scholars to Rake Bork Record," Legal Times, July 13, 1987, at 1, 10.

40. Again, I am not suggesting that the present is unique in any of these respects. Just as there have been earlier eras when legal "realism" dominated academia and the idea of role differentiation was consequently denigrated, and earlier presidents who concentrated hard on trying to figure out exactly how prospective nominees would vote in particular cases of interest to them, there have been stretches—notably, perhaps, the mid-nineteenth century—when the Senate rejected judicial nominees for raw political reasons. See, e.g., J. Hurst, The Growth of American Law: The Law Makers 143–44 (1950).

41. Dworkin, "From Bork to Kennedy," N.Y. Rev. Books, Dec. 17, 1987, at 40.

42. As for the also smooth post-Bork confirmation of Justice Kennedy, see page 359.

43. E.g., N.Y. Times, Sept. 19, 1990, at A1, col. 2.

44. See N.Y. Times, Sept. 18, 1990, at A1, col. 3, B7, col. 3.

45. The Recorder, Sept. 17, 1990, at 8, col. 4 (quoting Souter).

46. Democracy and Distrust 117.

47. But cf. N.Y. Times, Sept. 15, 1990, supra note 26 (Judge Souter indicating that his views on the morality of abortion could not properly affect his views on *Roe v. Wade*); id. at col. 1 (Souter expressing his view that judges "have not been placed upon courts in effect to impose our will. We have been placed upon courts to impose the will that lies behind the meaning of those who framed and, by their adoption, intended to impose . . . constitutional law of this country upon us all.").

48. See, e.g., id. at col. 5 (Senator Kennedy's pursuit of Souter's moral feelings with respect to abortion).

49. Bork, "At Last, An End to Supreme Court Activism," N.Y. Times, Aug. 29, 1990, at A21, col. 2.

50. Cf. N.Y. Times, Sept. 17, 1990, at A18, col. 6 (Bork expressing surprise at some of Souter's testimony).

51. In fact, we heard less about this point this time, presumably because wolf had been cried on the earlier occasion.

52. Wiley Rutledge was named that year. It's true he was a Circuit Court judge at the time of his appointment to the Supreme Court, but so were the four I mentioned in the text: my reference is to where the appointees in question had spent most of their careers. Felix Frankfurter and William O. Douglas were both appointed in 1939, the former directly from academia, the latter via a stint with the SEC.

53. It is difficult to postulate any other reason why Reagan would have been drawn to academics. The last pre-Reagan president who seems to have cared greatly about precisely how his nominees would rule, Franklin Roosevelt, was also the last pre-Reagan president to favor professors.

54. Legend has it that once Lana Turner was "discovered" sipping a soda at Schwab's, legions of lovelies took to hanging out there, sipping sodas and trying to look like Lana Turner.

55. In addition to the increased incentive toward overtly political "constitutional theories," the Schwab's phenomenon may exacerbate existing academic incentives not to build on, or even to acknowledge merit in, the work of others. Instead, an author is likely to cite as dispositive early criticism of the perceived rival, and then present his own theory (or, more likely, to sketch the outline of his own theory, as some sinister outside force habitually decrees that "this is not the place for a full presentation" of the author's own approach). Law teachers are caught in something of a whipsaw here, in that academia generally rewards originality, whereas the law generally rewards lack of originality—that is, the existence of precedent. The tension thus created probably helps account for the common scholarly slalom in which the author's theory is said to be immanent in a series of judicial decisions, though no prior academic commentator has even come close to apprehending it. There is little professional risk in acknowledging the possibility that certain judges may be idiot savants.

[It may also exacerbate the trend in the literature to report that while the author is clear that he is talking about what the Constitution requires, he is less clear on the issue whether the conclusions he is reaching should be judicially enforced. Of course there's nothing wrong in recognizing such a distinction: not all constitutional doctrine (though I would say most) needs to be judicially enforceable. It's the unexplained refusal to be clear about what falls into what category that raises the suspicion one may be attempting simultaneously to catch the President's eye and prepare for a Judiciary Committee hearing.]

56. One taking an "originalist" line might choose the latter combination and argue that, whereas the Constitution has absolutely nothing to say on the subject of abortion, the Fourteenth Amendment was intended to outlaw all racial classifications. It's a fair shot, but I believe it fails. Neither the overall theory of the Equal Protection Clause, see pages 269–75, nor the specific intentions of its framers, see Democracy and Distrust 61–62, suggest the unconstitutionality of laws discriminating in favor of powerless minorities. (What one can say in favor of the former combination, without resorting to some form of the claim that "these laws are good and those are bad" is more elusive still.)

A combination popular for a time with those running for the Reagan Court was that laws limiting campaign contributions should be invalidated under the First Amendment, but that few other laws should be.

57. I was asked after presenting a version of this article as the Sibley Lecture whether it constitutes a surrender. Certainly it is an admission that few people appear to agree with me, and that is a surrender of sorts. However, this article is intended to convey just as clearly the idea that today's consensus is wrong—the suspicious may even suppose that to be its principal point—and to suggest the likelihood that after a few decades the legal process ideal will experience a renaissance.

58. "The Politics of Anti-Politics," N.Y. Times, Sept. 26, 1990, at A24, col. 1 (editorial).

59. E.g., S. Smith, Call to Order: Floor Politics in the House and Senate (1989). The related decline in party affiliation as an important determinant of elections has in turn contributed further to the pressure incumbents feel to concentrate on constit-

uent (and other interest group) service. See M. Fiorina, Congress: Keystone of the Washington Establishment 112 (2d ed. 1989).

60. E.g., Choper, "The Supreme Court and the Political Branches: Democratic Theory and Practice," 122 U. Pa. L. Rev. 810, 830–32 (1974); R. Dixon, Democratic Representation: Reapportionment in Law and Politics 10 (1968).

61. The result of the combination is "a decentralized legislature, its fragmented party coalitions guided by tolerant party leaders, that [is] best suited to trafficking in particularized benefits." Jacobson, "Running Scared: Elections and Congressional Politics in the 1980s," in Congress: Structure and Policy 73 (M. McCubbins & T. Sullivan eds. 1987).

62. Although this characterization is mine, the system has been well documented by others. E.g., M. Fiorina, supra note 59; G. Jacobson, The Politics of Congressional Elections chs. 7–8, at 181–223 (2d ed. 1987); R. Davidson & W. Oleszek, Congress and Its Members 43–44 (3d ed. 1990). See generally T. Mann, Unsafe at Any Margin: Interpreting Congressional Elections 102 (1978) (examining link between electoral insecurity and accountability); D. Mayhew, Congress: The Electoral Connection 53–59, 108–10 (1974) (discussing benefits of constituent service).

A. Maass, Congress and the Common Good (1983), is a conspicuous presentation of the view that Congress frequently seeks to act for the common good rather than merely aggregating private preferences. However, Professor Maass is also clear to the effect that the president is the dominant influence in the legislative process, whereas the legislature plays the subservient role of criticism and "control." Id. at 10. "Control in this context means to exercise a check upon executive leadership, to oversee it, to criticize and influence it, and to approve, reject, or amend specific executive proposals." Id. at 11. See generally id. at 3–18 (modeling executive-legislative relations). (Various reforms of the early 1970s were calculated to beef up Congress's influence vis-à-vis the executive, but as Maass points out, they failed. Id. at 54–61.) In fact he makes the point that judicial examinations of "legislative history" would be more realistic if they shifted their focus from statements made in various congressional documents and debates to various records located in the executive branch, which is probably where the law was originated, almost certainly where the various alternative approaches were intelligibly weighed. Id. at 13–14. Maass's quarrel is thus with commentators like the early Robert Dahl rather than with Fiorina et al.

63. Even the rare dissenter from the proposition that casework matters importantly to one's chances of reelection agrees that congressmen think it does. Johannes & McAdams, "The Congressional Incumbency Effect: Is It Casework, Policy Compatibility, or Something Else? An Examination of the 1978 Election," 25 Am. J. Pol. Sci. 512, 516–17 (1981).

64. See, e.g., B. Eckhardt & C. Black, The Tides of Power: Conversations on the American Constitution 19–20 (1976); Democracy and Distrust 131; M. Fiorina, supra note 59, at 32–47, 53–67, 72, 86–90; A. Maass, supra note 62, at 228–30; D. Mayhew, supra note 62; M. Parenti, Democracy for the Few 195 (3d ed. 1980); "Image of a Senator: D'Amato Sticks to Local Interests," N.Y. Times, May 11, 1988, at B5, col. 5.

65. Fiorina takes account of the rapid growth in the influence of political action committees in his second edition, and correctly notes that, although it would now be a mistake to describe congressional casework as running only to the benefit of

geographical constituents, the rise of PACs serves only to reinforce his more general point. M. Fiorina, supra note 59, at 124–29.

66. In his second edition, Fiorina backs away from his earlier claim that the increase in casework had resulted in a decrease of legislative activity and suggests that, with increases in staff, it is possible that they both have been increasing. Id. at 91. He goes on to point out, however, that despite the staff increases the quality of legislative work remains in serious doubt. Id. at 91–92. Moreover, the statistical evidence that moved him on this issue—a showing that between 1958 and 1978 positive constituent evaluations on the basis of the representative's philosophy or ideology rose from 2 percent to 7 percent; on the basis of her stands on domestic policy, from 3 percent to 5 percent; and on the basis of her foreign policy stands, from 0 percent to 1 percent—also showed that over the same period positive evaluations on the basis of her attentiveness to her constituency rose from 11 percent to 25 percent. Id. at 89. Thus while one may not have been purchased at the expense of the other, 25 percent is still a lot bigger than 13 percent. The second edition also correctly cautions that the positive "policy" evaluations appear to have been based more on "position taking" than on actual legislative activity. Id. at 92–93; see also D. Mayhew, supra note 62, at 61–73 (discussing "position taking," the public enunciation of a judgmental statement on anything likely to be of interest to political actors).

67. M. Fiorina, supra note 59, at 68–69.

68. Id. at 9; D. Mayhew, supra note 62, at 14. On the connection, see, e.g., id. at 57, 69; M. Fiorina, supra note 59, at 35–36, 50–52. Admittedly, the existence of a strong causal connection can be questioned. Johannes & McAdams, supra note 63. But see Fiorina, "Some Problems in Studying the Effects of Research Allocation in Congressional Elections," 25 Am. J. Pol. Sci. 543 (1981) (rejecting findings of Johannes and McAdams); Yiannokos, "The Grateful Electorate: Casework and Congressional Elections," 25 Am. J. Pol. Sci. 568 (1981) (concluding that constituent service is important to reelection prospects). For a response, see Johannes & McAdams, "Does Casework Matter? A Reply to Professor Fiorina," 25 Am. J. Pol. Sci. 581 (1981). The important point for purposes of this article, however, is that congressmen allocate their attentions on the assumption that the causal connection exists. See supra note 63.

69. Actually, Congress seems to be getting less effective at logrolling and pork-barrel legislation (at least in up-front statutory form). See A. Maass, supra note 62, at 69. The tendency is thus toward "formula grants," often "controlled" by vague admonitions and thus respecting which the influence of members of Congress is more likely to be exerted at the administrative level.

70. Of course, Congress sometimes legislates in ways that are both quite directive and not explainable in terms of a desire to promote the interests of particular sets of members' constituents. The recent example most often cited is deregulation. See, e.g., M. Derthick & P. Quirk, The Politics of Deregulation (1985). Actually, this isn't a very clear counterexample to the Fiorina thesis—though it is to, say, the early Dahl—as leadership within the Ford and Carter administrations had a good deal to do with bringing deregulation about. But counterexamples certainly are possible: if I believed otherwise, I would not have concluded this article as I have. See pages 360–61.

71. Congress certainly exercises influence at the appropriations stage. Generally, however, that influence is felt at the level, say, of eliminating (or restoring) a particular weapons system as opposed to enacting or even proposing a competing general approach to an area such as defense. One reason for this is that thinking big generally has been left of late to the executive (and the judiciary). Another is that tinkering with the specifics of programs (including weapons systems) seems often to spring from constituent interests and other personal political agendas as opposed to any larger substantive vision. See, e.g., Owens, "Micromanaging the Defense Budget," 100 Pub. Interest 131 (Summer 1990); "Uprising in the House: Members Said No to Bush on Military without a Grand Design of Their Own," N.Y. Times, July 29, 1989, at A1, col. 4.

72. See, e.g., 122 Cong. Rec. 31,634 (1976) (statement of Rep. Levitas) ("When hard decisions have to be made, we pass the buck to the agencies with vaguely worded statutes."); Lobel, "Emergency Power and the Decline of Liberalism," 98 Yale L. J. 1385, 1407–9 (1989) (noting some 470 open-ended delegations to the President to deal with "emergencies"); T. Lowi, The Personal President: Power Invested, Promise Unfulfilled 52 (1985); McDowell, "Congress and the Courts," 100 Pub. Interest 89, 93–94 (Summer 1990); Schoenbrod, "Congress Must Spell Out Where the Burdens of Clean Air Fall," Wall St. J., July 5, 1983, at 22, col. 3.

73. M. Fiorina, supra note 59, at 69.

74. Cf. 122 Cong. Rec. 31,622 (1976) (statement of Rep. Flowers):

> [W]e stand back and say when our constituents are aggrieved or oppressed by various rules and regulations, "Hey, it's not me. We didn't mean that. We passed this well-meaning legislation, and we intended for those people out there . . . to do exactly what we meant, and they did not do it."

See also, e.g., Baker, "Not the Declaring Type," N.Y. Times, Nov. 10, 1990, at 23, col. 1 ("Later, after the President has played the hand, Congress can revel in the wisdom of hindsight and profit by passing crowd-pleasing judgments").

75. Actually, as we persist in divided government (president from one party, majorities in Congress from the other), this kind of influence on the part of the committee chairpersons probably will diminish to some degree—though it will always be significant—as that of the ranking minority members increases.

76. As Professor Fiorina has noted:

> The legislation is drafted in very general terms, so some agency, existing or newly established, must translate a vague policy mandate into a functioning program, a process that necessitates the promulgation of numerous rules and regulations and, incidentally, the trampling of numerous toes. At the next stage, aggrieved and/or hopeful constituents petition their congressman to intervene in the complex (or at least obscure) decision processes of the bureaucracy. The cycle closes when the congressman lends a sympathetic ear, piously denounces the evils of bureaucracy, intervenes in the latter's decisions, and rides a grateful electorate to ever more impressive electoral showings.

M. Fiorina, supra note 59, at 46–47; see also de Grazia, "Congressional Liaison: An Inquiry into its Meaning for Congress," in Congress: The First Branch of Government 297 (1966) (congressional oversight of the administrative process);

M. Fiorina, supra note 59, at 60–66 (suggesting that the decentralization of congressional power enables individual members to control specific policy decisions); Owens, supra note 71, at 141 (congressional oversight of the administrative process); Rabkin, "Micromanaging the Administrative Agencies," 100 Pub. Interest 116, 119 (1990) (same); R. Ripley, Congress: Process and Policy 251–52 (1st ed. 1975) (interaction between Congress and the bureaucracy). See generally K. Shepsle, The Giant Jigsaw Puzzle: Democratic Committee Assignments in the Modern House (1978) (study of committee assignments finds that freshmen representatives seek assignments to those committees in which their constituents have an important interest); A. Maass, supra note 62, at 40 (congressional oversight holds the bureaucracy accountable for administrative performance).

To give Congress its due, it did try to build a little more accountability into this routine by the device of the legislative veto (though in the process it hastened the trend toward flabby initial delegations). However, the legislative veto has been declared unconstitutional. INS v. Chadha, 462 U.S. 919 (1983).

77. M. Fiorina, supra note 59, at 68. The system has "produced a Congress that [is] inordinately responsive without being responsible." Jacobson, supra note 61, at 73.

78. See "Congress Agrees on Closing Bases but Leaves the Choices to a Panel," N.Y. Times, Oct. 13, 1988, at A1, col. 5.

79. One might wonder how these examples differ from the earlier creation of administrative agencies to handle various problems. The answer is that the distinction is not sharp: a desire to escape the political heat that comes with decision may have helped account for the creation of such agencies as well. In most such cases, however, a seemingly larger element was a desire to assign an entire set of problems to a group of "experts" who could study them over time and develop more detailed and sensible solutions than Congress itself could: faith in expertise was part of the New Deal religion. (In the recent instances I cite, the desire to escape accountability plainly predominates.) To the extent I'm wrong about this distinction, however, my broader point, unfortunately, is only reinforced.

80. 2 U.S.C. §§ 351–64, as amended by Act of Dec. 19, 1985, Pub. L. No. 99–190, 135 Stat. 1322 (1985).

81. N.Y. Times, Aug. 24, 1989, at A1, col. 4.

82. Balanced Budget and Emergency Deficit Control Act of 1985, 2 U.S.C. § 901 (1985).

83. The Supreme Court found unconstitutional this grant of executive power to an officer over whom Congress had removal authority. Bowsher v. Synar, 478 U.S. 714 (1986). I suppose we should be thankful that Congress doesn't have the full range of devices available to some state legislatures. In 1988 the California legislature, immobilized by conflicting pressures from two powerful interest groups (insurance companies and trial lawyers), placed on the November ballot four mutually inconsistent automobile insurance initiatives so complex and overlapping that the Stanford torts faculty was unable to explain either to their satisfaction, or to that of the rest of us, how even a person fairly clear of her goals should vote on them.

84. Of course every delegation to the executive or an administrative agency is indirectly a delegation to the courts that review their actions, but sometimes Con-

gress "cuts out the bureaucratic middleman" and makes its delegation directly to the judicial system. See McDowell, supra note 72, at 93–94.

85. Murphy & Tanenhaus, "Publicity, Public Opinion, and the Court," 84 NW. U. L. Rev. 985, 986–87 (1990) (footnote omitted).

86. The reasons here are various, including not only a desire to let the court system take the heat, but also, as noted earlier, the fact that it is easier to block legislation than to enact it. There are, of course, rare exceptions, such as Congress's amendment of Title IX of the Education Amendments of 1972, Civil Rights Restoration Act of 1987, Pub. L. No. 100–259, 102 Stat. 28 (codified at 20 U.S.C. § 1687 [1988]), in reaction to the Court's statutory holding in Grove City College v. Bell, 465 U.S. 555 (1984).

87. 50 U.S.C. §§ 1541–48 (1988).

88. See, e.g., Ely, "Suppose Congress Wanted a War Powers Act That Worked," 88 Colum. L. Rev. 1379, 1380–83 (1988); cf. Cole, Book Review, 99 Yale L. J. 2063, 2078–79 (1990) (similar experience under National Emergencies Act of 1976).

89. Those who find the distinction helpful might say that the "system of checks and balances" is working—to a degree at any rate—even if the "separation of powers" is not.

90. It has reached the point where senators and representatives, without evident sense of irony, can scold the executive for not having come up with a legislative program to deal with one or another pressing problem. See A. Maass, supra note 62, at 15, 170 (citing examples); Schoenbrod, "How the Reagan Administration Trivialized Separation of Powers (and Shot Itself in the Foot)," 57 Geo. Wash. L. Rev. 459, 460 (1989).

91. J. Sundquist, The Decline and Resurgence of Congress 306 (1981). Despite a good deal of post-Vietnam bravado, this pattern has persisted in the foreign policy area as well. "[M]ost of the major post-Vietnam foreign policy initiates, from detente under President Nixon to global anti-Sovietism under Reagan, still emanated from the executive. When Congress acted, it was to revise, endorse, or prohibit foreign policy proposals initiated by the executive branch." C. Arnson, Crossroads: Congress, the Reagan Administration, and Central America 12 (1989).

92. Perhaps this development is not as recent as I have painted it. Elements of it have surely existed for a long time, e.g., A. Maass, supra note 62, at 45–63, as have advocates (and specimens) of an overtly political judiciary. I have argued that as of 1991 we are witnessing a coincidence of "high" stages on each cycle. If you think I'm wrong about that, though—it is always difficult to place the present in historical context—please feel free to regard this as simply a rhetorical device. Even if each of these developments dated back to the dawn of the republic, the textual suggestion to which this footnote is appended might still be made (more forcefully, one would suppose)—and it would still be emphatically rebuttable.

93. Cf. E. Bronner, supra note 29, at 352:

There is an irony to the fact that fewer and fewer Americans participate in the political process, yet they turned out in massive numbers to play a role in the Bork controversy. Since the work of the Supreme Court has come to provide so much of the framework for social policy issues, democracy—in which citizens make choices through public debate, local referenda, and elected representatives—was replaced with a substitute form: debate over a nominee to the Supreme Court.

See also R. Bork, supra note 31, at 3 (instructive that pro-choice and anti-abortion demonstrators tend to picket the White House and the Supreme Court, but not Congress).

94. The argument is made in *Democracy and Distrust*. It entirely convinced its author.

95. Of course the Senate was originally conceived as something of an aristocratic counterbalance to the "democratic" House of Representatives, though the ratification of the Seventeenth Amendment in 1913 probably interred that rationale once and for all.

96. Chemerinsky, supra note 19, at 76.

97. An unusually circular version of the point—that no one could deny that the United States is a democracy, yet the United States Constitution (as construed by the commentator) incorporates a value-imposing judiciary—is rediscovered by every generation. E.g., E. Rostow, The Sovereign Prerogative ch. 5 (1962); Bishin, "Judicial Review in Democratic Theory," 50 S. Cal. L. Rev. 1099, 1112 (1977); Chemerinsky, supra note 19, at 77 ("[I]f one defines 'democratic' more broadly to reflect the actual nature of decisionmaking, all government institutions are, at least, somewhat 'democratic' . . .").

98. See Hall, "Progressive Reform and the Decline of Democratic Accountability: The Popular Election of State Supreme Court Judges, 1850–1920," 1984 Am. B. Found. Res. J. 345,362–65; J. Hurst, supra note 40, at 130–34.

99. We now kick our state judges out of office—I'm assuming that in this as in so much else, California is where the future happens first—and reelect 97 percent of our congressmen. I don't believe it's because they're better; instead I would suggest it's because both "branches" have evolved to the point where members of Congress have less to do with difficult and conspicuous political choices. (Incumbent governors, faced with tougher and more visible choices as Washington provides less and less financial help, have also become politically very vulnerable. See N.Y. Times, Nov. 8, 1990, at A1 col. 4.)

100. I'm not sure this account is correct. Roosevelt was not clearly a civil libertarian. At all events he was focusing on issues of federal power, on which Frankfurter's constitutional (as well as his political) views were well known and reliable. See also supra note 25.

101. Some might ask at this point whether members of the House of Representatives really have to stand for reelection any more, given that 98 percent of them were reelected in both 1986 and 1988, 96 percent in 1990, a year in which virtually all the pundits predicted a sizeable anti-incumbent backlash. For discussion of this question, see Tushnet, Schneider & Kovner, "Judicial Review and Congressional Tenure: An Observation," 66 Tex. L. Rev. 967 (1988). It's a fair question, but three observations are in order:

(1) Despite the statistics, congressmen worry about reelection. E.g., Jacobson, supra note 61; T. Mann, supra note 62. This is hardly a surprise: other officials, such as governors, senators, and presidents, certainly have to worry about reelection—on

senators, see, e.g., Dixon, "The Power of Incumbency Is a Myth," N.Y. Times, June 12, 1990, at A21 col. 2—and congressmen are not so coldly rational and self-confident as to sharply distinguish their own situation. Even at law schools that routinely grant tenure, people without tenure worry about getting tenure. Cf. R. Fenno, Home Style: House Members in Their Districts (1978) (recounting incumbent concern about reelection). This concern (whatever the actual statistical probabilities) is what gives congressmen incentives to take steps to adjust the process, or perhaps to ally themselves with constituent majorities in ways that unjustifiably disadvantage minorities, so as to ensure their reelection.

(2) It turns out that one of the few things that actually does affect an incumbent's chances of reelection, redistricting (see Tushnet, Schneider, and Kovner, supra, at 979), is on my theory the paradigm example of something the courts should carefully police. The argument of the cited article surely should qualify broadside allusions to "the countermajoritarian difficulty," and it points the way for much relevant research. While I don't pretend to have fully assimilated its implications (any more than its authors do), its negative implications for my own work seem (to me, and therefore predictably) attenuated. Indeed, my reaction to the authors' review of the actual occasions of judicial intervention was that in general the Court had been intervening roughly as *Democracy and Distrust* would have them intervene, where Congress appears to have been monkeying with the process so as to ensure the continued incumbency of its members (reapportionment, campaign finance, political speech), or reflecting a skewed version of its actual constituency (gender discrimination). See Tushnet, Schneider & Kovner, supra, at 987–90.

(3) Finally, one of the principal reasons there are so few electoral rejections of incumbent congressmen is that they have effectively taken themselves out of the business of legislating. See pages 350–54; Tushnet, Schneider, and Kovner, supra, at 977–78; see also M. Fiorina, supra note 59, at 7 (average congressional turnover per election in nineteenth century was 40–50 percent). It is the point of the instant article that the proper role of the courts is not to take the business of legislating over from them but rather to get them back into it.

102. Unlike Congress's, the Supreme Court's agreement is never affirmatively required before a given policy can take effect. However, again unlike Congress— and probably contrary to what most observers would abstractly describe as the contemplated system—the Court has not in general proved hesitant to involve itself in controversies it retains the legal discretion to avoid.

103. Thus, Professor Kamisar has suggested that the reason appointments to the Supreme Court have become more political in recent years is that they now are seen as more important than they used to be, which change in perception is presumably related to changes in judicial behavior:

The modern view . . . is that a president should get his pick once you satisfy considerations of ability, integrity and competence. People only recently have made a contrary argument. But it never came to a test before because presidents really never gave that much weight to ideology. With all respect, a Supreme Court appointment was not considered that important until 20 years ago.

Quoted in Wash. Post, July 1, 1987, at A9, col. 2.
104. Democracy and Distrust 46.

105. The Eleventh Amendment overruled Chisholm v. Georgia, 2 U.S. (2 Dall.) 419 (1793); the Fourteenth, Dred Scott v. Sandford, 60 U.S. (19 How.) 393 (1857); the Sixteenth, Pollock v. Farmers' Loan & Trust Co., 157 U.S. 429 (1895); and the Twenty-sixth, Oregon v. Mitchell, 400 U.S. 112 (1970).

106. The Twenty-sixth amendment was a development that Justice Black's opinion announcing the judgment of the Court in *Mitchell* quite clearly (and I have no doubt knowingly) invited, by leaving states that wanted to deny the vote to eighteen-year-olds the onerous task of enforcing one set of voter qualifications for federal elections, and another for state elections.

107. 491 U.S. 397 (1989).

108. United States v. Eichman, 110 S. Ct. 2404 (1990); 136 Cong. Rec. H4087 (daily ed. June 21, 1990); 136 Cong. Rec. S8719, S8736–37 (daily ed. June 26, 1990).

109. Clowns like Johnson and Eichman have gotten enough attention without our providing them another, still brighter spotlight.

110. Democracy and Distrust 47; see also, e.g., Friedman, supra note 37, at 1291–1302.

111. See page 345; cf. Democracy and Distrust 207 n. 18 ("At least with the benefit of hindsight, it seems in general the 'fault' [underlying 'mistaken' appointments] has lain in the limited sophistication of the appointive authority's predictive apparatus rather than in any drastic change in the appointee").

112. [So were Justices Thomas, Ruth Ginsburg, and Breyer, all appointed since the publication of this article.] True, Judge Souter hadn't yet actually decided any cases as a member of the First Circuit Court of Appeals, but he had served seven years on the New Hampshire Supreme Court.

113. From the dawn of the republic through Nixon, 103 men served on the Supreme Court (counting Hughes twice): only 37 of them (or 36 percent) came from lower courts, federal or state (counting Hughes, whose prior service was on the Supreme Court, and Thurgood Marshall, who came from the Solicitor Generalship but previously had served on the Second Circuit). There was, moreover, remarkable stability over time. From the turn of the twentieth century through Nixon, the figures were 44 and 15 (34 percent); for Franklin Roosevelt through Nixon, 25 and 9 (36 percent). Prior to Reagan and Ford (who went one for one) the only "hundred per-centers" (counting both state and federal judges) were Jefferson (three for three), Arthur (two for two), Tyler, and John Quincy Adams (both one for one). For collections of these and similar statistics on the Supreme Court, see A. Blaustein & R. Mersky, The First One Hundred Justices: Statistical Studies on the Supreme Court of the United States (1978); Congressional Quarterly, Guide to the U.S. Supreme Court (E. Witt 2d ed. 1990).

114. Thus of the twenty-two "surprises" Professor Friedman discusses (Story, McLean, Baldwin, Taney, Swayne, Miller, Davis, Field, Salmon Chase, Holmes, Day, McReynolds, Stone, Hughes, Reed, Frankfurter, Burton, Vinson, Clark, Warren, White, and Blackmun), Friedman, supra note 37, at 1292–1301, only three had previously served on federal courts and three on state courts. (I am again counting Hughes, as his "surprising" tenure apparently was his second!)

115. [So, apparently, does President Clinton: Ruth Ginsburg and Stephen Breyer were circuit judges when appointed to the Court, but had spent most of their adult pre-Court years as professors.]

116. In 1968 a combination of ethical problems forced President Johnson's choice to succeed Earl Warren as Chief Justice, Associate Justice Abe Fortas, to withdraw his name from consideration. (The next year he resigned from the bench entirely, upon disclosure of receipt of honoraria from a financier under indictment.)

117. See Freund, "Appointment of Justices: Some Historical Perspectives," 101 Harv. L. Rev. 1146, 1155–56 (1988).

118. Compare (Circuit Judge) Burger, "What to Do about Crime in U.S.," U.S. News & World Rep., Aug. 7, 1967, at 70, with (Professor) Bork, "Why I Am for Nixon," New Republic, June 1, 1968, at 19.

119. This may also help account for Souter's having had an easy time getting through. I hesitate to push the point too hard, however, because while it is true that no president since Cleveland has had his first nominee to the Court rejected, a total of only five nominees overall since then (counting [Douglas] Ginsburg) have gone down to defeat.

120. See, e.g., Lewis, "Souter and Senate: How Far Should Questions Go?" N.Y. Times, July 26, 1990, at A16, col. 1.

121. See N.Y. Times, Sept. 17, 1990, at A18, col. 4; N.Y. Times, Sept. 19, 1990, at A24, col. 3.

122. See N.Y. Times, Sept. 18, 1990, at B7, col. 2.

123. Miranda v. Arizona, 384 U.S. 436 (1966); see N.Y. Times, Sept. 18, 1990, at A1, B7, col. 1.

124. That is, the rule of Missouri v. Jenkins, 495 U.S. 33 (1990). See N.Y. Times, Sept. 19, 1990, at A24, col. 3. Judge Souter also suggested during the hearings that white collar criminals should be incarcerated following a first offense more often than they are now. See N.Y. Times, Sept. 15, 1990, at 10, col. 5.

125. See, e.g., infra note 129.

126. It doesn't come across that way from the transcript, but since I was just about as far away as anyone could get at the time without leaving the planet—in the Maldives, under about ninety feet of water—I guess I'll have to take the word of those who watched it on television.

When Souter's name was originally put forward by the President, Specter vowed to put him "under the microscope," N.Y. Times, July 24, 1990, at A19, col. 1, and was identified by the *Times* as one of the two "expected to be the most vigorous Senators in seeking precise answers from Judge Souter." N.Y. Times, July 26, 1990, at A16, col. 3.

127. N.Y. Times, July 27, 1990, at A12, col. 4.

128. Nat'l L. J., Oct. 1, 1990, at 3, col. 3 (quoting Biden referring to himself and to Senator Grassley).

129. On occasion Souter's flashing of his free pass was amalgamated with a claim that he hadn't really given the matter of *Roe v. Wade* much thought. This prompted the following September 14 interchange with Senator Herb Kohl:

[Q.] [D]o you recall your feelings about Roe v. Wade back when it was promulgated?
[A.] I frankly don't remember the early discussions on it. I mean, everybody was arguing it. . . .
[Q.] You had no—you had no opinion about it than just to say, "Wow"?
[A.] Oh, I doubtless—I doubtless had an opinion. No, I didn't just say wow.

[Q.] What was your opinion in 1973 on Roe v. Wade?

[A.] Well, with respect, Senator, I'm going to ask you to let me draw the line there . . . .

[Q.] O.K. With respect to Roe v. Wade just once more, is it fair to state even though you're not prepared to discuss it, understandably, that you do have an opinion on Roe v. Wade?

[A.] It—I think it would be misleading to say that. I have not got any agenda on what should be done with Roe v. Wade if that case were brought before me.

I will listen to both sides of that case. I have not made up my mind.

Quoted in N.Y. Times, Sept. 15, 1990, at 10, col. 3. Before his nomination, Justice Souter served as Attorney General of New Hampshire, on the New Hampshire Supreme Court, and, briefly, on the First Circuit Court of Appeals. He also apparently fills his free time with scholarly reflection upon the problems of his profession. As Professor Levinson noted in 1981, though: "*Roe v. Wade* was undoubtedly the most important constitutional decision of the past decade . . . . Not to have views on *Roe v. Wade* is equivalent to not having views on the nature of the Constitution itself or on the nature of the Supreme Court's role in a constitutional system." Levinson, "Should Supreme Court Nominees Have Opinions?" 233 Nation 375, 375 (1981). Souter's added twist is thus perhaps best read as an indication—and indeed this is what he seems to say—that while he (naturally) had a (privileged) opinion of whether *Roe v. Wade* was correct as a matter of constitutional interpretation, he was at the time of the hearing undecided about whether it should be overruled. [See also pages 304–5.] Aside from the claim of privilege, this strikes me as an entirely understandable position, albeit one—did no one pick this up?—that unmistakably signals his view of *Roe*. (Whether a correct decision should be overruled is not ordinarily a question that gives one pause.)

130. Of course a nominee should refuse to answer questions about particular pending cases: nobody disputes that. She should also feel free to indicate when she has not thought through a particular subject (though the claim here should be credible). She should feel free as well to point out that a judge's view of various issues is likely to be importantly affected by the substantive and procedural peculiarities of the cases in which they arise, and that any judge, herself included, is entitled, in fact duty-bound, to change her earlier views on a subject should counsel or her colleagues convince her that she should. It would also be a principled, if highly debatable, position to refuse to offer any opinion that might prove relevant to some future case. (Taken seriously, of course, this would mean basically that no nominee should testify to much of anything beyond her name, rank, and serial number, suggesting that a nominee thus disposed might better refuse altogether to appear. On the other hand, Justice O'Connor attempted to take, and by and large succeeded in taking, a position very close to this at her confirmation hearings. See Rees, "Questions for Supreme Court Nominees at Confirmation Hearings: Excluding the Constitution," 17 Ga. L. Rev. 913, 950–51 [1983].) It does not, however, seem consistent to share one's opinions about a number of contested questions of law that we all know perfectly well will come before the Court during the nominee's prospective tenure, but to withhold one's opinions about other such questions (or one other such question). When the opinion withheld respects what the nominee has reason to believe is the

subject the committee regards as most relevant to her confirmability, the drama builds. Convincing the committee that withholding that particular opinion (but not others) is somehow required by the ethics of our profession provides a final confirmation of the nominee's mastery of the situation.

131. Of course, Justice Kennedy—Bork's ultimate replacement—had also been easily confirmed. See page 359.

132. See N.Y. Times, Sept. 21, 1990, at A12, col. 6.

133. See also 3 Bork Hearings, supra note 30, at 2927 (testimony of Professor Henry Monaghan); E. Bronner, supra note 29, at 325 (remarks of Sen. Robert Dole to an aide: "I've been talking to folks on the floor, particularly Southern Democrats. They see a no vote as a no-lose proposition. They can please blacks, women, liberals. And in the end they figure the administration will get another conservative on the Court."). On each of the two occasions since 1930 when a nominee to the Supreme Court was rejected, the President's second choice was turned down as well. (Douglas Ginsburg's name was withdrawn before proceeding to the hearing stage, but that seems for present purposes not very different from a Senate rejection.) Each second choice had a fatal nonideological flaw, however: Judge Carswell seemed simply not qualified intellectually, and Judge Ginsburg was identified by informants as having smoked marijuana on a number of occasions. In addition, Carswell was plainly a "screw you" nomination in both style and substance, a caricature of the caricature of Haynsworth the Senate had refused to confirm. President Reagan indicated he was going to send that kind of replacement up for Bork, but didn't. (Ginsburg is conservative, but a good deal less contentious than Bork.) I suppose it is conceivable, though, that the Senate may fall into a pattern of "flexing its muscles" by rejecting two candidates every few vacancies. For the reasons developed in the text that too is not likely to matter greatly, except to the victims. (Curiously, President Cleveland lost two nominees too, when William B. Hornblower and Wheeler H. Peckham were both rejected in 1894. Thus on three of the four most recent occasions when a presidential nominee was rejected, two were. The exception was the rejection of nominee John J. Parker in 1930, followed by the nomination of Owen J. Roberts, who was confirmed. Parker and Roberts were not philosophically very different; if anything, Parker, defeated by liberals, probably panned out as somewhat more supportive of New Deal measures than his replacement. Freund, supra note 117, at 1155.)

134. See, e.g., Wash. Post, Nov. 13, 1987, at A11, col. 2 (quoting Sen. John McCain: "Nobody wants to go through that again. There's just too much blood on the floor").

135. See generally Chemerinsky, supra note 19, at 44–45 (noting that Justice Kennedy, in his first term, cast the fifth critical vote in a series of conservative decisions); James v. Illinois, 493 U.S. 307, 322–30 (1990) (Kennedy, J., dissenting) (joined by the other Reagan appointees on the Court, Kennedy argued that the impeachment exception to the exclusionary rule should be expanded). Despite ex-Judge Bork's criticism of the flag burning decision, it would not have been out of character for a *Justice* Bork to have joined the majority (as Kennedy did) in invalidating the Texas statute. Political expression was one right to which both Professor Bork and Judge Bork were prepared to give comparatively strenuous protection. See Bork, "Neutral Principles and Some First Amendment Problems," 47 Ind. L. J. 1,

20–35 (1971); Finzer v. Barry, 798 F.2d 1450 (D.C. Cir. 1986); Lebron v. Washington Metro. Area Transit Auth., 749 F.2d 893 (D.C. Cir. 1984). Ollman v. Evans, 750 F.2d 970 (D.C. Cir. 1984) (en banc) (Bork, J., concurring) is the only major case in which Bork and Scalia (who joined the Supreme Court majority in voiding the flag burning statute) voted differently while they were both on the Court of Appeals (they agreed 98 percent of the time, R. Bork, supra note 31, at 284), and it was Bork who came down on the side of the First Amendment. . . . Even Bork's ability to explain in clear terms what seemed to elude certain other commentators, that the (since-invalidated) statutory "fix" for *Texas v. Johnson* was not distinguishable in terms of the logic of the First Amendment from the law the Court had earlier struck down, N.Y. Times, July 20, 1989, at A14, col. 4, suggests at least the possibility of some deep sympathy with that logic, as thoroughgoing opponents of a position rarely are able to characterize it with much sensitivity. Finally, of course, Bork, as a narrowly confirmed "originalist," would have unusual incentives to enforce vigorously those rights that unarguably are to be found in the document.

I don't suppose I've lulled you into forgetting the troublesome datum that Bork has been critical of *Johnson* since it came down. See R. Bork, supra note 31, at 127–28. He seems to have chosen, however, to spend the next phase of his career as a sort of all-purpose conservative critic of the judicial scene, in which role criticism of the flag burning decisions seems de rigueur. I'm certainly not suggesting insincerity here—this does not appear to be an issue that Bork had previously addressed—only the understandable pull of the role he has assumed since his rejection (which choice in itself, by the way, is also quite understandable). My point is that the pulls on a *Justice* Bork would have been quite, perhaps dispositively, different. To the same effect, see Anastaplo, "Bork on Bork," 84 Nw. U. L. Rev. 1142, 1165 (1990). (Bork's criticism of *Johnson* has alluded to a purported distinction, between the substance of what was being said and the mode of saying it, R. Bork, supra note 31, at 127, that is so shallow and widely discredited that it is at least doubtful that he would have relied on it, after debate, had he been the deciding vote in an important Supreme Court case. Texas outlawed desecration of the state or national flag, as opposed to other pieces of cloth, because of the *sentiments* such desecration conveyed: that is the relevant First Amendment point. See pages 173–87.)

It is entirely possible that I am wrong in this speculation. (Neither I nor even Bork can be entirely sure about how he would have voted in *Johnson* had he become a justice, though I grant you he is the better witness by a fair margin.) In any event, the flag case, at least thus far, seems an isolated event: Kennedy does not generally seem to be evolving as significantly more "liberal" than Bork would have been (though if characterizations like this help encourage him to do so, that would be all right too). Cf. infra note 136 (possible effect of academic criticism on Blackmun).

136. Subsequent appointments "to his right" have moved him, as they have others before him, to the left. Moreover, the formative case for Blackmun plainly was *Roe v. Wade*, where his longtime association with the Mayo Clinic and consequent deference to the opinions of doctors seem to have overcome any "legal process" instinct he might have previously harbored toward distinguishing desirable policy from constitutional law: the opinion is a classic in its assimilation of the two. It thus was attacked not only from the political right, e.g., Epstein, "Substantive Due Process by Any Other Name: The Abortion Cases," 1973 Sup. Ct. Rev. 159, but also by liberal legal process aficionados, e.g., Ely, "The Wages of Crying Wolf: A Com-

ment on *Roe v. Wade*," 82 Yale L. J. 920 (1973) [pages 281–97], apparently leaving the Justice with little use for either perspective.

137. At the time of his appointment, Blackmun was reputed to have been Chief Justice Burger's recommendation. Whether or not this is true, the rumor was certainly known to the Senate. See N.Y. Times, Apr. 15, 1970, at 34 col. 6. During the 1971 term, Blackmun voted with Justice Rehnquist 81.0 percent of the time, with Justice Brennan 48.3 percent of the time. "The Supreme Court, 1971 Term," 86 Harv. L. Rev. 50, 301 (1972). For an enlightening look at the pre-*Roe* Blackmun (and in particular his concern for privacy), see Wyman v. James, 400 U.S. 309 (1971) (Blackmun, J., for the Court) [analyzed at pages 433–35, 437, 441–43]; see also, e.g., New York Times Co. v. United States, 403 U.S. 713, 759 (1971) (Blackmun, J., dissenting).

138. It is also my impression that the president generally wins games of chicken. Cf. Ely, "The American War in Indochina, Part I: The (Troubled) Constitutionality of the War They Told Us About," 42 Stan. L. Rev. 877, 915–16 (1990). In this context a stalemate will mean an empty seat on the bench, something there are legitimate pressures from all sides to avoid.

139. Obviously there are short-run ups and downs, but (somewhat contrary to my intuition) this number has not increased—and thus the number of appointments per four-year term has not decreased—over the long term.

140. From Inauguration Day 1869 to Inauguration Day 1989, 22 men served as president, yielding an exact average of three Supreme Court appointments per president. A president not serving out a term for which he was elected is almost certain to be replaced by a philosophical soulmate. (Indeed, as we are about to note in the text, *most* presidents are likely to be.)

141. See P. Herrnson, Party Campaigning in the 1980s (1988).

142. See Shepsle, "The Changing Textbook Congress," in Can the Government Govern? 238–66 (J. Chubb & P. Peterson eds. 1989).

143. Thus far, however, there is little evidence that floor-generated legislation proves any more coherent than committee-generated legislation. S. Smith, supra note 59.

144. E.g., M. Fiorina, supra note 59, at 76–77.

145. See, e.g., A. Bickel, The Least Dangerous Branch 143–56 (1962); Democracy and Distrust 131–34.

146. [The work alluded to became J. Ely, War and Responsibility: Constitutional Lessons of Vietnam and Its Aftermath (1993).]

147. 100 Yale Law Journal 1473.

148. Having implied some skepticism about citation studies, I should admit my awareness that Mr. Shapiro's list—I'll even grant it can't be a complete coincidence—is a very distinguished one. And if you promise not to tell—I have my reputation to think about—I was actually delighted to learn I was on it. Reich, Prosser, and Emerson are men it is an honor to finish even close to: in fact two of them—I never met Dean Prosser—were important influences on me not only as a scholar but also, I hope, as a person.

149. This talk was delivered on February 14, 1980, at the Yale Law Journal Symposium on Legal Scholarship: Its Nature and Purposes, as a response to the talk that became Brest, "The Fundamental Rights Controversy: The Essential Contra-

dictions of Normative Constitutional Scholarship," 90 Yale L. J. 1063 (1981). Much of it, as delivered, comprised my carping about Brest's carping about my work, and I wisely decided not to publish it. (Hey, we were young: had we realized that in the fullness of time and turn we would both reach the very summit of legal education, which is to say the deanship of Stanford Law School, it would all have been unnecessary.) Good sense and taste prevailed as swiftly for Brest as it did for me: the published version of his talk, while retaining some invalid criticisms of my work—a redundancy if ever I wrote one—was much fairer and, one must admit it, both good and important. Thus what is reproduced here omits what seemed at the time the essential defense of myself, though in the course of celebrating the joys and use of constructive legal scholarship it does decry what still seems to me a minor tragedy, Professor Brest's conversion from a liberal process-oriented scholar to a despairing—well, I'd be tempted to say critical scholar were it not for the fact that we know a dean can't be that.

150. [Admittedly, as of 1996 this campaign is licking its wounds and awaiting another, apparently distant, day. It was heroic nonetheless.]

151. To a "genuine reconstitution of society" (Brest, supra note 149, at 1109)? It is hard to take that as a serious suggestion, not because I don't think the effort worth making (well, depending on one's definition), but rather because if one had decided that was the goal she could most profitably pursue, there obviously would be less counterproductive ways to pursue it than debunking liberal legal scholarship.

152. A. Camus, The Myth of Sisyphus 91 (J. O'Brien trans. 1955). [This may suggest that the joys of a life of liberal legal scholarship are aesthetic joys, and indeed they are (at least I can't understand not making that part of the point). There's more, however. First, as the piece suggests, academic writing does influence judges—obviously rarely as much as the author would like (but who has that kind of influence?) Beyond that, those who respond to our work by noting that most constitutional issues will be settled by political compromise anyway, and inferring that it therefore must be pointless to try to shape the constitutional debate, are themselves missing a very big boat, that the constitutional debate itself can and often does contribute centrally to the nature of the political compromise, sometimes even helping to inject a little backbone into one of the branches.]

Index

The endnotes accompanying the listed pages should also be consulted.

Abington School District v. Schempp, 190, 192, 195

abortion, 7, 20, 21, 281–306, 345, 350; Republican platforms of 1980 and 1984's position on, 306n, 345. *See also Roe v. Wade*

"absolutist" approach to First Amendment, 183

abstention doctrine, 434n42

Abzug, Bella, 329

academics, as potential judges, 349–50, 357

accusatorial and inquisitorial criminal justice systems contrasted, 235–46

Adair v. United States, 414n179

Adams, John, 131, 142n

Adams, John Quincy, 490n113

Adarand Constructors, Inc. v. Peña, 275, 402n23

Adkins v. Children's Hospital, 290

administrative agencies, 409–10n133, 486n79

affirmative action, 19, 261–75, 304, 327, 350, 358, 389n191

age discrimination, 451n91

Agnello v. United States, 219–20, 222, 227

Agnew, Spiro, 141

aliens, discrimination against, 451n91

Allegheny Pittsburgh Coal Co. v. County Comm'n, 86–88

Allen, Layman, 33

Allstate Insurance Co. v. Hague, 70

amendment of Constitution; as method of overruling Supreme Court, 356–57; when appropriate, 299–300

American Communications Ass'n v. Douds, 112, 115–17, 123–24, 127, 130

Amish, right to keep children home from school, 196, 418n19

Amsterdam, Anthony, 439n89

Angel v. Bullington, 379n105

Annenberg, Walter, 329

anti-Communist legislation, 27–28, 96, 112, 115, 123–24, 127, 130–35, 321

antifederalists, 17–18

antimiscegenation laws, 468n157. *See also Loving v. Virginia*

anti-Tory legislation, 112, 116, 130–31

appropriations, legislative and executive roles respecting, 485n71

Aptheker v. Secretary of State, 463n70

Arizona v. Evans, 230

Armstrong, Scott, 188

Arnson, Cynthia, 487n91

Arthur, Chester Alan, 490n113

Articles of Confederation, 72

Austin v. New Hampshire, 69–72

automobile insurance initiatives, 1988 California, 486n83

Baade, Hans, 65

Bailey v. Richardson, 402n36

balancing tests, 176–78, 182–83, 185–86, 378n95, 419–20n30, 420n35, 422n50

Baldwin v. Montana Fish & Game Commission, 66–67, 71

Baxter, William, 64

Beale, Joseph, 86

Beaney, William, 201

Bentham, Jeremy, 14, 322–23, 415n185

Bergan, Francis, 61

Bernhardt v. Polygraphic Co. of America, 45

Betts v. Brady, 198–203

Bibfeldt, Franz, 476n16

Bible reading in public schools, 190, 192

Bickel, Alexander, 25–29, 137–38, 274, 447n30, 451n89

Biddle, Francis, 90, 95

Biden, Joseph, 346–47, 358–59

bills of attainder, 27, 89–136, 415n188; administrative adjudication and, 409–10n133; bills of pains and penalties included within prohibition, 112–13, 118, 128; declaration of guilt as supposed requirement thereof, 108, 111, 113, 115; inescapability as supposed requirement

bills of attainder (*cont.*)
thereof, 116–18; punishment as supposed
requirement thereof, 115–16, 127–29
Bird, Rose, 355
birth control, 279–81, 286–87, 312–14,
316–17, 326
Black, Charles, 32, 276
Black, Hugo, 25, 29, 96, 114, 295, 423n50,
479n31
Blackmun, Harry, 211–12, 282, 298–99,
301, 341, 359, 433–34n41, 434–35n42
Blom-Cooper, Louis, 164
Board of Education v. Allen, 195
Bodkin Adams, John, 165–66
Bolling v. Sharpe, 97, 479n31
border search, government attempt to assimi-
late rectal probe to routine, 210–11
Bork, Robert, 140–42, 147, 306, 345–50,
352–53, 357–59
Bosnia, 142–43, 150–51
Bowers v. Hardwick, 22
Bowsher v. Synar, 486n83
Brandeis, Louis, 44, 280, 474n8
Brandenburg v. Ohio, 178–79, 181–82, 184
Branzburg v. Hayes, 138
Braunfield v. Brown, 195
Breitel, Charles, 61
Brennan, William J., 23, 67, 349, 477n25,
495n137
Brest, Paul, 306, 308, 467n133, 468n157,
495–96n149
Breyer, Stephen, 490nn112, 115
Brilmayer, Lea, 61, 73, 389n192
Bronner, Ethan, 480n32, 487–88n93
Brown v. Board of Education, 4, 207, 273,
446n10, 448n40, 452n96, 453n100
Bruton v. United States, 222
Buchen, Phillip, 329
Buckley, James, 465n103
Buckley v. Valleo, 14
Buffo, 399n251
Burger, Warren E., 196, 211–28, 357–58,
495n137
Bush, George, 148–50, 337, 349, 356–57,
476n21
busing, as remedy for school segregation,
259–61, 268, 452n96
*Byrd v. Blue Ridge Electric Cooperative,
Inc.*, 40, 47, 50

Calabresi, Guido, 363
Califano, Joseph, 142–43

California v. Green, 441n96
Camara v. Municipal Court, 442n97
Camden & Suburban Ry. Co. v. Stetson,
383n133
campaign finance laws, 482n56
campus, application of Bill of Rights on,
232–35
Canadian constitution, 18–24
capital punishment, 23, 358, 368n28,
456n27, 462n70
Caplan, Lincoln, 304
Carolene Products footnote, 270, 288, 306–
7, 466n117
Carlswell, G. Harrold, 493n133
Carter Administration; civil rights policy,
258–60; leadership on deregulation,
484n70
Carter, Hodding, 480n34
Carter, Jimmy, 476n21
*Carter v. Jury Commission of Greene
County*, 254
case or controversy requirement, 119–20,
122–23, 134
Cassell v. Texas, 251–52
categorization approach to protection of
free expression, 178–84
Cavers, David, 86, 385nn150, 156,
392n205
Central Intelligence Agency, 333–34
Chafee, Zechariah, 406n90
Chayes, Abram, 384–85n146
Chemerinsky, Erwin, 476n19, 488nn96,
97
Chesterton, G. K., 172–73
Chisholm v. Georgia, 490n105
choice of law, 61–86
*Church of the Lukumi Babalu Aye, Inc. v.
City of Hialeah*, 197
City of Richmond v. J.A. Croson Co., 275,
399n250, 402n23, 453n101
Clark, Tom, 414n176
clear and present danger test, 183, 416–
17n9, 421n42, 422n50
clear mistake, rule of, 25–30
Cleveland, Grover, 491n119, 493n133
Clinton, William J., 142–43, 148, 150–51,
305n, 415n183, 490n115
Coast Guard Academy, admission of
women to, 258
Cohen, Marshall, 13
Cohen v. Beneficial Industrial Loan Corp.,
55–57, 375n70

Cohen v. California, 179–82, 184

Cohen, William, 86

Coleman, William T., Jr., 258–61, 330–31

Commerce Clause, 35, 38–39, 73, 371–72n42

commercial speech, 427n86

Communist Control Act, 131–32, 134

Communist Party v. Catherwood, 132, 410n134

Communist Party v. Subversive Activities Control Board, 115–18

"community" as defense of racial discrimination in school or voting district line drawing, 256

Comptroller General, 352

Concorde SST, 258, 329–31

Conformity Act, 383n134

conflict of laws, 61–86

Congress; passing off politically controversial decisions, 53; shift from policymaking to constituent casework, 350–54

congressional investigations, 97

consensus, as source of constitutional values, 23, 348, 354

contempt of court, as response to problem of pretrial publicity, 152–73

contraception. *See* birth control

contract, liberty of, 7, 290–91, 303

contractual capacity, 396–97n242

Coppage v. Kansas, 290, 414n179

Copyright Clause, 406–7n103

corruption of blood, 112

counsel, right to, 198–207, 231, 242, 378n95

countermajoritarian difficulty, 489n101

Countryman, Vern, 341

Court of Claims, constitutional status of, 93–95

Cox, Archibald, 137, 140, 142, 306, 415n188

criminal procedure, 198–246

critical legal studies, 22, 341–43, 475n16

Cromwell, Oliver, 116

cruel and unusual punishment, 87, 462n70

Cummings v. Missouri, 98, 113–15, 117, 128–29

Cuomo, Mario, 478n28

Currie, Brainerd, 61–62, 64–65, 67–68, 70, 76, 78, 86

Currie, David, 386n165

Dahl, Robert, 351n62

damage ceilings, 62, 85–86, 378n101, 388n188

Dandridge v. Williams, 290–91

Davis, Angela (D.C. Public Defender), 204

Davis, Kenneth Culp, 408n128

Days, Drew, 259, 261

Declaration of Independence, 346

Deerfield Park District v. Progress Development Corporation, 257–58

DeFunis v. Odegaard, 265–66, 268, 275

Dellums v. Bush, 148

Democracy and Distrust, 5, 6, 17, 19, 20, 26, 71, 247, 306–8, 310–11, 324, 340, 398n249, 399nn251, 399–400n255, 418n17, 449n66, 450nn80, 85, 452nn93, 97, 453n101, 467n147, 471n195, 488n94, 489n101

democracy, theories of, 9–11; direct and representative democracies contrasted, 368n22

Denning, A.T.D., 160

Dent v. West Virginia, 114

deregulation, 484n70

Dershowitz, Alan M., 211, 408n121

Descartes, René, 324

Desert Storm, 148, 150

Dickson, R. G. Brian, 20

Dies, Martin, 90

disadvantageous distinction model, defined, 250

discrete and insular minorities, 288–89, 298, 306

discretion in criminal charging and sentencing, 236–41

disorderly conduct, 424–25n72

diversity of citizenship jurisdiction, 39–61

divided government, 485n75

divorce, choice of law respecting, 396n242

doctor-patient privilege, 39, 60–61

Dodd, William, 89–111

Doe ex dem. Gaines v. Buford, 117

Doe v. Bolton, 66

Dole, Robert, 148–49

Donne, John, 310

double jeopardy, 27, 139

Douglas, William O., 250, 398n250, 423n50, 449n77, 481n52

Doyle, Arthur Conan, 159

draft card burning, 174, 176–77, 180, 182, 285

draft, military, religious exemption from, 188–90, 193–94
Dred Scott v. Sandford, 478n30, 490n105
Dreyfus, Alfred, 159
drugs, government regulation of, 283
due process, 20, 24, 29, 96–97, 99–100, 102–3, 106, 108–9, 122, 124, 279–328, 387n169, 412–13n173
Dukakis, Michael, 357
Durham v. United States, 203
Dworkin, Ronald, 261–66, 307, 311–28, 347

eavesdropping, electronic, 233–35
Edgerton, Henry, 402n36
Ehrenzweig, Albert, 65
Eisenhower, Dwight, 150, 477n25
Eisenstadt v. Baird, 459n53, 460n60
Eleventh Amendment, 490n105
Ellsworth, Oliver, 148
Ely, Richard, 10
Ely, Ron, 10
Emerson, Thomas, 179–80
Employment Division v. Smith, 196–97
England, approach to pretrial publicity, 152–73
Epstein, Richard, 29
Epperson v. Arkansas, 192–93, 428n4
equal protection, 49, 66, 86–88, 97–100, 102–3, 106, 108–9, 247–78, 327, 364, 387n169, 388n186, 464n90, 479n31; comparison of equal protection demands placed on federal and state governments, 275, 402n23
Equal Rights Amendment, 288, 335, 356
Erie R.R. v. Tompkins, 39–61
Escobedo v. Illinois, 217
Establishment Clause, 29
Estreicher, Samuel, 7
Estrich, Susan, 477–78n27
Everson v. Board of Education, 429n10
evolution, banning of teaching in public schools, 192–93
Ex parte Garland, 98, 113–15
ex post facto laws, 27, 87, 122, 128, 413n173, 468n157
executive power, 30, 480n31
executive privilege, 329–30
exhaustion of state remedies, 434n42
expression, freedom of, 29, 96–97, 99, 135–36, 152–87, 321

external/personal preference distinction, Professor Dworkin's, 261–66, 307, 311–28

Fairman, Charles, 29
federalism, 31–88
Federal Arbitration Act, 45
Federal Bureau of Investigation, 333–34
Federal Judiciary Act, 46
Federal Reserve, 352
Federal Rules of Civil Procedure, 41–43, 47, 50–60
Federal Rules of Evidence, 39–41, 60–61
Fein, Bruce, 478n28
Fickle, Stanley, 468n157
fighting words, 179
Finzer v. Barry, 480n31
Fiorina, Morris, 351, 483n62, 483–84n65, 484n66, 70, 485nn76, 77
Fitzpatrick, James, 204
flag burning or desecration, 147, 173–87, 353, 356–57, 465n106, 493–94n135
Fleming, James, 307, 368n30
Flemming v. Nestor, 130
Fletcher v. Peck, 113, 123, 128
Flowers, Richmond, 485n74
Ford Administration; civil rights policy, 258–61; leadership on deregulation, 484n70
Ford, Gerald, 477n25, 490n113
forum shopping, 47, 50
Fortas, Abe, 199, 202n, 203–4, 207–9, 357, 426n81, 491n116
Fourth and Fifth Amendments, impeachment by evidence taken in violation of, compared, 221, 440n92
France, criminal process in, 235–46
Frankfurter, Felix, 25, 46, 107–8, 110–11, 113, 115, 118, 124, 131, 223, 355, 403n52, 477n25, 481n52
Freund, Paul, 64, 385n150
Fried, Charles, 12, 16
Friedman, Richard, 490n114
Fuld, Stanley, 86
Full Faith & Credit Clause, 73
fundamental values, society's, as source of constitutional doctrine, 8, 18–24, 303–4, 354
Furman v. Georgia, 23, 462n70

Gall, John C., 96, 100–102, 105–8, 111
gender discrimination, 288–89, 304, 305,

334–35, 446n14, 452n93, 453n101, 461–62n65
Giamatti, A. Bartlett, 341
Gibbs v. Burke, 201
Gideon v. Wainwright, 198–209, 211, 242
Gideon's Trumpet, 203, 208
Ginsburg, Douglas, 349, 493n133
Ginsburg, Ruth Bader, 490nn112, 115
Giscard d'Estaing, Valéry, 444n102
Glennon, Michael, 399n252
Goldstein, Abraham, 239–40, 242–43, 245–46
Gomillion v. Lightfoot, 37–38, 248, 253
good faith exception to exclusionary rule, proposed, 228–30
Goodhart, Arthur, 152
Gordon, Jeffrey, 89
governmental encouragement of private acts of discrimination, 275–78
Graham, Billy, 424n71
Graham, Howard Jay, 29
Gramm-Rudman-Hollings Balanced Budget Act, 352
grand jury, power to call president before, 137–40
Grassley, Charles, 359
Green, John R., 201
Green v. Shumway, 405n78
Greene, Harold, 148
Grenada, 147
Griffin v. County School Board of Prince Edward County, 257
Griffin v. Illinois, 202
Grigg, Mary, 156
Griswold v. Connecticut, 279–81, 286–87
Grove City College v. Bell, 487n86
Guaranty Trust Co. v. York, 40n, 41, 46–47, 50, 59
guest statutes, 77–80, 82–83, 85–86

habeas corpus, 444n104; Supreme Court's contraction of, 206
Haiti, 142–43, 148–50
Hale, Leslie, 156
Hamilton, Alexander, 34–35, 38, 12
Hamilton v. Alabama, 202
Hanna v. Plumer, 40–43, 45–53, 56–57, 60
Hand, Learned, 425n74
handbills, laws banning distribution of, 175–77
Hanoteau, Claude, 235, 240, 242

Harlan, John Marshall (II), 41–43, 48, 51, 56, 179–80, 196, 211, 228, 276–77, 280, 418n23, 430n23
Harper v. Virginia Board of Elections, 399n250
Harris v. McCrae, 466n117
Harris v. New York, 211–28
Hart, Henry, 136, 373n59, 374–75n69
Hart, H.L.A., 314–15, 317, 319–22
Hawker v. New York, 114
Haynsworth, Clement, 357, 359
Heath, Edward, 329
Helms, Jesse, 148, 302–3, 465n108
Hentoff, Nat, 204–6
Heymann, Philip, 297
Hicklin v. Orbeck, 66–67
Hill, Anita, 334–38
Hippocratic Oath, 458n39
Hirshman, Linda, 477–78n27
Hogg, Peter, 19
Holmes, Oliver Wendell, 290, 474n8
homosexual acts, regulation of, 22, 283, 312–17, 324, 326, 468n157
homosexuals, discrimination against, 142–43, 452n93, 468n157
honesty, 329–39
Hoover, Herbert, 39
Hornblower, William, 493n133
Horsky, Charles, 95, 109–11
House v. Mayo, 202
Huber, Ulrich, 71–72
Hughes, Charles Evans, 490nn113, 114
Hughes v. Fetter, 62
Huguez v. United States, 210–11
Humphrey's Executor v. United States, 101, 403n50
Hunt, Linda, 340
Hunter v. Erickson, 276–77, 320
Hurtado v. Superior Court, 392n209, 394n224
husband-wife privilege, 39, 60–61
Hussein, Saddam, 148–49
Hutchinson, Allan, 340
Hyde Amendment, 466n117

Ickes, Harold, 92
impeachment of government officials, 101, 138–41; impeachment and attainder compared, 408n120
impeachment of witnesses, use of unconstitutionally obtained evidence for, 211–28

"impropriety, appearance of," 338–39
In re Gault, 203
incorporation of Bill of Rights in Fourteenth Amendment, 479–80n31
Indochina, 145–47, 150–51, 341
inquisitorial system. *See* accusatorial and
  inquisitorial criminal justice systems
  contrasted
INS v. Chadha, 30, 136, 486n76
interest analysis, 61–86
Internal Security Act, 133–34
interruption of speakers, prohibition of,
  183, 185–86
Iran, 143–47
Iraq, 146–48

Jackson, Robert A., 124, 272, 398n250
Jackson v. Denno, 214, 222
Jacobson, Gary, 483n61
jazz and constitutional interpretation com-
  pared, 342–43n
Jaworski, Leon, 142
Jay Burns Baking Co. v. Bryan, 290
Jefferson, Thomas, 34, 122, 490n113
Jenkins, Ed, 350
Johnson, Andrew, 137–38
Johnson, Frank, 254–55
Johnson, Lyndon, 143, 477n25, 491n116
Jones, Marvin, 102
Jones, Paula, 415n183
Johnson v. New Jersey, 433n33
Joyce, James, 341, 343n
judges, election of, 355
juges d'instruction, 235–46
jurisdiction of federal courts, Congress's
  power to limit, 136–37
jury selection, racial discrimination in, 250–
  52

Kamisar, Yale, 489n103
Kantianism, 367n12
Katz v. United States, 286
Katzenbach v. Morgan, 371–72n42
Kaufman v. United States, 439n87
Kay, Herma, 67–68, 386n165, 389n192,
  392n205
Kelman, Mark, 474n12
Kennedy, Anthony, 304, 306, 349, 359
Kennedy, Duncan, 342–43
Kennedy, Edward, 346–47, 477n26
Kennedy, John F., 332, 477n25
Kennedy, Ludovic, 159, 161

Kent v. Dulles, 463n70
Kerr, John, 90
Keyes v. School District No. 1, 259–60
Kilberg v. Northeast Airlines, Inc., 62
King, Cecil, 162
*Klaxon Co. v. Stentor Electric Manufactur-
  ing Co.*, 59, 374–75n69
Kohl, Herb, 491–92n129
Koppelman, Andrew, 327–28
Korea, 145, 147
Kovner, Mark, 488–89n101
Krash, Abe, 203–204, 207–209
Kurland, Philip, 40n
Kuwait, 149

*Lamb's Chapel v. Center Moriches Union
  Free School Dist.*, 197
Lamont v. Postmaster General, 136
Langbein, John, 240
law clerks, role of, 135–36, 188, 281
Lawson, James Francis, 35
*Lebron v. Washington Metro. Area Transit
  Auth.*, 480n31
legal process school, 340–41, 345, 355,
  357, 361
legal realism, 341–43, 345, 363–64, 481n40
legislative courts, 94
legislative vetoes, 30, 136, 486n76
Lehman v. City of Shaker Heights, 420n37
less restrictive alternative analysis, 175–77
Levi, Edward, 258–59, 329–30
Levinson, Sanford, 492n129
Levy, Leonard, 29
Lewis, Anthony, 203, 207–209, 416n2
Linde, Hans, 18, 425n73, 465n103
lobbies, constitutional effect of influence on
  legislation, 451–52n92
locals, preference for in choice of law, 61–
  86
Lochner v. New York, 26, 289–95, 309,
  312–13, 316, 324, 478n30, 479n31
Locke, John, 354
Lockley v. United States, 223
Lord Campbell's Act, 393n211
Lovett, Robert M., 89–111
Loving v. Virginia, 268, 451n90, 460n60
Lucas, J. Anthony, 261
Lynch v. Donnelly, 197n

Maass, Arthur, 483n62
McCain, John, 493n134
McCormick, Charles T., 409n132

503

McCray v. United States, 37–38
MacKinnon, George, 330
McLaughlin v. Florida, 268, 451n90
Macauley, Thomas Babbington, 407n118
Madden, J. Warren, 102
Maddox, Lester, 350
Madison, James, 14, 17, 34–35, 38, 120–
  21, 132
Maher v. Roe, 303–4, 398n249, 466n117
Mailer, Norman, 341
Marcus, Martin, 239–40, 242–43, 245–46
married women's statutes, 62
Marshall, John, 113, 123, 138
Marshall, Thurgood, 23, 67, 212, 435n42,
  441–42n96, 448n40, 490n113
Martin, James, 386n165
Martin v. United States, 211
Mason, George, 144, 148
Mattice v. Klawans, 382n132
meritocratic selection, 449n69
Merrill, Thomas, 26
Metro Broadcasting, Inc. v. FCC, 275,
  402n23
Meyer v. Nebraska, 460–61n60
Michelman, Frank, 364
Miguel v. McCarl, 400n7
military base-closing commission, 352
military police, author's experience in,
  208–9
Miller, Samuel, 113, 115
Mill, John Stuart, 14, 28, 308–9, 322–23
Miller, Arthur R., 376n79
Milliken v. Pratt, 62
Miranda v. Arizona, 207, 209, 211–28, 358,
  456n27, 462–63n70
Mishkin, Paul, 384–85n146
Mississippi Publishing Co. v. Murphree,
  60
Mississippi v. Johnson, 137
Missouri v. Jenkins, 491n124
mixed government, 354
Monaghan, Henry, 26
Montesquieu, Baron de la Brède et de, 120,
  354
Mortimer, John, 210
motivation, constitutional relevance of offi-
  cial, 36–38, 136–37, 191–97, 247–53,
  247–58, 275–78, 306, 362–64
Murphy, Frank, 29
Murphy, Walter, 352–53
Myers v. United States, 98, 101, 107, 110–
  11, 403n50

NAACP v. Alabama, 287
nativity scenes, governmental display of,
  197
natural law, 20
"Negro," use of term, 37n
Neumeier v. Kuehner, 77–80, 86
New York Times v. Sullivan, 302
newsman's privilege, 39
Nicholas, Samuel, 117
Ninth Amendment, 280, 307–8, 455n1
Nixon, Richard, 137–41, 145–46, 228, 295,
  329, 331, 357–58, 424n71, 477n25,
  497n91
Nixon v. Administrator of General Services,
  136
Nixon v. Sirica, 329–30
NLRB v. Jones & Laughlin Steel Corp.,
  369n11
Norris-LaGuardia Act, 414n179

Obligation of Contracts Clause, 122, 308–9,
  479–80n31
obscenity. *See* pornography
O'Connor, Sandra Day, 304, 306, 492n130
O'Fallon, James, 307, 310
*Oil, Chemical and Atomic Workers Interna-
  tional Union v. American Cyanimide*,
  478n30
Ollman v. Evans, 494n135
Oregon v. Mitchell, 371n42, 490nn105,
  106
Oswald, Lee Harvey, 170, 331
outcome determination test, 47, 49–50, 60
overbreadth, 421n40, 426n82

Palko v. Connecticut, 460n60
Panama, 147
Parker, John J., 493n133
Peckham, Wheeler H., 493n133
People v. Kulis, 213–14
Perkins v. Elg, 93
"perpetrator perspective" on constitutional-
  ity of governmental choices, 247, 362
Perry, Michael, 25
Persian Gulf, 143–48
personal autonomy, 306–28
personal preferences. *See* external/personal
  preference distinction
Peyrefitte, Alain, 236–37
Pierce v. Carskadon, 113
Pierce v. Society of Sisters, 460–61n60
Pinckney, Charles, 414–15n182

Planned Parenthood v. Casey, 304–6
platonic guardians, 7–8
plea bargaining, 238, 240, 243
Plessy v. Ferguson, 309, 451n89
pluralism, 14, 16–18
Poe v. Ullman, 279–81, 457n31
police brutality, 445n113
police power, 369n10
Pollock v. Farmers' Loan & Trust Co.,
    490n105
polygamy, criminalization of, 193
pornography, 179, 313–14, 316–17, 326,
    423–24n62
Portland, 399n251
Powell, Lewis, 136, 295, 341, 349
Powell v. McCormack, 415n184
pragmatism, 475–76n16
preemption, federal, 425–26n75
president, indictability of, 140–41
press, freedom of the, 152–73, 289
Prince v. Massachusetts, 182, 460–61n60
privacy, right to, 282, 285–87, 312, 338,
    347, 383n133, 455n3
Privileges and Immunities Clause (Article
    IV), 66–72
Privileges or Immunities Clause (Four-
    teenth Amendment), 29, 307–8, 387n169,
    455n1, 479n31
Profumo, John, 165
Projet Peyrefitte, 235–46
Prosser, William, 495n148
public defender, author's experience as,
    205–6, 209–11, 229, 242, 244
publicity, pretrial, 152–73, 458n43

Quincy, Josiah, 142n

racial discrimination, 247–78; in choice of
    public housing sites, 257; by decisions to
    close public schools, 257, in drawing
    school district and attendance zone lines,
    254–56; in drawing voting district and po-
    litical subdivision lines, 248, 253, 256; in
    jury selection, 250–52; in placement of
    public parks, 257–58; in residential
    zoning, 257; in teacher assignment, 254–
    55, 257
*Ragan v. Merchants Transfer & Warehouse
    Co.*, 56–57, 60
Railway Express Agency, Inc. v. New York,
    272, 398n250

rational basis test, 86–87, 97, 124–25, 269–
    70, 300, 364, 399–400n255, 420n32,
    479n31
Ratner, Leonard, 386n165, 392–93n209
Reagan, Ronald, 143, 341, 345–47, 349–50,
    357, 487n91, 490n113, 493n133
reapportionment, 489n101. *See also Rey-
    nolds v. Sims*
real estate tax assessments, 86–88
reasonable doubt standard, 230–33
recusal, occasions for, 403n52
Redlich, Norman, 197
Reed, Stanley, 107–8, 110, 477n25
Reese, Willis, 85
regulation of content/regulation of time,
    place and manner distinction, 181–82
Rehnquist, William, 184, 270, 282, 295,
    495n137
Reich, Charles, 495n148
Reitman v. Mulkey, 275–78
religion, establishment of, 188–87, 298,
    454n102
religion, freedom of, 188–97, 298, 424n69,
    454n102
removal power of executive, 96–103, 105–
    10
republicanism, 17–18, 475n16
residency requirements, durational, for wel-
    fare benefits, 388n186
Reynolds v. Sims, 4, 462–63n69
Reynolds v. Tennessee, 424n71
Rhode, Deborah, 232
right-privilege distinction, 129–30
Rintels, David, 204
Roberts, Owen J., 493n133
Roe v. Wade, 20, 281–306, 341, 343n, 345,
    358–59, 383n133, 398n249, 481n47; at-
    tempts to overrule by constitutional
    amendment, 297–301; attempts to over-
    rule by statute, 301–3, 480n31
Rogers, William P., 329
Roosevelt, Franklin, 92, 355, 477n25,
    481n53
*Rosenberger v. Rector and Visitors of the
    University of Virginia*, 197
Rousseau, Jean Jacques, 9
Rudman, Warren, 349
Rules Enabling Act, 40–42, 46–47, 50–61
Rules of Decision Act, 40–42, 44–53, 55–
    57, 59–60
Rutledge, Wiley, 29, 55, 481n52

sacrifice of animals, religious, 197
Sager, Lawrence, 312, 324, 368n22, 472n195
Salary Act of 1967, 352
Sandalow, Terrance, 468n157
Scalia, Antonin, 349, 494n135
Schattschneider, E. E., 10
Scheer v. Rockne Motors Corp., 392n205
Schlagenhauf v. Holder, 60
Schneider, Norman, 488–89n101
school desegregation, 258–61
school district and attendance zone lines, racial discrimination in drawing, 254–65
Schware v. Bd. of Bar Examiners, 463n70
Scopes "monkey" trial, 193
Seaton, Peter Donald, 19
Sedler, Robert, 64, 77–78, 393n209
self-incrimination, privilege against, 211–28, 240
self-regarding conduct, 308–11, 467n149
separation of powers, 31, 89–151
Seventeenth Amendment, 488n95
Seventh Amendment, 47
severability, 402n31
sexual harassment, 334–35, 415n183
Shapiro, Fred, 362, 363n
Shapiro v. Thompson, 388n186
Shelley v. Kraemer, 397n242, 479n31
Sheppard, Samuel, 170–72
Sherbert v. Verner, 193–97, 429n6
Sibbach v. Wilson & Co., 42, 46, 51, 58, 60–61
Sidgwick, Henry, 14
Simler v. Conner, 47
Simon, Paul (Senator), 478–79n30
Simpson, O. J., 230–32, 417n10
Sixteenth Amendment, 490n105
Skinner v. Oklahoma, 87, 460n60
Slaughter-House Cases, 479n31
Slesser, H. H., 161
Smith Act, 132–33
Smith v. Goguen, 184
Somalia, 142–43, 150
soundtrucks, regulation of, 182–83
Souter, David, 304, 306, 348, 358–59, 477n26, 490n112
Specter, Arlen, 358
speech-conduct distinction, 179–80
Spence v. Washington, 173
Spencer, Herbert, 308

Spock, Benjamin, 341
Stanford University, 232–33
stare decisis, 304–6
state action doctrine, 275–78, 300
statutes of limitation, 54–57, 375–76n70
Stevens, John Paul, 477n25
Stewart, Potter, 211, 215, 228, 290–91, 463n70
stockholders' strike suits, 56
Stone, Alan, 456n24, 457n37, 459n46, 461–62n65
Stone, Harlan Fiske, 270, 288–89, 298
Stone, Oliver, 333
Story, Joseph, 121, 135
Strauder v. West Virginia, 274, 454n103
Street v. New York, 184
strict scrutiny, 18–19, 268–75, 388n186
Stromberg v. California, 424n63
Struve, Guy, 419n27
substance-procedure distinction, 46, 51–55, 57–59, 61
substantive due process, 19–24, 27, 279–328, 418n21
Subversive Activities Control Act, 116, 133–34
Sundquist, James, 487n91
Sununu, John, 349
Supreme Court, as possible counterbalance to power of president, 356–60
suspect classifications, 19, 66, 364; immutability of classifying trait, and/or stigmatizing effect, as necessary or probative characteristic thereof, 450n85
Swain v. Alabama, 253–54
Swann v. Charlotte-Mecklenburg Board of Education, 268
Sweatt v. Painter, 262–66, 325
Swift v. Tyson, 44
symbolic expression, 173–74, 178, 184

Taft-Hartley Act, 115–17, 123, 127, 130
Takings Clause, 29
Tanenhaus, Joseph, 352–53
tax exemptions for religious organizations, 195–96
taxing and spending powers of Congress, 33–35, 37–38, 101–2, 105–8
Taylor, Telford, 89
Temple, Ralph, 204
tenBroeck, Jacobus, 29
Tenth Amendment, 36, 43–44, 308–9

territorialism in choice of law, 64–65, 86
Texas Monthly v. Bullock, 197
Texas v. Johnson, 187, 356, 494n135
textbooks, public distribution to parochial
  schools, 195
Thayer, James Bradley, 25–30
Thomas, Clarence, 334–37, 490n112
Tinker v. Des Moines School District, 178–
  19, 182
Third Amendment, 459n51
three judge district courts, 93–94
Tonkin Gulf Resolution, 147
Toomer v. Witsell, 66–67
Torcaso v. Watkins, 189
Totenburg, Nina, 338
Tower, John, 338
tradition, as source of constitutional values,
  20–21
Transportation, Department of, author's ex-
  perience as General Counsel, 31–32,
  258–61, 329–31
Trautman, Donald, 64, 389n191, 393n213
travel, right to, 388n186, 390n197
Traynor, Roger, 355
trial by newspaper, 152–73
Tribe, Laurence, 22, 298, 300–301, 343
Tripoli, 147
Trollope, Anthony, 341
Truman, Harry S., 477n25
Turner v. Fouche, 254
Turow, Scott, 210
Tushnet, Mark, 305n, 306, 341–43, 345,
  488–89n101
Twenty-sixth Amendment, 490nn105, 106
Twerski, Aaron, 61, 77, 79, 86

Union Pac. Ry. v. Botsford, 383n133
United States v. Brown, 114n, 135–36,
  398n249, 415n188
United States v. Burr, 138, 140
United States v. Butler, 369n8
United States v. Eichman, 187
United States v. Langston, 96, 100, 102
United States v. Leon, 230
United States v. Lovett, 89–111, 112, 114–
  15, 117, 129
*United States v. Montgomery County Board
  of Education*, 254–55
United States v. O'Brien, 174–87, 253
United States v. Robel, 419–20n30
United States v. Seeger, 188–90, 193–94
United States v. Vuitch, 455n6

United States v. Wade, 456n27
University of California v. Bakke, 275
"unprovided" cases in choice of law, 76–
  80
utilitarianism, 11–17, 262–66, 308, 311–
  28

vegetarianism, 16
vice president, indictability of, 140–41
"victim perspective" on constitutionality of
  governmental choices, 247, 362
Vietnam. *See* Indochina
volunteer army, 148
von Mehren, Arthur, 389n191, 392n209,
  393n213
voting district and political subdivision
  lines, racial discrimination in drawing,
  248, 253, 256

Wade v. Mayo, 199–200
Walder v. United States, 218–23, 227
*Walz v. Tax Commission of the City of New
  York*, 196
Walzer, Michael, 10
War and Responsibility, 143, 151, 495n146
war power, 143–51
War Powers Resolution, 143–46, 151,
  353
Ward, Stephen, 161, 165
Warren, Charles, 371n41
Warren Commission, 170, 209, 331–34
Warren, Earl, 3–5, 40, 135–36, 169, 188,
  281, 295, 332, 335, 477n25, 491n116
Watergate, 341
Watson, Goodwin, 89–111
"we/they discriminations," 271–73, 327,
  466n118
wealth discrimination, 248, 280–81, 303–4,
  311, 364, 441n96, 452n93, 462n69
Weinreb, Lloyd, 240
welfare department home visits. *See Wyman
  v. James*
Welsh v. United States, 193–94
West German Constitutional Court, 20
West, Robin, 340, 473–74n6, 476n19
West Virginia Bd. of Educ. v. Barnette,
  427–28n92, 430n25
Whaley, Richard, 102, 111
Whitaker, Samuel, 102
White, Byron, 22, 67, 184, 195, 211, 228,
  276, 282
white collar crime, 491n124

Wiggins, James Russell, 157
Williamson v. Lee Optical Co., 269–70
Wilson, James, 149
Wisconsin v. Yoder, 196, 418n19
Woods v. Interstate Realty Co., 55–57, 60, 375n70
Woodward, Bob, 188
Wormuth, Francis, 408n130
Wright, Charles Alan, 379n117, 380n124, 384n143
Wright, J. Skelly, 465n105
Wright v. Rockefeller, 253
wrongful death statutes, 62
Wyman v. James, 212, 433–34n41, 434–

35n42, 437n66, 441–42n96, 442–43n97, 464–65n102, 495n137
Wyman v. Updegraf, 27–28

Yale Law Journal, centennial celebration, 361–63
Yale University, 233–35
yellow dog contracts, 414n179
Yick Wo v. Hopkins, 281

Zimmerman v. Poindexter, 330
Zobrest v. Catalina Foothills School Dist., 197
Zola, Emile, 159

About the Author

Formerly the Tyler Professor of Constitutional Law at Harvard University and then Dean of Stanford Law School, JOHN HART ELY is the Richard A. Hausler Professor at the University of Miami Law School. His previous works include *Democracy and Distrust* and *War and Responsibility* (Princeton).